LETHAL MISTS:

AN INTRODUCTION TO THE NATURAL AND MILITARY SCIENCES OF CHEMICAL, BIOLOGICAL WARFARE AND TERRORISM

LETHAL MISTS:

AN INTRODUCTION TO THE NATURAL AND MILITARY SCIENCES OF CHEMICAL, BIOLOGICAL WARFARE AND TERRORISM

ERIC R. TAYLOR

Nova Science Publishers, Inc.
Commack, New York

Editorial Production:	Susan Boriotti
Office Manager:	Annette Hellinger
Graphics:	Frank Grucci and Jennifer Lucas
Information Editor:	Tatiana Shohov
Book Production:	Donna Dennis, Patrick Davin, Christine Mathosian, Tammy Sauter and Lynette Van Helden
Circulation:	Maryanne Schmidt
Marketing/Sales:	Cathy DeGregory

Library of Congress Cataloging-in-Publication Data

Taylor, Eric R., Ph.D.
    Lethal mists : an introduction to the natural and military sciences of chemical, biological warfare and terrorism / by Eric R. Taylor.
        p.   cm.
    Includes bibliographical references and index.
    ISBN 1-56072-459-5
    1. Chemical warfare. 2. Biological warfare. 3. Terrorism. I. Title.
UG447.T393   1998   98-44334
358'.3--dc21   CIP

Copyright © 1999 by Nova Science Publishers, Inc.
    6080 Jericho Turnpike, Suite 207
    Commack, New York 11725
    Tele. 516-499-3103   Fax 516-499-3146
    e-mail: Novascience@earthlink.net
    e-mail: Novascil@aol.com
    Web Site: http://www.nexusworld.com/nova

Printed in the United States of America

DEDICATED TO MY DAUGHTER, JENNIFER,
THE BEST OF THE WORLD.

THE MOTTO OF THE U.S. ARMY CHEMICAL CORPS

ELEMENTIS REGAMUS PROELIUM

WE RULE THE BATTLE THROUGH THE ELEMENTS

Gold and cobalt blue, the colors of the U.S. Army Chemical Corps, highlight any Chemical Corps insignia or emblem. The depiction of a battle-scarred tree comes from the Coat of Arms of the First Chemical Regiment of WWI. The dragon, a legendary fire breathing creature, symbolizes the destruction wrought by fire, chemical. Together these two symbols combine in the Regimental Crest shown above.

THE BRANCH INSIGNIA OF THE U.S. ARMY CHEMICAL CORPS

WORN BY ALL COMMISSIONED CHEMICAL CORPS OFFICERS UNDER GENERAL OFFICER RANK.

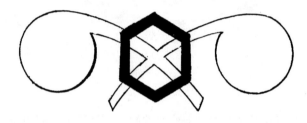

The bulbous devices on each end represent retorts, vessels used to distill or decompose chemical compounds. The hexagon represents the benzene ring, one of several dozen basic building block molecules from which all other industrial, commercial and military chemicals can be derived. The retorts are brass in color. When highly polished they have a golden luster. The hexagon ring is cobalt blue in color. Gold and cobalt blue are the Corps' colors.

CONTENTS

U.S. Army Chemical Corps Motto vii
U.S. Army Chemical Corps Insignia viii
Contents ix
In-depth Contents xi
Preface xix
Acknowledgments xxiii

PART I

INTRODUCTION 1
1. HISTORY 3

PART II

2. BIOLOGICAL MOLECULES 9
3. CHEMICALS 23

PART III

4. TOXIC CHEMICAL AGENTS 39
5. NERVE AGENTS 59
6. BLOOD AGENTS 71
7. CHOKING AGENTS 77
8. BLISTERING AGENTS 85
9. INCAPACITATING & DEFOLIATING AGENTS 93
10. INCENDIARIES & OBSCURANTS 105
11. ANTIDOTES 115

PART IV

12. MICROBIOLOGICAL ORGANIZATION 121
13. BIOLOGICAL AGENTS 135
14. ANTIBIOTICS, INTERFERON & VACCINES 169

PART V

15. EMPLOYMENT 185
16. DETECTION 197
17. PROTECTION 203

PART VI

18. TREATMENT 215
19. DECONTAMINATION 235

PART VII

20. THE CHEMICAL CORPS, U.S. ARMY 241
21. TRAINING & EDUCATION 253

PART VIII

22. FUTURE OUTLOOK, TWENTY-FIRST CENTURY CBW 259
23. CIVILIAN DEFENSE 281
24. CONVENTIONS, TREATIES, RULE of LAW and TERRORISTS 297
25. CONCLUSIONS 311

  FURTHER READINGS 317

  APPENDIX A: Glossary 331
  APPENDIX B: Addresses of Direct Sources 349
  APPENDIX C: How to Read Chemical Formulas 351

  INDEX 395

In-Depth Contents

U.S. Army Chemical Corps Motto
U.S. Army Chemical Corps Insignia
Table of Contents
Preface
Acknowledgments

Part I

INTRODUCTION
1. HISTORY
    The Sciences
    The Military

Part II

2. BIOLOGICAL MOLECULES
    Chemical Formula Notations & Conventions
    General
    Cell Components
        Proteins
        Lipids
        Nucleic Acids
        Carbohydrates
    Inter- & Intramolecular Forces
    Denaturation
    Chemical Agents and Inter- & Intramolecular Forces
        Proteins
        Lipids
        Nucleic Acids
        Carbohydrates

3. CHEMICALS
    The Pesticide Connection
    Household Agents
    Medicine
    Chemical Bonds- The Glue of Molecules
        Metallic Bonds
        Ionic Bonds
        Covalent Bonds
        Hydrogen Bonds
        Hydrophobic & Hydrophilic Interactions

Salt Linkages
Chemical Reactions
Injuries
Thermal Burns
Chemical Burns
Nature of Chemical Damage
Chemical Agents

PART III

4. TOXIC CHEMICAL AGENTS
General
Nerve Agents
Symptoms
Blood Agents
Symptoms
Choking Agents
Symptoms
Blistering Agents
Symptoms
Miscellaneous Toxins

5. Nerve Agents
General
Organophosphates
Carbamates
Mechanism of Reaction
Organophosphates
Carbamates
Nerve Impulses & Their Inhibition
Mixed Function Oxidases
Organophosphates
Carbamates

6. BLOOD AGENTS
General
Mitochondria
Electron Transport
Oxidative Phosphorylation
Mixed Function Oxidases

7. CHOKING AGENTS
General
Site of Action: Lungs
Miscellaneous Sites

8. BLISTERING AGENTS
    General
    Site of Action: Skin ..
        The Eye
        Respiratory Tract
    Mustard Systemic Toxicity
    Arsenical Systemic Effects

9. INCAPACITATING & DEFOLIATING AGENTS
    General
    Physical Incapacitants
        Lacrimators
        Vomiting Agents
    Psychoactive Agents
        Symptoms
    Defoliants
        Physical Toxicity
        Auxin-Like Stimulants
        Metabolic Inhibitors
        Photosynthesis Inhibitors

10. INCENDIARIES & OBSCURANTS
    General
    Incendiaries
    Fuel-Air Weapons
    Obscurants

11. ANTIDOTES
    General
    Nerve Agents
    Blood Agents
    Arsenical Agents

PART IV

12. MICROBIOLOGICAL ORGANIZATION
    General
    Eukaryotes
        Fungi
            Cell Wall
            Sporulation
    Prokaryotes
        Bacteria
            Cell Wall
            Cell Membrane
            Cytoplasm

Rickettsia
Viruses
    Nucleic Acid Synthesis
Basis of Pathogenicity
Infection Process
Cause of Symptoms of Disease
    Toxic Metabolites
    Specific Nutrient Requirements
    Facilitated Invasion
    Protection Against Host Defenses
Discrimination

13. BIOLOGICAL AGENTS
Background
General
Bacteria
Viruses
Fungi
Rickettsia
Viroids
Prions
Infectious Risks
Targets
    Military Vulnerabilities
    Civilian Vulnerabilities
Botulism
    Symptoms
Anthrax
    Symptoms
Cholera
    Symptoms
Ebolas
Hantavirus
Lassa Virus
Agricultural Diseases
Dissemination

14. ANTIBIOTICS, INTERFERON & VACCINES
General
Cell Wall Disruption
Cell Membrane Disruption
Protein Synthesis Interference
Nucleic Acid Synthesis Interference
Intermediate Metabolite Interference
Drug Resistance
Interferons
Vaccines

PART V

15. EMPLOYMENT
    General
    Munition Packaging
    Terrain
    Weather
        Continental USA Wind Patterns
    Nature of Target
    Persistence
    Agent Selection

16. DETECTION
    General
    Instrumentation
    Odor/Symptoms
    Chemical Indicators
    Miscellaneous

17. PROTECTION
    Warning
    Aerosol vs. Gas
    Protective Masks
    Protective Clothing
        Permeable
        Nonpermeable
        Miscellaneous
    Maintenance
    Vehicles
    Installations & Fortifications
    Biologicals

PART VI

18. TREATMENT
    General- FIRST AID
    Toxic Chemical Agents
        Nerve Agents
        Blood Agents
        Choking Agents
        Blistering Agents
    Incapacitating Agents
        Physical Incapacitants
        Psychoactive Agents
    Incendiary Agents
    Biological Agents

19. DECONTAMINATION
    General
    Materials
    Personnel
    Equipment
    Facilities
    Chemical Agents
        Nerve
        Blood
        Choking
        Blistering
        Arsenicals
        Incapacitants
        Smoking/Obscurants
    Biological Agents

PART VII

20. THE CHEMICAL CORPS, U.S. ARMY
    Origins
    Policy
    Organization
    Mission
    Research & Development
    Personnel
    Specified Commands and R&D Facilities
    Biosafety Levels
    Training
    Worldwide Distr. Cold War Chemical Units

21. TRAINING & EDUCATION

PART VIII

22. FUTURE OUTLOOK, TWENTY-FIRST CENTURY AGENTS
    General
    Key Points of Future CBWT R&D
    Biochemical Agents
    Physical Incapacitants
    Psychoactive Agents
    Smoke/Obscurants
    Biological Agents
    Likely Users & Targets

23. CIVILIAN DEFENSE
    General
    Chemical Agents
        Detection .
        Protection
        Decontamination
    Biological Agents
        Antimicrobial Chemical Agents
        Antimicrobial Nonchemical Agents
        Decontamination
    Sealed Room Design

24. CONVENTIONS, TREATIES, RULE of LAW and TERRORISTS
    General
    Principals of War (and Terrorism)

25. CONCLUSIONS
    Radiological Threats

FURTHER READINGS
APPENDICES
    Appendix A: Glossary
    Appendix B: Addresses of Direct Sources
    Appendix C: How to Read Chemical Formulas
        Chapter 2
        Chapter 3
        Chapter 4
        Chapter 5
        Chapter 6
        Chapter 7
        Chapter 8
        Chapter 9
        Chapter 10
        Chapter 11
        Chapter 14
        Chapter 18
        Chapter 22

INDEX

PREFACE

In 1917, the world was initiated to the specter of Chemical Warfare. Through the 1991 Persian Gulf War, the horror of chemical warfare loomed over the heads of troops who engaged each other on the battle field. With the 1945 detonation of two nuclear fission weapons over Japan, a new age in warfare dawned-- global nuclear war, potential annihilation of the human race.

Aside from nuclear war, nothing about modern war evokes more horror than the potential of chemical and biological warfare (CBW). Few in western society have ever experienced such warfare first hand. Though man's experience with nuclear war is confined to a few days in August 1945, historical accounts of nuclear war as seen from the ashes of Hiroshima or Nagasaki are the only official experience and record. The perception in the public consciousness of what CBW is holds horrifying images of badly blistered bodies, frozen in grotesque poses resulting from convulsing musculature in the death throes. In the minds of many, chemical and biological warfare does not evoke the same global concepts of instant, blinding death associated with nuclear war, but rather, of slow agonizingly painful death.

The fear that chemical warfare itself and now terrorism arouses in the minds of the public and even modern day troops is fueled by WWI newsreel footage of the carnage that took place in the trench warfare in France. Those troops were ill trained and ill equipped to deal with such assaults. More recently, the news films of the 1988 murder of Iraqi Kurdish civilians at Iraqi President Saddam Hussein's order using poison gas only heightened this psychological terror in the newsreel viewing public. Little thought is given to the fact that those unfortunate victims of a lunatic were themselves also ignorant of the facts of chemical terrorism, untrained and unequipped to deal with it. The absence of credible medical expertise and medicinals only guaranteed and sealed their fate. That publicized incident underscores the real vulnerability and fear laid bare in the consciousness of a grossly defenseless population.

The controversy over the use of defoliants in Vietnam and the resulting cases of cancer in the servicemen handling such chemical agents only added to the fear of chemicals as weapons of war. The classical symbol for poison is the skull and crossed bones. The image of chemical and biological warfare goes beyond that symbolism. CBW carries with it the very image of the Four Horsemen of the Apocalypse.

But why should chemical and biological warfare rival nuclear warfare in its promise of horror and misery? Perhaps because the public has become desensitized to nuclear war. Perhaps the dawning of a thaw and the seeming end to the Cold War with the introduction in the late 1980s of *glasnost* and *perestroika* and subsequent events in the whole Eastern Block, have raised hopes that nuclear war is now much less likely...

During the 1962 Cuban Missile Crisis, Americans old enough to remember it thought "so this is how it will end." Many Americans began to think that there is no defense (a view not held by U.S. Military Training). They felt they would be instantly incinerated in the blinding flash of the nuclear fireball itself.[1] A resignation, born of growing up in the shadow of the Bomb, led to a gradual,

---

[1] This is certainly true only if one is at ground zero or within the thermal effects radius of the incandescent fireball.

fatalistic acceptance of instant oblivion during the first few moments of a nuclear war.[2] As a result, the view that gradually and subconsciously emerged was that nuclear war for the vast majority of humanity would be mercifully instant death and the public has no control over any of it. CBW promised no such easy, quick end, though here too, the public has no control over any of it.

Biological warfare itself carries images born of human experience with general human disease. The thought of war weapons that not only make you "sick as a dog," but also, lead to one's inevitable death, lying in a pool of one's own vomit and excrement only added a sense of indignity to the agony of slow tortuous death. Movies such as the fictional *Andromeda Strain* or *OUTBREAK* emphasized the consequences of untreatable, run-away infections that disfigured, maimed and killed people in a hideous wholesale fashion. It underscored the inherent limitations of man's ability to perceive, understand and control the denizens of the microscopic world. The movies' ends, however, were pure Hollywood. Microbes are not so cooperative and not so easily defeated as our present experience with the HIV (Human Immunovirus) reminds us yet again, and they are perhaps much more adaptive than man can ever hope to be. This last point is underscored by the near panic in knowledgeable medical circles over the increasing resistance many bacteria are now displaying to decades old and tested antibiotics.

There are many books available on CBW. Regrettably, essentially all are written with a scientifically or militarily literate reader in mind. The majority of the public, educated as they are, are not chemists, microbiologists or physicians. Additionally, many of the books predate our present knowledge and understanding of the biochemical effects these agents have on the human, though that understanding remains largely spotty still. What few books that do address the biochemical specifics of injury are rather technical. Those with limited or no military or scientific background are swamped in the technicalities which assume a military or scientific background. The usual questions remain. When did its use begin? What is it? Why is it used? How does it work? What are the agents used? How do they affect the exposed person? Is there a treatment? A defense? Can one destroy these agents? What all these works omit is an integrated explanation of how chemical and biological agents affect the human system. As an example, toxic chemical agents cause chemical injuries. But what exactly is a chemical injury? Why is a chemical injury potentially lethal? Little wonder that the questions cited and still more abound in the public mind.

Lethal Mists intends to fill a broad gap in the subject of chemical and biological warfare and terrorism as usually presented. *Lethal Mists* attempts to draw together the selectively applicable body of information from diverse fields of science into one cohesive treatise. An integration of military science with the sciences of chemistry and microbiology is the focus of this work. Its goal is to present this broad, multidisciplinary subject in a concise, readable form, understandable to the educated and interested citizen regardless of his or her scientific or military background. This work will be basic to the knowledgeable scientist or military practitioner of modern CBW operations. Even so, it may put matters into a different perspective or raise a point or two not clearly considered or consciously recognized.

Lethal Mists intends to remove the mystery from and therefore, the blind terror of the unknown associated with CBW. This book will explain in the simplest terms possible, what CBW is. How it is used, what it can and cannot do, what defenses there are, why it was used and what its future use may be, what means of detection exist, treatment available, and the means for dealing with it by the armed forces and even, by extension, the public. A minimum of military and technical terminology

---

[2] There are classical psychological experiments with rats in which rats that must respond to a signal to avoid electroshocks manifest signs of stress. Those rats which have no control over the electroshock process adopt a passive, nonreactive behavior, taking the shocks as they come with seeming detachment.

is used and it is clearly defined when used.

What I do is explain the basis of chemical agent action on the body at the cellular level. This explanation is, to my knowledge, quite rare among the various works already on library shelves, many dated, others recent, but all generally neglecting this aspect of chemical agent action, certainly in lay terms. To better explain the chemical basis of injury, a small discussion of chemical bonding and interactions is required. Every attempt is made to keep it simple but technically correct within the confines of the imposed simplicity. Formulas and chemical properties of chemical agents and antidotes are also provided for a better understanding of these materials' chemical nature for those wishing to go that far.

Selected biological agents provide the reader with the properties and effects of these microbes on the body. The examples given are by no means complete. Rather they provide a sampling of the types of agents that are likely candidates for development as biological agents. That development will surely seek the advantages afforded by advances in genetic and bioengineering.

Medical aspects of agent treatment are for the most part brief but accurate in their scope. Exact details are not given. Rather, a general overview of symptoms and basic treatment methods are presented. The fundamentals are there, the nitty-gritty is not. The interested reader may access some of the details from any medical source dealing with such toxicological matters or from the technical memoranda cited under the Military History and Science section of the references.

Lethal Mists will not provide the details or ingredients for the formulation and manufacture of toxic chemical agents. Though this knowledge and information probably can be gleaned from the technical literature, it is not the author's intent to provide that information in concise form and by so doing aid the unscrupulous few in any society, who are otherwise incapable of understanding the technicalities, or lack the judgement and integrity to leave well enough alone, but who can follow recipes. Chemical and biological agents are not curios to be tampered with.

Lethal Mists is the story of chemical and biological warfare and terrorism, its agents, chemistry and biochemistry, training, equipment, doctrine, employment, treatment, detection, decontamination, and its future-- the Twenty-First Century threats.

Eric R. Taylor, Ph.D.
Biochemistry

ACKNOWLEDGMENTS

Certainly no book on a technical or controversial subject is uniquely and solely the labor of its author. Many people of varying skills and knowledge contribute a measure of themselves to the completed work, though they may not have contributed a single written line. It is to all such professionals of vastly different fields of expertise that I make acknowledgment of their assistance to the completion of this work.

My most heartfelt thanks are given to my wife, Jacqueline, who has been my inspiration since the day I met her and who encouraged me to write this book. I thank the following individuals for their contributions: Linda Randolph (owner) and Linnie LaFleur of Dixie Surplus of Lafayette, Louisiana for their cooperation and permission in the making of some of the photographs of the protective equipment shown in this book, Daniel E. Spector, Ph.D., Command Historian, U.S. Army Chemical School for historical reference material on the Chemical Corps, Joe A. Swischer, U.S. Army Chemical Research, Development and Engineering Center, Aberdeen Proving Ground, for supplementary information on carbon filters and other literature. I wish to acknowledge the kind permission of Williams & Wilkins, the publisher of Stedman's Medical Dictionary, 25th Ed. for permission to reproduce many of the definitions appearing in the glossary. I offer my appreciation to my colleagues who took time out from their many duties and responsibilities to read portions of the manuscript applicable to their field of expertise: Drs. August A. Gallo (Organic Chemistry) and Karen Wiechelman (Biochemist), Department of Chemistry, and Dr. Joseph Sobek (Microbiology), Professor of Microbiology, Department of Biology. I thank Mr. Charles F. Hamsa, and Anna Jane Marks, of the Dupre Library, University of Southwestern Louisiana for their assistance in acquiring many references and Mr. Nelson Robinson, former Meteorologist, KATC-TV, and Director/President, Alert Weather Services, Lafayette, LA. for the quarterly wind vector maps. Finally, I owe a debt of gratitude to Drs. Richard Perkins, Professor of Physical Chemistry, and James Wilson, late Professor of English, for reading the entire manuscript for its continuity and adherence to the rules of writing and the English Language. Any errors remaining are my fault. Finally a special thanks to Leslie Kinsland, Instructor of Chemistry, University of Southwestern Louisiana, who had the equipment and know-how to convert figures and photos to electronic media format.

PART I

Such I hold to be the genuine use of gunpowder;
that it makes all men alike tall.
            Thomas Carlyle, 1795-1881[1]

INTRODUCTION

In the book *CHEMISTRY*, W.B. Noyes, Jr. notes that World War I (WWI) has been called the chemists' war and World War II (WWII), the physicists' war. If the credit for the successes in war may be laid at the feet of any scientific discipline,[2] then Operation Desert Storm may be called the computer scientists' war. Smart bombs, cruise missiles, stealth and other sophisticated hardware certainly held the public and media spellbound to the graphic images of the successes of these electronic brain weaponry.[3] Numerous analyses of after action reports, films, etc. have questioned the idealized accuracy of such smart weapons since the end of the Persian Gulf conflict. The essentials of their successes probably hold within the limits of mass production quality controls. Every generation has sought the latest weapon to best its enemy on the field of battle-- regardless of whether that field is in fact a field, the sea, the air, or perhaps yet to come, the depths of space itself.

Man's history, and no doubt his prehistory as well, is heavily blood stained. The only animal on earth with the intelligence to plan his fellow specie's death, he has an ever growing list of conquests. From cave dwelling days when he used rocks and tree limbs to bash in his adversary's head, through the development of the lance, battle ax, bow and arrow, to the advent of gunpowder and the development of the firearm, the cannon and from these the aerial bomb and missile, man has devoted much of his intelligence and energy to finding a better and more lethal way to dispatch his enemies.

Each new weapon or weapon system has seen a further escalation by his adversary to develop a countermeasure. This does not necessarily have to be a new weapon, though it generally is. The Gatling gun and from it the machine gun answered the need for significant firepower to support troops in the defense and later in the attack. It was in WWI that the machine gun became just such a weapon. The tank evolved from a need for an armored vehicle that could provide protection against machine gun fire. And of course, man developed the antitank gun to neutralize the tank. But the need for a weapon that did not rely on the standard principles of direct (small arms) or indirect (artillery) fire, but could reach the enemy in entrenched positions, quickly surfaced in WWI. Poison gas complied with all these requirements. Inexpensive, effective and with the added benefit as a harassment and terror weapon, poison gas quickly gripped the trench warfare of France in its pungent, misty and lethal embrace.

Chemical, and to a historically lesser degree biological, warfare represents a further development in the age old quest to best an enemy on the field of battle. Chemical and biological warfare makes

---

[1] In *The Harvest of a Quiet Eye*, by Alan L. Mackay, Crane, Russak & Co., Inc., New York, 1977, p. 30.

[2] Such attributions on the surface appear to ignore the sacrifices of the foot soldier.

[3] The Patriot Antimissile missile system has certainly been one focus of controversy.

use of chemicals and biological microorganisms to poison, kill or incapacitate an enemy. A nation need not be a major power, militarily or economically, to field chemical weapons. In fact, a dissident group can field chemical and biological weapons. Such groups are called terrorists and their actions directed against unarmed, defenseless civilians, terrorism. All that is required is basic industrial chemicals and sources, knowledgeable experts and the determination to produce, package, stock and ultimately, use such weapons. For nations or lawless groups completely without the means to fund and pursue a nuclear weapons program, chemical, and to a lesser extent, biological weapons, give the "poor man" a significant boost in his military capabilities, and force major powers to take such nations as serious military threats, not to be casually dismissed.

Perhaps the most hazardous aspect to chemical weapon development is storage. Modern chemical weapons now come packaged as binary weapons, that is, two separate compartments each housing one of the two components that, when mixed, form the chemical weapon agent itself at the time of use. This method of packaging has increased the overall safety of storage and handling of such munitions.

Chemical warfare and terrorism (CW) is not just the poisonous chemicals used. CW is principles of employment, defenses against it, and methods of detoxifying or decontamination. It is the use of incendiaries, employment of incapacitating agents and the use of smoke munitions for concealment. Any war in which explosives, firearms, fuels, incendiaries, etc. are employed is the chemists' war. All these chemical components require research and development involving hundreds or thousands of chemists. By historical default, conventional munitions, though effective only because of the chemists' genius, are not classified as chemical weapons. It is not necessarily the explosive charge but the projectiles of such explosions that kill. Chemical weapons by their design and formulation are immediate agents of injury and death. They are designed solely to be so.

Biological warfare and terrorism (BW) does not necessarily have to be used against enemy troops only. BW actually is most effective against civilian targets and its employment against such targets becomes a strategic weapon whose aim is to destroy a peoples' ability and will to wage war or resist. In that regard, its use strikes at water supplies, food production capacity and general public health. BW rivals nuclear war in its potential for far-reaching and long term consequences, adversely affecting water and food purity, public health and equally as devastating, the public psyche. Just as those surviving nuclear war must face the onslaught of radiation poisoning and the popularized theoretical concept of nuclear winter, those surviving the initial firefights of war with biological weapons must face the onslaught of two prominent Horsemen of the Apocalypse-- famine and pestilence-- both always riding side-by-side with war and death.

If the employment of bombs, artillery and missiles with standard high explosive warheads is termed **conventional warfare** and the use of nuclear weapons, **nuclear warfare**, then the use of toxic chemical and biological weapons can be, and is, termed **unconventional warfare**. But warfare, however labeled, is deadly and indiscriminate. The innocent as well as the principal participants suffer the consequences of man's ingrained inhumanity to man.

Chemical warfare, for all its horrible images of WWI, does not tear arms or legs from its victim or blast fist size holes through a man's chest. To be sure, chemical agents can cause serious and even fatal injuries in unprotected persons. But chemical agents do give warning before they become lethal. Artillery, bomb, or missile shrapnel or the ever present bullet do not.

CHAPTER 1

HISTORY

To understand a science it is necessary to know its history.
-*Positive Philosophy*, Auguste Comte, 1798-1857[4]

Chemical and biological warfare has a history dating back thousands of years. The use of poison tipped arrows among prehistoric peoples, continuing even today in the jungles of South America and Southeast Asia was perhaps the earliest use. This use was by accidental discovery and reflected no understanding or planned search for such lethal or incapacitating substances. Man learned by pain of accidental experience what hurt him and he quickly recognized it could also be used to hurt (or kill) his game or enemy. In this regard, primitive man learned that fire was a useful defense against the wilderness and its denizens of the night. His observance of the destruction and death visited by forest fires also registered in his primitive mind. On a large enough scale, fire, too, is a weapon of mass destruction. When man established villages with wood, earth and grass structures, conflicts between villages or tribes often ended in the victor torching the domains of the vanquished. Thus was born incendiary usage in warfare. The huge volumes of choking smoke also registered with him when down wind. Perhaps such effluents could be used to drive into the open, enemies safely entrenched in enclosed fortifications.

It may have been a leap in primitive technology when other substances besides simple wood fire gases were used against an enemy. About 423 B.C. the Spartans burned sulfur and pitch to release the gas sulfur dioxide, today a component of smog, representing the first recorded use of gas in war. In the seventh century A.D. the Greeks developed what is called Greek fire, a deliberate formulation of probably rosin, sulfur, pitch, naphtha, lime and saltpeter. The material burned very well and floated on water. It proved very effective in naval battles. In 184 B.C., Hannibal, a brilliant ancient tactician, studied by all military students around the world, used earthen jars filled with poisonous snakes, tossing them into the ships of his Pergamene enemies. This may be taken as the first recorded use of biological weapons in war.

In the days of knights, the hot oil poured over castle walls on assaulting forces heralded perhaps the first regular use of antipersonnel incendiary chemicals directly against enemy troops. Though primitive by modern standards, it was nonetheless very effective on those receiving such showers. Torching of villages was a common practice and its employment constitutes incendiary warfare. Today's use of flamethrowers, napalm, thermite, phosphorus and other incendiary devices continues that military tradition and these devices also fall under the category of chemical warfare.

About 1854, Sir Lyon Playfair proposed the use of cyanide filled shells to end the siege at Sebastopol in the Crimean War. His suggestion was declined on humane grounds. Sir Lyon's reaction to the charge of its inhuman use was how much more humane are shells filled with molten metal producing "the most frightful modes of death." Interestingly, in 1862 during the American Civil War, John W. Doughty of New York, proposed the use of chlorine gas against Confederate forces. Some

---

[4] In Harvest of a Quiet Eye, p. 38

fifty three years later, the Germans would themselves use chlorine in France.

Modern chemical warfare has its roots principally in WWI where it enjoyed its first scientifically developed agents with specifically sought effects such as choking and blistering. This development came on the heals of the impressive growth of knowledge in inorganic chemistry of the late nineteenth century and the increasing knowledge of organic chemistry blooming during the early twentieth century. The Germans were the major players in the development of chemical knowledge as solutions to practical problems. Haber, a German chemist, developed the Haber process, essentially used today, in manufacturing ammonia from atmospheric nitrogen. The ammonia is a critical ingredient in fertilizers for agriculture and also a critical precursor in the manufacture of gunpowder and explosives. Some of the best chemists of the world were German. The German chemical industry and knowledge base and their ability to apply chemistry to the solution of practical problems, both civil and military was impressive. The German High Command, *Der Oberkommand des Heeres*, were receptive and quick to grasp new technology and weaponry.

On 22 April, 1915 at Ypres, Belgium, the Germans made the first large scale employment of chlorine against the French and British. The Germans also introduced the Allied Forces to phosgene in December, 1915. They released 88 tons of phosgene causing more than 1000 allied casualties. In 1917 the Germans used mustard gas for the first time. Throughout 1917 and 1918, both sides used mustard gas against each other in large quantities, causing some 400,000 casualties before the war's end. In July, 1916, during the Somme offensive, the French employed hydrogen cyanide filled artillery shells, its first known use in a war. Additionally, both sides employed tear gases which served a harassment role. Again, the Germans were principal players in developing tearing agents.[5]

WWII was free of poisonous gas use in the European Theater though the Asian Theater saw Japanese employment between 1937 and 1943 in China. The Italians used chemical agents[6] against the Ethiopians in the Abyssinian Campaign in 1936. It was during WWII that the Germans developed nerve agents which proved to be the most poisonous of the man-made chemical agents. The Germans never used them in combat. The reasons may be that Hitler himself suffered from mustard gas wounds in WWI, and they thought the US had similar nerve agents and would use them if the German forces employed them. FDR made it clear to Hitler what US response would be if toxic chemical weapons were used against Allied Forces.

The nerve agents were the product of the mind of the German chemist Dr. Gerhardt Schrader of the IG Farben works. The were developed as a pesticide to improve agricultural yields in the early 1930s. Its enhanced poisonous nature was discovered early on in its R&D when workers suffered severe and even lethal effects from the stuff. The first formulation was named Tabun. In 1938 Schrader's group synthesized Sarin, the second organophosphate of remarkable lethality. The third agent called Soman was made in 1944. It was these agents and their then unparalleled lethality that led to post war development of other nerve agents by the US military designated V-agents. The V-agents exhibited toxicities ten times that of Sarin. Sarin was used in March 1995 in a Tokyo subway against Japanese commuters. In 1958 the US Military selected a particular V-agent designated VX as its premier nerve agent. The original German preparations, were retained by the US Army but renamed GA (Tabun), GB (Sarin), and GD (Soman). A forth G agent with no formally recognized military name was named GF.

Though few documented cases have been made, charges were made that the U.S. used chemical

---

[5] The first tearing agent was named T-Stoff (German for T-stuff).

[6] Phosgene, mustard (see Chapter 4) and Lacrimators (see Chapter 9).

and biological weapons in Korea and China during the Korean War.[7] Additionally, the 1963-67 Civil War in Yemen found Egypt accused of using poison gas (mustard). There also have been charges of poison gas usage in the various brush fire wars in Laos, Kampuchea, Angola, Vietnam (between Vietnam and China), Afghanistan, Ethiopia, Iran vs. Iraq (mustard gas and Tabun nerve agent), El Salvador, Lebanon, and Thailand.

The use of chemical agents by the United States in the South Vietnamese War was in the form of defoliants, tearing and vomiting agents in addition to the traditionally acceptable phosphorus and thermite grenades as well as napalm.

Biological warfare in ancient times consisted chiefly of throwing diseased cadavers over fortification walls. The Tartars as an example, employed the dead of plague in the Crimea against the Genoese in 1346. Contamination of water holes and rivers with such bodies also was common practice. The American Indian was particularly susceptible to smallpox and millions died from it. Deliberate infection of enemy camps occurred in 1763 when the British Commander in the Colonies, Sir Jeffrey Amherst, proposed a smallpox infection of certain Indian tribes. The battle of Vicksburg of the American Civil War found retreating Confederate troops herding animals into ponds, killing them and leaving the carcasses to putrefy, thus denying advancing Union forces potable water. Japan according to at least one account was active in the development of biological weapons during WWII.[8] WWII Japan began an aggressive search for an effective biological warfare weapon in 1937 that continued to the end of the war in August 1945. The location of the laboratory facility, code named Unit 731, was about 40 miles south of Harbin, Manchuria. The biological microbes studied made up an infamous Who's Who of the deadly denizens of the microscopic world. Those agents included: anthrax, botulism, glanders, plague, small pox, tularemia, typhoid and typhus. The test subjects were not animals, but human, allied prisoners of war, nearly 1000 of whom died as a result of their guinea pig status with the Japanese. The work of Unit 731 may explain the 1940 outbreak of bubonic plague that befell China and Manchuria. Japanese planes overflew regions of those countries dropping infected fleas and grain. The grain served to attract rats which are excellent hosts for the fleas. Since rats inhabit human environments, the fleas were able to infest and pass on infections to people. There is at least one WWII account of the use of botulism toxin to assassinate Reinhard Heydrich, the *Reichsprotektor* of Bohemia and Moravia.[9]

The British experimented with anthrax themselves, contaminating the island of Gruinard of the coast of Scotland in 1942. To this day, the island is uninhabitable by man or beast. The US developed a method to isolate botulinus toxin, a natural product produced by the bacteria *Clostridium botulinum*. So toxic is this bacterial substance that 1000 molecules will kill a mouse. Means nothing to you? A pint, 1.1 pounds, 500 grams, of pure toxin will kill an estimated 100 million tons of animal life.

Perhaps the first modern-day, indirect employment of biological agents against enemy troops

---

[7] No Fire, No Thunder, Sean Murphy, Alastair Hay and Steven Rose, Monthly Review press, New York, 1989, p. 15-16

[8] Japan's Secret Weapon, Barclay Newman, Current Publishing Co., New York, 1944

[9] No Fire, No Thunder, p. 30-31

occurred in the Vietnam War. The Viet Cong had a practice of dipping punji sticks[10] in human and animal excrement, and other filth and placing those septic sticks point up, in small excavated holes along trails and along the shoulders of trails, covering these traps with thin brush coverings to conceal them. The hapless soldier, walking on the trail and coming under ambush fire, became impaled when diving for cover. These punji stick traps impaled an arm, leg or foot, or perhaps his abdomen. Even though the wound may not have been serious in itself, the resulting injury from the septic dip of the punji stick could cause serious, difficult to control infections.

Aside from these examples and others not cited here, biological agents, as a scientifically developed and deliberately employed weapon, have, to date, not been used. Much of the post WWII era has concentrated on treaty bans and international efforts to thwart third world development of CB weapons. U.S. efforts have centered on research and development. These pursuits have principally provided intelligence on agents, mode of action, capabilities, limitations, antidotes, treatment including vaccines and insight into the then Soviet or other potential adversary capabilities, activities and doctrine.

In *No Fire, No Thunder*, the authors provide a concise synopsis of international prohibitions against CBW.[11] On 16 December, 1971 the UN General Assembly approved a treaty drawn up by the 1971 Geneva Disarmament Conference. The United States signed on 10 April, 1972 and the U.S. Senate ratified it and the 1925 Geneva Protocol (to which the U.S. previously had not subscribed) on 16 December, 1974. However, on 25 November, 1969, then President Richard Nixon, on his own authority as Commander-in-Chief, had renounced the use of biological weapons by the U.S. He also ordered such U.S. stocks destroyed. To the extent that a Presidential Order made by one President is binding on succeeding Presidents, the U.S. has followed these Presidential and signed treaty bans at this writing. However, since WWI, neither the U.S. Armed Forces nor the American public have been deliberately attacked with chemical or biological agents. What U.S. policy and American public demands will become under such circumstances remains to be seen. A glimpse of likely US action toward a hostile state employing biological weapons against us may be found in the sentiment raised on the floors of the US House and Senate of the Congress. Nuclear retaliation may not be considered excessive.

THE SCIENCES

> There is no national science just as there is no national
> multiplication table; what is national is no longer science.
> -V. P. Pononarev[12]

Throughout the ages, man has consistently had one overriding question of the world around him: Why? He has always wondered at the sky. He saw points of light he later determined are stars,

---

[10] In Harvest of Death, the authors argue that the use of punji sticks appears to be only a defensive weapon. [This author's note: Any weapon may be defensively or offensively employed. It is still a weapon, and septic laden implements are then, by definition, the delivery systems for such biological weapons, however unsophisticated they may be.]

[11] No Fire, No Thunder, p. 76-87

[12] in *The Harvest of a Quiet Eye,* p. 33

essentially no different than the sun, though much larger, brighter and further away. He wondered why it rained. He wondered why he became ill. These and countless thousands of questions have and are still being asked and answered. As his knowledge increases, his questions become more probing, but remain the same-- Why?

He has organized his queries of nature and his self-made world into the sciences: astronomy, physics, chemistry, biology, medicine and engineering. He has learned much of the solar system and landed on the moon. He has learned the cause of his historical illnesses and through chemistry and biology, developed specific weapons (antibiotics) to attack these causes. He has learned to construct ships, automobiles and the airplane. He has learned how to construct dwellings that rival the Tower of Babel in size. Yet for all his genius and handiwork, he has not learned to control his fear, distrust and even hatred for his fellow man.

His automobile technology have spawned tanks. His airplanes now include bombers, rockets and missiles. His ships of trade brought forth battleships, aircraft carriers and nuclear submarines. His understanding of chemistry and biology has led to sophisticated poisons which he uses against his own kind as well as the vermin. The scientist in him sought, discovered and gave mankind tools to improve its lot. The predator in him has applied and furthered those tools to the use as weapons of human destruction. He has instituted governments for a better life and those governments have instituted war. What is supposedly a national secret cannot long remain so. Today's advantage of a nation against its rivals becomes the ability of its foe tomorrow. The scientific endeavor always seeks to push against the frontier of knowledge. The predator in man's institutions always seeks a military application.

THE MILITARY

On 19 August 1991, Mikhail Gorbachev, President of the Soviet Union, was deposed from office by elements of the KGB[13] and Soviet Army. The U.S. in particular has always prided itself in its own military forces remaining absolutely subordinate and obedient to the civilian authority, legitimately elected by we, the people. Additionally, the military of the United States has always followed a hands off policy with regard to the participation in the formulation of national policy. There are some examples which cast doubt on the U.S. government's sense of detachment and responsibility to the safety of its own members and the public as a whole.[14]

Perhaps because of its obedience, the U.S. military has always been the beneficiary of U.S. technology and the genius of its civilian scientists and engineers. Probably no better example of this benefit can be offered than the Manhattan Engineer District, 1941-1945, the development of the Atomic Bomb. More recent examples of the genius and competency of American scientists and engineers is found in the so-called smart weapons so dramatically showcased in the air war phase of the Persian Gulf Operation Desert Storm.

Only the most un-American American would begrudge the U.S. military for benefitting from the technical know-how of its scientific community. However, as with the 1945 Atom Bomb drops over

---

[13] Komitet Gosudarstvennoi Bezopasnosti, the state security police of the Soviet Union and its version of the CIA.

[14] Post WWII exposure of servicemen to direct radiation from nuclear burst tests, defoliant usage in Vietnam, the Tuskegee Syphilis experiments on Black men, and the tests of biological agent contamination of population centers such as San Francisco and New York.

Japan, the question will always arise: because we can, should we?

The decision to use some weapon systems is in part dependent upon circumstances and the overall cost.[15] Peacetime moralizations often collapse under the immorality of war's conduct and the desire of each side to bring its sons home alive and as well as possible. The actions of the U.S. military, sanctioned by its civilian authority during Operation Desert Storm was in keeping with the clear desire of the people and the political leadership to bring as many of our servicemen and women home-- alive and well. It is in this regard that weapons systems can be used to prevent harm-- by the perceived threat of their use, their availability.

Since the end of WWII, the proliferation of nuclear weapons and delivery systems on both sides of the Iron Curtain has prevented nuclear war by the principle finally named MAD-- Mutually Assured Destruction. Neither side could be absolutely certain that a preemptive strike would truly be preemptive. So too, the possession of chemical weapons as well as nukes by the U.S. may well have stayed the hand of Saddam Hussein in using any chemical weapons capabilities he possessed simply because the U.S. possesses the ability to retaliate with more devastating chemical or even in the extreme, nuclear counter attack.[16] The point to be kept in mind is that whatever the weapon system in the hands of the military, that weapon can potentially be used given sufficient provocation. The possession of a weapon system can also be a deterrent. The deterrent value of a weapon system is only as strong and effective as the resolve to use it if provocation and escalation necessitates its use.

---

[15] The post WWII period witnessed a dramatic increase in the number of births in the U.S. alone. It is estimated that some 37 million baby-boomers were born in the period 1945 to 1950 or so. The decision to drop A-bombs on Japan was based in part on the clear fear of suffering one million casualties (probably dead) among U.S. servicemen if storming the beaches of mainland Japan were undertaken. The casualties taken by U.S. force in the island hopping campaigns of the Pacific and the steadily increasing bloodiness of the island invasions the closer to the mainland we came, raised horrifying prospects. A Normandy style invasion of Japan was considered to result in a slaughter of unimaginable proportions. Though some 200,000 Japanese died as a result of the two A-bombs dropped, certainly one million American servicemen's lives were spared by so doing. I and many of those 37 million others live and breath today solely because the use of the A-bomb was a decision made in favor of human life... both Japanese and American.

[16] There were suggestions, ever so subtly made by some U.S. political leaders that if Saddam Hussein employed chemical and/or biological weapons, the U.S. should consider tactical nuclear strikes against his forces.

PART II

CHAPTER 2

BIOLOGICAL MOLECULES

CHEMICAL FORMULA NOTATIONS & CONVENTIONS

Though it is not possible to present a course in chemistry and formula notations and conventions here, a limited explanation of the notations and conventions followed will be helpful to the inexperienced chemical literature reader. The Periodic Table of the Elements among other information provides the symbols of the elements used by all chemists around the world. The most common elements found in abundance in biological molecules are carbon (C), oxygen (O), nitrogen (N), sulfur (S), phosphorus (P) and hydrogen (H).

Each element possesses a specific number of covalent bonds. Hydrogen can form a single covalent bond with another element. Oxygen can form at most, two covalent bonds with another element and can also form a double bond with some others. The number of bonds an element may possess is often referred to as its valency and elements are referred to as being monovalent (one bond), divalent (two bonds), trivalent (three bonds), tetravalent (four bonds), etc. Thus, hydrogen is monovalent; oxygen, divalent. Carbon is tetravalent and nitrogen is trivalent[1] or tetravalent. Sulfur and phosphorus are capable of much more complex valencies for reasons which concern the electronic structure of the element and their ability to accommodate many more bonding electrons. In biological systems, sulfur is divalent[2] in some cases, hexavalent[3] in others. Phosphorus is only found in the pentavalent[4] state in the form of phosphate in biological systems. Trivalent phosphorus (known generically as phosphines[5]) are quite toxic to biological systems.

---

[1] Nitrogen can be tetravalent when employing its lone electron pair, usually with a positively charged specie such as a hydrogen ion or a carbocation (positive carbon specie). Such tetravalency leads to the forming of a fourth bond between nitrogen and another element of the moiety, giving rise to what is called coordinate covalent bonds- bonds in which the electrons necessary for the bond are exclusively provided by the nitrogen. Such tetravalent nitrogen species are themselves positively charged (cations).

[2] Sulfur is divalent in the amino acids cysteine and methionine as well as certain other important intermediate metabolites.

[3] Sulfur is hexavalent in the sulfate moiety which finds use in certain detoxifying processes.

[4] Phosphorus is pentavalent in the phosphate moiety commonly found in the nucleic acids, both in monomer units such as ATP and the polymers such as RNA and DNA.

[5] The parent compound is phosphine, PH_3. As P is a member of group V of the Periodic Table, this compound bears similarities to the nitrogen analog, ammonia, NH_3.

Additionally, certain chemical groups are often treated as a single entity in chemical formulations. The naming scheme (nomenclature) of organic compounds follows the rules established by the IUPAC (International Union of Pure and Applied Chemists). Examples include: the methyl groups (-CH_3 or H_3C-), the methylene group (-CH_2-), the ether linkage (C-O-C), the thioether group (C-S-C), the hydroxyl group (-OH), the thiol group (-SH), the primary amino group (-NH_2 or H_2N-), and the secondary amino group (C-NH-C). Also certain amino compounds have a nitrogen-carbon double bond. This specie is called an imino group (-C=N-). The subscripted numbers mean that the element or group of atoms of a polyatomic[6] system preceding the subscript is taken that many times in the formula notation. Thus the methyl group consists of one carbon and three hydrogen atoms in a covalent moiety. When all bonds between carbon and the other elements to which it is bonded are single covalent bonds, the maximum number of attached atoms (ligands) is four. An example of this is natural gas, methane (CH_4). Such carbons possessing four other attached atoms in single covalent bonds are referred to as saturated.

Unsaturated carbon compounds are those in which multiple bonds[7] exist on the carbons. Simple examples of these types of compounds are ethylene (CH_2CH_2) and acetylene (C_2H_2) in which a carbon-carbon double bond and carbon-carbon triple bond occur respectively. Compounds may also possess doubly bonded oxygen, sulfur or nitrogen to a carbon.

Furthermore, certain cyclic systems are given specific names. The pentagon shaped ring composed of five saturated carbon atoms is cyclopentane [I]. Saturated six membered rings are cyclohexanes [II]. Saturated four carbon member rings are cyclobutanes [III] and the smallest possible cyclic carbon ring system is that of the saturated three carbon member ring of cyclopropane [IV].

The convention followed in the writing of these structures is to omit the attached hydrogens. Thus for cyclopentane [I] there are two hydrogens on each carbon; the carbons are represented by the vertices of the geometric figure drawn. An attached non-hydrogen atom or group of atoms is represented by that atom or group symbol. The other hydrogen present remains omitted.

A further point that is important to the biological activity of a particular compound is its shape, referred to by chemists as its conformation. Cyclic ring compounds are generally drawn as flat geometric structures on paper. In fact, only cyclopropane is literally flat in its conformation of the ring system. Cyclobutane [V], cyclopentane [VI] and cyclohexane [VII] are nonplanar in conformation. As the number of carbons comprising the ring system increases, such ring compounds can approach planarity but because of bond angle constraints or thermal energy motions, almost never completely achieve it.

Unsaturated cyclic ring systems follow specific nomenclature schemes also formalized by the IUPAC. The above named saturated ring systems if possessing a single carbon-carbon double bond are known generically as cycloalkenes. The parent name is changed by dropping the -ane suffix and ending the root with -ene. Thus a monounsaturated derivative of cyclopentane is called cyclopentene. Diunsaturated cyclic compounds are termed cyclic dienes. A six carbon member ring with two carbon-carbon double bonds is called cyclohexadiene. A special case is the three carbon-carbon double bonded six member ring. This compound is not cyclohexatriene for complicated chemical reasons. It behaves vastly different from what chemists would expect of such a cycloalkene. This

---

[6] Meaning made up of more than one atom.

[7] Multiple bonds are two or three such covalent bonds between two elements.

special case is named benzene [VIII] and it the simplest member of a unique class of cyclic organic compounds generically known as aromatics.[8]

Another point concerning aromatics is the structural representation on paper. One of the points concerning the unique properties of aromatics is the phenomenon of resonance. Simply put, compounds whose structures can be written two or more different ways and yet represent the same compound exhibit resonance. Resonance actually addresses the behavior of bonding electrons in the compound. Benzene provides the simplest example of this process. Benzene can be written either as structure [VIII] or structure [IX]. Both representations signify the same compound-- benzene. The only difference between the two representations is the location of the single and double bonds. These two representations suggest a mobility of the bonds. In reality, the drawn representations as given in [VIII] and [IX] reflect the inability to draw a benzene structure in an accurate depiction using discrete single and double bonds. The convention often employed to better represent the actual bonding electrons distribution in the benzene molecule is given in [X]. The hexagon ring with an inscribed circle reflects the mobility of the electrons within and about the carbon-carbon bonding array. The circle denotes the delocalized nature of the doubly bonding electrons. It is this phenomenon of delocalized bonding electrons that is the basis of the incredible stability of benzene and other aromatic compounds to the usual chemical reactions that would assault normal double bonded systems such as in the cycloalkenes. Aromatic ring system compounds can be quite large, made up of two, three, four or more fused ring systems. Finally, aromatic ring systems are planar so long as no single bonds join two otherwise separate ring systems.

Element atoms other than carbon may be part of the closed ring systems of the examples above and if so, entirely different names are applied to these derivatives. Thus the elements of oxygen, nitrogen, and sulfur typically occur as a constituent of closed cyclic ring compounds found in biological systems and also in certain antibiotics, either naturally acquired or synthetically produced. Such cyclic compounds consisting of carbon and some other element are generically called heteronuclear cyclic compounds reflecting the inclusion of some other non-carbon atom as part of the ring system.

GENERAL

Since the human body is made of millions of chemical compounds, a number of chemical substances can chemically react with many of the biochemicals comprising its cells. Though external exposure brings skin into contact with harmful chemical agents, even inhalation or intravenous exposure[9] results in chemical agents coming first into contact with cell surfaces which are membranes. If the chemical agent can penetrate the membrane to reach the internal structures of the cell, the agent has a wide selection of structures or organelles with which to interact. The cells of all organisms

---

[8] Aromatics was the name given to these types of compounds because they often exhibited distinct fragrances. The term aromatic has now taken on special meaning to the chemist because of the unique chemical properties of this class of compounds. The electrons involved in the bonding of aromatic compounds (regardless of their having an odor or not) are not as susceptible to chemical reaction as other unsaturated carbon-carbon compounds. Aromatics are among some of the most unreactive or very difficult to react compounds and require very special conditions for chemical reactions on them.

[9] Blood is a protein rich medium and those proteins, albumin, globulins, etc., also may interact with blood dissolved chemical agents.

consist essentially of four main chemical groups. They are the proteins, carbohydrates, nucleic acids and the lipids.

Lipids and proteins constitute by far the majority of biochemical compounds of the animal body and its cells. This is because they serve so many and diverse roles in the cell for which these two classes of biomolecules turn out to be uniquely suited and thus, have been selected by evolutionary design. Additionally, these two classes are intimately involved in the structural framework of the cell. However, whereas protein is a class of biomolecules having a distinct chemical nature[10] consistent among all proteins, lipids are a general, broad and operational classification which rests not on a unique chemical nature, but rather similar chemical properties among several different chemical types that all behave, under certain conditions, alike. The conditions under which these kinds of compounds behave similarly is in their extraction with what are called "fat solvents". Such solvents are ethyl alcohol, chloroform, ether, petroleum ether and benzene. Thus the class of so-called lipids includes such diverse chemical species as fatty acids, triglycerides (body fat), and steroids such as cholesterol, its derived bile acids, and steroidal hormones such as the sex hormones.

Nucleic acids occur in two principal forms. They may be monomer units primarily used as an energy carrier[11] or they may serve as the building blocks for much larger systems known as polyribonucleotides (RNA) or polydeoxyribonucleotides (DNA). The DNA is the genetic storehouse. It codes the information for every minute facet of the cell and by extension, the entire organism. The RNA is the means by which the coded information of the DNA is translated to protein synthesis. RNA is a limited copy of the DNA. It is made by a process termed transcription. The RNA is the means by which protein is made in a process called translation.

Carbohydrates[12] are essentially an immediate energy source. They are used to derive ATP, the often called currency of life. Glucose and fructose (monomers) and sucrose (table sugar, a dimer of glucose and fructose) are the more common carbohydrates though more complex forms exist as polymers. Starch and glycogen are polymers of glucose as is cellulose. The difference between starch or glycogen and cellulose is that the former two are covalently chained in what is called an $\alpha(1-4)$ glycosidic linkage while cellulose is chained in a $\beta(1-4)$ glycosidic linkage.[13]

---

[10] The nature of chemical classes is actually referred to by chemists as the functional group which gives the class its unique form and properties of only that particular class of compounds.

[11] ATP, adenosine triphosphate, is the typical , but by no means the only example.

[12] Fats are a valuable energy source but serve as a reserve or emergency source of energy in times of fasting or starvation. When carbohydrate is available in sufficient quantity, fats are not metabolized for energy production.

[13] It is the $\alpha(1-4)$ linkage of starch that permits humans to digest starch. The enzyme found in saliva is called α-amylase which is active only on $\alpha(1-4)$ glycosidic linkages. The $\beta(1-4)$ linkage is not touched by α-amylase and therefore, polysaccharides possessing $\beta(1-4)$ glycosidic linkages are indigestible by humans. Foods containing cellulose serve only as roughage or fiber and have only a chemomechanical benefit in the human diet but no nutritional value.

CELL COMPONENTS

PROTEINS

Proteins are derived from individual monomer amino acid units, chained together in sometimes huge molecules generically termed polymers. Because proteins are formed by the condensation of a carboxylic acid end of one amino acid with the amino end of another amino acid, a chemically special unit is formed called an amide linkage. In biochemistry, this unique amide unit (derived solely from the condensation of amino acids) is termed a peptide linkage. Proteins are then also known as polypeptides in recognition of the polymerization of many peptide linkages.

Each amino acid unit of the protein possesses its own identity in the form of the so-called side chain that marks the distinction between the 20 common amino acids. This fact is shown in the general structure of an amino acid [XI].

The side chain denoted by the "R" in the generalized amino acid structure is the variant among the different amino acids and the differences between the amino acids arise as a consequence of these "R" group differences. There are at least five distinct classes of the amino acids based upon the unique chemical functional group properties of the "R" groups. Amino acids can be classified as polar, nonpolar, acidic, basic, and aromatic. These distinctions are for ease in noting the properties of the various amino acids and there is some overlap of these classes. One classification scheme can place the "R" groups of the common amino acids into the following divisions:

Table 2-1: A Classification of Amino Acids				
Acidic	Basic	Polar	Nonpolar	Aromatic
Aspartic Acid Glutamic Acid	Lysine Arginine Histidine	Serine Threonine Glutamine Asparagine Cysteine Glycine	Methionine Alanine Proline Leucine Valine Isoleucine	Phenylalanine Tyrosine Tryptophan

The sequence of amino acid groups comprising the protein is called its primary structure [XII]. When amino acids are written in the sequence in which they occur in a protein, their abbreviations are used. The amino acid and its abbreviation appear in Table 2-2.

The amino and carbonyl groups of the polypeptide chain fold about a "helical axis" resulting in a right handed helix. Some proteins adopt a form resembling corrugated sheet metal, called a pleated sheet in biochemistry. The pleated sheet or the helix are each examples of the secondary structure of a protein. It is the "R" groups of the amino acid units in the protein that give the protein its unique structural properties and most importantly, its functional role in the cell.

Proteins serve a wide range of roles in the cell. They are structural, that is, they provide support for body mass and such functioning proteins comprise bone, cartilage, and muscle. Others serve transport roles, that is, they are like conveyor belts in that they carry or afford the passage of critical materials through cell membranes or for that matter in the blood. Hemoglobin is a case in point. As a protein, globin covalently binds the heme unit which carries the iron atom, itself the binder of oxygen. Still others are important in a defense role for the body. The immunoglobulins, or antibodies, are the infantry of the immune system and are constantly on patrol, attacking and destroying foreign molecular materials inadvertently ingested or deposited to the blood. There are other roles served by proteins in the cell and body, but regardless of the protein's role and location in the cell or body, it is subject to chemical reaction with a wide variety of chemical agents which can destroy a protein, either its chemical integrity or its ability to serve its functional role.

Table 2-2: Abbreviations of Amino Acids	
Amino Acid	3-Letter Code
Alanine	Ala
Arginine	Arg
Asparagine	Asn
Aspartic Acid	Asp
Cysteine	Cys
Glutamic Acid	Glu
Glutamine	Gln
Glycine	Gly
Histidine	His
Isoleucine	Ile
Leucine	Leu
Lysine	Lys
Methionine	Met
Ornithine[14]	Orn
Phenylalanine	Phe
Proline	Pro
Serine	Ser
Threonine	Thr
Tryptophan	Trp
Tyrosine	Tyr
Valine	Val

LIPIDS

Lipids as a classification serve very diverse roles in the cell. Besides their major role in membrane composition and structure, lipids serve an energy source role and also a body insulation role as an adjunct to their energy role. Additionally, some hormones[15] are classified as steroidal lipids as they are essentially derivatives of cholesterol, the preeminent steroid. It is the lipids' role in membrane function that brings them into play as targets for toxic chemical agents. Membrane lipids consist primarily of what are called phospholipids [XIII]. Phospholipids possess a unique dual property in such a small molecule. It is both hydrophobic and hydrophilic. One end of the phospholipid is quite water soluble while the other end is quite water insoluble. It is this unique property of the phospholipids that make them ideally suited as the building blocks for membranes.

---

[14] Ornithine is not one of the 20 common amino acids found in proteins. It is an amino acid and is used in other biochemical processes.

[15] Examples include testosterone (male sex hormone) and estradiol and estrone (female sex hormones).

Phospholipids [XIII] consist of four components: a base, a phosphate group, a glycerol moiety and fatty acids. Of the three components, only the latter, the fatty acid constituent, is water insoluble. The solubility of the base end (called head) is enhanced by attached cationic bases or highly hydrophilic, neutral bases. Some examples are ethanolamine (cationic) [XIV], choline (cationic) [XV], glycerol (neutral, hydrophilic) [XVI], and inositol (hydrophilic, neutral) [XVII]. The lipid components of the cell membrane interact through hydrophobic interactions (see Forces section below). The tail portions of the phospholipids form what can be called a sea of hydrocarbons. Though there is no rigid structure to these hydrocarbon tails within the membrane, the forces interacting between the hydrocarbon tails of the phospholipids exclude water and this stabilizes the membrane architecture. Certain other lipids, notably cholesterol as an example, modify the fluid characteristics of the membrane. The embedded proteins, soluble in the hydrocarbon membrane sea because of surface hydrophobic groups, function in the membrane's overall permeability of various substances through it.

NUCLEIC ACIDS

Monomer nucleic acids consist of three components-- a phosphate, a sugar and a base. The bases are derivatives of two parent aromatic compounds, purine [XVIII] and pyrimidine [XIX]. Nucleic acids are best known as the DNA and RNA. But nucleic acids serve a much broader role in cell activity than simply the storing of genetic information (DNA) or the coding of protein amino acid sequence (RNA). Smaller nucleic acids, the monomers, serve as the building blocks for the larger polymers of DNA and RNA and also as energy carriers (ATP and GTP[16]). Additionally, certain biological compounds serve as coenzymes[17] which consist in part of monomer nucleic acids. The most common example is NAD$^+$ (nicotinamide adenine dinucleotide). The most important nucleic acids from the standpoint of damage from toxic chemical agents are the polymers, DNA and RNA.

DNA and RNA are very much alike except for a handful of specific differences which make all the difference to the cell. DNA employs the sugar deoxyribose [XX] while RNA employs the sugar ribose [XXI]. DNA contains the aromatic bases of adenine with thymine [XXII] and guanine with cytosine [XXIII]. RNA contains the base uracil [XXIV] in place of the thymine. Additionally, DNA [XXV] is generally found as a double stranded structure while RNA is generally single stranded. The double stranded nature of DNA derives from base pairing. The adenine-thymine pair [XXII] employs two hydrogen bonds (see Forces section below) and the guanine-cytosine pair [XXIII] utilizes three hydrogen bonds. Furthermore, since the base pairs of DNA stack on each other, the double stranded helical nature is enhanced by the added stabilization derived from the hydrophobic interactions and aromatic bonding electron interactions arising between any two adjacent base pairs [XXV]. RNA is produced from DNA as a single strand during the process of transcription.[18] Finally, the overall conformation of the two polymers is different owing to the conformations of the two different sugars comprising the backbone. Both polymers possess phosphate as the bridging moiety of the sugars. The

---

[16] GTP: Guanosine Triphosphate

[17] Coenzymes are small molecular weight molecules which play a central role in the transport of electrons from metabolites (such as food stuffs) and the subsequent derivation of energy in the form of ATP.

[18] DNA production, called synthesis, is accomplished by the process known as replication.

bases are covalently attached to the sugar. Of the two polymers, DNA is by far the more important as concerns damage from interaction with toxic chemical (alkylating) agents.

CARBOHYDRATES

Carbohydrates serve a number of roles in the human animal. Their primary role is that of a energy source. The metabolism of carbohydrates to carbon dioxide and water results in the production of ATP. Carbohydrates find use as components of antibodies of the immune system and as adducts in detoxification processes mediated by the liver, as well as components of specialized membrane lipids.

Carbohydrates occur as monosaccharides, disaccharides, and polysaccharides. Examples of the more common monosaccharides are glucose [XXVI], fructose [XXVII], ribose [XXI] and deoxyribose [XX]. Sucrose [XXVIII] is common table sugar, a disaccharide.

Glucose is stored in man as the animal starch glycogen deposited in the liver and muscle. The importance of glucose to man is that it is the primary energy source for the brain and the glycogen stores of the liver are utilized to maintain blood glucose levels for the brain.[19]

Fructose, fruit sugar, arises from the hydrolysis of sucrose in the diet or as an activated intermediate[20] in glucose metabolism. Glucose can be converted to ribose through a series of metabolic reactions. Ribose is used primarily for the synthesis of RNA. Additionally, ribose is convertible to deoxyribose for DNA synthesis.

Polysaccharides are typified by glycogen, starch and cellulose. Cellulose is a structural material of plants. It provides incredible strength and mass support for its weight. Carbohydrates are without doubt the most predominant material of the plant world. Were it not for cellulose, certainly trees as large as the California Redwoods could not support such massive weights.

Considering that cells consist of a myriad of chemical compounds, what holds the cell together? The forces that hold a cell together are the same forces that hold molecules together.

INTER- & INTRAMOLECULAR FORCES

Intramolecular forces are forces that act within a molecule. Intermolecular forces are forces that act between two separate molecules. There are principally five kinds of molecular forces that determine the interactions between biomolecules or between distantly separated portions of the same

---

[19] In starvation, glycogen reserves are depleted to the point of nonexistence. The brain can switch to what are called ketone bodies derived from fatty acid metabolism when glucose availability is low or absent. The fatty acids are derived from triacylglycerols (triglycerides) from fat storage cells of adipose tissue.

[20] Activation of monosaccharides is principally a phosphorylation of the native monomer.

biomolecule. They are: (1) apolar, (2) polar, (3) hydrogen bonding, (4) covalent disulfide linkages[21] and (5) salt type interactions.

Apolar or hydrophobic interactions are interactions that exclude water and other polar solvents and materials. Molecules consisting of only carbon and hydrogen (such as gasoline) are typical of the kinds of molecules associated with each other through apolar or hydrophobic interactions. Any amino acids which possess side chains consisting exclusively of hydrogen and carbon are the main amino acids engaging in apolar interactions. These amino acid residues (as they are called) are usually found buried within the interior of a folded or globular protein. One exception is in the membrane bound proteins where such apolar amino acid residues are found on the protein surface, interacting with the phospholipid components of the membrane and thus stabilizing the protein in the membrane.

Polar interactions, also called hydrophilic interactions, are interactions between the water soluble amino acid components of the protein and the water-based medium. Other polar molecules of the cell can interact with the polar side chains of the protein. For proteins found in the cytoplasm, blood, or aqueous regions of the digestive tract, polar amino acid residues tend to reside on the surface of the protein. Such associations can enhance the apparent solubility of the protein in the medium.

Hydrogen bonding interactions are central to the secondary structure of many proteins and DNA as well. The helical form of many proteins is due to the interaction arising from hydrogen bonding between amino and carbonyl groups several residues away. These kinds of forces assist in holding the secondary structure together much as the railing of a spiral staircase is held in position to the stairs by the spaced, vertical rungs. Hydrogen bonding, however, goes well beyond just the secondary structure of a protein. It also plays a role in maintenance of the tertiary and even quaternary structures of other more complex proteins. Additionally, hydrogen bonding plays a role in some interactions between the protein and other smaller molecular species with which the protein may interact. Hydrogen bonds are very weak interactions, though summed over billions, can lead to very strong and stable structures.

Disulfide bridges or linkages are the result of two distantly placed cysteine amino acid residues coming together, as a result of protein folding dynamics, forming a covalent bond and stabilizing the subsequent protein tertiary structure. Such systems are important in the folding of proteins which then brings other amino acid residues into close proximity for further stabilization of the protein's final tertiary or quaternary form. These linkages are susceptible to reducing agents which break the disulfide bond, generating the native cysteine side chain. Under such a circumstance, the protein has lost its native form and activity if it is an enzyme[22].

Salt formation is a process in which acidic and basic components of a protein interact. The anionic side chain of aspartate[23] could associate with the cationic side chain of lysine forming in essence, a salt. Such electrostatic interactions are quite strong and valuable to protein tertiary and

---

[21] Disulfide linkages arise from two cysteine amino acids covalently joining at their thiol group (-SH). These types of linkages are significant in the folding of protein on itself. Such kinds of linkages are responsible for the curling of hair. The treatment received at a hair salon requires first the reduction of such linkages (breaking the -S-S- linkage) to regenerate the free cysteine side chains (-SH). Setting the hair in the desired curl pattern is followed by an oxidizing agent treatment which regenerates the disulfide linkages but the linkages formed are not likely the natural ones.

[22] Enzymes are biological catalysts.

[23] Biochemists have developed the habit of referring to various bio-acid compounds by the anionic name of the acid. Thus aspartic acid becomes aspartate.

quaternary structure. Often times such interactions are found in close proximity to or in the active site of an enzyme where binding of its substrate alters the interactions of these salt interactions, facilitating the enzymatic activity on the substrate. The process of altering a biomolecule's shape and thus its activity through the disruption of any one or all of these inter- and intramolecular forces is called denaturation.

DENATURATION

Denaturation is the process by which a protein (or nucleic acid[24]) can undergo partial or complete unfolding of its native form. Denaturation of a protein always alters the functional activity of a protein. Extreme denaturation destroys protein function completely. It is the folding of the polypeptide chain upon itself and the resultant proximity of the amino acid side chains to each other that gives a protein its unique three dimensional form called its tertiary structure. For the majority of proteins, the tertiary structure is the final form of the protein rendering it active in the cell. Two or more separate proteins may come together to form larger, more complex protein aggregates. This level of protein organization is the quaternary structure of such proteins. The tertiary and quaternary structures of a protein are all important. These levels of organization of a protein are determined by the amino acid sequence (the primary structure) of the protein. Altering the amino acid side chains (and hence the sequence) or the tertiary or quaternary structure of a protein can have disastrous effects on protein native activity. Any chemical agent that can interfere with the forces that hold any large molecule in a particular shape, including proteins, can cause the disruption of the protein's native form.[25]

The simplest and most easily seen examples of this disruption of native protein form and its consequences are typified by the action of acids (such as vinegar) or alcohol on milk, or the cooking of meat.

Milk consists of a number of proteins and fats in a colloidal suspension. This colloidal suspension is a delicately balanced juggling act between complicated forces that suspend the components and the forces that tend to disrupt this suspension. Left standing at room temperature, milk sours. This process is a result of bacterial action and temperature. The by-products of bacterial action causing the disruption of complex structure and form of apparently dissolved materials comprising milk can be simulated more rapidly by the use of acids and organic solvents.

---

[24] Though nucleic acids are acted upon by certain chemical agents, nucleic acids are buried deep within the cell in the nucleus, an organelle of the cell. The nucleus has its own membrane called the nuclear membrane by cell biologists and physiologists. Generally, the only chemical agents which penetrate the cellular and nuclear membranes to reach the DNA are alkylating agents. These chemical agents are not so much immediately lethal, though they may be quite toxic for other reasons concerning proteins and membranes, as they are harmful in a long term sense. Alkylating agents are also known as carcinogens- chemical compounds that in altering DNA, lead to cancers. From the standpoint of a chemical war agent, alkylating agents targeting DNA only are not fast acting enough to afford their military use. Toxic alkylating chemical agents such as the mustards are rapid acting on skin and components of the skin. They may be absorbed and reach the DNA where they can alkylate the DNA. Alkylation of DNA, however, is a militarily ineffective process.

[25] Some commonly used denaturants for proteins are: potassium perchlorate ($KClO_4$), perchloric acid ($HClO_4$), urea, guanidinum salts, 2-mercaptoethanol and ionic detergents.

Acids can hydrolyze proteins. In fact, this is the major reason the human stomach secretes hydrochloric acid after a meal. The acid content provides hydrogen ions[26] (H^+) which will protonate any element possessing what are called lone electron pairs. Oxygen and nitrogen possess such lone electron pairs, which are ideal targets for hydrogen ions provided by any acid; strong acids provide copious quantities of the hydronium ions. These hydronium ions protonate, as it is called, the electron rich elements such as oxygen and nitrogen of proteins. Under very strong acid treatment, disruption of the bonding in proteins can result, fragmenting the polypeptide into smaller units. Even without breaking the polypeptide backbone or primary structure of the protein, the susceptible side chain groups are affected. These hydronium ions can protonate the anionic carboxylic acid side chains of such amino acids as aspartate or glutamate, generating a neutral side chain. If the ionized form of the side chain is important to the tertiary structure of the protein, then disruption or weakening of this level of protein organization results. Similarly, the basic amino acid side chains such as lysine, which may be positively charged under the normal solution conditions for the native protein, may become deprotonated by bases and the subsequent neutral specie also contributes to disruption of the protein's tertiary structure. Otherwise neutral but polar amino acid side chains are also affected by acid treatment. The amino acid side chains of serine and threonine may become protonated. Such protonations have serious chemical consequences to the identity of the amino acid side chain.

Protonations of hydroxyl group bearing compounds results in a cationic water moiety which results in the excellent leaving group, water[27]:

$$\text{--C-OH} + H^+ \longrightarrow \text{--C-O}^+H_2 \longrightarrow \text{--C}^+ + H_2O$$

The elimination of water from such protonated amino acid groups results in a positively charged intermediate carbocation which is not long-lived and can lead to rearrangements or other additions to the transient cation. Base treatment of proteins causes the opposite effects of acid treatment. That is, bases tend to remove labile hydrogen atoms from native proteins and these reactions can generate anionic or neutral intermediates from the native neutral or cationic specie respectively. In any case, the effects on the proteins are dramatic. Milk treated with acid curdles and the resultant visible particles precipitate.

Treating milk with strong organic solvents also disrupts protein structure and native form but by a different means. Many organic solvents interfere with the hydrogen bonding within proteins. Additionally, some are very hygroscopic, that is, they dehydrate materials. They remove water from the material. Water removed from protein adversely affects its tertiary structure as all proteins possess some water of hydration which, through hydrogen bonding, stabilizes their tertiary structure. Alcohol, in high concentration, is such a solvent. Generally, non-water soluble portions (hydrophobic) of the protein are buried within the protein while its water soluble (hydrophilic) portions are exposed to the aqueous solvent medium. Organic solvents such as alcohol disrupt this partitioning of hydrophobic versus hydrophilic portions. As organic solvent concentration increases, the tendency for hydrophilic

---

[26] Hydrogen ions in aqueous (water-based) solutions are given the special name hydronium ions.

[27] Leaving groups are those molecular species which arise in a compound as a result of chemical reactions and can detach from the parent structure (leave). As the example shows, a protonation reaction of an alcohol results in a charged water molecule fragment. Water is a stable entity by itself and so, it detaches from the parent molecule. The charge that was present remains behind on the parent molecule.

surfaces of protein to interact with aqueous media decreases. At the same time, the hydrophobic interior portions of the protein are capable of solvating in the organic solvent. Though not entirely an accurate portrayal of the outcome, one can loosely say the protein tends to turn inside out. Native protein tertiary structure and function are clearly lost and as a result, so too is the solubility characteristics of the protein. Milk treated with strong alcohol solutions will also show similar curdling but the mechanism in the case of organic solvent treatment is different from that of acid/base treatment. The milk is of course still spoiled.

Heating also causes the denaturation of protein. Overheating milk for the evening hot chocolate results in a skim or thin film of denatured milk proteins rising to and forming at the surface. Heating increases molecular motions, specifically vibratory and translatory motions. Smaller molecules are particularly responsive to this increased energy input. Water molecules are significantly excited in their vibratory and translatory motions. A thermal dehydration occurs to the proteins which release some of their water of hydration. The loss of water of hydration alters their tertiary structure. The loss of native tertiary structure leaves the protein vulnerable to further denaturing damage by heating. Continued heating only aggravates the process. Other examples of denaturation of protein by heating are cooking of an egg (hard or soft) or meat. The same general points noted above also apply.

Charring often occurs during the cooking process. Charring is a process that goes well beyond the disruption of the forces that hold a protein in its tertiary or quaternary state. Severe cooking with charring is the destruction of the protein itself. Such extreme cooking conditions is technically known as pyrolysis. In pyrolysis, the protein's primary structure is assaulted. Pyrolysis does not simply break peptide bonds, though this certainly does occur, but rather wholesale regions of the polypeptide including its vast side chain network are being superheated and chemical rearrangements take place. Browning and charring provide clear evidence of burning. Pyrolysis leads to new, heat produced compounds. These compounds can be simple, such as water or carbon dioxide, or complex, such as polycyclic aromatic hydrocarbons.

Denaturation of lipids does not produce the same consequences as denaturation of proteins, though pyrolytic processes can destroy a lipid. Because of this, denaturation is a term generally not applied to lipids. However, lipids with long flexible chain components such as fatty acids or lipids possessing fatty acids such as the phospholipids, can experience a localized disruption of their hydrophobic conformational "structure" by exposure to the so-called "fat solvents" noted previously. Additionally, heat will increase thermal molecular motions of these long-chained components, adversely affecting overall lipid system properties.

Polymeric nucleic acids, specifically double stranded DNA, are also sensitive to a range of denaturants such as organic solvents, salt solutions and heat. Organic solvents tend to disrupt the water of hydration associated with DNA. Solvents such as absolute alcohol[28] are particularly effective in this regard. Such solvents appear to cause a congealing of DNA in solution, enabling the DNA to be removed from solution on a glass rod, wound up and about the rod much in appearance as a mucous-like spaghetti strand.

High salt concentrations, typically sodium chloride (table salt), cause a reversal of the helical sense of DNA. These interactions, electrostatic in nature, interfere with the charged phosphate groups and the normal counterions[29] associated with the stabilized DNA backbone.

---

[28] 95% ethyl alcohol

[29] Counterions are positively charged metal ions such as sodium (+1) or magnesium (+2).

Heating of solutions of native double stranded DNA provides the most quantitative means of following the denaturation process of DNA.[30] As heat is applied, thermal molecular motions increase. The most susceptible forces affected by this energy input are the hydrogen bonds holding both strands together via the paired bases. Sufficient heating leads to diminished duplex structure of the DNA, finally resulting in two separate strands of DNA. The higher the number of guanine-cytosine base pairs (called the GC content), the more heat energy is required to completely denature the native DNA.

Denaturation of carbohydrates, specifically polysaccharides, is applicable to cell systems which employ such components as structural units. This is the case for plants, but animals also employ carbohydrates in varying levels of complexity for such purposes. In fact, animals have developed systems for digesting or breaking down polysaccharides into smaller monomer units for further metabolism. As a result, no further consideration of carbohydrate denaturation is warranted.

CHEMICAL AGENTS & INTER- AND INTRAMOLECULAR FORCES

PROTEINS

A good example of the interference of a toxic agent with the covalent state of a protein is the action of the anticholinergic nerve agents discussed in Chapter 3. Enzymes such as acetylcholinesterase are known as serine series enzymes because they possess the amino acid serine at the active site. The hydroxyl group of the serine side chain is intimately involved in the enzymatic action of the enzyme on acetylcholine. The organophosphorus nerve agents covalently bind to the hydroxyl group by replacing the hydrogen atom. The resultant phosphate linkage at the active site [XXXII] is very difficult to hydrolyze, particularly on a time scale lethal to human life. Such a covalent bond between the protein (an enzyme in this case) and the toxic agent inactivates the protein and destroys its functional role within or between cells.

LIPIDS

Toxic agents that are fat soluble are capable of penetrating and interacting with the membrane lipid constituents including as well any membrane-bound proteins. These agents can either react covalently with susceptible biomolecules or can effectively dissolve within the membrane lipid sea. Such dissolution reactions will undoubtedly affect the membrane's integrity and structural dynamics. Disruption of membrane structural integrity can lead to weaknesses in membrane permeability and in the extreme cases, also lead to cell lysis and death. Magnified over hundreds or thousands of cells, tissue damage becomes a major consequence. Such injuries will manifest themselves as chemical burns such as are caused by the vesicants (blistering agents) like mustard agent.

---

[30] This means of DNA denaturation is called melting and is followed spectroscopically. A plot of absorbence of light energy versus temperature yields a characteristic sigmoidal curve.

NUCLEIC ACIDS

DNA is the principal target for a class of compounds known as alkylating agents. These compounds have the ability to chemically attack certain DNA bases. In so doing, the agent forms a covalent bond with the targeted base and particular atoms[31] of specific base ring structures which are very susceptible to this kind of reaction. Mustard agents are an example of compounds that are alkylating agents. Such compounds are or have been suspected to be chemical carcinogens-- chemical compounds which chemically alter the DNA and after repeated exposures over several years can cause malignancies.

CARBOHYDRATES

For the same reasons that denaturation of carbohydrates was not discussed, so too, interaction of carbohydrates with toxic chemical agents is omitted. Though reactions in some cases may occur, they do not have the same level of importance in terms of injury value or lethality that attaches to proteins, lipids of membranes and even to DNA.

---

[31] N(7) and N(2) of guanine, N(7) and N(6) of adenine and to a lesser extent, O(6) of guanine are the principal atoms targeted by alkylating agents.

CHAPTER 3

CHEMICALS

Life is a partial, continuous, progressive,
multiform and conditionally interactive self-
realization of the potentialities of atomic
electron states.
    - *The Origins of Life*, 1967[1]

THE PESTICIDE CONNECTION

Chemical agents are not uncommon in everyday experience. Parathion [I] and Malathion [II] are technically known as organophosphates, only one class of toxic chemical war agents, though the public knows them only as insecticides. Parathion is so poisonous that it is not generally available. The less poisonous Malathion[2] serves as a substitute for public use. Additionally, veterinarians may administer oral nerve agents to pets severely infested with fleas or other parasites. The standard flea dip of pet care and grooming businesses also employs similar substances but under controlled conditions of application. Some fumigants are industrially important compounds and are also pesticides, some having found military application. Cyanide, a member of a second class of toxic war agents, is used as an insecticide and rodenticide fumigant in warehouses and other nonhuman habitable buildings and ships.

Though chemical weapons research and development was not necessarily the original focus of industrial chemical or pesticide research, it did evolve from such research[3] and the two now go virtually hand-in-hand. Many industrial and pesticide compounds can be altered chemically, thus enhancing their toxic or other properties for specific applications and uses. Replacement of a single

---

[1] In The Harvest of a Quiet Eye, p. 17

[2] Malathion is hydrolyzed to nontoxic by-products by mammalian liver.

[3] The Germans discovered the nerve agents during the course of their insecticide research. Dr. Gerhardt Schrader, a chemist, was a principal researcher of organophosphates with the I.G. Farbenindustrie (I.G. Dye Industry), 1936. The same company later developed Zyklon B, the gas used in the gas chambers of the Nazi concentration camps.

atom in the molecule[4] with an atom of another element[5] can have significant impact. An example is that of water [III] consisting of hydrogen and oxygen. At room temperature and pressure, it is a liquid. Replacement of the oxygen with sulfur leads to the highly poisonous and repugnantly odorous hydrogen sulfide [IV] (the odor of rotten eggs), a substance in many respects more dangerous and poisonous than cyanide. The sulfur atom imparts chemical property changes. In addition to being very poisonous, it also leads to a compound that is gaseous at room temperature and pressure. For very small molecules such replacements impart drastic changes in properties. For larger molecules, the changes can be less drastic, though no less important or significant to the intended use of the compound.

The relationship between pesticide research and chemical warfare agent research naturally follows from the efforts to develop pesticides that are considered "safe for human use". This concept of "safe for human use" is at best a relative concept, and technically, nonsense. Any pesticide, by definition, is poisonous to the pest and since biochemical reactions of living cells are virtually identical for the human and the pest, the pesticide is poisonous to humans as well. The distinction is in the dose required to kill, which depends on body weight. The importance of dose or more correctly, the lethal dose that kills 50% of the targeted animals, LD_{50}, is central to the effectiveness of a pesticide and by extension, to humans. It is also a factor in a formulation's effectiveness as a chemical weapon in war. The LD_{50} is but one factor in a list of requirements that a prospective chemical weapon for war must meet.

HOUSEHOLD AGENTS

In addition to the household insecticides, many household cleaning chemicals are potentially dangerous, particularly if mixed in the wrong combinations. Some of these household cleaning agents release fumes which can cause the same symptoms on unprotected exposure as bonafide war gases. For example, many people in cleaning the bathroom with bleach [V] or even worse, a bleach with ammonia [VI] combination, overexpose themselves to fumes released by these products in a confined space. The small quantity of hydrazine gas (one time, a rocket fuel), the fumes released, is an example of a third class of toxic war agents. Overexposure results in sore throat, tightness in the chest, and mild, labored breathing, all early symptoms of choking agent exposure. Anyone who has peeled onions has experienced tearing. The causative chemical substance of this tearing is propanethiol [VII], an example of a mild tearing agent.

Finally, though not a household chemical, the toxins of poison ivy, poison oak or poison sumac are good examples of a common vesicant or blistering agent. Though the reaction to the toxins of these poisonous plants is considered an allergic reaction, which in some hypersensitive individuals can be very hazardous, it nonetheless elicits the same kinds of delayed and eruptive physiological symptoms with skin as a war mustard gas, though on a smaller scale. The parent compound of the irritant substances from these plants is the generic urushiol [VIII] compound which differs in the R group from one plant to another. Poison ivy, for example, has a fifteen carbon side chain with from zero to three double bonds, while poison oak possesses a seventeen carbon side chain with from zero

---

[4] The smallest unit of a substance made up of two or more (covalent) bonded atoms which retain the properties of that substance.

[5] An element is a pure substance that cannot be separated into simpler substances by chemical means.

to three double bonds. The exposure to these plant toxins leads to reddening, itching[6], burning and finally, blistering and, depending upon the individual's allergic sensitivity, in about the same time frame as a response to a war mustard gas. Though the reaction to these poisonous plant toxins is commonly viewed as an allergic response, any injury or foreign substance will elicit the same kinds of responses. Allergic responses are the mobilization of the body's immune system to invasion. Hay fever is a typical example of such a response. Allergic response is simply the reaction of the body to a foreign substance and injury and is also part and parcel of what is called the inflammatory response by the body to any foreign substance or injury.

Table 3-1: Common Poisonous Plants	
Common Name	Scientific Name
Poison Ivy Poison Oak Poison Sumac	*Toxicodendron radicans* *Toxicodendron diversilbum* *Toxicodendron vernix*

MEDICINE

Anyone who has had an infection or other ailment probably has taken a prescription drug. Many antibiotics are derived from bacterial fermentors, wherein hundreds of gallons of bacterial soup are fermented and the sought antibiotics extracted for concentration and purification. Some antibiotics are man-made. They are all chemicals and are specifically designed to attack particular cells. Even anticancer (antineoplastic) drugs are chemicals of potent toxicity, administered by physician's order and closely monitored. They are all examples of a chemical warfare directed at cells and tissues that threaten human life. Medical use of chemicals represents an application in the reverse order, that is, rather than kill the person, we seek to kill the cause of the patient's misery. It is nothing more than a focused application in a limited chemical war where knowledge is central to recognizing hazards and preventing harm.[7] Overdoses of medication kill. Overdoses of military chemical agents kill, too.

---

[6] Itching is actually a mild pain.

[7] One example of the use of a medicinal to kill a pest occurred in Mexico. The vampire bats were a problem in spreading disease, most particularly rabies, among domestic livestock on which the bats fed.
Anticoagulants were spread on the backs of captured vampire bats and released. These treated bats returned to the communal roost where the bats, both treated and untreated, cleaned each other, ingesting fatal doses of the anticoagulant.

Chemical Bonds- the Glue of Molecules

Glue of one kind or another is a common material used for minor repairs and other uses around the home. As a generic substance, glue binds[8] two materials together by very different means dependent upon the specific kind of glue. Some glues function as adhesive intermediates through physical associations[9]. Others penetrate materials that are porous and then harden upon drying forming a kind of reinforced lattice work of glue fibrils throughout the immediate surface depths of the materials they bind. This is much like reinforced steel mesh in concrete. Though this type of binding can consist of chemical interaction processes, such a binding is as much or more a physical, nonchemical process, or a hydrophobic process which is relatively weak. Still other glues actually function through a chemical reaction with and between the two materials they bind. These glues actually form chemical bonds[10] and are the strongest glues.

One of the most fundamental considerations in chemistry is the chemical bond. The nature of chemical bonds, the reason for molecules being held together, is central to the properties of molecules and is responsible for many of the reactions that can or cannot take place. This discussion will facilitate the explanations in the next section dealing with chemical injuries, the result of the actions of chemical war agents.

Chemical bonds are classified by chemists into four major groups. They are **metallic bonds[11]**, **ionic bonds[12]**, **covalent bonds[13]** and the weaker (by comparison) **hydrogen bonds[14]**. Regardless of the specific type of bond under consideration they all share one important feature: they all are a product of the interaction between electrons and between electrons and the nuclei of the atoms the bond 'binds' together. A fifth means of holding molecules together includes the **hydrophobic, hydrophilic, and salt linkage interactions** (a special kind of ionic bond).

---

[8] The term bind will be used rather than bond since bond will have a very specific meaning in a chemical sense.

[9] Physical associations do not entail any chemical reactions involving the breakage or formation of chemical bonds. They consist of hydrophilic or hydrophobic interactions, much like oil dissolved in gasoline. As such, separation of the two components joined by such interactions is accomplished by physical means. As applies to adhesive glues such as labels, peeling them off overcomes these attractive, nonbonded forces.

[10] A chemical bond can be defined as that state of attraction between two atoms in which the forces of attraction make the close association of the atoms more favorable than as separate and apart atoms. These forces are regarded as Coulombic in nature. Coulombic attraction is the attraction between two opposite charges. The force of this attraction has the form:

$$F \propto e^- e^+ / r^2$$

[11] Linus Pauling, *The Nature of the Chemical Bond*, 3rd Ed., Chapter 11, Cornell University press, New York, NY, 1962

[12] ibid, Chapter 19

[13] ibid, Chapters 2,3,4

[14] ibid, Chapter 12

METALLIC BONDS

Metallic bonds are not germane to the discussion of chemical war agents, but are so very common to everyday life and experience. The shininess of metal is due to the properties of this type of bonding. The principal feature of metallic bonds is the existence of a sea of electrons freely moving about a matrix of metal atom nuclei. It is the freedom of mobility of electrons that gives metals their characteristic shiny luster. It is also responsible for their excellent electrical current and heat conductivity.

IONIC BONDS

Ionic bonds arise from the complete transfer of one or more electrons from one atom to another. This total transfer of an electron from one atom to another leads to positively charged ions (cation, the ion resulting from loss of an electron) and negatively charged ions (anion, the ion resulting from the gain of an electron). The resulting charges on the two atoms are opposite in sign and attract each other much like two magnets, but with much more force of attraction. The most common example of such ionic bonding is in table salt, sodium chloride. In this substance, the sodium exists as a positively charged sodium ion (cation). The chlorine atom exists as a negatively charged chloride ion (anion). This property of table salt, its ionic nature, is why table salt is such an excellent conductor of electrical current when dissolved in water. It also is the reason why table salt cannot be melted on the kitchen stove. The force of the bonding (technically referred to as the electrostatic force between the two ions) is much greater in energy than can be overcome by the heat input from the kitchen stove. Epsom salts is also an ionic substance composed of the metal magnesium and the nonmetal sulfur in combination with oxygen ($MgSO_4·7H_2O$). All ionic substances exhibit the same basic property of conductance of electrical current when dissolved in water, as well as high melting and boiling points (in the hundreds of degrees Celsius) and usually are crystalline in appearance. Such ionic bonds can only be disrupted by other substances possessing very high polar properties such as water. This is because ionic substances exist in a network[15] of associated cations and anions, each dependent upon the presence of the others for its stability in form. This is why such materials are often crystalline in form and appearance. Polar substances such as water are able to surround each ionic specie and stabilize it in dissociated form from the complementary ion. Ionic substances will not dissolve in nonpolar substances such as oil or gasoline. These latter substances cannot disrupt the strong electrostatic forces which bind the ions together.

In animal and plant tissues, ionic bonds arise as cationic and anionic components of protein molecules. Such cationic and anionic species are found as acidic and basic groups which have an attraction for each other in a fashion similar to that of the metals and nonmetals noted above.

COVALENT BONDS

Covalent bonds (the most common and strongest type) arise from the sharing of electrons between two atoms. Simple examples are found in water and carbon dioxide. In covalent substances the molecules are capable of independent existence. They are not necessarily associated with each

---

[15] technically called a lattice, a three dimensional array of cationic and anionic particles.

other for existence as is the case with the ions of ionic substances. The sharing of the electrons is between the nuclei of the two atoms involved. Neither atom has sole possession of the electrons and so the electrons reside between the nuclei. This sharing of the electrons leads to a closer approach of the two atoms' nuclei than occurs between the nonbonded atoms. In organic substances this is evidenced by a much lower melting and boiling point. Many organic substances decompose upon heating at or before the melting point and most cannot be heated to boiling as they are destroyed by such high energy input. Cooking is an example of this process and is most significantly observed in the cooking of meats. The browning and charring is evidence of a destructive rearrangement of covalent bonds before the melting point is reached. The destructive rearrangement of covalent bonds leads to significant chemical changes in the substance. The substance is no longer what it was before such treatment.

Covalent bonds can exist in a multiplicity of types. Many organic molecules posses double and triple bonds. Each single covalent bond by definition consists of two shared electrons. Double covalent bonds possess four shared electrons and triple covalent bonds, six shared electrons. The greater the multiplicity of the covalent bond, the greater the energy of the bond and the closer together are the two bonded atomic nuclei.

Covalent bonds can be viewed as behaving like rubber bands between two atoms. As a result, the bonds can undergo stretching, twisting and bending. There is a practical limit to the extent of stretch a covalent bond may experience. Like the rubber band, a covalent bond can be stretched beyond its 'elastic limit', at which point it breaks and the two atoms are no longer bonded to each other.

HYDROGEN BONDS

Hydrogen bonds are the weakest and the most difficult to characterize of the four. These are special types of bonds that result from particular atoms' attraction to electrons belonging to other particular atom. The best example of hydrogen bonding is seen in water. Though individual water molecules are covalently bonded molecules, there exists forces of attraction between any two water molecules that do not rely on the transfer or sharing of electrons as discussed above. Water on Earth under normal conditions is liquid because of hydrogen bonding. Such bonds primarily arise between nitrogen and oxygen atoms, one of which must have a hydrogen atom covalently bonded to it. Because the hydrogen atom has a slight positive charge character, it is attracted to any element with high electron attracting ability (referred to by the chemist as electron density and electronegativity). These hydrogen bonds derive their name because hydrogen is an active participant in this type of attractive force between atoms. They are very weak and easily broken. Heating of water to the boiling point does demonstrate the cumulative strength these bonds have when summed over trillions of molecules.[16]

Tissue is held together by all these types of bonds (except metallic bonding) but to varying extents. DNA, for example, is held together by covalent and hydrogen bonding. Proteins are held together by covalent, ionic and hydrogen bonding also to varying extents dependent upon the specific protein in question.

---

[16] One ounce of water possesses at least 1.9×10^{24} hydrogen bonds.

HYDROPHOBIC AND HYDROPHILIC INTERACTIONS

Hydrophobic interactions rely on electron attractions occurring between the electron clouds of two molecules. These interactions arise from molecules associating with like kind. Water insoluble organic compounds will generally dissolve in each other. There is no hydrogen bonding, no ionic bonding, no covalent bonding between such independent molecules; rather, a complex interaction between electron clouds[17] of one molecule with that of another are the basis of this interaction. Such interactions are responsible for the solubility of oil in gasoline but not water in gasoline. These interactions are based in part on the nonpolar character of such molecules. These interactions are particularly significant in the formation of membranes of cells which consist mostly of fat-like molecules. These interactions also play a role in the stability of the structure of DNA,[18] structural proteins, enzymes, etc. Typically these hydrophobic interactions exclude water even when water is present. That's why gasoline forms a separate layer of liquid on top of the lower water layer, the water being more dense than gasoline.

Hydrophilic Interactions are those interactions between polar molecules such as water. In these interactions, attractions are a result of hydrogen bonds, electrostatic attractions, or electronegative element components of molecules. These interactions are usually associated between water-soluble or polar molecules and water.[19]

SALT LINKAGES

Salt linkages arise as the electrostatic attractions between two oppositely charged organic functional groups. These are ionic bonding in character. These types of bonding interactions occur to a significant extent in proteins, stabilizing protein tertiary and quaternary structure. Salt linkages typically exist between an anionic carboxylic side chain of one amino acid residue with the cationic amino side chain of a second amino acid residue:

$$-COO^- \cdots H_3N^+-$$

where the ⋯ represents the ionic interaction force between the two species. These interactions are also observed in enzymatic active and allosteric sites. Disruption of salt linkages in proteins by other potent cationic or anionic species significantly alters the proximate location of the natural salt linkage moieties. This disruption alters the shape of the protein, which in the extreme case can denature and inactivate the protein's biological function.

---

[17] Though electrons are particles with mass, they do not necessarily behave as particles within atoms and molecules. The term electron cloud is used to describe the physical characteristics of an electron in an atom as deduced from mathematical and experimental studies of electron behavior. The concept of an electron cloud is best described by way of an example. A fan blade is a particle with mass. Yet when the fan is on, the fan blade is not seen as a blade but rather as a blur which defines the region of space occupied by the fan blade. A similar idea applies to the description of the electron cloud.

[18] DNA: **deoxyribonucleic** Acid, the genetic material of life and found within all living cells and certain viruses.

[19] Hydrophilic means water loving.

CHEMICAL REACTIONS

The world is a gigantic chemical reactor. Chemical reactions take place in the atmosphere, the depths of the oceans, in soil, and in the multitude of living organisms, including of course the human animal. All chemical reactions are nothing more than a rearrangement or redistribution of electrons in matter. The nature of these rearrangements or redistributions of electrons in matter and how these processes occur comprises the basis of the science of chemistry.[20] Some reactions result in the sharing of electrons between two atoms, while others involve the complete transfer of electrons from one atom or group of atoms to another. The former materials are referred to by chemists as covalent substances while the latter are called ionic[21] substances. Table sugar is an example of a covalent substance (technically called a compound) and table salt is an example of an ionic substance.

There are hundreds of millions of chemical reactions. Chemists have generally categorized chemical reactions into at least three distinct classes. They are combination, decomposition and displacement (also known as replacement) reactions. Additionally, a few have taken on special significance all to themselves as they signify unique processes. These few are neutralization or acid/base reactions, hydrolysis reactions and reduction/oxidation or redox reactions. Acid/base reactions are a subset of displacement reactions while redox reactions are a subset of combination reactions. Thus, the reaction of vinegar (an acid) with baking soda (a basic salt) is a replacement reaction and also an acid/base or neutralization reaction. The reaction of sodium metal with chlorine gas to produce sodium chloride, table salt, is a combination reaction and also an example of a redox reaction in which sodium is oxidized and the chlorine reduced. Decomposition is typified by the conversion of limestone, calcium carbonate, to lime (calcium oxide) and carbon dioxide by the agency of applied heat.

All chemical reactions entail a redistribution of electrons among the reacting materials. Chemists call the initial starting materials the reactants and the final materials produced, products. A cardinal requirement for a chemical reaction to take place is that the reaction converting reactants to products must be favorable in the direction of products. Technically, this means the energy possessed by the products must be less than the energy possessed by the reactants. This concept acquires a mathematical form in the science of thermochemistry and is designated the free energy. It is possible to calculate this free energy of a chemical reaction to determine if it is favorable[22] before actually mixing the reactants. This ability to predetermine the favorability of a reaction is so well established by the availability of tables of thermodynamic data, that a wide and varied range of reactions can be calculated in advance, including chemical reactions unique to living systems. Concentrations of reactants and products play a critical role in the free energy of a reaction and even determine which way the reaction will go-- towards products or back toward reactants. It is the concentration of reactants and products that determines the overall direction of many biological chemical reactions within the cell. Such concepts even play a role in processes of absorption and diffusion of nutrients into and out of cells lining capillaries.

---

[20] There are several fundamental fields of chemistry: general, inorganic, analytic, organic, and physical chemistry. Other areas of chemical study are mixtures or hybrids of two or more of these fundamental fields of chemistry. Hybrid fields of chemistry include pharmaceutical, medicinal and biochemistry.

[21] Ionic substances bear small positive and negative charges in their structure, though the overall charge (sum) is zero. Ionic substances conduct electrical current when dissolved in water.

[22] Technically called the spontaneity.

In biological systems, toxic chemical agents, as reactants, must react with one of four specific classes of biomolecules. They are: proteins, carbohydrates, lipids or nucleic acids. The latter is the most difficult to reach as it is buried deep within the cell[23] inside the nucleus, principally as DNA. RNA is found throughout the cell. However, toxic chemical agents make contact with gross structures, the tissues.

Tissues are composed of a network of cells all working in concert to perform specific tasks definitive of the tissue. Thus it is the cell surfaces that experience the initial toxic chemical agent. Cell surfaces are the membranes known as a lipid bilayer. Consisting primarily of lipids and proteins, the proteins are dispersed on both sides of the membrane as well as imbedded within it. The membrane serves a range of functions for the cell; not least of these functions is that it is a barrier designed to be selective in what it allows to pass through.

It is however, the very chemical properties of biological molecules such as lipids and proteins that facilitate reactions with toxic chemical agents. These reactions are damaging to the chemical identity of the biomolecule and by consequence, lethal to the cell.

INJURIES

THERMAL BURNS

Injury to tissues, cells, etc., involves chemomechanical damage. A broken bone is a mechanical injury, but also a biochemical injury as the chemical forces that once held the bone together at the break have been disrupted. Healing is the reestablishment of these chemical forces in bone tissue. A cut is a mechanical injury too, but also a chemical injury for similar reasons. Biochemical forces and the integrity of molecular systems of tissue are destroyed or disrupted at the lesion site. Additionally cells were killed or died as a result of the injury. Death, too, is a very biochemical intensive process.

Thermal burns of the skin represent an example of oxidation of the skin which falls into the subcategory of a combustion chemical reaction. In severe, third degree burn cases, the damage and oxidation products are visually evident. The charring of the skin in third degree burn cases is an example of pyrolysis of organic matter-- just like burning a wood log or overcooking the weekend barbeque steak.. One of the consequences of pyrolytic reactions is that chemical bonds are rearranged and the identity of compounds is altered.

In lesser degree thermal burns, the damage and evidence of oxidation is less obvious. In such milder cases of thermal burns, the damage is not as penetrating though it may be nonetheless extensive in surface area affected. Such thermal burns (second degree) lead to cell death in the afflicted tissue but not to the depth and severity as found in third degree burns. Second degree thermal burns damage the integrity of skin, creating lesions in which the skin's barrier properties are degraded. This is most noticeably evidenced by blistering, which if burst, can lead to severe opportunistic infections. Such burns are responsible for biological membrane destruction in cells with subsequent lysis[24] in addition to the body's immune response to rush blood and lymph fluids to the site of injury.

---

[23] John W. Hole, Jr.'s book Human Anatomy and Physiology, William C. Brown Co., Dubuque, IA, 1979, Chapter 3, pp. 35-62, provides a general description of the (human) cell as considered in this work.

[24] Meaning bursting, loss of cell fluid, and cell death.

First degree burns are the least dangerous and represent the least damage, usually only a slight reddening of the area. This reddening is indicative of both mild, limited cellular and tissue damage, as well as a rush of blood to the area as part of the immune response to any injury. The reddening is due in part to an increased quantity of blood below the surface at the site of injury.

CHEMICAL BURNS

Overall, chemical injury can affect more than skin. But the simple explanation of the damage to skin in thermal burns carries over to what are called chemical burns. These burns are not thermally caused but are every bit as difficult to heal. Chemical burns are a result of a reaction taking place between the cellular or tissue site in contact with the offending chemical agent. Such reactions can be of several different types dependent upon the chemical nature of the offending chemical agent. For example, the acid of lead storage batteries[25] has high water absorbing (desiccator[26]) properties, and first dehydrates the region of skin with which it is in contact. The loss of water of hydration in tissue molecules alters the environment of cells in that tissue. Loss of water from cells can lead to cell death.

Acids are also excellent proton donors. That is the definition of acids as it certainly applies to the common mineral acids.[27] Protein is rich in nitrogen which is an excellent proton acceptor. Alteration of the state of protonation of protein alters its three dimensional shape, chemical properties, and function. On the other side of the coin, bases such as sodium hydroxide[28] are excellent proton acceptors. They have the ability to remove certain hydrogens from protein and similarly can alter the three dimensional shape, chemical properties, and function of the protein.

Other chemical agents can oxidize protein. Household bleach[29] is an oxidizing agent, meaning that it can remove electrons (and certain chemically bound hydrogen atoms) from cellular chemical substances such as protein. This kind of reaction process is noticeable, for example, in bleaching colored materials. On skin, the reaction is evident by a strange slimy feel to the skin surface during initial contact with the bleach due also to the mild alkaline properties of the bleach. Prolonged exposure leads to damage not only of the dead skin surface but eventual penetration to the underlying living tissue.

Various organic substances are capable of skin necrosis.[30] These compounds are able to dissolve in the skin, chemically attack cells and the protein components leading to addition reactions which destroy the identity and function of the protein or other biological compounds with which they react. They can dissolve in the membranes of cells disrupting the permeability properties of membranes. Additionally, they may even penetrate to and through the nuclear membrane and reach the DNA and

---

[25] Sulfuric acid

[26] Removes water.

[27] Sulfuric, hydrochloric (muriatic), nitric, phosphoric acids.

[28] Commonly known as lye, the active ingredient of Draino.®

[29] Sodium hypochlorite.

[30] Meaning death.

cause addition reactions to the DNA which in turn can lead to carcinogenesis. Other compounds can react in addition reactions with specific proteins to prevent their function as enzymes.

NATURE OF CHEMICAL DAMAGE

Damage done to cells is damage done to the molecules of the cell. The damage done to such molecules consists of alterations made to the molecules. These alterations consist of changes to the chemical character of the molecule. As an example, an acidic molecule may be changed to a basic molecule, or a reduced molecule is oxidized or vice versa.

Oxidizing a molecule is the basis for the action of bleach on a stain. The stain molecules becoming oxidized by the bleach molecules often change color, going from an observable color such as brown, red or blue to a near white or colorless. This process changes the chemical identity of the stain molecules. This may manifest itself as a more soluble stain molecule which is then removed from the garment by the dissolving process of washing. Alternatively, it may just render the stain transparent-- colorless, restoring the near original color of the garment at the stain site.

Damage to tissues and therefore cells, can also lead to discolorations as a result of these chemical changes. Fresh, oxygenated blood is bright red in color. This is due to the chemical identity or state of the iron atoms as +2 in charge and normal globin protein structure. Old, dried blood is brown. This is due to the oxidation of the iron which then is +3 and denaturation of the globin protein.

The first material likely to come in contact with harmful chemical agents is the skin.[31] Skin is composed of several layers (see Chapter 8). The outermost layer consists of dead and loosely held cells. These cells have been keratinized, that is, the cellular fluid, cytoplasm, was replaced with the protein keratin as the cell died and the cell was pushed to the surface. Deeper penetration to the underlying layers of living cells brings the chemical agent into contact with cellular membranes of live cells. Additionally, connective tissues such as collagen are present and these too are proteins. The nature of the chemically damaged skin depends upon the chemical nature of the agent as well as the chemical nature of the specific cellular compounds it contacts. It all is a matter of chemistry.

Proteins are made of subunit molecules called α-amino acids. Amino acids are both a base and an acid all in the same molecule. Chemists call such molecules amphoteric. By oversimplification, amino acids can be viewed as a derivative of acetic acid (vinegar) or of ammonia. Because an amino acid has properties of both an acid and base, it reacts chemically under appropriate conditions as either an acid or a base. What makes the 20 common amino acids different from each other is the so-called side chains.

The side chains are molecular fragments which themselves can be neutral, acidic or basic in chemical character. It is the side chains that play the determinative role in the folding and function of a protein. It is the side chains that primarily interact with a chemical agent. Generally, acidic, basic or hydrophilic[32] side chains are aligned or associated with the water-laden regions of the cell while

---

[31] Skin is not a tissue but an organ system. An organ system consists of two or more organs each of which consists of tissues. Other organ systems are the skeletal, muscular, nervous, endocrine, digestive, respiratory, circulatory, lymphatic, urinary and reproductive systems.

[32] hydrophilic: meaning water loving, water seeking

the neutral or hydrophobic[33] side chains tend to reside away from water regions, buried usually in the internal folds of the protein. One exception is in proteins either partially or completely embedded within cellular membranes. In such circumstances, the hydrophobic side chains are associated on the outer surface of the protein, interacting with the hydrophobic lipid molecules comprising the membrane itself. The hydrophilic side chains are located generally on the interior regions of such membrane bound proteins providing channels for exchange of water soluble materials between the interior of the cell and the external environment. Such water soluble materials include sodium and potassium ions and glucose which can cross the membrane through the channels or holes in the membrane protein. Think of these holes as tunnels. Some water soluble components such as sodium and hydrogen ions require assistance to cross the membranes via an energy-- coupled process known to biochemists as active transport.

In proteins, amino acids are joined together in a head-to-tail fashion which combines the acidic group of one amino acid with the basic group of the following amino acid. This joined portion is designated the peptide[34] bond and is a rather strong bond. It can, however, be broken by acid hydrolysis (such as in the stomach), by digestive enzymes or with extreme heating.

The more toxic chemical agents such as nerve or mustards are hydrophobic in chemical character. They are soluble in hydrophobic solvents such as gasoline and thus are soluble in the hydrophobic media of cells such as membranes and the hydrophobic portions of proteins. The most immediate consequence of these agents' interaction with cellular molecules is inactivation or denaturation[35] of a protein or disruption of the permeability structure of membranes and membrane bound proteins. These interactions can be exclusively physical associations, covalent adduction[36], or a combination of both. Three examples of these processes will be noted: (1) in enzymes, (2) in nonenzymatic proteins and, (3) membrane structure.

Enzymes are biological catalysts.[37] Hundreds of reactions in a living cell occur only because of the presence of specific enzymes which increase the rate of the reaction. This provides a "real-time" response in cells and even in whole animals to a range of stimuli and the means to instantly generate the energy required to respond. However, some chemical substances can interfere or even stop completely an enzyme's activity by interacting with the enzyme. This interaction usually takes two

---

[33] hydrophobic: meaning water shunning

[34] A peptide bond or group is chemically known as an amide linkage but in proteins the special designation peptide is used.

[35] Denaturation is the term applied to the process by which the overall shape of a molecule is altered. The molecule is in a state of disfigurement.

[36] Covalent adduction is the process of adding one molecular fragment to another molecule by way of a distinct chemical reaction, the result of which is the formation of a covalent bond between the two components. Separation of the two components requires chemical degradation.

[37] A catalyst is a chemical substance that facilitates the rate of a reaction but is itself not a reactant or a product of the reaction. It is not consumed in a reaction as reactants are. An example of the utility catalysts are to chemical reactions is that of the reaction between hydrogen and oxygen gases to produce water. By themselves in a closed container, the reaction rate is exceedingly slow. Yet a catalyst of finely divided palladium when sprinkled into the gas mixture results in a reaction with explosive violence.

forms. The chemical agent can associate with the protein in a noncovalent manner at the active site,[38] thus blocking access of the normal reactant (called substrate) to the active site. Such interactions usually arise from chemical agents that are very nearly like the normal substrate. Generally, an equilibrium exists for given concentrations of normal substrate and the chemical agent such that the chemical agent may not be strongly held and it comes off. Normal substrate can then bind to the active site and react to yield the product. As the product comes off, either another substrate binds or perhaps another chemical agent binds. This can go on for some time until the chemical agent is itself removed from the cell by degradative and detoxifying processes that all cells possess. The worst case scenario is that of a covalent bond formed between the chemical agent and the enzyme active site.

In the covalent adduction of the chemical agent to the enzyme active site, a chemical reaction has occurred in which one or more of the unique amino acid side chains composing the active site has reacted with the chemical agent. The result is a covalent bond which is not easily or quickly broken by reversal of the process. Generally, once formed, the covalent bond that results is fast and can only be broken, restoring normal enzyme activity, by other chemical treatments-- provided that such treatments are themselves not destructive of the protein or the cell as a whole (see Toxic Agents Chapters-- Nerve Agents, and Treatment Chapter-- Nerve Agents).

For nonenzymatic proteins, such as structural proteins of muscle and bone, or transport proteins of membranes, or the blood, the interaction with toxic chemical agents can also be a physical association or covalent adduction process. In either case, however, the consequences to the protein are essentially an alteration of the conformation[39] of the protein and thus its inability to function optimally if at all. Particularly in the case of transport proteins embedded in membranes, changes in the conformation by either physical or covalent interactions can alter significantly the shape of the protein, the size and shape of protein channels and even interfere with the proximal displacements of charged groups of such channels, altering and interfering with their ability to permit critical, biologically important ion exchange. However, membrane-bound proteins are not the only subject of attack by hydrophobic toxic chemical agents. The membranes themselves can be adversely affected.

Membranes consist of mostly lipids-- phospholipids[40] to be specific. Phospholipids possess two distinct and separated regions in the molecule. One end is hydrophilic or charged, and the other end is neutral and hydrophobic, a hydrocarbon much like vegetable oil in chemical characteristics. Though membranes[41] are seemingly rigid they are not. There is considerable flexibility and elasticity to a membrane including movement of the hydrocarbon portions or tails, as they are known to biochemists and cell physiologists, comprising the internal region. The hydrocarbon tails form a relatively loosely aligned network that in simple terms resembles the fingers of the hands loosely intertwined. The membrane surface is not smooth but possesses many inward and outward folds, greatly increasing the

---

[38] The active site of an enzyme is the location in the folded, native form protein where the chemical reactions occur. It is the side chains of the particular amino acid units comprising the active site that determine the chemical activity of the active site.

[39] Simply meaning a substance's physical shape and form.

[40] Phospholipids consist of four specific groups in covalent association. They are a phosphate group, glycerol, an aliphatic lipid (also known as a long chain aliphatic carboxylic acid), and what is called a base (ethanolamine, choline, inositol, etc.).

[41] Cellular membranes are incredibly thin, visible only with the electron microscope.

surface area of the membrane. Embedded, partially or completely[42] in this sea of hydrocarbon are the membrane-bound proteins. The fine structure and composition of membranes is critical to the permeability and barrier functions of the membrane. It serves to keep the internal cellular materials-- the cytoplasm-- inside, and the rest of the world outside, or put another way, keeps the cytoplasmic contents from spilling out into the rest of the environment about the cell. With the aid of the membrane-bound proteins, the membranes provide what is called selective permeability. Only certain materials may enter or leave the cell. Typically, nutrients and oxygen enter and wastes including carbon dioxide (in chemically bound form) exit. Membrane permeability is such that it is as though minuscule pores exist in the membrane affording greater permeability to a select few biologically important materials. Upset the delicate composition and construction of the membrane and the existence of the cell is in jeopardy. How might this delicate structure be disrupted by toxic chemical agents? By the same kinds of interactions affecting proteins, but in a different setting.

Hydrophobic chemical agents are soluble in the membrane. As a result, they will alter the internal fine structure of the membrane so critical to its selective permeability. Though the membrane can essentially 'heal' itself, extensive damage can lead to cell death by a process akin to bleeding known as lysis. Defects such as holes in the membrane which can not be resealed are the ports of leakage of cytoplasm from the cell. This is analogous to the hydrodynamic pressure exerted by the water of a dam against a crack or hole in the dam wall. A lysed cell is a dead cell. A tissue with millions of lysed cells is a dying tissue. One class of toxic chemical agents undoubtedly functions initially and primarily on the membranes of cells of the skin leading to blisters (see Chapter 8).

CHEMICAL AGENTS

What makes a chemical a good choice as a war agent? The characteristics of a chemical agent are its chemical and physical (referred to by chemists as its physicochemical) properties. A sampling of these physicochemical properties are:

1. toxicity (LD_{50})
2. physical state
    a. gas
    b. liquid
    c. solid
3. density
4. color
5. odor
6. portal of entry
    a. lungs
    b. eyes
    c. skin
    d. digestive tract
7. low freezing point, volatility

---

[42] Some researchers believe that membranes consist of a sandwich morphology, in which protein lines the outer surfaces of the lipid component, the lipid material residing between the two protein layers.

8. moderate vapor pressure
9. stability to environmental effects, storage
   a. humidity
   b. temperature
   c. sunlight
10. inexpensive
11. nonflammable

The physical state of a chemical agent is important for the packaging of it as a munition. Gaseous agents are broadly unsatisfactory as they are gases under normal temperature and pressure conditions on the battlefield, require liquefaction[43] for packaging, and are too easily removed from the battlefield by winds. This translates to the diminished time of duration over the target. Solids are also less desirable for the opposite reasons. They are very dense, they settle to the ground too quickly and generally are removed from the air unless kicked up by passing troops and vehicles. Also they may be more identifiable on the ground and serve to alert enemy forces to their presence. Liquids are perhaps the best form of agent for weapons use since they are easily packaged and, in fact, all chemical agents are currently packaged in liquid form. On dispersal over the battlefield they are in the form of an aerosol (fog is an aerosol) or dense vapor which settles to the ground slowly, disperses more evenly than gases or solids and covers a larger area in higher concentrations. In conjunction with low freezing points and moderate vapor pressures of the agent, chemical agents remain liquid or aerosol under cold temperatures. Their volatility, the ability to vaporize[44] under environmental conditions, assures reasonable evaporation of liquid pools and the maintenance of a militarily effective vapor concentration in the area of dispersal.

Density[45] is important since any agent lighter than air will be displaced by air near the ground where air density is greatest. This results in the aerosol or vapor state never reaching the ground where troops are. An agent should be as dense if not more dense than air so that its aerosol or vapor form will hover above the ground no higher than man height or settle to the ground slowly with time. Dense agents are particularly effective on defensive positions since they settle to the lowest points on the ground, i.e. foxholes, trenches, bunker emplacements, valleys, revetments, any place troops seek cover (defined as protection from direct, line-of-sight fire).

Color is important since a colorful agent immediately signals its presence. Ideally, chemical agents should be colorless so as to mix with the air and become indistinguishable from the air. Practically speaking, agents may be colorless in pure form but in concentrated liquid form with other materials mixed with them (impurities, etc.) may have a slight color. Upon dispersal over a target area, however, they become invisible after the initial placement and spread with the air currents.

Portal of entry means simply where the agent enters the body. The most effective and fastest acting agents are those designed and intended to be inhaled-- entering through the lungs. Entrance through the lungs immediately places the agent into the bloodstream, rapidly spreading it to all parts of the body. This is without question the optimum manner of entry and many of the most lethal of the chemical agents are so intended to enter via the lungs. The eyes are also effective portals of entry

---

[43] To condense a gas to liquid form.

[44] To become gaseous or vapor.

[45] Mass per unit volume.

though slower in absorption than the lungs. From a military protection standpoint, if the lungs are protected, so too are the eyes via a protective mask.

The skin is a deliberately designed barrier of the body against penetration of a wide range of foreign particles, both inanimate and animate. However, some chemical agents can be absorbed through the skin and some chemical agents are designed solely for and act directly on or through the skin. Though much slower absorbing than the other portals of entry, skin, nonetheless, is a specific target for some agents and a secondary target of others. Breaks in the skin, i.e., cuts, open wounds, increase the effectiveness of skin-acting agents.

The digestive tract is another portal of entry. Ingestion of poisonous substances is effective though the body's defensive mechanism is vomiting, a not so absolute and correct response for all poisons. This means of agent use is quite slow and, generally, no chemical agent is designed specifically for ingestion by enemy troops. However, such action may arise from accidental ingestion of agent-contaminated water or food or contact of agent-contaminated fingers with the mouth.

Stability of the agent to environmental destruction is critical to agent usefulness. An agent that hydrolyzes (destroyed by water) is less effective than one that is water stable. Humidity in the air, over time, can and will destroy agents that are water reactive. Susceptibility to photochemical reaction (chemically altered by sunlight) is yet another environmental test a proposed chemical agent must pass. Over time, humidity, sunlight, rain, wind, etc., will slowly dilute and destroy chemical agents, removing them from the target site. Most of these properties have an impact on what is called the persistence of the agent. Effective agents persist, that is they remain stable over a period of militarily significant time (defined as lasting for 24 hours), are not destroyed quickly by environmental conditions over and on the terrain during deployment, and possess properties of volatility and density affording maximum concentration at dispersal for optimum casualty performance.

The cost of the chemical agent is also a factor. Particularly in this era of "smart" weapons, chemical agents are very cost effective, that is, a "better bang for the buck." They generally are very inexpensive compared to the cost of conventional artillery rounds, smart bombs and certainly a nuclear weapon. If the potential agent is not a generally available industrial chemical, its manufacture must be cheap enough to justify its use. Additionally, they have the advantage of imposing potentially high casualties on an unprotected and unsuspecting enemy force without imposing any structural or real estate damage as do conventional and nuclear weapons. Chemical weapons in particular, and to a lesser extent, biological weapons, are systems ideally suited to use by less technologically advanced military nations. Such nations may not possess the resources for or the technical expertise (engineers, physicists, etc.) to support a nuclear weapons program or even a "smart weapons" program, but chemistry is a near ubiquitous technology that only the most impoverished nations (economically and intellectually) cannot afford or pursue.

Finally, and critical to the agent's application to the battlefield in a munition, it must be nonflammable. Since munitions will burst from an internal explosive charge, the heat and flame of the explosion should not ignite the agent. Furthermore, the heat of munition detonation also provides a means for instant vaporization of liquid agent, placing it into aerosol form for dispersal down wind.

Chemical agents fall into three broad categories: lethal or toxic, incapacitating, and incendiary. Each category has immediate destructive effects on enemy forces. Smoking agents are chemical agents though a miscellaneous category. Of the former two categories, the separation between lethal and incapacitating is a matter of degree. Generally, there are four classes of toxic chemical agents (excluding incendiary types) intended for use as weapons to either kill or severely injured. These classes are *nerve, blood, choking, blistering* and they follow this order in decreasing lethality and delay in onset of effects. The classification "blood" agent is a misnomer. However, it is still found in the literature and many such agents have been discussed in this connection.

PART III

CHAPTER 4

TOXIC CHEMICAL AGENTS[1]

Science has nothing to be ashamed of, even in
the ruins of Nagasaki.
  -*Science and Human Values*, Julian Messner[2]

GENERAL

Stocks of various U.S. toxic agents in reserve are considered classified information. Estimates, however, place these supplies of lethal munitions at about 150,000 tons.[3] This mass of lethal agents is distributed among artillery shells (105 mm GB, 155 mm GB & VX) and GB aerial bombs (500 lb & 750 lb).

In the sections that follow, the discussion of various agents presupposes their military or terrorist use as opposed to any industrial accidental exposure. As such, military exposure places a practical limit achieved on the quantity or concentration of an agent in the air (for aerosol or vapor agents) or fine droplets and very minuscule puddles on the ground (for liquid agents). Thus, from a military or terrorist employment standpoint, agents are intended to be inhaled or to settle on personnel as a fine mist (aerosol). Industrial accidental exposure can entail much higher concentrations than may be practically achieved in the field under combat and environmental conditions.

Agents principally act through absorption in the lungs (inhalation) or through the skin. Though the skin is a very effective barrier against a wide range of particulate matter (particularly microorganisms), it is less effective as a barrier against chemical substances. This is because skin is

---

[1] Toxic agent is the correct term to use in describing war chemicals. The term gas was introduced in WWI, but is technically incorrect, certainly in the description of the majority of such chemical agents. The book The War Gases, Chemistry and Analysis by Mario Sartori, D. Van Nostrand Co., Inc., New York, 1940, examines various classes of chemical compounds for their suitability as war agents. Though dated and a number of the compounds cited have found little use as war agents, the work nonetheless offers the reader a view of chemical properties and reactions of such candidate agents.

[2] in *The Harvest of a Quiet Eye,* p. 25

[3] This is the total weight of munitions, not just the weight of the agents themselves. [Ref.: M. Meselson & J.P. Robinson, "Chemical Warfare and Disarmament", *Scientific American* **242(4)**, 38-47 (1980)]

a nearly hydrophobic[4] material. Skin is a complex system (organ) consisting of dead (surface) and living (interior) cells in a protein matrix (collagen of connective tissue). The membranes of cells are themselves very hydrophobic in nature. As a consequence, most aqueous systems experience little or no absorption by the skin.[5] Most industrial chemicals and certainly most chemical war agents are hydrophobic substances. They are soluble in materials possessing the same characteristics: like dissolves like. Therefore, some chemical agents are able to dissolve into the skin, be absorbed, and affect exposed personnel through that mechanism. (See also Blistering Agents.)

NERVE AGENTS

Nerve agents are the most lethal and derive their classification from their action on the body. They interfere with the transmission of nerve impulses. Specifically, they are known as (acetyl)cholinesterase inhibitors. Nerve agents act by binding, irreversibly[6] in most cases, to an enzyme, specifically acetylcholinesterase, important in nerve impulse transmission regulation. This is by far not the only susceptible enzyme.

There are two principal classes of anticholinergic[7] compounds. They are organophosphates and carbamates. The carbamates (derivatives of carbamic acid [I]) are a more recent development in insecticide formulations. Both types find widespread use as insecticides though the organophosphates are perhaps the best known.

Prior to WWI and the development of nerve agents, gas warfare was viewed as a tactical approach to gaining the upper hand over an enemy force on a localized battlefield. With the inception of nerve agents, the application of gas warfare shifted from the tactical realm to the strategic realm. Nerve agents, because of their high toxicity and rapidity of action, now make it practical to assault civilian population centers as generally civilians are, due to government laws and prohibitions, less likely to possess the means to defend themselves against enemy attacks of any kind, much less chemical attack.

SYMPTOMS[8]

Nerve agents are generally odorless and colorless. They are principally lung active agents, that is, they are intended to be inhaled and distributed throughout the body via the cardiovascular system. This is the most advantageous means of dosing personnel. Nerve agents also are skin active, that is, they can be absorbed through the skin and distributed also by the cardiovascular system, though this is a much slower mechanism.

---

[4] Literally, fear of water, meaning water repellent.

[5] Skin wrinkling in dishwater or in sea water is due largely to dehydration of what water is on or in the skin matrix.

[6] Meaning cannot be easily undone, if at all.

[7] Substances that interfere with nerve impulse transmission.

[8] Handbook of Poisoning, Robert H. Dreisbach, Lange Medical Publications, Los Altos, CA, 1983.

Generally, the main effects of nerve agent poisoning appear as visual impairment, respiratory impairment and gastrointestinal hyperactivity. Significant manifestation of symptoms can appear as late as 30 minutes and peak as late as eight hours after exposure. Specifically, nerve agent poisoning falls into three levels of severity.

Mild exposure manifests itself as dizziness (vertigo), headache, weakness, anxiety, anorexia, tremors of the tongue and eyelids, visual acuity impairment,[9] substernal pain, and miosis[10] from direct eye contact. These symptoms can alert the exposed and knowledgeable soldier of his exposure at which time he should self-administer his atropine injector and alert his unit medical personnel. These are the earliest warnings he receives directly from the agent. These effects occur seconds after exposure and peak about 15 to 20 minutes after removal from exposure.

Moderate exposure hazard is revealed by worsening of the above symptoms and by excessive salivation and sweating, abdominal cramps, diarrhea, nausea, vomiting, tearing and muscular fasciculation. At this point in the process, the soldier knows that he is in trouble.

Severe exposure is signaled by pinpointing, unresponsive pupils to light; significant, labored respiratory impairment; convulsions and seizures; involuntary and uncontrollable urination and defecation; cyanosis (due to lack of oxygen); respiratory paralysis; flaccid paralysis and coma. Without emergency care intervention, death follows.

The following table lists some of the common nerve agents and some of their properties.

TABLE 1

SPECIFIC MILITARY CHEMICAL AGENTS BY TYPE					
NERVE	BLOOD	CHOKING	BLISTER	INCAPACITANTS	INCENDIARY
SARIN SOMAN TABUN VX	CYANIDE CYANOGEN CHLORIDE	CHLORINE PHOSGENE	S-MUSTARD N-MUSTARD LEWISITE	TEARGASES CS CN URANIUM	WHITE P NAPALM THERMITE

---

[9] Effects on the eyes generally arise from direct eye contact with vapor or droplets.

[10] Contraction of the pupil. Not to be confused with meiosis.

TABLE 4-1: NERVE AGENTS		
COMMON NAME	TABUN	SARIN
CHEMICAL NAME	DIMETHYLPHOSPHORAMIDOCYANIDIC ACID, ETHYL ESTER	METHYLPHOSPHONOFLUORIDIC ACID, 1-METHYLETHYL ESTER
MILITARY SYMBOL	GA	GB
CLASSIFICATION CHEMICAL MILITARY	ANTICHOLINERGIC ORGANOPHOSPHATE, NERVE AGENT	ANTICHOLINERGIC ORGANOPHOSPHATE, NERVE AGENT
PHYSICAL STATE/COLOR	LIQUID/COLORLESS TO LIGHT BROWN	LIQUID/COLORLESS
BOILING/MELTING POINT (°C)	240/-50	147/-57
DENSITY (AT °C)	1.08 (4)	1.1 (4)
ODOR	FRUITY, BITTER ALMOND, NONE WHEN PURE	VIRTUALLY NONE WHEN PURE
HYDROLYSIS	QUICKLY, NONTOXIC ORTHOPHOSPHATE COMPOUNDS, HCN HAZARD	ORTHOPHOSPHATE COMPOUNDS
LETHAL CONC.	0.01 MG/KG	0.01 MG/KG
PERSISTENCY	NO	NO
PRIMARY SITE OF ABSORPTION	LUNGS	LUNGS
SECONDARY SITE OF ABSORPTION	EYES, SKIN	EYES, SKIN
DECONTAMINATION METHODS	BLEACHING POWDER, ClCN HAZARD	BLEACHING POWDER, WATER, BICARBONATE, SODIUM HYDROXIDE SOLUTIONS
ANTIDOTE	ATROPINE, OXIMES	ATROPINE, OXIMES

TABLE 4-1: NERVE AGENTS CONTINUED		
COMMON NAME	SOMAN	VX
CHEMICAL NAME	METHYLPHOSPHONOFLUORIDIC ACID, S-[2-[BIS(1-METHYLETHYL)AMINO]]	METHYLPHOSPHONOTHIOIC ACID, S-[2-[BIS(1-METHYLETHYL)AMINO]] O-ETHYL ESTER
MILITARY SYMBOL	GD	VX
CLASSIFICATION CHEMICAL MILITARY	ANTICHOLINERGIC ORGANOPHOSPHATE, NERVE AGENT	ANTICHOLINERGIC ORGANOPHOSPHATE, NERVE AGENT
PHYSICAL STATE/COLOR	LIQUID	LIQUID
BOILING/MELTING POINT (°C)		
DENSITY (AT °C)	6.33 (VAPOR)	9.2 (VAPOR)
ODOR	FRUITY, CAMPHOR ODOR IN PURE FORM	ODORLESS IN PURE FORM
HYDROLYSIS		
LETHAL CONC.	0.01 MG/KG	AS LOW AS 10 MG/KG
PERSISTENCY	SLIGHTLY	YES
PRIMARY SITE OF ABSORPTION	LUNGS	SKIN
SECONDARY SITE OF ABSORPTION	EYES, SKIN	EYES, LUNGS
DECONTAMINATION METHODS	BLEACHING POWDER	BLEACHING POWDER
ANTIDOTE	ATROPINE, OXIMES	ATROPINE, OXIMES

TABLE 4-1: NERVE AGENTS Continued		
COMMON NAME	MALATHION	PARATHION
CHEMICAL NAME	[(DIMETHOXYPHOSPHINOTHIOYL)THIO] BUTANEDIOIC ACID, DIETHYL ESTER	PHOSPHOROTHIOIC ACID, O,O-DIETHYL O-(4-NITROPHENYL) ESTER
MILITARY SYMBOL	NONE	NONE
CLASSIFICATION CHEMICAL MILITARY	ANTICHOLINERGIC ORGANOPHOSPHATE, INSECTICIDE, NONE	ANTICHOLINERGIC ORGANOPHOSPHATE, INSECTICIDE, NONE
PHYSICAL STATE/COLOR	LIQUID/BROWN TO YELLOW	LIQUID/PALE BROWN YELLOW
BOILING/MELTING POINT (°C)	156/2.9	375/6
DENSITY (AT °C)	1.23 (25)	1.26 (25)
ODOR	YES	YES
HYDROLYSIS	VERY SLOWLY, HEPATICALLY METABOLIZED	INSOLUBLE IN WATER
LETHAL CONC.	1375 MG/KG (MALE RAT)	13 MG/KG (MALE RAT)
PERSISTENCY	MODERATE	YES
PRIMARY SITE OF ABSORPTION	SKIN	SKIN
SECONDARY SITE OF ABSORPTION	EYES, LUNGS	EYES, LUNGS
DECONTAMINATION METHODS	BLEACHING POWDER, STRONG BLEACH	BLEACHING POWDER, STRONG BLEACH
ANTIDOTE	ATROPINE, OXIMES	ATROPINE, OXIMES

APPENDIX A: NERVE AGENTS Continued	
COMMON NAME	**DIAZINON**
CHEMICAL NAME	PHOSPHONOTHIONIC CID, O,O-DIETHYL O-[6-MWTHYL-2-(1-METHYLETHYL)-4-PYRIMIDINYL] ESTER
MILITARY SYMBOL	NONE
CLASSIFICATION CHEMICAL MILITARY	ANTICHOLINERGIC ORGANOPHOSPHATE INSECTICIDE, NONE
PHYSICAL STATE/COLOR	LIQUID, PALE BROWN TO YELLOW
BOILING/MELTING POINT (°C)	83/-
DENSITY, G/ML (AT °C)	**1.12 (20)**
ODOR	YES
HYDROLYSIS	SLOWLY
LETHAL CONC. OR DOSE	
PERSISTENCY	NO
PRIMARY SITE OF ABSORPTION	SKIN
SECONDARY SITE OF ABSORPTION	EYES, LUNGS
DECONTAMINATION METHODS	BLEACHING POWDER, STRONG BLEACH
ANTIDOTE	ATROPINE, OXIMES

BLOOD AGENTS

The term Blood agents is a misnomer. Historically such agents were thought to affect the blood. They do not. However, for ease of classification we will retain the term though it has no basis in scientific fact.

Blood agents rival nerve agents for lethality and rapidity of action. Some blood agents act against the body's ability to absorb oxygen in the blood (carbon monoxide[11] , a true blood agent, in the hemoglobin of red blood cells, Figure 4-1) or in the body's ability to metabolize oxygen to water in the cell[12] (cyanide[13] within the mitochondrion). They are effectively lung active agents. Generally, blood agents are cyanide based and releasing compounds. The principal and best known blood agent is hydrogen cyanide [II]. This is the compound used in the California Gas Chamber in capital punishment executions. Hydrogen cyanide, a volatile, colorless liquid, has a sweetish odor sometimes characterized as that of almonds (though not detectable by all). It is an unstable compound in concentrated form and can decompose with explosive violence. It is not irritating to the eyes, nose or throat.

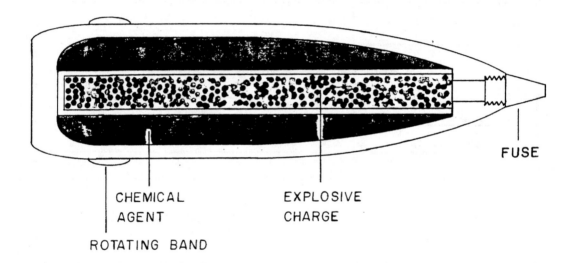

FIGURE 4-1 The configuration of a single composition chemical munition shell for an artillery gun.

---

[11]   Carbon monoxide has an affinity for hemoglobin that is over 200 times greater than oxygen. It binds to the iron +2, Fe(II).

[12]   The enzyme system responsible for this is called cytochrome oxidase.

[13]   Cyanide, CN⁻, dissolves in the blood plasma and is carried in the blood to the capillaries where cyanide passes into cells to reach the mitochondria. Cyanide binds to the iron +3 state, Fe(III), which in hemoglobin is a very small fraction, constituting less than 1% of total hemoglobin. It does not form a stable complex with Fe(II) of hemoglobin.

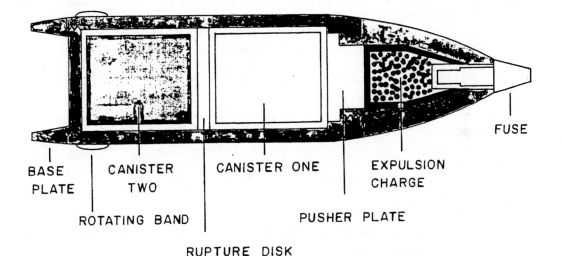

FIGURE 4-2 The configuration of a binary munition shell for artillery. This method provides for a safer handling and storage of the chemical munition. The lethal agent is generated only after firing of the round from the gun tube. The instant acceleration of the shell down the tube bursts the rupture disk separating the two reactants that mix and produce the lethal agent while the shell is in flight to target.

Cyanogen chloride [III], also a blood agent, acts similarly to hydrogen cyanide. First used by the French in October, 1917, it was found very effective in penetrating the German protective mask but not the American mask. Its drawbacks are that its vapor has poor density compared to air and it is immediately irritating[14] to the eyes and nasal passages. The agent also is unstable and tends to polymerize.[15] This process can be retarded by the use of stabilizers such as sodium pyrophosphate.

All blood agents act essentially the same way. They interfere with the ability of the cell to metabolize oxygen to water. This process is vital as it is a major means of producing energy in the form of ATP[16] [IV] and takes place within the mitochondria (Chapter 6). The essential feature of this inhibition to metabolize oxygen to water is the interference with the transport of electrons from fuel molecules (food) to the receiving oxygen molecule.

The following table lists some data on Blood Agents.

---

[14] On contact with water, it hydrolyzes to hydrogen cyanide and hypochlorous acid (the acid form of bleach), the latter very irritating to and destructive of mucous tissues.

[15] Polymerization is the process by which small molecules of the same kind react with each other to form longer molecules made up of the smaller repeat units.

[16] ATP: Adenosine TriPhosphate, commonly and accurately portrayed as the currency of life. The transfer of the terminal phosphate to other molecules is the process by which those molecules are activated for use in metabolic pathways.

TABLE 4-2: BLOOD AGENTS		
COMMON NAME	PRUSSIC ACID	CYANOGEN CHLORIDE
CHEMICAL NAME	HYDROGEN CYANIDE	CYANOGEN CHLORIDE
MILITARY SYMBOL	AC	CK
CLASSIFICATION CHEMICAL MILITARY	CYTOCHROME OXIDASE INHIBITOR, BLOOD AGENT	CYTOCHROME OXIDASE INHIBITOR BLOOD AGENT
PHYSICAL STATE/COLOR	GAS OR LIQUID/COLORLESS	LIQUID
BOILING/MELTING POINT (°C)	25.6/-13.4	13.8/-6
DENSITY (AT °C)	0.687 (4)	1.19 (4)
ODOR	SWEETISH, FAINT ALMONDS	IRRITANT VAPORS
HYDROLYSIS	NONE	HCN, HOCL
LETHAL CONC.	50 TO 60 MG	13 MG/KG
PERSISTENCY	NO	NO
PRIMARY SITE OF ABSORPTION	LUNGS	LUNGS
SECONDARY SITE OF ABSORPTION	EYES	EYES
DECONTAMINATION METHODS	NONE, DISPERSES IN AIR	NONE, DISPERSES IN AIR
ANTIDOTE	SODIUM NITRITE, THIOSULFATE, AMYL NITRITE	SODIUM NITRITE, THIOSULFATE, AMYL NITRITE

SYMPTOMS

Essentially, signs of blood agent poisoning are rapid respiration, convulsions and coma. Absorption of a quantity near the LD_{50} leads to vertigo, headache, palpitations, deep, rapid breathing (tachypnea), drowsiness, nausea with or without vomiting. Increased absorption progressively worsens these symptoms rapidly and leads to respiratory difficulty or distress, paralysis, unconsciousness, convulsions, respiratory arrest and death. A bluish color to the skin (cyanosis, not always apparent), due to the lack of oxygenation in the blood vessels. This condition can progress to a dull grayish pale color, usually a sign of imminent death.

CHOKING AGENTS

Choking agents, such as chlorine and phosgene, attack the respiratory tract and are thus lung active. Phosgene, colorless and slightly denser than water, dissolves in the moisture inherent in the lungs and releases hydrochloric acid and tissue acylating molecular species which lead to rupturing of the capillaries of the air sacs (alveoli) of the lungs. The severity of exposure is not evident for about three or four hours after inhalation. This in turn leads to bleeding and the filling of the lungs with fluid in more advanced exposure. Suffocation from fluid-filled lungs follows in extreme exposure often called dry land drowning. These agents are not immediately irritating when inhaled and vary in odor depending on the agent used. Chlorine smells characteristically like household bleach, while phosgene's odor is that of mown or moldy hay.

The following table lists some choking agents and their properties.

TABLE 4-3: CHOKING AGENTS			
COMMON NAME	PHOSGENE	CHLORINE	DIPHOSGENE
CHEMICAL NAME	CARBONYL CHLORIDE	CHLORINE	TRICHLOROMETHYL CHLOROFORMATE
MILITARY SYMBOL	CG	CL	DP
CLASSIFICATION CHEMICAL MILITARY	ACYLATING AGENT, CHOKING AGENT	OXIDANT, CHOKING AGENT	ACYLATING AGENT, CHOKING AGENT
PHYSICAL STATE/COLOR	GASEOUS/COLORLESS	GASEOUS/GREENISH YELLOW	
BOILING/MELTING POINT (°C)	8.2/-104	-34.1/-102	128/-
DENSITY (AT °C)	1.37 (20)	1.4 (20)	
ODOR	MOWN HAY, CORN	PUNGENT, BLEACH	MOWN HAY, CORN
HYDROLYSIS	CO_2, HCL	HCL, HOCL	HCL (SLOW)
LETHAL CONC.	0.1 PPM	1.0 PPM	
PERSISTENCY	NO	NO	MODERATE
PRIMARY SITE OF ABSORPTION	LUNGS	LUNGS	LUNGS
SECONDARY SITE OF ABSORPTION	EYE IRRITANT	EYES, SKIN	EYES, THROAT
DECONTAMINATION METHODS	STEAM, ALKALINE SOLUTIONS	ALKALINE SOLUTIONS	ALKALINE SOLUTIONS
ANTIDOTE	NONE	NONE	NONE

SYMPTOMS

The outcome of choking agent poisoning is respiratory and circulatory failure. Symptoms of exposure begin within 24 hours. Initially, a burning sensation in the throat and irritation of the eyes and nasal passages (high concentrations) progresses to constricted feeling in the chest, violent coughing, painful breathing, and nausea, retching and vomiting. Cyanosis may also be evidenced in advanced cases along with bloody sputum and finally death.

BLISTERING AGENTS

Blistering agents are generally not as rapidly lethal as the other agents, though more modern blistering agents rival earlier developed nerve agents for toxicity on inhalation.[17] They are, nonetheless, potent in their ability to at least severely incapacitate those so exposed. They are the slowest acting, exhibiting their effects between one to twelve hours after exposure. Their potential value was not fully appreciated during WWI, though since then they have become recognized as one of the significant chemical agent threats. This class of agent is principally intended as a skin active agent, though inhalation of its aerosols and vapors can also lead to severe respiratory injury that can threaten life.

They are severe vesicants, causing blisters (chemical burns) generally, and particularly of moist areas of the body such as between the fingers, toes, armpits, behind the knees, waistline, crotch and anal region, the eyes, and skin in general.

During WWI, only about 2% of those exposed to the blistering agent mustard[18] (a sulfur containing compound) died. This statistic can only be attributed to the ineffective and inefficient experience and means for its dissemination on the battlefield in WWI. Its value to the military rests on its high toxicity to skin as well as the eyes and lungs. Other blistering agents or mustards may be formulated using the element nitrogen and are known as nitrogen mustards.

Secondary infection due to the ulcerations (blister rupture of the skin) is a serious complication. Severe exposure of the eyes can lead to blindness in heavily exposed, delayed treatment cases. In WWI the most significant cause of injury to the exposed soldiers and reason for delay in returning them to duty was severe eye damage, requiring weeks or months of care. Another consequence of severe exposure is infection of the bronchial passages (bronchopneumonia).

Nitrogen mustards are well suited for offensive use as they are much more rapid acting than the sulfur analogs. They are hydrolyzed by water but the products of hydrolysis are themselves also quite toxic. As these substances may be viewed as derivatives of ammonia, they have a characteristically fishy odor, though a few are odorless. They produce similar injuries and effects as the sulfur based mustards with some variations, but have thus far found greater use in medicine as chemotherapeutic agents in cancer treatment rather than as a war gas.

Recent studies show that mustards[19] (blistering agents), as the sulfur compounds are specifically known, have strong alkylating properties.[20] That is to say these compounds combine with DNA, the genetic material of the cell, and can or are suspected to be chemical carcinogens. This property has no military value, though from the standpoint of industrial workers producing such munitions, it can

---

[17] See Chapter 8: Blistering Agents

[18] bis(2-chloroethyl)sulfide: $ClCH_2CH_2SCH_2CH_2Cl$

[19] The term mustard originated from the odor of some of the sulfur compounds, reminiscent of mustard.

[20] Certain chemical compounds are known to be carcinogenic in that they chemically react with the DNA of a cell. This reaction leads to an alteration of the chemical identity of the DNA component with which the chemical has reacted. This process is known to the chemist as alkylation and the compounds that so react, alkylating agents.

have dire consequences five, ten or twenty years later. Nitrogen mustards[21] like the sulfur mustards also attack the DNA.

Arsenicals such as Lewisite[22] are irritating compounds whose injuries are very painful. Lewisite is the more lethal blistering agent developed in WWI but never used. Lewisite is particularly hazardous as it is extremely toxic and a respiratory and systemic poison. The nerve agents and modern sulfur mustards largely render this agent obsolete as it is more easily neutralized by water and wet clothing than the other agents.

Sulfur based mustards of military use generally have little or no odor or sweet agreeable odors, some smelling like garlic, and the odors often can be masked by use of smoke munitions in conjunction with the mustards. Lewisite in particular smells like geraniums.

Another agent is phosgene oxime [V], a urticant.[23] This, too, produces severe blistering and is immediately painful upon contact.

The following table lists several blistering or vesicant agents and some of their properties.

---

[21] The first nitrogen mustard was developed in 1935 by Kyle Ward, Jr.: *Journal American Chemical Society* 57, 914-916 (1935).

[22] Named after Dr. Winford Lee Lewis, director of the team of chemists who developed it in 1918.

[23] A stinging compound, acts like a corrosive.

TABLE 4-4: BLISTERING AGENTS		
COMMON NAME	MUSTARD GAS	LEWISITE
CHEMICAL NAME	BIS(2-CHLOROETHYL)SULFIDE	DICHLORO(2-CHLOROVINYL)ARSINE
MILITARY SYMBOL	HD, HS	M-1, L
CLASSIFICATION CHEMICAL MILITARY	ALKYLATING AGENT, BLISTERING, VESICANT AGENT	ARSENICAL, BLISTERING, VESICANT AGENT
PHYSICAL STATE/COLOR	OILY LIQUID	LIQUID
BOILING/MELTING POINT (°C)	216/14.4	190/-18.2
DENSITY (AT °C)	1.27 (20)	1.88 (20)
ODOR	GARLIC	GERANIUMS
HYDROLYSIS	HCL, NONTOXIC ORGANOSULFIDES (SLOW)	ARSENIC OXIDES, SYSTEMIC HAZARD
LETHAL CONC.	20 MG/KG	0.5 TO 2.0 ML
PERSISTENCY	YES	ARSENICAL HAZARD YES
PRIMARY SITE OF ABSORPTION	SKIN	SKIN
SECONDARY SITE OF ABSORPTION	EYES, LUNGS	EYES, LUNGS
DECONTAMINATION METHODS	LIME, SODIUM SULFIDE SOLUTIONS	WATER, ALCOHOLIC SODIUM HYDROXIDE
ANTIDOTE	NONE	BAL: BRITISH ANTILEWISITE (2,3-DIMERCAPTOPROPANOL)

TABLE 4-4: BLISTERING AGENTS CONTINUED		
COMMON NAME	NITROGEN MUSTARD	ETHYLDICHLORARSINE
CHEMICAL NAME	2-CHLORO-N-(2-CHLOROETHYL)-N-METHYLETHANAMINE	ETHYLDICHLORARSINE
MILITARY SYMBOL	HN	ED

CLASSIFICATION
  CHEMICAL
  MILITARY
	AMINE, ALKYLATING AGENT, BLISTERING, VESICANT AGENT	ALKYLATING AGENT, ARSENICAL, BLISTERING, VESICANT AGENT

PHYSICAL STATE/COLOR	LIQUID	LIQUID
BOILING/MELTING POINT (°C)	87/-60	156/-30
DENSITY (AT °C)	1.12 (25)	1.7 (20)
ODOR	HERRING	FRUITY
HYDROLYSIS	TOXIC QUATERNARY AMMONIUM SALTS	HCL, ETHYLARSENIOUS OXIDE (SYSTEMIC HAZARD)
LETHAL CONC.	1.1 MG/KG (RATS)	
PERSISTENCY	YES	ARSENICAL HAZARD
PRIMARY SITE OF ABSORPTION	SKIN	SKIN
SECONDARY SITE OF ABSORPTION	EYES, LUNGS	EYES, LUNGS
DECONTAMINATION METHODS	BLEACHING POWDER, SODIUM THIOSULFATE	SOAP/WATER, SODIUM HYDROXIDE SOLUTIONS
ANTIDOTE	NONE	BAL

Symptoms

These agents, depending on the concentration and time of unprotected exposure take effect in two to three hours and symptoms begin with tearing and irritation of the eyes, nose and throat, developing into conjunctivitis, coughing, eyelid irritations, reddening and inflammation of the skin, severe itching, ulcerations[24] of the skin and membrane tissues, necrosis of exposed respiratory tract and skin. Ingestion causes nausea and vomiting.

Skin effects are classified as mild erythema[25] progressing to sensitivity to touch and tiny blisters. Significant exposure leads to severe erythema, severe blistering and systemic toxic effects.

Eye injuries arise by reddening, conjunctivitis, a gritty sensation under the eyelids, tearing and sensitivity to light. Significant exposure of the eyes leads to corneal edema[26] and clouding, edema of the eyelids and photophobia with severe blepharospasm[27] and temporary blindness. Severe exposure of the eyes gives rise to corneal damage, possible ulcerations and secondary infections. These symptoms can progress, if untreated, to loss of vision, severe pain, severe corneal damage and perforations as well as systemic effects.

Respiratory tract symptoms begin with irritation of the nasal passages and hoarseness. Upper respiratory tract exposure exhibits sneezing, lacrimation, rhinorrhea[28], epistaxis[29], sore throat. Lower respiratory tract involvement exhibits tracheobronchitis[30], hacking cough, tachypnea, pulmonary edema and bronchopneumonia. Also edematous[31] changes are evident in the pharynx, tracheobronchi with necrotic bronchopneumonia. Death often arises through secondary infections in this instance.

Systemic effects arise as a loss of taste and smell, nose bleeding, sore throat. Chest pain, wheezing and dyspnea[32] follow. Additionally the severely exposed individual experiences increased susceptibility to lingering bronchitis, bronchial asthma, hoarseness and hypersensitivity to smoke, dust, fumes and respiratory infections. There is increased vulnerability to various carcinomas, particularly lung cancer.

Lewisite is immediate acting. Immediate pain and injury of the exposed eyes results upon contact. Serious and permanent damage can result if not decontaminated quickly and completely. Contact with

---

[24] The ulcerations or blisters can become immense in size.

[25] Inflammatory redness of the skin.

[26] An accumulation of excessive watery fluid in cells, tissues or serous cavities.

[27] A spasmodic winking of the eye caused by certain eye muscles contracting uncontrollably. Facial, jaw and neck muscles may also be involved.

[28] Discharges from the nasal mucous membranes.

[29] Nose bleeding, nasal hemorrhage.

[30] Inflammation of the mucous membranes of the trachea and bronchi.

[31] Typified by edema.

[32] Shortness of breath, difficulty in breathing.

the skin results in immediate pain increasing in severity. After about five minutes, graying of the skin occurs with blister formation. Lewisite produces more severe injury and tissue death than sulfur mustards in much shorter time span. The respiratory tract exhibits burning sensation and irritation of the nasal passages.

MISCELLANEOUS TOXICS

A number of other nonmilitary poisonous substances also arise incidental to military operations. Many of these miscellaneous toxics occur to varying extents in civilian environments. A few of the more significant miscellaneous toxics are carbon monoxide (CO), ammonia (NH3), hydrogen sulfide (H2S), nitric oxide (NO), nitrogen dioxide (NO2) and dinitrogen tetroxide (N2O4).

Carbon monoxide results from the incomplete combustion of organic matter and fuels. The most common source is from the internal combustion engine. It is produced by other means such as burning gunpowder, explosive bursts, and smoldering materials. The gas is colorless, odorless[33] and less dense than air. It diffuses rapidly in open air, but in confined spaces, it builds in concentration. The lethal character of carbon monoxide is its ability to chemically combine with the hemoglobin of blood. It binds to hemoglobin some 300 times more readily than oxygen. This capacity of carbon monoxide is responsible for the asphyxiation it produces. Symptoms of carbon monoxide poisoning are headache, templar throbbing, vertigo, yawning[34], dyspnea, diminished visual acuity, bright pink patches on the skin, significant weakness, coma and finally death.

Ammonia is not a military agent but can arise from the same causes as noted for carbon monoxide. It is a colorless gas with a very characteristic odor (household ammonia is a water based solution of ammonia) and is about half as dense as air. It is very water soluble. Exposure to ammonia leads to immediate, high irritation of the eyes and respiratory tract. The irritations of the eyes and respiratory tract in high concentrations is significant burning sensations, lacrimation, sneezing, chest pain, severe coughing, swelling of the mucous membranes of the larynx and trachea, and asphyxia. Direct skin contact with liquid leads to blistering.

Hydrogen sulfide[35] is a colorless gas with the characteristic rotten egg odor. It is denser than air and thus will settle to low lying areas and depressions. It is detectable in very small, harmless concentrations, but prolonged exposure leads to olfactory fatigue- the inability to detect it. This olfactory fatigue poses the hazard to the presence of hydrogen sulfide as its concentration increases to lethal levels. The gas is generated by the same kinds of sources as carbon monoxide. The gas irritates the eyes, nose and throat. High concentrations produce pulmonary edema and paralysis of the respiratory center. Lethal levels induce increased panting breathing which is rapidly followed by unconsciousness and respiratory cessation. Convulsions may also be present.

---

[33] The odor of internal combustion exhausts is not carbon monoxide. The odor associated with such exhausts are other organic and inorganic molecules discharged from the engine.

[34] Yawning as experienced by everyone is not a sign of fatigue as commonly thought. It is a sign of mild oxygen insufficiency and the body reacts to such by yawning, a mechanism intended to intake more oxygen.

[35] H_2S is poisonous to the enzyme phenolase (monophenol monoxygenase). This enzyme is involved in the oxidation of tyrosine to dopa, a precursor of melanin and epinephrine.

Nitric oxide is a colorless gas with a pungent odor and only very slightly more dense than air. The gas forms in air by high energy electrical discharges such as electric arcs and lightning. It also can form in the course of high pressure fuel combustion in air and as a result of nitro-based explosive detonations. The gas can build in concentrations in enclosed areas such as in gun pits, tanks, ship magazines, and in mining and tunneling operations. Nitric oxide poisoning tracks similarly to that of phosgene poisoning as regards symptoms and probable mechanism of action on tissues.

Nitrogen dioxide is a reddish-brown gas, about 50% more dense than air, and has a pungent odor. It is one of the chief components of smog. The gas can combine with itself to form dinitrogen tetroxide (colorless) in an equilibrium manner:

$$2\ NO2 \longleftrightarrow N2O4$$

It is highly poisonous and also tracks similarly to phosgene in its symptoms and probable mechanism of action on tissues.

The nitrogen oxide gases are capable of forming nitric acid in moist tissues. They produce a yellowish discoloration[36] of exposed mucous membranes, irritations of the eyes, throat, nose and lungs. Pulmonary edema develops in significant exposures.

---

[36] Nitric acid will yellow the skin. This is due to the nitration of certain amino acids such as tyrosine or phenylalanine which are aromatic amino acids. The yellowing of exposed mucous membranes to these nitrogen oxide gases probably results from the formation of nitric acid and the subsequent nitration reactions of the aromatic biomolecules.

CHAPTER 5

NERVE AGENTS

GENERAL

There are two principal anticholinesterase class agents commonly known and used commercially. These are the organophosphates and the carbamates, the former also having found potential use as toxic chemical weapons for military use, both used as insecticides for various species of insects. Both will be discussed here though not in profuse detail or as military weapons, but in a more general context and for reasons of their general use by the public as pesticides. The reader is directed to the PESTICIDES heading of the reference section where specific literature appears and in more detail than will be given here. Generally speaking, military organophosphates (nerve agents) are about 100 to 500 times more toxic than insecticidal compounds such as Malathion.

ORGANOPHOSPHATES

Organophosphates find principal commercial use as pesticides. Only the few specific compounds dedicated to military use as chemical weapons grade formulations have been dubbed nerve agents. The term organophosphate generically applies to any organic compound possessing a phosphorus atom, though more specifically organophosphates consist of a phosphate-like group, that is, a pentavalent phosphorus atom.

Phosphate itself [I] is an inorganic polyatomic moiety consisting of phosphorus and four oxygen atoms in covalent association. It is commonly associated with energy activation processes of the cell. Additionally, it is the bridging moiety between sugar units (ribose or deoxyribose) found in polymeric nucleic acids (RNA or DNA, respectively). This form of organophosphate is nontoxic, certainly in the concentrations and chemical forms found in the cell and, in fact, absolutely essential to the cell. Such compounds of the living cell are termed esters of an alcohol (generic term) and phosphoric acid (the source of the phosphate moiety). Typically cellular organophosphates have the form given in [II]. The R group is a biological molecule such as glycerol, adenosine, or creatine. The negative charges shown on this structure [II] are normally present and countered by a positive metal ion such as magnesium (counterion). These ionic forms aid in the water-solubility of the overall molecule. Furthermore, they serve as a recognition point for specific enzymes[1] that process such compounds. The innocuous nature of these kinds of organophosphates is lost when carbon is directly bonded to the phosphorus atom [III].

Organophosphates with direct carbon-phosphorus bonds exhibit vastly different chemical action in the cell. These variants can have a multiplicity of chemical structures as suggested by the general structure [IV]. The R groups, R', R'', R''' may be any combination of atoms or groups as shown by the

---

[1] These enzymes are known generically as kinases, phosphorylases, and dephosphorylases.

possible substituents of R', R", R'". Typically, R" is oxygen or sulfur. R'" is typically oxygen or possibly another carbon. R' offers the labile group, the attached atom which exhibits the chemical reactivity associated with the mechanism of toxicity of organophosphates.

Organophosphates are subject to alkaline hydrolysis and thus, inactivation. That means that as pH increases above 7, the rate of hydrolysis increases. It is only at pH values above 7 that hydroxide ion (OH⁻) concentration becomes significant.[2] The more electronegative[3] the group, the greater is the susceptibility of the organophosphate to alkaline hydrolysis. Thus the more electronegative the atom bonded to phosphorus, the greater the pull of the electrons toward that atom and therefore away from phosphorus. This has the effect of establishing a slight or partial positive charge on the phosphorus atom. This partial positive charge on phosphorus renders it more susceptible to what is called nucleophilic attack by a specie bearing a negative charge (or high, unpaired electron density). In structure [IV], if R' is a fluorine atom, the phosphorus is a greatly enhanced target for a nucleophilic agent such as hydroxide. Even neutral, covalently bonded oxygen atoms of biological molecules serve as nucleophilic agents.

The serine hydroxyl group (-OH) is just such a specie and it is this property, located at the active site of the cholinesterase enzyme, that results in the toxic nature of the so-called nerve agents. For such nucleophilic attacks[4] on the phosphorus atom of organophosphates to occur, an attached atom or group on the phosphorus must concomitantly leave. That is, those groups on phosphorus must be good leaving groups. Fluorine (F)[5] and the cyano group (-CN) covalently attached to phosphorus are such examples. Reaction with the serine hydroxyl oxygen results in the serine hydroxyl group losing the attached hydrogen, leading to simultaneous release of HF or HCN during the covalent reaction between the serine oxygen and phosphorus of the organophosphate nerve agent. The enzyme's serine at the active site is now covalently attached to the phosphorus atom of the organophosphate. This is in effect a phosphorylation reaction of the enzyme and it inactivates the enzyme. The leaving group may or may not be toxic itself. If the leaving group is F⁻ or CN⁻, then HF or HCN are released as well, each one a potent poison in its own right.

CARBAMATES

Carbamates, too, are anticholinergic agents, but unlike organophosphates, carbamates contain no phosphorus. These compounds have for the present not been adopted for any purposeful military use as nerve agents so far as any literature notes. Carbamates come in two versions-- medically useful and

---

[2] The pH of human blood hovers around 7.35 to 7.45. Blood is the universal carrier of toxic substances in the body.

[3] Electronegativity is a dimensionless measure of the electron attractive ability of an atom in a covalent compound. Fluorine is the most electronegative element (4.0); oxygen, 3.4; chlorine, 3.2; nitrogen, 3.0; sulfur, 2.6; carbon, 2.5; phosphorus, 2.2.

[4] Generally, the enzyme is regarded as the target of the organophosphate. The organophosphate is the reagent. I am viewing the enzyme here as the agency for chemical reaction. It "initiates" the reaction on the organophosphate as though the organophosphate were the substrate, a point of considerable importance as the organophosphate chemically "appears" to be a substrate to the enzyme.

[5] Fluoride anion released by fluorine containing organophosphates also presents a poison hazard. For example, fluoride is poisonous to the enolase enzyme of glycolysis.

insecticidal. Medically useful carbamates possess a basic or quaternary nitrogen group while insecticidal carbamates do not. The basic or quaternary nitrogens in a carbamate bind to the anionic site of the cholinesterase enzyme. Such ionizable moieties impede the compound's penetration of insect exoskeleton and their nerve sheaths.

All carbamates are derivatives of the parent compound carbamic acid [V]. Their identity and toxicity were known as early as 1925.[6] It wasn't until the discovery of acetylcholinesterase that the specific nature of their toxicity was uncovered. There are a number of carbamates employed as insecticides or in medicine, the better known being Sevin [VI] and prostigmine [VII].

Carbamates exhibit variable toxicity against various insects and this together with their slower acting nature, in part, is probably why they have enjoyed virtually no interest as military toxic chemical agents. Though some difference of scientific thought exists concerning the mechanism of action of carbamates, it is clear that they do act on the cholinesterase type enzymes. This is presumably at the serine hydroxyl group just as with the organophosphates. In fact, advantage can be taken of carbamate activity with cholinesterases to protect such enzymes from irreversible inactivation by military organophosphate (nerve) agents.

Pyridostigmine[7] is in use by the U.S. Military forces as a pretreatment aid against exposure to nerve agents. It binds to the acetylcholinesterase and, in so doing, prevents the binding of nerve agent. This is particularly useful in reducing the effects of Soman (GD) [VIII] as Soman-enzyme complexes age rapidly compared to those of Sarin (GB) [IX] or VX [X]. Only about 20 to 40% of the total acetylcholinesterase available need be bound in this method to afford significant benefits against GD poisoning. Another military nerve agent is TABUN [XI].

One carbamate that has been examined for its toxicity compared to military organophosphates is the one represented by [XII]. This aryl (aromatic) carbamate is reported to be 10 to 30 times[8] more toxic than Sarin (GB). The fact that it has quaternary amino groups renders it less valuable as an insecticide for the reasons previously cited.

MECHANISM OF REACTION

The mechanism[9] of reaction of anticholinesterase agents all appear to follow a set sequence of processes categorized as (1) complexation, (2) phosphorylation (organophosphates) or acylation (carbamates), (3) rearrangement (facilitated by water) and (5) regeneration of the active enzyme.

---

[6] This was an outgrowth of interest in the poisonous Calabar beans, seeds of *Physostigma venenosum*, used by West African natives in primitive justice trials by ordeal.

[7] Pyridostigmine is issued to each soldier as a "blister pack" of 21 tablets (30 mg each). Upon command of Division or Corps Commanders in light of intelligence estimates of impending nerve agent use by enemy forces, one tablet is taken each eight hours. It should not be taken beyond seven consecutive days.

[8] The order of toxicity depends upon the reference frame for the comparison. For example, toxicity can be compared on a mg or a molar basis and these two reference frames provide differing levels of toxicity comparison.

[9] Mechanisms in chemistry are formalized sequential steps that describe the exact (sometimes only postulated) change in reactive species as the reaction proceeds from reactants to products.

ORGANOPHOSPHATES

The first step is the formation of what in biochemistry is called the enzyme-substrate complex.[10] The formation of the enzyme-substrate complex, ES, requires the normal substrate to bind to cholinesterase at two distinct loci of the enzyme's active site-- the esteratic and the anionic sites. Normally, acetylcholine binds to the active site such that the ester portion of the molecule binds to the esteratic site and the cationic quaternary amino group binds to the anionic site. The organophosphate compound binds analogously with the esterified portion binding to the enzyme's esteratic site and the anionic site may or may not be occupied, depending upon the structure of the organophosphate.[11]

The second step of the process (and a rapid one) results in the transfer of the hydrogen atom of the serine moiety, located at the esteratic site of the enzyme, to the leaving group of the organophosphate. The remainder of the organophosphate attaches to the serine amino acid group. This is called phosphorylation.[12]

The third and fourth steps are fast in acetylcholine involvement. These steps entail the water present at the active site to attack the acyl-enzyme complex, releasing the acid form of the acyl group. In the case of the acetyl group, it is acetate. This occurs by OH^- from the water: $HOH \dashrightarrow H^+ + OH^-$. The hydronium ion restores the hydrogen atom to the serine oxygen, regenerating the serine moiety at the active site, preparing the enzyme for yet another round of reactions. If the organophosphate is the substrate, a substituted phosphoric acid specie is released,[13] but this is a very slow process and is the basis for the very quick toxic nature of the toxic organophosphates. While the organophosphate-enzyme complex exists, acetylcholine builds up, leading to the characteristic symptoms of organophosphate (nerve agent) poisoning. It is these last two steps that are speeded up by antidote in nerve agent poisoning. The administration of oximes such as 2-PAM with its quaternary amino moiety binds to the anionic site, enhancing the rate of restoration of the active enzyme by enhancing the hydrolysis process. The longer the organophosphorylated enzyme complex exists, the more difficult is the removal of the organophosphate moiety. This is believed due to what is called "aging", a process in which the substituents of the phosphorus atom are replaced, over time, with hydroxyl groups, altering the chemical properties of the covalently bound phosphate unit. Atropine binds to the acetylcholine receptor[14] thus blocking the binding of acetylcholine. This blocking of the acetylcholine receptor inhibits or reduces the frequency of nerve impulse transmissions until restored enzyme activity destroys the neurotransmitter.

---

[10] Normally an inhibitor forms an enzyme-inhibitor complex, EI, with the enzyme. For this discussion we will forego the fine distinction between it and the enzyme-substrate complex as the anticholinergic material is the substrate for the enzyme here. The normal biological substrate is actually acetylcholine.

[11] Those organophosphates which possess no anionic group, bind only to the esteratic site. [A. Goldstein, *Arch. Biochem.* **34**, 169 (1951)]

[12] If the substrate is acetylcholine, the process results in the choline moiety receiving the hydrogen atom, the acetyl group (an acyl group) is bound to the serine oxygen. This is called acylation.

[13] known as dephosphorylation

[14] Known as muscarinic sites, named after muscarine, a cholinergic substance meaning it mimics acetylcholine in action.

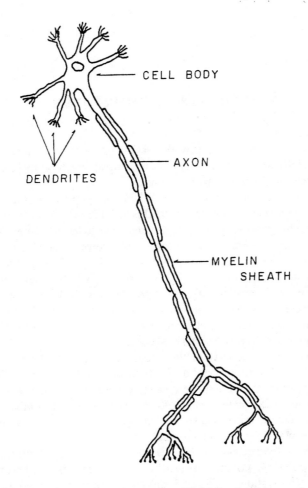

FIGURE 5-1 Illustration of a nerve cell with its dendrites and axon.

CARBAMATES

Carbamates generally exhibit the same cholinesterase toxicity as organophosphates. However, the chemical mode of action with cholinesterase is different in two ways. The first difference is in step (1) above, the complexation step. It is reversible for carbamates. The second difference is in step (3), the rearrangement or hydrolysis[15] of the carbamate from the enzyme-carbamate complex. This step is much faster for carbamates than it is for organophosphates. These two differences lead to enzyme inhibition that is reversible for carbamates. Under high acetylcholine concentrations, the carbamate will eventually be hydrolyzed, a point that does argue against carbamates[16] serving a

---

[15] known as decarbamylation

[16] Carbamates act less as inhibitors and more as alternate substrates with a higher binding affinity for the enzyme. [A. Goldstein, *Arch. Biochem.* **34**, 169 (1951); D.K. Myers, *Biochem. J.* **52**, 46 (1952), *Biochem. J.* **62**, 556 (1956)]

general military use. Quaternary ammonium carbamates bind to both the esteratic and anionic sites of the cholinesterase.[17]

NERVE IMPULSES & THEIR INHIBITION

To better understand how nerve agents work to inhibit (stop) nerve impulse transmission controls, it is useful to very briefly look at what a nerve is, its general structural make-up, and some simple electrochemistry concerning a nerve's working state.

Figure 5-1 is a simplified drawing of a nerve cell. For our purposes it consists of essentially five components. The first component is the cell body. This includes the nerve cell cytoplasm, the nucleus and associated internal organelles. The second component is the dendrites. These are numerous branched strands radiating out from the cell body. They receive signals from other nerves, such as sensory nerves of smell, taste, touch like sharp, heat, cold and so on. The third component is the axon. This is the long tubular structure of Figure 5-1. The axon ends in the fourth component called the synaptic knobs. These are the small dot-like structures shown at the lower right of Figure 5-1. These synaptic knobs make contact with other nerve cell dendrites, muscle or glandular cells for example. The fifth component is the myelin sheath. The myelin sheath is like the rubber insulation of an electrical wire though the analogy is a very simple one.

So what happens to trigger a nerve to "fire" as it may be called? Some stimulus be it external such as extreme heat or a thought to move a muscle stimulates the dendrites. These in turn cause a nerve impulse to move along the axon to the synaptic knobs which in turn release a chemical called a neurotransmitter to be released at the synaptic knobs. These neurotransmitters bind to a receptor in a target tissue such as muscle and cause some kind of action. In the case of muscle, it causes the muscle to contract. How is this process mediated?

Figure 5-2 illustrates the process that initiates the nerve impulse. A resting nerve (one that is not "firing") is said to be *polarized*. Polarized means that the nerve axon is charged on the outside surface with positive charge. This is shown in Figure 5-2(a) which shows an axon with a cutaway view in its facing side. Sodium ions (Na^+) are pumped out of the interior to the exterior of the axon by specialized proteins lining the axon membrane. These "sodium proteins" only pump sodium ions. At the same time that sodium ions are pumped out, potassium ion (K^+) are pumped in. The "potassium proteins" only pump potassium ions. There are more sodium ions pumped out than potassium ions pumped in. The net effect of this process is to establish a net positive charge on the outside of the axon while the interior has a net negative charge. Negative ions do not easily move across the membrane. In the resting nerve axon this establishes the polarized state. The nerve in now primed or cocked so to speak (using a gun analogy). It does not yet transmit a nerve impulse.

[17] A. Goldstein, *Arch. Biochem.* **34**, 169 (1951); D.K. Myers, *Arch Biochem.* **27**, 341 (1950).

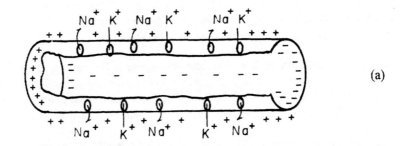

(a)

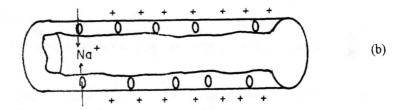

(b)

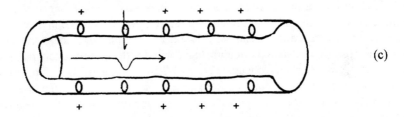

(c)

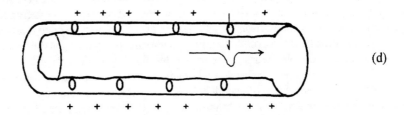

(d)

FIGURE 5-2 A schematic representation of a resting nerve and the effects on that nerve when excited. See text for full explanation.

(a) A resting nerve is polarized or charged. A higher sodium ion concentration resides on the exterior surface of the axon than inside. Thus the outside is slightly positive and the interior is slightly negative.

(b) When stimulated, sodium ions flow into the interior of the nerve axon at the point of stimulus, thus depolarizing the axon. This stimulatory process proceeds along the axon with sodium ions moving into the axon at each point of stimulus. This reduces the exterior positive charge, and decreases the interior negative charge sequentially at each point along the axon.

(c) The result of the process in (b) is to set up a nerve impulse or self-propagating wave of charge shown by the arrowed line with the wave. As the sodium ions flow into the axon sequentially along the axon, the nerve impulse moves along the axon from the left (c) to the right (d) in the illustration.

(d) As the nerve impulse moves to the next location along the axon, sodium ions are immediately pumped out to the exterior of the axon at the previous point of stimulus, reestablishing its polarized state and recharging the nerve for the next "firing".

Figure 5-2(b) illustrates what happens when the nerve is excited, meaning stimulated to "fire" a nerve impulse. In this illustration the sodium ions move into the cell while potassium ions move out at the point of stimulation. The bulk of charge transfer is into the nerve axon. Thus, the nerve is *depolarized*. This results in a lessening of the exterior positive charge on the exterior surface of the axon. This difference in charge creates a nerve impulse or self-propagating wave along the entire length of the axon. This influx of sodium ions due to external stimulation is very short-lived. As soon as the sodium enters, a transient potential is created at that discrete location and the impulse moves toward the synaptic knob and the sodium that entered is then immediately pumped back out. This is illustrated by comparing the sequential Figures 5-2(b), 5-2(c) and 5-2(d). Notice that in Figures 5-2(a) through (d) a vertical arrow pointing from the exterior of the axon to the interior notes the entry of sodium ions. The horizontal arrow with the wave component within the axon represents the nerve impulse moving from the figures' left to right ends. How fast is this impulse transmission?

The speed of nerve impulse transmission along an axon depends on the diameter of the axon, the thickness of the myelin sheath about the axon (see Figure 5-1), and the separation between myelin sheath regions. The larger the diameter of the axon, the faster the impulse speed. The speed of impulse transmission ranges from 0.5 meter per second (1.1 mph) to 100 meters per second (224 mph) depending on the axon in question. What does the nerve impulse do once it arises within the axon?

Figure 5-3 illustrates the events attending a nerve impulse arriving at the synaptic knob. In Figure 5-3(a), a firing, or depolarized axon is shown terminating at its synaptic knob (SK). Within the synaptic knob are numerous vesicles each containing thousands of neurotransmitter molecules. The best understood system is that of acetylcholine. Acetylcholine is made up of two components. One is of acetic acid (vinegar) and the other a positively charged amine called choline. In combined chemical form they are acetylcholine and active. Figure 5-3(a) also shows a nerve impulse (the horizontal arrowed line with a wave in it) traveling toward the synaptic knob.

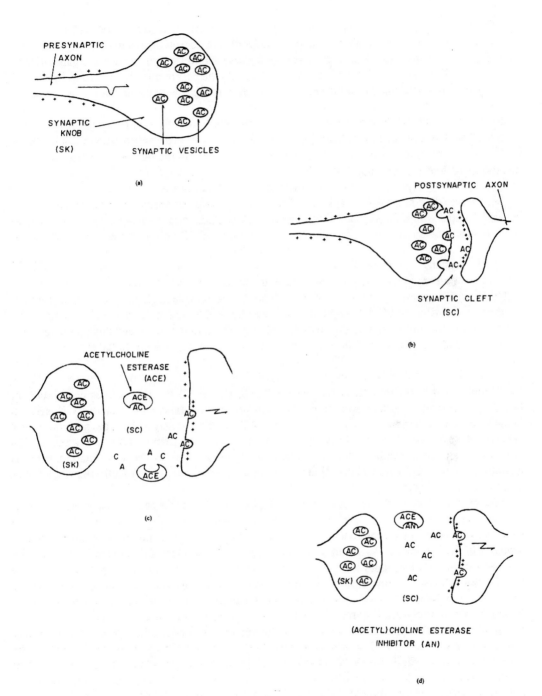

FIGURE 5-3 A schematic representation of the action of nerve impulse transmission it normally occurs (a)-(c) and as occurs in the presence of a cholinergic agent such as organophosphate or carbamate (d).

(a) A resting nerve axon and synaptic knob. The structures marked synaptic vesicles are numerous in number and contain thousands of molecules of neurotransmitters. Neurotransmitters are biological chemicals which transmit a nerve impulse across the synaptic cleft, a gap between to nerves. The nerve impulse cannot jump this gap, but the neurotransmitters do and in effect transmit the nerve impulse to the next nerve by stimulating it and depolarizing that nerves receptor.

(b) The synaptic cleft is shown with the neurotransmitter (AC) released from the presynaptic axon. These neurotransmitter difuse across the very narrow space to bind to neurotransmitter receptors on the postsynaptic axon membrane surface. In binding the receptors, the neurotransmitters alter the shape of the receptor protein and permit influx of sodium ions into the postsynaptic axon in a mechanism much like that discussed in Figure 5-2.

(c) Nerves do not normally continue to fire because the neurotransmitter is destroyed by an enzyme located within the synaptic cleft, here shown as ACE, acetylcholine esterase. The enzyme cuts the neurotransmitter, AC, acetylcholine, into two biologically inactive pieces, A, acetic acid, and C, choline.

(d) In the sequences (a) through (c) all is normal as it occurs in nerves. In the presence of a nerve agent such as an organophosphate or carbamate, the nerve agent acts as an inhibitor of the enzyme ACE of (c). The nerve agent (AN) covalently binds to the enzyme ACE and prevents its binding of the neurotransmitter AC. Consequently, the neurotransmitter is not destroyed and continues to bind the its receptor protein on the postsynaptic axon membrane surface and this continues the firing of the postsynaptic nerve, leading to twitching or convulsions in the extreme.

Upon arrival of the impulse at the synaptic knob, Figure 5-3 (b), the vesicles containing the neurotransmitter merge with the membrane of the synaptic knob at the synaptic cleft (SC). This results in the neurotransmitter, in this case acetylcholine (AC), being discharged into the synaptic cleft, a very small space between the presynaptic axon and the postsynaptic axon or receptor. The acetylcholine neurotransmitter diffuses across the synaptic cleft to the postsynaptic axon or neurotransmitter receptor a special receptor protein associated with the postsynaptic axon membrane. This is shown in Figure 5-3(c).

The postsynaptic membrane is itself polarized prior to binding of the neurotransmitter. At binding of the neurotransmitter, here the acetylcholine, the neurotransmitter alters the shape of the neurotransmitter receptor protein to which it binds. This change in shape of the neurotransmitter protein triggers the influx of sodium ions into the postsynaptic axon, represented by the positive charges shown on the synaptic cleft side of the postsynaptic axon. Under normal nerve impulse activity, this influx of sodium ions, due to neurotransmitter binding to the postsynaptic axon protein, creates a nerve impulse (called an excitatory postsynaptic potential) in that axon, shown as the lightning shaped arrow. All is normal under these circumstances. Nerve impulses do not continue to fire indefinitely. They stop. This termination of impulse occurs by the action of the enzyme acetylcholine esterase (ACE shown in Figure 5-3(c). As represented here, the acetylcholine neurotransmitter is hydrolyzed by the enzyme, meaning it is chemically cut in half yielding to inactive products, one the acetic acid component (the A species shown) and the other the choline amine component (the C species shown). This hydrolysis of the neurotransmitter terminates the initiation of a nerve impulse in the postsynaptic axon. The axon then returns to its resting or polarized state, essentially being reprimed or recocked for another round of firing when more neurotransmitter binds. Now, what is the problem created by military or insecticidal nerve agents?

Figure 5-3(d) illustrates this abnormal event. Nerve agents are inhibitors of the acetylcholine esterase enzyme (ACE). The nerve agent is represented by the specie AN in Figure 5-3(d). Such agents are referred to as anticholine esterase inhibitors. When nerve agent enters the picture, the agent covalently bonds to the enzyme. This bond is very strong and not easily broken if at all. The organophosphate agents are more tenacious in bonding to the acetylcholine esterase than the carbamates. Since the covalent bond between the enzyme and nerve agent is so strong and on practical grounds irreversible, the enzyme is inactivated. That means it cannot hydrolyze any acetylcholine inhibitor present in the synaptic cleft. Consequently, the neurotransmitter continues a cyclic binding to and dissociation from the receptor and thus continues an unending firing of the postsynaptic axon or receptor. If the receptor is a muscle, the muscle continues to contract and relax cyclically which manifests itself as twitches or in the extreme convulsions.[18]

Given that muscles are a prime target of nerve agent poisoning, binding of these poisons leads to eventual paralysis of the muscles and consequent cessation of breathing.

MIXED FUNCTION OXIDASES

Mixed function oxidases (MFOs) are enzyme systems which require NADPH as a reducing agent and an electron transport system employing cytochrome P_{450}. These enzyme systems generally operate as a means for detoxifying substances. These systems catalyze a broad range of reactions intended to do essentially two things: (1) detoxify and (2) increase substance polarity and thus aqueous solubility for excretion in the urine.

MFOs act to catalyze such diverse reactions as deaminations, demethylations, dealkylations, hydroxylations of aromatic ring systems, alkyl and N-hydroxylations, breakdown of esters, epoxidations, oxidations of organosulfides and oxidations of aldehydes and alcohols to carboxylic acids to name several. Although generally intended to detoxify a substance, occasionally the processing of a substance can lead to its enhanced toxicity compared to the parent compound. Examples of this arise in the epoxidation of benzo[a]pyrene to its epoxide derivative (a carcinogen) or of aflatoxin,[19] also thought to be oxidized to an epoxide, and a very potent hepatic carcinogen. Examples of MFOs enhancing the toxicity of organophosphates are known.

ORGANOPHOSPHATES

In the processing of organophosphates, MFOs can bring about oxidations ($P=S \rightarrow P=O + SO_4^{2-}$), N-dealkylations ($O=P-NR_2 \rightarrow O=P-NH_2$), oxidative degradations of arylorganophosphates such as parathion, hydroxylation of side-chains as in Diazinon [XIII], and even isomerizations. Such reactions which result in a derivative of equal or enhanced toxicity are referred to as activation.[20]

---

[18] Curare, a plant poison applied to arrow tips by South American Indians, also binds to the acetylcholine receptor. However, it does not induce a nerve impulse in the postsynaptic axon. Thus bound to the acetylcholine receptor, the curare prevents acetylcholine binding and consequently paralyzes the muscles. A drug with similar curare action is Pavulon, used in surgery to relax muscles.

[19] Aflatoxin is a toxin secreted by the mold *Aspergillus flavus*.

[20] See Toxicology of Insecticides, Matsumura, pp. 206-228 for a concise discussion of these processes.

CARBAMATES

Carbamates appear subject to only oxidative degradation by MFOs. There is no definitive pattern by which the toxicity of the by-products can be correlated with enhanced or diminished toxicity compared to the parent compound. Generally, the by-products are not less toxic than the parent.

CHAPTER 6

BLOOD AGENTS

GENERAL

Blood agents (now a somewhat archaic term) are general chemical agents which act through or in a few specific cases on the blood itself. The latter type of compounds are typified by carbon monoxide which binds to the hemoglobin of red blood cells preventing the uptake of oxygen from the lungs. This leads to anoxia or the lack of oxygen and in high enough doses can lead to death, though the first symptom is usually headache. Another type is carried in the blood to the cells where they passes through the cellular membranes into the cytoplasm on to the mitochondria. These compounds interact with specific coenzymes (cofactors necessary for the enzyme's activity) such as the cytochromes which are electron carrying biomolecules.

In order to better appreciate the effects of blood agents, it is useful to briefly examine the mitochondrion of the eukaryotic cell.

MITOCHONDRIA

Mitochondria (Figure 6-1) are often called the 'powerhouses' of the eukaryotic cell. They are the organelles responsible for the vast majority of energy (in the form of ATP) produced within the cell. They function in performing a process known as oxidative phosphorylation which is, simply stated, the addition of phosphate to specific molecules. The mitochondrion can be 'dissected' into three specific components: the outer and inner membranes and the matrix. It is in the mitochondrion that a range of enzymes exists, insulated as they are from high water concentrations found in the cytosol. Various metabolic processes are compartmentalized between the inner, outer membranes and the matrix. Many different enzymes are internalized within the matrix that is bordered by the inner membrane. Thus such enzyme systems responsible for the metabolism in the Tricarboxylic Acid Cycle (TCA) and fatty acid oxidations (β-oxidation) are found in the matrix. Certain enzymes required for phospholipid biosynthesis are located at the outer membrane. The inner membrane contains many of the enzymes responsible for the electron transport chain.

From a biologically historical point of view, mitochondria are though to be bacterial cells that benevolently invaded other, larger cells establishing a cooperative (symbiotic) agreement in which each assists the other in survival. One of the most important biochemical reaction processes taking place within the mitochondria is that of electron transport. In grade school you were probably taught that you eat to live. That is true in a macroworld sense, but in fact you eat to acquire two very essential components from the food you ingest. You eat to gather electrons and hydrogen ions from the food in order to use those two species to make energy. That energy is a molecule uniquely represented by the letters "ATP". Biochemists call it adenosine triphosphate. It is a very high energy molecule which is the biological equivalent of gasoline. The loose analogy ends there, however. Your body cells must make ATP and they use the electrons and the hydrogen ions to do so. This is where electron transport enters the picture.

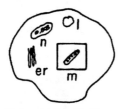

Eukaryotic Cell

l = lysosome
n = nucleus
er = endoplasmic
      reticulum
m = mitochondrion

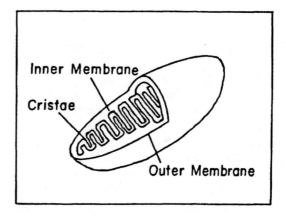

Mitochondrion

FIGURE 6-1 A diagram of the location of mitochondria within the eukaryotic cell and the internal fine structure of the mitochondrion.

ELECTRON TRANSPORT

The electron transport chain in fact does just that, it transports electrons removed from specific food molecules and transports them along this system to oxygen (Figure 6-2). Some of the hydrogen ion or protons (H^+ ions) released in metabolism as well are used to provide the hydrogen for the making of the water (H_2O) from the oxygen. It is this very reaction that explains why you, as an animal, breath air.

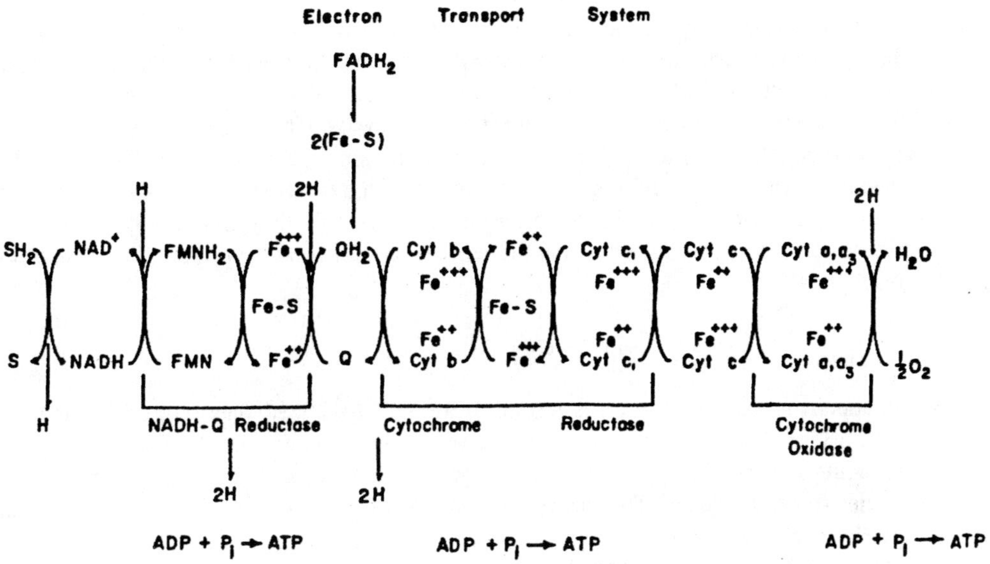

FIGURE 6-2 The Electron Transport System. A reduced (hydrogenated) molecule (substrate) enters the system shown at the left of the diagram as SH_2. Its hydrogens are transferred to NAD^+ (nicotinamide adenine nucleotide), a carrier molecule yielding its reduced form, NADH plus an extra H^+. The electron and hydrogen are transferred to FMN (flavin mononucleotide) yielding its reduced form, $FMNH_2$. An iron-sulfur protein (Fe-S) is associated with the FMN, the combination of the two known as NADH-Q reductase. The Q is shorthand notation for a compound known as ubiquinone. The electron and hydrogen are transferred to ubiquinone to give dihydroubiquinone (QH_2). The electron is transferred to a composite system called cytochrome reductase, composed of cytochrome b and c_1 which are bridged by an iron-sulfur protein. Cytochrome c receives the electron and passes it to cytochrome oxidase (a,a_3). The electrons and two hydrogens are combined with the oxygen from the blood to yield water. Cytochromes are electron carrier systems, which possess a chelated iron (or copper in some cases) in a structure very similar to the heme of the blood's hemoglobin. The transfer of the electron is noted by the changes in the number of positive charges on the iron (Fe) atoms of the respective cytochrome. Each time an iron goes from a +++ (+3 ionic charge) to a ++ (+2 ionic charge) an electron was gained by that cytochrome or iron-sulfur protein. These individual proteins are coupled in such a way that as the iron of one is reduced (gain of an electron) the other next to it to the left is oxidized since it donated the electron. At three particular places along the sequence, ATP is synthesized. These locations are at the NADH-Q reductase, cytochrome reductase and the cytochrome oxidase steps. So-called blood agents bind to the cytochrome oxidase stopping the flow of electrons there.

The cytochromes[1] are approximately similar to the hemoglobin of blood. They possess a heme group and protein and are more complex. They are vastly different from hemoglobin in function. Hemoglobin carries oxygen. The cytochromes transfer electrons between themselves. This transfer is performed by changes in oxidation state of the coordinated central metal atom, usually an iron atom coordinated to the nitrogens of a porphyrin ring system. Some cytochromes also have copper atoms which are coordinated with sulfur atoms, usually from the amino acid cysteine. The iron, whose chemical symbol is Fe, is critically important in this electron transfer process of the cytochromes. Cytochromes play a central role in electron transport. The reactions they facilitate simply entail the change in oxidation state (ionization state) of the centrally coordinated metal atom. In the case of the iron, the reaction is:

$$Fe^{2+} \leftarrow\!-\!\rightarrow Fe^{3+} + e^-$$

What happens is that an electron is passed to the Fe^{3+} (oxidized state) converting it to Fe^{2+} (reduced state). This electron can then be passed to yet another cytochrome whose iron is also in the 3+ state, reducing it to 2+. Each time the cytochrome passes an electron it is oxidized. Each time it receives an electron it is reduced. This process becomes a biological version of the hot potato game, wherein the electron is passed off.[2] The end player in this process is oxygen, which with protons (H^+ ions) gains the electrons to form water. This biological game ends well with the formation of water. Life continues. With cyanide, it doesn't.

The blood agents cyanide [I] and cyanogen chloride [II] block the transfer of electrons to oxygen, as shown in Figure 6-2, at the cytochrome c oxidase step. Cyanide binds to the oxidized iron (Fe^{3+}) preventing the transfer of the electron to oxygen and prevents the subsequent reduction of the Fe^{3+} to Fe^{2+} for yet another cycle. Since incoming electrons now are stuck on the preceding enzyme sites, these components of the electron transport system become saturated with electrons and are unable to pass them off to the next component. This process also stops the production of ATP. The cessation of electron transport has rapid acting and lethal consequences.[3]

OXIDATIVE PHOSPHORYLATION

The other need for the hydrogen ions is for the enzyme ATP synthase. This enzyme is located on the matrix side of the inner membrane. As electron transport takes place some hydrogen ions are pumped into the space between the outer and inner membrane. This space becomes very acidic (high

---

[1] Cytochromes (**cyto**: cell, cytoplasm; **chrome**: color, pigment) are heme proteins which serve as the site of electron transfer in mitochondria. They are generally colored complexes or exhibit absorption of specific colored light frequencies. They are nearly primordial proteins, believed to be as old as 2 billion years. They have, over evolutionary time, experienced very little change.

[2] Figure 20-13, page 539 of Biochemistry by Donald Voet and Judith G. Voet, John Wiley & Sons., New York, 1990, offers a simple, but beautiful representation of this process.

[3] The CN^- anion is also poisonous to the catalase enzyme. Catalase is the enzyme responsible for the hydrolytic destruction of hydrogen peroxide generated within cells due to certain biochemical reactions. The hydrogen peroxide formed is a potent oxidizing agent of cell components.

acid or hydrogen ion concentration). At the same time the matrix becomes alkaline (low hydrogen ion concentration and therefore high OH⁻ concentration). As the difference in acid and base concentration across the inner membrane increases, the hydrogen ions begin to flow (like water in a river) through the ATP synthase. It is this flow of protons (an electrical current, and electricity is energy remember) through the ATP synthase that drives a process that makes the ATP. This process, called oxidative phosphorylation, is an energy mediated process, that is, the energy released by electron transport is not lost but stored via phosphorylation. This occurs through the aid of the enzyme ATP synthase. This process is also referred to as energy coupling as the energy potential of electron transport is coupled to that of the phosphorylation of ADP to yield ATP, the energy currency of life. Some blood agents can decouple this process. Certain insecticidal and acaricidal (ticks, mites) formulations have been shown to do this.

MIXED FUNCTION OXIDASES

Just as discussed in Chapter 5, mixed function oxidases can act on various complex compounds that otherwise interfere with electron transport and oxidative phosphorylation. This is particularly evident in numerous insecticide studies. Again, the by-products may or may not exhibit toxicities comparable to the parent compound.

CHAPTER 7

CHOKING AGENTS

GENERAL

Choking agents (now called pulmonary agents by the US Army) derive their name from the physiological effect they have on the human respiratory tract. They are agents which are inhaled and dissolve in the fluids of the lungs liningf the bronchial tubes and the alveoli (air sacs). They react upon contact with susceptible biomolecular groups resulting in an acylation[1] of such compounds. The resultant reaction on respiratory tissues causes fluid seepage and fluid build-up in the alveoli.

The body's response to this abnormally high fluid build-up is to cough, a mechanism which nature designed to bring up and expel the excess offending fluid present. The choking occurs due to significant liquid fluid[2] increase and the difficulty in expelling the liquid fluid because of its presence, greater density than air and continuing build-up.

The importance of choking agents may lie not in military use but as the result of fires in civilian settings. Many building materials are or were composed of chlorinated organics. These materials, when subject to intense heat or pyrolysis, burn with the release of phosgene. Smoke in such fires may be heavily laden with phosgene. The odor of phosgene, mown or moldy hay, may be masked by other odorant constituents in the smoke.

Common choking agents are phosgene (CG) [I], chlorine (Cl) [II] and diphosgene (DP) [III]. The small amount of phosgene which dissolves in water forms carbon dioxide and hydrogen chloride.[3] Any substance with a labile hydrogen (a replaceable hydrogen on an other atom) will be reactive to such agents. The reaction for simple hydrolysis with water is:

$$H_2O + COCl_2 \dashrightarrow CO_2 + 2HCl$$

The hydrochloric acid formed is not high enough in concentration to account for the physiological damage done to respiratory tissues by phosgene inhalation.[4]

The reaction of the choking agent phosgene appears more complicated than simple hydrolysis

---

[1] Acylation is the adding of an acyl group, R-C=O, to another molecule.

[2] Gases or liquids are both fluids in a physical chemistry sense.

[3] Hydrogen chloride gas dissolves in water to yield hydrochloric acid:
$$HCl + H_2O \dashrightarrow H_3O^+ + Cl^-$$

[4] Phosgene is about 800 times more toxic than an equivalent amount of hydrochloric acid (hydrogen chloride gas inhalation).

with release of hydrochloric acid.[5] Phosgene acts through acylation as the means of its toxicity. The understanding of this point emerged from comparative studies using ketene [IV] which also causes similar injuries to the lungs but does not hydrolyze to release hydrogen chloride.

Since the lungs consist of proteins possessing amino, hydroxyl and thiol groups as well as other components[6] also possessing labile hydrogens, the reaction of phosgene with lung tissue is diverse and complicated. The acylation of these components leads to derivatives of the parent compounds. These derivatives possess chemical properties very different from the native compounds intended by nature, and thus alter the physicochemical characteristics of the chemically modified tissues. Permeability and integrity of membranes certainly is affected by such acylations. The reaction of phosgene undoubtedly entails the cross-linking of some biomolecules with the carbonyl moiety of phosgene as the bridging unit.

The site of action of choking agents principally is the lungs though any mucous-like or moist tissues are susceptible. These tissues include the eyes, nose, sinus and the throat. The principal cause of the injuries sustained are due to tissue acylation reactions by phosgene. Acylation reactions require susceptible, labile hydrogen atoms attached to relatively electronegative elements such as nitrogen, oxygen and sulfur. The labile group of phosgene in acylation reactions is the chlorine atom and there are two of them. Thus phosgene can react with two susceptible hydrogen atoms, one from each of two different contributing molecules:

$$\begin{array}{ccc} Cl & & NH\text{-}R \\ / & & / \\ O{=}C & + 2H_2N\text{-}R \longrightarrow O{=}C & + 2HCl \\ \backslash & & \backslash \\ Cl & & NH\text{-}R \\ & \text{Amine} & \end{array}$$

Amino acids of proteins that are susceptible are lysine and the amino group involved in the peptide bond defining a protein.

$$\begin{array}{ccc} Cl & & O\text{-}R \\ / & & / \\ O{=}C & + 2HO\text{-}R \longrightarrow O{=}C & + 2HCl \\ \backslash & & \backslash \\ Cl & & O\text{-}R \\ & \text{Alcohol} & \end{array}$$

The amino acid serine possesses an alcohol side group susceptible to this reaction scheme.

---

5 The Mechanism of Action of Phosgene and Diphosgene, A.M. Potts, F.P. Simon and P.W. Gerard, *Arch. Biochem.* **24**, 329 (1949), and Phosgene Induced Edema: Diagnosis and Therapeutic Countermeasures, 1985

6 Amide (-CONH$_2$), carboxylic acid (-COOH)

$$\underset{\text{Thiol}}{O=C\overset{Cl}{\underset{Cl}{\big<}}} + 2\text{HS-R} \longrightarrow O=C\overset{S\text{-}R}{\underset{S\text{-}R}{\big<}} + 2\text{HCl}$$

The amino acid cysteine possesses a thiol group susceptible to this reaction scheme. These reactions could be mixed:

$$O=C\overset{Cl}{\underset{Cl}{\big<}} + \text{H}_2\text{N-R} + \text{HS-R} \longrightarrow O=C\overset{NH\text{-}R}{\underset{S\text{-}R}{\big<}} + 2\text{HCl}$$

or

$$O=C\overset{Cl}{\underset{Cl}{\big<}} + \text{H}_2\text{N-R} + \text{HO-R} \longrightarrow O=C\overset{NH\text{-}R}{\underset{O\text{-}R}{\big<}} + 2\text{HCl}$$

or

$$O=C\overset{Cl}{\underset{Cl}{\big<}} + \text{HS-R} + \text{HO-R} \longrightarrow O=C\overset{S\text{-}R}{\underset{O\text{-}R}{\big<}} + 2\text{HCl}$$

These reactions of phosgene with the amino ($-NH_2$), hydroxyl ($-OH$), and thiol[7] ($-SH$) groups occur much more rapidly than with water alone.[8] The reactions given are simply stated. Phosgene reacts with primary (1°) and secondary (2°) alkyl or aryl amines to yield initially carbamoyl chlorides:

1°: $R\text{-}NH_2 + COCl_2 \longrightarrow R\text{-}NH\text{-}COCl + HCl$
2°: $R_2NH + COCl_2 \longrightarrow R_2N\text{-}COCl + HCl$

The carbamoyl chlorides of primary amine origin can easily be dehydrohalogenated to yield isocyanates:

---

7 Also called a sulfhydryl group.

8 Chemical Reactions of Diphosgene of Biological Significance, in *Fasciculus on Chemical Warfare Medicine*, p. 147; Recent Research on Respiratory Irritants, Chapter XXXVII, in *Science in World War II*.

$$R\text{-}NH\text{-}COCl \longrightarrow R\text{-}N=C=O + HCl$$

Even isolated amino acids in solution react easily with phosgene to yield an oxazolidine-2,5-dione:

$$
\begin{array}{c}
NH_2 \\
| \\
R\text{-}CH\text{-}COOH + COCl_2 \longrightarrow
\end{array}
\qquad
\begin{array}{c}
R\text{ - }CH\text{-}C=O \\
/ \qquad \backslash \\
H\text{ - }N \qquad O \qquad + 2HCl \\
\backslash \qquad / \\
C=O
\end{array}
$$

Carboxylic acids react with phosgene to yield acyl halides:

$$R\text{-}COOH + COCl_2 \longrightarrow R\text{-}COCl + CO_2 + HCl$$

The amino acids aspartic and glutamic acids possess side chain carboxyl groups susceptible to this reaction type. The acyl halide is a very reactive group which also is capable of reaction with any compound possessing a labile hydrogen:

$$R\text{-}COCl + H_2N\text{-}R \longrightarrow R\text{-}CONHR + HCl$$
$$\text{Amide}$$

$$R\text{-}COCl + HO\text{-}R \longrightarrow R\text{-}COOR + HCl$$
$$\text{Ester}$$

$$R\text{-}COCl + HS\text{-}R \longrightarrow R\text{-}COSR + HCl$$
$$\text{Thioester}$$

The reaction of phosgene with amides leads to nitriles:

$$R\text{-}CONH_2 + COCl_2 \longrightarrow R\text{-}CN + CO_2 + 2HCl$$
$$\text{Nitrile}$$

Since tissues possess biomolecules exhibiting all or most of these reactive chemical group types, phosgene has a range of cellular chemical targets with which to acylate.

Chlorine reacts with water to form hydrochloric [V] and hypochlorous acids [VI], the latter being the acidic form of household bleach (an oxidizing agent, one of the potent oxidants among the chlorine oxyacids):

$$Cl_2 + HOH \longrightarrow HCl + HOCl$$

The hypochlorous acid oxidizes susceptible tissue molecules. Hypochlorous acid reacts with a variety of organic molecules yielding carbon-- and nitrogen-chlorinations, additions and esterification reactions. One of the possible forms of damage done to the alveoli is an addition reaction to certain protein and lipid constituents possessing unsaturated sites, C=C. Since the double bond between carbons is an alkenyl moiety, it can undergo what is called an addition reaction with agents such as chlorine or its hypochlorous acid hydrolysis product. Some phosphatidylcholines[9] and certainly the sphingomyelins possess such unsaturated C=C and the addition and oxidation across these sites alters such molecules' surfactant properties as well as of those found as integral components of the membranes. Such addition reactions of water based (aqueous) chlorine across the C=C yield compounds called chlorohydrins:

$$\text{HOCl} + \underset{/\quad\backslash}{\overset{\backslash\quad/}{\text{C=C}}} \quad\text{-----}\rightarrow\quad \underset{\overset{|\quad|}{\text{Cl OH}}}{\overset{|\quad|}{\text{-C-C-}}}$$

Proteins also may undergo substitution reactions with chlorine or oxidation reactions with it or the hypochlorous acid. The mechanism of the reaction of chlorine or hypochlorous acid with tissue is not clear but may be similar to that which is believed to occur with microorganisms.

Chlorine and its hypochlorous acid hydrolysis product are believed to destroy microbes by penetration of the cell wall and reaction with microbial enzymes. Thus the reaction of chlorine or hypochlorous acid with the lung tissue enzymes responsible for the surfactant deposition may be likely.

Hydrochloric acid is a strong acid and dissociates completely in water to yield hydronium ions:

$$\text{HCl} + \text{H}_2\text{O} \quad\text{-----}\rightarrow\quad \text{H}_3\text{O}^+ + \text{Cl}^-$$

But hypochlorous acid is a weak acid:

$$\text{HOCl} + \text{H}_2\text{O} \quad\text{-----}\rightarrow\quad \text{H}_3\text{O}^+ + \text{OCl}^-$$

with a dissociation constant of 2.95×10^{-8}, a pK_a of 7.53.[10] Thus in a medium liberating both acid forms, HCl and HOCl, the HCl dissociation will increase the hydrogen ion concentration. This hydrogen ion concentration tends to drive the reaction of hypochlorous acid dissociation to the left in the previous equation. That is, dissociation of HOCl is suppressed by the hydrochloric acid present.

Hypochlorous acid solutions are known to exist in an equilibrium state with chlorine monoxide (dichlorine oxide), Cl_2O [VII]:

$$2\text{HOCl} \quad\leftarrow\text{-----}\rightarrow\quad \text{Cl}_2\text{O} + \text{H}_2\text{O}$$

Chlorine monoxide is called hypochlorous acid anhydride. Very small quantities of chlorine monoxide are present at equilibrium in dilute solutions of hypochlorous acid.[11]

---

9 The unsaturated alkenyl units of phosphatidylcholine would be found in the fatty acid side chains.

10 $K_a = [\text{H}^+][\text{OCl}^-]/[\text{HOCl}] = 2.95 \times 10^{-8}$, or $pK_a = -\log(K_a) = 7.53$

11 The characteristic yellowish color of household bleach, sodium hypochlorite, may be due to very small quantities of chlorine monoxide if not other impurities:

$$\text{NaOCl} + \text{HOH} \quad\leftarrow\text{-----}\rightarrow\quad \text{Na}^+ + \text{OH}^- + \text{HOCl}$$
$$2\,\text{HOCl} \quad\leftarrow\text{-----}\rightarrow\quad \text{Cl}_2\text{O} + \text{HOH}$$

SITE OF ACTION: LUNGS

The lungs are the site of gas exchange between the body cells and the external environment. The lungs can be viewed as an elastic balloon, though this is very oversimplified. In fact, the lungs are more accurately described as thousands of miniature balloons all connected to converging branches that culminate at the trachea. The alveoli (singular: alveolus) appear as grapes clustered on a stem network called bronchioli (singular: bronchiolus). The bronchioli converge to form the secondary bronchi which in turn converge to form the bronchi (singular: bronchus) and these converge to the trachea.

The bronchioli possess no cartilage but rather are composed of smooth muscle and elastic fibers. The diameter of the bronchioli is about 1 mm. The alveoli or air sacs terminate the bronchioli. It is the alveoli that are lined on their external surface with capillaries, the site of gas exchange.

The alveoli undergo cyclic expansions and partial collapses during the course of breathing. It is in these structures that gas exchange and oxygen transfer to the blood occurs across the membranes separating alveolus and capillaries. This cyclic movement of the alveoli can be impeded by the surface tension created by the thin film of water normally lining the interior surface of the alveoli. The presence of surfactants[12] reduces this surface tension without interfering with gas solubility/exchange properties afforded by the moisture present or the volume properties of the alveoli. Lipid surfactants consist of various phosphatidylcholines, the major one being dipalmitoylphosphatidylcholine [VIII]. Sphingomyelins [IX] also occur.

The role of surfactant in lung function is critical. The surfactants secreted into the alveoli and coating them are produced by an enzyme simply known as acyl transferase.[13] Phosgene toxicity is associated with an inhibition of acyl transferase activity.[14] A more recent examination of this relationship between phosgene toxicity effects and acyl transferase activity suggests that acyl transferase activity is increased due to the phosgene after an initial period of inhibition. The view is that the increased fluid build-up caused by phosgene reactivity with respiratory biomolecular cell components of the alveoli serves as a signal for the increased synthesis of surfactant (anti-edematogenic) compounds.

Breathing rate is dependent upon three factors: oxygen, carbon dioxide and hydrogen ion concentrations. If oxygen[15] concentration falls or carbon dioxide or hydrogen ion[16] concentrations

---

12 The surfactants are lipids mixtures.

13 1-acyl-2-lysophosphatidylcholine:acyl-CoA acyltransferase

14 *Amer. Rev. Resp. Dis.*, (Suppl.) **117**, 234 (1978)

15 Oxygen concentration has little direct and immediate effect on breathing rate, playing only a minor role by itself as long as oxygen concentration remains in a specific range.

16 It probably is hydrogen ion concentration that has the most direct impact upon breathing rate. In blood carbon dioxide and hydrogen ion concentration are related by the relationship:
$$HCO_3^- + H^+ \longleftrightarrow H_2CO_3 \longleftrightarrow H_2O + CO_2$$
As biological activity results in metabolism of fuels, acid (hydrogen ions) is released to the blood where it combines with latent bicarbonate to form carbonic acid. This is one of three buffering mechanisms to maintain a constant blood pH. In the lungs, oxygen concentration is high and carbon dioxide concentration is low at inhalation. The carbonic acid at the capillary/alveolus junction decomposes to carbon dioxide and

increase, breathing rate increases. It is chemoreceptors located in specialized cellular structures of the carotid and aortic arteries that sense increased carbon dioxide and hydrogen ion concentrations.

The increased carbon dioxide and hydrogen ion concentrations detected by the chemoreceptors of the carotid and aortic arteries result in impulses sent to the respiratory center causing the increase in breathing rate clinically observed. Though the hydrogen chloride is not the primary source of injury, its presence leads to increased lung tissue and blood acidity, a condition known as acidosis. Acidosis stimulates increased breathing (hyperventilation) resulting in increased inhalation of phosgene contaminated air.

Physiologically, the consequence is coughing. Dependent upon the quantity of phosgene inhaled, the coughing can become very hacking and forceful. This severe coughing can become so repetitive and deep as to lead to further damage, rupturing of delicate capillaries already weakened by damage from the agents and results in bleeding into the alveoli. Extreme cases of this process result in a pinkish to reddish frothing cough. The foaming observed is due to soluble proteins in the edemic fluid. The labored breathing and the resulting foaming leads to a mechanical suffocation. Of civil note is the occasional report that several firemen were treated for smoke inhalation. The carbonized material of smoke is generally acrid and itself quite irritating to nasal and lung tissues. But if the fire, as is typical, involves a modern building where plastics are a major structural or decorative component of the structure, the firemen have also inhaled phosgene.

MISCELLANEOUS SITES

The eyes, nose, sinuses and throat are minor sites of action of choking agents. As these organs and areas are bathed in moisturizing and lubricating aqueous body fluids, they are susceptible to the hydrolysis products of choking agents. The effects of choking agents on these organs and tissues do not constitute a life-threatening hazard. However, the hydrolytic action of the choking agents on these areas contributes to the discomfort of the afflicted under significant exposure. The action on these tissues is delayed because of the general bathing of these tissues by fluids that are constantly flushed over them. This is most true in the case of the eyes. Generally the concentrations as experienced in the open in the field are not high enough to result in any serious, permanent injury to such tissues. Liquid agent splashes to the eyes can present significant, and nearly immediate reaction by tearing.

water vapor to be exhaled.

CHAPTER 8

BLISTERING AGENTS

GENERAL

Blistering agents are fat soluble compounds. They are heteroaliphatic compounds consisting of a hydrocarbon main chain or cyclic ring system with chlorine, sulfur, nitrogen or arsenic. The sulfur containing agents are known simply as mustards while those possessing nitrogen in place of sulfur are termed nitrogen mustards. The arsenic containing compounds are arsenicals, a best known example being Lewisite.

Blistering agents are designed to attack the skin though they are equally effective in causing injury to the eyes and lungs.[1] They are externally active compounds, requiring no ingestion, inhalation or other internal absorption through blood to bring about their effects. Though topical exposure can be very serious and debilitating if the agents are not cleansed from the skin soon after contact, they are the slower acting toxic agents of the persistent variety. If removed from the skin immediately, little or no injury is sustained.

The immediate injuries caused are chemical burns which yield serious blisters. The hazard arising from blistering agents even in treatable cases is the serious damage done to the barrier properties of the skin and the subsequent opportunistic infections that invariably result. The nature of the injury to skin occurs in three phases: erythema (reddening), blister formation and necrotic lesion development. The latter is susceptible to opportunistic secondary infections as the dermis of the skin is penetrated.

The sulfur mustards are bifunctional alkylating agents. This means that each molecule can react twice with target biomolecules. The sulfur mustards are only slightly soluble in water. It is, however, the dissolved mustard that undergoes hydrolysis and brings about its physiological reactions. An intermediate specie is formed, a cyclic ethylene sulfonium cation [I].[2] This ionic specie has been observed through spectroscopic techniques.[3] The sulfonium cation is believed to arise by the mechanism shown in reaction equations (1) and (2).[4] The sulfonium cation is a transient specie with insufficient half-life for isolation and characterization. Dilute mustard reacts with water to form

---

[1] An excellent book titled "Medical Defense Against Mustard Gas" offers the most in-depth discussion of the effects of mustard agent under one cover.

[2] The nitrogen mustards possibly yield an analogous ionic specie, the cyclic ethylene imonium cation.

[3] NMR, Nuclear Magnetic Resonance spectroscopy

[4] A full and detailed discussion of this process is presented in Medical Defense Against Mustard gas: Toxic Mechanisms and Pharmacological Implications.

thiodiglycol[5] [II] and hydrochloric acid.

Sulfur mustards are subject to oxidation. The oxidation products are classified as sulfoxides [III] and sulfones [IV]. The sulfones exhibit significant vesicating (blistering) propensities and toxicity. Sulfones do not react with protein under physiological pH and temperature. Some sulfones are quite unstable and decompose to other alkylating species. The importance of oxidized sulfur mustards arises as a consequence of the detoxification processes of the body (notably residing in the liver) and the subsequent toxic products that result.[6]

The reactivity of sulfur mustards shows an enhanced preference for groups with available electrons and this includes anionic species as well. Thus, sulfhydryls (-SH), phosphates, aromatic nitrogens, carboxylic groups (-COOH) of amino acids, and so on are susceptible to attack by sulfur mustards. The sulfhydryl groups show the greater susceptibility.[7]

SITES OF ACTION

SKIN

Skin is a multilayered organ of the body. The surface layer consists of dead skin cells, hair, and pores. Figure 8-1 diagrams the composition and layered structure of skin. The epidermis is the outer layer of skin visible to the eye. The deepest portion of this layer is found at a level called the *stratum germinativum*. This region is located at the top of the dermis and is supplied with nutrients by the dermal blood vessels. As cell growth in this region continues, older cells are pushed toward the surface of the skin: the cells increasingly further from the dermis receive increasingly less nourishment and eventually die. As these cells are pushed toward the surface, they are keratinized, a hardening which is due to the build-up of protein (keratin) in a fibrous matrix throughout the cells' cytoplasm. These dead, keratinized cells form the surface of the skin and constitute a dead, waterproof surface coat that we see as the skin. This outer layer is technically called the *stratum corneum*. The intervening layers or strata, *stratum lucidum, stratum granulosum*, and the *stratum malpighii* are progressively deeper layers of epidermal skin which represent increasingly significant changes in cellular composition as the cells are pushed from the *stratum germinativum* to the *stratum corneum*. Skin growth and the thickness of the outer layer of dead skin are closely regulated by the growth of the underlying strata, and skin growth is more pronounced in areas where skin wear, rubbing and pressure are high. This prevents the outer *stratum corneum* from wearing away completely in otherwise healthy individuals. This increased growth of skin in such regions is the basis for calluses and 'corns' on the palms, toes and heels.

---

[5] bis(hydroxyethyl)sulfide

[6] This problem is not unique to mustards. Many foreign compounds ingested are processed by detoxification mechanisms of the body. These detoxification processes are a way the body attempts to remove toxic materials from the system. Typically, detoxification results in creating a more soluble compound by hydroxylations, or conjugation reactions with glucose, sulfate or glutathione. On occasion, an "allegedly" detoxified substance is rendered more dangerous. This is the case in point with polycyclic aromatic compounds such as benzo[a]pyrene which is oxidized to a diol epoxide, exhibiting carcinogenic properties. Sometimes the body's good biochemical intentions cause more harm than good...

[7] In Medical Defense Against Mustard Gas: ..., these groups are discussed in terms of what is called competition factors. The groups have different competition factors.

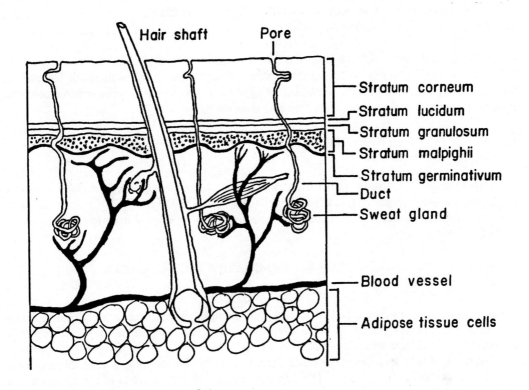

FIGURE 8 Diagrammatic structure of skin showing the various layers and component morphology.

Skin is nearly always moist from perspiration and other secretions. The sweat glands secrete oil-like fluids which serve as biological lubricants for the skin. These fluids are excellent solvents for the blistering agents. These dead skin cells and protein network act as a biological armor-like surface coating of the skin. Drying as well as microscopic cuts violate the integrity of this protective coat which is otherwise replaced on a continuous basis as surface layers peel, are washed off, etc. Additionally, abrasive effects from wear and tear of the skin due to clothing, rubbing, bruises, etc. also weaken the integrity and protection afforded by surface skin, exposing the living, vulnerable under-layers. The pores are holes in this barrier through which the agent is able to penetrate down into the gland channels where the tissue is composed of live, sensitive cells which are significantly more susceptible to damage by the agent. Thus it is these sites of microscopic damage and access that serve as the nucleation sites for the blisters that arise from unprotected exposure.

Mustards will chemically react with a broad range of biological compounds. The basis of these reactions is the functional groups found in biological compounds: sulfhydryl, imino, amino, and

enzymes such as the proteases.[8]

Interactions with sulfhydryl units presumably follows a reaction as[9]

$$R\text{-}SH + ClCH_2CH_2SCH_2CH_2Cl \longrightarrow R\text{-}S\text{-}CH_2CH_2SCH_2CH_2Cl + HCl$$
$$\text{mustard}$$

where the second chloro (Cl) unit can react with another sulfhydryl or other susceptible unit. Sulfhydryl groups in proteins exhibit a less reactive susceptibility to sulfur mustard. The smaller molecular weight sulfhydryl compounds such as cysteine, glutathione and methionine demonstrate greater reactivity. Imino groups, $=N\text{-}H$, may also react similarly:

$$R_2C=N\text{-}H + ClCH_2CH_2SCH_2CH_2Cl \longrightarrow R_2C=N\text{-}CH_2CH_2SCH_2CH_2Cl + HCl$$
$$\text{mustard}$$

again where the second chloro group may react with another susceptible group. A similar reaction can occur with the amino groups, $-NH_2$, where the product is $-NH\text{-}CH_2CH_2SCH_2CH_2Cl$. The reaction of a mustard with hydroxyl groups, particularly at the active site of an enzyme leads to an ether product $(C\text{-}O\text{-}C)$:

$$R\text{-}OH + ClCH_2CH_2SCH_2CH_2Cl \longrightarrow R\text{-}O\text{-}CH_2CH_2SCH_2CH_2Cl + HCl$$
$$\text{mustard}$$

It is the reaction of a mustard agent, in high doses, with an enzyme such as acetylcholinesterase that leads to symptoms similar to nerve agent poisoning. The reaction of sulfur mustard with biomolecules of the membranes is possible, in principal.

The reaction of both chloro ends of mustard is responsible for the cross-linking ability of such agents. This cross-linking reaction in DNA results in a double helical strand of DNA that can not undergo replication since the cross-linking by mustard prevents their separation during the replication process. The molecules of agent that reach the DNA add onto it, a process known as alkylation. Because of the structure of mustards, they can cross-link two different guanine bases of the DNA. This cross-linking prevents replication of DNA.[10] If replication is inhibited, cell division is inhibited. This invariably leads to cell death. Thus the regenerative capacity of skin in the region of the agent lesion is significantly degraded and in part explains the lengthy time required for healing (10 to 30 days). The nitrogen mustards also alkylate DNA. Unlike the sulfur mustards, for which no significant evidence yet exists, the nitrogen mustards have been shown to cross-link protein to DNA as well.[11]

Though there are no immediate clinical signs of exposure (no immediate sensations of burning, stinging or reddening of the skin) the mustards become 'fixed' to tissue biomolecules such as proteins, membranes, etc. It is later that clinical effects arise. In interacting with cellular components, the

---

[8] enzymes that degrade protein.

[9] R is the organic chemist's way of designating a nonspecific hydrocarbon group.

[10] This presumably occurs at the exocyclic nitrogen of guanine ($-NH_2$) designated as N(2).

[11] Eukaryotic cells possess special proteins associated with DNA in its packaged nucleosomal form. These proteins are referred to as *histones*.

mustards will also penetrate the cell and reach the nucleus, the site of DNA.

The toxicity of mustards is believed to be highest in rapidly dividing cells and skin, with its daily wear and replacement. It is here in this rapid growth and production of skin that mustard agents work their harm. For a much more medically founded discussion of the effects of mustard the reader is directed to the text:. *Medical Defense Against Mustard Gas: Toxic Mechanisms and Pharmacological Implications.*[12]

The eyes and respiratory system also are subject to injury from mustards. In extreme cases, the eyes are ulcerated with opacification[13] of the cornea. The respiratory tract exhibits irritation of the trachea and bronchi. Advanced effects include alveolar hemorrhage usually followed by infection.

THE EYE

The chemical nature of the biomolecules found in the eye is not that drastically different from that found in other biological tissues. That is, the functional group characteristics are the same. As a result the biological compounds of the eye are subject to the same type of reactions possible with skin. The consequences are perhaps a shade more serious if for no other reason than the importance attached to eyesight. The eyes are without doubt more sensitive organs and their ability to sustain injury less tolerant. The subsequent inflammation and damage to the eyes has all the more seriousness than injury to skin. Typically a form of conjunctivitis evidences eye exposure to mustard.

RESPIRATORY TRACT

The respiratory tract is no less similar in biochemical functional group characteristics to skin and eye biomolecules. However, unlike the skin, the respiratory tract is much more sensitive to contact with atmospheric contaminants than the skin. This is certainly in part due to the actively living and metabolizing nature of the tissues within the respiratory tract in marked contrast to the surface layer of dead, nonliving keratinized skin.

The nature of reactions of respiratory tract tissues to exposure to mustard agents is not significantly different from that of skin. That is, tissue alkylations occur and though blistering is observed on skin, such injuries are not observable within the lungs. The results on respiratory tract tissues is essentially the same, manifested principally as pulmonary edemas. The susceptibility to infection also is present and, generally, it is the respiratory tract infections that pose the ultimate crisis to the blistering agent casualty in unprotected respiratory tract cases.

---

[12] Injury & Description of Lesions: Chapter 2; Molecular Cytotoxicity: Chapter 7; Toxicodynamics: Chapter 4; Histo and Cytopathology: Chapter 3.

[13] The process of rendering the eye impervious to light.

MUSTARD SYSTEMIC TOXICITY

Because sulfur [V] (and nitrogen [VI]) mustard agents also react with a host of other biomolecules other than skin, eyes or respiratory tract, they can trigger other effects not directly intended by their use. For example, the ability of the sulfur mustards in very high, absorbed concentrations to react with certain enzymes arises in symptoms very much like those attributed to organophosphate nerve agents. Thus, the mustards in attacking the skin, eyes or respiratory tract with all the attendant symptoms and complications is but a prelude to other serious, less easily characterized, internal injuries. The mustards have an effect on the entire animal system and therefore pose a systemic toxicity in high absorbed concentrations.

ARSENICAL SYSTEMIC EFFECTS

Some typical arsenicals are cacodylate [VII] (pentavalent arsenic); ethyldichloroarsine [VIII], Lewisite [IX], and Adamsite [X] (trivalent arsenic).[14] The action of mixed function oxidases on arsenicals yields arsenious acid [XI] from trivalent arsenicals and arsenic acid [XII] from pentavalent arsenicals. In tissues, these materials exist as their respective salts: arsenites and arsenates.

Arsenic acid [XII] bears a striking resemblance to phosphoric acid [XIII]. This leads to one of the problems arising with arsenic poisoning, the potential utilization of arsenious acid and in some instances, arsenic acid, as the adduct to ADP instead of phosphoric acid.[15]

Arsenic poisoning arises through three processes: (1) arsenolysis or the uncoupling of oxidative phosphorylation (see Chapter 6), (2) -SH enzyme poisoning (inactivation), and (3) protein denaturation also called precipitation. The latter is unlikely to be important in arsenic poisoning as the gross protein subject to denaturation by arsenic is too great in quantity to be systemically affected by the small quantities of arsenic required for the LD_{50}. The most likely effect on proteins is case (2), the inactivation or inhibition of the so-called -SH enzymes, those enzymes which have critical thiol groups at the active site or which participate in tertiary protein structure and which undergo oxidation reactions.

Enzymes possess specific shapes (called conformations) which bring certain amino acid residues into close proximity to each other. Some of these specific amino acid residues comprise the active site, the region of the enzyme in which reactions take place. Many enzymes facilitate their conformation by utilizing cysteine, an amino acid with the thiol group (-SH), to form a -S-S- called a disulfide bond with another cysteine. These -S-S- linkages are very susceptible to disruption by heavy metals such as lead, mercury and arsenic. Such metal-cysteine complexes lead to denaturation of the enzyme and in the extreme cases, inactivation. Additionally, some enzymes require what are

---

[14] Only ethyldichlorarsine and Lewisite are vesicants.

[15] Addition of arsenic acid to ADP is termed arsenolysis while the addition of normal phosphoric acid to ADP is termed phosphorylation. The latter results in the formation of ATP. The former results in an ADP-arsenic moiety complex, $ADP-As(OH)_2$, which is unstable and spontaneously hydrolyzes to ADP and $As(OH)_3$. No net ATP synthesis results. Other susceptible biomolecules are glyceraldehyde and glyceric acid which normally exist as the phosphorylated derivative. An enzyme susceptible to arsenic acid poisoning is glyceraldehyde 3-phosphate dehydrogenase, an enzyme of the glycolysis system.

called coenzymes,[16] moderate molecular weight organic molecules that serve a critical role in the enzyme's activity on its substrate. Many of these coenzymes are themselves dependent upon the thiol group in their structure for their chemical activity in conjunction with the enzyme. One example of many is the component lipoic acid [XIV] which possesses two thiol groups in the reduced state.

The pyruvate dehydrogenase multienzyme complex consists of several distinct enzymes which act together to yield acetyl-CoA units.[17] One of these is dihydrolipoyl dehydrogenase which possesses a lipoic acid moiety in amide linkage to the ϵ-amino group of a lysine residue of the enzyme. In contributing hydrogen atoms for reduction of a substrate, the lipoic acid moiety is oxidized to a five-membered heterocyclic ring system [XV]. Arsenic can react with the reduced sulfurs of these kinds of enzymes and components. In so doing, the -SH is not available for the reversible reactions in which they normally participate. The enzymatic activity is impeded or stopped dependent upon the concentration of enzyme and arsenic.

Furthermore, Coenzyme A, the acetyl unit carrier, also possesses a thiol group in its terminal β-mercaptoethyleneamine [XVI] moiety. Arsenic complexation with this unit can frustrate acetyl-CoA synthesis. In principal, any biomolecule which possesses a thiol group can be "poisoned" by arsenic.

Because of these diverse effects of arsenic on cellular processes and the nonspecific nature of a targeted system, arsenic affects a wide range of processes in the cell and body as a whole. It is this broad spectrum of effects on the whole organism that earns arsenic the title systemic poison.

TABLE 2

DOWNWIND VAPOR HAZARD FROM HD[18]

TYPE OF TERRAIN	DOWNWIND DIMENSION OF TARGET AREA (IN METERS)	DISTANCE DOWNWIND OF HD CONTAMINATED AREA THAT VAPOR HAZARD MAY EXIST (IN METERS)	
		HOT, HUMID WEATHER (ABOVE 80°F)	WARM WEATHER (60° TO 80°F)
OPEN GRASSLAND	200	900	1600
	500	2200	4100
BARREN SOIL OR SAND	200	1100	2100
	500	2700	5200

[16] Many vitamins are coenzyme precursors.

[17] Acetyl-CoA units arise from glucose and fatty acid metabolism and are initial players leading to the Tricarboxylic Acid Cycle (Krebs Cycle) for the derivation of ATP.

[18] From FM 3-5, Chemical, Biological and Radiological (CBR) Operations, September 1961, p. 69

CHAPTER 9

INCAPACITATING & DEFOLIANT AGENTS

GENERAL

Incapacitating agents are classified principally as physical incapacitants and psychoincapacitants. They attack particular body systems and thus reduce one's ability to function either physically or mentally.

The central advantage to the use of chemical agents (excepting incendiaries and smoking) is to avoid destruction of facilities, penetrate well fortified positions and at the same time, eliminate enemy resistance by incapacitation, either temporarily or permanently by death. Such agents enjoy advantage in use by civil and military authorities, but are unlikely to be used by terrorists as the object of the terrorist is to terrorize and that means kill in a spectacular manner. The lethal use of agents are accomplished by the toxic agents: nerve, blood, choking and blistering.

Incapacitating agents have found principal use in crowd or riot control among civilian populations where cultural, moral and ethical principles prevent the use of lethal force, though they have military advantages when used on enemy troops dispersed among a civilian population. Additionally, even among exclusively military troops, circumstances may be such that the use of lethal force on troops also violates moral and ethical as well as international agreements. One such example applies to prisoners of war who, under the Geneva Conventions, are under the protection of the national forces holding them, though these Geneva Protocols clearly are not adhered to by all nations, even those who have signed such protocols.

The U.S. found it necessary to reestablish order in a POW camp in South Korea during the Korean War when North Korean POWs rioted. The use of physical incapacitants in restoring order avoided the political and ethical problems posed by the use of lethal force in such circumstances.[1] Their effects and actions on the body are as varied as the agent types.

PHYSICAL INCAPACITANTS

Physical incapacitants are the principal incapacitating agents used world wide. These agents are generally considered nonlethal (though nontoxic is understating their potential hazard) as the lethal dose is rarely achieved in practical, field application. The distinction between a lethal agent and a nonlethal (incapacitating) agent is somewhat based upon types and numbers of casualties achieved in its field use. Incapacitating agents generally are designed not to kill, injure or even have lasting side effects. Deaths from these agents usually arise from hypersensitivities, heart attack or respiratory failure owing to their significantly overpowering effects in high concentrations in susceptible

---

[1] The use of riot control agents at the POW camp did evoke propaganda charges against the U.S. in the UN on 8 May, 1951.

individuals, or use in confined, poorly ventilated areas. Physical incapacitants, as their name suggests, affect a person's ability to function physically. Such individuals when in contact with such agents generally offer little or no resistance to public authority personnel using the agent. Of the physical incapacitants, the lacrimators (tearing) and vomiting agents are prominent.

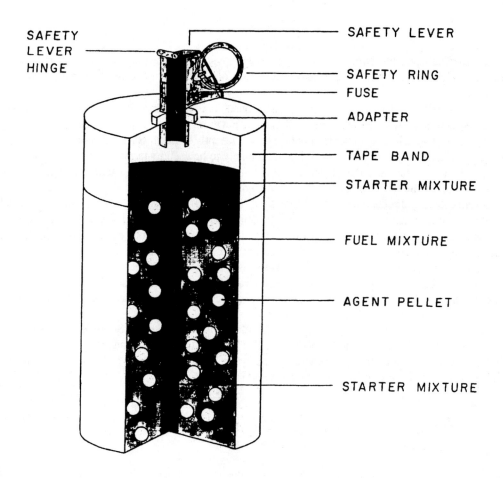

FIGURE 9 A schematic diagram of a teargas grenade. The material is ignited by pulling the ring pin at the top of the grenade. This starts the burning of the fuel which is mixed with the tearing agent material. The heat of the burning fuel vaporizes the tearing agent. The agent vents through the tube located along the center axis of the grenade can. The agents also vents through a tape band which burns away. Phosphorus grenades have a similar construction and appearance though such munitions do explode to propel the incandescent pieces of burning white phosphorus out radially from the grenades explosion point.

LACRIMATORS

Lacrimatory or tearing agents (a.k.a. tear gas) are very irritating to moist tissues such as the eyes, nasal and throat passages. The tear gases CS [I] and CN [II] are the best examples of this class of chemical agents which affect the eyes and breathing. Lacrimatory compounds are o-chlorobenzylmalononitrile [III], chloropicrin [IV] and bromobenzyl cyanide [V], benzyl bromide [VI], and the xylyl bromides [VII(a,b)]. Some of these compounds generally are of such a chemical composition that upon contact with water they are hydrolyzed, releasing products that are quite irritating. One product of such hydrolysis could be an acidic compound. The irritation is so great that the body's response is to immediately suspend breathing, a catching of one's breath, and flood the affected region in fluid secretions to flush the irritant away. This usually aggravates the condition as further hydrolysis of agent in the area continues. Rubbing of the eyes and nose only further aggravates the condition by imposing mechanical abrasions to the sensitive tissue of the eyes and nose in contact with the tearing agent. A burning or stinging sensation can also arise on the skin. This is due to microscopic cuts, abrasions and minuscule water vapor in close proximity to the skin. The microscopic cuts and abrasions partially expose pain-sensing nerve endings that respond to the hydrolytic agent assault. Any disorientation as a result of significant exposure is a result of individual side-effects and usually leads to immediate halting of the breath, panicked closing of the eyes and inattention to one's location and direction of flight from the area as well as any allergic hypersensitivity to the agents. Once the agent is flushed from the eyes, nose and throat, symptoms subside relatively quickly and no permanent injury is expected in the majority of otherwise healthy individuals so long as the aerosol material is the only contact. Exposure of eyes to massive doses can lead to corneal burns. Concentrated quantities in direct contact with the skin can lead to discoloration. Headache and vomiting is not uncommon.

VOMITING AGENTS

One of the better known vomiting agents is Adamsite [VIII]. This material is chemically classified as an arsenical, a compound formulated on the element arsenic. This vomiting-inducing agent is lacrimatory in its function but is more severe in its effects: any pain, headache or tightness in the chest induced by the conventional tearing agents are amplified by exposure to Adamsite. Though permanent injury from the standard tearing agents is not an expected problem, Adamsite is not without its risk for causing permanent injury. As an arsenical, Adamsite is a potential systemic poison. The use of Adamsite as a crowd control agent-- civilian or military-- is therefore hazardous since deaths could easily result.

PSYCHOACTIVE

Probably the most famous psychoactive chemical is the mind altering drug LSD [IX].[2] Though research continues on chemicals that affect the mind, they have thus far never been used in any crowd control or ethically sanctioned military setting. Aside from the objections for use of such agents on

---

[2] LSD's chemical name is **L**y**S**ergic acid **D**iethylamide

moral and ethical grounds, their unpredictability and incredible potency are perhaps the best reasons for their lack of use. Psychoactive agents require only the most minuscule quantities for their activity and such dose control can not be practicably achieved in the field. The likely concentrations that normally would arise from field dispersal would be vastly higher than tolerable, probably rendering their use lethal. Additionally, the side effects vary from little or none to bizarre and even have led to psychotic episodes and death. Many of the psychoactive chemicals induce time and sensory distortions which can not even be generalized in scope of activity among all potential subjects exposed. They are quite unpredictable and remain principally of psychiatric interest rather than for general military field applications at the present time. Given the desire of terrorists to control their victims and the event they have initiated, it is also remote that they would resort to use of such agents in terrorist attacks in which they the terrorist are collocated. The potential bizarre behavior of the hostages would create uncertainties which even the terrorist would recoil from. The bottom line, a dead hostage is a poor bargaining chip.

SYMPTOMS

The effects vary among the different psychoactive agents. Generally, they manifest, in part or in whole, hyperexcitability, convulsions, psychotic episodes, psychopathic disorders, homicidal and suicidal tendencies, mental dissociations, coma and even chromosomal damage.

DEFOLIANTS

Defoliants, or herbicides, are poisonous chemicals to plants. They are toxic to humans and in high enough dosage will kill humans, though they are intended and designed to be toxic only to plants. Their value as a chemical agent is twofold. They may be used to destroy agricultural capabilities of the targeted country or they may be used to destroy vegetation affording concealment.[3] The former is a strategic employment while the latter is principally a tactical employment. Defoliants come as a wide range of herbicides, specific for particular plants or for particular types of plants such as all broad leaf plants. Their military use has been significant only in the Vietnam War.

The successes cited in defoliant use in Vietnam had little effect on the course or the outcome of the war. As a "nonlethal weapon system" used against enemy troop activities, it may have been a tactical success, but also a dismal strategic failure of political magnitude. The cases of cancer among American servicemen who handled the materials claimed considerable political and media attention for several years following their use. Those afflicted with the medical problems attributable to the various defoliants are either dead from cancers and leukemias or suffer today still other debilitating consequences. Some of the news reports that have filtered out of postwar Vietnam suggest that many former enemy troops may also suffer adverse effects of exposure to the aerial sprays of these agents. But their use for whatever reason changed nothing of the war's progression. We still lost the war. Killing trees is no substitute for killing enemy troops.

---

[3] This was the purpose for the use of Agent Orange in the Vietnam war. The agent was sprayed from aircraft overflying known or suspected supply routes of the Viet Cong and North Vietnamese Army regulars (NVA). The intent was to destroy the dense jungle canopy that concealed movements of those forces under it.

Use of defoliants in military operations has five basic purposes. They are to: (1) enhance security; (2) improve military intelligence; (3) reduce enemy resistance; (4) increase number of troops available for combat, by reducing casualties; and (5) facilitate movement of military supplies.

Enhanced security arises from the removal of dense foliage that obstructs fields of vision and fire. By clearing away undergrowth, dense brush, etc., installations, fire bases, and such have wide and open perimeters. Enemy advances and attacks are less likely to occur by surprise and the absence of such vegetation denies the enemy forces any concealment.

Military intelligence improves by the removal of dense areas of forests and jungles in uninhabited or unfrequented regions by exposing terrain features for improved maps, as well as military plans and operations.

Reduction of enemy resistance by defoliation presumably results from exposure of enemy supply depots, base camps, and lines of communications. Defoliation also leads to more effective air strikes against such targets. Fewer friendly forces are required to carry out these tasks compared to the needs in operations in fully vegetated areas.

Defoliated perimeters afford increased security and also less manpower to man the security posts. Additionally, defoliated friendly supply routes deny the enemy concealment and open fields of view for convoy security forces. Such open fields of view, and thus open fields of fire, discourage enemy attacks. With such open areas, any attacks are seen as early as possible and casualties can be reduced, the enemy having been denied the element of surprise, one of the ten principles of war.

Defoliation of supply routes facilitates the movement of supplies. The primary advantage is the clear fields of view. The reduction of foliage along river banks and bays renders shipping channels and harbors safer for use.

Defoliation also places logistical burdens on enemy forces. Herbicides used on enemy food crops deny them an essential materiel. Additionally, more of the opposing enemy manpower must be dedicated to supply defense, food acquisition, etc.

Defoliants kill plants by four different methods: (1) physical toxicity, (2) auxin[4]-like stimulants, (3) metabolic inhibitors, and (4) photosynthesis inhibitors.

PHYSICAL TOXICITY

Physical intoxicants are chemical compounds which disrupt physical (as compared to chemical) processes of plants. These agents are active on such levels of plant organization as the cellular membranes. The disruption is not a chemical reaction but a physical action such as dissolving one material in another. Various petroleum products do damage by dissolving in membranes, altering their integrity and permeability. The barrier properties of the membrane are disrupted, leading to cell death. Compounds such as the bipyridylium ionic compounds are soluble in water, yielding ionic by-products which through photosynthetic reactions in the presence of oxygen yield hydrogen peroxide, an oxidizing agent, as well. These compounds are derived from the bipyridyls [X(a-f)].

---

[4] Auxins are plant growth hormonelike substances. These substances are found mostly in young, physiologically active regions of plants such as roots and shoots. An example is indoleacetic acid, enzymatically synthesized from the amino acid tryptophan. Auxins regulate tissue and organ growth, cell division in some tissues, partly regulate abscission of leaves, flowers and fruits, development of fruits from flower ovaries, ripening of seeds and function in the so-called tropisms of plants (phototropism, geotropism, and chemotropism).

Serious cell and chloroplast[5] membrane damage is done leading to cell and plant death.

AUXIN-LIKE STIMULANTS

Auxin-like substances do not appear to affect mitochondrial processes such as oxidative phosphorylation or reactions of the chloroplasts. These substances derive their classification from auxin, a plant hormone, in that they mimic auxin. Their biochemical effects vary from one plant type to another.

Phenoxyaliphatic acids [XI] generally increase cell division, activate phosphate metabolic reactions, and increase RNA and protein syntheses. Arylaliphatic acids stimulate cell elongation, tissue growth, increased and sporadic root growth and induce fruit maturation in the absence of fertilization.

METABOLIC INHIBITORS

Several metabolic processes are affected by metabolic inhibitors. Various phenolic derivatives interfere with oxidative phosphorylation by an uncoupling mechanism. Nitroaniline [XII(a-c)] derivatives impede growth by limiting root growth. Another class of herbicides, the nitriles [XIII], are potent inhibitors of oxidative phosphorylation as well as carbon dioxide fixation. The nitriles are a class of organic compounds possessing the -CN moiety. One feature of these compounds is the release of CN⁻ which is poisonous to the cytochrome c oxidase of the electron transport system.

Another metabolic interference arises with the arsenicals. As noted in previous chapters, arsenicals can release arsenic which mimics phosphorus. Uncoupling of phosphorylation by arsenic (arsenolysis) and binding to and denaturation of thiol group (-SH) enzymes and proteins are the principal effects of arsenicals in plants as they are in animals. Specific enzyme inhibitors are available. These inhibitors can block respiratory, photosynthetic and protein syntheses processes.

Inhibitors of plant nucleic acid and protein syntheses follow the same general mechanistic pattern as found in animals. Various substances affect these processes and include the carbamates [XIV], thiocarbamates [XV], and the chlorinated aliphatic acids.

PHOTOSYNTHESIS INHIBITORS

Finally, photosynthesis, specific to green plants, is an excellent target for such specific agents. Various agents which act against particular photosynthetic reactions are triazines [XVI], triazoles [XVII(a-b)], urea [XVIII] and uracil [XIX] derivatives.

The commercially available defoliants used in Vietnam are agents ORANGE, BLUE and WHITE, so named because of the identifying color markings of their respective shipping containers.

---

[5] Chloroplasts house the photosynthetic components necessary to synthesize sugars from carbon dioxide and water.

Agent ORANGE is a 50:50 mixture of 2,4-D[6] [XX] and 2,4,5-T[7] [XXI] with trace dioxin [XXII]. The agent is liquid at room temperature and the grade used has a reddish brown color. It is insoluble in water but soluble in organic solvents such as diesel fuel, a common solvent used by the military for cleaning equipment as well as its fuel use. ORANGE is found useful against woody and broad-leaf plants.

Agent BLUE is commercial grade sodium cacodylate [XXIII] known as Phytar 560G. As an organoarsenical, it poses a systemic poison hazard to humans.[8] The grade used is a reddish or brownish colored liquid. It is soluble in water[9] and alcohol, insoluble in oils. It is effective on woody, broad-leaf, and grassy plants.

The third agent, WHITE, is 20% picloram[10] [XXIV] and 80% 2,4-D. These active ingredients were complexed with triisopropanolamine [XXV] to form the organic salts of the agent components. The formulation offers a viscous, dark brown liquid. This agent, too, is effective on woody and broad-leaf plants. It is soluble in water, insoluble in oils.

The following table lists several incapacitant (antipersonnel) and defoliant compounds and some of their physicochemical properties.

---

[6] 2,4-D: n-butyl-2,4-dichlorophenoxyacetic acid.

[7] 2,4,5-T: n-butyl-2,4,5-trichlorophenoxyacetic acid.

[8] The poison is most toxic through ingestion as the gastric acid releases inorganic arsenic.

[9] This property restricts its use as rain will flush the material from targeted plants.

[10] 4-amino-3,5,6-trichloropicolinic acid

Table 9-1: **INCAPACITANTS & DEFOLIANT AGENTS**			
Common Name	MACE	CAMITE	TEAR GAS
Chemical Name	2-chloroacetophenone	bromobenzyl cyanide	o-chlorobenzylidene malononitrile
Military Symbol	CN	BBC	CS
Classification Chemical Military	lacrimator incapacitating agent	lacrimator incapacitating agent	lacrimator incapacitating agent
Physical State/Color	solid/white	solid	solid/white
Boiling/Melting Point (°C)	244/59	242/-	310-315/-
Density (at °C)	1.3 (20)		
Odor	sharp, penetrating	sharp, penetrating	sharp, penetrating
Hydrolysis	none	none	
Lethal Conc.	0.34 ppm	0.9 mg/L	0.05 ppm
Persistency	yes	yes	yes
Primary Site of Action	eyes, respiratory tract	eyes, respiratory tract	eyes, respiratory tract
Secondary Site of Action	skin (direct contact)		skin (direct contact)
Decontamination Methods	hot caustic soda solution	flush w/water	flush w/water
Antidote	none	none	none

Table 9-1: **INCAPACITANTS & DEFOLIANT AGENTS Continued**			
Common Name	ADAMSITE	DIPHENYLCHLO RARSINE	DIPHENYLCYA NARSINE
Chemical Name	10-chloro-5,10-dihydro-phenarsine	diphenylchlorarsine	diphenylcyanarsine
Military Symbol	DM	DA	DC
Classification Chemical Military	arsenical vomiting agent incapacitating agent	arsenical lacrimator incapacitating agent	arsenical lacrimator incapacitating agent
Physical State/Color	solid/canary yellow	solid	solid
Boiling/Melting Point (°C)	410/195	383/44	
Density (at °C)	1.65 (20)	1.4 (20)	
Odor			
Hydrolysis	HCl & DM oxide, systemic poison hazard	HCl & DA oxide, systemic poison hazard	HCl & DC oxide, systemic poison hazard
Lethal Conc.	0.65 ppm	0.60 ppm	
Persistency	systemic effects	systemic effects	systemic effects
Primary Site of Action	respiratory tract	respiratory tract	respiratory tract
Secondary Site of Action	skin, ingestion	skin, ingestion	skin, ingestion
Decontamination Methods	bleaching powder, Cl gas	caustic soda, Cl gas	caustic soda, Cl gas
Antidote (Systemic Effects)	BAL	BAL	BAL

Table 9-1: **INCAPACITANTS & DEFOLIANT AGENTS Continued**			
Common Name	CHLOROPICRIN[11]	BENZYL BROMIDE	ETHYLIODOACETATE
Chemical Name	trichloronitromethane	bromophenylmethane	ethyl iodoacetate
Military Symbol	PS		

Classification
  Chemical
  Military
	lacrimator
	incapacitating agent
		lacrimator
		incapacitating agent
			lacrimator
			incapacitating agent

Physical State/Color	oily liquid	liquid	
Boiling/Melting Point (°C)	112/-64	198/-3.9	
Density (at °C)	1.656 (20)	1.44 (22)	
Odor			
Hydrolysis		slowly	
Lethal Conc.			
Persistency	yes	yes	
Primary Site of Action	respiratory tract, eyes	respiratory tract, eyes	respiratory tract, eyes
Secondary Site of Action	skin	skin	skin
Decontamination Methods	soapy water solution	soapy water solution	soapy water solution
Antidote	none	none	none

---

[11] Also has choking agent qualities.

Table 9-1: **INCAPACITANTS & DEFOLIANT AGENTS Continued**		
Common Name	3-QUINUCLIDINYL BENZILATE	LSD	AGENT WHITE
Chemical Name	1-azabicylo [2.2.2]octan-3-ol benzilate ester	9,10-didehydro-N,N-diethyl-6-methyl-ergoline-8β-carboxamide	2,4-dichlorophenoxy-acetic acid (2,4-D), 4-amino-3,5,6-trichloropicolinic acid (picloram)
Military Symbol	BZ		
Classification Chemical Military	atropinemimetic psychoactive incapacitant	psychomimetic psychoactive incapacitant	chlorinated herbicide defoliant agent
Physical State/Color	solid, white	solid/white	solid
Boiling/Melting Point ($^\circ$C)	-/164		
Odor			
Hydrolysis			weathering
Lethal Conc.			
Persistency			
Primary Site of Action	mind	mind	
Secondary Site of Action			
Decontamination Methods			
Antidote			none

Table 9-1: **INCAPACITANTS & DEFOLIANT AGENTS Continued**		
Common Name	AGENT ORANGE	AGENT BLUE
Chemical Name	(a) n-butyl-2,4-dichlorophenoxyacetic acid (2,4-D derivative) (b) n-butyl-2,4,5-trichlorophenoxy acetic acid (2,4,5-T derivative) (c) 2,3,7,8-tetrachlorodibenzo[b,e][1,4]dioxin (DIOXIN[12])	sodium cacodylate
Classification Chemical Military	chlorinated herbicide defoliant	arsenical herbicide defoliant
Physical State/Color	solid	solid
Boiling/Melting Point (°C)		320-325/195
Odor	odor is that of solvent in which dissolved	odor is that of solvent in which dissolved
Hydrolysis		inorganic arsenic, systemic poison hazard
Lethal Conc.		1.25 g/Kg (mice)
Persistency		arsenical hazard
Decontamination Methods	weathering	weathering
Antidote	none	BAL

---

[12] DIOXIN is a contaminant in the manufacture of AGENT ORANGE.

CHAPTER 10

INCENDIARIES & OBSCURANTS

Iacta alea est.
The die is cast.
- Julius Caesar, 102?-44 B.C.[1]

GENERAL

On 25 February 1945, 172 B-29 Superfortress bombers attacked Tokyo, Japan in the first incendiary raid on that nation. The raid was ordered by then Major General Curtis LeMay, Commander of all B-29 forces in the Pacific Theater. Gen. LeMay after the end of WWII became the first commander of the USAF Strategic Air Command or SAC. The B-29 was the brainchild of General 'Hap' Arnold, senior Army Air Corps commander in Washington when the air power was still part of the US Army prior to and during WWII. It was a strategic bomber of greater capacity than the B-17s and B-24s used in both the European and Pacific Theaters.

The results of that mission were indeed illuminating to General LeMay. An ardent supporter of high altitude precision bombing, he and his command had experienced little success in previous high explosive (HE) precision attacks on Japan. The reasons for this lack of success which frustrated the reason for development of such a high altitude heavy capacity bomber in the first place was that with the B-29, we could attain very high altitudes and thus we ran head long into the Jet Stream, a current of high velocity air that the other bombers didn't experience because of their lower operating ceiling. The Jet Stream played havoc with bombs falling from such heights, blowing them this way and that during their fall, and effectively blew them off their target aim point in spite of using the Norden bomb sight.

Records of that lone incendiary mission captured at the end of the war revealed that some 28,000 buildings had been destroyed in a square mile of city. Estimates place the number killed at 97,000, the injured at 125,000, and the homeless at 1,200,000.[2] That damage was caused by a raid at about 30,000 feet altitude. It was only a prelude to the destruction and death that was to rain from the skies over Japan over the next several remaining months of the war. The effectiveness of incendiary bombs didn't require the pinpoint accuracy of high explosive bombs because the wood construction of the major portion of Tokyo's buildings succumbed to fires. These fires were called fire storms because of the high winds generated by the immense fires developing, drawing in air with a ravenous appetite. The idea for such bombing occurred to Lemay as a result of his experiences and knowledge of such bombing in Europe, notably Dresden and Hamburg Germany, and the pressures put on him by Arnold for results.

---

[1] Dictionary of Quotations, The Oxford University press, Crescent Books, New York, 1985, p. 120

[2] Contrast that loss with that caused by both A-bombs; on Hiroshima: 75,000 killed, Nagasaki: 40,000 killed.

During the 9-10 March raid on Tokyo, at an altitude of 8,000 feet, the bombers had destroyed 16.8 square miles, 83,793 killed, 40,918 wounded, and 267,171 buildings incinerated, leaving a million people homeless. About 18% of Tokyo's industrial capacity was obliterated from the face of the earth, all in one massive raid. The destruction was second only to the 1923 earthquake which also targeted Tokyo.[3] The death and destruction by incendiary attacks continued unabated, targeting major industrial centers of Japan up to and including the destruction of Hiroshima (6 August 1945) and Nagasaki (15 August 1945) by nuclear bombs, the biggest incendiaries of them all.

Incendiary use in the European Theater during WWII was very effective (Dresden, Hamburg) but the wooden built structures in Japan were an irresistible invitation. Incendiary bombing in Europe and Japan during WWII had well established the roll and benefit of incendiary use by the U.S. Air Forces to reach seemingly unreachable or vastly dispersed target areas. Because of WWII experience and successes, incendiary use continued in the Vietnam conflict. Incendiaries come in different forms such as metal, pyrotechnic, oil-based, oil-metal, and pyrophorics.

INCENDIARIES

Metals which burn easily (it is actually a rapid oxidation) are particularly well suited as incendiaries though they must be stable until ignition. Most high school students have seen demonstrations of sodium metal reacting with water or air. This metal is problematic as an incendiary metal since it instantly reacts on contact with a wide range of substances including water and air. Metals such as magnesium and aluminum are excellent components as their oxidation in the air generates enormous quantities of heat per pound of metal. Uses of these metal incendiaries are against metal targets such as vehicles; trucks, tanks, armored personnel carriers, and even aircraft on the ground.

Thermite is the best example of the pyrotechnic class of incendiaries. It is a mixture of iron (ferric) oxide and powdered or granular aluminum, which when ignited can produce a temperature of 2400°C. Its use is found as an igniter for magnesium bombs and also in other incendiary bombs and hand grenades.

Oil-based incendiaries can produce temperatures between 800° to 1200°C. A good example is that of napalm. Napalm derives its name from the ingredients originally used to formulate it: aluminum naphthenate and aluminum palmitate. It was invented by professor Louis Fieser of Harvard in 1942.[4] The palmitate component was actually a number of different fatty acids of coconut oil, palmitate itself constituting only 8.2% of the mix. The name, however, stuck. Another brand of napalm, napalm B, contains 50% polystyrene and 25% each of benzene and gasoline.[5] In 1954 the U.S. Army lifted some of the secrecy surrounding napalm when it discussed the chemical structure

[3] Iron Eagle: The Turbulent Life of General Curtis LeMay, by Thomas M. Coffey, Avon, 1986

[4] The Scientific Method: A Personal Account of Unusual Projects in War and Peace, L.F. Feiser, Reinhold, New York, 1964.

[5] Chemical and Engineering News, March 14, 1966.

properties of the incendiary.[6]

Also commonly known to Vietnam veterans is the formulation known as fougasse[7], a jellied gasoline in 55 gallon drums, ignited by an explosive charge under the bottom of the drum. These incendiary devices were commonly used in perimeter defenses in Vietnam and were also in use during WWII by the British. The advantages of this incendiary form are the increased burn time realized over that of petroleum only fuels, a more even spread on contact compared to the metal types, their ease and safety in flamethrower use and an ability to stick to target surfaces such as walls and personnel.

The advantages of oil-based and metal incendiaries are combined in the oil-metal class of agents. They generally provide the excellent spreading properties of the oil-based group and the intense heat production of the metal group. This type of incendiary has the special name of pyrogels. The temperatures they generate can be as high as 1600°C.

The pyrophoric class of incendiary employs processed elements as the agent. White phosphorus (WP)[8] [I] perhaps is the best known agent and is easily recognized in war film footage as the spectacular explosion of white, filamentous fingers radiating outward from the blast center. These munitions come in the form of grenades and bombs. White phosphorus is insoluble and unreactive in water. Water immersion is a way of extinguishing any such burning debris on personnel. It is soluble in carbon disulfide, an organic liquid solvent, and is sometimes formulated in such solvents for use in artillery shells and bombs. WP on ignition emits large plumes of dense white smoke[9]. The resultant smoke of its oxidation in air is irritating to the mucous membranes, forming phosphoric acid on contact with water. WP is used both as an incendiary and smoke agent. The irritating properties of the WP smoke is, however, an added benefit as it also is injurious to enemy troops.

Though red phosphorus (that of match heads) is not absorbed or poisonous, the white phosphorus is quite poisonous. It is easily absorbed and can lead to tissue damage, interference of carbohydrate, fat and protein metabolism within the liver. White phosphorus poisoning appears as jaundice, fatty deterioration of the liver and kidneys with their eventual destruction, as well as gastrointestinal tract erosion and hemorrhage. White phosphorus on the skin spontaneously ignites on exposure to air and causes second and third degree thermal and chemical burns that are very slow to heal. The chemical reaction of the combustion product, phosphoric acid, with tissue leads to chemical burns superimposed upon the thermal injury. Respiratory absorption of the white phosphorus vapors exhibits effects one to three days later. These symptoms are nausea, diarrhea, cardiac arrhythmia and the breath and excrement smell of garlic.

The metal zirconium in fine powder form also possesses pyrophoric properties. Such materials emit sparks when struck and are useful as ignitors in other incendiary weapons. Gas lighters employ cerium as a flint material for spark generation. Zirconium is used in HE and armor-piercing incendiary rounds.

Uranium (depleted, nonradioactive) is used in some armor-piercing rounds. The 30 mm antitank rounds of the A-10 tank killer aircraft of the U.S. Air Force employ such uranium cased rounds. These rounds with the uranium hull are able to penetrate the armor plate of tanks and other armored

---

[6] Chemical & Engineering News **32**, 2690 (1954)

[7] From the French fougade formerly meaning, in warfare, a small mine charged with (gun)powder and covered with earth or stones.

[8] This is known in the military parlance as Willie Peter.

[9] The smoke is actually tetraphosphorus decoxide, P_4O_{10}, a very corrosive and irritating compound.

vehicles because of the greater density of uranium (greater than lead) over that of steel. These warhead munitions on penetration emit copious sparks of high temperatures, and inside a tank can ignite the tank's own ammunition or fuel, leading to catastrophic destruction of the vehicle.

Certain chemical compounds have incendiary properties. Many incendiary compounds are oxidizing agents, and the chlorinating formulations are good examples. STB (Super Tropical Bleach) and DS2 are two examples to be discussed later. One compound of extreme danger is chlorine trifluoride [II]. This substance even in dilute concentrations will spontaneously ignite glasswool, clothing and similar materials.

In addition to the destruction of real property and other military targets susceptible to fire, incendiaries can be used to decontaminate routes through areas contaminated with toxic chemical agents. This works because of the volatility and combustibility[10] of the toxic chemical agents under high temperature conditions.

FUEL-AIR WEAPONS

This incendiary device received some press coverage during the Persian Gulf Crisis in Operations Desert Shield and Desert Storm, but its principle is well founded on the experiences of decades of handling highly flammable fumes. It is a well-established fact of chemistry, physics and front page reports that highly flammable substances, when in vapor or aerosol form, explode with an unparalleled fury and rapidity, greatly in excess of what the victim ever expected or anticipated. This is well-publicized in the accidents in which grain storage silos explode from ignition of the fine dust suspended in the air within, or the unthinking weekend backyard bar-b-quer pouring gasoline over the charcoals and strikes a match.

The essential elements of fuel-air explosives are a highly volatile and combustible liquid component and a delayed ignition device. The munition is deployed by bomb, for example, in such a way that the fuel is dispersed as a dense vaporous cloud. After some seconds of dispersal, the fuel is ignited. The result is an instantaneous explosion of incredible force for the weight of munition used. This device establishes a very high overpressure or shock wave that emanates outward from the explosion epicenter. The concussion wave can cause severe personnel injuries, bursting the ear drum of troops near it, overpressure injuries to the lungs, etc., or cause the premature detonation of pressure sensitive land mines at the ground zero[11] of the explosion. These types of incendiaries were considered for use in Operation Desert Storm in the Persian Gulf as one means for clearing avenues of approach for the allied forces through some of the mine fields lining the Iraqi-Saudi and Kuwaiti-Saudi borders. An excellent scene at the beginning of the film *OUTBREAK*, a movie about the dreaded Ebola virus, shows a military transport plane overflying a jungle hospital area and dropping a bomb with parachute delay. The bomb in that scene is a fuel-air weapon. The parachute delays the

---

[10] The reader will recall that one of the desirable traits of a chemical agent is its non-inflammability. The combustibility of a chemical agent is not quite the same thing. Given high enough temperatures, toxic chemical agents will burn and incendiaries certainly can attain those very high and sustained temperatures to volatilize and burn off the agents.

[11] Ground zero, as the reader knows, is usually used in connection with nuclear explosions. However the use here is also appropriate since, as with nuclear air bursts, the ground and immediate environs are directly below the explosion center and are therefore ground zero by definition.

fall of the bomb which is triggered by an atmospheric pressure sensitive detonator. The delay allows the plane to get out of the radius of effects of the bomb.

OBSCURANTS

Obscurants or smokes are chemical agents and are generally nontoxic in field concentrations. They are used not only in training but in actual combat operations. They serve as a means of concealment when natural means are not available- such as under flat-as-a-table desert operations- naval sea battles or to signal friendly forces. However, those obscurants whose action is based upon chemical reaction with the air can, and many do, give off highly irritating and in some cases, toxic by-products.

Smokes are released by artillery shells, bombs, smoke pots and generators. They were even released through the engine exhaust of fossil fueled naval ships in WWII to provide a covering screen to the flotilla and to conceal the approach to shore of troop-landing barges. Aircraft deployment of aerial smoke also took place.

Various substances can be used to provide the smoking agent. Dense oils are used in oil burners. Black smoke does not have the obscuring, concealment value of white smoke.[12] A common agent used to emit a dense, white smoke is titanium tetrachloride[13] [III] which reacts with water moisture in the air to release a complex mixture of dense, finely suspended titanium compounds. This agent does have the tendency to clog such smoke emitters. White phosphorus also produces much smoke. A mixture[14] of sulfur trioxide [IV] and chlorosulfuric acid [V] also produces excellent dense smokes. All of these smoke agents produce by-product vapors that are acidic and thus corrosive to metals and very irritating to mucous membranes.

Smokes are used essentially as visual concealment or screening devices. There are four kinds of smoke screens used: a blanket, a haze, a curtain, and blinding smoke. Smoke blankets are a defensive device. They are deployed over friendly areas and lines to impede enemy visual observation from the air, to hinder bombing precision or to hinder the effectiveness of direct fire. They form a dense smoke cloud which can extend down to the ground. They hamper friendly movements and increase risks of accidents within friendly lines, but offer the most screening protection.

Smoke hazes are principally used in the combat zone. They conceal friendly forces' activities from observation by enemy forces. Hazes as suggested by the term are less dense than blankets and offer limited concealment.

Smoke curtains are employed on the forward edge of the battle area (FEBA). Curtains are vertically-oriented smoke walls. They are deployed between enemy and friendly positions. Curtains restrict only direct ground observation of the disposition and movement of friendly forces. They do not prevent enemy overflight observations.

Blinding smoke is smoke deposited directly on enemy positions. It prevents direct observation of friendly forces and impedes safe movement of enemy forces within their own lines. It frustrates

---

[12] Black colored items actually represent the absorption of all frequencies of visible light, thus no reflected light manifests itself as black. White colored items reflect all visible frequencies of light.

[13] Known as FM, this is no longer used.

[14] The mixture is called FS in the Army.

coordination among ground units and individual troops and raises the anxiety level among them.

Smoke screening operations come in three types: large area smoke screens, small area smoke screens and dummy screens. Large area smoke screens are used to conceal: (1) road and bridge complexes, (2) artillery positions, (3) construction of battle fortifications, (4) supply and service areas, (5) troop and vehicle assembly areas, (6) troop movements, either attacks or withdrawals, and (7) river crossing sites or bridge construction.

Small area smoke screens conceal: (1) recovery of wounded, (2) recovery of damaged vehicles and equipment, (3) patrol activities, (4) assaults on strong points, (5) breaching of mine fields (enemy or friendly), (6) relief of combat units, (7) airstrips or helipads, (8) road construction, (9) specific areas of the FEBA, and (10) landing of (air) assault units.

Dummy smokes are smoke screens used to confuse the enemy about the intentions of friendly forces. To fool the enemy into thinking an attack is beginning on one flank, a dummy smoke screen may be laid down on that flank. The idea is that the enemy will (1) believe an attack is in progress at that point, (2) cause him to strip forces from other areas, particularly the real assault point, to bolster strength at the smoked area, and (3) reduce enemy visibility of the area, further confusing the situation for him.

Colored smokes rely on colored dyes packaged with the smoke agent itself and released through any of the commonly used smoke munitions. Grenades are very common for signaling use by ground troops, aircraft delivery, and artillery shells to mark targets or friendly positions.

Smoke generators, such as the M3 Smoke Generator, are used to disperse smoke over large areas. Such mechanical smoke generators employ an engine fueled by gasoline or diesel which vaporizes a fog oil sprayed by injectors into the engine exhaust tube. The M3 vaporizes between 25 to 50 gallons of fog oil per hour. The XM56 in development provides smoke obscurant dissemination employing smokes that provide visual, infrared (IR) and millimeter wavelength obscuration. It is a modular system employing a gas turbine engine power source. The M157 Smoke Generator Set is an improvement of the M3 series smoke generators. It provides large area screening-smokes in the visual and IR spectrum.

Smoke pots are either burning type or thermal generator type devices. The M1 Smoke Pot using HC[15] munition is a 10 lb device while the ABC-M5 is a 30 lb pot. These are for exclusive use on land. The M42A2 is an HC smoke pot used on either water or land. The AN-M7 and the AN-M7A1 use SGF2, a special petroleum oil base. These two smoke pots are usable on either land or water.

Flares are difficult to assign to a category. They are pyrotechnic devices, but generally used as aerial signals for ground observation and not intended as an incendiary, but rather as illuminaries. They are not smoke agents in use or operation. They have colored illumination due to the impregnating of the flare fuel agent with metal salts which impart characteristic colors as seen in the spectacular 4th of July fireworks displays.

Terrorists have not made use of smoke agents. However, such use of these agents can draw on the military advantages. Copious amounts of smoke in a building can raise the specter of fire and serve as a means of redirecting emergency authorities' attention, creating a diversion, while the terrorists carry out their main mission elsewhere.

The following table lists the physicochemical properties of some incendiaries and obscurants.

---

[15] Hexachloroethane, producing a dense grayish-white smoke. It is toxic in high concentrations.

Table 10-1: **INCENDIARY & OBSCURANT AGENTS**			
Common Name	WHITE PHOSPHORUS	ZIRCONIUM	URANIUM
Chemical Name	phosphorus (white)	zirconium	uranium
Miltary Symbol	WP		
Classification Chemical Military	nonmetal element incendiary, smoke	metal element incendiary	metal element incendiary
Physical State/Color	waxy solid/white, colorless	solid/bluish-black, grayish white luster	solid/silver white
Odor	matches	none	none
Boiling/ Melting Point	280/44.1	3577/1857	-/1132
Density (at °C)	1.83 (20)	6.5 (20)	19.05 (20)
Combustion Products	P_4O_{10}: forms H_3PO_4 with water in air	metal oxide	metal oxide
Toxic Hazards	WP vapor toxic, combustion byproducts irritating to mucous membranes	reported low toxicity	highly toxic
Uses	as smoke, antipersonnel, antimaterial incendiary	explosive priming, explosive mixtures	antiarmor munitions

Table 10-1: **INCENDIARY & OBSCURANT AGENTS Continued**			
Common Name	NAPALM	CHLORINE TRIFLUORIDE	TITANIUM TETRACHLORIDE
Chemical Name	mixture of hydrocarbons	chlorine trifluoride	titanium tetrachloride
Miltary Symbol			FM
Classification Chemical Military	- incendiary	- incendiary	salt smoke/obscurant
Physical State/Color	gelatinous/color of solvent	gas/colorless liquid/yellow green	liquid/colorless
Odor	gasoline or other solvent	sweet, suffocating	acrid
Boiling/Melting Point		11.8/-76.3	136.4/-24.1
Density (at °C)		1.8 (25)	1.7 (25)
Combustion Products	CO_2, water vapor, CO & sooty compounds	depends on material it reacts with, violently hydrolyzed by water	complex titanium oxides, HCl gas
Toxic Hazards	solvent vapor hazard	highly irritating to eyes, skin, mucous membranes	HCl respiratory hazard
Uses	antimaterial, antipersonnel	incendiary against glass wool, other organic matter (not used militarily)	smoke/obscurant

Table 10-1: **INCENDIARY & OBSCURANT AGENTS Continued**			
Common Name	SULFURIC ANHYDRIDE[16]	CHLOROSULFURIC ACID[1]	THERMITE
Chemical Name	sulfur trioxide	chlorosulfuric acid	a mixture
Miltary Symbol	FS component	FS component	TH
Classification 　Chemical 　Military	acid anhydride smoke/aboscurant	acid smoke/obscurant	incendiary incendiary
Physical State/Color	solid	liquid/slightly yellow	solid, power/whitish
Odor	acrid	acrid	
Boiling/Melting Point	62.3/1.9	152/-80	
Density (at °C)	1.9	1.76	
Hydrolysis Products	violent, hot reaction with water, forms sulfuric acid	forms sulfuric and hydrochloric acids with water	
Toxic Hazards	respiratory irritant	respiratory irritant	
Uses	smoke/obscurant fogs, skin vessicant, lung irritant	smoke/obscurant fogs, skin vessicant, lung irritant	incendiary mixture starter component

[16] These two compounds are utilized together as a single smoke formulation: FS.

CHAPTER 11

ANTIDOTES

ANTIDOTE:
A substance that counteracts the effects of a poison or toxin.

GENERAL

Presently, because of the nature of the action of the various toxic chemical agents, only nerve and blood agents have been amenable to antidote treatment. The choking agents undergo hydrolytic chemical reactions with the body cells and tissues, generally producing acid by-products and acylated biomolecules. Blistering agents, though they can undergo very slow hydrolysis, generally interact with lipid or protein based or other hydrophobic biomolecular components of cells and tissues, particularly membranes and associated proteins. These interactions are initially physical associations like mixing oil with gasoline rather than chemical reactions. Chemical reactions between the mustard agents and biomolecules occur over several hours.

Antidotes generally are effective because they cause a chemical reaction between themselves and the targeted toxic agent or the toxic agent's target. The nature of choking and blistering agents does not presently render them destroyed or counteracted by an antidote. Additionally, antidotes are essentially internally taken substances, active on internally absorbed poisons and effective on poisons that specifically react with distinct biochemical species like enzymes such as acetylcholinesterase or cytochrome c oxidase. Choking and blistering[1] agents are not specific for a unique biochemical target. It is the unique biochemical specificity of nerve and blood agents that makes them so rapidly lethal and thus subject to immediate counteraction by an antidote.

One class of agents, the arsenicals, represented by Lewisite or Adamsite, present a systemic poisoning hazard. The cause is the inorganic arsenic released from metabolism of the organoarsenical agent. The inorganic arsenic compounds are subject to reaction with specific organosulfur compounds such as BAL[2], the means of detoxification as noted below.

---

[1] Principally topically active

[2] British AntiLewisite

NERVE AGENTS

Atropine [I] is perhaps the oldest known antidote for what is now recognized as cholinesterase poisoning.[3] It had first proven effective in treatment of eserine (a carbamate) poisoning. To this day it serves as the first agent used and the most often employed therapeutic for such poisoning.

Atropine is an alkaloid[4] obtained from *Atropa belladonna*. It is a toxic substance that must be used discriminately. Atropine functions by competing with acetylcholine for the anionic site of the acetylcholine receptor. Since acetylcholine mediates nerve impulse transmissions, its build-up during anticholinergic agent poisoning continues the 'firing' of the impulses. Acetylcholine in very high concentrations leads to muscular twitching and convulsions initially, followed by paralysis.[5] Atropine, by blocking the receptor to acetylcholine, prevents acetylcholine binding and impulse transmission. Thus atropine counteracts acetylcholine concentration build-up. Atropine has no effect upon the inactivated enzyme which cannot destroy the acetylcholine neurotransmitter.

Atropine is not sufficient alone to reverse the effects of nerve agent poisoning in severe cases. It has no effect on restoration of activity of the organophosphate compromised enzymes. Though it is true that the enzyme-agent complex, in most cases, will hydrolyze over time and thus restore enzymatic activity, the patient does not have the time to wait it out. Oxygen starvation of the brain begins certainly after four minutes, and enzyme-agent complex breakdown is measured in hours. Since one of the sites adversely affected by nerve agents is the lungs, breathing becomes a serious medical emergency. Some compounds have been found that restore enzymatic activity. The oximes are such compounds.

Oximes are compounds possessing the -CH=NOH group. They react in two ways: (1) with the enzyme-agent complex,

$$RCH=NOH + EA \longrightarrow RCH=NOA + EH$$

where E is the enzyme, or (2) with the native nerve agent,

$$RCH=NOH + AX \longrightarrow RCH=NOA + HX^{[6]}$$

where A is the toxic agent, and in so doing, either restore native enzyme activity, (1), or inactivate the nerve agent before it reacts with the native enzyme, (2).

---

[3] L. Kleinwachter, *Berlin Klin. Wachschr.* 1, 369 (1864)

[4] Nitrogenous organic, mildly basic compounds of bitter taste derived from plants.

[5] Nicotine poisoning acts similarly and this is believed to also act on acetylcholine receptors usually referred to as nicotinic sites. Heavy smokers often exhibit a twitching of the musculature of the hands and fingers due to the excessive nicotine absorption and action on such receptors of the muscles.

[6] If the X group of the nerve agent is the cyano group, -CN, hydrogen cyanide may be released. This can also be released as the nerve agent reacts with the enzyme thus enhancing its toxicity. The hydrogen cyanide can be detoxified by the body's detoxification mechanisms though in high concentrations a blood agent antidote may also be necessary (see blood agent antidotes).

Some enzymes are completely inactivated by certain organophosphates. The organophosphates that do so, possess very bulky alkyl groups which block access of the critical enzyme-organophosphate linkage (E-O-P) to the oxime. Another reason is believed to be the very rapid aging of such enzyme-agent complexes. Generally though, the oximes work well.

Atropine and oxime therapy are most enhanced when jointly applied. The enhancement is many times that of either one alone and depends upon the particular organophosphate involved. Though there are many oxime formulations to choose from, the more common one used is 2-PAM [II].

BLOOD AGENTS

Blood agents are also rapid acting though their targets are different biochemical sites of the body. Typically cyanide or cyanide releasing compounds bind to cytochromes such as cytochrome c oxidase, the last component in a series of electron transfers that ultimately passes the electrons to oxygen. It is the iron atom of the cytochromes which bind the cyanide moiety very tightly.

The reaction utilizes hydrogen ions (H^+) generated in metabolism of fuel compounds to provide the hydrogen for the water (H_2O). The rapidity of these sequences of reactions in the production of water from oxygen and the concomitant production of ATP is critical to the biological activity of the air-breathing, oxygen-using organism. Stop electron transport and one kills the organism.

The importance of electron transport to life itself is modeled by an internal combustion engine. Consider for a moment that the gasoline in the fuel line is the flow of electrons in electron transport. As long as gasoline flows to the engine cylinders, energy is produced that runs the engine, propels the car, provides electrical power, etc. Electron flow in electron transport leads to the production of energy (ATP) through the coupled oxidative phosphorylation. The ATP is the energy that 'runs' the cell, as long as the electrons flow. Stop the flow of gasoline to the engine cylinders and what happens? The car runs as long as the fuel in the carburetor lasts-- which isn't very long, a few minutes maybe. The car sputters, shudders, and dies-- quits. The same is essentially true of stopping the flow of electrons in electron transport for a cell and on a larger scale, the organism. It uses up its residual ATP and dies.

A number of antidotes have been found useful. The antidotes appear to work in two different ways. Sodium nitrite [III] functions by converting hemoglobin to methemoglobin within the blood. The methemoglobin combines with cyanide to form a nontoxic cyanmethemoglobin.[7] This is a temporary detoxification of cyanide. However, the cyanmethemoglobin releases cyanide to other tissues. Sodium thiosulfate [IV] along with the liver enzyme rhodanese[8] converts cyanide to the much less toxic thiocyanate[9] [V] which is excreted in the urine. The mechanism of thiosulfate/rhodanese action is believed to be:

---

[7] One gram of methemoglobin reacts with 2.9 mg of cyanide to form the cyanmethemoglobin. [Detoxication Mechanisms, p. 394]

[8] Enzyme names usually end in "ase". Rhodanese is thiosulfate sulfurtransferase.

[9] About 200 times less toxic than cyanide.

```
    S                          S
    /                          / \
    E   + S=SO₃⁻²  ----→  E   S   + SO₃⁻²
    \                          \ /
    S                          S
```

```
    S                          S
    / \                        /
    E   S + CN⁻  ----→  E   + SCN⁻
    \ /                        \
    S                          S
```

Residual quantities of cyanide remaining are removed by exhalation (hydrogen cyanide gas), conversion to hydroxocobalamin for formation of vitamin B_{12}, oxidation to formic acid and carbon dioxide and reactions with the amino acid cysteine. The reaction of CN⁻ with cysteine yields iminothiazolidinecarboxylic acid. These latter methods are not sufficient in extent or rapidity to detoxify lethal doses of CN⁻. They operate on very small quantities of CN⁻ which normally arise from a number of means.

ARSENICAL AGENTS

It has been known as far back as 1908 and the work of Paul Ehrlich[10] that trivalent arsenic is more toxic than the pentavalent form. Many poisonous arsenic compounds are of the trivalent variety and the poisonous military agents based upon arsenic adhere to this principle.

The best known antidote for arsenical poisoning arose as a treatment for Lewisite poisoning. The antidotal compound is BAL [VI].[11] The reaction of arsenic is typical of many other poisonous heavy metals such as lead and mercury. These metals have a high reactivity with chemically active sulfur such as in the sulfhydryl (-SH) form. Reaction of Lewisite with BAL entails the reactivity of the reduced sulfhydryl moieties for metals such as chemically active arsenic. The reaction can be represented as follows:

---

[10] Paul Ehrlich and his coworkers developed an arsenical called Salvarsan as the first successful chemical treatment for syphilis. Ehrlich, because of this work and other previous work on chemicals as "magic bullets" in the treatment of infectious disease, is often referred to as the "Father of Chemotherapy."

[11] 2,3 dimercapto-1-propanol

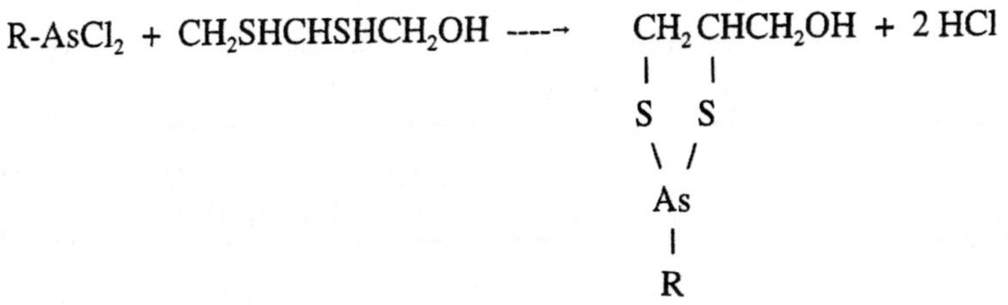

R-AsCl$_2$ + CH$_2$SHCHSHCH$_2$OH ----→   CH$_2$CHCH$_2$OH + 2 HCl
                                           | |
                                           S   S
                                            \ /
                                            As
                                            |
                                            R

The reaction with the Lewisite hydrolysis product Lewisite oxide can be represented as follow:

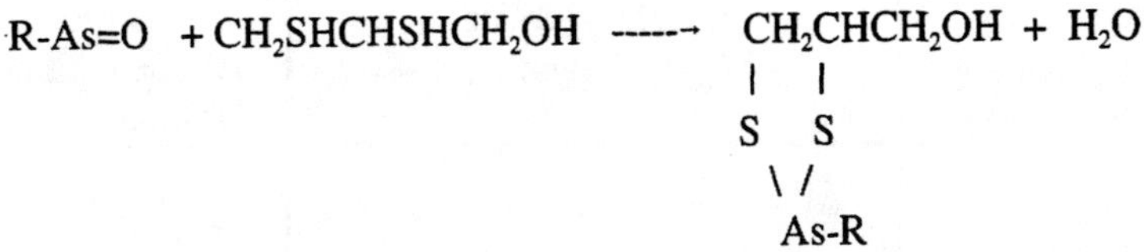

R-As=O + CH$_2$SHCHSHCH$_2$OH ------→   CH$_2$CHCH$_2$OH + H$_2$O
                                          | |
                                          S   S
                                           \ /
                                          As-R

The reactions portrayed above are in fact general for any arsenical poisoning treatment employing mercapto compounds. One reason for this reactivity is that the sulfhydryl group exhibits a greater acidity than the hydroxyl group. Thus, the sulfhydryl hydrogen atoms are more labile and are slightly more ionizable, generating a small concentration of the corresponding sulfide anion. Other military agents possessing an arsenic atom in the molecule are also subject to this kind of treatment approach. These agents include ethyldichlorarsine [VII] and diphenylchlorarsine [VIII].

Generalized treatments of heavy metal poisoning may also employ substances known as chelating[12] agents. Typically the metal atom is in ionic form (a cation) and the chelating agent possesses two or more polar groups on a single molecule. This method is particularly useful in removing high concentrations of very soluble metal cations such as calcium in blood using EDTA.[13]

The following table lists the more common antidotes of historical usage.

---

[12] from the Greek meaning claw

[13] ethylenediamminetetraacetic acid

Table 11-1: **ANTIDOTES**			
Common Name	AMYL NITRITE	ATROPINE (SULFATE)	SODIUM NITRITE
Chemical Name	amyl nitrite	α-(hydroxymethyl)benzene-acetic acid, 8-methyl-8-azabicyclo[3.2.1]oct-3-yl ester (sulfate)	sodium nitrite
Antidote for	cytochrome oxidase inhibitors (blood agents)	anticholinergics (nerve agents)	cytochrome oxidase inhibitors (blood agents)
Molecular Weight	117	289.38 (694.82)	69
Melting Point		114-116 (190-194)	271

Common Name	SODIUM THIOSULFATE	2-PAM	BAL
Chemical Name	sodium thiosulfate	pralidoxime chloride; 2-pyridine aldoxime methyl chloride; 2-[(hydroxyimino)methyl]-1-methylpyridinium chloride	2,3-dimercapto-1-propanol
Antidote for	cytochrome oxidase inhibitors (blood agents)	anticholinergics (nerve agents)	systemic arsenical poisoning
Molecular Weight	158.13	172.63	124.21
Melting Point		235-238 (decomposes)	

PART IV

CHAPTER 12

MICROBIOLOGICAL ORGANIZATION

GENERAL

Microorganisms come in a variety of kinds, types, sizes and shapes. There are essentially two kinds[1] of microorganisms-- the cellular and the viruses.[2] Additionally, as pertains to the cellular kind, there are two. They are designated prokaryotic and eukaryotic cells. Both classes have members that are pathogenic. The cellular microbes come in several types, simply designated as yeasts[3] (eukaryotic) and bacteria (prokaryotic). Bacteria is a rather broad term but includes what are called mycobacteria and rickettsia, both with unique requirements for survival, different from classically viewed bacteria.

To understand the basis of microbe pathogenicity, one must understand something of their nature, structure, composition and functioning. This chapter examines the types of microorganisms. It examines their composition, organization and finally, the basis of the pathogenicity exhibited by those that trouble mankind without mercy.

---

[1] The classification or taxonomy of microorganisms follows the scheme applied to all living creatures: Kingdom, Phylum, Subphylum, Class, Order, Family, Genus, Specie.

[2] One other possible addition to this classification is the prion (**proteinaceous infectious** particle). Prions are believed to be pathogenic proteins devoid of any nucleic acid genetic information. This makes such particles the smallest nonliving pathogens, smaller than viroids. This belief rests on specific digestive tests which destroy nucleic acids but leave proteins intact. Such pathogenic proteins are believed responsible for scrapie in sheep and goats, transmissible mink encephalopathy, and chronic wasting disease in mule deer and elk. In man, Creutzfeldt-Jakob disease first observed in the 1920s by Hans Gerhard Creutzfeldt and Alfons Maria Jakob is also suspected of being a prion caused disease. This disease is a transmissible spongiform encephalopathy- that is, it gives a spongy appearance to brain and neuron tissues of those afflicted and is typical of the dementia associated with such diseases. Two other diseases of the same genre are kuru and Gerstmann-Strassler disease. The verdict is still out on the existence of prions and will not be considered further here.

[3] True fungi of the family Saccharomycetaceae.

EUKARYOTES

Eukaryotic cells are those which have a distinct nucleus. Such cells are the basic unit of animal cells including human cells. The nucleus of a eukaryotic cell is an enclosed organelle with a membrane separating it from the bulk of the cell fluid (cytoplasm). The nucleus houses the DNA in what is called chromosomes-- a prepackaged, tightly folded form of DNA associated with certain proteins called histones.[4] These chromosomal units are subdivided into what is called nucleosomes-- regions of basic protein (histones) and about 140 base pairs of duplex DNA.[5]

Typically, eukaryotic cells comprise higher forms of life such as animals and associate in aggregate formations designated as tissues which in turn comprise organs. There are eukaryotic microorganisms and the best known are the fungi.[6]

FUNGI

Fungi are eukaryotic organisms, and there are some 80,000 species.[7] They are found virtually anywhere on earth, though they are primarily encountered as terrestrial living creatures serving a critical role in the breakdown of dead organic matter for the return of organic carbon to the soil. As a group, fungi are probably the single most severe economic problem of agriculture causing the majority of the crop damage. Though some are pathogenic to man, they are less a problem than the bacteria (excluding the nuisance yeast infections women occasionally contract, the ever present athletes foot, or bathroom molds). Fungi bear some unusual structural characteristics compared to prokaryotic organisms.

The vegetative form of fungi, the thallus, consists of filaments called hyphae (singular: hypha). Mycelium are simply a mass of hyphae. Growth of fungi occurs by the extension and innervation by hyphae throughout the growth medium and results in visible whitish threads. Mycelial cells secrete enzymes which facilitate digestion of the dead host material.

Numerous nuclei are found segmented along the cytoplasm of the hyphae and there is general cytoplasmic flow toward the tips of growing hyphae. These nuclei become part of what is termed

---

[4] The packaging of DNA in eukaryotic cells is an example of the action of many intermolecular forces discussed in Chapter 2. DNA is an anionic polymer while the histones are a cationic polymer. The electrostatic forces between these two oppositely charged molecules plays a central role in the packaging of the DNA around the histone core.

[5] To give you some idea of the incredible compactness with which nature can pack the DNA consider these facts: (1) human DNA consists of about 3×10^9 base pairs, or two helices of 3×10^9 bases wrapped about each other, (2) the human DNA is divided up into 46 chromosomes, (3) each DNA strand is about 20 Å in diameter or 7.87×10^{-8} m which put another way means that 12,700,000 strands lain side-by-side measure one inch wide, (3) and if all the DNA of one cell were placed head to tail to each other like the cars of a train, they would measure about 1.0 m or 39 inches in length. If there are one trillion cells in the human body, then all the DNA in length is one trillion meters long or about 600 million miles long. The distance to the sun from earth averages 93 million miles.

[6] Others are yeasts, diatoms, and the protozoa: paramecium and euglena.

[7] Only about 50 species are pathogenic to man.

fruiting bodies-- a propagative mode of fungi. This is an important feature in the growth and invasiveness of pathogenic fungi. Additionally, fungi have cell walls that differ markedly from bacterial cell walls.

CELL WALL

One of the distinguishing characteristics of fungi is the cell wall composition. There are four principal components comprising fungal cell walls: (1) cellulose,[8] (2) chitin,[9] (3) and β-1,3- and β-1,6-glucans. Additionally, various other polysaccharides are also associated with these components.

SPORULATION

Sporulation is a characteristic process of fungi. Its purpose is to (1) enable the spread of the specie to new and distant locations (the spores are carried on the wind and air currents) and (2) a means of survival during harsh environmental conditions, unfavorable for growth and life of the fungi. Spores come in two types-- asexual and sexual.

Asexual spores exhibit resistance to drying and radiation, but are not particularly heat resistant. They germinate upon the availability of moisture. This sometimes occurs even when nutrients are absent. Sexual spores exhibit greater heat resistance. Fungal spores in general are less tolerant of heat than bacterial endospores. The sexual spores display dormancy, germinating only under specific stimuli such as particular chemical triggers.

PROKARYOTES

Prokaryotic cells are cells which lack a distinct and separate nucleus. The DNA is located in the bulk cell fluid (cytoplasm) absent of any confining organelle such as the nucleus of eukaryotes. Additionally, prokaryotic cells do not associate in more complex systems such as tissues and organs as is found in the case of eukaryotic cells of animals. Prokaryotic cells are separately living, independent cells and comprise the bacteria, mycobacteria, and rickettsia.

BACTERIA

Bacteria are unicellular microorganisms, lacking a nucleus, and grow and divide. They come in a variety of shapes and sizes. There are six principal shapes observed in the bacterial realm-- coccus, coccobacillus, bacillus, vibrio, spirillum, and spirochetes. Coccus bacteria are spherical; coccobacillus are short rods nearly elliptically shaped; bacillus are long, cylindrical rods; vibrio are comma shaped;

---

[8] β-1,4-glucan, the most abundant polysaccharide on earth.

[9] Polymeric N-acetyl-D-glucosamine in β-1,4 glycosyl linkage, like cellulose. It is the second most abundant polysaccharide on earth, commonly observed as the exoskeleton of insects, crabs, etc.

spirillum, a nearly stretched out spring shape; and spirochetes are tight helically shaped organisms.

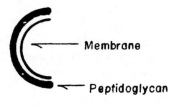

Gram-positive Bacteria

FIGURE 12-1   Diagram of the cell wall composition and location of gram-positive bacterial cells. The cell wall composed exclusively of peptidoglycan is thick and encloses the cell membrane.

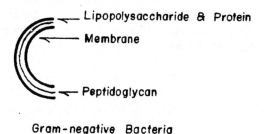

Gram-negative Bacteria

FIGURE 12-2   Diagram of the cell wall composition and location of gram-negative bacterial cells. The peptidoglycan component is thin compared to gram-positive organisms and is externally covered by a lipopolysaccharide and protein layer.

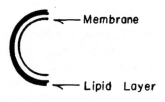

Acid-fast Bacteria

FIGURE 12-3   Diagram of the cell wall composition and location of acid-fast bacterial cells. Note the absence of peptidoglycan; the cell wall consisting essentially of a lipid layer.

Bacteria that are actively metabolizing and growing are referred to as vegetative. The converse of this is nonvegetative. A form of bacteria that is believed by some to be a protective means against harsh conditions is the endospore.[10] Endospores are metabolically inert and are quite resistant to high heat,[11] radiation and even several toxic chemicals. The endospore is not a means of reproduction for such bacteria. Additionally, endospore-forming bacteria are saprophytic soil organisms, and their pathogenicity to man is only incidental.[12] Though endospores are simply called spores, they should not be confused with spores as related to fungi. Additionally, bacteria exhibit a variety of external features.

Flagella (singular: flagellum), cilia (singular: cilium), pili (singular: pilus) and fimbriae (singular: fimbrium) are observed on many bacteria. Flagella are a long whiplike external appendage used as a means of locomotion. Generally bacteria are equipped with one to several flagella. Cilli are much smaller structures in length but are much like flagella in their purpose. There are many of these appendages lining the external cell wall regions. They have the appearance of the multiple oars of an ancient trireme. Pili are very small hollow tubes, similar to flagella. They do not serve a locomotive function, but rather serve as a means of genetic material exchange (conjugation). Fimbriae are like pili except they serve as a means of attachment to other cells or even to the surface regions of water immersed bodies. The fimbriae are significantly employed by pathogenic bacteria, enabling them to adhere to host cells such as red blood cells of mammals.

CELL WALL

Bacteria exhibit three primary distinguishing cell wall compositions. These compositions differentiate a further classification distinction among bacteria. The designated Gram[13] stain discriminates between gram-positive and gram-negative organisms. Gram-positive bacteria exhibit a relatively thick cell wall (Figure 12-1) of peptidoglycan[14] overlying the cell membrane. Gram-negative bacteria also contain peptidoglycan, but in significantly thinner quantity. The peptidoglycan

---

[10] Some researchers hold that endospores are actually part of the normal life cycle of vegetative bacteria and have little to do with survival of the bacterium during adverse conditions. However, in bacteria that sporulate, *Bacillus & Clostridium*, sporulation occurs during times of plenty and under favorable environmental conditions. Furthermore, should conditions become unfavorable, sporulation is not possible if not already done.

[11] One genus of bacteria producing endospores is that of the *Clostridium*. These anaerobic bacteria produce very potent toxins and are often associated with spoilage of canned foods improperly prepared before sealing. Proper sterilization of canning materials requires heating to boiling in a pressure cooker to elevate the boiling point of water above the normal atmospheric 100°C.

[12] B. anthracis is a possible exception.

[13] So-named after the Danish bacteriologists, Christian Gram, who developed the method for distinguishing between bacteria of different cell wall composition.

[14] Consisting of N-acetylglucosamine and N-acetylmuramic acid.

is enclosed by a lipopolysaccharide[15] (Figure 12-2). So-called acid-fast bacteria lack significant peptidoglycan composition. These bacterial types have the membrane enclosed by a lipid layer (Figure 12-3).

Bacterial cell walls are responsible for the shape of a bacterium. The semirigid nature of the cell wall serves as a kind of exoskeleton for the microbe, providing support and containment of the internal structures. It is very porous, permitting free-flow of materials into and out of the bacterial cell. The major component of the cell wall is peptidoglycan. This material consists of N-acetylglucosamine and N-acetylmuramic acid in an alternating polymeric array which is significantly cross-linked by a tetrapeptide.[16] This creates a biological net-like matrix of significant strength. The cell wall is the thickest in gram-positive bacteria.

Gram-negative bacteria have another component called the outer membrane, consisting of lipopolysaccharide[17] attached to the peptidoglycan cell wall component and making it an integral part of the cell wall. Lipoproteins are covalently attached to peptidoglycan though embedded within the outer membrane.

Acid-fast bacteria, the mycobacteria, have a thick cell wall like the gram-positive variety. It contains much lipid and less peptidoglycan. These organisms grow quite slowly owing to the difficulty of materials to pass through the thick-layered lipid cell wall.

The cell wall, particularly in those microbes with much peptidoglycan, is the target of antibiotics which interfere with cell wall synthesis. Details of this therapeutic approach to infection appear in Chapter 14: Antibiotics, Interferon & Vaccines.

CELL MEMBRANE

The cell membrane, a.k.a. plasma membrane, is a biological component, that is, it is part and parcel of a living material that defines the demarcation between the cell and its environment.[18] Unlike the cell wall which is static in nature, unchanging, the cell membrane is in a constant state of flux or change. The identity of particular molecules comprising it does not remain the same over the life time of the cell. Additionally, its dynamic permeability changes with changing environmental conditions or cellular needs. All biological membranes, regardless of whether prokaryotic or eukaryotic, are essentially alike in morphology and physiology. They are fluid-mosaic in nature.

The fluid-mosaic model of the cell membrane holds that a membrane is a lipid bilayer. Two layers

---

[15] Lipopolysaccharide is a compound or complex of lipids and carbohydrates, or their derivatives. It is an integral part of what is called the outer membrane of all gram-negative bacteria and an important identifying feature.

[16] A tetrapeptide consists of four peptide bond units made from five amino acid units bonded together in a chain.

[17] Lipopolysaccharide is also known as endotoxin and is the responsible material for the toxic response elicited by gram-negative pathogenic bacteria. The outer membrane material is responsible for the symptoms associated with bacterial infections- fever and dilatation of the blood vessels being two pronounced effects. The endotoxin responsible is released in greater quantity upon cell death, exacerbating the pathologic effects on the host.

[18] One can loosely view the cell wall in bacteria as the armor plate of the bacterial cell, much in purpose as the armor vests worn by knights.

of lipids associate in such a fashion that the hydrophobic portions of both lipid layers form the interior of the membrane. The outer surfaces which bound the hydrophobic interior consist of the hydrophilic portions of the two lipid layers. Thus, one hydrophilic surface is exposed to the cell interior aqueous fluid, the cytoplasm, the other to the external environment. The membrane exhibits selective permeability, a property unique to living systems, and which is the ability to allow only certain molecules to pass through. The membrane is another target in the chemotherapeutic treatment of infection.

CYTOPLASM

The cytoplasm[19] is the internal aqueous fluid of the cell. It is viscous, likened to thinned syrup and has no rigid form other than that imposed upon it by the confinement afforded by the cell membrane and wall of the microbe. The cytoplasm houses all the critical internal metabolic and sustaining structures and systems or organelles of the cell including its DNA. The cytoplasm contains the polyribosomes (responsible for protein synthesis), the DNA, vacuoles and such. The cytoplasm is the third site of antibiotic attack in treatment of infection. Antibiotics can interfere with protein or DNA synthesis as well as other intermediate processes critical to cell viability.

RICKETTSIA

Rickettsia are very small bacteria. They live only intracellularly[20] in a host cell, usually mammals, and are at some time in their life cycle associated with vectors[21] such as fleas, lice, ticks, mosquitos, etc. Rickettsia are in form and organization like any other bacteria. Typically they are Gram-negative coccoid or bacillus shaped cells possessing both cell wall and membrane. Many lack certain biochemical processes, presumably acquiring needed intermediates, cofactors and other nutrients from the host cell, absorbed through the rickettsial membrane which is much more porous to such needed materials than usual membranes.

Rickettsial microbes penetrate host cells in an active process which means the host cell must be actively metabolizing (alive). They multiply within the host cell cytoplasm, continuing their increase in numbers until the overburdened host cell ruptures, releasing the rickettsial bacteria into the surrounding tissue fluids. They exhibit dependence upon host cell environment[22] for survival and probably die in air.[23]

---

[19] a.k.a. cytosol

[20] Technically called obligate intracellular parasites.

[21] A bloodsucking arthropod or insect that carries a microbial parasite, transmitted to an animal through its bite.

[22] Host cell cytoplasm is full of degradative enzymes which normally attack and destroy foreign prokaryotic cells.

[23] One noted exception is *Coxiella burnetii*, the cause of Q fever.

VIRUSES

Viruses are not cells as they are not capable of independent function apart from a cellular organism. Viruses are nonliving microbes in the sense that they do not perform respiration or biosynthetic functions of their own accord. Though they come in many sizes and shapes, they consist simply of nucleic acids (RNA or DNA) and protein (coat or capsid) and a few types have lipid coats associated with them. The nucleic acid genetic material is enclosed by the capsid. A single virus particle is also called a virion. Viruses are strictly pathogenic to animals or plants and even to bacteria.[24] They sometimes are agents of hereditary information exchange or contamination, often times incorporating new genetic information into themselves and/or imparting part of their genetic information to the host.

Virally infected cells exhibit increased cell membrane permeability. Thus, substances that would not otherwise likely enter a noninfected cell will enter a virally infected cell. This has significant potential chemotherapeutic value in treating viral infections.

Viruses require the commandeering of host cell biosynthetic machinery to produce new virions. This often leads to the eventual death[25] of the host cell and release of hundreds of new virus particles to infect adjacent cells. Other times, they infect a cell and remain dormant[26] until some as yet uncertain stimulus results in their activation. The lysis of host cell (particularly bacterial cells) is mediated by a lysozyme-like enzyme coded for by the virion's nucleic acid.

Virus multiplication has six steps. First, the virion must attach itself to a susceptible host cell. This is followed by penetration of the host cell membrane by the virion's nucleic acid.[27] Third, replication of viral nucleic acid material ensues. The fourth step (simultaneous with the third) is the production of viral protein coat components. The fifth step is the combining of the genetic and protein coat material in an assembly of new native virions. Finally, the intact viruses are released from the host cell.[28]

NUCLEIC ACID SYNTHESIS

Viruses are categorized into two groups characteristic of the nucleic acid content. They are RNA and DNA viruses. Both the RNA or the DNA nuclear material may be single or double stranded. The mechanism for the production of new virion nucleic acid material depends upon whether the host is

---

[24] Bacterial viruses are called bacteriophages or simply phages.

[25] Nonpermissive infection.

[26] Permissive infection.

[27] In prokaryotic infections by viruses, the genetic information (RNA or DNA) enters the cell by way of a kind of injection process. In eukaryotic infections by viruses, the entire virion enters the cell by phagocytosis or pinocytosis.

[28] In prokaryotes, lysis of the bacterial cell is the means of release of the new virions. In eukaryotic cells, release occurs without lysis of the host cell, possibly by a reversed pinocytosis. The release of viral particles from eukaryotic cells may or may not kill the host cell.

prokaryotic or eukaryotic as well as whether the virion is an RNA or DNA type.

RNA or DNA synthesis occurs within the cytoplasm of the host prokaryotic cell. Certain RNA viruses (known as retroviruses) use the RNA as a template to make a DNA copy by an enzyme that is referred to as a reverse transcriptase.[29]

In animal eukaryotic cells, two sites of synthesis of viral nucleic acid material exist depending upon whether the virion genetic molecule is RNA or DNA. The RNA variety synthesized in the cytoplasm also employ a reverse transcriptase to make a complementary DNA template. The DNA variety find the virion DNA making its way into the cell nucleus where normal replicative processes of the host cell perform the synthesis.

In the DNA versions, the DNA must be used to synthesize a mRNA for the synthesis of protein capsid coats. The mRNA crosses the nuclear membrane into the cytoplasm where viral proteins, including virus-specific enzymes are produced. Viral coat proteins find their way to the nucleus where assembly of the virions occurs. The completed virion passes through the nuclear membrane into the cytoplasm where it makes its way to the cellular membrane. Here it is released into the environment of the cell by a process known as budding, in which a portion of the host cell membrane serves as a further coating of the completed, native viral particles, ready for infection of new host cells.

BASIS OF PATHOGENICITY

Pathogenicity can be defined as the ability to produce disease. Contrary to common perceptions and experiences, disease is not the focus of microbial life, it is the exception. As put forward by Lewis Thomas, 1974, "disease usually results from inconclusive negotiations for symbiosis,[30] an overstepping of the line by one side or the other, a biological misinterpretation of borders."[31] However it may be between man and the microscopic realm, disease does occur and it does serious damage. The single most significant question always asked by scientists and by all afflicted with a disease is, Why? What is it about those microscopic creatures that they can fell an elephant and certainly man?

One of the principles of war is mass-- bringing as much force to bear on the target as possible. A second principle is surprise-- no warning whatsoever. As relates to disease, a biological condition of war exists between man and the tiny chemiotaxic[32] denizens of the microscopic world. Microbes as a matter of happenstance effectively employ both military principles to the utmost. Like an invading army, they make a crucial breakthrough-- a breakthrough at the weakest point of the host.

---

[29] The normal route of biological information follows a fundamental tenet of molecular biology (Central Dogma of Molecular Biology) which simply states that information flow is: DNA → RNA → protein. In RNA viruses, the production of new viral RNA must some how use a DNA complementary copy of the RNA. This is accomplished by the use of an enzyme, reverse transcriptase, which uses RNA to make a complementary copy of the viral RNA made of DNA. The DNA then serves as the normal template for the synthesis of the viral RNA.

[30] Meaning co-habitating in a harmless, yet mutually beneficial manner.

[31] Microbiology: Principles & Applications, Joan G. Creager, Jacquelyn G. Black & Vee E. Davison, Prentice Hall, Englewood Cliffs, NJ, 1990, page 377.

[32] Responds to chemical triggers or stimulants.

This breakthrough serves as a biological salient. Rather than pour more pathogens through it as would be the case of human armies, bacteria do the biological equivalent-- they grow and multiply rapidly and in large numbers. The surprise element exists by virtue of their minuscule size. They are unseen with the naked eye. There is no warning or sign of exposure to them or of their presence-- until they have gained a tactical foothold.

Against this assault, man's body is armed for defense. He possesses an immune system, a complex system consisting of essentially two components-- cellular and chemical.[33] The immune system is much more adept at its function than the most sophisticated man-made weapons systems. The cellular system consists of an array of specialized cells specifically designed to kill by phagocytosis invading foreign cells. In fact, some bear the name "killer cells" for this reason. However, just like man's confrontation with invading armies, the body must first know that an enemy is present and attacking. The immune system has specially developed cells that act as sentinels. They detect a pathogen. The process is complex and takes time to develop.[34]

The chemical component is the antibodies or immunoglobulins-- moderate molecular weight proteins of specific conformation and possessing specific receptors that are specific for a particular antigen.[35] The antibodies are like biological cruise missiles. Their structure and chemical-receptor identity, complementarity, to an antigen-- provides a kind of biological guidance system, a specificity for a particular antigen. These antibodies are secreted by certain cells under specific circumstances once recognition of the invader is made. Usually antibodies attack biological poisons (toxins), binding with the toxins, form insoluble aggregates and render the toxin impotent. Until the immune system can effectively respond to an infection, the symptoms and effects of the infectious microbe's presence serve as the biological equivalent of a Pearl Harbor-- a serious tactical defeat, but not yet a strategic defeat.[36] But what is required for a disease to occur? What causes the characteristic symptoms and reactions typifying a disease?

INFECTIOUS PROCESS

To become infected, several factors must come together, though not at all simultaneously. First of course, one must come into direct contact with a pathogen. The contact must be infectiously specific, that is, the contact must be at a site of the body which is a penetrable locale for the pathogens. A cut, puncture wound, inhalation, or ingestion is sufficient. Second, sufficient numbers of the pathogen must be introduced at the infection site to survive the body's leukocytes and phagocytes initial attack and ingestion of the foreign cells and particles. Some must escape this fate for infection to take hold. Third, the host must be the right host-- species specific. For example, plant

---

[33] Technically referred to as the humoral (fluids) system.

[34] About 5 to 14 days for each pathogen species and strain.

[35] A chemical substance usually secreted by a bacterium.

[36] A biological strategic defeat due to infection is permanent damage, even death.

pathogens do not infect people.[37] Additionally, even after some of the microbes escape destruction by the host immune system, the environment required by the pathogen must be provided by the host body. The human body clearly is an excellent environment for microorganisms pathogenic to man. Fourth, the organism must not be so lethal that it kills its host in minutes or hours such that it has little or no time to reproduce progeny pathogens for spread to other hosts or vectors, etc. Fifth, the best pathogens must be able to survive in the terrestrial environment, separate, even isolated from susceptible hosts. Many pathogenic bacteria and fungi in fact are soil inhabitants, only inadvertently infecting man. It is their metabolic by-products or metabolically active substances such as extracellular enzymes which, when secreted into human cells or blood, are toxic.

CAUSE OF SYMPTOMS OF DISEASE

One principal problem of infection that leads to the manifestation we call disease is the toxic substances which microorganisms release as a result of their own normal metabolism. Another is specific requirements of a pathogen. A third is preparing the host medium for nutrient value. A fourth problem is to aid the spread of progeny microbes and finally, protecting the microbe from host defenses.

TOXIC METABOLITES

Many examples of microbial toxic metabolites are known or suspected, but the better known examples are the neurotoxin of botulism, tetanus, the aflatoxins, and the enterotoxin of cholera. The problem facing medical and microbial scientists is why these substances are produced by the microbe- - though in the case of the cholera toxin, it may serve an obvious beneficial value to the success of the microbe's growth and reproduction. Some toxins are thought to have counter-microbiotic[38] value.

SPECIFIC NUTRIENT REQUIREMENTS

The best studied example of this problem in infection is found in cattle. Cattle are subject to organ specific infections by *Brucella abortus*, the cause of brucellosis (infectious abortions). The *B. abortus* organisms specifically infect the fetus, placenta and amniotic fluids of the gestating cow. The reason for this localization of infection here is that the bovine uterine contents are rich in erythritol, a four-carbon alcohol. The *B. abortus* microbe grows well within these specific organ cells of the cow because of the presence of this alcohol. Other tissues and organs of the cow lack this specific alcohol and, as a matter of fact, so too does human female and associated reproductive organs and tissues, including the human fetus. Infections of humans are not uterine localized and do not cause infectious abortion.

---

[37] It is important to realize that though plant pathogens do not infect people, some of the metabolic by-products of plant disease pathogens are quite toxic to people. Example: ergot.

[38] I am coining this term to mean that one microbe may secrete a substance to kill or inhibit its microbial competitors.

FACILITATED INVASION

Certain microbes[39] produce enzymes that break down tissue. The enzyme is hyaluronidase which hydrolyzes hyaluronic acid.[40] Also species of Clostridia that cause gas gangrene release collagenase into tissues. This enzyme destroys collagen, a major connective and supportive protein of tissues.

Another means is employed by Streptococcal bacteria. Sometimes a body defense measure is to isolate the pathogen, seal it off from surrounding cells and tissues. Blood clotting at the site of injury and infection is one means of doing this. Streptococci secrete an enzyme called streptokinase, a fibrolytic enzyme, which digests blood clots and clears the way for further spread of the pathogen.[41]

PROTECTION AGAINST HOST DEFENSES

Staphylococci on the other hand secrete an enzyme called coagulase which purposely promotes blood clotting. The fibrin of clots is deposited about the Staphylococci bacteria culture in what may be interpreted to be a defense measure of the pathogen against attack by the host's immune system. The localization of the infection to such lesions as pimples may be explained by this process.

DISCRIMINATION

One of the most crucial abilities of the body's defenses is discrimination-- the ability to distinguish between its own cellular components and those of an invader. This is no minor ability. Were it not for this ability, a person's own body cells and tissues would be killed by the immune system.[42] However, this defense discrimination, an "identification friend or foe" mechanism, also tolerates many microorganisms that by themselves, in their proper place, present little or no pathogenic threat.

There is a virtual menagerie of resident flora in and on the human body.[43] No less than five major species inhabit the skin; seven, the upper respiratory tract; fifteen, the mouth; 23, the intestine (at least two are protozoa); and eight, the urogenital tract. Many of these organisms are pathogenic only under

---

[39] Streptococci, staphylococci, pneumococci and certain clostridia.

[40] A dimeric polymer of glucuronic acid and N-acetylglucosamine, in that sequence, in β-1,3 glycosyl linkage. It associates much water, making it an excellent lubricant, shock absorbent as well as a kind of tissue glue. It is also found in synovial fluid, vitreous humor and the umbilical cord.

[41] Streptokinase or variants of it are used in treating some heart attack and stroke victims. The enzyme hydrolyzes (destroys) minuscule blood clots traveling in the blood stream that, if left in tact, would clog an artery in the heart or brain.

[42] This problem is exactly the problem faced by a patient who is the recipient of an organ transplant. Several drugs are in use to try to suppress the immune system to the extent that it will not attack and destroy the transplanted organ. Such suppressions of the host immune system, however, invite opportunistic infections.

[43] Microbiology: Principles & Applications

certain circumstances. Skin penetration wounds account for many localized infections by such agents as Staphylococci, commonly called staph infections. This is a major concern in hospitals, particularly problematic among patients recovering from surgery. *Candida albicans* (fungi) and other yeasts can flare up as a result of antibiotic treatment for bacterial infections, a common problem among women. The examples are numerous. Most infections arise as a result of a preexisting condition and opportunistic infections by the very normal flora associated with the human body. They proliferate beyond normal static levels as a result of some stimulus that weakens the person. Stimuli that weaken a person's immune response are stress, serious invasive injury, chemotherapy (antibiotic or anticancer) and so on.

A final comment about pathogens is in order. Their activity as a pathogen is all chemistry-- biochemistry to be specific.

CHAPTER 13

BIOLOGICAL AGENTS[1]

Half of the secret of resistance to disease is cleanliness;
the other half is dirtiness.
-advertisement in the *Philosophical
Transactions of The Royal Society*[2]

BACKGROUND

There isn't a society or an army of recorded history that has not suffered more casualties from disease than from direct enemy action though to be sure, much of the disease endured was a result of injury, wounds or other factors stemming from engagement with the enemy. One could say that each and every army going into battle fights a two front war, one officially recognized, the other unofficial, silent, covert. The first is against the human enemy before it, but the second is always the microbe within its ranks and even off the battlefield. Wherever man has lived, fought, or traversed, he has always stumbled upon the microbial denizens of that area. Microbes by virtue of their incredibly tiny size are invisible to the human eye and thus exhibit stealth of which aeronautical engineers can only dream. They are remarkable in their adaptability to their environment. Generally lying dormant in soil or nooks and crannies of objects, they are opportunistic to a fault. The slightest breech of the skin, inhalation, or ingestion is all they require. The most deaths in war traditionally have been from infections arising from wounds sustained in combat or the close overcrowding of troops systemic to armies. Antibiotics, first widely used in WWII provided seemly magic cures from various forms of sepsis that in a few years earlier were a death sentence to the soldier. Whole armies in recorded history were stopped in their tracks by disease. Armies that were invincible before other human armies were defenseless and ruthlessly humbled before the microbial armies that spread throughout and ravaged their ranks. Their unique feature compared with other nonbiological weapons is the ability to produce themselves and spread. What an effective weapon.

Disease was and is one problem associated with war that spans the history of mankind regardless of weapons technology. It was disease and the experiences of armies in war that led to a further quantum leap in unconventional weapons or weapons of mass destruction. Organized biological warfare. And such a weapon in the hands of an educated and dedicated terrorist state or group would be near Biblical Apocalypse come true.

Disease is a companion of progress in peace as well as war. In 1968, the Aswan hydroelectric dam project resulted in a huge lake up stream called Lake Nasser. The result of all this was that a certain fresh water snail population exploded as a result in the significant decline in Nile River water

---

[1] For definitions of terms, see Glossary.

[2] in The Harvest of a Quiet Eye, p. 3

flow rate. The snails are the vector of a parasite called Schistosomiasis. The problem now affects not only Egypt but also Sudan and Ghana, countries that have also build large hydroelectric dams. But the problem of increased disease risk is greater than the Schistosomiasis. Rift Valley fever, a viral disease, prior to the dam project almost never affected people, but rather livestock. Since completion of the dam, the fever also afflicts many people as well. The disease is spread by a mosquito vector. Madagascar, Mauritania and Senegal have experienced their own increased disease outbreaks resulting from dam projects. Overcrowding and the rise of vast metropolises around the world have increased the need for effective sanitation, but effectiveness of such is lacking in many countries around the world, particularly in Africa, South America and the Pacific Asian Rim. About 50 years ago, the Earth's population was about 2.5 billion people. Now it is some 6 billion and growing more rapidly than ever. Humans are an excellent culture medium for pathogenic microbes and our growth in population is their growth. Bon apetit.

Thanks to geographic location and the medical prowess of its medical, biological, and medicinal scientists, the US has relatively little experience anymore with serious infectious diseases or epidemics. During the latter half of the 20th century, we all but wiped out even the common childhood diseases of measles, mumps and such through vaccination programs and in particular, world wide incidences of small pox disappeared through a major immunization campaign implemented by the World Health Organization of the UN in 1967 under the leadership of physician Donald Henderson. Another disease, and also viral in basis is polio. Polio was a terror for parents, and scarcely a summer went by in the years following WWII that parents didn't fear its striking one of their own. Many parents of that era remembered too well that FDR suffered from polio. Of course, thanks to the medical giants Salk and Sabin who developed vaccines against polio, mostly through private funding efforts of Rotary International, summers now come and go with not a thought of polio much less any concern. But now since 1980, we have AIDS, Acquired Immune Deficiency Syndrome to worry about. But AIDS, believed by many in the medical community to be caused by the HIV, Human Immunovirus, isn't the only serious viral infectious disease threatening the human specie. Others, presumably coming out of dense, impenetrable tropical rain forests are slowly making themselves known with unique calling cards. One such example is Ebola to be discussed later. The real problem with disease is not what Mother Nature springs on us, but what we have the capacity to do to ourselves. And military use of biologicals is not the major problem here. Terrorists are the real problem.

When President Nixon occupied the White House he issued one particular Executive Order to which no one regardless of political philosophy or agenda had any real objections. Effective on 25 November 1969, he rescinded US use of biological weapons. He ordered any stocks destroyed and restricted US Military R&D to strictly defensive purposes. The major agency engaged in this R&D work is the US Army's facility at Ft. Detrick, MD. Known by its military acronym USAMRIID-- United States Army Medical Research Institute of Infectious Diseases. The facility is located at the base of the Catoctin Mountains. USAMRIID is the center of military oriented biological agents research. The CDC-- Centers for Disease Control and Prevention-- is the civilian agency that has responsibility for monitoring and intervening when serious infectious diseases rear their heads so to speak anywhere in the US. There is close coordination between the two agencies, particularly on infections that are new, previously unknown, especially lethal, and viral in nature. USAMRIID came into the public eye during the mid 1990s through a book by Richard Preston titled *The Hot Zone*, and a movie titled *OUTBREAK* starring Dustin Hoffman. In both media, the subject of concern was a virus, specifically a particular type designated by virologists as Ebola, a *filovirus*, which is highly contagious and equally lethal.

GENERAL

Biological agents take the form of microorganisms such as viruses, rickettsiae, bacteria and fungi. The agents chosen must cause disease. Their potential value in modern warfare arises from the experiences of man in war throughout history. Historically, many more troops die of disease acquired on and off the battlefield than die of wounds directly inflicted at the hands of an enemy. In fact, even in the case of traditional wounds by gunfire, artillery and bombs, infection is often times the most serious problem to surmount for the wounded's recovery. It is the breaking of the skin, the body's first line of defense against infection, that is the second means of infecting a person. Inhalation of such agents dispersed in the air is the intended and primarily most effective means of infection.

Biological agents are not as straightforward in lethality as chemical agents since factors such as immunity (natural or acquired), means of entry into the body (inhaled, puncture wound, ingested), incubation time and treatment means available all alter the effectiveness of a given biological agent. Several disease organisms are potentially available for use as biological weapons, one of the most significant being the causative organism of plague, *Pasteurella pestis* or *Yersinia pestis*. Untreated, 50% mortality is expected, while treated, only about 10% mortality is expected. Not all those exposed to the disease will contract it.

Biological agents are susceptible to destruction by exposure to sunlight and air drying effects. Their use is restricted by such environmental decontamination means as well as human health potentials of a physically fit soldier or civilian population and the vast resources and expertise of the target nation's medical and health personnel. However, given these marginal impediments to an effective use of germ warfare and terrorism, what are the targets, what are the problems in preventing and defending against such attacks?

Below are some of the types of microorganisms and their definitions[3]. These are the likely agent types in biological warfare.

BACTERIA

-- unicellular prokaryotic microorganisms that usually multiply by cell division and have a cell wall that provides a constancy of form; they may be aerobic or anaerobic, motile or nonmotile, and free-living, saprophytic, parasitic or pathogenic

Bacteria are ubiquitous creatures, found in all nooks and crannies of the earth, on land, in the seas, even in arctic regions. They live in locales otherwise inhospitable to man where temperatures fall to subzero or rise to over 180°F, and even at depths of the Pacific near hot vents known as smokers where temperatures are searing and pressures bone-crushingly high. They are perhaps the most adaptive of living organisms on earth. They are categorized simply by shape. Rod shaped bacteria are bacillus; spherical shaped, coccus; and coiled or spiral shaped, spirochetes, so on.

The public generally views bacteria as vile, disease producing organisms, the cause of infections and misery. This is in fact true for many bacteria as human experience throughout history has been

---

[3] Definitions are taken from Stedman's Medical Dictionary, 25th Edition, Williams & Wilkins, 1990, in part or in whole with permission.

made miserable because of the pathogenic variety. As a group, they are the cause of such terrifying diseases as plague, leprosy, cholera, botulism, tetanus and typhoid fever to name a few. The effects of infection such as fever, nausea and diarrhea are the result of rapid, nearly uncontrolled growth of the infectious bacteria and the high concentrations of toxic waste products they produce and release into the blood stream, intestinal tract, etc.

Bacteria take in food materials, discharge waste products, grow, reproduce and die, too. Bacteria are participants in the decay of all dead creatures from even the gnat to the elephant. However, many bacteria are harmless or even directly beneficial to man such as those found in the intestinal tract or used to manufacture yogurt.[4]

Table 13-1: Diseases and Causative Microorganisms	
Disease	Microorganism
Plague	*Pasteurella (Yersinia) pestis*
Leprosy	*Mycobacterium leprae*
Cholera	*Vibrio cholerae*
Botulism	*Clostridium botulinum or parabotulinum*
Tetanus	*Clostridium tetani*
Typhoid Fever	*Salmonella typhii*
Urogenital Tract	*Escherichia coli*
Athlete's Foot	*Epidermophyton floccosum*
Endocarditis,	*Candida albicans* (a yeast)
Septicemia,	*Rickettsia prowazekii, typhi, &*
Meningitis	*tsutsugamushi*
Typhus	

Were it not for bacteria, life as we humans know it would probably cease. At the same time, some are a threat to human life itself. Just as there are good and wicked people, there are good and pathogenic bacteria.

VIRUSES

-- a term for a group of microbes which with few exceptions are capable of passing through fine filters that retain most bacteria, and are incapable of growth or reproduction apart from living cells. They have a prokaryotic genetic apparatus but differ sharply from bacteria in other respects.

Viruses, like bacteria, are also ubiquitous microorganisms. They, too, like bacteria, come in a range of sizes and shapes but orders of magnitude smaller than the smallest bacterium. They are more

---

[4] Lactobacillus bulgaricus, acidophilus and Streptococcus lactis

often associated with disease in man though they are often species specific, infecting all types of animals and even bacterial life forms. The common cold, distemper in dogs and cats, rabies, cold sores, encephalitis, yellow fever and most recently learned, AIDS[5], are all virally caused diseases. The unique feature of the viral life-style is that it cannot sustain itself independent of a host. Viruses do not eat in the sense normally attributed to cellular organisms. They do not release waste products of their own manufacture. They do not reproduce themselves by asexual or sexual means. A virus must infect a cell, either bacterial, plant or animal, and commandeer the cell's reproductive biological machinery to make new virions. Such infections sometimes result in the death of the host cell, at which time, new virus particles by the hundreds are released to infect other cells.[6] On the other hand, some viruses after infection of the host cell do not kill the cell. They remain dormant until some other stimulus triggers their lethal development within the host cell.[7] As a consequence of the virus' dependence upon a living cell for the means to reproduce itself, it is apparent that all viruses are only pathogenic to cellular organism.

FUNGI

-- a division of eukaryotic organisms that grow in irregular masses, without roots, stems, or leaves, and are devoid of chlorophyll or other pigments capable of photosynthesis. Each organism is unicellular to filamentous and possesses branched somatic structures surrounded by cell walls containing cellulose or chitin or both. They produce sexually or asexually (spore formation), and may obtain nutrition from other living organisms as parasites or from dead organic matter.

Fungi are also microorganisms that can cause disease. Mushrooms and athlete's foot are perhaps the most commonly known examples. Other fungi inhabit the human intestinal tract, but can cause serious, life threatening infections due to other illnesses or injuries. But like bacteria, some fungi are pathogenic, others serve man. Yeasts are fungi and find use in baking and brewing of beers and wines. Still others have served man in his eternal combat with bacterial infection.

Table 13-2: Beneficial Microorganisms	
Application	Microorganism
Brewing Penicillins	*Saccharomyces cervisiae* *Penicillium notatum or chrysogenum*

---

[5] Acquired Immune Deficiency Syndrome. A few researchers question the sole responsibility of the Human Immunovirus as the cause of AIDS. These few suspect specific mycobacteria as well.

[6] This process is known as nonpermissive infection.

[7] This process is known as permissive infection.

RICKETTSIA

-- a group of bacteria containing small (nonfilterable), often pleomorphic, coccoid, to rod-shaped, Gram-negative organisms that usually occur intracytoplasmically in lice, fleas, ticks and mites but do not grow in cell-free media; pathogenic species are parasitic in man and other animals.

Rickettsial microorganisms are a special class of bacteria that often are parasites, living within a host cell. These organisms are often transferred by vectors.[8] One example of such organismic disease is that of typhus.

VIROIDS

-- an infectious pathogen of plants that is smaller than a virus and differs from viruses in that it consists only of a single-stranded closed circular RNA. Viroids lack a protein coat (capsid) and are low molecular weight RNAs; replication does not depend on a helper[9] virus, but is effected autonomously by the DNA-dependent polymerase of the infected host cell.

Little is known or understood of viroid microbiology. Though no presently known diseases are caused by viroids in humans they are known to cause a number of plant diseases.[10] Thus their potential as a biological agent weapon is limited to plants and even then, the process for their artificial production and genetic engineering would be possible.

PRIONS

One does not see the virus coming. Viruses are orders of magnitude smaller than bacteria cells. Viruses do not carry out any self contained metabolism. They must reside within a host cell, taking control of the host cell's biochemical processes to make more virus. There are a few antiviral agents in use, but very restricted in their use against only certain viruses. Essentially mankind is defenseless against the virus. But the pathogenic bacteria and viruses may not be the only threat to human life. Another one has emerged, born of scientific disbelief and amazement and still in some doubt. That threat is the prion.

Prions (pronounced pree-ons) is short for proteinaceous infectious particles. These proteins are

---

[8] Vectors are insect transmitters of pathogenic microorganisms.

[9] Some viruses experience fragmentation through repeated multiplications. The fragments possess some of the genetic information of the original native virus but are produced only during production of the mature virus or helper virus.

[10] Potato spindle tuber disease, chrysanthemum stunt, cucumber pale fruit disease, and at least one disease of the tomato

small in mass and are believed to induce normal, harmless protein to change shape and become dangerous to the host cell. The host cells in all cases of prion infections are brain and neuron cells. Several known and well characterized diseases are believed to be caused by prions. They include scrapie of sheep and goats, so named because of the itchiness caused in some animals, leading them to scrape their hide against objects to relieve the ever present itch, transmissible mink encephalopathy, chronic wasting disease (of mule deer and elk), feline spongiform encephalopathy, bovine spongiform encephalopathy, Kuru, Creutzfeldt-Jakob disease, Gerstmann-Straussler-Scheinker disease and fatal familial insomnia. All of these diseases, the last four found in humans, are fatal and are classified by the medical community as spongiform encephalopathies due to the holing or pitting observed throughout the brain.

The first suggestion that a protein was the initiator of a disease rather than the genetic DNA or RNA of viruses arose in the early 1980s with Stanley B. Prusiner[11]. Met with disbelief and ridicule as evidenced by some of the humorously suggested causes such as linoleum or kryptonite, the skepticism diminished in the ensuing 20 years when extensive biochemical and medical tests revealed that no nucleic acids (the stuff of genes) was present or identifiable in prepared extracts of the diseased tissues yet the extracts elicited the disease when administered to test animals. It was Gerald A. H. Wells and John W. Wilesmith of the Central Veterinary Laboratory in Weybridge, England who noted the mysterious effects of a disease striking cattle in England in 1986. The feed provided the cattle proved to be the source of the pathogen, consisting in part of scalp flesh and bone material from slaughtered sheep. In 1988 Britain outlawed the use of animal-derived supplements for use in feed. The outbreak in 1996 of the same disease among English cattle revealed a problem in the controls.

The body of evidence shows that prions are genetically coded proteins found in some animals such as sheep, goats, cows and mice and presumably in humans as well. It also appears that the same protein may have two different shapes, one that is harmless, the second pathogenically lethal. The protein coded for by the gene and produced in protein synthesis is called prion protein or simply PrP.

The basis for the complete skepticism with which Prusiner's assertion was initially met is reasonable in light of the then existing doctrine of molecular biology. The so-called Central Dogma of Molecular Biology holds that information flow is from DNA to RNA to protein. That means that the DNA of the host codes for the RNA which codes for the amino acid sequence which makes up the protein to be synthesized. This dogma holds true in every case involving prokaryotic (bacterial) and eukaryotic (animal) cells from the E. coli within the human large intestines to the plant cells to the cells of the whales and giraffes and so on. It also holds true for DNA viruses. The one exception is with the RNA viruses the so-called retroviruses such as the HIV virus of AIDS notoriety.

Retroviruses have RNA not DNA as the genetic material. Within a host cell they produce a DNA copy of the viral RNA. The DNA copy then is used to make more viral RNA. But even here, there is a consistency of sorts with the Central Dogma of Molecular Biology, the virally ordered DNA is used to make viral RNA. Some research suggests that RNA preceded DNA in the birth of life in the prebiotic Earth. Another consistency even with the retroviruses is that nucleic acid information codes for protein information. Thus for a disease to arise, nucleic acid must be the final 'smoking gun' if you will, in the process. But this is where prions depart the norm as we understand that norm.

With the issue of the prion, some wonder if proteins with an ability to produce themselves through an as yet unknown and unimagined mechanism didn't precede RNA. Though prions appear to have a genetic origin, once made, and they are thought to be made in many copies once the gene is expressed, the prions go their own way. That is to say that the pathogenic type appears to induce the nonpathogenic type to undergo a change in shape which produces from that process much more

---

[11] see "Prions" by Stanley B. Prusiner, *Scientific American*, October 1984.

pathogenic prions. Additionally, prions extracted from an afflicted animal and injected into a test animal stimulates the occurrence of the disease. There is some question about prions being able to breech the species barrier.

The matter of a species barrier arose from work of Pattison done in the 1960s. Pattison found that extracts of sheep brain infected with scrapie (a prion disease) could not illicit the same disease in rodents. This seemed reasonable in that the gene for the PrP must be present. Then any prions produced by that host gene would be susceptible to changes in shape by pathogenic shaped PrP on inoculation. But the barrier could be penetrated. A colleague of Prusiner's, Michael R. Scott, managed to insert a PrP gene for the Syrian hamster into mice. The difference between Syrian hamster PrP and mouse PrP is only about 16 amino acids out of 254. Normal mice without the hamster gene when inoculated with hamster PrP remained normal-- no disease manifested. But the genetically altered mice, transgenic mice, when inoculated with hamster PrP, developed the disease.

The message here has significant potential. Though no known cases of prion diseases afflicting animals have been proven transmittable to humans, the fact that the genes of one specie can be incorporated into another, thus rendering the gene recipient susceptible to the disease of the gene donor strikes at the heart of viral infections. Viral gene segments can be incorporated into host genes, and vise versa. Could viral genes incorporate a prion gene?

The species barrier to prions then is perhaps only a barrier as good as the specie's ability to sustain a defense against infections by viruses that constantly undergo changes in their genetic identity. Though it is rare that a virus that affects some animal may also affect humans, there is at least one case well documented. Rabies. It is perhaps no small coincidence that rabies also attacks the brain. There may be little concern at present about the possibility of a virus acquiring prion based genetic information and thus spreading to other animals or humans. What is of concern is that The Human Genome project seeks to map the human DNA genetic map. That knowledge permits selectivity not by nature as much by man. If one knows on what chromosome the PrP gene resides and can selectively excise that gene via the multitude of restriction enzymes available for cutting DNA at exact places along its sequence, one can remove that gene, and splice it into another DNA of anything one wishes, including DNA viruses. Conversely, synthesis of the complementary RNA sequence permits splicing that sequence into an RNA virus.

More down to earth is the question of cases in which humans who have worked around known infected prion diseased animals have developed a prion disease themselves. In Britain in 1996, it appears that there were two farmers whose cattle had the Mad Cow (prion) disease. These two farmers shortly died of Creutzfeldt-Jakob disease (a human prion disease). There is no evidence that the disease of cows is communicable to humans, however, the concern in these two cases has amplified the importance of the question of the impenetrability of the species barrier. There have been studies examining if there is any particular region of the PrP molecule especially important in penetrating the species barrier. It appears from several studies that the greater the difference in the PrP gene sequence between species, the greater the difficulty of transspecie transmission.

One last point that bears mention. If the prion must enter the brain for expression of the disease and the host animal must also possess such a gene, how then does feeding animals with a feed that contains the prion enter the brain? The prion is a protein. Proteins are subject to denaturation, a process that alters the overall shape of the protein and in the extreme destroy its biological function. Additionally, proteins are subject to digestion in the stomach and small intestines. Proteins are hydrolyzed by enzymes such as chymotrypsin, trypsin, pepsin and so forth. Hydrolysis of proteins breaks them down into smaller fragments, amino acids, which presumably renders them biologically nonfunctional compared to their native state. What is the mechanism that permits ingested prions to survive the digestive tract and finally trigger consequences in the brain. Is the shape and composition of the prion less susceptible to digestion? Is it a statistical problem; a few whole prion molecules survive the hydrolytic processes of digestion? How does it enter the brain cells? In humans for example, the belief is that prion contaminated tissue such as eye cornea in transplants may be the means of inoculation of the recipient. This is quite reasonable given that the eye is essentially an extension of the brain exposed to the environment. But in the case of animals such as the cows in England, they ingest feed contaminated with prion matter. The only way for such material to enter the brain is from absorption into the blood stream and then passage to the brain. How does the prion, a protein, survive digestion?

INFECTIOUS RISKS

Viruses pose perhaps the greatest risk of infection and treatment. Their very nature makes them the most difficult microorganisms to isolate and study. Development of vaccines is difficult and methods applicable to one group of viruses may not be applicable to others. Viruses are also subject to antigenic mutations and variation; that is, they can undergo changes in genetic characteristics that make them nearly new and different organisms, yet elicit essentially the same disease, or they can have certain genes expressed in one host, and repressed in another. Antigenic mutation is part of the problem with developing a vaccine for the common cold, caused by rhinoviruses, and also a significant feature of the AIDS viruses and the search for a vaccine for it.

Viruses too, like bacteria, can infect a range of cells, tissues and organs of the human body. They manifest their pathologic presence in a multitude of signs. They can cause disease of the respiratory tract, skin, the central nervous system (CNS), the eyes, ears and throat, cardiovascular system, joints, gastrointestinal tract, urogenital system[12], and hepatic (liver) to name a few sites. There are three primary routes of infection: through the skin, ingestion and inhalation.

---

[12] mumps, herpes, acute hemorrhagic cystitis

| Table 13-3: A Few Disease Causing Viruses in Humans ||
Disease	Location
Viral Pneumonia, Influenza, Croup	Respiratory Tract
Eruptions and Rashes	Skin
Rabies, Polio, Encephalitis, Meningitis	Central nervous System (CNS)
Certain Conjunctivitis, Measles, Mumps	Eyes, Ears, Throat
Myocarditis, influenza, mumps, Measles	Cardiovascular System
Arthritis, Mumps	Joints
Diarrhea, Gastroenteritis	Gastrointestinal Tract
Mumps, Herpes, Acute Hemorrhagic Cytitis	Urogenital System
Hepatitis, Jaundice, Yellow Fever, Infectious Mononucleosis	Liver (Hepatic System)

Penetration by pathogenic microorganisms, regardless of their type or size, arises through inhalation, ingestion or breaks in the skin. These breaks can be cuts, punctures, ruptured blisters or abrasions. Entry through pores is also a possible site of infection. Generally, secretions through the pores serve as a flushing flow, minuscule as it is, that provides an against the flow route, generally very difficult for microorganisms to pass through. Clogged pores, either partially or totally, do offer less resistance to invasion than freely flowing pores. Once the skin's epidermal layer of dead skin is breached, the underlying live tissue of the dermis and the rich nutrient environment of that tissue with its copious blood supply is an ideal environment for pathogenic microbiota. Penetration of the capillaries and invasion of the blood leads to most serious kinds of infection, septicemia, regardless of the route-- whether initially through the skin, gut or lungs.

Ingestion is another favored means of infection of the host by microbes. Once ingested, the organisms have a choice of the stomach, small or large intestines to incubate and proliferate, secreting as well vast quantities of toxins, themselves responsible for the range of effects experienced. These effects include nausea, vomiting and diarrhea. Generally, the very acidic conditions of the stomach kill most if not all microbes ingested, though some apparently survive to cause such ailments as cholera, gastrointestinal anthrax, influenza, etc.

The pulmonary route is perhaps the easiest means of infection. The repetitive breathing, some 16 times per minute, draws in large quantities of air-borne particles, including microbial matter in the air. Aerosolized microbes such as viruses, bacteria, and spores are tiny enough to travel on air and wind currents. The human body is equipped to filter such debris with varying success. The nose as well as the bronchial passages are lined with very tiny hairs that are intended to trap such particulate matter, usually imbedding the debris in thick mucous. However, no system, be it mechanical or biological, is perfect and some pathogens manage to avoid entrapment and enter the lungs. The usual signs of congestion in the chest signal the invasion of the lungs by foreign material. In the case of animate particles such as bacteria, fungi or viruses, the lungs also provide an ideal environment of microbial growth and proliferation. Again the toxins and waste products generated and secreted by these pathogens lead to symptoms as in the other two cases, such as fever, fatigue, congestion, etc.

TARGETS

MILITARY VULNERABILITIES

A natural target for any weapon system, including biological weapons, is the military forces. Life in a combat zone is far from sterile. One of the most significant contributors to the barbaric life style of the field soldier is limited water. Usually the only potable water a modern day soldier has is in his canteen. If he is on a front line, he will see no extra water for bathing, and even shaving can become a problem. Though modern American military field sanitation principles recognize the need for cleanliness, as a matter of practicality, it is in a combat zone that this fact of civilian or garrison life is one of the first to suffer rigorous, daily attention. Attention is given to minimum sanitation but nothing like that found in peacetime. This statement is not a condemnation of commanders' concern for their troops or a lack of responsibility on their part. It is a recognition that in the field, especially under fire for prolonged periods of time, and particularly if isolated and cut off from friendly forces, the civilized amenities of life just cannot be transported to the front lines like ammunition, medical supplies and replacements. It is the living conditions of the combat soldier that make him a logical target for possible biological warfare.

Throughout history, man's record of combat with his own kind has not only recorded his conquests, but also the less glorifying defeats at the instigation of infections. No military force, including the U.S. Armed Forces, has ever gone to battle and fought only man. The record of U.S. Pacific Island campaigns is littered with the ravages of disease, taking as much a toll in the military's combat effectiveness, if not more so, than the Japanese. Any time man enters a different environment, or call it a different world, from which he came, he confronts the flora and fauna of that environment which are totally alien to him. His resistance to disease is immediately challenged. Though anyone who served in the Armed Forces remembers the battery of inoculation shots he received before going overseas, he also well remembers those of his friends and comrades in arms who suffered from flu, trench foot, festering sores and all manner of so-called jungle rot.

Though the military forces are an obvious target, the nature of a microbe's mechanism of virulence actually mitigates its effectiveness. Microbes are not instantaneously injurious as a bullet or bomb. If one is attempting to stop an attacking force, one does not have several days for the incubation of the organism to manifest the disease. It is this practical, time dependent problem of biological warfare that places significant limitations on its applicability against a maneuverable military force. Such a force can reek untold havoc on its enemy before any symptoms of infection by biological agents take hold. The enemy using biological weapons against an attacking force can be defeated before illness stops the attackers in their tracks. The mobility of modern troops is also a significant factor impeding the usefulness of biological weapons. No longer do modern military forces engage in the classic set piece siege warfare of previous centuries. Additionally, modern military forces, especially the western powers, are equipped and trained to deal with such threats. But civilian populations, the backbone and sinew of a nation's military might, are fixed in place and quite vulnerable if not totally unprepared.

> Today's city is the most vulnerable social
> structure ever conceived by man.
> -Urban Guerilla[13]

CIVILIAN VULNERABILITIES

Perhaps the greatest threat and most useful employment of biological agents is against civilian population targets. It follows that civilian populations are the easiest targets for assault. They are generally not prepared, mentally or physically, for the rigors of war and combat[14] and equally naked before determined terrorist attacks. Civilians generally do not possess the means for defense against a well-trained and equipped army or terrorist group and this is usually the result of their government's laws and regulations imposed on the population arising from that government's desire to control the population as a whole and certainly the more lawless elements among them. Biological weapons employment against civilian targets does not necessarily mean the use of human pathological agents directly against people. Any biological agent that affects civilian populations in some strategic sense is useful. The destruction of food crops, textile crops, etc. can have overwhelming consequences to civilian economies, health, stamina and the will to oppose an aggressor nation and its military force as well as adversely affect that population's support of its own government and military forces engaged with the aggressor nation and forces. Terrorist attacks with seemingly impunitive success will also reap political consequences beyond measure.

However, it is not likely that any aggressor nation willing to employ biological agents against such strategic targets as agriculture would confine its weapons to nonhuman pathological systems. Terrorists would be more interested in the short term, immediate and spectacularly wonton death that toxic biologicals have on people, not crops or livestock. A terrorist nation would, in all likelihood, employ a combination of biological agents, some of which undoubtedly will attack both agricultural targets and human targets. The best example of potential human pathological biological weapons arises not from actual historical use of such agents in war (there have been none), but from accidents

---

[13] In The Harvest of a Quiet Eye, p. 114

[14] It is interesting that in the late 1960s, the U.S. Government effectively suspended any serious thought or efforts concerning civil defense for the American public against a nuclear attack. The early development of fallout shelters and stocks of cracker-like protein wafers, medicinals and sanitation materials was discontinued and even removed from once designated shelters by the mid 1970s. (While at Ft. Bliss, I was the Officer-in-Charge of the removal of all such materials from downtown El Paso buildings.) The same attitude has prevailed with respect to chemical and biological warfare. This particular disregard is perhaps more serious as such warfare could easily be waged against the American public in a very covert manner at the outset. Most importantly, any thought of educating the public to the hazards of such warfare and measures that they may take on their own behalf has been left essentially unpublicized. More interesting is that though the Congress and the Presidency have largely abandoned and written the public off, provisions had been made and in place for such protection of the creme de la creme of the Washington establishment, including high ranking military officials. A 3 June 1992 National Network broadcast announced the existence of a bomb shelter for members of Congress which cost some $14 million a year to maintain. So much for the officially pandered view that bomb shelters for the public provide little protection and are too expensive to construct and maintain. Apparently not so for politicians! The lack of civilian preparedness does not extend to the military, where US Army doctrine educates the soldier in ways to protect himself against such attacks (nuclear, chemical, biological). The public is left to its fate. Of further interest is that the former USSR and even Switzerland do not share the belief that civil defense preparedness is too expensive and unlikely to reap rewards in the event of nuclear [chemical, biological] attack.

of nature, disease decimated populations. Though it is true that modern medicine has conquered a wide range of historical diseases, modern biological warfare and terrorism will undoubtedly utilize newer and more virulent strains of historically lethal pestilences. These new strains will have no established treatment or vaccine standards to combat them. One such candidate is that of bubonic plague, the Black Death. There have been no less than four pandemics of plague recorded: 542 to 600 A.D.; the 14th century; the 15th, 16th, and 17th centuries; and the present which began in 1894 and is receding. The 14th century outbreak was responsible for the estimated deaths of 25 million people, about one fourth of the European population. The plague period of the 15th, 16th and 17th centuries ended in the Great Plague of London from 1664 to 1665. The present period is believed to have landed initially on American shores on 27 June, 1899 with the arrival of the Japanese ship *S.S. Nippon Maru* in San Francisco. The outcome of this inoculation of the U.S. was some 523 recorded cases from 1900 to 1951.

The number of cases in the U.S. during 1900 to 1951 does not appear alarming. But cognizance must be noted that during this time, the U.S. had experienced two World Wars neither of which saw battle on American soil. The resources of the health agencies of the U.S. and the various states were not taxed by the destruction of resources as was the case in Europe, Asia and the Pacific Islands. The consequences to a modern country in the grip of an epidemic or a continent in the grip of a pandemic is best exemplified by the 14th century death rate. At that time, medicine was primitive by today's standards. It lacked not only knowledge of the cause of disease but also effective medicinals, sanitation, and vector controls. Failure in these areas underscores the potential threat today of all-out war on a nation's soil and the introduction of germ warfare. Without the peacetime controls of sanitation, disease outbreak will naturally occur. An enemy bent upon achieving his agenda can exacerbate such natural events and the cost and effort to him is minuscule compared to the havoc and suffering he can impose on his enemy's population.

Another telling example of the overwhelming loss of human life imposed by biological agent infections is the experiences at the end of WWI with influenza (flu). Within six months of its end, flu claimed 20,000,000 lives, 550,000 of these in the U.S. This level of loss of life can only be attributed to the serious damage done the European countries, their agricultural ability, nutritional standards, public health capabilities and sanitation facilities, all of which suffered from four years of war. The level of deaths in the U.S., though not attributable to similar problems, represents the lack of preparedness and the lack of medical technology to confront such a virulence. Modern biotechnology and advances in genetic engineering may present a similar unpreparedness in future wars (nationally organized or terrorist group inspired) where biological weapons, if used, will present virtually insurmountable detection and treatment problems.

Oddly, the greater risk to domestic populations may arise from their own government's experimentations. During WWII the British conducted a study in which *Bacillus anthracis*, the causative microbe of anthrax, was dispersed on Gruinard Island just west of Scotland. As late as 1981, a scientific team could detect the presence of viable *B. anthracis* spores to a concentration as little as three spores per gram of soil.[15]

Another incident of government experimentation to the potential hazard of its own people occurred in September 1950. The U.S. Navy tested an allegedly harmless bacteria by releasing it from two minesweepers off the San Francisco coast. The microbes contaminated an estimated 117 square miles of the Golden Gate city, exposing some 800,000 residents. Other tests involved Virginia and

---

[15] *Bacillus anthracis* on Gruinard Island, R.J. Manchee, M.G. Broster, J. Melling, R.M.Henstridge & A.J. Stagg, *Nature(London)* **294**, 254-255 (1981)

the subways of New York City.[16]

The introduction of biological warfare or terrorism does not necessarily require intercontinental weapons delivery. The easiest and perhaps the most efficient means of introducing germ warfare (BW) is through sabotage, guerilla, and terrorist warfare. A free society is ripe for such assaults. Vast open borders are virtually impossible to seal in national emergencies. The effort to do so strips valuable resources that otherwise would be devoted to more massive and conventional military force deployment at the front lines. Even such an impossible task as sealing a nation's borders completely, if successful, does not create impenetrability to winds, bird migrations, insects and even rivers flowing from one country through another.

The disadvantage to biological warfare is that it can not necessarily be confined to only a given geographic region. The factors noted above, winds, birds, vectors, rivers, all unwittingly conspire to spread the affliction across borders, and across continents. Also, the more advanced the society, the better prepared it is to deal with the first signs of such outbreaks. So long as the resources of that society are in place and the population understands the nature of the actions taken to confine and eradicate the disease, all could end well... Could end well. It requires a lot of a people not to flee in the face of what, in a germ warfare setting, appears to be certain death. Panic, the bonus to enemy employment of germ warfare, can thwart health officials' efforts to contain and destroy an outbreak. The populations' general ignorance and lack of education and preparation for measures necessary to combat germ attacks will work against officialdom. Pestilence, a Horseman of the Apocalypse, has absolute range over the earth, despite man's efforts.

The vulnerabilities faced by both military and civilian populations to germ warfare are actually two different ends of the same spectrum. The military field forces by their very life style-- hit and run, attack, stay and defend, etc.-- makes securing hygienic conditions virtually impossible. At the other end of the spectrum, the civilian population whose daily lives center on sustaining their forces in the field, find their lot worsened. If, as is likely in all-out war, they are subject to attacks, as the resources for the war effort become compromised, they will find themselves also doing without. The depletion of medical personnel, the urgency of need for medicinals and other medical materials in the front line army will eventually create seriously diminished domestic availability of these stocks. Attacks that lead to the destruction of reservoirs, sewage treatment facilities, etc., place an added burden on the raw materials necessary for repair or reconstruction. These same materials are in priority demand by the armed forces for fortifications, airfields and shipping installation construction.

Add to the materiel shortages, the introduction of bioengineering which looms in the near future. The ability of an inhuman and unscrupulous power or group to marshal its biotechnology to engineer man-altered pathogens sets the stage for a war of incredible pestilence. The techniques that allow the probing of the gene, the removal of DNA from one cell and placing it into another, permit the ability in the future to remove disease-causing genes from one organism and place them into a totally different organism, otherwise nonpathogenic in man, taking advantage of cell surface immunity factors. There is no predicting the enumerable possibilities of such Jekyll and Hyde microbe

---

[16] No Fire No Thunder

technology.[17] It is perhaps this potential of a future adversary that argues for the continued research and development by U.S. Military laboratories, such as USAMRIID, in biological warfare with an emphasis on treatment and immunizations. Though treaties such as the Biological Warfare Convention (see Chapter 25) are an ideal, human nature is not so ideal. Regrettably, a nation such as the U.S. must be prepared to deal with the actions not only of the Hitlers, Stalins and Saddams of the world, but the rogue extremists cloaked in political and religious outrage. To place too much credit in the words of nations or renegade groups is to ignore the potential application of bioengineering to military and terrorist use of biological weapons of mass destruction because of treaties, mere paper. To ignore man's predatory nature is to invite the very horror we wish to forestall by these treaties.[18]

BOTULISM

Botulism is caused by *Clostridium botulinum*[19] which secretes the neurotoxin botulin, a protein of about 1500 amino acid residues. There are some six botulin types characterized as A, B, C, D, E, and F by microbiologists and toxicologists. The toxin interferes with neuron impulse transmission, being a cholinergic synaptic inhibitor. The animal exposed to the toxin dies of respiratory paralysis, essentially the same cause of death resulting from chemical nerve agent exposure. It acts on the presynaptic and postsynaptic neuromuscular junctions. Its actions inhibit the release of acetylcholine from the presynaptic vesicles. It is not clear what the exact effect the toxin has on the postsynaptic membrane, though evidence suggests a change in the membrane. The changes are thought to be due to interference by the toxin with other biochemical compounds involved in the stimulation of the postsynaptic membranes.[20]

Between 1950 and 1979 some 90% of botulism cases arose from home canning, and home processed foods. One quarter of those afflicted with the toxicosis died. Principal means of contracting botulism are: food-borne, wounds, and unknown causes.

The bacterium is an anaerobe, meaning it has no tolerance for oxygen (or air). As soil bacteria,

---

[17] As serious a potential future threat as this may be, the public must be cautioned about damning the scientists who have developed the technologies later applied to these futuristic bio-horrors. It is not the scientists, in general, who are at fault, but the politicians and power-hungry world leaders who apply, what was otherwise, a gift for the improvement of humankind's lot, to the destruction of humankind. Only very close supervision of national leaders and other policy makers can hope to stay their errant agendas. A supervision that, regrettably, is all too lacking under the all powerful pen of state secrets.

[18] The reader is directed to the book Gene Wars by Charles Piller and Keith R. Yamamoto, Beech Tree Books, New York, 1988 for a fine presentation of biological warfare as seen by molecular biologists.

[19] *C. botulinum* is ubiquitous, found in soil naturally.

[20] Postsynaptic Effects of Botulinum Toxin of the Neuromuscular Junction, Lawrence C. Sellin, pp. 81-92 and Pharmacological Studies on the Cellular and Subcellular Effects of Botulinum Toxin, Lance Simpson, pp. 35-46 in Biomedical Aspects of Botulism, George E. Lewis, Jr. , Ed., Academic Press, New York, 1981

these microorganisms exist as spores[21] in their dormant state which are very difficult to kill. The spores are carried on the wind and find their way in the home, onto dishes, pots and pans, etc. When canning, the cooking of foods kills bacteria as well as driving off any dissolved oxygen in the cooking water. The temperature of boiling water at normal atmospheric pressure is not generally high enough to kill bacterial spores. Thus pressure cooking foods raises the temperature to or above 250°F. Cooking at that temperature for 30 minutes will kill the spores. Any growth of *C. botulinum* in food results in the release of the neurotoxin into the food medium. The toxin is also itself susceptible to air oxidation and destruction by cooking. Such contaminated food may not evidence any tainted signs by mere taste or smell.

It was van Ermengen who discovered and named the disease cause. Van Ermengen isolated cell-free extracts which produced the identical symptoms of botulism as the bacterial laden media. Thus, he discovered the botulism toxin. From the quantities isolated, van Ermengen calculated the quantity of toxin necessary to kill an animal. He determined that 50 mg of his (crude) toxin extract would kill 100,000 Kg of rabbits. The pure toxin is about 1000 times more lethal than the crude extract prepared by van Ermengen. It is estimated that 500 mg of pure botulinum toxin would kill one million tons of animal life![22]

The genus *Clostridium* harbors some of the most deadly anaerobic microorganisms known. This group of bacteria is responsible not only for botulism, but also tetanus (*C. tetani*), gas gangrene (*C. perfringens*), a specie associated with wounds of war (*C. cochlearium*), and appendicitis (*C. fallax*). In summation, the genus Clostridium is anaerobic and is responsible for or intimately associated with a wide range of infections, nearly all of them being acutely fatal if not detected and treated quickly.

Because of the potential threat of BW in the Persian Gulf during Operations Desert Shield and Desert Storm, concern over biological weapons use led the U.S. Army to accelerate and field various newly developed remedies. Among those remedies was the antitoxin for botulism. The antitoxin is developed by dosing a test animal with minute quantities of the toxin. Increased dosages over time leads to the build-up of immunity in the test animal against such toxin assaults. The toxin antibodies produced by the test animal can be extracted from its blood, processed and serve as the basis for the production of a human vaccine against the toxin.

As a historical note, a horse was used in the production of antitoxin for human use against botulism. Its name was *First Flight*, a 21 year old Army thoroughbred quartered at the University of Minnesota. This particular horse has given about 1000 liters of blood over its lifetime.[23]

SYMPTOMS

Symptoms can appear as soon as two hours or as late as several days after exposure to the toxin. Treatment begins with timely, accurate diagnosis, followed by administration of antitoxin. First signs of botulism arise in the digestive tract, signaled by nausea and vomiting. Some 12 hours after toxin

---

[21] Spores are an inactive, dormant, nonliving state of many bacteria, particularly soil-borne anaerobic microorganisms. A thick polysaccharide coat comprising the spore 'hull' is nearly impenetrable by a wide range of agents.

[22] *Cholera*: The American Scientific Experience: 1947-1980, W.E. Heyningen and John R. Seal, Westview Press, Boulder, CO., 1983, p. 43

[23] *Newsweek*, July 15, 1991, p. 4

ingestion, neurological disturbances begin. Early signs of this effect are fatigue, headache, dizziness, blurred vision and even double vision. Mucous tissues of the mouth and throat become dry and there is a feeling of constriction in the throat. Difficulty in swallowing attends these manifestations as well as difficulty of speech. Advanced symptoms arise with respiratory distress, leading to respiratory paralysis and finally death from anoxia. Several improvements are proposed based upon experimental volunteer studies.[24] Principal importance in treatment is the neutralization of free, as yet unbound toxin and the maintenance of adequate ventilation opposing the onset of respiratory paralysis.

ANTHRAX

Anthrax is caused by the bacterium *Bacillus anthracis*. Also known as splenic fever, black bain, charbon, malignant pustule and murrain, it is a disease that is transmittable to man from a wide variety of domestic and wild animals. The disease has been described by Hippocrates, Virgil, Pliny and Galen. It was Robert Koch, the eminent German bacteriologist, who conclusively proved the rod-shaped bacterium *B. anthracis* the cause of the disease. On 2 June, 1881, Louis Pasteur introduced his successful vaccine preventing infection with anthrax bacilli. This was a monumental step in the history of medicine as a science as anthrax was the first disease shown to be caused by microorganisms and the first disease for which a preventative vaccine was specifically prepared.

Anthrax is a world-wide disease, though a more prevalent problem in the Mediterranean region, Africa and Asia. The first human case diagnosed in the U.S. was recorded in Philadelphia in 1834. The microbe's tenacity is directly attributable to its ability to form spores, a nonvegetative form of the bacteria which are the dormant state. The spores are highly resistant to chemical, heat and radiation destruction. The spores are destroyed by heating to 120°C for 15 minutes. Spores in the environment can remain a threat to live stock for more than a decade.

Periodic outbreaks still occur in the United States. States with significant livestock, and ranching commerce are the primary sites of concentration. These areas encompass Louisiana, Oklahoma, Colorado and California. As a historical note, the Fifth and Sixth Plagues of Egypt as noted in Exodus are thought to have been anthrax. It has been estimated that 10 grams (about 1/3 ounce) of anthrax can potentially kill as many people as one ton of the nerve agent Sarin.

SYMPTOMS

Infection by *B. anthracis* leads to symptoms caused by the exotoxin secreted by the microbe. The exotoxin is composed of three protein components. Each protein component by itself is nontoxic. The bacteria enter the animal by one of the three possible means. The first is called cutaneous anthrax and arises by bacterial contact with cuts or abrasions of the skin. Flies and mosquitoes also may cause cutaneous anthrax through their bites. This vector method of spread of the disease has been observed in Africa. The second form of the disease is termed pulmonary anthrax as the infection originates in the lungs from inhalation of the bacterial spores. The third form is intestinal or gastrointestinal anthrax and arises from ingestion of infected meat or meat products. In this version of infection, the

---

[24] Approaches to the Prophylaxis, Immunotherapy and Chemotherapy of Botulism, pp. 261-270, George E. Lewis, Jr. in Biomedical Aspects of Botulism.

bacteria invade the gastrointestinal mucosa.

Cutaneous anthrax infection comprises 95% of all cases of the affliction. Symptoms arise two to five days after inoculation. Signaled by a small papule at the site of exposure, it develops to a vesicle laden with a dark bluish-black fluid. Rupture of this vesicle exposes a black eschar[25] at its base. This eschar is surrounded by a distinct inflamed ring. This wound morphology gives rise to the name malignant pustule. Such wounds typically appear on the hands, arms or head. They are painless. They are very seldom found on the torso, legs or feet.

Pulmonary anthrax, acquired by inhalation of spore laden dust, most generally afflicts those who handle contaminated hides, wool or hair. The infection arises from inhalation of the spores which lodge in the smallest reaches of the lungs (alveoli) and germinate to active, reproducing bacteria. Symptoms initially imitate typical respiratory infections exhibiting fever, malaise, cough and muscular pain (myalgia). Within several days the infection worsens considerably, manifested by respiratory distress and cyanosis. At this stage of the infection, death follows in 24 hours.

Intestinal or gastrointestinal anthrax manifests nausea, vomiting and diarrhea. Occasionally blood appears in the stool and or in the vomitus (hematemesis). Advanced infection also leads to extreme exhaustion, shock and finally, death.

All three means of infection can lead to invasion of the blood (septicemia) and localization of the infection in the membranes covering the brain or spinal cord (meninges) resulting in fatal meningitis. Once in the blood, systemic anthrax results in rapid fatality. Toxin production rapidly climbs in the lymph nodes and spleen. Destruction of these organs and the spleen, most notably, discharges large quantities of toxin and bacilli into the blood and inter-organ cavities. In a few hours, shock, coma and death follow. Destruction (necrosis) of the walls of small blood vessels results in hemorrhage and the discharge of blood from the mouth, nose and anus. The large numbers of bacilli so released contaminate surrounding areas, leading to infection of other animals and people.

Treatment of anthrax initially begins with making the correct diagnosis. Often times, anthrax is not suspected and the misdiagnoses leads to the wrong, ineffective antibiotic prescribed. This is a problem in the United States where the disease is so rare in spite of the occasional occurrence. If the infection is believed to be a staphylococcal infection, any incision and drainage of the pustulant debris may lead to a serious spread of the anthrax bacilli contained in the wound. Once the disease is correctly diagnosed, particularly the pulmonary version, treatment must begin immediately with massive doses of intravenous antibiotics. Penicillin is most effective, though for patients with penicillin intolerance, other antibiotics work as well, such as tetracycline, erythromycin, chloramphenicol or gentamicin.

Usual treatment consists of 500 mg of penicillin V administered orally every six hours for five days. Alternatively, 600 mg of procaine penicillin can be administered by intramuscular injection every 12 to 24 hours for the five days. Severe cases may require as much as 1200 mg of penicillin G administered intravenously every six hours. Once the patient's condition improves, continued medication by the intramuscular injection dosage is followed.

---

[25] In medicine, a thick scab resulting from a chemical or thermal burn or other physical cauterization of the skin.

CHOLERA

Cholera is a disease of the gastrointestinal tract. It exhibits its pathology as an acute diarrhea. The cause of cholera is the bacteria *Vibrio cholerae*. Such bacteria are comma-shaped with a single flagellum.[26] The site of action by *V. cholerae* is the jejunum and ileum, the last two portions of the small intestine. The disease manifests itself a few hours to five days after ingestion of the microorganisms. A water-borne pathogen, *V. cholerae* are ingested through contaminated water supplies where drinking water and sewage water sources are one and the same. Historically cholera was unique to Asia, almost exclusively to India. However, in the 19th century, between 1817 and 1899, cholera spread to Europe, Africa and the Americas.

The British physician John Snow established cholera's water-borne nature in 1854 during an outbreak in London of that year. Through careful mapping of the incidences of cholera, he isolated a particular public water pump in London as the source of the infection. It wasn't until 1883 that the renowned German bacteriologist Robert Koch identified the bacterial cause. In 1884, Koch suggested a specific poison secreted by the bacteria within the gut is responsible for the pathology. It was S. N. De of India who discovered the cholera exotoxin[27] in 1959.

V. cholerae is not the only specie[28] of Vibrio bacteria. There are no less than nine Vibrio specie that are pathogenic to man. These pathogens are generally food-borne.[29] The nature of the harm caused varies from gastrointestinal, wound and ear infections, to septicemias. Foods that are natural host carriers of Vibrio pathogens are crabs, shrimp, turtles, oysters, crawfish, lobsters and fish. The most common pathogen in the U.S. is *V. parahaemolyticus* and invariably arises as a result of mishandled, cooked seafood.

Until recently, some question surrounded the natural state survivability of the Vibrios, *V. cholerae* in particular. It was not clear whether *V. Cholerae* existed exclusively within the human gut and transiently in human feces, or if it could survive in the environment independent of a human host. Studies in Australia and the U.S., however, have established *V. cholerae*'s ability to live free and multiply in fresh water and brackish coastal waters. *V. parahaemolyticus* on the other hand is clearly a free-living microorganism, independent of human host and is not sewage dependent. Generally, all the Vibrio pathogens are water-borne, either coastal, fresh or estuarine in habitat. Of the Vibrios, *V. vulnificus* is considered the most lethal and individuals subject to liver disease are at a greater risk of death if these bacteria are ingested through raw seafood.

---

[26] Flagella (singular: flagellum) are long whip-like appendages on the exterior surface of a bacterial cell used by them as a means of locomotion.

[27] Exotoxins are usually proteins and are produced within the bacterial cell but secreted into the environment about them. For gastrointestinal bacteria, the environment is the stomach and intestinal tract. For cholera, the toxin is specifically classified as an exo-enterotoxin.

[28] Classification schemes list genus first, followed by specie such as *Vibrio cholerae*. Genus is capitalized, specie is not.

[29] Vibrios in the Environment, Rita R. Colwell, John Wiley & Sons, New York, 1984.

Symptoms

Cholera is typified by profuse, painless and effortless diarrhea which leads rapidly to severe dehydration. The diarrhea arises in the small intestine. The cholera diarrhea is described as "rice-water stool" owing to its light-grey, watery stool containing minute particles of mucous matter. There is no blood or pus associated with this type of diarrhea. Most sufferers also experience sudden vomiting and muscular cramps usually of the extremities. Severe dehydration is signaled by sunken eyes, dryness of the tongue, mucous membranes, and hoarseness. Additionally, the skin of the hands, face and feet appears drawn and withered, becoming cold and clammy to the touch. The lips assume a bluish hue. These symptoms stem from the action of the cholera toxin on the gut, specifically, the small intestine.

The small intestine[30] appears as a cylindrical column about 280 cm long and 4 cm in diameter. This translates to an apparent surface area of about 3300 cm^2. However, the small intestine is not a smooth-walled organ but rather possesses incredibly complex convolutions lined with finger-like projections called villi. Between the villi are regions of cells called crypts. The villi are in turn lined with microvilli. The net effect of this complex architecture is to provide an organ for absorption with an effective surface area of some 2 million cm^2. This is the same surface area as provided by a rug measuring a little more than 65 ft X 32 ft.

Across this surface area passes about 16 liters (about 4 gallons) of electrolyte solution per day. This transfer of fluid occurs repeatedly in a back and forth fashion that amounts to a flow of 100 liters per day. This volume of fluid flow is over 2 million cm^2 surface area, resulting in what equates to one drop per cm^2 per day, an easily managed rate of fluid flow. An imbalance of any kind such that net fluid flow is into the intestine results in fluid accumulation that greatly exceeds the small intestine's capacity.

The cells lining and comprising the microvilli have a life-time of about one week. As a result, about 250 g (half a pound) of cells are released from the gastrointestinal tract each day. They are replaced continuously. It is this life-time limit that places a limit on the duration of cholera. The toxin bound to the cell is removed through the cell's death and replacement. However, incubating and growing *V. cholerae* continue to release toxin. Absorption occurs in the villous cells and secretion occurs in the crypt cells. The cholera toxin impedes absorption and stimulates secretion, hence the diarrhea.

The tremendous fluid loss through cholera mediated diarrhea requires fluid replenishment. This replenishment can be as much as 60 liters per day. Prior to the discovery of the specific action of *V. cholerae* and oral methods of treatment, fluid replenishment was done exclusively by intravenous addition. In poor, underdeveloped countries with primitive sanitation provisions, the logistics of this treatment easily overburden the similarly primitive transportation and supply networks. Hardest hit by cholera are children and the very old.

Today after diagnosis and early i.v. restoration of fluid loss, oral supplementation of electrolyte fluid is administered along with antibiotics such as tetracycline, chloramphenicol or streptomycin. Tetracycline in sufficient quantities will kill the bacteria. A cholera vaccine is available, but its effectiveness is only about 50% and its protective life-time is about three to six months. When the disease does arise in a vaccinated person, it is every bit as debilitating as in an unvaccinated person. The best preventative against cholera is a pure water supply and a separate and effective sewage

---

[30] The reader is directed to Cholera: The American Scientific Experience, 1947-1980, W.E. van Heyningen and John R. Seal, Westview Press, Boulder, CO, 1983, pp. 215-218 for a concise, and simple discussion of gastrointestinal tract morphology.

removal/treatment system.

EBOLA VIRUS

In July 1976 in Southern Sudan the first recorded case of what became known as Ebola hemorrhagic fever occurred. Of 250 cases, 140 died. In September 1976, the same disease reared its viral head in about 50 villages along the Ebola River in Northern Zaire. The Zairean infection struck 318 people and killed 290. The name of the virus derives from the river and was coined by researchers at the Centers for Disease Control and Prevention known commonly by its acronym CDC. The name hemorrhagic fever is given because a very high fever attends the infection and because the patient hemorrhages profusely near the end. The loss of blood volume from the multitude of bleeding sites, both internal and external, results in a fall in blood pressure, a rapid heart rate initially.

Ebola is one of several causes of hemorrhagic fevers by very different viruses, but the Ebola version is considered, thus far of all viral infections presently known, the more lethal. The Zairean Ebola outbreak killed some 500 people giving the virus a 90% mortality rate. The infection is so rapid in disease development and outcome (death can come in as little as five days) that the outbreak burned itself out due to depletion of victims. It is this rapidity of disease progression that is the Achilles' heal of the virus. In 1979, the viral outbreak struck the Sudan and the same Northern Zairean region yet again. The Sudanese outbreak infected 34 and killed 22. Mode of transmission was declared human-to-human contact.

The disease exhibits its first signs about three to seven days after infection. Typically a headache starts, a throbbing pain located behind the eyes. The pain grows in intensity, with an apparent spreading to the temples and seemingly permeating the head. The eyeballs, or the whites of the eyes assume a bright red color. The face becomes yellowish in pallor, while bright red, pinpoint sized, star-shaped speckles (called petechiae) blotch the surface. As time progresses, the red speckles begin to merge taking on the appearance of nasty looking bruises of a purplish color, a sign of blood under the skin. The surface layer lining of the tongue, back of the throat and the trachea separate and slough off with considerable pain attending such. The skin takes on the black and blue color of someone having lost all his rounds with the heavy weight champ of the world. Muscle tone of the face is lost and the face shows drooping because the tissue is dissolving, becoming gelatinous or liquid and the connective tissue is separating from its bone attachment points. Vomiting is prevalent, and the characteristic color of dead, dying and rotting tissue and oxidized blood gives generates a black colored tarry soup, giving the vomitis the name *vomito negro*. This black material is a sure sign that the virus has amplified itself, it is being replicated in such vast numbers so large as to have commonality only with astronomical numbers. The body, trying to fend off and fight the infection undergoes herculean efforts to seal damaged arteries and veins. Clotting is so rampant that it is clogging the very arteries and veins intended to be shored up by the process. The clots are also a result of the viral proteins generated which exhibit biological similarity to the natural clotting factors of the blood. These clots impede blood flow and lead to a rapid death of organs. The liver is generally the first to go, but kidneys, intestines and stomach are dying rapidly and simultaneously as well.. Intestinal lining is being sloughed off *en mass* and results in liters of blood soaked material draining from the intestines through the anus. This virus also attacks the heart, brain, hands, feet, all regions and sites of the body essentially a massive body-wide stroke. Blood seeps from the nose, around the eye sockets and ears as well, any orifice of the human body to include the vaginal orifice. The liquefaction as it is of the tissues of the body gives the phrase *melt down* a whole new meaning. The patient is in the "bleeding out" phase. All such fluids are highly contaminated and virulently infectious. Throughout the latter stage of the disease, the patient is in considerable, all encompassing and all enveloping pain.

The foregoing is the process called hemorrhagic fever commonly observed in Ebola and in another related filoviral hemorrhagic fever disease called *Marburg* which flared up in Marburg and Frankfurt Germany in 1967 in workers handling infected African Green monkeys. The 25 primary infections resulted in seven deaths, the five secondary infections ended in full recovery.

In 1989 a similar Ebola virus, but one which allegedly infects monkeys only, arose in a group of monkeys housed under import quarantine in Reston, Virginia. The facility's animals were destroyed and the facility itself was thoroughly decontaminated and destroyed under the authority of USAMRIID. Then in April 1995 another Ebola outbreak fell on Zaire yet again. The city of Kikwit with a population of 600,000 suffered about 250 infected though exact deaths are not definitively known. The source or host for the virus is not known. It could be an animal such as bat or monkey, or a rodent, perhaps an arthropod, or even an aquatic creature fished and eaten by people in the endemic regions. Virologists just don't know. The virus appears transmitted by contact with body fluids such as blood, saliva or other excretions. It is not clear if it could ever be airborne, spread by aerosol such as sneezing. There is presently no known cure. Prognosis of infection is discouraging for primary cases, somewhat hopeful for secondary and beyond cases.

Viruses are truly the microbial world's stealth killers. They are the terrorists of the microbial world. They infect other cells and generally kill the host cell. Viruses respect no geographical boundaries, national borders or man-made laws. They have no regard for race, sex, age, religious affiliation and ignore political correctness. If they had a mind, they would be single-minded in their determination to proliferate themselves at the expense of the host. Of all microbes, none are more difficult to detect, treat, and cure, or present the greatest threat to human life than the virus.

HANTA VIRUS

The Ebola hemorrhagic fever is only one of many difficult, lethal and tenacious viral diseases. In Albuquerque, New Mexico an outbreak of another hemorrhagic fever virus occurred. This virus is called the *Hantavirus*, and is believed spread through aerosolic particles of dust in part consisting of deer mouse droppings and urine in which the virus is excreted. The pulmonary form is the more dangerous, exhibiting about a 65% mortality rate. Like Ebola, Hantavirus is a class IV biological agent and can only be cultured in totally isolated environments available at the CDC or USAMRIID.

LASSA VIRUS

In 1969 Nigeria hosted a totally new disease. This disease was called *Lassa* fever and killed about 67% of those who contracted it. The first case reportedly was a missionary who died ten days after becoming ill. Many attending nurses and physicians treating similarly afflicted patients themselves contracted the disease. In an effort to determine the nature and cause of the disease, a patient was flown to New York for observation and study. Shortly after arrival, two Yale researchers working at the arbovirus laboratory became ill. One had not come in contact with any diseased specimens and the fear this disturbing fact generated led to the immediate termination of all study of the disease. In March 1976, another Lassa fever victim landed in Dulles Airport. Some 300 other passengers were exposed and Public Health officials were obliged to track them all down in 17 states.

AGRICULTURAL DISEASES

At about 350 B.C. Aristotle was perhaps the first human to record plant diseases. In biblical times, the Old Testament describes mildews and blights of crops. The Ancient Romans sacrificed red dogs as an offering to the god of wheat in a bid to ward off the red rust that afflicted that crop. Even Shakespeare notes the disease of wheat in his *King Lear*. Though pestilence cursed man's every step through life, it wasn't until Anton von Leeuwenhoek designed and built the first crude microscope that man finally perceived his microbial foe and realized a chance against his age-old and previously invisible nemesis. Ever since, man has relied upon the microscope, either the light microscope or the electron microscope, to see what his naked eye could not. To this day, with all the biochemical and genetic techniques for identifying and classifying the microbiota, the scientist still wants to see his quarry-- a picture taken with the aid of the microscope and evidence of his game's physical existence. Yet today as the world prepares to enter the Twenty First Century, disease of man, livestock and crops still haunts him. All his technology and knowledge enables him to fight only a delaying action at best against disease. The microbes have as their only weapon, adaptability. They use this weapon with unfailing precision and success.

Any number of factors can be cited as necessary for the development of communal societies. Civilization as we know it is certainly made more pleasant and comfortable by such innovations as indoor plumbing, central heating and air conditioning, sewage treatment and because of the latter, replacement of the outhouse with the commode. But population centers, though dependent upon these common, everyday conveniences, are only possible because of the developments and advances in modern, technological agriculture. The biological tie to the land, if not genetic in man, is certainly at least psychological. In western societies millions of people have gardens, either for growing beautiful flowers and foliage to decorate their homes, or to grow supplemental fresh vegetables for their tables. A small vegetable garden does not provide the food to feed a family for a year. Thus the dependence upon farmers is significant, but unconsciously recognized. Estimates place the food reserves of the world at about 200 million metric tons.[31] It is postulated that this reserve would feed the present world population for approximately eight weeks. Surprisingly, it is the rich nations of the world that import food, not the poor. If total failure of a season's crops befell a nation, the result to that nation is

---

[31] A metric ton is 1000 Kg or 2200 lb.

summed up in one word. FAMINE.

The impact famine can have directly on the country it strikes, and indirectly on another country is illustrated by the Great Potato Famine of Ireland in the mid to late 19th century. This particular historical famine led to one of the greatest influxes of immigrants to the U.S. It all centers on the importance of the potato to the Irish. The potato was a diet staple of the Irish and was difficult for the British occupation forces of that time to discover and destroy. Carefoot and Sprott[32] provide the historical perspective of this unique crop and both its geopolitical and dietary importance to the Irish in their struggle with British absentee landlords.

The unique crop properties of the potato were known back as far in time as the Inca civilization. Historical records credit Spanish sailors with the provisioning of their ships with the potato for the return voyages to Spain. Additionally, cultivation of the potato in Europe dates back to about 1570 in Spain, France and Italy. As populations increased throughout Europe and the favored grain crops became spoiled with smuts[33] and rusts[34], a new source of food was actively sought and the potato emerged a suitable substitute. The potato gained favor with plentiful cultivation throughout Europe and harvests were bountiful. Until 1845. The summer of that year was an unqualified disaster for potato crops. A number of factors contributed to the potato famine but by no means insignificant was the weather. Unusual weather for the season and particularly cold rains fell over Ireland. The potato, a reasonably hearty plant, has its limits and it could not endure such conditions. On the heels of potato crop failure came hunger, starvation, disease and death. The cause of the potato crop loss was the fungus *Phytophthora infestans*. The disease is spread by spores that are carried on the wind from plant to plant, field to field, and even across national boundaries as occurred on the European Continent. The reasons for the starvation in Ireland over a single food crop are geopolitical and complex as Carefoot and Sprott narrate. Because of these factors, the potato was the singly most important and abundant staple of the Irish diet at that time. Its failure could only spell doom to an already poor and tired nation. The disease of the Irish potato famine would strike again and again, but it would be 1916 Germany, embroiled in war, that would suffer the consequences of a failed potato crop at a most critical juncture of its history. Some 700,000 Germans would starve to death because of this potato fungus. Not one human being had been infected by it, but hundreds of thousands died because of it. The serious loss of the potato crop of 1916 is believed to be a contributing factor to the eventual defeat of Imperial Germany.

It is the absolute dependence upon technological agriculture that places all nations at risk to the unreasoned actions of an instigator of BW against a target nation's agriculture. The less developed and less technologically adept a nation, the more profound the consequences. With the world's population approaching 6 billion people and increasing by the tens of millions each year, the dependence by many nations on a few to supply additional food stuffs only deepens. A near total loss of the agricultural output in grains and livestock of Canada, the United States and Argentina would have world-wide repercussions. In spite of all our technology, we still fight, at best, a break even battle against plant diseases. Fungus infections of crops alone destroy enough each year to feed about

---

[32] Famine on the Wind: Man's Battle Against Plant Disease, G.L. Carefoot and E.R. Sprott, Rand McNally & Co., 1967, Chapter 4.

[33] Smuts are fungal diseases of plants which characteristically produce a blackened appearance due to the large mass of spores produced by the fungal pathogen.

[34] Rusts are also fungal diseases but derive their name from the characteristic reddish-brown color of the microbe and spores formed. This coloration has the same general appearance as the color of rusting iron.

300,000,000 people per day.[35] Protection of agriculture against natural disease is frustrating enough. Protection of agriculture against deliberate terrorist microbiological attack is of paramount strategic importance to any nation and the most difficult to guard against, particularly as crop lands dwindle with population increases.

With one estimate citing a world population of 50 billion people by the year 2047[36], the need for crop lands will be an emergency issue. The Western and even developing nations are using potential farm lands for cities, shopping centers, airports and parking lots. Superimpose on these pressures, the man-made horror of biological warfare against agriculture to gain an upper hand or victory over an enemy and the outcome is anyone's call. Agricultural BW pathogens will undoubtedly be resistant strains of existing natural pathogens. The selection is a smorgasbord.

The most important cereal crops of world agriculture are wheat[37] (15.3%), rice[38] (13.6%) and corn[39] (12.7%) in this order of abundance and importance. Together they constitute 41.6% by mass of all food production. Potatoes[40], classified as a root and tuber crop, leads the list (12.7%) of these types of food stuffs. Wheat is the major grain crop of the former Soviet Union while in the United States, corn is the major grain crop. In the U.S. most of the corn is used as fodder for livestock, only a small fraction of the total tonnage grown being directly consumed by humans. Rice constitutes the major grain crop of Asian countries such as China, India, and the Southeast Asian countries of Vietnam, Laos, Indonesia, etc. As shown in the table, the importance of these crops to various regions of the world is illuminating.

---

[35] Famine on the Wind: Man's Battle Against Plant Disease, G.L. Carefoot and E.R. Sprott, Rand McNally & Co., 1967. Pages 13-20 provides a concise discussion of population increase and the pressure it places on agriculture.

[36] ibid, p. 14

[37] Triticum aesativum

[38] Oryza sativa

[39] Zea Mays

[40] Solanum tuberosum

Table 3-4: Major Crops of the World			
Region	Millions of Metric Tons		
	Wheat	Rice	Corn
North America	86	9	188
South America	12	15	30
Former USSR	98	3	10
Africa	9	8	27
Asia	130	362	83
Totals	338	397	338
World Total	444	400	392

The types of disease[41] producing microorganisms of plants are as varied as they are for man. They fall into the following groups: bacteria, fungi, mycoplasmas[42], nematodes[43], rickettsia, spiroplasmas[44], viruses and viroids.[45] The multitude of diseases, signs and methods of their spread among some of the more common and important crops of the world, appears in a book by Robert F. Nyvall.[46] In the natural scheme of plant disease, disease is spread by several factors. They are: wind, water, vectors and plant to plant contact.

Winds are probably the single most significant means of plant pathogen spread. Spores, as an example, traveling on the wind can attain altitudes as high as 10 Km and distances of over 1000 Km down range of their origin. Strong winds such as storm fronts can easily carry spores, insects, nematode eggs and bacteria hundreds of kilometers.

Water as rain run-off can carry bacteria, spores and other infected debris along routes of drainage to rivers, streams, ponds and lakes. Fields free of infection can become inoculated by run-off and irrigation waters which are infected. High winds can drive infected rains laden with pathogens to

[41] There are some 50,000 known plant diseases of economically important plants alone.

[42] Mycoplasmas are bacteria-like microorganisms but generally smaller than bacteria, lack the rigid cell wall and variable in shape. Dissemination is by insect from plant to plant.

[43] Nematodes are microscopic, nonsegmented worms, found mostly in soil.

[44] Spiroplasmas are similar to mycoplasmas, but are helical shaped microorganisms. Dissemination is by vector means.

[45] Viroids are virus-like but differ in that they are smaller in mass, consist only of small molecular weight RNA and lack the usual protein coat found in true viruses. Dissemination is by mechanical means such as on tools used to till the soil.

[46] Field Crop Diseases Handbook, Robert F. Nyvall, AVI Publishing Co., Inc., Westport, CT, 1979. This book concisely lists the diseases caused by the previously noted microbes for alfalfa, barley, buckwheat, cotton, crambe, field beans, flax, millet, oats, peanut, rapeseed & mustard, red clover, rice, rye, safflower, sorghum,soybeans, sugar beets, sugarcane, sunflowers, tobacco, wheat, and wild rice.

fields previously free of disease.

Insect vectors play a crucial role in crop disease spread. Aphids can carry viral diseases of potatoes and sugar cane. Flying insects in particular can cover large distances in a day. Honey bees, wasps and flies carry bacteria that cause fire-blight of apples and pears.[47] To make matters worse, some viruses and mycoplasmas only reproduce within the insect vector. The seriousness of insect/vector damage and loss of crops is underscored by the following facts: the white fly infestation that struck California crops in the 1981 and 1991 seasons caused $500 million in damage, the Russian wheat aphid destroyed $600 million of wheat, and the Mediterranean fruit fly destroyed $900 million of crops. In man's feeble effort to stay one step ahead of the pests, agriculture shells out $7 billion on pesticides. That's $7 billion of your grocery bill each year.

Plant to plant contact arises in transplants of cuttings or in the harvest and transport of early-stage infected plants through other fields where debris falls off and settles to the ground.

Plant disease development depends on overall environmental factors. Winds, temperature, moisture, light, nutritional factors, soil and its pH[48] all play a contributory role. All organisms have an optimum temperature range in which they grow and prosper well provided other needs are met. As a result, such diseases as bacterial wilt occur in warm weather while potato late blight arises in cool weather. Even overnight temperatures are key to the pathogen's survival and proliferation.

Moisture is important as the state of humidity can be life giving or life threatening to certain pathogens. Everyday experience in the home illustrates this point. Mold grows in bathrooms along the tub caulking because of the generally cooler temperatures and high humidity normally found in the bathroom. Mold seldom if ever is found growing on the kitchen walls where temperatures are most generally higher and the humidity much lower.

Light conditions also affect pathogen growth. The amount of sunlight (therefore, shortwave ultraviolet light) received by a plant determines not only its own health from the standpoint of photosynthesis of needed materials, but also influences the growth or death of pathogens. Some fungal spores are killed by one hour's exposure to sunlight. Shading and dense foliage crops can restrict the amount of sunlight received overall by the crop plants.

Nutrition encompasses the soil content. Minerals, nitrogen and phosphorus levels are important to plants for the production of strong cellular walls, leaves, stalks, etc. Too high a nitrogen content leads to delayed maturity of the plant but nonetheless, rapid growth. The rich tissue composition provides excellent media for pathogenic microbes which attack immature, rapidly growing plants. Diminished nitrogen content of the soil leads to slower growth, but rapid maturation (aging). The weaker condition of the plant leaves it vulnerable to attack by pathogens attacking slow growing plants.

The soil and its pH are a dual factor. Certain pathogens tolerate less well soil which is rich in organic matter. As organic matter includes acidic and alkaline compounds, the pH of the soil is also affected. Nematodes are an example of a pathogen sensitive to and inhibited in growth and proliferation in organic matter rich soils. The state of porosity of soil contributes to how well it drains after rains or how long it remains water soaked. All pathogens have an optimum temperature and pH range in which they can efficiently metabolize. Some can not tolerate acidic soils while others can not tolerate alkaline soils. Interestingly, crop plants exhibit the same pH sensitivity.

---

[47] *Erwinia amylovora*

[48] pH is the negative of the logarithm of the hydrogen ion concentration (acidity). pH = -log[H$^+$]. A pH below 7 is acidic; above 7, alkaline; at 7, neutral.

DISSEMINATION

The virulence[49] and lethality of a microorganism is of no use if it cannot be delivered to the target. How it is effectively delivered to the target depends upon what the target is and the obstacles placed before the aggressor in making his biological attack. There are three particular targets for biological weapons: military, civilian populations and agricultural targets.

These three targets do overlap but are not one and the same in nature. Though military targets evoke thoughts of soldiers, in fact, military targets can be facilities or materiel. Destruction of fuel depots is a military objective that does not necessarily require the killing of a single soldier, but can immobilize an army, particularly mechanized and armored units. Attacking petroleum refineries can cripple commerce. Attacking civilian populations can be considered a military target in that the civilian population provides the hardware and manpower upon which armies are built. Attacking agricultural targets such as corn fields and cattle ranches can appear an attack on civilian populations, but it is an indirect attack. It likewise is an indirect attack on the military, a military commodity-- the very food that fields the army. The division here into three distinct target groups is for convenience in describing the methods that are used to attack each. In total war, as was the case in WWII, the distinction between a military or a civilian target is a political nicety. For those on the receiving end of the attack, it is an academic distinction. Clearly, terrorists avoid military units and installations as they can shoot back. Civilians generally can't for one reason or another.

Military targets by their very nature in Twentieth Century warfare, with the exception of the trench warfare in France of WWI, are mobile. Military units from squad to corps do not stand clustered in place for very long, most particularly since August 1945 when the nuclear attack on Hiroshima clearly demonstrated the destruction and carnage to which a static target is subject. Military targets must be struck instantly, without warning and with overwhelming force. This has been the rule in conventional warfare. This practice has utilized artillery and, in modern aerial warfare, bombs. With the missile and rocket age in full bloom, these ballistic munitions also provide a massive, lightning quick strike.

The dispersal of military forces, and the concealment and cover they routinely pursue to protect themselves from conventional and even nuclear attack all make the task of an aggressor the more difficult. Hardened fortifications when used are capable of enduring unimaginable punishment from systematic shelling and bombing as was learned by the U.S. Marines in the island hopping campaigns of the Pacific in WWII from Guadalcanal to Okinawa. Since a conventional attack on a defending force requires two or three times the forces by the attacker, how does an inferior military force attack a superiorly numerous and/or well armed defender? This is, of course, the very situation a Third World nation, or for that matter, a terrorist organization, faces if it confronts any of the superpowers' military forces. Clearly, such a confrontation stimulates the inferior forces to seek the weaknesses of the superior forces. For most nations of the world today, conventional arms sales and purchases leave little to want. Less developed nations do not generally have the resources to fund a nuclear weapons program.[50]

---

[49] The toxicity of disease evoking ability of the microorganism for a particular host.

[50] Iraq's and more recently, Iran's, designs for a nuclear program is one exception to this rule, but then, their vast oil holdings and petrodollars provides the resources for such pursuits... if they can find a seller.

Chemical weapons programs are much less costly to pursue but still require competent technical know-how and the raw materials for such formulations, as well as installations for production and packaging. Many of the industrial chemicals required for chemical weapons manufacture are closely monitored by the Western Powers to prevent their use in such production. This has not been absolutely successful. Even beyond the acquisition and formulation of chemical weapons, the packaging and delivery systems required are unto themselves a technical hurtle to overcome. Most Western nations are equipped and their forces trained to deal with a chemical attack on their military forces. Little can be gained in chemical weapons use against a Western military power by an aggressor but to invite reciprocal and more devastating counterattack. Chemical attacks are by their nature obvious and impossible to conceal.

Biological weapons require a higher degree of technical expertise. Their very nature entails much greater risks to the user in just the research and development phase. Additionally, any attempt to use a common pathogen is doomed to failure as the Western nations have vaccines and corrective medical procedures in place for the common variety of diseases. What is required is a pathogen that is genetically different from its common forerunner. This requires considerable knowledge of genetics and bioengineering. It also requires very specialized facilities to conduct the work in an environment that is safe to those doing the work and the host nation as a whole. Again, the specialized equipment and materials will evoke a suspicious eye of Western governments, particularly when such unique equipment is bought in large quantities by nations of established hostility and questionable integrity. But, suppose they have accomplished all these tasks. How do they use the stuff?

Packaging the pathogen can be accomplished in a number of ways. For short ranges, artillery is fine. For longer distances, aerial bomb or even rocket or missile will suffice. An aerosol spray is effective, but requires the user to be close to his intended target, though certainly up wind, and detection is likely. The drawback with biological weapons as noted earlier is that an incubation time is required for the microorganism to begin its disease producing work. Most microorganisms have incubation times of a few days to a few weeks. In a siege like setting, that may not be a problem, but modern warfare does not stand still and sieges are only in the history books. No military force can expect to dig in, remain static and expect to win. Advance, attack, take ground, etc., are the modern tenets. These ideas couldn't have been more graphically demonstrated in recent consciousness than in the Persian Gulf during Operation Desert Storm. Iraq dug in. The Allied forces went on the offensive: attack, advance, take ground, etc. Though military forces and installations would appear likely targets, priority preparation, including expert medical personnel and medications are on the side of the Super and Western nations in countering such attacks. The best targets are not military but civilian, including agricultural centers.

Agricultural targets are easy prey for biological attack. Vast fields of corn, wheat, barley, etc. are usually unattended for long periods of time, deserted overnight and a saboteur can easily lose himself in such fields, unseen as he spreads the crop pathogen. This kind of attack will not risk human life as a rule since plant diseases are not communicable to humans. However, many plant pathogens release toxins, such as ergot, which have profoundly lethal effects on humans when ingested. Any foe with the ability and capacity to wage a biological war against its enemy's agriculture certainly can acquire sample crop plants for research and development of a strain of pathogen devastating to that crop. A simple drive through the rich farm lands of the targeted country and tossing a harmless enough looking litter, laden with crop pathogenic microorganisms is simple, easy and effective enough to do the job.

The drawback to this kind of attack is that time is required for the incubation and spread of the crop disease to all the plants in the field. Though routine examination of the field by the farmer will reveal a problem, it may not be recognized that the disease is "man-made" and the usual treatment methods may not then be effective. Though discovery that the crop disease is not a natural strain may eventually occur, the winds will have spread the multiplying pathogens to other fields. A last ditch effort to destroy the disease by burning the crop field or plowing under may have some limited use. By such time, the "cat is out of the bag." Whether by pathogen destruction by burning or other method, the enemy may still achieve his purpose-- destruction of the host nation's crop(s). In the extreme case of no food crops and little or no reserves from previous seasons, hunger will settle quickly on the host nation's civilian population as what little food is available will be priority dedicated to its military forces, certainly under the conditions of a war, or as is the popular practice since WWII, a police action. Hungry civilian populations find it difficult to support and sustain the nation's military adventures as was amply demonstrated in Japan and Germany toward the end of WWII. In the extreme case, starvation diverts a population's attention from the perceived foreign threat to the domestic competition for food. The domestic competition is the next door neighbor, the family on the other street, or the community in the other town, or next state. What little food is available is not enough to feed all who have need of it. The seed for unparalleled civil unrest, even civil war or rebellion, is planted.

The nature of civilian populations leaves them ripe for biological attack (see Civilian Vulnerabilities above). Specific biological agents such as cholera and anthrax against human targets as well as the specific agricultural diseases directed at such targets as corn, wheat, etc., set the stage for effective use of biological agents against these targets. An enemy force is not required. No armies, navies or air forces need be involved. Point of fact, their presence would have triggered preparatory actions by a confronted nation to the hostile presence. Covert attack is the best means. It is less costly than fielding an army. It arouses no suspicion as does a naval armada. No declared hostility is necessary, and is in fact, counter productive. Slipping one or several dozen agents into a country, either covertly or under diplomatic passport is all the manpower required. The biological agents can be contained in diplomatic pouches, immune to scrutiny certainly by Western governments who are sticklers for diplomatic protocol. Biological agents in vials in whatever form appropriate for the survivability in transport of the particular pathogen can be surreptitiously transferred to fifth columnists who can scatter to the four corners of a country, and most likely, undetected. They can discharge their lethal material into water supplies, crop fields, airports, subways, shopping malls, etc., depending on the biological agent and the target. But the biological agents cannot be the usual, common organisms of disease. They would have to be genetically engineered. They would have to possess a virulence far surpassing any natural pestilence. Those that are intended to be water-borne, must be able to survive water treatment practices of the Western nations. They must be unique: no previous experience with them that led to the development of a vaccine or treatment regimen. An ideal biological agent would have the certain and unpreventable fatality of AIDS, but the rapidity of botulism for it to be militarily or strategically effective. It must overwhelm the targeted nation's social, political, medical and military machinery. It must spread like a wildfire. If the using nation has any intelligence, it will have developed a vaccine along-side the development of the agent to protect itself and, perhaps, use the vaccine as a bargaining chip for protecting itself against political and military reprisals. Such a nation will also have to have exhibited uncanny stealth of purpose and intent to deflect suspicion from itself. These last points, both scientific and political, are far from easy to achieve. Most nations make their animosity toward others obvious. But such an agent under such crafty circumstances would easily be the biological equivalent of Pearl Harbor, providing a likely newer historical date of paramount infamy...

A classic example of the vulnerability of civil populations to attack by either chemical or biological agents was amply demonstrated on 20 March 1995. The people of Tokyo went about their business as any other people around the world. They engaged in commerce, went to work, were shopping, etc. Public transportation, the goal of all governments for the movement of large numbers of people about the city, is the main means of transportation in Tokyo. It also fits the criteria for an excellent target for a chemical or biological attack. On that day, a fanatical religious cult planted separate canisters of the nerve agent Sarin in five different cars of the subway train. Being under ground, the subway complied with one of the requirements for use of a chemical agent: a low lying, enclosed, contained area. The agent released began its lethal work. It killed at least 11 people virtually immediately. It injured some 5500 others. Fast acting chemical agents such as the organophosphates act on people within minutes of exposure. But consider for a moment what the outcome could have been had the cult used canisters of anthrax or some other bioagent. Those 5500 infected people would have spread the agent over the next several days to weeks and the outcome, as bad as it was for a chemical agent, could have been much worse.

The following table offers a small selection of pathogenic microbes that present man no end of trouble.

Table 13-5: **BIOLOGICAL AGENTS**				
Disease	ANTHRAX	CHOLERA	DENGUE FEVER	DIPHTHERIA
Organism Name	*Bacillus anthracis*	*Vibrio cholerae*	*Dengue*	*Corynebacterium diphtheriae*
Host Targeted	humans & other mammals	humans	humans	humans
Type of Microbe	bacterial	bacterial	viral	bacterial
Tissue Targeted	lungs, skin, digestive tract	small intestines		pharynx, systemic
Treatment	vaccines, antibiotics	rehydration therapy		vaccines, antibiotics
Lethality in Humans (untreated)	yes, respiratory form	yes		yes
Method of Exposure	see text	see text		respiratory secretions

Table 13-5: **BIOLOGICAL AGENTS Continued**			
Disease	ERGOTISM	HEPATITUS	INFLUENZA	PLAGUE
Organism Name	*Claviceps purpura*	*Hepatitus A, B*, etc	*Influenza*	*Yersinia pestis (Pasteurella p.)*
Host Targeted	humans	humans	humans	humans
Type of Microbe	fungal	viral	viral	bacterial
Tissue Targeted	nervous tissues	liver	lungs, digestive tract	lymph nodes, blood stream, lungs
Treatment				vaccines, antibiotics
Lethality in Humans (untreated)				yes
Method of Exposure	ingestion			vector bite

Table 13-5: **BIOLOGICAL AGENTS Continued**			
Disease	POTATO BLIGHT	Q FEVER	TRENCH FEVER	TYPHOID FEVER
Organism Name	*Phytophthora infestans*	*Coxiella burnetii*	*Rochalimaea quintana*	*Salmonella typhi*
Host Targeted	potato	humans	humans	humans
Type of Microbe	fungal	bacterial	bacterial	bacterial
Tissue Targeted				
Treatment		antibiotics	antibiotics	antibiotics
Lethality in Humans (untreated)	none			
Method of Exposure	windborne spores			

Table 13-5: **BIOLOGICAL AGENTS Continued**		
Disease	RIFT VALLEY FEVER	SMALL POX
Organism Name	*Bunyavirus Phlebovirus*	*Variola*
Host Targeted	humans	humans
Type of Microbe	Arbovirus	virus
Tissue Targeted	nonspecific hemorrhagic, hepatitis, encephalitis	skin, spleen, lungs
Treatment	supportive therapy	supportive therapy, antibiotics for secondary infections
Lethality in Humans (untreated)	varies	15% to 100%
Method of Exposure	vector	respiratory, infected materials

CHAPTER 14

ANTIBIOTICS, INTERFERON & VACCINES

ANTIBIOTICS

A substance produced by microorganisms (or artificially synthesized) and capable of inhibiting or killing another microorganism. Such substances are themselves often potent toxins and are given in dilute form.

GENERAL

In 1910, Paul Ehrlich, renowned German chemist who was by education a physician, announced to the world the first man-made chemical substance[1] specifically synthesized for the treatment of a disease. The chemical, Salvarsan, was the first synthetic drug, an arcenical, shown effective in the treatment of syphilis. Paul Ehrlich's lifelong dream of applying chemistry to the synthesis and production of drugs as "magic bullets" that seek out and selectively kill the pathogenic microbes that have plagued man for centuries finally emerged as a realistic solution to disease. Salvarsan,[2] however, had its own side effects and particular toxicity to its human subjects and thus fell short of the idealized "magic bullets" envisioned by Ehrlich. But it marked the first step on a long road that has seen the development of a wide range of pharmaceuticals used today.

Modern pharmaceuticals represent thousands of man-hours and multimillion dollar investments in the pursuit of these "magic bullets" envisioned by Ehrlich. Many of the modern drugs are antibiotics or derivatives of antibiotics. What does an antibiotic do? They should first of all, kill bacteria or other microbes for which intended. They should not pose a significant toxic threat to the patient under clinical dosages. An ideal antibiotic is a broad spectrum drug, that is, it is effective against a wide range of bacteria. It should not be allergenic.[3] Large doses should not be harmful to the host. It should be active in whatever body-target medium used, i.e. blood, other body fluids, etc. It should also be water-soluble, stable and permit attainment of high concentrations rapidly and sustainable for long periods.

Unfortunately, the ideal antibiotic is yet to be discovered. Many are too toxic for internal use and are confined to topical application. Others, though used internally, are restricted in dosage and

---

[1] chemotherapeutic

[2] Prior to Salvarsan, mercury salts were used in the treatment of syphilis. Mercury salts are notoriously poisonous to humans and even the small doses applied to the treatment of syphilis left many unpleasant side effects. One of the more offensive side effects though not in itself dangerous to the patient was the development of a very malodorous halitosis.

[3] Causing allergic reactions which can, in some cases, be life threatening.

duration of use due to their long term toxicity or cumulative effects. Still others are allergenic and many people cannot tolerate intravenous contact with them. Few are easily soluble in water and their concentrations in blood, for example, build slowly and are quickly removed, requiring repeated dosages taken regularly. So how do they work with all these restrictions and problems?

Antibiotics fall into five classes based upon their specific modes of action against the microorganisms. They interfere with (1) cell wall synthesis, (2) cell membrane function, (3) protein synthesis, (4) nucleic acid synthesis, and (5) intermediary metabolism of the targeted microbes. It should be emphasized that cell walls and cell membranes of microorganisms are two very different structures of the cellular microbes.

CELL WALL DISRUPTION

One way to kill bacteria is to interfere with cell wall construction. Cell walls of bacteria can be likened to the exoskeleton[4] of insects. Cell walls provide form and support for the bacterial cell mass. The cell wall protects the delicate cell membrane from osmotic and mechanical damage.[5]

Bacterial cell walls are made of a complex chemical called peptidoglycans [I].[6] Peptidoglycans form a polymeric, cross-linked network that in physical form and function acts like a rigid mesh net enclosing the cell. Any chemical that interferes with the bacterium's ability to synthesize the peptidoglycan results in a cell wall structure laden with defects- holes. Such a cell wall does not provide the rigid, confining support required for the cell membrane and the cell's interior fluids. Rupture of the membrane through these holes under the high osmotic pressures from within the cell cytoplasm leads to lysis and cell death.[7]

Antibiotic interference with cell wall production arises only when cells are growing and actively synthesizing new cell wall. Interference with cell wall synthesis can occur at several different places along the biochemical pathways of peptidoglycan construction. Some of the antibiotics found useful in interfering with cell wall biosynthesis are: the penicillins [II], penicillin G (benzyl penicillin) [IIa], ampicillin [IIb], and amoxicillin [IIc]; cephalosporin [III]; and bacitracin [IV]. Any cell lacking a cell wall is immune to the effects of such antibiotics. This includes mycoplasmas and all eukaryotic cells such as yeasts and, of course, human tissue cells.

---

[4] The exoskeleton of insects consists of chitin.

[5] Consider a thin skinned balloon within a strong net. The balloon serves as a model for the cell membrane; the net, the cell wall. If a water source is applied to the balloon to fill it with water, this represents the osmotic pressure exerted against the membrane, a pressure pushing out against the membrane. Such a membrane (balloon) will expand continuously until it is restricted by some enclosure (the net or cell wall), or until the pressure ruptures it. Mechanical damage to the balloon is prevented by the tough net. The cell wall provides an analogous protection to the cell membrane.

[6] Peptidoglycan consists of N-acetylglucosamine and N-acetyl-muramylpentapeptide in a polymeric matrix.

[7] Our earlier example of the net and balloon model for cell wall and membrane illustrates the lysis process if one cuts many of the strands of the net (without cutting the balloon). The constant pressure of the internal water against the balloon causes it to expand against and through the holes of the net until the balloon fabric can not longer support the pressure. It ruptures, spewing the fluid contents about. This is lysis.

CELL MEMBRANE DISRUPTION

The cell membrane serves the role of a biological traffic cop. It controls, by its component composition and structure, the passage of materials across the membrane. Beyond its control of nutrient absorption and waste products excretion, it also plays a role in certain respiratory and biosynthetic processes. Unlike the case with cell wall synthesis where interference arises only during new cell wall production, cell membrane interference can occur at any time in a cell's life and is independent of cell growth. Thus when an antibiotic that inhibits cell membrane function comes into contact with cell membrane, the adverse effects begin immediately. Additionally, cell membrane inhibitors (as such antibiotics are generically known) are less discriminate about which cell membrane they attack. They are an equal opportunity inhibitor in that they will as easily inhibit host cell membranes as well as pathogenic cellular membranes. This results in an innately greater toxicity of the cell membrane antibiotics compared to the cell wall antibiotics. Consequently, few such membrane antibiotics find use in medicine. One such antibiotic that is of value is miconazole [V]. Others are generically known as polymixins, polyenes, azoles and triazoles.

PROTEIN SYNTHESIS INTERFERENCE

Protein synthesis begins with the process of transcription[8] followed by translation.[9] The synthesized mRNA arises from the action of a DNA-dependent RNA polymerase, an enzyme. This process affords three foci for the activity of antibiotics that inhibit protein synthesis during the transcriptional phase. The antibiotics can interfere with (1) the DNA template role or (2) with the RNA polymerase itself. A third opportunity is at the translational step. Either case dooms protein synthesis to failure.

Inhibiting the DNA template step is the mode of action of the antibiotic actinomycin D [VI]. Actinomycin D associates with the DNA in a process called intercalation. Intercalation is the process of a smaller molecular specie inserting itself between two adjacent base pairs of the DNA. This is often described as a sandwich in which the actinomycin D serves the role of a slice of bologna and the two DNA base pairs, the bread slices.

The two pentapeptide moieties of Actinomycin D are aligned on the external surface of the DNA, the so-called minor groove. The RNA polymerase reads the DNA in the minor groove. Since the biological action of actinomycin D is effective on both pathogenic and host cells, it is not used clinically. Its intercalatory action is, however, typical of other similar compounds designed as

---

[8] Transcription is a complex process involving the DNA as a template from which a complementary sequence of RNA is produced. The RNA produced is a continuous strand incorporating in its sequence subcomponents which, when separated by biological hydrolytic enzymes, result in separate and distinct molecules of transfer RNA (tRNA), ribosomal RNA (rRNA) and messenger RNA (mRNA). The mRNA serves as a kind of tape in which is the specific sequence of three nucleotide units (triplet code) each triplet coding for a particular amino acid. The mRNA then codes for as many as hundreds of amino acids in a sequential fashion.

[9] Translation is also a complex process in which a protein is initiated, elongated and terminated, all by the coded information contained in the mRNA. Simply put, protein synthesis involves the translation of a sequential genetic coded information into sequential amino acids comprising the finished polypeptide chain.

intercalators, many of which are utilized as antineoplastic agents in chemotherapy against certain kinds of tumors.

Rifampicin [VII] inhibits protein synthesis by a different mode of action. It binds to the DNA-dependent RNA polymerase, preventing chain initiation. Any RNA synthesis already in progress is not affected. The binding of rifampicin induces a change in shape (conformation) of the enzyme to illicit its inhibitory effects. It is effective on prokaryotic RNA polymerase but ineffective against DNA-directed RNA polymerase of eukaryotic cells. Hence its clinical value.

The mRNA is processed by organelles of the cell called ribosomes.[10] Synthesis of a protein from the coded information of mRNA is called translation-- translating the genetic (nucleic acid sequence) code into amino acid sequences. This process requires ribosomes which consist of subunits designed as 30S and 50S for prokaryotes.[11] The overall process of synthesizing a protein entails three stages-- initiation, elongation and termination. Any antibiotic that interferes with protein synthesis at any one of these stages inhibits such synthesis. However, antibiotics which attack the 70S ribosome of prokaryotic microbes are ineffective in inhibiting protein synthesis of eukaryotes which possess 80S ribosomes.

Streptomycin [VIII] and tetracycline [IX] attack prokaryotic 30S ribosomal subunits. Chloramphenicol [X] and erythromycin [XI] inhibit the function of the 50S ribosomal subunit.

NUCLEIC ACID SYNTHESIS INTERFERENCE

When any cell grows, it is preparing to divide. Such division results in two cells (daughter cells) from the one (parent cell). Among all the cell components and materials that may be doubled in preparation for cell division, doubling of the DNA content is critical as the DNA possesses the genetic information necessary for the new cells formed to function. The production or synthesis of DNA, replication, is a critical point in cell growth and represents a time when significant lethal damage can be done to the cell. This is the role of a third class of antibiotics, those that inhibit DNA synthesis. Though there are several antibiotics that inhibit DNA synthesis and lead to cell death, two are too toxic for clinical use and one is used in urinary tract infections. They are mitomycin C [XII], novobiocin [XIII] and nalidixic acid [XIV].

Mitomycin C is metabolized by the targeted pathogen to an alkylating agent that covalently bonds the two strands of DNA together via the mitomycin C metabolic byproduct. Such DNAs are not capable of further replication as the process stops at the covalent site (called lesion by molecular biologists). Additionally, numerous monoalkylations occur on the individual DNA strands. The attempt by the pathogen's repair systems to remove (called excision) such alkylated DNA segments, results in massive fragmentation of the cell's DNA. Mitomycin C also attacks host DNA as well. Its lack of specificity to only bacterial cells has obviated its use in humans.

Novobiocin, too, interferes with a number of cellular biosynthetic processes including DNA

---

[10] Ribosomes can loosely be likened to the heads of a tape player. The heads decode the magnetic codes of the tape as electrical impulses which are manifested as music. The ribosomes in a complicated process, decode the amino acid codes contained in the sequence of the mRNA, converting that coded information into a sequence of covalently linked amino acid residues resulting in a polypeptide chain, a protein.

[11] These subunits combine to form a complete 70S unit. No, the numbers are not additive as the 30S and 50S subunits reflect a density of each and the 70S unit a density of the combined subunits.

synthesis. It particularly inhibits the stage of DNA production referred to as supercoiling of the finished DNA. Supercoiling is a process in which the DNA is wound into a final packaged form. Like mitomycin C, novobiocin has found no clinical use as yet.

Nalidixic acid finds use as a therapeutic for urinary tract infections. It interferes with DNA synthesis, but at a different stage of that from novobiocin.

Another medicinal, a viricide, ribavirin [XV] is an effective inhibitor of viral-encoded nucleic acid polymerases and is effective against several viruses.

INTERMEDIATE METABOLITE INTERFERENCE

The previous methods cited by which antibiotics inhibit or kill cellular microbes at various biological levels of organization can be likened to military attacks on human constructs. Antibiotics that attack cell wall or membranes are analogous to attacks on installations and fortifications. Breach the battlements. Antibiotic attack of protein synthesis is analogous to attacks against troops-- the fundamental strength and backbone of a military organization. The targets of antibiotic action so far discussed are, in biological terms, tactical targets. But attack against nucleic acid synthesis is an attack against the microbe's command and control centers. It is much like attacking the White House, the Pentagon, SAC[12] and the Congress in one stroke-- strategic attacks. Attacks against nucleic acid synthesis then represent a strategic attack against microbes by antibiotics. Then what is intermediate metabolite interference?

Intermediate metabolite interference on the microbial level is much like attacking ammunition, fuel and food stores, power facilities, etc. of an army. It is a logistical war on an army's supply trains and lines of communications. Interference with intermediate metabolite usage in microbes represents to the cell an analogous logistical attack against its materials for daily support. These capabilities of the microbe are energy production, molecular building blocks synthesis, etc. Though these processes for the purpose of explanation and analogy to armies appear subsidiary in nature, they are far from insignificant to the overall viability of the cell. As an example, all cells have need to carry out what are referred to as one-carbon transfers. These one-carbon transfers are conducted by an intermediate metabolite called tetrahydrofolate (THF).[13] Tetrahydrofolate is synthesized by the enzyme dihydrofolate reductase.

It is apparent that if the means for effectuating one-carbon transfers is inhibited or prevented, any process which must utilize one-carbon units cannot occur. An antibiotic which inhibits THF synthesis at the dihydrofolate reductase enzyme is trimethoprim [XVI], which has a very high preference for the bacterial enzyme. Such medicinals can act as competitors of the normal substrates of the enzyme. By competing for the active site of the enzyme, the bound antimetabolite excludes the binding of the normal substrate.[14] Binding of the antibiotic results in a significant reduction in the concentration of the needed product, here THF. This reduction in the pool of THF results in an intolerable impedance

---

[12] Strategic Air Command, the nuclear armed side of the U.S. Air Force.

[13] Tetrahydrofolate is an essential cofactor in the synthesis of thymidylic acid (TMP) and the purine base moieties adenine and guanine, precursors of DNA synthesis, the synthesis of the amino acid glycine from the amino acid serine and the synthesis of the amino acid methionine.

[14] For this particular case, the normal substrate of dihydrofolate reductase is dihydrofolate.

of one-carbon transfer reactions mediated by the THF. The greatly reduced THF concentration cannot meet the demand required. Bacterial cell growth fails, bacterial cell death follows, the patient recovers.

Another useful tact is to prevent synthesis of folic acid, the precursor of THF. This can be accomplished by using an antibiotic that mimics any one of the precursors of folic acid itself. One precursor of folic acid is the compound p-aminobenzoic acid, PABA [XVII]. Sulfanilamide [XVIII], a sulfonamide drug, is one such antibiotic. The utility in this approach is that the folic acid pool in human tissues does not pass through bacterial cell membranes. Bacteria must synthesize it from its precursors, one of which is the aforementioned PABA. Additionally, humans cannot synthesize folic acid from PABA. Since bacteria do, sulfonamides [XVIII] are effective in inhibiting folic acid synthesis, leading to bacterial cell death.

A final example is flucytosine [XIX] used as an antifungal agent. This medicinal undergoes metabolic processing that results in its incorporation into RNA, or an inhibitor of DNA synthesis. It is not yet clear whether flucytosine activity is due to protein synthesis defects or impaired DNA synthesis.

DRUG RESISTANCE

Animals have an immune system. This system consists of essentially two components-- a cellular component and a biochemical component. The cellular component is typified by the leukocytes or white blood cells. The biochemical component comprises the antibodies or immunoglobulins-- proteins. These two systems serve the animal as its defense against disease or other foreign matter. Antibiotics are foreign matter to microbes and they too exhibit what can be very loosely called a bacterial level development of immunity to certain chemical substances. This is specifically called resistance. That bacteria become resistant (they no longer are killed) to certain antibiotics is typified by the now alphabetic series of penicillins.[15] Each succeeding penicillin derivative was developed as a previous formulation no longer exhibited bacteriocidal action on particular strains of microorganisms.

Resistance to a given antibiotic arises from principally two means. (1) Repeated use of a particular antibiotic on a specific microbe eventually selects what are called new strains of that microbe. These are drug-resistant mutants. Such resistance arises from genetic mutation[16] (independent of antibiotic exposure) in the microbe population. As antibiotic sensitive microbes succumb to the action of the drug, the resistant ones increase in population as they grow and divide, unhampered by the antibiotic to which they are resistant. Over time, susceptible microbe strains perish from the scene; only resistant ones remain alive and thriving. (2) Another means of acquiring resistance to a specific antibiotic is by genetic exchange in which one microbe exchanges[17] a

---

[15] Penicillin BT, G, N, O, P-12, S, V

[16] Mutations are slight changes in the genetic information of an organism and arise spontaneously (though perhaps initiated by environmental factors) as 1 in 10^5 to 10^{10} cell divisions.

[17] In addition to native chromosomal DNA (rarely exchanged), bacteria possess secondary DNA known as plasmids which possess the resistance traits. It is principally plasmid exchange that takes place between microbes.

resistance trait contained in its DNA with another. As many microbes develop multiple resistances,[18] the potential for difficult or impossible-to-treat infections arises. But what is the basis of this resistance? It's biochemical.

Drug resistance in microbes arises from one or more of the following factors: decreased cell permeability to the antibiotic, enzymatic inactivation of the antibiotic, modification of the antibiotic receptor such that the medicinal no longer binds to the site where previously active, or the development of an alternative synthetic pathway which is much less sensitive to the antibiotic. Herein lies the problem with biological weapons developed by genetic and bioengineering techniques.

Culturing a certain pathogen in a medium laden with a potent antibiotic isolates the antibiotic resistant strain. In addition plasmid exchange work can also select a resistant and very virulent strain of the microbe.[19] Plasmids are circular DNA distinct and different from the host genetic DNA. The resistance factors for antibiotics reside in the plasmid DNA. Taking advantage of antigenic factors of a microbe coupled with unnatural pathogenic traits incorporated into the microbe can result in a horrifically pathogenic creature. A simple example of the inherent potential of global disaster is in using a microbe as common as *E. coli*, a common human intestinal bacterium. Imagine the problem facing man if such an organism, alike the normal intestinal *E. coli* in every respect, possessed the added genetic ability of causing anthrax or secreting tetanus or botulinum toxin[20].

INTERFERONS

Interferons is the name given to a particular family of cellular proteins. The property of interest of these proteins is their antiviral actions. Additionally, they have demonstrated effects on cell multiplication, differentiation and even anticellular activity.[21] Interferons are subdivided into three distinct types denoted as α, β, and γ (alpha, beta, and gamma, respectively). Their importance here is as antiviral agents. Interferons arise in detectable quantities only in unhealthy cells. They are species-specific host components.

Interferons are about 145 amino acid units long. The genes coding for them are suppressed in healthy cells. Synthesis of interferons arises through several stimuli: (1) viral infection,[22] (2) heat inactivated viruses, (3) double-stranded RNA.

Interferons interfere with viral multiplication (hence the name). The mechanism of interference appears to be the inhibition of translation of viral mRNA or the degradation of the viral mRNA. The unique nature of interferons is evident in their ability to not affect host cell protein synthesis while

---

[18] As an example, certain strains of *Shigella dysenteriae*, the causative agent of bacillary dysentery, are resistant to chloramphenicol, sulfanilamide, tetracycline and streptomycin. This was observed in Japan in 1957.

[19] It isn't quite as easily done as said.

[20] It is not a simple matter to engineer such a microbe, but techniques are developed each year that put such abilities closer to hand. The wisdom of doing so is another matter for consideration of scientific ethicists.

[21] This ability of interferons has received much attention in recent years as it makes interferons potentially antitumor agents.

[22] RNA viruses appear better at inducing interferon synthesis than DNA viruses.

at the same time interfering with viral protein synthesis.

VACCINES

Vaccines are presently the only effective means of preventing viral mediated disease. There are three kinds of antiviral vaccine methods employed: (1) inactivated virus vaccines, (2) attenuated viral vaccines and (3) subunit vaccines. Viruses may be viewed immunologically of consisting of two components: the infective component (the viral nucleic acid- RNA or DNA) and the antigenic component (the viral proteins).

Inactivated virus vaccines are most difficult to produce as the trigger for immunity in host. Antigenicity[23] of the viral proteins is often subject to destruction by the means used to inactivate the virus' infectivity. However, in such cases where effective inactivation can be accomplished, immunity to a specific viral infection is optimum.

Attenuated active virus vaccines are weakened viruses, sometimes of a different variety. An example of this type of vaccine is the cowpox virus used to immunize against smallpox, a much more serious disease. The usual method of attenuating viruses is by repeated infection of another host animal. Such an approach leads to the selection of a human virus of greatly reduced virulence, but excellent immunogenicity against the normal, virulent human pathogen.

Subunit vaccines employ components of a virus to induce immunity of the host. Usually, viral proteins are extracted and used as the vaccine, the host developing antibodies to the viral protein in use. Contact with the pathogenic virus leads to host production of antibodies against the very proteins the virus produces and against which the host was immunized. The drawback with this method is that the entire virion, including the infectivity factor, viral nucleic acids, is not present in the vaccinating medium and the full range of immunologic protection is absent.

The following table lists several antibiotics and some of their properties.

---

[23] Antigenicity is associated with viral proteins which are subject to chemical, radiation and other means of alteration, denaturation or destruction.

Table 14-1: **ANTIBIOTICS**				
Antibiotic Name	Actinomycin D	Amphotericin B	Bacitracin	Cephalosporin C
Discovery Date of First Isolate	1954	1956	1945	1948
Microbes Most Susceptible	neoplastic cells, gram + bacteria	fungi	bacteria	bacteria: gram ±
Medicinal Action	inhibits RNA synthesis	binds to cell membrane sterols, leads to lysis	inhibits cell wall synthesis	inhibits cell wall synthesis
Molecular Weight	1255.47	924.11	1421	415.45
Antibiotic Group	actinomycins	polyenes	polypeptides	cephalosporins (β-lactams)
Typical Dosage (approximate)		50 mg vials, 3% suspensions		
Original Source	*Streptomyces parvulus*	*Streptomyces nodosus*	*Bacillus subtilis & licheniformis*	*Cephalosporium*
Physical Form	i.v. injection	i.v., lotions, creams, ointments	topical ointments	

Table 14-1: **ANTIBIOTICS Continued**			
Antibiotic Name	Chloramphenicol	Erthythromycin (A, B, C, D, E)	Flucytosine	Miconazole
Discovery Date of First Isolate	1948	1952	1957	1969
Microbes Most Susceptible	bacterial, rickettsial	bacterial	fungi	fingi (*Candida albicans*)
Medicinal Action	inhibits protein synthesis, trans-peptization reaction	inhibits protein synthesis, esp. in streptococal & pneumococcal infections	metabolized to 5-fluorouracil, inhibits DNA/RNA synthesis	inhibits ergosterol synthesis of fungal cell wall
Molecular Weight	323.14	733.92	129.09	416.12
Antibiotic Group	nitrobenzene derivative	macrolide, basic	pyrimidine	imidazole derivative
Typical Dosage (approximate)	50, 100, 250 mg	250 mg	250, 500 mg	10 mg/mL, 2% cream
Original Source	*Streptomyces venezuelae*	*Streptomyces erthyeus*	synthetic	synthetic
Physical Form	1% cream, oral suspensions	capsules, solutions	capsules	ampules, topical ointments

Table 14-1: **ANTIBIOTICS Continued**			
Antibiotic Name	Mitomycin C (A & B)	Nalidixic Acid	Novobiocin
Discovery Date of First Isolate	1958	1962	1955
Microbes Most Susceptible	neoplastic cells	gram (-) bacteria	bacterial
Medicinal Action	inhibits DNA synthesis	inhibits DNA replication	inhibits chromosomal DNA synthesis, DNA gyrase enzyme
Molecular Weight	334	232.23	612.65
Antibiotic Group	mitomycins	naphthopyridines	glycosidic
Typical Dosage (approximate)	10,20, 40 mg vials	250, 500, 1000 mg	
Original Source	*Streptomyces caespitosus & verticillatus*	synthetic	*Streptomyces spheroides, niceus, niveas*
Physical Form	i.v. injections	caplets, suspensions	pale yellow crystals

Table 14-1: **ANTIBIOTICS Continued**				
Antibiotic Name	Amoxicillin	Ampicillin	Carbenicillin	Penicillin G
Discovery Date of First Isolate	1964	1961	1964	1929
Microbes Most Susceptible	bacterial	bacterial	gram (-) bacteria	bacterial
Medicinal Action	inhibits cell wall synthesis	inhibits cell wall synthesis	inhibits cell wall synthesis	inhibits cell wall synthesis
Molecular Weight	365.41	349.42	378.42	356.38
Antibiotic Group	penicillins (β-lactams)	penicillins (β-lactams)	penicillins (β-lactams)	penicillins (β-lactams)
Typical Dosage (approximate)	250, 500 mg 125, 250 mg/ 5 mL	125, 250, 500, 1000 mg	1, 2, 5 g vials 382 mg	125, 250, 500 mg
Original Source	semisynthetic	semisynthetic	semisynthetic	*Penicillium chrysogenum*
Physical Form	capsules suspensions	i.v., i.m., capsules	injection, tablets	injection, tablets

Table 14-1: **ANTIBIOTICS Continued**				
Antibiotic Name	Nafcillin	Oxacillin	Penicillin V	Ribavirin
Discovery Date of First Isolate	1961	1961	1953	1972
Microbes Most Susceptible	bacterial: penicillinase resistant, only staphylococcal infections	bacterial: staphylococcal infections	bacterial	virus (broad-spectrum)
Medicinal Action	inhibits cell wall synthesis	inhibits cell wall synthesis	inhibits cell wall synthesis	
Molecular Weight	436.46	401.44	350.38	244.21
Antibiotic Group	penicillins (β-lactams)	penicillins (β-lactams)	penicillins (β-lactams)	nucleosides
Typical Dosage (approximate)	0.5, 1.0, 2.0 g; 250, 500 mg 250 mg/5 mL	250, 500, 1000, 2000, 4000 mg vials	125, 250, 500 mg; 125, 250 mg/ 5 mL	6 g vials
Original Source	semisynthetic			synthetic
Physical Form	tablets, capsules, suspensions	injection, suspensions	tablets, suspensions	injection, inhalation

Table 14-1: **ANTIBIOTICS Continued**

Antibiotic Name	Rifampin (Rifampicin)	Streptomycin	Sulfanilamide	Tetracycline
Discovery Date of First Isolate	1966	1944	1908	1953
Microbes Most Susceptible	bacterial, esp. tubercular	bacterial, aerobic gram (-) bacilli	bacterial	bacterial (broad-spectrum)
Medicinal Action	inhibits bacterial RNA synthesis		inhibits DNA synthesis	inhibits protein synthesis
Molecular Weight	822.56	581.58	172.21	444.43
Antibiotic Group	macrocyclic naphthalene	aminoglycoside	sulfonamides	tetracyclines
Typical Dosage (approximate)	150, 300 mg; 20 mg/mL	1 g/ 2.5 mL vial 500 mg	4 oz.	250, 500 mg; 125 mg/5 mL
Original Source	*Streptomyces mediterranei*	*Streptomyces griseus*	synthetic	*Streptomyces aureofaciens & viridifaciens*
Physical Form	capsules, syrup	i.v., i.m. injection	tube applicator, suppositories	capsules, suspension, i.v.

Table 14-1: **ANTIBIOTICS Continued**			
Antibiotic Name	Trimethoprim	Amantadine	IDU (5-Iododeoxyuridine)	Methisazone
Discovery Date of First Isolate	1962	1960	1959	1960
Microbes Most Susceptible	bacterial	influenza A_2	herpes simplex	viral
Medicinal Action	dihydroreductase inhibitor	prevents virus penetration of host cell	inhibits pyrimidine nucleotide synthesis	inhibits virus protein synthesis
Molecular Weight	290.32	151.26	354.12	234.29
Antibiotic Group		tricycloalkyl	pyrimidine nucleoside	
Typical Dosage (approximate)	100, 200 mg			
Original Source	synthetic	synthetic	synthetic	synthetic
Physical Form	capsules			

Table 14-1: **ANTIBIOTICS Continued**		
Antibiotic Name	Acyclovir	AraC (1β-D-arabinosylcytosine)
Discovery Date of First Isolate	1974	1959
Microbes Most Susceptible	herpes virus	herpes simplex, antineoplastic
Medicinal Action		inhibits DNA chain propagation during synthesis
Molecular Weight	225.21	243.22
Antibiotic Group	acyclic purine nucleoside	pyrimidine nucleoside
Typical Dosage (approximate)		
Original Source	synthetic	*Streptomyces antibioticus*
Physical Form		

PART V

CHAPTER 15

EMPLOYMENT

We shall have to learn to refrain from doing
things merely because we know how to do them.
-Sir Theodore Fox, 1899-1977[1]

GENERAL

One consideration concerning employment of toxic chemical or biological agents is the target. Is it military or civilian? The effects of toxics on the two is quite different. One study[2] hypothesized that over a million civilian casualties would result from the use of Sarin in a general chemical war against troops in Germany under the prevailing weather conditions. The hazard to civilians would exist for about 40 kilometers downwind. This war game scenario underscores the hazard presented to civilian populations left naked in the face of chemical weapons use particularly by an adept and resourceful terrorist group. The use of biological weapons potentially ups the ante as witnessed by the concern of the Israelis during the Gulf War with Saddam's Scud missiles raining on Tel Aviv.

The dissolution of the Warsaw Pact alliance in late 1990 and indeed the dissolution of the Soviet Union itself throughout 1991, does not automatically eliminate the threat of chemical and biological weapons use against civilian populations anymore than they reduce the threat of nuclear attacks. The mere existence of such weapons leaves a "window of vulnerability" open for even an accidental miscalculation or a deliberate use by terrorist groups coming into possession of such weapons. Even nationally orchestrated aggression or terrorism (is there a difference?) by the likes of Iraq, Iran, Syria or Libya so long as there are Saddam Hussein types in power, is the real danger emerging in the shadow of the death throes of international communism. The bombing of the World Trade Center in NYC certainly illustrates that terrorism is far from dead along with the former USSR.

The proposed Biological Weapons Convention and the Chemical Weapons Convention (see Chapter 25) are attempts to remove the physical existence of such weapons from humans hands altogether at the state and individual levels. There is much heated debate on this point in political circles concerning the attainment of such a goal. But as regards terrorists, and their acquisition and use of such weapons, several incidents with chemical weapons have already occurred. Will laws and

---

[1] In *The Harvest of a Quiet Eye*, p. 58

[2] M. Meselson & J.P. Robinson, "Chemical Warfare and Disarmament", *Scientific American* **242(4)**, 38-47 (1980)

other international agreements really secure security against these devices? Do existing laws prevent the murders that occur? So what can one look for as ripe conditions for chemical or biological attack?

When cultures founded on diverse political or religious grounds go toe to toe with each other, even the concept of MAD backed by impressive nuclear deterrent might does not serve as a deterrent. Non-western socioreligious cultures are not swayed by western concepts of life, liberty and the pursuit of happiness. The road to heaven is a road to be paved in the blood of the enemy of those cultures. As is true of any culture, the bad apples not only draw all the attention, they can cloud the innate goodness of the general group.

For starters, there is a misconception in terminology usage of the nature of chemical and biological weapons depending upon your definitions. Many believe and characterize chemical and biological weapons as weapons of mass destruction. To characterize a weapon as a mass destructive weapon is to mean, literally, that it is capable of total and indiscriminate destruction. Nuclear weapons certainly fall into this category. Chemical and biological weapons really do not. They may kill people and livestock on a wholesale basis but they do not destroy real property. The rendering of land unusable is usually measured in days, weeks or months, not decades or centuries as it is with nuclear weapons. Chemical and biological weapons are weapons only of mass "animicidal" destructiveness. However the term mass destruction is in the literature and we will not depart from that label. The effectiveness of such weapons depends upon the type of weapon, the nature of the target, the weather conditions and the means for its dispersal, and who uses them. Let's look at traditional military doctrine first, then terrorist use, second. There are many rogue nations out there who have chemical and biological weapons technology capabilities. The fact that they have not used them against the US is no guarantee that they won't use them in the future regardless of treaties they sign (see Chapter 25). Many points explicitly mentioned as applicable to military forces also apply with some modification to terrorist groups choosing such weapons. The difference between the two is that military units may be confronted with defense against such agents, while terrorists will be the aggressors utilizing such agents.

Chemical agents (and biological agents) are dispersed as aerosols or in liquid form depending on the type of agent used, the terrain, the environmental conditions under which they are to be used, their volatility, etc. The most rapidly acting agents are intended to be inhaled. Some are potentially lethal (nerve and mustard agents) if contact with skin is achieved and left on the skin for absorption. All agents are in liquid form within the munition (bomb, artillery shell, mine, rocket or missile) and are delivered to the target by means dictated by munition packaging. The chemical agents are generally denser than air, and this is one property of a good agent. The agent is intended to settle to the ground and be dispersed by the air (diffusion). Ideally little or no wind is desired, as high winds will rapidly disperse and dilute the agents thus significantly reducing their effectiveness if not totally eliminating them from the area on which they are deposited. Chemical weapons are thus an area weapon rather than a point weapon such as a bullet or shrapnel (against humans) or an antiarmor round (against a tank or heavily fortified position). Agents such as the nerve agents can be used to cover tens of square miles. All chemical agents can be deposited by explosive burst or by spray and are to be deployed on or just upwind of the target area. Thus any slight wind which is almost always present gently blows the agent throughout or across the target area.

Given their density, chemical agents are most effective against targets which are defensive since the vapors settle to the lowest point-- e.g., a foxhole, trench or bunker, basement, subway, etc. They may also be used on terrain through which enemy forces may advance either to deny use and access to such avenues of approach or, if the enemy does proceed through, to subject the enemy to the dire effects of the agent if they are unprotected. Such terrain denial usage would probably be most advantageous if the agent were a nerve agent with very low volatility which exists as droplets on the ground and vegetation after dispersal; these droplets appear much like dew if disseminated at appropriate hours of the day.

Since all modern recognized military powers have CB warfare capabilities, including defensive/protective means, chemical weapons use is principally a harassment weapon in that its use, and the enemy's recognition of its use, requires the enemy forces immediately to interrupt their activities to take protective measures (don protective mask and suits, etc.). The protective measures include either changing direction (if in the attack) and leaving the area to relocate in a safe location to begin decontamination procedures or (if in the defense) completely decontaminate all equipment and facilities. Until such decontamination is accomplished, the soldiers must remain masked and suited and this reduces their combat effectiveness due to limitations in vision, mobility and hearing while so protected. Successive chemical attacks and decontamination cycles affect morale and combat efficiency and preparedness. It is physically and psychologically draining. It is a major harassment tool when used against military forces, a kind of playing with the enemy's head.

Terrorist use is different. They are not really concerned with denying avenues of approach to anyone. They want to kill. The more the better in their view. The use of chemical or even biological agents against civilians is more than harassment. It is terror itself. Chemical agents give near instant gratification to terrorists, much like detonating a bomb does. Deaths begin within minutes and it becomes news nearly as fast. Chemical weapons would serve strictly a tactical role for terrorists. It has localized effects, creates unbridled confusion among the victims followed by terror as symptoms rapidly progress. Agents used would probably be the more lethal such as the nerve or blood agents. Terrorists are not subtle. In addition to the terror they seek to create, they want razzle dazzle. They want to see their handiwork on the evening news.

However, the more educated, deliberate, thoughtful and sinisterly minded terrorist will seek the use of biological weapons. The use of biologicals will most certainly be a strategic employment. It will be a strategic use because of the nature of the weapon. Time released death. Inhale now, die later. The strategic component here is that you spread the biological to many others. The effects of the weapon are nearly geometrically magnified.

MUNITION PACKAGING

Militarily speaking, the means of packaging CB agents is dictated by the employment. There are three principal methods for dissemination of agent and not all methods are suitable, particularly in the case of biological agents. These methods are: explosive, vaporization and spray.

Explosive dissemination provides the greatest variety in munition packaging, from mine to ballistic missiles and all the intermediate choices. Essentially the agent is packaged around an explosive charge which when detonated by some means, ruptures the munition hull, forcibly ejecting the agent material in aerosol form. It does not provide for uniformity of particle size, however, and thus the larger particles precipitate to the earth, under the influence of the earth's gravitational pull, very quickly and close to the ground zero site of munition detonation. This method is useful for dissemination of the agent as liquid droplets. The explosive charge method achieves a rapid vapor concentration. Such munitions are found packaged as land mines, artillery shells and missiles. These devices do not explode with the ferocity of the standard high explosive (HE) munition of the same type.[3] The explosive is a diminished charge since much of the weight of the warhead is the agent. The explosive sound from such munitions delivery appears muffled to the experienced combat soldier and the thick cloud remaining and lingering over the munition ground zero is a tip-off that a chemical attack may be in progress. Usually simultaneous conventional HE attack is used to conceal the chemical agent munitions use. Chemical shells, etc., do not sound as loud as the regular HE rounds.

The vaporization method relies on heating the agent so it essentially boils off, resulting initially in a vapor which cools and forms minuscule droplets. In this method, the agent can be packaged in the fuel of a munition such as a rocket motor which vaporizes the agent as the fuel propels that munition toward and over the target. Some grenades operate on this principle. This is in fact the basis of the teargas grenade. Clearly the agent must not be biological and it must not burn during the firing of the propellant charge.

Another means of dissemination is the pressure method. In this method an agent reservoir is attached to a pressure nozzle device which ejects the agent in a fine spray of particles of very good size uniformity. Gases such as compressed nitrogen, compressed air or carbon dioxide serve as the propellent in such systems. This method is especially well suited for dissemination of biological agents because it avoids the clear problems of potentially killing the biological agent by the heat generated by the other means discussed.

Other agents such as hydrogen cyanide, a blood agent, when disseminated, form an expanding vapor cloud which is cooling as it expands, causing a cloud of greater density than air. A sense of the cooling effect of an expanding vapor cloud can be felt if one opens a carbonated soda bottle twist cap slowly, paying attention to the temperature of the fingers about the cap as the gas escapes.[4] It is also the basis of air conditioning and refrigeration units.

Terrorists would become very obvious carrying an artillery shell of any kind through an airport let alone a chemical agent shell. To employ enough agent to be effective would require (1) a very toxic agent, (2) a nonexplosive release mechanism and (3) planting it in a well traveled, highly populated area, preferably an area that is noisy to mask any sounds emitted by the release mechanism. A train, subway or subway car will do nicely as was the case in March 1995 in Tokyo Japan where a religious cult released Sarin nerve agent. Noisy and odorous environments only aid in the effective dissemination of such agents for obvious reasons.

TERRAIN

One of the important considerations for any military force is terrain. It is also true for terrorists. Military leaders spend much of their time examining and studying the effects the 'lay of the land' has had on the conduct of a battle throughout history. The experiences of the U.S. Marines during the island hopping campaigns of WWII in the Pacific exemplify this study principle. The ability of Japanese soldiers to hole-up in seemingly inaccessible nooks and crannies on and around hills and mountains led to costly casualties among the marines ferreting out these entrenched Japanese. Learning from the first few such engagements, new tactics were developed and implemented, and

---

[3] Chemical filled munitions on detonation provide about half the shrapnel hazard of the equivalent HE round.

[4] This is a demonstration of the Joule-Thomson effect, a method employed in the liquefaction of many industrially important gases. Some gases cool upon expansion.

even the employment of unconventional weapons such as the flamethrower became essential.[5]

Terrain encompasses much more than just the hill and dale elevations. Vegetation, rivers, lakes, villages, towns and cities are all part and parcel of this subject. Weather is an important corollary to terrain since much of the earth's weather is influenced by terrain: mountains, great lakes, deserts. However, weather will be considered separately.

A chemical or biological agent's use is subject to the advantages that can be taken of terrain. Often, it is a question dependent upon the agent's use as a defensive or offensive weapon and also dependent upon the role played by the forces involved: defensive or offensive. Chemical weapons can clearly serve as powerful offensive weapons, and this was amply demonstrated in the trench warfare of WWI where any seeming ineffectiveness was due more to ignorance and inexperience of the user than a failing on the part of the agent. In that kind of war, fought over essentially flat or very gently rolling countryside, perforated with a complex trench network and heavily fortified with machine gun and mortar emplacements, and with supporting defensive artillery fire, the use of gas was not only very effective, it was, militarily speaking, brilliant. It provided a weapon that did not require direct line-of-sight contact with the enemy but could reach deep into the very defensive holes that made conventional frontal assault on them suicidal.[6]

Rolling hills are a mixed blessing for armored units, as their visibility is seriously degraded. Additionally, such terrain can conceal to attacking forces the laying and deposition of chemical agent along avenues of approach. With no apparent sign of such deposition, approaching forces walk into a trap of silent death. By the time any signs of unconventional weapons use is apparent-- over exposure-- it may well be too late for the hapless unit traversing the area. This is one manner of employment for chemical weapons. Deny the enemy land on which to maneuver.

Open, flat terrain can be vegetated land such as the central plains of the United Sates or the flat to rolling expanses of desert such as the southwestern United States, the Middle East or North Africa. Vegetation low to the ground is ideal as it captures droplets of agents (particularly the denser nerve agents and mustards), retaining them in shaded areas of the growth. The persistent (see below) agents will remain dormant in absence of erosive and weathering effects for some time. As troops travel over and through such contaminated areas, they stir up the agent, vapors of which rise quickly and the exposed troops are subject to the injurious, even lethal effects.

Desert conditions present a different situation. Liquid agents will seep into the underlying strata of the sand. That portion at the surface is exposed to the sun and can be evaporated quickly under the high temperatures experienced in desert climates. Any winds, however slight, will tend to disperse the airborne agent, diluting it and blowing it away. The agent in the underlying layers of sand will remain relatively stable. Any traffic, either foot troops or vehicles, crossing the area will churn the sand, exposing agent which will evaporate and become kicked up into the air adhering to fine sand particles. Again, troops may not recognize the hidden attack until significant exposure and casualties

---

[5] The Island hopping campaigns saw a drastic change in the importance of the battleship. The advent of the aircraft carrier made obsolete the battleship and its huge 16 inch rifled guns in the classical set piece naval battles. With the formidable defenses of Japanese held islands facing U.S. Marines, the dreadnoughts found for themselves more valuable roles to play in naval warfare-- support of amphibious operations. Their heavy calibered guns proved an excellent though not foolproof means of softening up the very defenses the Japanese thought impregnable. As an added benefit, the battleships bristling with all kinds of guns proved unexcelled antiaircraft fire platforms.

[6] Interestingly, the first use of gas warfare by the Germans in WWI created serious disorder among the trench lines of the French and British in addition to the high casualties. The Germans, fortunately for the Allied Forces, didn't realize this breech made in Allied lines.

begin.

Jungle climates would appear to be the least favorable terrain, for the jungle vegetation, particularly the dense canopy, would serve as a filter for agent, retarding its reaching the ground or significantly diluting its military concentration in reaching the ground. Also, the high humidity of the jungle places limitations on the type of chemical agent that can be used. Those agents that are particularly susceptible to hydrolysis would be poor candidates for such terrain environments. However, agent that reaches the ground is shaded from the sun. Winds are slight in such dense vegetative environments and the agent remains present and toxic for much longer periods of time than in open areas.

Arctic conditions frustrate the problem at the other end. In addition to the significant amounts of snow and ice which can destroy hydrolysis sensitive agents, the temperatures can be very close to the freezing points of some agents. Also the regularly high winds thwart effective use. Snow can trap agent and even shell bursts of agent munitions in snow drifts, banks and packs will be swallowed up by the overlying snow pack.

Agent clouds (as they exist) will follow the terrain, passing around hills, buildings, and other obstructions in their path. As they do so, they are broken up and diluted due to the effects of friction that terrain naturally has on cloud systems.

Cities present a multiplicity of problems and benefits. The concrete jungle absorbs heat from the sun, storing it for release into the air at night. Buildings break up wind currents and even create unique patterns among buildings. Such erratic shearing wind patterns are detrimental to effective agent dissemination (chemical or biological). Pavement can absorb some chemical agent as noted by anyone who observes the floor of a service station where motor oil changes are performed. Oil stains the floor. In sunlight some of this chemical agent will be vaporized creating a residual vapor hazard. Generally atmospherics will dictate whether any agent can be used outside in a big city. Locations like Chicago, known as the windy city, would frustrate any meaningful attempt at dosing the city. Calm days are another matter.

WEATHER

Regardless of the means of delivery (artillery shell, bomb, missile, rocket, spray) of the chemical or biological munition, each of these means results essentially in a cloud of agent suspended in the air above the ground. As such, the cloud is subject to weather. Three conditions affect the behavior and dispersal of the agent cloud: wind (turbulence), ground friction with the cloud, and thermal effects (heated ground causing warmed air to rise, cooler air to descend). The initially concentrated cloud begins moving along the air or wind currents present. As it does so, it begins spreading out, not only along the axis of wind travel but laterally as well due to diffusion principles operating on all concentrated substances in either the gaseous or liquid state. Very high winds or erratic winds (constantly shifting in direction) all contribute to the tearing apart of the cloud which translates to the rapid and destructive dilution (rendering it militarily ineffective). A slight breeze of about three to five mph is optimal wind for effective dispersal. Biological agents require different wind conditions. As many biological agents are susceptible to destruction by air and sunlight, higher wind velocities help to disperse such agents quickly, providing greater area coverage in the minimum of time. Winds as high as 30 mph or greater are actually an advantage so long as the site of application is far enough down wind to carry the agent cloud across the target site.

Friction between the ground and air varies with altitude above the ground. Friction is greatest at ground level while virtually zero at altitudes as high as 2500 feet. As a result the speed with which a cloud travels and disperses is height dependent, the cloud layer closest the ground moving the slowest, the topmost layer, moving the fastest. At the same time, realize that agents are by their military nature denser than air; thus the cloud (within constraints of wind effects) is also settling with distance traveled down wind. Therefore, as the cloud travels, its speed of dispersal and the distance it will cover in the presence of wind decreases. This causes the cloud to travel much as an ocean wave breaking upon the shoreline, an internal roiling over itself motion. Additionally, the lay-of-the-land features of the terrain on which agent clouds are dispersed also lead to changing directions of the cloud. Hills, buildings, gullies all affect the progression of agent clouds over the land, creating turbulence that break it up, trap it (depressions) and otherwise dilute or concentrate the presence of agent.

Thermal effects have a solely destructive impact on the agent cloud. As land heats up under warming by the sun, the warmer air rises due to its lesser density compared to air above it. The cooler air will sink to the ground as the warmer air rises. Agent cloud caught in such thermals will be broken up. These effects are most pronounced between sunrise and sunset. As a result, the use of agents during these hours (most particularly biological agents) is much less effective even in the absence of high winds. Employment of agents (again, particularly biological agents) is most advantageous during night hours or an hour or two before sunrise. During these hours winds are usually minimal and, in the case of biological agents, the destructive effects of the sun are absent or lessened. For chemical agents, conditions may also be favorable an hour or so before noon or early evening when atmospheric conditions are more stabilized than during the day. If agents are intended to cover areas in size much greater than tens of square miles, the effects of turbulence and wind shear on the cloud are significantly diminished, or even helpful in spreading the toxic cloud. Cloud size is significantly dependent upon target size as well as the distance from the site of release. A cloud that is a hundred miles across will retain military potency over very long distances down wind as it traverses the terrain.

CONTINENTAL USA WINDS PATTERNS

The data for the winds patterns maps shown herein were provided by Mr. Nelson Robinson, former meteorologist of KATC-TV3 and the president and director of ALERT WEATHER SERVICES, INC. of Lafayette, Louisiana.

The maps are the resolutions of numerous surface/boundary layer micro-wind vectors utilizing data for 1950 through 1990. The resolved patterns are average continental vectors from zero to 1500 feet altitude. There is considerable variation of localized winds across the entire United States. The patterns given are general flow patterns. These general flow patterns represent the overall flow of air masses over and across the continental United States. The broad, half arrow head wind vector plots designate winds of 3 to 15 MPH while the thin, full arrow head vectors designate winds of 15 to 27 MPH. There are four separate maps, each one corresponding to a seasonal period: January-March, April-June, July-September and October-December.

The January-March Map:

The continental wind pattern entering the US from the Washington State/Oregon Pacific and traveling along the eastern edge of the Rockies represents average wind currents that track through the Cheyenne Mountain region of NORAD (North American Air Defense Command) and down along central to east central New Mexico (numerous military installations such as White Sands Missile Test Ranges). This pattern also tracts across northern Texas and Louisiana (Barksdale AFB) up along central Mississippi into the Tennessee valley, across central Kentucky (Ft. Knox, the Armor School) and then across the coal rich West Virginia region and across central Virginia and across to Washington, D.C.

The continental wind pattern entering the USA from western Canada and traveling across the north central plains of Montana to the Dakotas and northern Nebraska bring currents across numerous strategic regions such as ICBM sites and Omaha and Offutt AFB, former SAC (Strategic Air Command) Headquarters. The winds then divert east across the industrial heart of the USA into Illinois, Ohio and western Pennsylvania, up across east central New York, on to northern Massachusetts. A number of military installation lie along this path including Wright Paterson AFB, a major research facility.

The continental wind pattern entering the US along northern California, southern Oregon and tracking down through Nevada, dipping into Mexico and then back across western Texas to central Texas and into the Gulf of Mexico brings such winds across many military installations such as Edwards AFB, Ft. Bliss, and so on. This wind pattern reenters the US from the Gulf just west of New Orleans and travels across southern Mississippi, into northwestern Alabama, along the Tennessee/Georgia border across northern South Carolina and out to the Atlantic.

The continental wind pattern entering from central Canada blow through Minnesota, across central Wisconsin and Michigan and along the Great Lakes region and crossing the northern most of New York into Maine.

Florida is covered by two Gulf Winds patterns that enter to the southern and northern regions of the state, east of its panhandle. A number of military installations are found throughout Florida, and the former Homestead AFB is in the southern most region of the State, a once important continental air defense sentinel outpost monitoring Cuba.

THE OTHER PATTERNS MAPS:

The other continental winds patterns maps for April-June, July-September, and October-December show the alteration of the continental winds as a function of the specific time of year. Though there is a generalized change in overall direction and flow course, the winds still run along routes that bring the air masses over and across regions of either dense population or of strategic importance such as military installations, industrial centers, or rich agricultural regions.

Any attempt to introduce a strategic CB agent to the US must take into account the exact meteorological conditions for the day and time of day during which the agent is to be released. As a practical matter, chemical agents will be dispersed and effectively destroyed by diffusion and dispersal forces of the micro-meteorological winds in a given geographical region. The use of chemical agents would have very limited value for those reasons. Biological agents, however, will enjoy an enhancement of their dispersal though the effectiveness of the agents is also dependent upon actual doses encountered. Generally, the best application is at densely populated regions such as in cities. Agricultural bioagents would benefit from release upwind of a cultivation. In large enough releases or numerous, dispersed releases, an effective saturation could be achieved.

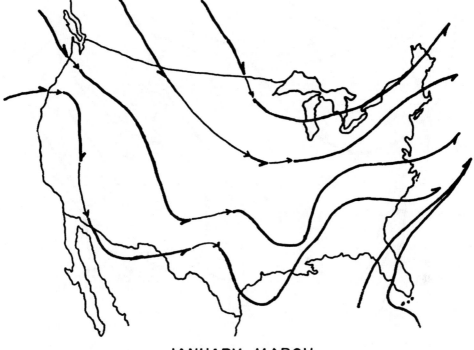

JANUARY - MARCH

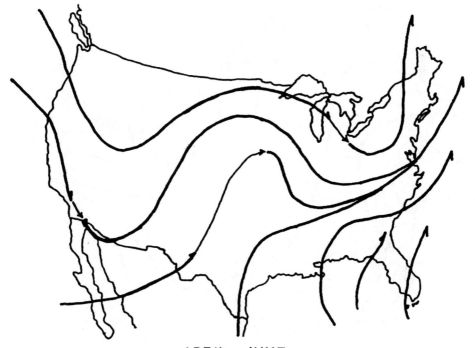

APRIL - JUNE

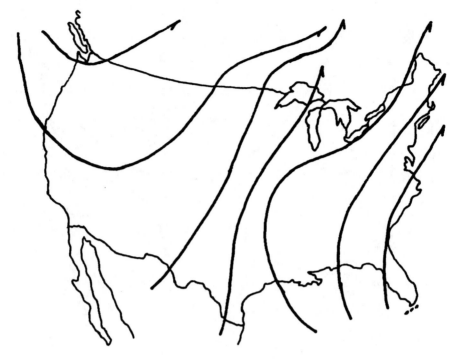

JULY - SEPTEMBER

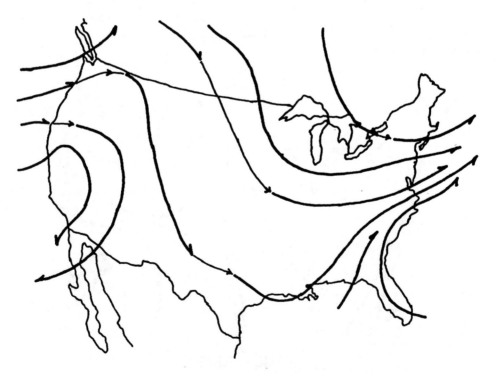

OCTOBER - DECEMBER

Nature of Target

Any man-made structure, habitat or occupied area is a potential target for chemical and biological weapons. The most significant advantage of chemical and biological weapon use over that of conventional HE weapons is that CB weapons do not cause destruction of the materiel aspects of the target, but do kill or incapacitate personnel. The targets can be tactical (platoon, company, battalion, brigade, even division) size forces or strategic (Army groups, civilian centers, rear supply and staging areas such as airfields, depots, industrial centers, capital city, etc.) They can be used to deny enemy forces access to specific areas of land such as avenues of approach utilized by attacking maneuver elements and can serve as significant tools for terror and harassment of both military and civilian targets.[7]

Persistence

Persistence is a term often used to describe chemical agent staying power. It concerns the very character of an agent in terms of its stability to environmental destruction and retention of the dispersed form as a vapor or liquid. Generally agents that exist solely as a vapor or aerosol when released are termed nonpersistent since these physical forms are easily removed from the target site by winds. Examples are hydrogen cyanide and cyanogen chloride (blood agents) or phosgene (a choking agent). Agents which are liquid in physical state for their action are termed persistent since they remain liquid longer, evaporate slow enough to maintain a hazardous concentration in the area of application and generally are intended as liquid for their use. Examples are mustards and the less volatile liquid nerve agents.

Agent Selection

The choice of agent used is dependent upon factors of terrain, weather and persistence for the application (target) in mind. It depends upon whether the target is a defensive or offensive (attacking) target.

Defensive targets, i.e. dug-in troops in well fortified positions, are not going anywhere and so present no urgency as regards inflicting casualties within any particular time frame. Employment of chemical (and to a lesser extent, biological) agents, which are fast acting, is not an immediate issue. Slower acting agents, those with little or no odor, considerable persistence, stability to the environmental conditions in existence at the target site as well as the extent of coverage required and the cost of such agents essentially preselect the type best used. The state of readiness of defending forces against chemical attack also offers a premium consideration. Mustards are particularly well suited for use against defending troops, as was amply demonstrated in the trench warfare of WWI.

---

[7] This was in fact the principle outcome for the conventionally armed Scud missile attacks on Tel Aviv and Riyadh though Iraqi President Saddam Hussein's purpose was to entice Israel to attack him in hopes of shattering the Allied alliance in Operation Desert Storm.

Attention must also be given to the possession of the target site after the attack. If the forces employing chemical agent attack intend to take and occupy the positions currently held by the defenders, then persistent agents such as mustards or rapidly toxic agents such as nerve may not be used because of the decontamination measures that must be implemented before friendly forces can occupy the site. Choking agents may be of use in that regard as they are much less persistent than nerve or mustard; they are destroyed by water and humidity at the target site and quickly vacate the site. Any preparedness the defending forces have only complicates the choice of agent.

Attacking troops present an urgent requirement. If not stopped, they can overrun a position and win the battle. If conventional means do not appear effective or expensive conventional weapons systems are to be conserved, chemical agent (not biological) provides an effective defensive weapon used against offensive troops. In this case the time urgency of effect dictates an agent that acts rapidly and is very lethal. Nerve and blood agents fill this requirement. These agents are designed for and generally effective only if inhaled; since advancing troops are generally winded, breathing heavily from exertion, they will inhale such agents quickly and deeply into their lungs. Recognition of agent use can be masked by conventional artillery use on them while some rounds are chemical in nature. Any detection of such agents by the targeted force requires them to stop temporarily, to don protective gear. They cannot easily return fire while doing so, making them momentarily easier targets for defending forces' direct fire.

CHAPTER 16

DETECTION

You don't know, my dear boy, with what
little reason the world is governed.
-Axel Gustafsson [Count] Oxenstierna
1583-1654[1]

GENERAL

Given man's aggressive nature, he will use whatever weapon he can lay his hands on against his adversary. If the word will suffice, fine. If not, force, even lethal force is his resort. Given that many chemical and all biological agents are odorless and colorless, a means for detecting them is essential. To this end, technology has provided many different ways to determine the presence of such agents. Excluding the unfortunate case of an individual succumbing to an exposure as a first warning of such contact, there are two principal means available. The first is simple chemical detector kits employing chemical indicators that offer a color change when exposed to particular agents. The second and more sophisticated is the electronic detection instrumentation.

INSTRUMENTATION

The U.S. Armed Forces have sophisticated electronic instrumentation capable of chemical agent detection and identification (as to class of agent). In conjunction with military assessments and alerts provided to subordinate commands and units, these instruments would be placed within units on the front lines. Chemical personnel monitor these instruments and provide the earliest possible warning of chemical agent use and presence prior to and/or during a battle engagement. Older instruments are given to the national guard and reserve units essentially for peacetime training purposes. Newer instruments are retained by the regular U.S. Army.

One such older instrument is the M8 Chemical Agent Alarm. This alarm consists of the M43 Detector Unit and the M42 Alarm Unit. The alarm system uses the M229 consumable supplies, allowing continuous operation for 15 days. The M229 kit includes 30 solution reservoirs, two cell-sensitivity check bottles and 60 air filter packages. The unit is run for about 12 hours before battery replacement is advisable. The M8 Alarm provides warning of vapor or aerosol presence of nerve, blood and choking agents.

An interesting nerve agent detection instrument is a British unit that employs butyryl thiocholine substrate which continuously flows over an immobilized cholinesterase enzyme. Sampled air passing

---

[1] In The Harvest of a Quiet Eye, p. 115

over the system inhibits the enzyme, resulting in a change in the voltage across the electrochemical cell, triggering an alarm.[2] Future U.S. Army detection will be high technology based. A prototype mass spectrometer is under testing for use in the detection of chemical and biological agents. Use of antibody technology will find application in biochemical reaction detectors.

The M1 Chemical Agent Monitor (CAM) is the latest hand-held device about the size of a geiger counter. This unit can detect chemical agent contamination on both personnel and equipment. Microprocessor technology is used in this device to detect molecular ions generated as a result of sampling of the air. This unit is intended for use in detection of nerve and blister agents.

The XM21[3] Remote Sensing Chemical Agent Alarm (RSCAAL) is an automatic scanning, passive infrared (IR) sensor. This device detects nerve and blister agent vapor clouds by changes they produce [in absorption/reflectance] by remote objects or the sky. A tripod mounted system, it scans a 60° horizontal arc in less than one minute. The alarm consists of an IR energy sensor detector, a microcomputer, visual and auditory alarms. Deployed for operation, it can monitor automatically for at least twelve hours. The XM21 will be issued to each NBC Recon Platoon. It can be mounted to the NBC Recon System XM93E1 Fox for stationary contamination reconnaissance during brief halts.

The XM22 Automatic Chemical Agent Alarm (ACADA) employs ion mobility spectroscopy (IMS) technology to detect and identify all nerve and blister agents by type and concentration (low, medium, high). The detection can be accomplished locally or by transmission to a battlefield information network (MICAD). The XM22 consists of the XM88 Chemical Agent Detector, a battery box, and the M42 Alarm. Additionally, the system employs an XM279 Surface Sampler, XM278 Maintenance Kit, a Collective Protection Equipment (CPE) adapter, XM28 power supply for use with generators. It is mountable to vehicles.

The XM22 ACADA will replace or complement the M8 series alarms. It is intended primarily as a point detection, area warning device. It can be used on the move as well as in stationary mode within Collective Protection Equipment.

The Chemical Agent Detector Network (CADNET) provides automatic, remote alert of chemical detector alarms on a real time basis. The system receives alarm warnings over existing command and control radio frequency nets, utilizing the Miniaturized Intrusion Detection System (MIDS) transmitters and receivers.

CADNET consists of two major components, the XM23 and the XM24. The XM23 consists of the MIDS transmitter and an interface between the detector and the transmitter. The XM24 consists of the MIDS receiver and an interface to an attached radio.

MICAD, Multipurpose Integrated Chemical Agent Detector, is a microprocessor capable of processing signals from chemical agent detectors to initiate collective protection systems. The system is capable of providing continuous [real time] information on the concentrations of chemical agent vapors inside and outside of collective protection systems as well as compromises of collective protection system integrity.

For detection of CB contamination over vast areas, the experimental XM93E1 Nuclear, Biological, Chemical Reconnaissance System (NBCRS) is under cooperative study by both the U.S. Army and Germany. Appearing as a slightly flattened armored personnel carrier (APC) with six wheels rather than two tracks, this vehicle is intended to range over the area of operations of a couple battalions, detecting and marking locations of contamination. Such prelocated contaminated areas can

---

[2] M. Meselson & J. P. Robinson, "Chemical Warfare & Disarmament", *Scientific American* **242**(4), 38-47 (1980)

[3] The "X" designation prefixing military model numbers means that the item is in the experimental/development stage.

then be bypassed by friendly military forces.

ODOR/SYMPTOMS

There is a saying in the military: stay alert, stay alive. This couldn't be more true concerning chemical agents. Though most chemical agents offer some kind of odor, a few do not. But even in these cases as in those that do, they all offer some indication of their action on the individual early on in the exposure prior to achieving lethal, body absorbed concentrations.

Nerve agents do not generally have an odor, but the nature of their action is an important clue to their presence and one's exposure to them. The eyes are basically an extension of the brain, a piece of the brain exposed to the environment. They are the first organs affected and they offer the first signs of nerve agent presence. The pupillary constriction, twitching, and excessive salivation are the early signs of initial exposure and if heeded by the affected individual further serious effects can be prevented by prompt corrective action at the time as well as medical evacuation (medevac) to a military field hospital. If nerve agent is suspected or known, administration of the atropine antidote injector should alleviate symptoms.

Blood agent such as cyanide will not affect the pupils as does nerve agent, though difficulty in breathing is common to it as in nerve agent. Significantly, early signs of blood agent poisoning are headache, vertigo, nausea and vomiting, all of which arise due to the oxygen deficiency the agent causes. It also tends to cause increased deeper breathing leading to further inhalation of more agent.

Choking agents are slower acting initially and due to the nature of their action few known antidotes exist or can be devised. However, odor is an important key to their recognition though not a foolproof means of detection. If shortly after a chemical attack and after troops have donned protective equipment, soldiers experience irritation of the eyes, nose and throat accompanied by constriction in the chest, chances are they have been exposed to a choking agent. Medical evacuation may be called for by the unit medic or corpsman.

Blistering agents, generally the slowest acting of all chemical agents, are much less immediate in action on the exposed soldier. However, irritation of the eyes and eyelids, reddening of exposed skin, and itching are signs of such exposure.

The bottom line to alertness and detection of chemical agent attack or exposure is awareness of the environment around you, particularly its odors. On the battlefield one expects to smell the products of war and combat: gunpowder, cordite, diesel, the coppery odor of blood, burned and decaying flesh, etc. What one does not expect to smell is hay, flowers, fruit, cut grass, etc. These are unnatural odors on a battlefield and should elicit the immediate donning of the protective mask and the alert signal to others in the area.[4]

---

[4] The signals for chemical/biological agent attack follow the donning of the protective mask. One yells "GAS" and at the same time extends both arms out horizontally from the shoulders, palms up, bends the arms at the elbows, touching the extended fingers to the shoulder. This is done several times.

CHEMICAL INDICATORS

Prior to the electronic age, the only way to detect toxic agents were by odor (a very hazardous practice as some have no odor) or by on-the-spot chemical paper indicators. These chemical indicator methods employed various dyes which were specific for mustards. Even crayons which were impregnated with dyes could register the presence of mustard and Lewisite on surfaces. Many of these early, post-WWI, pre-WWII, chemical indicators were developed by the British.

Other kits, as they were designated, were dyes packaged in tubes containing silica gel. A small hand pump was used to draw air samples and expose the tube contents to the air samples taken. These kits were able to detect the presence of mustards, phosgene and cyanogen chloride.[5]

The M9 Chemical Agent Detector Paper provides evidence of the presence of liquid agents only. It does not identify the type of agent. This item is carried by the soldier in his mask carrier for use as needed. This detector paper can be used under all climatic conditions. It is designed to affix by sticking to clothing, vehicles and other equipment and thus readily indicates liquid agent exposure.

The M256 Chemical Agent Detector Kit provides prepackaged, finger crushable ampules for spot tests of suspected vapors of nerve, blister and blood agents. The kit includes three instruction cards, 12 individually packaged sampler/detectors and a booklet of M8 Detector paper. The M256 kit is provided per fire team (4 to 5 men) or squad (11 to 12 men).

The M8 Detector paper is a specific agent detector paper. It detects and indicates by specific color changes, blister or H agents (pink), V nerve agents (green) and G nerve agents (gold). One kit per protective mask carrier is issued.

MISCELLANEOUS

In the early pre-electronic instrument days of mining, miners would frequently take canaries with them into the depths of the mine they were working. The reason for this practice was that canaries were sensitive to many of the poisonous but odorless gases that may be uncovered during the drilling, blasting and excavation of ores sought. The method depended upon the canary dying first as a warning to the men that a toxic gas was uncovered, giving them time to evacuate the shaft presumably in time and without harm.

In gas warfare, animals have been used in the testing of such agents and even on the front lines as a means for detection and early warning of an agent passing through on the winds. This practice has some practicality though it is significantly dependent upon the sacrificial animal's greater susceptibility to the agent(s) for which it is used.[6] Additionally, animals, just like man, have a threshold level of agent required in the air for them to respond symptomatically. This level may in all

---

[5] This agent is classified as a blood agent, but can be a product of decontamination of the nerve agent Tabun (dimethylaminoethoxycyanophosphine oxide). Cyanogen chloride may not be suitable as a war gas as it is very irritating on contact with the eyes and other mucous and moisture laden tissues, thus giving an immediate warning of its presence.

[6] In the U.S. involvement of Operation Desert Storm in the Persian Gulf, some Arabic Allies of the U.S. used animals as an early warning measure. This approach must be utilized cautiously and is dependent upon animals of greater sensitivity than man.

probability by too high and risk human injury. The advent of electronic chemical detection has replaced the practice of animal detectors and has improved the time for advanced warning of combat concentrations by the instruments' greater sensitivity to much lower concentrations. Other detection means even discriminate between different classes of toxic agents.

Though the sacrificial animal detector method suffers from numerous flaws in effective early warning, it is better than nothing. If such a means is the only means of detection of toxic agents, then maximum warning can be approached by positioning the animal well up wind, some distance from the main body of troops. Close monitoring of the animal's behavior by alert and reliable observers, perhaps from some distance themselves with binoculars, may be the best and only warning of a chemical hazard carried down wind if a threat condition exists.

CHAPTER 17

PROTECTION

Till now man has been up against Nature;
from now on he will be up against his own
nature.
                    -Dennis Gabor, 1900-1979[1]

WARNING

The first measure of protection against chemical agents is warning. To this end, the vast resources of modern military and civilian intelligence agencies constantly seek information concerning the enemy's plans. Today's armed forces have the benefit of reconnaissance satellites[2] in addition to the traditional spies within enemy ranks or lines, aircraft reconnaissance[3] overflights of enemy forces and individual unit patrols seeking prisoners for interrogation.

Additionally, the training of soldiers emphasizes the signs of chemical attack and the kinds of auditory and visual signals to give exclusively for chemical attack. Soldiers are trained to immediately mask up at the first sign or suspicion that a chemical attack is in progress and then immediately give the signals themselves. In conjunction with any early warning of chemical attack, the donning of the protective mask will provide the best possible protection that the foot soldier has against airborne chemical agent attack. The protective mask is also effective against airborne biological agents. Even in a nuclear environment, the protective mask is effective in filtering out radioactive dust from entering the lungs. Of course, the filter elements must be changed ASAP and even the mask requires thorough cleaning and decontamination afterwards. The types of masks issued to troops for protection against chemical and biological agent attack are correctly called *protective masks* as distinguished from *gas masks*. There is a significant difference, a difference as markedly distinct as the difference between day and night. Either ignoring or not knowing the technical difference between the two types of masks, many people, both civilian and military, will refer to a protective mask as a gas mask. Part of the reason for this stems from WWI experience when the chemical agent weapons were referred to as *gas attacks*, and the masks issued were logically called gas masks. The concept of *aerosols* was not as well understood then as it is now. Before discussing the protective mask and its

---

[1] In The Harvest of a Quiet Eye, p. 61

[2] The imaging KH-9 Bigbird (1971) and the newer KH-11 Keyhole (1976), and radar satellites such as the Lacrosse, Whitecloud, and the RORSAT satellites.

[3] RF-101 Voodoo (low altitude), the Lockheed U-2 and the Lockheed SR-71 Blackbird, the fastest (MACH 4) and highest flying (over 80,000 ft). Recently, versions of the F4 Phantom and the F-111 have seen use in low altitude, aerial photo reconnaissance.

chemimechanical filtering ability, let us first establish clearly in our minds what the difference is between a gas and an aerosol. It does make a big difference.

AEROSOL VS. GAS

As terrestrial animals, humans are air breathers. We breath gas. That gas is the atmosphere about us and consists of several kinds of gas, the most common being nitrogen (78.08%) and the most important to us, oxygen (20.95%), and others such as argon (0.93%), carbon dioxide (0.033%) all values referring to percent by volume. There are trace amounts of many other gases such as various oxides of nitrogen, ammonia, various sulfur oxides, hydrogen sulfide and so. Most dictionaries of chemistry or physics will define a gas something as 'a fluid state of matter in which the matter concerned occupies the entire volume of its container regardless of the quantity of gas present and is easily compressible'.

A gas is a collection of independently existing molecules with very little forces of attraction between them. The key word here is molecules. Molecules are the as small as you go without breaking it down into its constituent atoms. The size of molecules varies with the type of molecule, that is oxygen or nitrogen molecules are smaller than carbon dioxide molecules because there are only two atoms of oxygen or nitrogen in a molecule of each, while carbon dioxide consists of three atoms, one of carbon and two of oxygen. The LPG, liquid propane gas, is made of three carbons and eight hydrogens. It is larger than carbon dioxide. In terms of dimensions, gases are less than 10Å (3.9×10^{-8} inches). DNA is about 20Å in diameter.

Aerosols are generally defined as 'an aggregate of solid or liquid particles suspended in a gas phase or medium'. The pump hair spray bottle with its small valve on top disperses a spray of contents in a mist. That mist is an aerosol. Fog is an aerosol of water and dust particles suspended in the air. Aerosols are particles measuring between 10Å to 100μm (3.9×10^{-3} inches). The latter dimension is the size of airborne dust or fog particles. For the sake of comparison, if we compare the upper most size of a gas, something less than 10Å to a fog or dust particle of about 100μm we see that aerosol particles are about 100,000 larger. A green pea is about 0.25 inches in diameter. If a gas molecule were the size of a pea, a fog aerosol particle would be 25,000 inches in diameter. Put another way, a gas molecule compares to a larger end aerosol particle as a pea compares to almost 7 football fields put end to end.

Another important point about aerosols is that they are collections of solid or liquid molecules held together by weak forces. They are denser than air molecules and so will settle to the ground with time if not broken up by shearing forces of air currents buffeting them about. The larger and thus denser the aerosol particle the heavier and the quicker it settles to the ground by the force of gravity acting on it. Gas molecules do not respond to gravity anywhere as easily. If you spray a bottled or can preparation such as hair spray and watch the particles in the air, you will see them slowly fall to the floor. Gases do not do that. Inhalants prescribed by physicians for those with respiratory or allergic problems are aerosols.

With the particle sizes in mind, gas masks filter out certain gas molecules. Protective masks do not filter out gases, they filter out aerosolic particles, species about 10,000 to 25,000 times larger than gas molecules. Now let's examine how protective masks work.

PROTECTIVE MASKS

Primary personal protection is the protective mask (erroneously called a gas mask). The protective mask consists of a chemical resistant rubber type body which fits over the face sealing about the forehead, down either side of the face in front of the ears and under the chin. The mask is fitted with shatter resistant lenses for vision and a filter element of some type. More modern masks also provide a vibrating diaphragm element for voice communication and in some even a specially fitted tube for attachment to a canteen in a chemically contaminated environment.

Filter elements once consisted of activated charcoal[4] and soda lime layered in a crisscrossed fiber matrix screening to filter out both aerosol chemical agent, dust and other particulate matter (as for example, biological agents). The arrangement of activated charcoal and fiber filter material is such that the fiber filter traps particulate matter and aerosol components. The activated charcoal adsorbs any finer vapor that is not trapped by the filter material. The activated charcoal component adsorbs large quantities of the chemical agent vapor. The filter elements typically are further treated with other substances such as copper,[5] silver[6] or chromium.[7] The soda lime[8] component (once used) destroyed any toxic material released from the earlier activated charcoal component. The filter elements can exist as a canister that screws into place on either side of the mask or in front. These methods of mounting the filter element can interfere with the combat soldier's ability to hold and fire his rifle. The post WWII U.S. Army and Marine protective masks have two oblong discoid filter elements which fit within cheek pouches (one per side) accessible on the inside of the mask, thus providing the U.S. military forces with an ambidextrous mask for right or left handed weapon use. The canister elements are somewhat easier to change. The mask provides total protection of the wearer's eyes and lungs when properly worn.

---

[4] Activated charcoal or carbon is made by heating animal bones or certain types of vegetable charcoal to high temperatures (800° to 900°C) in a stream of steam or carbon dioxide. This treatment leads to a very high porosity, a very high surface area. The surface area can be as high as 2000 m^2/g. The grade of activated carbon presently used in U.S. Military protective masks is 900 - 1000 m^2/g.

[5] Copper complexes react with hydrogen chloride and chlorine which would otherwise pass through the filter element.

[6] Silver complexes oxidize phosphine (PH_3) and arsine (AsH_3) which also may pass through the charcoal filter element.

[7] Chromium complexes react with the cyanide type agents such as hydrogen cyanide and cyanogen chloride which have low adsorptive properties on activated carbon alone.

[8] Soda lime is no longer a component. It was used because it was effective in removing phosgene and hydrogen cyanide that could eventually penetrate the activated charcoal used in the filter elements between WWI and WWII. Now 100% impregnated activated charcoal is used. The impregnants can be silver, copper and chromium compounds though the latter is being phased out because of its toxicity on fine carbon dust particles inhaled and its carcinogenicity.

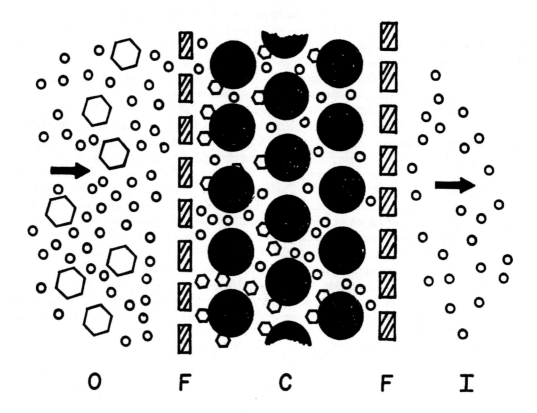

FIGURE 17 The mechanical filtering action of the chemical agent protective mask. The region marked "O" is the outside air with air gases (small open circles) and chemical agent (large hexagons). The region marked "F" is the filter fiber mesh network schematically illustrating the spaces in the mesh network for gas and aerosol passage. "C" is the region of the activated charcoal adsorbent. The inside of the mask where a person's face is, is represented by the region designated as "I". Finer particles of chemical agent aerosol impact with the charcoal particles in a collision process that results in the agent's adsorption onto the charcoal surfaces.

Figure 17-1 is a schematic blowup of the essential components and arrangement of those components in the filter element. The region marked "O" is the outside air in which small open circles represent the air molecules, principally of interest, oxygen. The large hexagons represent the aerosol particles of a chemical agent as dispersed in a chemical attack. The regions marked "F" are the filter fiber mesh network (hatched vertical rectangles). This component is intended to filter out dust and other macroscopic particles (not shown). The spaces between the filter fiber mesh network represent the microscopic spaces within the mesh network through which air passes. As the soldier, wearing the mask, inhales, air is drawn in which also contains chemical agent. Coarser aerosol particles of agent upon contact with the filter fiber mesh network are broken up into smaller particles by the force of the mechanical action of inhalation. These finer particles (the smaller hexagons) enter the filter element region containing the activated charcoal particles (large solid black circles) located in region "C". The charcoal particles allow the air gases to pass through. The finer chemical agent aerosol particles, however, collide with the charcoal particles, thus becoming adsorbed onto the activated charcoal particle with which they collided. The extent of adsorption is represented by the small hexagons attached to or partially imbedded in the large black circles of the activated charcoal. As the soldier continues to breathe through the mask, the air gases proceed through the filter element and emerge into the interior of the mask where the soldier's face is, represented here by the region designated as "I". Notice that on the outside the air gases are more numerous, while on the inside, the representation shows the concentration of air gases reduced. This is a pictorial representation of the difficulty to breath through such a filtering system indicating the slightly reduced air intake compared to the unmasked ease of breathing. Removal of toxics by the filter element is not 100%. A very small amount does get through, but is so small in concentration as to be inconsequential.

The filtering of toxic vapors or of biological agents is but one critical (albeit very critical) requirement of a protective mask. It must not pose significant resistance to breathing. The activated charcoal filter component particles cannot be too fine (increases resistance to breathing) or too coarse (failure to filter at all). The mask must function properly under all weather and temperature ranges from arctic to tropical to desert. It must prevent water from rain entering the mask filter elements and clogging the fine porosity leading to increased resistance of and labored breathing. The lenses must not fog, particularly in cold climates, and to this end, protective masks generally are designed to afford air flow on inhalation across the lenses to remove and prevent condensation.[9] Additionally, exhaled air from the lungs, heavily laden with moisture, must not be directed toward and over the lenses to cause fogging. The mask must fit tightly and snug about the face to provide total seal when properly worn.[10]

Several different protective masks exist in the military inventory, each specific for a different mode of combat use by the soldier. The older protective mask types are the M17/M17A1/M17A2 Chemical & Biological Protective Mask, the M25/M25A1 Tanker's Chemical & Biological protective Mask, and the M24 Aircraft Crewmember's Chemical & Biological Protective Mask. They all are termed tactical masks and are designed specifically to protect the wearer's face, eyes, and respiratory tract against CB agents in field concentrations.

The M17 series mask consists of the rubber face piece and head harness, carrier, waterproof bag, a pair of eyelens outserts and two replaceable M13A2 filter elements (color coded green- toxic agents). The filter elements of the M17 series masks are located within the cheek pouches on the inside of the mask and can only be replaced in a safe, uncontaminated area. One set of green M13A1 filters is to be installed and two sets held on reserve, sealed in the factory packaging. The M17A1 and M17A2 permit drinking water in a contaminated environment using the M1 canteen cap. Additionally, the M17A1 is fitted with a resuscitation tube assembly located within the mask at the back of the voicemitter outlet valve.

The M25/M25A1 Tanker's Protective Mask couples to a gas particulate filtering unit (GPFU) via a hose. This unit filters outside air drawn through the GPFU and the unit services all crewmembers.

---

[9] This is much in principle like the defroster of automobile windshields.

[10] Beard growth will frustrate mask seal and therefore shaving regularly is critical in a potential gas warfare environment.

When crewmembers leave the vehicle, they must disconnect from the GPFU system and attach the hose of the mask to the M10A1 canister. The M25/M25A1 masks consist of a face piece, hose assembly, carrier, canister and antifog kit.

The M24 Aircraft Crewmember's Protective Mask provides detoxification and filtering of air to the user. A CB mask oxygen adapter can be coupled to the mask canister when high altitude flight is undertaken requiring oxygen. Two sealed replacement canisters per M24/M25 series masks are required on hand.

The newest mask in the inventory is the M40/42 series Protective Mask. The M40 is for use by the foot soldier and the M42 is for armored vehicle crewmembers. The M40 employs a canister filter element located on the external cheek surface of the mask face. The new mask offers improved protection, significantly better voice communications and vision and has greatly improved compatibility with optical instruments such as the night vision devices used by ground troops for night fighting.

The M43 Protective Mask is the latest replacement for use by aircraft crewmembers. The mask is completely integrated with the aircraft communications system, compatible with optical instruments and provides filtered, blown air for the user.

Civilian chemical masks are very similar in design and function to the military masks. Filter elements come in several different types dependent upon the type of chemical material to be filtered. Some are designed for filtering organic vapors such as paint and other solvent fumes while others are designed to filter inorganic chemical gases such as ammonia, sulfur dioxide, hydrogen chloride, hydrogen sulfide or various nitrogen oxides (true gas masks). Some civilian masks are complete in that they cover the entire face while others are half masks, covering only the respiratory orifices. The later type of masks requires a separate eye goggle protection. Such civilian chemical masks, like their military counterparts, are not intended, designed or safe for use in high chemical vapor concentrations and definitely not when oxygen concentrations fall below about 19%. Such toxic vapor conditions require oxygen source systems that isolate the user's respiratory system completely from the outside contaminated air.

PROTECTIVE CLOTHING-- PERMEABLE

In addition to the mask, some agents require protective clothing. This is particularly true of nerve and blistering agents which are also effective on exposed skin of the arms, neck, and legs. The uniform (fatigues or the more modern term battle dress uniform, BDU) of the field soldier can provide some protection but not for long if it is not specially treated. Specially treated uniforms are termed permeable protective clothing and have been treated with chemicals which retard penetration by and interact with and destroy those agents which can act on or through the skin. They are permeable since they do allow for some air flow and excess body heat and moisture radiation. They are effective in this regard since chemical agents as dispersed on the battlefield are not true gases like air, but rather aerosols or fine particulate vapors which become lodged in the clothing fiber and then chemically react with the protective treatment substances.

A newer permeable clothing is available which is water-repellent. It is a double layered suit of which the inner layer has a bonded activated charcoal layer. It permits 'breathing' for air flow and heat and perspiration exchange.

NONPERMEABLE

The utmost in clothing protection is the nonpermeable protective suits so named since they are impenetrable by even air. These suits consist of a double layer of rubber like material between which is a thin layer of charcoal. These suits, though providing excellent protection, place a limitation on their continued wear over long periods of time since they do not afford a means for body heat and moisture buildup to escape. This disadvantage is of paramount importance in tropical or desert environments where temperatures and/or humidity can climb to high levels. The risk in their prolonged use in such a contaminated environment is heat exhaustion and in the extreme, heat stroke, both in themselves medical emergencies.

MISCELLANEOUS

Gloves, boots and hoods covering the hands, feet, head and neck are available with either permeable or nonpermeable protective clothing. Also made of rubberized materials, these gear provide obvious protection. The gloves can reduce manual dexterity and the hoods can reduce one's ability to hear. However, they are absolutely necessary for handling chemical agents or in dealing with massive chemical attack with very lethal (nerve) or vesicant (blistering) agents under prolonged contact.

Other clothing generally in the possession of the soldier is also useful as protection against agent contact. The raincoat and even the military poncho are ideal coverings to use in event of spray dissemination of agents, particularly mustards or the denser droplet nerve agents. These garments can be draped over the soldier and provide a barrier between him and the liquid droplets. After the attack has passed, discarding of the contaminated garment is an option or cleaning it as per decontamination procedures.

The shelter halves, half of a two man tent, that soldiers may also have is an excellent covering. Any materials such as blankets, canvas, even paper or cardboard that can cover the soldier completely can be used and will establish a barrier shield under which the soldier is protected from direct contact with agent droplets.

Protection for the soldier on the modern, Twenty-First Century battlefield must address a wide range of threats. In addition to small arms (ballistic) and CBW threats, technological weapons advances expose the foot soldier to other hazards not faced by his grandfathers. These hazards include lasers. The U.S. Army is developing and fielding a whole body, integrated protective suit called the Soldier Integrated Protective Ensemble or SIPE. This suit has the outward appearance of the protective flight suits worn by the astronauts. The limited description available suggests the suit consists of a helmet and visor intended to protect the soldier's head, face and eyes against ballistic and laser threats while providing respiratory, visual and audio abilities. The visor is compatible with optical night vision devices. The suit is self contained in its ability to control internal temperature and humidity. Future plans call for a global positioning system enabling the soldier to determine and know his/her exact location. A computer system planned for incorporation into the suit will provide the ability to transmit and receive images and information to and from external sources. The suit, helmet, boots and gloves are made of the latest materials affording protection not only against CBW hazards, but also against flame and laser threats. If ever fielded, one can only imagine what the cost per suit will be.

Finally, ointments, cremes and absorbent pads are provided along with the protective mask and stored in the mask carrier. These items are useful in blotting up and neutralizing such agents as blistering and nerve. The absorbent pads are used to blot up the droplets[11] on the skin and the ointments and cremes then applied. These methods are particularly effective in use against mustard agents which are the slowest acting agents. Skin contact with nerve agents is a less effective means of causing casualties than through inhalation. But in the case of nerve agent exposure, the soldier also has an atropine injector (antidote) which he can self-administer at the first signs of nerve agent toxicity.

Water flushing of exposed areas of the skin is the minimum method of removing droplet agent. Even better is the use of soaps and detergents which are ideal solvents for emulsifying these agents and flushing them off the skin. Some agents are also subject to hydrolysis on contact with water as well.

MAINTENANCE

A word about maintenance is in order. Like any equipment in either civilian or military life, things break down, repairs are required, even replacement. Equipment like the protective mask in particular and the nonpermeable protective clothing, hoods, gloves and boots all demand attention to what is called serviceability. Clearly any cracks in the rubberized surfaces render the item unserviceable. But many potentially lethal defects are not apparent by simple topical examination of the gear. One area of critical importance is the valve units which allow air to be drawn in and exhaled in the proper direction of air flow through the filters and mask body. These valves are small circular pieces of rubberlike material. They fit snugly over the openings they close and are rather delicate compared to the heavier rubberized material of the mask body. They are subject to compromise by excessive manhandling and beyond that, can become ill-fitted by the growth of mold (in tropical climates), excessive freezing condensation (in arctic climates) and sand grit (in desert climates). Just as the soldier is drilled ad nauseam about care and cleanliness of his rifle, in environments where a protective mask is required, he must also be very meticulous in his attention to the care and cleanliness of his protective mask. It must be checked daily in such environments where foreign debris can prevent a valve from closing properly and thus allow deadly chemical agent vapors to enter through the wrong valve opening. Straps used for tightening must be checked as well for signs of minuscule tears from sand as should the lenses for cracks or sand blast effects which will decrease his vision more than just from the innate mask field of vision limitations. Such defects also can be leak points. The filter elements should be checked for sand deposits (in desert environments), mold (in tropical environments), and signs of freezing (in arctic environments). Any damage to the filter's pore integrity can either impede breathing through it (difficult enough when in excellent condition) or fail to trap and filter chemical agent vapors completely (problems potentially likely in tropical or arctic environments). Any hose systems used with a protective mask must also be checked for signs of cracking, wear of the hose body, etc.

Lifetime or shelf-life of the toxic agent filter elements depends upon the environmental conditions. Once the filter elements have been removed from their factory sealed package they must

---

[11] Don't smear the droplets across the skin as this tends to rub them into the pores. Rather, dab or blot the droplets, followed by ointment or creme application with rubbing in of these preparations on and about the area initially in contact with the suspect droplets.

be replaced every two months in tropical climates (such as Central, South America). In temperate climates (such as Europe, USA) they are good for 12 months. In Arctic climates, their shelf-life is 24 months.

VEHICLES

Most military vehicles are not airtight conveyances. Some however, by their very nature are or can easily be made air tight. Pilots of fighter and bomber aircraft have oxygen masks to provide oxygen for high altitude use. These personnel are not likely to encounter chemical agents while on missions given the unique employment properties of such agents exclusively at ground level and the aircraft's rapid approach and egress from their targets even in ground support rolls. The rapid flow of air of the slipstream across the airframe removes completely any telltale agents encountered in a close support ground operation. Their systems are useful while on the ground during takeoff and landings. Once on the ground, the pilots, too, must be provided protection as applies to the ground personnel.

Tanks and armored personnel carriers (APCs) provide obvious protection to a wide range of munitions though certainly, specialized antitank munitions can destroy the tanks and APCs. Chemical and biological munitions do not cause materiel damage, but rather personnel injury. Though these munitions will not harm the tank or APC, they can seep into the interior of a tank or APC and attack the respiratory system of the crew members. Many U.S. armored vehicles are either equipped or are becoming equipped with CBW air filtration systems. These capabilities are especially common on tracked vehicles previously expected and designed to fight a war in Europe with the former Soviet and Warsaw Pact military forces. These systems draw outside air through similar filtering media as found on individual protective masks; however, they maintain an over pressure within the vehicle thus preventing outside air from leaking in.

INSTALLATIONS & FORTIFICATIONS

The protection of installations and fortifications where troops and other military personnel are massed presents special problems. Areas located well back from the front lines of combat are not necessarily safe from any kind of attack, let alone chemical and biological attack in this day and age of ballistic and cruise missiles. Command and Control centers and headquarters are strategically important and lucrative targets. The vulnerability of military installations such as supply and storage depots, command and control centers, harbors, airfields, etc. is expected by such personnel because of their clear military importance to the war effort. Additionally, major military facilities such as the MASH[12] units (field surgical hospitals) and even naval hospital ships are also likely targets. All western nations regard such medical facilities as inviolate to attack. Unfortunately, not all past, present and future enemies of the western world have felt or will feel the same way. But the vulnerability of medical facilities is troublesome from the standpoint of western ethical principles as well as from the psychological impact on the essentially helpless wounded confined to the MASH and

---

[12] Mobile Army Surgical Hospital

unable to take defensive actions for themselves. Western nation's wounded have always regarded themselves out of the war (at least until recovered) and such facilities as off limits as a military target. Attacks on such facilities imparts an added continuum of the horror and terror experienced on the front lines and chemical and biological attack further raises the psychological terror ante imposed upon the wounded as well as their medical saviors who must then fight the threat posed by attack in addition to the fight to save lives.

Military installations are seldom established concrete and brick structures though advantage of these in an area is certainly made. The most difficult facility to establish and maintain is perhaps the field medical hospital or MASH. These consist exclusively of tents in which are established the traditional components of the concrete and brick civilian hospitals: surgery, X-ray, intensive care, pharmaceutical and other wards. They must maintain absolute cleanliness and sterility in spite of the filthy, germ ridden countryside around them and the deplorable hygiene of the wounded brought to them for treatment, most of whom are on an emergency basis. The combination of this conventional warfare environment with superimposed chemical and biological warfare hazards clearly requires some procedure and facility capable of dealing with contaminated casualties.

Tents are in the U.S. Military inventory which provide for air tight isolation from the outside environment. These tents are equipped with air conditioning units against the heat and humidity of the summer months and heating against the damp and cold of winter. Additionally, these portable facilities are equipped with filter units on air pressure lines which filter gases and aerosols in incredible quantities of air drawn in, and expel internal air through one-way valve exhaust systems. A positive, over pressure within is maintained to prevent outside air from leaking in. Entrances are double sealed, providing an air lock system between the outside and the controlled inside environments. Areas are set aside for initial determination of a wounded patient's contamination with a chemical agent. Provisions are made to decontaminate the wounded prior to entry into the sealed MASH facility providing first a preliminary whole body cleaning of the wounded, thus minimizing further injury from agents as well as protecting the medical personnel inside, awaiting the wounded's delivery to their expert care. All water and food storage systems are protected and kept sealed. Washing of materials brought from the outside with decontaminant methods and closed system water sources are all available to the field MASH unit for CBW operating conditions. Similar enclosure systems are also available to nonmedical field installations such as headquarters, command and control centers, etc.

Modular Collective Protection Equipment (MCPE) is a group of equipment consisting of gas particulate filter units (CPFU), protective entrances (PE) and several installation kits. This system is designed to provide positive pressure protection for a variety of military vans and shelters.

Chemically and Biologically Protected Shelters (CBPS) systems are used with specially designed tents to provide 72 hours continuous operation. These systems are mobile, expandable and self-contained. The CBPS consists of the XM1097 HMMWV[13], SICPS hard shelter, a 300 square feet soft shelter and mobility trailer.

The Collective Protection Equipment (CPE), NBC, Simplified, M20 consists of four components: a gas particulate filter unit; a protective entrance or airlock; a support kit composed of a motor blower assembly, room sealing materials and miscellaneous supplies; and a liner kit containing three vapor impermeable disposable room liners of 200 square feet each.

Civilians even without a mask, if under a chemical attack can take certain measures to minimize exposure. This is also true if one lives close to or down wind of a chemical plant where an explosion has occurred. Wearing rubberized rain coats buttoned up completely with similar hats, plastic bags

---

[13] High Mobility Multipurpose Wheeled Vehicle (pronounced "hum-vee").

draped over the head, wearing gloves, even cloth, will minimize direct skin contact with any chemical aerosol droplets falling on you. In evacuating in a car, keep the windows rolled up tightly and close the air inlet vents. For infants, place them in the common carriers with handles, and drape a light blanket over the entire carrier for the time they are out in the contaminated air. Breathing slowly and minimally, minimizes the amount of any contaminated air inhaled. Placing damp washcoths over the nose and mouth will help filter aerosolic particles. In an airborne chemical emergency, dampening a cloth with baking soda may afford added filtering protection. Anything that you can wear or put between you and the agent cloud, or air will help a little. It is that little bit of less exposure that will make the difference. Above all else, do not panic. In any emergency situation, my personal view is that panic can kill.

BIOLOGICALS

Biological agents are not neutralized or destroyed by the protective mask, but they are filtered. Thus the mask is an excellent and a first line of protection against inhalation exposure to them. Clothing serves well in protection as a barrier between skin and the agent. However, clothing is no substitute to unbroken skin which is the best protection from injury (infection) by biological agents. This last point may be too optimistic a hope on the battlefield where abrasions from running and jumping for cover, falls, etc. or injuries from small arms fire and shrapnel wounds violate skin's protective integrity. However, immunization against various disease organisms is another means of preventative protection for the combat soldier against biological agents. This mean's only flaw is that a vaccine must exist for the agent and have been administered by medical personnel prior to commitment of the soldier to the combat zone. It is not at all likely, in this day and age of looming biotechnology, that common pathogenic agents will be used. The emphasis on chemical and medical personnel to acquire agent samples, identify them, and then develop a vaccine is a time consuming process requiring months if not years; time an exposed military force does not have. The search for in-the-mean-time treatment, such as an antibiotic spectrum, is in itself a time consuming process which takes place by experimenting until identification is made. Undoubtedly, fatalities will be incurred during this hit-and-miss phase. Bacterial, fungal and rickettsial agents will be more easily fought on the medical battlefield than viruses. The unique biological nature of viruses makes them the most difficult to identify and treat since the methods of identification are technology intensive (facilities not available to the field combat medical services) and also antiviral medications are difficult to devise. Most antiviral substances are too toxic to administer orally and even topical, skin application, invites more harm to the skin than effectiveness against viral contamination.

Present Army research promises vaccines for hepatitis A, shigella and malaria. As Desert Shield became Desert Storm, the U.S. Army accelerated research and development to field centoxin, a monoclonal antibody medication for gram negative bacterial septicemia and endotoxic shock. These problems are indeed the most serious consequences of invasive wounds. Additionally, an antiviral therapeutic called Ribavirin was fielded for the treatment of hemorrhagic fever. In the development stages are a botulinal toxoid, an anthrax vaccine and a nonspecific immune enhancing drug.

PART VI

CHAPTER 18

TREATMENT

Primum non nocere
(Above all, do no harm)
-guiding principle of the physician

GENERAL- FIRST AID

The discussions that follow concern the methods available for treatment of chemical and biological agent exposure. There is no intent or attempt in this work to present these methods and treatments on what may be considered a rigorous medical foundation. The exact nature of a treatment is determined by qualified medical personnel attending to a specific toxic agent exposure, the casualty's own peculiar response to the agent, any known allergies to medications, and supporting chemical antidote or antibiotic regimens available.

First aid treatment of chemical agent victims is not simply common sense. It is only common sense if one understands the biochemical effects and the medical reasons behind such immediate actions. Such knowledge and understanding is hardly common. Immediate, general first aid treatment of chemical exposed individuals include:

1. Evacuate the person to an uncontaminated area, ideally to the open air if originally indoors.
2. Remove contaminated clothing as soon as possible. Cover patient (loosely) with blankets or other coverings to conserve body heat, guard against shock.
3. Wash any agent contaminated skin with soap and water. Summon medical assistance (ambulance if civilian; medics, corpsmen if military). Prepare patient for transportation to a medical facility.
4. The victim must be kept still, in a resting position, either lying down or partly so, but comfortably, inclined. Do not allow the patient to move around or talk needlessly. Reassure patient. A person under the effects of chemical poisoning will be quite anxious and fearful. Epinephrine (formerly called adrenalin) is flowing. The person's heart rate and blood pressure will, in the beginning stages, be increased. This only exacerbates the spread of the poison. Reassurance is intended to calm the patient. If he believes he will be OK, that he is in good hands, much of his anxiety will be diminished. Psychologically, this is very helpful until expert medical help takes over. If breathing is difficult and oxygen equipment is available, administer oxygen.
5. If phosphorus burns are the injury, cover the affected area with water. A soaked cloth may be helpful for areas too large to immerse in water. Immersion of hands, feet, and lower arms is best.

Toxic Chemical Agents

Nerve Agents

For nerve agents, administration of an antidote available in several types is the first course of action. For a chemical attack with nerve agent, the individual soldier's atropine injector carried within his mask carrier is his earliest treatment. The atropine injector is a magic marker sized device that is spring loaded. The soldier strikes its head against his thigh (intramuscular administration) with a force of two to eight pounds. The needle is thrust into the muscle, autoinjecting the antidote. The use of atropine counteracts the build up of neurotransmitter (acetylcholine), though it is limited in its effects. However, atropine is itself a poisonous substance.[1] The field soldier is cautioned not to take more than three such injector treatments himself. Each autoinjector consists of 2 mg of atropine [I] sulfate and 600 mg of 2-PAM[2,3] chloride [II] or iodide.[4] Case histories indicate that as much as 12 mg can be administered within two hours. His training alerts him to the fact that when he has had enough, he will experience a dry mouth, flushed face and widely dilated pupils.[5] The atropine is absorbed slower in the presence of 2-PAM and this shortcoming is under research resolution.

Another chemical formulation known as TAB[6] is available as well for intravenous injection for more serious cases.[7] The recommended normal dose is 1 g i.v., slowly. This treatment can be performed twice in 24 hours. These oxime preparations work by removing the nerve agent from the enzyme[8]. The combination of the two is most effective in reversing the effects of the nerve agent, though the sooner applied, the better. Clearly the stronger an enzyme inactivator the nerve agent is, the more difficult to effect a breakdown of the nerve agent-enzyme complex[9]. In cases where exposure is advanced and life threatening, the most significant threat and cause of death in untreated

---

[1] Atropine was at one time a commonly used cockroach poison.

[2] Pyridine-2-aldoxime methylchloride.

[3] Pralidoxime chloride

[4] Another version is pralidoxime methosulfate (P2S).

[5] Medically known as atropinization.

[6] TAB: **T**rimedoxime [III], **A**tropine, **B**enactyzine [IV]. Benactyzine is similar in effects as the atropine.

[7] PAM and other oximes are not effective as an antidote for carbamate poisoning as they appear to enhance the toxicity of such anticholinergic substances.

[8] With the atropine/PAM treatment, the body is able to return to normal neuromuscular states over time during which the excess neurotransmitter, acetylcholine, is destroyed by the restored levels of active enzyme (acetylcholinesterase) accomplished by the PAM treatment.

[9] The term complex is used by biochemists and aptly describes the physicochemical combination of a substrate (compound normally acted upon by the enzyme) or inhibitor (substance that retards enzyme activity for its substrate) with the enzyme.

victims is asphyxia (lack of oxygen) due specifically from paralysis of the lung muscles and diaphragm.

FIGURE 18-1 *Protective Gear*: A mannequin dressed out in protective mask, impermeable overgarment, rubberized gloves and hood with rubberized boots. Note that the hood covers over the shoulders. Straps are provided for tying under the armpits. Also, the trousers seal around and below the top of the rubberized over-boots. [Courtesy Dixie Surplus, Lafayette, LA]

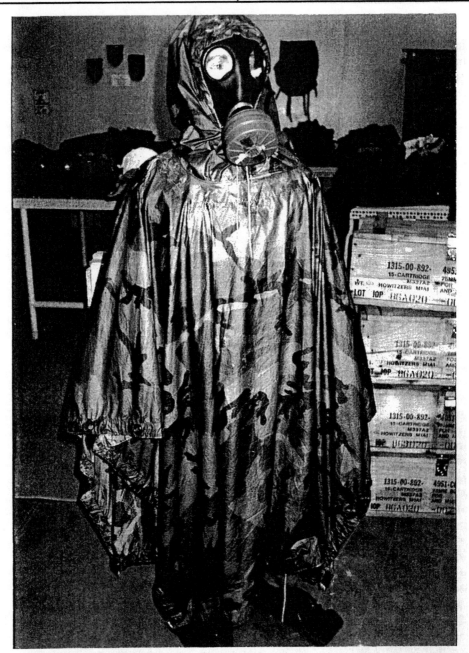

FIGURE 18-2 An alternate overgarment protection method used in absence of regular issue protective overgarments. The rain gear or poncho which is rubberized, can be worn over the battle dress uniform (BDU). Though not as effective as the rubberized impermeable overgarment, the poncho provides protection against direct contact with droplets of toxic agent falling from the air. The poncho can be decontaminated for reuse or discarded, dependent upon tactical circumstances and the availability of decontamination materials and a suitable decontamination site. [Courtesy Dixie Surplus, Lafayette, LA]

FIGURE 18-3 Close-up of one type of protective mask with chin-type filter element. Notice that the hood is worn over the mask and sealed tight around the mask with draw-strings in the hood. As seen here, visibility is expected to be lessened during the wearing of the mask. Additionally, hearing will be degraded by the wearing of the hood. Air is drawn in through the underside center of the filter canister and exhaled through a one-way valve in the mask body above the right top of the canister. [Courtesy Dixie Surplus, Lafayette, LA]

FIGURE 18-4 Close-up of a rubberized over-boot which is worn over the combat boots. The eyelets on the toe, heal and sides of the boot are used to tie the over-boot securely around and over the combat boots. [Courtesy Dixie Surplus, Lafayette, LA]

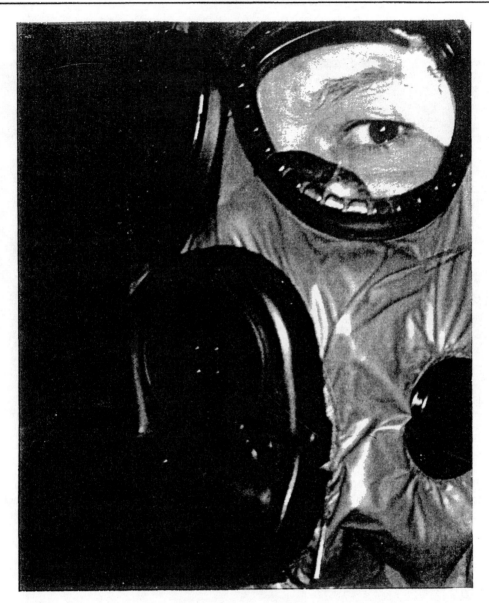

FIGURE 18-5 The M17A1 Protective Mask as worn by a real soldier. The black circular object in front of the mask at the nose of the wearer houses the voicemitter and the exhaust valve is below the voicemitter under the black rubber cover flap at the bottom. The long object just below the voicemitter is a drinking tube which attaches to the canteen under combat conditions. The smaller black circular object to the right of the picture under the eye piece is the intake valve assembly cover. Air enters through it, passes over and through the toxic agent filter element located within each cheek pouch of the mask body and the air passes into the interior of the mask by flowing over the transparent eyelens. This airflow arrangement is intended to act as a defogger to permit clear vision through the eyelenses. [Courtesy U.S. Army]

FIGURE 18-6 A close-up of the face piece of the M25A1 Protective Mask for tanks and other tracked vehicles. Note the hose attached to the chin portion of the mask body. This hose attaches to either a self-contained air filtering system organic to the vehicle or to a man-portable filter element canister. [Courtesy U.S. Army]

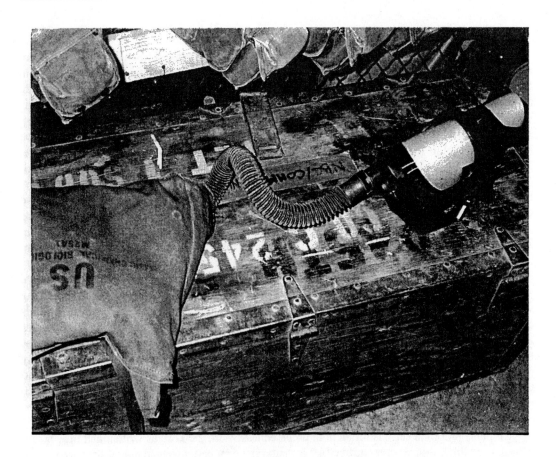

FIGURE 18-7 A view of the entire M25A1 Protective Mask system showing the mask, attached hose and the canister carrying case. The carrying case has a belt and leg straps for wearing the unit at the hip while outside of the vehicle. [Courtesy U.S. Army]

A different formulation is reported to provide preventative protection to the toxic effects of nerve agents. This formulation is called pyridostigmine [V]. It is in pill form and when taken shortly before exposure is alleged to improve the chances of preventing the poisoning effects of nerve agents in conjunction with the use of the autoinjector formulations.[10] The pyridostigmine is designed to provide a minimum of 12 hours of protection against exposure to nerve agent. A future goal is to expand this window of protection to a full 24 hours.

A newer anticonvulsant is in use by the U.S. Army. Known as the Convulsant Antidote for Nerve Agent (CANA), this material is available as an autoinjector and contains diazepam [VI], a sedative. The sedative serves to calm the individual down. The calmer one is, the slower the absorption rate of the toxic agent. The CANA is a buddy-aid device. That is, for the soldier who is incapacitated by nerve agent poisoning, a buddy can administer the CANA autoinjector for him. Each soldier will have one CANA issued along with the three atropine/2-PAM autoinjectors.

Atropine is also in the form of an aerosolized inhaler called Medical Aerosolized Nerve Agent Antidote (MANAA). This device looks much like the inhalers used by asthmatics but is issued to medics for use on nerve agent exposed troops to conserve the autoinjectors.

Though antidote preparations undoubtedly have been administered to severely exposed nerve agent casualties, time is required for antidote absorption to counteract the nerve agent, time during which the patient must somehow breathe or die despite the antidote. As a result, medical facilities anticipating nerve agent casualties must have respirator and oxygen equipment on hand. This creates a logistical problem however. The nerve agent exposed patient will have to remain on the respirator for some time until the antidote has taken effect and cholinesterase enzyme levels are functionally restored. This could require 48 hours. The first four to six hours of treatment is critical. It is estimated that a patient under rigorous care at the onset of symptoms can recover from doses as high as 100 times the lethal dose (LD_{50}). In a gas warfare environment, there easily could be more agent toxified patients than there are respirators.

Civilians present a serious problem in preparedness. With the laws as written and the present climate over illicit drug use, the proverbial ice cube stands a better chance in hell than we private citizens do of being allowed to carry antidote formulations against possible terrorist attacks. Two things can be said about such license. Had the people in the Tokyo Japan been (1) better educated about the effects of such agents and (2) been carrying antidote, there probably would not have been 11 deaths and 5500 injuries from the Sarin attack they suffered. However, were it not for the criminal predation of their fellow man even this paragraph would be moot. So what are you the private citizen to do? Know the symptoms of nerve agent poisoning. When the initial stages develop, have yourself taken immediately (by friend, coworker, family member, or ambulance) to the nearest emergency room and inform the staff, if still conscious, of your suspicions. They'll do the rest, including determining first if you are correct in your suspicions.

BLOOD AGENTS

For blood agents, the antidotes are sodium nitrite [VII] and sodium thiosulfate [VIII]. Amyl nitrite [IX] ampules are effective and at one time were issued and available to the combat soldier in the field. The ampule (about 0.2 ml each) was crushed and placed in the mask so the exposed individual inhales the vapors. Treatment consists of one ampule each five minutes to a maximum of

---

[10] M. Meselson & J.P. Robinson, *Scientific American* **242(4)**, 38-47 (1980)

three.[11] Medical personnel may need to monitor blood pressure as the amyl nitrite can depress it. For this reason and others, amyl nitrite is no longer the personal, field blood agent antidote. Since blood agents can interfere with the oxygenation of the blood, anoxia[12] is a problem even during treatment. No doubt, such an afflicted individual, in addition to the antidotes administered by medical personnel in the field, may require evacuation for ventilation with pure oxygen.[13] This may have limited effect for severe cases as the blood is then significantly dosed, and very little oxygen capacity exists under such conditions. Hyperbaric[14] oxygen therapy may be called for. Promptness of diagnosis and intervention is absolutely essential. At a MASH facility, administration of 3% sodium nitrite solution, i.v., is called for. This is followed by 25% sodium thiosulfate solution, i.v. If the patient lives through the first four hours, recovery is usual.

A gain as above concerning civilians and antidotes, know the symptoms of blood agent poisoning. If you suspect you have been exposed by initial symptoms, get thee with utmost haste to the nearest emergency room.

CHOKING AGENTS

In 1939 it was learned that the compound HMT (hexamethylenetetramine [X]) was effective in preventing lung tissue destruction from exposure to phosgene. This compound reacted with the phosgene upon its entry into the lungs and inhibited its action.[15] It offered a preventative to accidental exposure of factory and laboratory personnel but offered little value for troops who could not easily be inoculated with it on a regular basis in the field.

Usual treatment of exposure to choking agents consists of first removing the victim from contaminated area and administering oxygen as soon as possible. Cortisone acetate (1 mg/Kg) given orally one to three times a day appears to reduce tissue damage. Other steroids may also work well, a physician's call. The fluid build up (pulmonary edema) requires correction as it interferes with oxygen absorption in the lungs. Medically routine procedures apply in this therapy.

Unlike nerve and blood agents, you have a larger time window to respond to initial symptoms of choking agents. You must know the symptoms first. As an interesting point about choking agents and civilians, you have a greater chance of exposure to these as a result of fire than from deliberate terrorist attack. Phosgene, the more likely choking agent threat resulted from the chlorinated plastics so common in building construction materials and furnishings. As such materials burn, the process of pyrolysis converts some of the chlorine content to phosgene. However, though phosgene has a characteristic odor of cut grass or hay, you will not smell it. The sooty components of smoke mask

---

[11] The use of amyl nitrite is still warranted in the absence of the injections of sodium nitrate or sodium thiosulfate. For civilian treatment, the ampule contents are deposited onto a gauze pad or clean cloth and held to the victim's nose for inhalation of the vapors for three minutes. This process is repeated every five minutes to a maximum of three such exposures.

[12] Oxygen starvation

[13] Normal air mixes contain about 21% oxygen by volume.

[14] Oxygen under higher pressure than normally applied.

[15] MD (EA) MR 81, "Therapeutic and Prophylactic Value of HMT in Phosgene Poisoning", 19 March, 1943.

its odor. Firemen who are admitted to hospitals for smoke inhalation injuries, probably have suffered some injury from phosgene in fire involving such chlorinated plastics. Its very uncomfortable. It can be very scary with the labored breathing, but quick, effective monitoring and intervention treatment if required offers excellent prognosis to the victim.

BLISTERING AGENTS

Mustards provide a different threat to life compared with the previous three toxic agent types. Historically, the experience with mustard has been that it is not itself a particularly lethal agent (though it certainly can be lethal under certain conditions) but rather a severe (toxic) incapacitant. The principal problem confronting the injured and the medical personnel treating such wounded is the blistering and from that the very real hazard of secondary opportunistic infections. Inhalation injury usually results in infections in the form of bronchopneumonia. The advent of penicillin alleviated much of the risk of death particularly for sulfa drug resistant strains of bacteria. Blistering agent burns must be treated as third degree burns of thermal causes. Early use of sulfadiazine ointment was effective and now, petrolatum salves containing silver nitrate [XI] are also effective therapeutics. Today silver formulations are specifically designed for third degree thermal burn, antibacterial treatment.[16]

Arsenicals such as Lewisite are also systemic poisons in addition to being vesicant agents. As such, their absorption manifests signs of arsenic poisoning. BAL (British AntiLewisite[17]) [XII] is an effective antidote for arsenic and other heavy metal poisons. Treatment consists of administration of 3 mg/Kg dosage every four hours for the first 2 days; for the next 10 days, 2 mg/Kg every 12 hours.

The combat soldier is issued an Antidote, Arsenical, Self-Aid (I-BAL) package. The package contains a gauze swab soaked in 3 to 5% BAL. This is suitable for treatment of eyes and skin.

Civilian exposure to blistering agents is no different to them than it is for troops. Same time course of symptom development will result. Initial symptoms are the same and a warning of more serious damage if not treated. Infection is the real problem if the exposure continues, assuming the stuff has not been inhaled.

One area of caution is due a related class of chemicals, also chlorinated. That class is the chlorinated hydrocarbons, many of which are or have been used in dry cleaning preparations, paint removers, and so forth. One in particular is methylene chloride. Methylene chloride has or still is a component of paint remover. You brush it on, let it stand and the solvent properties along with its volatility leads to separation of the paint bond with the surface of the material. This shows up as a bubbling of the paint skin. Methylene chloride is a potential carcinogen and is also absorbable by the skin. Its blistering ability is questionable, but its innate toxicity is not. Handle this stuff out of doors, with the wind to your back, with care.

---

[16] One preparation, Silvadene, silver sulfadiazine, a prescription medicinal, is a very effective bactericide for a wide range of bacteria.

[17] dimercaptopropanol

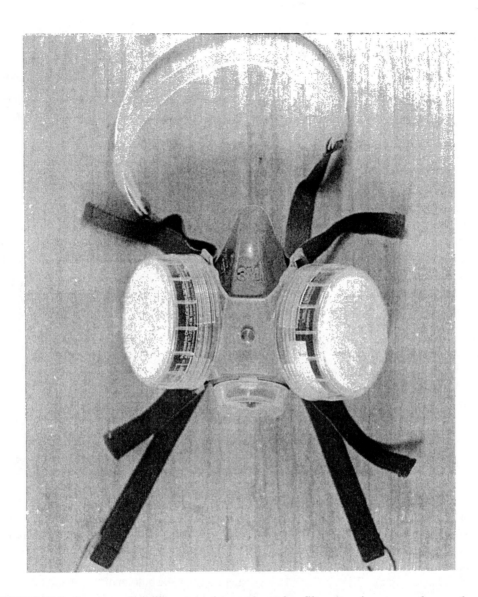

FIGURE 18-8 One type of civilian protective mask used to filter organic vapor and aerosols of paint. This type of mask provides only respiratory protection from organic solvents commonly employed to solvate paint formulations. It does not provide eye and face protection. The mask is worn over the nose and mouth using the clear plastic strap shown at the top of the picture across the top back of the head. The two loose-end straps fasten at the back of the neck after passing them across the cheeks and jaws under the ears. The large white surfaces are dust particle filters and the black region below the white fabric dust filter material are the activated charcoal components. The smaller black circular object at the bottom is the exhaust valve. Air is drawn in through the white fabric dust filter, across the activated charcoal and into the interior of the mask for inhalation.

FIGURE 18-9 A close-up of the civilian painter's mask. The two large white objects are the filter element showing a fabric dust filter. Air is drawn in during breathing through the two filter elements directly to the nose and mouth. Unlike the military protective masks, this type of mask with no eyelenses does not require passage of the intake air across the lenses for defogging as there are no eyelenses. The smaller, black circular object at the bottom of the mask is the exhaust valve assembly (the plastic cover opened).

FIGURE 18-10 A close-up view of the interior of the filter element housing with the element removed to expose the air inlet channel. The small black circular object is the inlet valve. The O-ring is seen around the outer edge of the filter element housing which provides a seal for the element body.

FIGURE 18-11 A filter element unit showing the thin fabric (white) cover over the activated charcoal component. The white circular object is the cover assembly which screws onto the mask filter element housing, holding the filter element securely in place.

INCAPACITATING AGENTS

PHYSICAL

General first aid treatment of exposure to incapacitating agents consists chiefly of leaving the area and facing into the wind and washing away fine particulate agent from the face with water. Removal of the clothing is optimally effective as clothing will trap fine agent aerosol particles within its fiber mesh construction, allowing such particles to vaporize and continue exposure. This is particularly true of heavy concentrations exposure such as being very close the source of the agent release. The eyes are the most important organs subject to serious injury and should be washed with copious amounts of water. Washing the skin with soap and water also removes any fine particles of agent.

FIGURE 18-12 A close-up of the interior structure of a civilian protective painting mask. The two black objects are the filtered air intake valves which open into the mask cavity upon inhalation. On exhalation, these valves close from the exhaled air overpressure and at the same time open the exhalation or exhaust valve (not shown here) which is located at the base of the chin piece.

These agents generally present no lethal threat to exposure in the majority of people, though they clearly are very irritating. They do pose a problem to medical personnel attempting to treat exposed patients for whatever reason. The material can be on clothing and the fine particles stirred up into the air by handling of the patient. Thus emergency care personnel may require protective gear. Treatment entails essentially removal of all contaminated clothing and thorough washing of exposed skin with soap and water. Eye exposure discomfort is alleviated by washing of the eyes with water or even a normal saline solution for about 15 minutes. Eye injuries may require examination by an ophthalmologist.

The vomiting agents such as Adamsite pose a serious poisoning threat because of their breakdown products. These breakdown products are arsenicals and as such are potential systemic poisons. Thorough washing of the skin and clothing with soap and water are important to remove the agent and its hydrolysis products.

PSYCHOACTIVE

Treatment principally begins with 0.1 mg/Kg oral dose of diazepam. This medication assists in the control of convulsions. Coma, etc. must be treated as well through specified therapies and may vary depending upon the specific psychoactive agent involved.

INCENDIARY AGENTS

Injuries from incendiaries are essentially thermal burns that must be treated as such. There is added concern when the incendiary material is imbedded in the wound. Some of these materials are themselves quite poisonous. A case in point is that of WP, white phosphorous. This material is highly combustible in air and oxidizes to tetraphosphorus decoxide, P_4O_{10}, which reacts with water to form phosphoric acid. Under water, the WP is inert as far as combustion is concerned, but the poison hazard remains. Such injuries have been treated by removal of the WP particles under a copper sulfate solution. The copper sulfate is effective in removing the fine particles of WP on the skin.

For inhalation of WP fumes, treatment consists of those applicable to the treatment of pulmonary edema and shock. Ten milliliters of 10% calcium gluconate [XIII] is given to maintain calcium levels in the blood. Observance for hepatic failure is cautionary.

Care must be exercised around metals such as magnesium and aluminum. Metal objects made of these if heated to the ignition point yield fire of incredible ferocity and heat.

BIOLOGICAL AGENTS

Treatment of infections depends upon the nature of the infection as well as the patient's susceptibility to allergic reactions to any medication administered. Because of the unique differences between bacteria, rickettsia, fungi and viruses, the approach taken for one is not likely effective for the others. Additionally, some infections lead to susceptibility for opportunistic infections by secondary pathogens which must also be guarded against or simultaneously treated as the need arises. Even in the case of bacteria alone, the differences between what are called gram-positive and gram-negative bacteria are significant and determine specific medicinal treatments. Furthermore, what is effective on cocci bacteria most likely is not effective on spirochetes and so on.

One would think in this day and age of modern medicine with the advanced knowledge, diagnostic techniques and the wide selection of medicinals available, that bacterial infections alone would be nothing more than a passing nuisance. In fact, modern medicine has, with its antibiotic interventions, complicated the stage of microbial pathology. Resistant strains of bacteria (see Chapter 14) are now an ever present frustration in the treatment of infection and it has gone a step further with much of the human population developing hypersensitivities to the very potent antibiotics that would otherwise be the cure.

Even the diagnostic tests to identify a particular organism may be either expensive or very time consuming to run, or both. Multiply these two factors over the hundreds of thousands of people seeking medical help for a variety of infections from the toes to the urogenital tract to the rare brain infections, and the problems take on gargantuan proportions. Such intense diagnostic tests are only run for those suspected infections for which no obvious pathophysiological medical history is known and are acutely lethal if existing treatments don't work.[18] Usually, a physician's experience and knowledge of the kinds of infections that frequent various parts or organs of the body leads him to make an on-the-spot educated guess pending any specific diagnostic culture he may order.[19] But sometimes, the microbes outsmart the "doc."

In dealing with infections, often times several different microbes will exhibit similar symptoms, most particularly in the early stages of the infection. Additionally, the rarity of some infections in western society can often be mistaken for some other less lethal infection. As noted in Chapter 13, anthrax is one example of a microbe that can be misdiagnosed by even the competent, but unsuspecting physician. Pulmonary anthrax leaves little room, if any, for a second guess or opinion. Diagnostic medicine is an art as much as it is a science.

In the event of a biological war agent use, the knowledge and diagnostic talents of the medical community will be taxed. This is all the more true if genetically engineered microbes are used which poses one set of immunologic traits and yet another set of pathogenic traits. Any resistance factors incorporated into such "man-made" creatures will only enhance the difficulty of their identification and treatment. As a result, the study and research into microbial sciences assumes a greater importance not only in the study of the kinds of genetic "monkeying" that can be done, but also in the area of antibiotic methods for treatment. The latter will lag behind the former.

One example of the problem of antibiotic resistant microbe selection arose in NYC in early 1992. Tuberculosis, which was under control for many decades, suddenly arose in near epidemic proportions, particularly among the more susceptible segment of the population, the homeless, vagrants, the socioeconomically deprived. The specifics of the tuberculosis microbe's life cycle is such that antibiotic treatment must continue for many weeks, often months, perhaps into a full year after the patient is "feeling quite well". Cessation of medication before complete treatment leads to a relapse of the disease and significantly as has occurred, by strains resistant to the normally used antibiotic treatment.

Viruses as has been noted in Chapters 12 and 13 present the worse case or nightmare senerio. There are very few antiviral agents the medical community can draw on. With rather exotic and new

---

[18] Sometimes, regrettably, the cause of the infection and death is not determined until after an autopsy.

[19] Sore throat, fever, and coughing often lead the physician to tentatively diagnose Strep throat for which a throat culture specimen is taken. Pending results of the culture, appropriate antibiotic treatment is prescribed for about ten days.

viruses popping up such as the Hantavirus, Lassa virus and the Ebola virus, our first line of defense is a good offense in the form of the US Army's USAMRIID and the CDC. They are charged with the responsibility to intercept, identify, and crush an outbreak of these nonliving, biological stealth killers. The US may have unilaterally renounced use of biological weapons in any war, but we better not renounce R&D into the these little monsters.

As relates to terrorist attack with biological agents, there may be some time before terrorist groups can make the quantum leap from gunpowder, cordite, Semtex, or even Sarin to cultivated Ebola or some other exotic microbial, real world Andromeda strain agent. Present technology requirements to do such R&D and proposed and pending international agreements may make it more difficult for such groups to acquire the equipment and materials, but that's not the same thing as impossible. One major weapon against civilian victimization against any terrorist attack is an effective intelligence apparatus which makes use of all forms of intelligence, including HUMINT to uncover the plans and intentions of these groups. The balancing act is between a government's desire and willingness to know what everyone is doing, harmless or criminal, versus say Constitutional rights in the US. Its going to be a touchy if not tough juggling act.

CHAPTER 19

DECONTAMINATION

Out, damned spot! out, I say!
Lady Macbeth, in *Macbeth*, Act V, Scene I,
William Shakespeare

GENERAL

Once the individual or military unit has been exposed to chemical or biological agents, they must decontaminate themselves and all equipment including facilities if they are occupying a defensive position. The methods and equipment are standardized and permit decontamination of any known agent. Identification of the particular agent type (nerve, blood, choking, blister) is best as this permits the selection of the optimum and most effective and economical methods and materials for decontamination.

However, some agents are not long-lived once exposed to the environment. Choking agents, as an example, are with time easily hydrolyzed by water or humidity in the air. Their significant nonpersistence also is due to their easy dispersal by winds. For agents such as persistent nerve or mustards, specific and thorough decontamination must be accomplished before the personnel may unmask and the area declared safe. The methods and materials described below are general and applicable to any and all levels of military organization and structure, from the squad to the Army Group or depot. Thus decontamination is that process by which people or equipment or an area is rendered safe for unprotected personnel. It is not necessary to decontaminate the vapor hazard as this is like chasing air. What is sought is the elimination of any liquid pools of agent in the area where personnel work, live, even fight.

MATERIALS

Various decontamination materials and kits are available to the individual soldier and to company size units. These materials are essentially industrial strength chemical cleaning agents. Principally four types of decontamination materials are available: the M258A1 Skin Decontamination Kit, DS2[1], STB[2] and a general purpose detergent. Storage of DS2 and STB requires adequate separation of the two as their mixing in pure form constitutes a serious incendiary hazard.

The M258A1 Skin Decontamination Kit is used by the individual soldier on himself. This kit is stored in the mask carrier for ready availability under field combat conditions. The kit consists of

---

[1] Consists of 70% diethylenetriamine, 28% ethylene glycol monoethyl ether and 2% sodium hydroxide.

[2] Possesses about 30% available chlorine.

chemically impregnated, absorbent pads or towelettes for blotting up suspicious droplets on the skin. The chemical impregnate reacts with and neutralizes mustard and nerve agents. A small tube of ointment or creme also is provided for rubbing into the skin areas exposed to droplets after blotting. The kit towelettes can be used for minor decontamination of personal equipment such as the individual weapon.

A new decontamination kit was rushed into service for use in Operation Desert Storm. This new kit is a resin-based, nontoxic, noncorrosive, and nonirritating skin decontamination material. It is reported to be effective against a broad spectrum of chemical agent types. Designated the M291 Personnel Casualty Decontamination System Skin Decontamination Kit (PCDS SDK), this kit contains six individual decontamination packets. Each packet contains 2.8 g of formulated decontamination resin in a laminated fiber material.

An Individual Equipment Decontamination Kit (IEDK), XM295, is under evaluation. The XM295 consists of four mitt-like wiping cloths. The mitt consists of a nonwoven polyester material and a polyethylene film backing. An absorbent resin permeates the nonwoven polyester material. The resin and nonwoven polyester padding are the active decontamination ingredients.

DS2, Decontaminating Solution 2, is an all-purpose decontaminant, effective against all known military toxic chemical agents. It comes packaged in 1⅓ quart cans or 5 gallon pails. When using DS2, the protective mask must be worn as the material is quite corrosive and irritating to tissue. STB, Super Tropical Bleach, comes in 8 gallon pails and 50 lb drums and consists of chlorinated lime and calcium oxide in powder form. This material is effective against mustard, Lewisite and nerve agents.

A newer decontamination material, Improved Chemical Biological Agent Decontaminant Decontaminating Agent: Multipurpose (ICBAD/DAM) will replace bulk DS2 in September 1999. The DAM is safer for personnel and also environmentally safer to use compared to DS2. As the sole decontaminating agent, it will replace both DS2 and STB, reducing logistical burdens of supplying many different decontaminating agents.

PERSONNEL

Decontamination of a person usually involves thorough washing with soap or detergent and water. This is effective as the persistent chemical agents are organics which are solvated by the soap or detergent and rinsed away with the water. This also is effective in general antibacterial cleaning of the skin.

Other formulations effective in removing and even destroying chemical agents on the skin are solutions of baking soda, mild bleach and sodium thiosulfate. These chemicals actually react with the chemical agents to destroy them as well as remove them and the hydrolysis products.

EQUIPMENT

In addition to the usual brooms, mops and buckets, heavier duty equipment designed specifically for decontamination of toxic chemical agent contaminated heavy tactical equipment is available. The ABC-M11 Portable Decontamination Apparatus uses DS2 in 1½ quart quantities. This apparatus utilizes a refillable cylinder, a spray head and is affixed to a vehicle. Nitrogen gas from a source cartridge provides the pressure to force decontaminant through the spray head. This device is used to decontaminate driver controls and surfaces of vehicles.

A recent development is the M17 Lightweight Decontamination System (LDS). The LDS is a small engine powered pump and water heating unit. The system consists of a 1580 gallon, collapsible water tank, two spray wands, connecting hoses and a shower rail. The unit can produce hot water or steam. Water can be drawn from any available source. The water is forced through a nozzle under moderate pressures and controlled temperature. Plans called for the purchase and distribution of 550 of the LDS during FY92.

Another development under testing is the Modular Decontamination System (MDS), XM22. This item mixes and dispenses a continuous flow of Improved Chemical/Biological Agent Decontaminant (ICBAD) from two spray wands. Powered by a 7.5 HP diesel JP-8 engine, the XM22 will be mounted on the same trailer as the XM21 Remote Sensing Chemical Alarm. The system provides as much as 1200 psi adjustable water pressure at 5 gallons per minute flow rate. Used in conjunction with the M17 LDS, high pressure hot water is available.

The Modular Decontamination System (MDS)- Decontaminant Power/Scrubber, XM21 (DP/S), is a DS2 dispensing unit providing a field expedient application through two spray wands. It is powered by a 7.5 HP diesel/JP-8 engine which also powers two scrubbers. The XM21 is transportable on a 1.5 ton trailer.

FACILITIES

Decontamination facilities in the field are impromptu expedients, established as needed due to chemical agent exposure and dependent upon the agent encountered. Such facilities consist of a location far removed from and down wind of troop habitable areas. The facility essentially is a series of points along a short route through which vehicles and heavy equipment pass to be decontaminated. DS2 and STB decontamination formulations are used, followed by water/detergent and finally water rinses. Such facilities are applicable to large motorized or mechanized units which may have many such vehicles consisting of trucks, tanks, APCs, artillery pieces, etc. Such facilities may also be established by battalion or brigade headquarters and run entire motorized companies through in serial fashion. Much heavier decontamination equipment is required for such large and wholesale unit decontaminations. The former Soviets, for example, were known to have large jet engine powered decontamination equipment[3] for large, mass scale decontamination of armored units.

CHEMICAL AGENTS

NERVE

DS2 and STB are the principal decontamination agents used, though DS2 in bulk use is replaced by the newer DAM. Additionally nerve agents on equipment or on the ground are hydrolyzed (destroyed) by water, sodium hydroxide (lye) and sodium carbonate yielding reduced toxicity by-products.

---

[3] This equipment is now undoubtedly distributed among the various republic military forces.

BLOOD

Blood agents generally are nonpersistent. As such they are volatile and removed from the area by winds. They seldom form pools of liquid agent in warm climates and will evaporate quickly if they should. They are soluble in water and thus will dissolve in bodies of water. Reaction with soil and other soil borne materials effectively removes them and leads to their decomposition. General washing of any splashes on the skin of these agents with soap or detergent water solutions will neutralize and remove them from the skin.

Reaction with water leads to slow decomposition. Any compound with the cyano group (CN) is subject to release of hydrogen cyanide which will dissolve in the water.

CHOKING

Choking agents, like blood agents, are nonpersistent. They are almost always gaseous or aerosols in nature and are quickly removed from the area by winds and breezes and require no site decontamination. Additionally, their very chemical nature makes them highly susceptible to destruction by humidity and rain as well as any moisture or water pools on the ground. Hydrolysis products are generally hydrogen chloride (which dissolves in water to form dilute hydrochloric acid under field conditions) and carbon dioxide for phosgene and diphosgene; hydrogen chloride, chlorine dioxide and hypochlorous acid (all dilute and relatively harmless under field conditions) for chlorine gas.

BLISTERING

There are chemical materials which can absorb and destroy such agents suspected or known to be on the skin. Such remedies as bleaching powder and sodium thiosulfate solution are quite effective. Additionally, the soldier has kits such as the M258A1 Skin Decontamination Kit or the newer resin-based kit with specially treated absorbent pads with his mask carrier for blotting up (do not smear) suspicious liquid droplets he finds on himself. Application of the ointment or creme provided with the kit is the follow-up action to blotting of suspicious droplets on the skin. Prompt action in blotting up such droplets will effectively remove the threat of any harm.

Hydrolysis with water of blistering agents is a slow process under moderate conditions. The products that do result over time are hydrogen chloride and nontoxic organosulfides from mustard HD. For ethyldichlorarsine, the hydrolysis products are ethylarsinous oxide (poisonous if ingested) and hydrogen chloride. Lewisite is also hydrolyzed by water and the principal hydrolysis by-product is also an organoarsenic compound of systemic toxicity if ingested.

Nitrogen mustards are hydrolyzed by water and the by-products are also toxic. Soap or detergent, baking soda, and mild bleach solutions can aid in removing a nitrogen mustard from the skin. More concentrated solutions of these preparations can be used to decontaminate washable objects.

ARSENICALS

Most if not all of the military arsenical agents are subject to hydrolysis by water. The hydrolyzates are often water soluble and can be washed away. They do present a systemic poison hazard and precautions must be taken to avoid contamination of ingestibles such as drinking water and foods. Canned items can be decontaminated by washing in soapy solution and rinsing before breaking the seals.

INCAPACITANTS

Some tearing agents are hydrolyzed by water to various by-products depending upon the specific chemical identity of the agent. Diphenylchlorarsine (DA) hydrolyzes in water to yield hydrogen chloride and the organoarsenical oxide (a poison hazard if ingested). Bromobenzylcyanide slowly hydrolyzes to release hydrogen bromide and other by-products. Diphenylcyanarsine (DC) and chloroacetophenone (CN) are virtually insoluble in water so no discernible hydrolysis is observed. Chloropicrin is not easily hydrolyzed and it is only slightly soluble in water. However, even in cases of incapacitating agents not soluble in or hydrolyzed by water, thorough washing with strong soap or detergent water solutions can remove them from the skin and objects.

SMOKING/OBSCURANT AGENTS

Smoking agents generally function by reaction with air and the water moisture inherent in the air. These reactions liberate in most cases very irritating fumes which are essentially acidic in nature. For example, titanium tetrachloride reacts with air to release hydrogen chloride, anhydrous[4] hydrochloric acid, which dissolves in the moisture of air to form the acid. Sulfur trioxide reacts with water to form sulfuric acid fumes and chlorosulfuric acid releases both hydrogen chloride and sulfuric acid fumes.

These can be neutralized by treatment with baking soda. Any skin contact with any mists or droplets of these smoking agents should entail cleansing with water as a minimum.

BIOLOGICAL AGENTS

Decontamination of biohazards depends upon what is to be decontaminated. For human decontamination, we learned as youngsters to wash our hands with soap and water. This is the minimum action and probably the most required under normal microorganism exposures encountered in everyday life. Today specially formulated antibacterial soaps are commercially available.

Under conditions where a serious, potentially lethal microorganism threat exists, soap and water washing of the body and hands may not leave one completely confident. Usually soap and water washing if not thorough, fails to remove bacteria under the fingernails and under finger rings. Soaps used by surgical personnel of a hospital are very good. A mild bleach solution is also effective as long

---

[4] Anhydrous means devoid of water.

as the solution is not too strong.[5] Rubbing alcohol is effective and is still used to disinfect skin surfaces before injections are given. Various specialized disinfectants are also available such as a betadine solution and soap.

Decontamination of objects is much easier. Metal objects such as eating utensils and dishware, pots and pans, etc. can be very thoroughly disinfected with a stronger bleach solution than used on the skin. Tin cans used in food storage also can be treated this way (do not heat up sealed cans) prior to opening. Sunlight is rich in ultraviolet radiation. This will kill many vegetative microorganisms if they are exposed to it for several hours, though some spores are resistant.

Boiling water is the classical, and a really simple yet effective, way to kill bacteria. The water must boil for a minimum of 30 minutes. Water for drinking can be treated with a few drops per gallon of bleach, iodine, HTH, or halozene if boiling is not possible. The usual means of washing and cleaning in everyday life generally is sufficient so long as it is thorough.

---

[5] Too strong a bleach solution will injure the skin, effectively acting as a blistering agent.

PART VII

CHAPTER 20

THE CHEMICAL CORPS, U.S. ARMY

No plan survives contact with the enemy.
-Field Marshal Helmuth Carl Bernard Von Moltke,
1800-1891[1]

ORIGINS

The present day Chemical Corps has its roots in WWI. General John J. Pershing, Commander of the American Expeditionary Force (AEF) created the Gas Service as a result of German use of chemical weapons. The creation of the First Gas Regiment was a direct outgrowth of the Gas Service.

Between WWI and WWII responsibility for CBW[2] was divided among several U.S. government agencies: Bureau of Mines; Medical Department, Ordnance Department, Signal Corps, and Corps of Engineers of the U.S. Army. However, on 28 June 1918, the first steps at unifying overall responsibility for CBW was taken. All the responsibilities of these diverse agencies were combined into one with the name Chemical Warfare Service (CWS), National Army. By act of Congress, the CWS became a permanent branch of the Army on 20 September 1920. The CWS assumed responsibility for biological warfare in 1942. On 2 August 1946, the latter was redesignated the Chemical Corps, U.S. Army. The insignia of the Chemical Corps was adopted in 1917.

On 27 June 1986, the Chemical Corps was established as a Regiment[3] under the U.S. Army Regimental System. The home of the Chemical Corps is Ft. McClellan, Alabama. The Commandant of the Chemical School is the Chief of the Chemical Corps and Deputy Commanding General of Fort McClellan. The rank of the senior chemical officer of the U.S. Army is Major General.

In the few years preceding 1976, the U.S. Army studied and contemplated the elimination of the Chemical Corps as a separate branch by absorbing it and its roles and functions into the Ordnance Corps. In 1976 all thought of such an absorption of the Chemical Corps into the Ordnance Corps was dropped as a result of increased awareness of and concern over then Soviet NBC operations capabilities. The spread of CB technology to the Third World Countries further emphasized the need for continuation and strengthening of the U.S. Army Chemical Corps. This point was amply clear as

---

[1] In *The Harvest of a Quiet Eye*, p. 155

[2] CBW is an outdated term. The military now uses NBC which stands for Nuclear, Biological and Chemical.

[3] A regiment is a military unit consisting of several battalions. A battalion consists of a headquarters element and two or more companies (infantry) or batteries (artillery).

a result of captured Soviet vehicles and equipment in the 1973 Yom Kippur war between Israel and Egypt. That equipment clearly demonstrated the then Soviet superiority in preparedness to wage a chemical war and the seriousness and determination of their technology to pursue such preparedness.

POLICY

U.S. Government and U.S. Army policy concerning NBC operations are defined as follows:[4] The United States

(1)   will not be the first to use chemical weapons;
(2)   will continue efforts to negotiate a verifiable ban on production and stockpiling of chemical weapons;
(3)   will maintain protective measures against chemical attack;
(4)   will deter, by threat of retaliation, chemical attack by an adversary; and
(5)   may use chemical weapons in retaliation to enemy first use of chemical weapons.
(6)   the United States has renounced the use of biological weapons.

The U.S. Army is designated the Executive Agent for chemical and biological defense. This means all R&D concerning CB preparedness is under the direction and authority of the U.S. Army. Thus, the preparedness and means for dealing with CB threats by the U.S. Navy, Marine Corps, Air Force and Coast Guard originate with the Army and through the expertise of the Chemical Corps.

ORGANIZATION

The Chemical Corps is headed by a Major General. He is responsible for all facets of U.S. Army preparation, training, installations, research and development, production, procurement, storage, etc. concerning chemical warfare matters. The officers of the Chemical Corps are generally those with degrees and training in various related fields such as civil, electrical, mechanical, and chemical engineering; chemistry; biochemistry; microbiology; physics; and metallurgy.

MISSION

The mission of the Chemical Corps is "To prepare the Army to win in NBC warfare operations."

---

[4] Specific declarations made to the author in a letter dated 20 May, 1991 by then Colonel David R. Moss, GS, Chief, Chemical Division, Department of the Army, Deputy Chief of Staff for Logistics, Washington, D.C. 20310-0500.

RESEARCH & DEVELOPMENT

Research and development is conducted by the U.S. Army Chemical Research, Development and Engineering Center (CRDEC). The CRDEC is an element of the U.S. Army Armament, Munitions and Chemical Command, which is itself one of ten major subordinate commands of the U.S. Army Materiel Command. The CRDEC is headquartered in the Edgewood Area of the Aberdeen Proving Ground located in Maryland. Nearly 70% of the 1300 civilian and 100 military personnel work in the Maryland complex. About 39% of the CRDEC employees have bachelors degrees, 10% have masters and 7% have the Ph.D. The Mission of the CRDEC is "to provide materiel for defense against chemical and biological (CB) attack and to provide a deterrent and retaliatory capability against the first use of chemical weapons by our adversaries." They "also have responsibility for conducting the Army's technology base programs in smoke/obscurants and flame weapons."

Areas of particular interest and research at the CRDEC are

1. receptor technology
2. aerosol science
3. alternatives to animal testing
4. hazardous waste management
5. decontamination/contamination avoidance
6. molecular modeling and display
7. plasma technology
8. mass spectrometry
9. respiratory test technology
10. stress physiology

These areas are all of practical and commercial importance to the private sector as well.

Of the priority objectives of the CRDEC, four are of particular importance in a CB environment. They are:

1. to reduce current dependence on charcoal in filters for defense against chemical agents,
2. to reduce the physiological effort in the use of respiratory protection,
3. to develop versatile multi-agent detectors that cope with future and unknown agents,
4. to develop alternatives to lethal agents

PERSONNEL

Chemical personnel of the Chemical Corps are assigned to all major and subordinate commands of the U.S. Army around the world including the Continental United States Army commands down to and including as low as battalion level. These personnel are responsible to the commander for all training and preparedness of subordinate units concerning nuclear, biological and chemical warfare (now called NBC in the Army).

A division level chemical company is authorized 167 personnel. These personnel are organized into four decontamination platoons, one mechanized smoke platoon and one reconnaissance platoon.

FIGURE 20-1 The M17 Lightweight Decontamination System (LDS). The LDS is a portable, lightweight, compact, engine-driven pump and multifuel-fired water heating system that produces hot water at 80°C and at 100 psi pressure delivered at a flow rate of 5 gpm. It can be used as a vehicle rinse and for personnel showers. The system is used during hasty and deliberate decontamination procedures. It draws its water from any source and delivers at moderate pressure and at controlled temperatures. Aside from the pump and heating unit, the system comes with a 165 lb. accessory kit which contains hoses, spray wands, and personnel shower hardware. The system also includes a rubberized fabric, self-supporting, collapsible tank, top center of picture. [Courtesy U.S. Army Chemical Research Development and Engineering Center]

FIGURE 20-2 The XM56 Motorized for Dual Purpose Unit-- Mechanical Smoke Generator. This system is mounted on the XM1097 High Mobility Multipurpose Wheeled Vehicle. The system will provide stationary or mobile smoke in the visual, infrared, and millimeter wave regions. The generator will produce 60 minutes of visual smoke and 30 minutes of infrared smoke on the battlefield. It is modular and uses a gas turbine engine as a power source to disseminate obscurants. It includes a control panel to allow operation "on-the-move" from the cab of the vehicle. [Courtesy U.S. Army Chemical Defense Research and Engineering Center]

SPECIFIED COMMANDS AND R & D FACILITIES

USAMRMC

On 3 November 1994 the U.S. Army Medical Research and Materiel Command (USAMRMC) was established at Fort Detrick, Maryland. The purpose of this action and the reorganization that it embodied was to improve the Army's ability to prevent illness and injuries in deploying forces, to equip and better train the Army's medics in caring for combat casualties among other goals. Accomplishments claimed under the reorganization include among others:

1. hepatitis A vaccine licensing for immunization of US Forces overseas deployments
2. support of Ebola virus and other highly infectious disease investigations (spearheaded by USAMRIID) in cooperation with the World Health Organization (WHO) of the UN.
3. support of investigations into Venezuelan Equine Encephalitis (VEE) epidemics in Venezuela and Columbia
4. product licensing of Tularemia Live vaccine

Various military laboratories exist that are at the forefront of R&D into both chemical and biological warfare agents. This work is, so far as is known and in accordance with Presidential and statutory strictures, aimed at defensive rather than offense capabilities development.

USAMRICD

The U.S. Army Medical Research Institute of Chemical Defense (USAMRICD) was established in 1981 and is now located at Aberdeen Proving Grounds, Maryland. It is subordinate to the USAMRMC. USAMRICD is the lead agency of the US Army with development, testing and evaluation of medical treatments of chemical agent exposure. It also develops, tests, and evaluates materials for prevention of chemical agent casualties. It covers the range of chemical agent concerns from actual agents likely used, antidote research, skin protectants development and decontamination formulations. Several biological agent threat agents are also studied.

USAMRICD origins trace back to WWI elements of the US Army Medical Department responsible then for development of medical defenses to chemical weapons being used in the trench warfare that so characterized that period of warfare.

USAMRIID

The U.S. Army Medical Research Institute of Infectious Diseases (USAMRIID) has previously been mentioned in earlier chapters. USAMRIID is a Biosafety Level 4 installation (see below). That means that it (and the Centers for Disease Control and Prevention, CDC) are the only agencies permitted to handle and study viruses of such extreme communicability, lethality and for which no effective treatment regimen exists. USAMRIID is also located at Fort Detrick, Maryland. USAMRIID came into full view with the discovery of a filovirus infection in monkeys housed at the Reston Primate Quarantine Center once located in Reston Virginia. The Center was operated by Hazelton Research Products, a division of Corning, Inc. This outbreak was the subject of the book *Hot Zone* by Richard Preston. This true story is well worth reading as it gives the reader unschooled in the biological sciences an excellent view of the threat viruses pose to humans and the extremely good luck that fell on the United States in October 1989. To put is bluntly, we were damn lucky.

The role of USAMRIID is to develop countermeasures against potential biological weapon agents as well as natural disease threats. USAMRIID is the military agency charged with that responsibility. The CDC is the civilian agency similarly charged. Additionally, USAMRIID serves as a biological resource to the WHO headquartered in Geneva, Switzerland, and to the CDC in Atlanta, Georgia. USAMRIID's keynote distinction is its responsibility for responding to the diagnosis and treatment of unusual diseases wherever they occur. This means essentially exotic, rare viral diseases such as the Ebola filoviruses among others such as Hanta and Lassa viruses. These are Biosafety Level 4 organisms and are not open to general medical or university research organs because of their incredible, hyperinfectivity and hyperlethality.

WRAIR

Walter Reed Army Institute of Research (WRAIR) also has a hand in infectious diseases. Their principal areas of interest and activity have been in malaria and other tropical diseases as well as hepatitis, and HIV/AIDS. Walter Reed Army Hospital was named after the U.S. Army bacteriologist and physician who was instrumental in determining the cause of Yellow Fever spread by the mosquito *Aëdes aegypti*. Yellow Fever was to be a problem for construction crews during the construction of the Panama Canal in the early 1900s under President Theodor Roosevelt. WRAIR operates overseas research labs and units in Thailand, Brazil, Germany and Kenya. The Hepatitis A vaccine development noted above (USAMRMC) was accomplished with the aid of the Thai Armed Forces Research Institute of Medical Sciences.

BIOSAFETY LEVELS

Biosafety Level (BSL) is a classification of precautions taken when working with biological pathogens. There are four such levels enumerated one through four. One is the lowest level and presents the least or no viable threat to human health and life, while four is the highest level and represents the most serious and most lethal level of pathogenic threat to humans.

BSL-1 concerns organisms that are not pathogenic to humans or at least not known to cause any diseases. These are the type of microbes handled by college microbiology undergraduates in general microbiology courses. Typically such agents are handled in the open air, at lab bench tops, employing standard microbiological practices of cleanliness and safety. No special equipment (meaning containment) is required for their study.

BSL-2 concerns microorganisms which do cause disease in humans and present hazards of an autoinoculation, ingestion, or mucous membrane exposure risk. Provisions for such study includes not only the standard microbiological practices, but also added precautions such as warning signs for use of sharps (needles, etc.), limited access to personnel directly involved with the studies, specified waste handling, decontamination procedures of laboratory facilities, equipment and such. Certain containment devices are also required for working with such microbes. The wearing of lab coats, gloves and face protection against splashes are required as needed.

BSL-3 begins dealing with the more serious pathogenic microbes. These are microbes that not only are indigenous or exotic, but also have a potential for airborne dissemination in aerosol form.

They have the added distinction of causing very serious infections and of being lethal. Practices for working with these biologics is based upon BSL2 procedures supplemented with controlled access, strict decontamination of all wastes and lab clothing *before laundering*. The requirement for protective clothing as in BSL2 is also in force.

BSL-4 addresses procedures for working with the most lethal (nearly always), nearly or exclusively aerosolic transmitted pathogens, or those of unknown transmission risks. Viruses such as Ebola, Hanta and Lassa viruses are a group that populate this class of safety precaution. Here BSL3 precautions are a mandatory starting point. In addition, workers must change out of street clothing and don specially designed suits, the space suit type of personal isolation, before entering specially designed rooms within which the microbe may only be studied. The rooms typically operate under a slightly lower atmospheric pressure so that air can only seep in, not out of the containment room. Special anterooms or locks are provided for preentry to the "hot room" where the microbes are kept and stored. Completion of work requires the worker to enter a lock where decontamination procedures include very short wave UV light and highly microbially toxic chemical decontamination spray of the outer "space suit". The specialized suits are pressurized to minimize if not prevent entry of the pathogen into the suit should a puncture or cut of the fabric occur. An air supply via hose for each suit is provided isolating the worker completely from the room atmosphere. Strict procedures for access to the hot room are followed. One's life does in fact depend on it.

TRAINING

Training includes use of protective gear (mask, clothing, etc.), detection of chemical agents, symptoms of agent exposure, first aid treatment, decontamination procedures, and employment. Additionally, Chemical Personnel train lower echelon or unit chemical officers and noncommissioned officers who are appointed to serve as the unit chemical personnel. This usually occurs at the company level. These appointed personnel attend military post schools staffed by Chemical Corps officers and NCOs and provide the unit with in-house experts for the lowest level commands. They remain up-to-date in the latest developments, policies, doctrines and training techniques provided by the installation or major command Chemical Corps personnel. The unit chemical personnel additionally are charged with primary responsibility to the unit commander for the serviceability of all unit NBC equipment and materials.

Unit training includes classroom instruction on NBC principles, hands-on practical experience in protective equipment, measures and procedures, decontamination procedures, and gas chamber training employing the protective mask with tearing agents.

Training with live agents, the GB and VX nerve agents, is conducted at the Chemical Decontamination Training Facility located at Fort McClellan in Alabama. This facility is the only one of its kind in the Free World. All soldiers in the Chemical Military Occupational Specialty (MOS) train at this facility. This includes enlistees for the Chemical MOS and extends to senior officers in the Senior Commanders Course (colonels and general officers) as well as Navy and Marine Corps courses offered at the Chemical School. Additionally, about 60 soldiers each year from the German Army have attended the school. Some State and Federal level civilian employees have also attended the course offerings.

WORLDWIDE DISTRIBUTION OF COLD WAR CHEMICAL UNITS

The following maps display the locations of the cold war regular U.S. Army and National Guard Chemical Units throughout the Continental United States (CONUS), the Pacific Basin (Hawaii, S. Korea), and in Europe (former W. Germany to include W. Berlin within E. Germany). The units are located by capital alphabetic letters enclosed by a hexagon. The legend for such unit locations is given below for each map.

Map 1. Active CONUS Regular Army Units:
        A-- Ft. Meade, MD: 82 JA DET (NBCE)(JA)
        B-- Ft. Bragg, NC: 21 ABN/AA CO (82 ABN DIV), 101 DECON CO (CORPS),
           1 JA DET
        C-- Ft. Stewart, GA: 91 CM CO (24 ID)
        D-- Ft. Campbell, KY: 63 ABN/AA CO (101 AA DIV), 36 JA DET
        E-- Ft. Polk, LA: 84 SG CO (MTZ)(-), 45 CM CO
        F-- Ft. Riley, KS: 1 PLT 172 SG CO (MTZ), 12 CM CO (1 ID)
        G-- Ft. Hood, TX: 46 SG CO (MTZ), 181 DECON CO (CORPS), 68 CM CO (1
           CAV), 44 CM CO (2 AD), 2 CM BN, 51 JB DET
        H-- Ft. Sill, OK: 83 JA DET
        I-- Ft. Carson, CO: 172 SG CO (MTZ)(-), 31 CM CO (4 ID)
        J-- Ft. Bliss, TX: 1 PLT 84 SG CO (MTZ), 507 FA DET, 63 JA DET, 89 LA DET
        K-- Ft. Lewis, WA: 164 SG CO (MTZ)(-), 9 CM CO (MTZ)(9 ID)
        L-- Ft. Irwin, CA: 1 PLT 164 SG CO (MTZ)

Map 2. Active CONUS National Guard Units
        A-- Lexington, MA: 272 CM CO (NBC DEF)(26 ID)
        B-- Brooklin, NY: 42 CM CO (NBC DEF)(42 ID)
        C-- Seagirt, NJ: 50 CM CO (HVY DIV)(50 AD)
        D-- Philadelphia, PA: 128 CM CO (NBC DEF)(28 ID)
        E-- Frankfort, KY: 141 CM CO (HVY DIV)(35 ID)
        F-- Houston, TX: 449 CM CO (HVY DIV)(49 AD)
        G-- Terre Haute, IN: 438 CM CO (NBC DEF)(38 ID)
        H-- Northfield, MN: 447 CM CO (NBC DEF)(47 ID)
        I-- Long Beach, CA: 140 CM CO (HVY DIV)(40 ID)

Map 3. The Pacific Basin: Regular U.S. Army Units-- Hawaii & S. Korea
        A-- Schofiled Barracks, HW: 71 CM CO (25 DIV)
        B-- Camp Casey, S. Korea: 4 CM BN
        C-- Yong Song, S. Korea: 38 JA DET

Map 4. U.S. Army Chemical Units- W. Germany (preunification)
        A-- W. Berlin (in former E. Germany): 43 FA DET
        B-- Fulda: 19 FA DET, 54 LA DET
        C-- Katerbach: 69 CM CO (1 AD)

D-- Nurnberg: 17 CM DET (DECON)(FA), 20 CM DET (NBCE)(JB), 87 CM DET (RECON)(LA)
E-- Wurzburg: 92 CM CO (3 ID)
F-- Karlsruhe: 10 DECON CO (CORPS)
G-- Stuttgart: 16 JB DET
H-- Nellingen: 51 DECON CO (CORPS), 11 DECON CO (CORPS), 242 JB DET
I-- Pirmasens: 98 FB DET (59 ORD BDE)
J-- Kaiserslautern: 26 JB DET
K-- Bad Kreuznach: 25 CM CO (8 ID)
L-- Darmstadt: 247 FB DET (32 AADCOM)
M-- Frankfurt: 22 CM CO (3 AD), 503 JB DET
N-- Giessen: 95 DECON CO (CORPS)

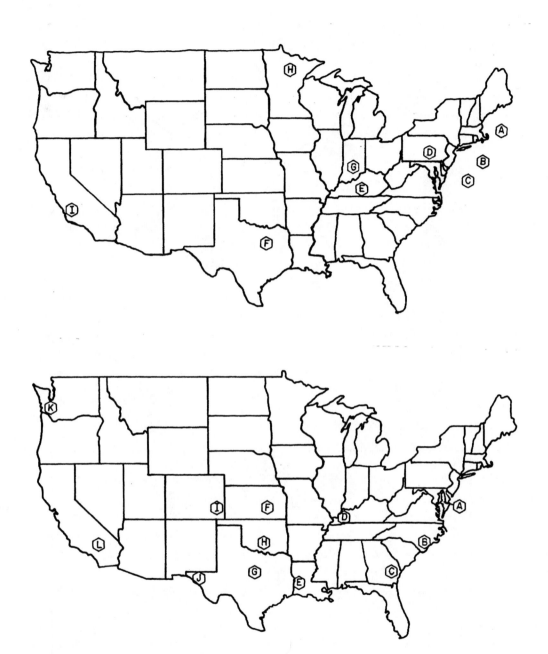

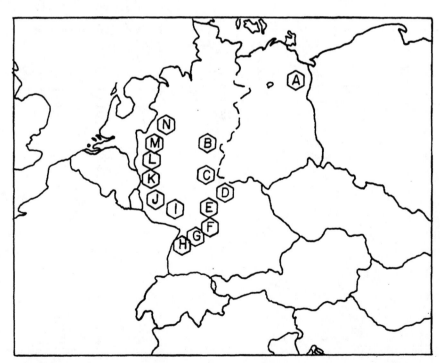

CHAPTER 21

TRAINING AND EDUCATION

Before a war military science seems a real
science, like astronomy; but after a war it
seems more like astrology.
-Rebecca West, 1892-1983[1]

Two essentials are paramount to the effectiveness and survivability of not only a military unit, or the individual soldier but also of a civilian. These two essentials are training and attitude. Thorough training is no guarantee.

For the soldier the term training brings to mind images of firing ranges for small arms familiarization. It also includes hand-to-hand combat, survival, escape and evasion and a range of other lesser known subjects. But training goes well beyond the skills of personal soldiering. It is much more than the techniques of killing and personal survival. These subjects enable the soldier to protect himself. Training also includes aspects dependent upon the individual's own conduct and choreographed with many other soldiers as well.

Without training, the soldier or the military unit to which he belongs does not know what to do. They must know the established routine or 'plays' for the conduct of their particular method of battle at their level of organization. It is in the training of the soldier and his unit that such terms as employment, fire and maneuver, escape and evade, hit and run, envelopment, interdiction, air assault, airmobile, and a host of other military jargon take on special meaning and mean very specific actions to be taken by the soldier or his unit. It matters not if the soldier and his unit are squad, platoon, company, battalion, brigade or division in size, he must know the list of 'plays' just as the football team member must know the repertoire of team plays. It is because of this need for each man (or woman in today's military) to know their niche and role in the conduct of battle that the Department of Defense spends tens of millions of dollars a year on unit training from the squad level on up to the division. Occasionally, such training is combined arms[2] training. These rehearsals go on year round. One of the reasons for this repetition is that the soldier must be able to react to a wide range of circumstances he may encounter under the heat of battle, without hesitation, or prolonged confusion. He must also remain flexible to the unforeseen. His life and that of his unit members literally depends on his instant, automatic 'knee-jerk' reactions. The training is repetitive. That is, his response to fire or orders must be instinctually habitual in nature. When incoming artillery barrages are dropped on you there is no time to stop, think and weigh options. That is the method of disaster in combat. Thus training is the intent to instill in the soldier, automatic spit-second reactions to do the right thing without having to think too long or too hard about it. Clearly, there are circumstances where time is

---

[1] In *The Harvest of a Quiet Eye*, p. 159

[2] Combined arms are integrated Army, Air Force and Navy exercises. Such exercises can last weeks.

available, and a little thought is well worth the time spent. This is in fact reflected in the OPORD (Operations Order) issued to all subordinate commands.[3] The automatic reactions desired by the military are the kind that minimize casualties and enhance the probability for successful accomplishment of the mission. Training is the preparation for saving lives and the accomplishment of the mission, though the importance is not necessarily in that order. The training is applied to private and company commander alike, enlisted to officer throughout all levels of command. This is and should be no less true for training in NBC. This brings us to attitude.

Attitude is critical to the ability of a soldier or military force to carry out their mission. Ten dedicated, well trained, and spirited soldiers can reek more havoc against an enemy force four or five times their size if the opponent force is poorly trained and demoralized, regardless of their materiel advantages. This was shown very clearly and effectively in the Vietnam war. The Viet Cong had little by way of logistics and they seldom operated in large unit operations, but they were very effective for their size. Our Green Beret and Navy Seals were as much a product and spirit of that fact as any other. They, too, were small (about six to twelve men) units operating essentially off the cuff while in the field. Attitude begins and ends with the commanders and leaders of any military unit regardless of size. The officers are the brains behind the brawn of a unit. If the brain does not function well neither does the body. If the officer has a poor attitude, poor morale, one cannot seriously expect the unit under that officer's direction to fare any better. Attitude has a very direct impact on training. If the troops see and understand that the officers take the training seriously and approach it with determination and example, the troops will get the message.

Fear in battle is normal. It can also be paralytic and lethal. Training intends to minimize fear by instilling confidence in the soldier of himself, his equipment, his leaders, and yes, his training. If training is lacking in any area that directly impacts on the soldier's ability to survive and function under the heat of battle, fear takes over, and fear can lead to panic under fire.

An armored officer would not dream of training for engagement of Soviet armored units in Europe and not include in that training Soviet armored equipment capabilities and weaknesses as well as recognition of his own equipment abilities and weaknesses. The infantry officer would not consider himself qualified to close with and fight a Soviet platoon or company without having learned something of Soviet small unit tactics, order of battle, and weapons systems available and how to employ his own men and materiel resources against such a foe.

Any enemy will seek to determine your weaknesses. He will plan to capitalize on those weaknesses. He will use those weaknesses against you. This applies not only to materiel weaknesses, but to training weaknesses. Remember, one of the intelligence gathering techniques is to take prisoners while on patrols. Regardless of official, national level press releases concerning a military force's preparedness, the truth comes from the mouths of POWs. A skillful, expert intelligence officer can sort out the facts from the fiction.

Training in the armed forces entails intimate familiarity with weapons and equipment. Live firing exercises are designed to zero weapons from small arms to big bore heavy artillery guns. This training also instills confidence in the soldier for his weaponry. He sees first hand that it works. NBC training does not enjoy the same sense of near reality training. Standard US small unit NBC training consists of three components: classroom instruction, gas chamber exercise, and an NBC component usually integrated into an overall FTX (Field Training Exercise) of the unit.

Classroom instruction consists of a detailed disassembly and reassembly of the protective mask, its components, its care and maintenance, its use. Also, the soldier learns about the different agents,

---

[3] Operations orders detail the mission, units to carry it out, support available, logistics, the time and date of commencement, and a summary of the situation as it affects the mission, and actions of adjacent units.

lethal and incapacitating, symptoms of exposure, antidotes and treatments applicable, decontamination procedures, detection of agents, etc. This type of detailed training is essentially academic in nature, complete with field and training manuals available to students be they the rank and file troops or unit NBC officers and NCOs attending a post NBC school. They take the lessons back to their units and hold unit level classes for their personnel. This naturally leads to a dilution of the knowledge and expertise. This phase of the training usually ends with a graduation exercise held at the post gas chamber where they undergo a practical exercise in the protective mask's use in a teargas environment.

FTXs are branch oriented, specific field training. That is, armored units conduct armored tactics, infantry, infantry tactics, and airborne units jump out of perfectly good aircraft in simulated airmobile assaults. NBC training in the field is integrated with these conventional training scenarios. This consists of an alert to gas attack to which the unit's response is monitored and judged along with other FTX subject matter. (Units sometimes know the schedule of such tests...) This training usually entails masking up and going through the motions of a contaminated environment operation. If decontamination materials are about to expire in their shelf-life, and need to be replaced, these materials may then actually be used to go through a "dress rehearsal" decontamination of the unit. This is rarely done, though. It is here that the contrast between traditional training and off-the-cuff NBC training experiences a chasm in reality training. Conventional training is hands-on. Troops fire weapons; operate tanks; move, setup, fire, move again; artillery batteries set-up, zero and fire; airborne troops jump with real parachutes. Yet in NBC training, the closest they come to the real value and purpose of the protective mask is in a post gas chamber filled with CS (teargas). It remains difficult to understand how a soldier can believe and have confidence in his mask's ability to really protect him against lethal agents when he is exposed only to teargas which produces relatively minor symptoms of tearing, stinging of the eyes and runny nose. He learns first hand that his mask is good against teargas. If the enemy uses teargas, the soldier's confidence is at a peak. What about the lethal stuff?

Training with live ammunition is dangerous. Accidents do happen. Even Airborne assault exercises from time to time experience a death from a parachute failure. But live jump exercises are still conducted for the simple reason that there is no other way to simulate a realistic air assault parachute jump. Additionally, the more jumps a soldier gets, the more confident he is of his ability to do so. The training makes the mechanics of jumping automatic. It frees his mind for what is 100 % hazardous to him-- the enemy at the jump zone.

Armored exercises are fraught with danger. Sixty ton tanks rampaging across the countryside and maneuvering on a dime with infantry about runs the risk of a soldier being run over by such a tank. Accidents of this kind have happened though thankfully not very often. But how else do you train combined arms tactics to armor and infantry without such hazardous field training? Use a simulator? If only wars were fought with simulators.

There are safety precautions to be taken to minimize if not eliminate accidents, especially lethal accidents. But softening the training in the name of absolute safety (which can never be attained) is to expose the soldier to the greater risk of death at the hands of a future enemy for lack of thorough, effective and near realistic training. Old timers seasoned in battle of WWII or Korea often say, a pound of sweat in training saves a pint of blood in battle.

The few soldiers and officers who receive real lethal military chemical agent training is not enough. Just as each soldier is required to qualify on the rifle range, each soldier must be required to qualify in a realistic lethal chemical agent exercise. The former Soviet military practiced this principle regularly. The exercise does not have to be in the open air during an FTX. It could be a gas chamber type exercise in which the soldiers clearly see that they are in a lethal environment, protected quite well by their protective masks and whatever other protective clothing is required by the nature of the agent. No better demonstration of the lethal contents of the air is necessary than to have a sacrificial rat[4] removed from its protective, airtight cage after some time. The sight of the animal dying before their masked eyes will tell more in that picture than thousands of words uttered in a classroom. It also will reinforce the classroom stated importance of the protective mask. Decontamination exercises with lethal agents also is a valuable training lesson. It's one thing to tell a soldier that the antitank round will knock out a Soviet tank. It's something else more demonstrable to see a tank destroyed in a training exercise by that very type antitank round. So too, the use of decontamination materials to decontaminate a surface that is contaminated with a lethal agent is valuable. The soldier graduating from such exercises **will** have confidence in his NBC equipment. He is, after all, living proof that it works. As in any training exercise with equipment and materials that are potentially dangerous or lethal, the instructors must be present and closely monitor and supervise each step of the training exercise. It is done with live ammo firing of small arms, artillery, tank, grenades, flamethrowers, etc. It can be done with toxic chemical agents, too. Training with chemical agents does not mean that they must be used in combat. It merely trains the soldier in recognizing the real stuff and how to handle and deal with it on a hot battlefield. As any veteran of combat will tell you, the battlefield is no place to learn the basics. The battlefield is no place for on-the-job training of beginners.

The U.S. government spends billions of dollars every year for the latest in techno-armament. It is quite revealing then to read that the U.S. Military forces of Desert Shield/Storm operated in the theater in less than fully prepared manner as it pertains to NBC operational threats.[5] This state of affairs perhaps illustrates the lagging behind of NBC equipment compared to the high tech variety.

In the civilian world, education is no less important. Education prepares the individual for the requirements of the chosen career. Attitude is also important. If you feel "I can't do this," you will perform in such a way as to prove it so. Education should include the minimum basic knowledge. Laws require a basic background in mathematics (so you can balance your check book), reading (so you can read traffic signs, etc.) and English (so you can communicate orally and in writing). In a society such as ours, is a basic knowledge of simple chemistry and physics no less important in light of all the chemicals in the home and in the workplace?

Hundreds of people suffer injuries at home or in the workplace from chemical related accidents. Often times, these accidents result from the mixing of two or more incompatible materials. Sometimes, just ignorant contact with a single chemical is all that is required for injury. The simplest explanation for this is the lack of education on the part of the user. We live in a very chemically oriented society. In fact one of the distinguishing characteristics, if not the distinguishing characteristic, between a modern technologically advanced society and the underdeveloped societies is the intensity and degree of chemical technology in place. You have but to look around you to see it.

Chemical technology is not just under the kitchen sink with all its household cleaners. Take electricity for example. Were it not for chemical technology, we would not have electricity. The wires which carry the current are insulated. Chemical technology gave us the rubberized and plasticized insulation of the wires. The wires themselves are a product of chemical technology. Modern sewage treatment also is a result of modern chemical technology. Certainly our state of national health, too,

---

[4] For those who object to the use of even the lowly rat as a sacrificial example, perhaps a cage of roaches would suffice. Certainly there isn't a Society for the Prevention of Cruelty to Roaches? Death in such gas chambers would be quick for any creature.

[5] "Chemical Warfare Protective Equipment Needs Upgrading", *Chemical & Engineering News*, 25 May 1992, page 13.

is a product of chemical technology. All the medicinals at the finger tips of the physician, the antibiotics, the anesthesia for surgeries, the rubber gloves, the discardable surgical gowns, all is a result of chemical technology. Much of the comfort and safety of the automobile is a product of chemical technology. Our agriculture also is a chemical technology dependent endeavor. Our foods are processed, packaged and prepared in accordance with the abilities afforded by chemical technology.[6] Even our homes are a product of the means permitted by chemical technology. Simply put, take chemical technology *completely* out of American society and our comfortable, safe, well fed, healthy way of life would collapse.

With the all pervasive role of chemical technology it is unfortunate that our educational system does not emphasize a better foundation in the chemical sciences than it presently does. The vast majority of high school graduates are not required a course in chemistry for graduation. Even our colleges and universities do not require any course in chemistry for the bachelors degree. We do require reading skills, but what good do those skills do if one does not also understand the chemical hazard residing in the identity of two chemical compounds found in the home? Simple concepts of acid and base, oxidizing and reducing agent are lost to the majority of the public. Most accidents are a result of ignorant and haphazard mixing of acids and bases or oxidizers with reducers. Explosions or toxic fumes can result.[7]

----

[6] It is true that in the past 10 to 20 years growing concern about various additives has occurred. With some exceptions, generally chemical technology has enhanced the nutritional value of our foods: vitamin D added to milk and vitamin enriched breads as two examples.

[7] As an example, concentrated sulfuric acid should not be used to clean clogged sewage drains as has been done. The reason is that sulfuric acid releases hydrogen sulfide, rotten egg odored gas, which is quite toxic and most especially within a confined space. Diluting concentrated sulfuric acid by pouring water into it leads to an extremely hot reaction of the acid with water, causing the water to boil or spatter and with the spattered water, droplets of acid ejected like a volcanic eruption. Mixing household ammonia with bleach leads to release of hydrazine, a poisonous lung irritant.

PART VIII

CHAPTER 22

FUTURE OUTLOOK: TWENTY-FIRST CENTURY CBW

... he that increaseth knowledge, increaseth sorrow
-Ecclesiastes 1:18

GENERAL

Chemical and biological warfare and terrorism (CBWT) is the subject of this book. That is, on the one hand, too broad a classification and on the other hand an arbitrary one. For example, many authors consider the use of toxics (poisons of biological origin) as chemical warfare. With today's knowledge of chemistry and biology, a better classification is needed. I make the following distinctions.

Any chemical substance which has a generalized reaction that affects nearly every part of the body by an underlying common reaction process is a chemical agent. Examples are the choking and blistering agents. The choking agents as previously noted generally react by acylation processes, also releasing acidic or corrosive by-products. Most vulnerable are the lungs because of their central importance in oxygen/carbon dioxide exchange. Blistering agents, also alkylating reagents, are broad spectrum agents, similarly affecting skin, eyes, lungs, etc. alike. These substances are man-made chemical agents and their use constitutes classical chemical warfare.

The blood agents and the nerve agents form a very special group of chemical agents. These compounds, as noted in previous chapters, attack very specific biochemical processes of the body, in particular key enzymatic reactions. They interfere and block these processes. Thus, these compounds are better classified as biochemical agents and their use constitutes what should be termed biochemical warfare. The use of an extracted toxin (such as botulinum or tetanus toxins) from a bacterial source which interferes with a specific biochemical process of man is also considered here a biochemical agent of biochemical warfare, both because of its biological origin and its unique biochemical reactivity. In the two specific examples cited in the previous sentence, they act on the nerves.

The use of biological agents is defined here as specifically requiring the presence of that causative microorganism to bring about the desired effects. Remember that in previous chapters dealing with pathogens and biological agents, the pathogens generally secreted toxins which cause the symptoms manifesting the infection. Though it is these toxins that bring about the serious consequences we call illness or disease, the host organism is itself present to secrete these toxins. Therefore,

> chemical agents .... chemical warfare
> biochemical agents ..... biochemical warfare
> biological agents .... biological warfare

What does this apparent splitting of hairs have to do with the future of CBWT? It is a matter of the advance of technology and knowledge. Consider the past.

Previous chapters have examined the past and present technology of chemical and biological warfare. Past chemical agents have been man-made and general or broad spectrum agents. That is, they have toxicities that affect a wide range of tissues and organs yet their actions are most pronounced on specific tissues and organs. Most particularly for the subject of this chapter and as a historical note, chemical agents have been essentially man-made compounds, that is, they are chemicals most generally not found naturally as such in other organisms. The case of toxins, poisons of biological origin, will be considered separately.

With the numerous international treaties and protocols against the use of chemical and biological agents, what possible future is there for what the military classifies as nuclear, biological and chemical warfare (NBC) and terrorism? There are laws against murder, but people still commit murder. At the international level, wars are still started by those with designs of conquest and power. The future of CBWT will probably follow the direction set by the nerve and incapacitating agents. However, these directions are but a few of the many directions which classical CBWT could follow. The capabilities of CBWT in the next century will be far from classical.

KEY POINTS OF FUTURE CBWT R & D

Because of the increased learning curve enjoyed by those seeking to take advantage of technology in the design and use of weaponry, particularly as regards terrorist groups keeping pace with those advances is all important for governments. Put simply, they must know what the opposition knows and can do. Also, as populations increase, natural resources decrease and food stocks become increasingly burdened with the demand, governments will have to be mindful of maintaining order and control over populations that may become less inhibited of government authority in light of socioeconomic stresses on those populations. The use of incapacitating agents for so-called riot control will become a more important factor as a means of control without causing undue harm. Recent upheavals in the Middle East with the use of the "rubber bullets" as a means of subduing unruly crowds will become increasingly under fire for the serious injury and death these projectiles cause.

Chapter 20 very briefly outlined a few of the current major interests of the U.S. Chemical Corps' research and development plans for the future. The interests of the military are guarded as far as public knowledge is concerned. One can make some educated guesses, estimates or put a different way, guesstimates of specific future developments required to bring CBWT capabilities up-to-date for the Twenty-First Century.[1] These developments must of necessity take into account what foreign interests are doing and the direction their efforts are or will take, even in light of treaties, conventions and other international laws. The order of presentation here in no way is intended to suggest a priority of effort. Each point presented has it own unique importance to the overall solution of many individual CBWT problems as realized by historical use, present developments, and future knowledge and technology.

---

[1] The reader is directed to *The Problem of Chemical and Biological Warfare: Vol. II, CB Weapons Today* for an early discussion of several of the possible directions of future CBW R&D. In this presentation, I expand slightly on some of the details or alter the ideas offered by others to fit my view of the direction of CBW R&D efforts for the future.

There are several major concerns as relates to CBWT agents, equipment, utilization, and operations in the future. Some of the interests and solutions sought are or will be dictated by domestic and geopolitical considerations and national policies. National policies themselves may well change several times over the course of decades along with who controls the political institutions of the U.S. or for that matter, another nation. It should be noted at the outset that any and all military developments and policies concerning CBWT capabilities will remain essentially very secret and subject only grudgingly to the most minimal disclosure and even then, for essentially political reasons.[2]

One of the most vexing problems associated with any CB agent use is the effects of weather on the agent. The problems posed to effective agent use by weather or more generally, the environment, are threefold: hydrolytic and sunlight (ultraviolet[3]) degradation of presently known and existing agents, destruction of agent cloud concentrations by winds, and temperature effects on the volatility of the agent itself. Little can be done about agent volatility under a given temperature without altering its other characteristics. Likewise, the hydrolytic susceptibility of an agent is a function of its chemical identity. The development of an agent with low susceptibility to hydrolysis is not an insurmountable problem. Even in cases of a desirable agent with poor resistance to hydrolysis, methods that protect the agent from weathering effects are also likely foci of study.

Will the agent perform as designed and intended? This calls the agent's reliability into question and it is the second area of interest. As pertains to toxic agents, there is little question of their reliability. But when biological agents are examined, reliability becomes important. At present, biological agents are not very reliable. A given bioagent may or may not perform as intended. It may not have the incapacitating or even lethal effects originally thought in field applications. It may even produce effects not desired by the user. The bioagent may be susceptible to the human immune system when originally thought not. Ebola has been observed to decrease in lethality with subsequent serial infections. An effective antibiotic may be quickly developed by the opponent. And worst of all possible cases, the bioagent may get out of control. It may spread more rapidly and over much larger areas than intended and may come back to infect the user's nation. In order to have reliability, there must be some effective control.

A third concern of significance to military and civilian populations alike is protection against CB hazards. Protection is double edged. There is individual protection and there is collective protection. Present protective gear such as the masks and suits or the collective protection tents provide protection, but it is protection that is not absolute and certainly not foolproof. One of the weak links in this area is the means of filtering hazardous agents, the charcoal filter elements. There are problems in uniformity of the particles, packing within the filter housing, and even serious questions of charcoal's ability to filter all possible toxic agents, and it is the unknown agent that worries the military thinkers grey-headed.

Protection on the battlefield for the soldier takes on a Buck Rogers appearance in light of other perceived future threats very different from even the CBWT concerns. Military planners are concerned about the electromagnetic threats such as LASERS.[4] Chapter 17 referred to a futuristic

---

[2] Recall earlier mention of US Military experiments with biological agents in San Francisco and New York, most of which to this day remains largely cloaked in secrecy.

[3] A particularly significant problem of biological agents.

[4] Light Amplification through Stimulated Emission of Radiation.

protective BDU[5] to be worn by field troops-- the SIPE, Soldier Integrated Protective Ensemble. How far such designs will go from the drawing board remains to be seen, but the imagined threat is not entirely fictional. Our knowledge of LASER technology and their capabilities has come a long way since their first appearance in the late 1960s. The idea of a LASER weapon for destroying a tank, aircraft or reentry vehicle warhead from space is not entirely unlikely, *a la* Jules Verne.[6] Though a credible threat such as the now defunct USSR does not provide an immediate impetus to continued R&D efforts at previous breakneck pace, the R&D will undoubtedly continue. Such R&D may well make antipersonnel LASER weapons more workable for close range use (within a thousand meters) long before they are practical for antiarmor, antiaircraft applications.[7] There are three critical advantages to such weapons: (1) line-of-sight "ballistics", (2) speed of light effectiveness, and (3) in principle, stealth; no sound of detonation as with conventional armaments or the telltale signature of firing as with smoke and flame trails associated with chemically propelled munitions. This brings us to the fourth factor-- technological surprise.

Surprise has always been and will continue to be one of the ten principles of war. Throughout history, not only armies but nations have fallen because of effective use of surprise-- falling prey to what was totally unexpected, even considered impossible. The surprise attack on Pearl Harbor by the Imperial Japanese Naval Air Forces on the morning of 7 December 1941 was nothing if not a complete surprise.[8] It was both a tactical and strategic success and at the same time a tactical and

---

[5] Battle Dress Uniform

[6] Jules Verne wrote stories that entertained, marveled and stimulated the imagination of his readers down through the century. He also, as it turns out, wrote stories that were prophesies. He wrote of lighter than air ships (Zeppelins), travel to the moon (Apollo Astronauts, 1969), and of course who can forget Captain Nemo and his *Nautilus*, the imagined forerunner of today's nuclear powered, ballistic missile submarines. The first nuclear powered submarine (U.S. Navy) in fact was named *Nautilus*. And remember the underwater breathing gear Nemo's crew wore? In WWII (1943) Jacques-Yves Cousteau and Émile Gagnon invented the aqualung-- a steel cylindrical tank of compressed air fitted with a valve and regulator for underwater breathing. The sport is known as scuba diving-- self-contained underwater breathing apparatus. Man has long thought of breathing underwater and particularly in this century the though of doing so through liquid rather than air has been an active interest of research. The perfluorohydrocarbons bring us closer to realizing this possibility. The fictional movie *The Abyss* included this very idea in its plot. What man can imagine, man can probably find a way to do... given time and the advance of knowledge and technology. There are limits of course. Man can imagine flight under his own muscle power, but human anatomy and physics are against that particular dream.

[7] One of the more vexing technical problems with LASERS as a weapon is beam spread. In the atmosphere, air and water molecules as well as dust particles all interfere with the focused, concentrated beam diameter which can be as small as 0.1 mm. As the distance from the LASER increases, the beam experiences scattering which diffuses or spreads the beam out, also diminishing its power with distance. One solution: find a lasing material that is not affected appreciably by air. Not very likely and certainly not very easy.

[8] Historians have, since the day after the attack it seems, argued about how much of a surprise the attack was. It is a moot point insofar as the forces at Pearl Harbor had no idea of a planned attack against them. No one seriously entertained the notion that Japan would dare strike the U.S. Pacific Fleet at its Pearl Harbor lair. But remember, surprise is one of the principles of war. [*The Pacific War: 1941-1945*, John Costello, Quill, New York, 1982]

strategic failure.[9] Similarly, the use of the nuclear bombs by the U.S. on Hiroshima and Nagasaki were also surprise attacks. They were surprises because (1) the Japanese had very little, if any, idea about nuclear weapons actually being in existence, (2) each raid was carried out by only a few of B-29 bombers (only one was the weapon craft, the others were observer aircraft) and the Japanese had been lulled into complacency by reconnaissance flights of a few aircraft for months and (3) the magnitude of destruction visited by a single bomb was overwhelming to the human psyche. The nuclear bomb drops over Japan were by any definition a technological and strategic surprise. That fact was not lost on U.S. military planners. So what is the CBWT counterpart to the surprise WWII nuclear attack?

An effective technological surprise in CBWT matters has two faces: a (bio)chemical advance or a biological advance. Much has been made of the critical role of the stealth fighters during the Persian Gulf Operation Desert Storm. What better air weapon than an aircraft that is (nearly) invisible to any detection by the target. For chemical warfare, what better agent than one that is highly toxic or incapacitating, odorless, colorless, holds-up to environmental factors, easily packaged as a munition, unresponsive to any known antidote or treatment regimen, undetectable by present chemical agent detectors, difficult to identify[10], penetrable of all known protective systems and measures, and so rapid in effects as to give no warning of its presence until it is too late to react against it?

Efforts to prevent a technological surprise of a (bio)chemical nature will include broad and far reaching research into natural products toxicity as well as opportunistic synthetic discoveries. Presently well-known toxin examples illustrate the severe threat from use of such *hypertoxic* substances. Substances such as botulinum toxin, aflatoxin [I], ricin, and shellfish toxin, to name a few, possess incredible toxic potency which at least rival synthetic organophosphates toxicity if not exceed them.[11]

The above points introduce the fifth concern of future CBWT operations, that of detection and warning. This aspect of CBWT operations is of paramount importance to both military and civilian personnel. There is an axiom that goes, "know your enemy." It matters little whether the enemy is a man or man-made. In order to know your enemy, that is, to know the nature and character of the enemy, one must first have identified the enemy. Detection is the key here. One major concern of military tacticians and strategists of future CBWT operations is the unknown. How do you devise a method or system to detect that which does not yet exist or for which there is no known analog? For chemical agents, one way to reduce the probability of missing detection of a lethal chemical agent is to devise detection methods based not on specific cases or even specifically known classes of agent types but on marker chemical properties (such as chemical functional groups); or actions on or

---

[9] The Japanese did effectively destroy the U.S. Pacific Fleet stationed at Pearl, but they missed their primary target-- the U.S. carriers. The Japanese did totally destroy the battleship arm of the fleet, but they also left intact, the dry docks, fuel tank farms, and other facilities necessary to salvaging and repairing the damage. They also left the U.S. submarine fleet at Pearl intact which for the first six months before the Battle of Midway, raised hell with Japanese shipping throughout their Co-prosperity Sphere including the home islands as well.

[10] This last point of difficulty of identification is not a significant problem. Advances in analytical chemistry keep pace with advances in synthetic chemistry. Numerous analytical instruments presently exist and are being further refined in sensitivity and discriminatory ability as well as new instrument development and combinations. Such instrument systems are the Gas Chromatograph (GC), the Mass Spectrometer (MS), the Nuclear Magnetic Resonance Spectrometer (NMR), and the Fourier-Transform Infrared Spectrometer (FT-IR). Additionally, extensive computer based data banks of spectra of molecules and molecular fragments exist and grow in variety with each passing day. Our knowledge and ability to isolate and identify biologics also advances in a like pace.

[11] At the present state of knowledge, many other toxins are as toxic as the known organophosphates.

reactions with model systems that respond in measurable ways to various inhibitory or poisonous substances. Electronic means may provide the means for detection of incredibly minuscule quantities of hazardous chemical agents. Such means may rely on enzyme mediated reactions whose by-products are in some fashion detected by the instrument and subsequently signal agent presence by auditory and/or visual indications. Such systems are presently in use and under further study and development but will have to enjoy considerable advances in technology to be effective on a real-time basis and to truly detect toxics absolutely, let alone discriminately.

Detection of biological agent hazards provides even more difficult problems for resolution. Presently various biochemical and, in the extreme, molecular biological fingerprinting[12] tests, are required to identify a microbe. With the wide variety of microbes and the eventual possibility of genetic engineering modifications in the near future, detection and identification of pathogenic organisms will be difficult and complicated. For any detection test to have timely value in a military or public defensive sense, it must be rapid (within a few hours) and discriminate between nonpathogenic and pathogenic microbes. The detection of viruses will require methods vastly different from those of cellular organisms. The dependence of quantity of organism present in the sample for the detection system will be a critical factor directly tied to the sensitivity of the method of detection.

Even with detection, warning methods must be rapid and efficient. Communications will be a factor in future CBWT operations and preparedness. The dissemination of threat information and the effective and timely utilization of such information by both military and civilian authorities will play significant roles in the success in thwarting successful use of CB agents by enemy forces or enemy covert agents.[13]

In spite of the best detection and warning methods available or in development, the use of CB agents inevitably means that casualties will be taken. That fact brings us to the sixth area of concern of future CBWT operations-- up-to-date treatments and even in the ideal case-- prophylaxis. One of the more fascinating areas of medical research into treatment of toxic agent exposure is in preventing susceptibility to the toxic agent effects. The idea is simple enough but the execution is another matter. Prophylaxis entails the use of some other chemical compound or formulation that will react preferentially with the toxic agent absorbed and neutralize it before it can react with targeted cellular or tissue systems or serve to protect the cellular target from reaction with the CB agent. The work done with HMT, hexamethylenetetramine, after WWI was such a case of a prophylaxis against the choking agent phosgene. However, the preventative suffered from a few drawbacks, the most significant one being the requirement to take the prophylaxis agent several times during a day. This requirement of "taking your medication" every four or six hours poses serious operational problems under combat conditions, not to mention a further logistical headache.

---

[12] Biochemical tests consist in the simplest form as metabolism by-products analysis or microbe composition (as for example Gram-positive vs. Gram-negative cells) whereas molecular biological fingerprinting consists of elaborate DNA typing and matching analyses.

[13] Recently it was revealed in news reports that the site where American forces destroyed munitions stores and now believed to have stored mustard and nerve agent munitions was not only unknown to the US forces engaged in that destruction, but was known to the CIA as soon as 1989. Yet the CIA did not, as alleged in the reports, notify the US forces in Iraq of said threat. The right hand once again may not be talking to the left hand.

Another example of a pretreatment is the use of a carbamate preparation for GD poisoning.[14,15,16] Pyridostigmine {Treatment (Chapter 18), [V]} is a carbamate which when taken before exposure to the nerve agent lessens the effects of the nerve agent on the nervous system. Carbamates generally are more easily hydrolyzed from the serine hydroxyl group at the active site of the cholinesterase-like enzymes (about 30 minutes) than are the organophosphate adducts (over four hours if at all). The principle is that the carbamate binds to the active site and thus blocks binding of the organophosphate. Administration of the atropine/oxime antidote system then diminishes the effects of and neutralizes the organophosphate itself and over the time course of these two chemical processes, the carbamate is hydrolyzed from the enzyme. The hydrolysis of carbamate from the serine hydroxyl group is faster than the hydrolysis of the organophosphate moiety. The desirable utility of a pretreatment or prophylaxis agent that will confer some effective level of protection against toxic agent exposure will certainly be an area of active research. This will be more so as newer toxic agents are discovered and probably encountered, perhaps likely in a civilian-industrial R&D setting as a result of accidents.

Because uptake of toxic agents is nearly if not exactly directly proportional to the level of metabolic activity and thus the state of stress and fear[17] of the individual, various sedatives may provide modest reduction of enzymatic inactivation by anticholinergic substances. One candidate sedative is diazepam {Treatment (Chapter 18), [VI]}. The intent of any such medicinals in countering the effects of toxic agents is merely to chemically calm (sedate) the individual. By so doing, the individual's breathing rate, blood pressure[18] and pulse rate are minimized and therefore, reduce the

---

[14] USAMRICD Technical memorandum 90-1, p. 10

[15] J. Amer. Med. Assoc. **262(5)**, 649-652 (1989)

[16] Military Medicine **155(11)**, 527-533 (1990)

[17] It is important to note here that in combat, stress and fear are at a maximum and these human states are significantly influential on metabolic rate through the agency of adrenaline (now called epinephrine). Thus, blood pressure, pulse rate, glucose metabolism, glycogen metabolism, fat mobilization, protein metabolism, neuronal metabolism, etc. all increase markedly. All these processes translate into deeper and increased rapidity of breathing which is the means by which most toxic agents can be maximally absorbed and deposited directly to the blood stream.

[18] Blood pressure is a very significant factor. The increased pressure within the capillaries increases the pressure sensitive diffusion processes of exchange of materials across the membranes between capillaries and cells. Many physicochemical processes are pressure sensitive as relates to equilibrium of a given reaction. A simple example of this pressure sensitivity is offered by the physicochemical dissolution of carbon dioxide in water (such as in a carbonated beverage bottle). The reaction equilibrium is represented as:

$$H_2O(l) + CO_2(g) \dashrightarrow H_2CO_3(aq)$$

where (l) is liquid, (g) is gaseous and (aq) is aqueous condition. The equilibrium can be mathematically described by:

$$K_{eq} = [H_2CO_3]/P_{CO2}$$

Because this equilibrium has a set numerical value, imbalance in any of the three components leads to an adjustment of the relative measures of each such that the overall numerical value of the constant, K, is reestablished. Put another way:

$$[H_2CO_3] = K_{eq} \times P_{CO2}$$

which states that the concentration of the H_2CO_3 in solution is directly dependent upon the pressure of the CO_2. Increase CO_2 pressure, one increases the concentration of the H_2CO_3 in solution.

amount of toxic agent inhaled. This can buy significant time for treatment methods to be applied effectively and reduce the overall consequences of the agent's toxicity.

A seventh area of concern nearly complements the sixth. Decontamination is a defensive and preventative method that, if carried out early and effectively, reduces the risks of casualties from contact with toxic agents. One of the pressing problems with current decontamination agents is their own innate toxicity and environmental hazard. There is a new decontamination agent in the pipeline for use in the closing years of the twentieth century (see Decontamination: Chapter 19). Future studies on the decontamination materials will undoubtedly require components which are so-called environmentally safe.[19] Of greater importance is the need for decontamination agents which present as little hazard to human use and contact compared to the standard STP and DS2 of the post-WWII era. The requirement for the decontamination agent to actually destroy and remove a toxic agent from personnel, equipment or facilities requires a material which will react with the toxic substance. Since the most effective destruction of toxic agents is by oxidation, hydrolysis or destructive fragmentation of the toxic agent molecules, decontamination agents must be able to act in one of those ways with the toxic agents. For decontamination to be effective on a real-time scale, the decontamination agent must react quickly. Only harsh chemical substances can be expected to chemically react so quickly and completely. The selection of universal decontamination agents requires the agent to react with and destroy a wide range of toxic agent types which undoubtedly have diverse chemical functional group properties. On a simple level, if one wishes to decontaminate an acid, base is used. But base will not decontaminate a base; an acid must be used. To destroy either an acid or a base with one decontaminating agent, the agent must be able to react chemically with either an acid or a base. Such a compound that is environmentally safe is not so easily found. Finally, the by-products of decontamination must also themselves be nontoxic and environmentally safe.

The eighth point of study for future chemical or biological agents is improved means of dissemination. This not so much for first use of such agents as currently banned by treaties and conventions, but for an understanding of the means employed by a hostile adversary. Given that munitions types will not significantly deviate from their historical forms (explosive, grenade, bomb, missile, artillery, sprays, etc.) the improvement in dissemination means will probably follow improved packaging. Problems with spray systems center around clogging of nozzles, hose lines, etc. Better ways of packaging agents for spraying will require means to prevent them from clumping up, sticking to surfaces, absorbing moisture, etc.

The dissemination of agents by explosive means also presents problems with uniformity of particle size and thus concentration. Particle sizes can range from minuscule aerosolic particles to that of a small stone for the solid materials. For liquid form agents, the problem is that of minuscule liquid mist (aerosol) particles to large splashing quantities. The intent of liquid agent dispersal is not to leave a pool of liquid on the ground that draws attention to its presence. Aerosol science is one of the specific interests of the U.S. Army Chemical Research, Development and Engineering Center (CRDEC). Improved ballistic performance of agent during detonation of the munition will also depend upon packaging advances and characteristics of the agent. The stability of the agent to storage is a factor that has an impact on dissemination when the agent is used on the battlefield or in a civilian population. Some of the traditional agents can polymerize on storage and added components minimize this problem. Additionally, binary agent systems have found use with the organophosphate nerve

---

[19] The term environmentally safe is a laudable sounding term but also a loaded term. In small enough quantities, most anything will be absorbed and processed by nature to its degradation and disappearance. It is when the material is dumped into the environment in huge quantities that environmental overload occurs and pollution and damage arises. This overload can be a localized phenomenon or a global phenomenon.

agents. Newer developed agents will also be subject to packaging and storage studies aimed at producing a consistency at the time of use and point of delivery to maximize uniform dispersal and minimize evidence of agent presence, as well as enhance storage shelf-life. Again these points do not suggest that western nations will do so for employment, but rather for understanding the capabilities of an adversary.

Packaging raises the ninth point of future CBWT agent development[20]-- micro-encapsulation. This subject may have greater impact on biological agents than on chemical agents given the susceptibility of various biologics to the destructive effects of air and sunlight. Micro-encapsulation entails the packaging of microscopic particles of a substance within a protective or encasing wrap.[21] The possibilities are numerous as to the properties of the microencapsulant. Such systems can be devised to be slowly photodegraded or slowly hydrolyzed by moisture or even degraded by body enzymes once ingested, inhaled, etc. Such microencapsulant degradative specificities can provide a uniquely targeted time and site of release of agent after contact with the micro-encapsulated agent.

Encapsulation methods drawing on recent studies of such exotic substances as buckminsterfullerene[22] may offer a starting point of design of agent delivery means that protect agent against environmental effects, but release the agent within cellular or tissue environments. The literature has many references to these kinds of encapsulation means for delivery of insulin, antibiotics and such for useful, future medical purposes such as time-release processes.

As noted in chapter 20, there are several areas of immediate concern to the U.S. military as concerns CBW developments. Considerable interest presently centers on: receptor technology, aerosol science, alternatives to animal testing, hazardous waste management, molecular modeling and display, plasma technology, mass spectrometry, respiratory test technology and stress physiology and decontamination/contamination avoidance. Some of these areas of interest have been considered above.

Receptor technology is concerned with the three dimensional fit of molecules on what are called receptor sites. Biologically speaking, receptors are locations on cell surfaces which bind a particular molecule. The molecule which binds to the receptor initiates specific biochemical processes of the cell. A simple example is the hormone insulin. Insulin binds to specific receptors on cells which trigger specific processes which utilize glucose (glycolysis), suppress fatty acid breakdown (β-oxidation), suppress proteolysis (breakdown of body proteins) and enhance uptake and utilization of dietary amino intake (amino acid metabolism) and glucose absorption. The importance of this specific receptor process is evidenced in the absence or greatly diminished production of insulin as typified by the disease insulin-dependent diabetes (juvenile onset or Type I diabetes). The importance of receptor technology is particularly significant in the action of some of the most toxic substances known to man such as botulinum toxin, tetanus toxin, most any bacterial, animal or plant toxin. Understanding the biochemical dynamics of receptor-toxin interaction can offer clues to the development of effective antidotes and even in the ideal, prophylaxis measures.

---

[20] The use of binary agents is already in place, applied to the nerve agents.

[21] The process of micro-encapsulation was first used commercially in 1954 for carbonless "carbon" copy paper. This innovation was introduced prior to WWII by the National Cash Register Co. (NCR). [*The Problem of Chemical and Biological Warfare; Vol. II CB Weapons Today*]

[22] Buckminsterfullerene is a molecule of carbon forming a spherical cage-like molecule of some 30 or more carbons whose center or internal region is vacant, but available for insertion of some smaller molecular specie.

Alternatives to animal testing is twofold. First it was noted in previous discussions on detection, chapter 17, that earlier methods of detection utilized animal subjects. This was an outgrowth of turn-of-the-century coal mining operations where canaries were often used in the depths of a mine to alert miners to the presence of poisonous gases during drilling and blasting. As was also stated, the method relies on the equal or increased sensitivity of the test animal to the poison compared to humans. This is not always the case, though decades of experience has revealed a number of animals that do provide reasonably good warning. However, as the toxicity of man-made military agents increases, methods are required that reveal the hazard before a lethal dose arises in advance of specific responses of the test animal. Additionally, it has always been a problem in translating the LD_{50} for an animal to that for a human. Finally, the animal rights groups have become more vocal, even violent in their idealization of man's stewardship and dominion over "the birds of the air and fishes of the sea."[23] There is consideration of developing animal computer models for use in testing and developing medicinals and procedures that historically required real, air breathing animals. I remain skeptical about the computer-modeled animal substitute.

Hazardous waste management would seem an issue of political and commercial importance, but it has importance to the military forces as well. The U.S. Armed Forces are perhaps the single most significant producer of wastes ranging from the munitions plants to the installations and their various spills of one kind or another. The technology that they may develop will most certainly have immediate benefit to the civilian sector. Much of what the military must be concerned about is also a headache for the commercial industrialist.

Molecular modeling and display is an ongoing endeavor in the scientific community. With increased computer capacity and speed, we are able to model and display increasingly more complex molecular systems including reactions. This is particularly important to those involved in accessing explosives and their characteristics at detonation. These reactions take place in milli- or microseconds and are too fast to easily observe and record with high speed film though such records are made for visual cues. As our understanding in the area of fluid dynamics, kinetics and a range of other technical fields increases, we will be better able to factor in and model the complexities associated with these and other presently difficult processes to study. Modeling will include improvements in dynamic flow of air masses applicable to the study of agent cloud dispersal and it will also have a meteorological benefit in weather forecasting.

Plasma is thought by most laymen to be a component of blood, the straw-colored liquid remaining after the removal of the cellular fraction. Plasma technology in the military has nothing to do with blood, though the Medical Corps certainly is interested in blood plasma. A plasma, in physics, is a superheated ionic gaseous state in which there are electrons and positively charged atoms. The overall system is electrically neutral. Such a state of matter[24] is viewed absolutely essential to the development

---

[23] I don't wish to appear intolerant of the views and philosophies held by another group. Even I recognize that there are some medical experiments performed on animals that stretch the imagination's acceptance of medically useful data. At the same time, as a scientist, I do not feel the extremists of these groups appreciate the importance of early animal medical research that developed the medicinals and vaccines that gave them their excellent health which enables them to set booby traps for humans-- a serious warp in their claimed "sense of humanity."

[24] There are three classical states of matter: gas, liquid and solid. A plasma is a fourth state.

and harnessing of fusion[25] reactions for electrical power generation. On a more earthly basis, plasma research presumably will be applicable to the detection and analysis of toxic agents by small devices that convert a micro-sample of agent to a (quasi)plasma state. Along this same line of charged particles analysis, the mass spectrometer is a device in use by chemical scientists for the identification of compounds.

Mass spectrometers are instruments that take a small sample and ionize it by a fragmentation process. Each polyatomic molecule has a characteristic fragmentation pattern or fingerprint including what is called its molecular ion[26] that uniquely identifies it. By developing mass spectrometer units that take advantage of microchip computer technology and data bases, a sample of a suspected agent in theory can be quickly identified.

Respiratory test technology is a vital area of interest in elucidating the dynamics and kinetics of lung-active inhaled agents. Particularly important is the physicochemical dynamics of absorption across the membranes between the alveoli and capillaries. The understanding of these processes will have a marked impact not only on the development of chemical agents but also on the development of improved respiratory therapies and treatments for any number of chemically induced, respiratory based intoxications. It will also be a benefit in the treatment of the more common and troubling respiratory ailments afflicting millions in society.

The role of stress physiology is another area of importance to combating various poisonings. Stress increases blood pressure, pulse rate, and metabolism across the board. Such responses only speed the absorption and spread of toxics throughout the body. In its simplest consideration (and by no means the only) any methods that can be developed, be they chemical or psychological, that can put the patient at ease, to calm him physiologically, will buy invaluable time for the effectiveness of applied antidotes and therapeutic regimens.

Other areas of interest for future CBWT operation research and development include improved incapacitating agents; bioagent sampling and detection and natural products toxins; and the future of smoke/obscurants. These areas will be discussed below under their respective headings.

BIOCHEMICAL AGENTS

Nerve agents represent the ground-breaking advance in toxic chemical agents. They are designed to attack a specific biochemical process, a critically rapid acting process (as for example nerve impulse transmission) that, if blocked, leads to rapid death. These types of agents are more than just toxic chemical agents. They may be classified as biochemical agents since they directly compete with

---

[25] Fusion, also called thermonuclear, reactions are reactions that take place in stars. They are the combining of two smaller nuclei, typically two isotopes of hydrogen, into a heavier atom. Thermonuclear or fusion processes generate about a thousand times more energy on a weight for weight basis than the fission reactions which entail the splitting of a heavy nucleus into two or more smaller nuclei. Fusion reactions are considered somewhat cleaner in that not as much radioactive by-products are produced. Fusion weapons require tremendous instantaneous pressures and high temperatures to initiate them. A fission device is used to trigger the fusion process. In fusion power plant designs, powerful magnets are considered the means for containing the plasma for the sustained fusion reaction.

[26] The molecular ion as the name suggests is the molecule less an electron. This specie is observed on a detector and provides the molecular weight of the compound.

or inhibit specific natural biochemical substances of the body and block their action. More advanced compounds, though not necessarily organophosphates, also exhibit extreme neurotoxicity. Whereas the classical chemical weapon nerve agents kill in milligram quantities, these other compounds can kill in the microgram[27] quantities. These kinds of *hypertoxic* agents (the tenth area of R&D) may someday be man-made but presently are usually of biological origin.[28] These kinds of super lethal chemicals are metabolites produced by microorganisms or certain plants or animals. These compounds and specifically man-made versions of them will usher in a new chapter of CBWT-biochemical warfare and terrorism, which had its origins with the use of blood agents in WWI and the development of the first organophosphate insecticides in Germany in the 1930s. Presently, most of these microbial toxins present technical problems for their acquisition, synthesis or use. But research on them continues in any chemically competent laboratory in the world. This research effort presently is more of a medical necessity than any immediate military need or terrorist application. However, we are slowly building a catalog of these very *hypertoxic* substances and it is only a matter of time before an incisive breakthrough permits thinking of these agents in a military or terrorist context.

There are a number of well known toxins, poisons of biological origin. In this genre are such *hypertoxic* compounds as botulinum toxin[29], aflatoxin[30], ricin[31], tetanus toxin[32], the less popularly known shellfish toxin[33] and puffer toxin[34] to name a few. These particular examples will probably serve as model toxins for the search, extraction and development of other biologically produced

---

[27] A microgram is 1/1000 of a milligram.

[28] Such compounds as botulinum toxin (a protein) can have very complex chemical structures. How some are synthesized by the host organism may not yet be understood. Others are more simple in structure such as aflatoxin B_1, which is more toxic than even cyanide. Our knowledge of biochemical synthetic processes in microorganisms is advancing steadily. So too is our ability to either synthesize the simpler compounds or "farm" the microorganisms which naturally produce these *hypertoxic* substances in a broth batch.

[29] A protein from *Clostridium botulinum*

[30] From *Aspergillus flavus*, a substituted coumarin [for a brief review see M. Bonnett & E. R. Taylor, *J. Biomolec. Struct. & Dyn.* **7**, 127-149 (1989)]

[31] Ricin is a very toxic lectin and hemagglutinin isolated from the castor bean, *Ricinus communis*. Lectin is a protein, typically of plant seeds, though also found in animals and has properties resembling specific immunoglobulin (antibody) in that it affects precipitation, agglutination or other similar antibody actions. It is not an antibody as it is not a result of antigenic stimuli required from immunoglobulin synthesis. Hemagglutinin is an antibody or other chemical material that leads to the agglutination of red blood cells. This process may be immunologically or non-immunologically mediated.

[32] A protein from *Clostridium tetani*, a protein

[33] Typically from bivalved molluscs. The toxin is a neurotoxin (saxitoxin) produced by the dinoflagellate algae *Gonyaulax catanella* which is ingested and filtered by the shellfish. These algae are associated with the "red-tide" seasonally observed around the U.S. coasts.

[34] From a number of similar fish: toadfish, puffer, blowfish, porcupine-fish, balloonfish, etc.; an amino perhydroquinazoline. [For systemic effects see *Dangerous Marine Animals of the Indo-Pacific Region*, Carl Edmonds, pp. 176-179]

toxins, and some years down the road, artificially synthesized. As medicine and biochemical research ever seeks newer tools in studying biochemical processes as well as newer compounds to use medicinally, the discovery or refinement of biologically produced toxins will undoubtedly come from those areas of research, and only the more promising toxins and derivatives which can fit the list of requirements for a (bio)chemical agent (Chapter 3) will enjoy any serious military scrutiny.

PHYSICAL INCAPACITANTS

It is the physical incapacitants which will likely see the greatest interest of the US military for future research, development and eventual usage. With regard to riot control agents such developments will have direct impact on and utility for civilian law enforcement agencies. The most potent incapacitants would not, as the reader may think, be the teargas type agents, though they certainly will be the mainstay of any law enforcement agencies required to confront unruly and highly charged mobs. Rather, the most potent incapacitants will be those that exert a psychological action, agents that lead to significant short term (a few hours) disorientation, loss of mental coordination of thought with action and so on.

PSYCHOACTIVE AGENTS

Toxic agents are not the problem that earlier discussions may suggest. Perhaps a more menacing, more frightening threat looms in the future as our understanding of the action of psychoactive drugs grows. As noted in chapter 9, psychoactive drugs have thus far proven of more interest in psychiatric medicine. The incredible potency of these formulations in minuscule amounts has made their military application risky. Controlling the field concentration of these preparations is a small problem to overcome with time and research. The real hazard rests in their psychoactivity. LSD as an example has recognized mind altering powers. It is the perception of the exposed individual that is the issue. How and why a person so dosed responds to the mental images created in his mind is a matter for psychologists and psychiatrists, not a biochemist. But the ability of such a drug to create fantastic images and perceptions of an unreal and warped world raises the possibility of developing a drug that is less extreme in its effects, but no less convincing to the exposed, unsuspecting victim. The object is not to create an obviously unreal "reality" but a slightly altered reality that retains all the qualities of what appears as a normal, conscious contact with reality-- a kind of chemical hypnosis.

Hypnosis evokes images of a person acting like a chicken or feeling warmth when in fact an ice pack is applied to a hand. Though a legitimate tool in certain cases of mental illness treatment, the popular view of hypnosis is well off the mark from what it really is. Hypnosis cannot easily make a person do that which is against their fundamental moral beliefs. For example, a person cannot be hypnotized to commit acts of violence if such is against their normal conscious will without some in-depth work setting the stage.[35] But what about chemical substances that can alter a person's view of his surroundings or more significantly, his perception of normal reality and relationships, slightly

---

[35] Personal communication, Allan Campo, MS-Psychology, Clinical Mental Health Councilor, Psychotherapist, Lafayette, LA, 24 December 1991.

altered, specifically, his view of those around him, his sense of right and wrong or his analysis of situations around him? Such substances would have "chemohypnotic" properties.

Technically a hypnotic is a substance that induces sleep. A "chemohypnotic" is defined here as a substance that alters a person's perception of reality through a chemical agent without the act of psychological hypnosis administered by a hypnotherapist. A chemohypnotic then is considered a chemical agent that short-circuits the normal view. That is, a friend appears as the enemy, an enemy appears as the friend or what is right appears wrong and what is wrong appears right. Such futuristic chemical agents are indeed far in the future. The development of such agents requires detailed knowledge and understanding of the workings of the human mind. What is a thought? How is it stored? What constitutes the recognition of right and wrong? The answer to and the understanding of these questions requires us to understand the "biochemistry" of the mind, not just the neurobiochemistry of the brain. There is a difference though they are interrelated. However, in the interim, agents may be developed that induce confusion or cause psychological paralysis-- a mental inability to receive or process information as acquired by the mind. These contradictory states are perhaps oversimplified here, but again, there is some precedence for that already. LSD does instill an anti-reality in the user and it impairs the user's ability to process information received by the mind. Another compound of less drastic effects is BZ to be discussed below. Sociological circumstances can also be an added stimulus to any alteration of perceptions.

The Nazis in assuming power in pre-WWII Germany, employed socio-environmental distresses to alter the perceptions of the German people. Through the upheavals of the Depression, violence in the streets, and instabilities and inabilities of post WWI German governments, the Nazis laid the seeds, the ground work for convincing the German people that the Jews were the problem (the enemy) and the Nazis the solution (the friend). Such a mass hypnosis (call it mass brainwashing if you prefer) requires years and a series of well orchestrated events and significant manipulation of the mass media to bring about success. That it was successful is historically amply clear! On an individual level, there are many examples from wartime "brainwashing".

During the Korean war many American servicemen were subjected to barrages of propaganda and harsh living conditions. Over many months of such incessant, intense programming, many soldiers came to regard their captors as in the right and their home country as in the wrong.

On a more clinical level, an individual can be "programmed" over time with carefully orchestrated alterations of material facts and fabricated scenarios. In combination with untrue situations presented as real, an individual can be hypnotized into believing that another person in a specific context or situation poses a material threat to himself or a loved one. The unthinkable act of violence against that "threat" then becomes a "logical" solution. The use of a drug to slightly alter the perception of realities is only a next logical step and various existing drugs aid in the altering of perceptions.[36]

However, for drug induced alteration of perceptions to work effectively in a military or civil authority and control context, the dosed individual cannot be aware of the drug's action. At all times, the dosed individual must experience no sensations of consciousness alterations, side effects, etc. that would otherwise suggest he has been drugged. Also important, there must be no signs of drugging of the individual to the casual bystander, no behavioral characteristics suggestive of an altered consciousness in the dosed victim. All would appear normal... on the surface. Such agents for military or police mass applications would ideally be lung active, that is, they pass into the blood stream from inhalation or absorbed through the skin or ingestible through food or water. This last means of delivery makes entire civilian populations as much if not more so a target than a military force. These

---

[36] In addition to LSD there are peyote (mescaline), Mexican Mushrooms (psilocybin), and so on.

agents would also have to pass through the blood-brain barrier which is otherwise impenetrable by most other substances or perhaps be metabolized to a direct acting, blood-brain barrier penetrable second metabolite. They would have to take effect within minutes and be active for several hours before being biochemically degraded by the body. Such agents render the need for fifth-columnists obsolete. Such an Orwellian ability would have distinct advantages over bullets and bombs. It would open the door to what I call psychochemical or chemopsychological warfare-- a fourth level of unconventional warfare. Unlikely you say. Who in 1945, even with the knowledge of the German V-2 rocket, would have bet his life on the US putting a man on the moon and bringing him back, alive and well, in 1969? Who would have given legitimacy to the proposed idea, particularly in light of WWII German concentration camp experiments on helpless Jews and other East European peoples, that the US would embark on medical experiments on American citizens without their knowledge no less? I am speaking of the Tuskegee Experiments on Blackmen suffering from syphilis. Or how about the radiation experiments on retarded children carried out by the US? Such things do not happen in the land of the free and home of the brave? Tell the victims! Noting the US government's insistence of foreign governments' adherence to human rights of their citizens, no one involved in these incidents has been held accountable in a criminal or civil manner for these breeches of American citizen human rights.

The side-effects problem is no small hurdle to overcome. Presently any psychoactive substance exposes itself to the individual and those around the subject by a series of side-effects. Some of the side-effects of present psychoactive drugs are: dizziness, nausea, headache, visual distortions, and sensory distortions to mention a few.

Presently the psychoactive agents for the most part enjoy medical applications (excluding illegal usage) though one has seen some specific interest in a military context as will be discussed below. The psychoactive agents come in a variety of chemical types with a variety of psychological and physical effects on the exposed individual. One classification scheme places the psychoactive agents into five categories:

(1) CNS[37] depressants,
(2) behavioral stimulants and convulsants[38],
(3) opiates[39],
(4) antipsychotic agents[40] and,
(5) psychedelics and hallucinogens.[41]

---

[37] Central Nervous System

[38] Amphetamines (benedrine, methedrine); clinical antidepressants; cocaine; convulsants (strychnine); caffeine; nicotine

[39] narcotic analgesics: opium, heroin, morphine, codeine, Percodan, Demerol

[40] Thorazine, reserpine derivatives, Haldol, lithium

[41] LSD, mescaline, tryptamine derivatives (bufotenin), cannabis substances (marijuana, hashish, tetrahydrocannabinol)

This classification is based upon physiological and/or psychological effects. Individual agents can be placed into chemical groupings based upon the parent compounds from which the specific members are derived.

Phenothiazines are derivatives of the parent compound phenothiazine [II] exemplified by Thorazine [III] an antipsychotic. Another parent compound is indole [IV] or tryptamine derivatives [V] and the hallucinogenic derivative LSD [VI]. A further broad group is the heterocyclics such as tetrahydrocannabinol [VII] or THC, the active ingredient of marijuana, hashish and other such psychedelics or hallucinogens. Aromatics are typified by such parent compounds as phenylethylamine [VIII], phenylacetic acid [IX], diphenylmethane [X] and benzoic acid [XI]. Finally, there are various other psychoactive agents viewed as derivatives of aliphatic glycols[42], carbamates, wood alcohol[43], amines, amides, and hydrazine [XII] derivatives. The intent of this presentation is not, and certainly does not represent, a complete description of the various psychoactive agents.[44] Such is well beyond the scope of this book. Rather, it illustrates the diverse chemical nature of various groups and specific examples of more or less everyday common examples.

One psychoactive agent that has received enough military interest to include the stockpiling of it is 3-quinuclidinyl benzilate known since 1961 by its military designation BZ [XIII]. BZ is an atropinemimetic[45] intended for inhalation, though evidence suggests a topical contact hazard also exists. BZ causes some of the same kinds of symptoms as associated with atropinization, acting on the central and peripheral nervous systems. BZ specifically causes anticholinergic psychotomimetic[46] symptoms. The effects of BZ begin about one half hour after exposure and can peak within about six or eight hours. The effects of BZ can last for as long as four days. Physically, within the first four hours, the exposed individual exhibits dry nose, mouth and throat. His skin is dry and flushed.[47] Headache and vomiting may occur. Vision becomes blurred, equilibrium is altered as evidenced by dizziness, and the person may be confused and sedated, even to the extent of stupor. Additionally, the exposed individual may stagger or wander aimlessly about, nonsensically mumbling or speaking with a slur. Later, the effects of BZ lead to disorientation, visual and auditory hallucinations, an incapability to effectively interact with his environment. Memory loss is not uncommon. Though the person will recover, this requires several days during which time he may be erratic in behavior. Clearly such an afflicted individual can offer no effective, coordinated resistance, either militarily or otherwise. However, BZ, like other psychoactive substances, is not entirely predictable in its effects

---

[42] dihydroxyalcohols such as propanediol: $CH_3CHOHCH_2OH$

[43] methanol: CH_3OH

[44] See for example *Psychotropic Drugs and Related Compounds*, *A Primer of Drug Action* or *The Botany and Chemistry of Hallucinogens* in the references for a reasonably concise compilation, dated as they may be.

[45] A mimetic is a substance that imitates another, that is, it causes symptoms of a disease or condition attributable to some other recognized causative agent.

[46] A substance that induces various psychological and behavioral alterations associated with psychoses. Psychosis is a mental affliction in which the individual exhibits gross distortions and disorganization of mental capacity, reduced affective response to environmental and interpersonal interactions, incapacity to recognize reality, reduced ability to communicate or relate to others and generally a diminished capacity to cope with life's everyday demands and pressures.

[47] These symptoms are similar to atropinization.

on individuals under stress, or for that matter, under combat conditions. Individuals in such circumstances exhibit a wide range of behavioral differences. It is an article of faith among combat forces that plans and actions of the individual and entire units are founded upon the accepted and predictable, if not established, actions and reactions of opposing forces under a given set of conditions. Use of psychoactive agents that result in unpredictable behavior of an enemy is sensibly avoided like the plague. But such agents are not without potential if the unpredictability can be removed from their effect on personnel. Research in such agents as incapacitants will undoubtedly continue in search for the ideal psychoactive incapacitant. In fact, the US Military is interested in the development of new, more effective (physical) incapacitants to replace toxic agent usage altogether.

Such research is not going to be public. It will be done in the most secretive setting possible, most likely a federal installation and probably at that, in a government medical facility. In such a facility safeguards can be taken to prevent or minimize accidental deaths or contain experimental subjects (voluntary or involuntary) from creating a stir and drawing unwelcomed public attention. Any attempt to uncover the goings-on at such a facility will undoubtedly, as has happened in the past with other supersecret military endeavors, invoke national security interests to frustrate probing inquisitors, both journalistic and legislative.

One can often tell when a line of research has hit upon a possible military use by following technical and scientific journals. An example of this is pre-WWII research into nuclear processes. By the time Germany invaded Poland in 1939 and with the bombing of Pearl Harbor at the end of 1941, all meaningful and significant works referring to and papers concerned with nuclear studies disappeared from such publications (ours as well as others). The same fate befell any and all references to organophosphate insecticide work in Germany during the same time frame. Intelligence experts sift through foreign journals for just such sudden ends to references to particular subjects. Another tact is to follow the articles that are published, looking for signs of less and less significant results or a sudden departure from a previous direction of the research to one that appears abrupt and seemingly tangential to the direction previously followed. It is a blinking red light that something is in the wind-- so to speak.

With the varied views of what is patriotic among US citizens, it is not likely that researchers will be easily swayed from their original line of work because a government agent approaches them about its possible military value or attempts to exert pressure on them. Scientists view research and knowledge as something of the public and even international domain. But since the Manhattan Project of the 1940s, many scientists have come to regard themselves as having a responsibility to mankind. This view places patriotic values sometimes at odds with professional ethical and even humanitarian values. Of course, if federal monies sponsor the research, the government has a large stick to use for leverage in getting its way.

Other countries may not harbor the same moral concerns that may exist in the US or for that matter generally throughout the Western societies. So-called third world countries struggling for their own niche in the world, culturally, economically, militarily, even religiously, may not find it morally difficult to justify development of weapons systems which they fully intend to use against centuries-old adversaries. NBC is an area of weapons development that is subject to these same concerns and prejudices. Whereas the US may research and develop nonlethal, psychologic agents, other morally less hindered cultures may seek *hyperlethal* agents. One can argue that research in the US on chemical and biological agents is a must if for no other reason than to keep technically abreast of the developments and potentials of these weapons systems in the wrong hands. Where to draw the line in research activities is a social and political judgment which must factor in the military issues facing a nation for a sensible decision.

SMOKES/OBSCURANTS

The utility of smokes or obscurants (a more general term) in military operations is an accepted fact. Just in training exercises alone, smokes are stand-ins for a range of simulated munitions. But their real importance is in providing concealment of one kind or another for military forces in actual combat operations (see chapter 10). The problem with the smoke munitions of the WWII era type is that they obscured observation only in the visible spectrum. They do not obscure observation in the ultraviolet (UV), infrared (IR), and microwave (MW) regions of the spectrum. Today's modern military forces have optical instruments that literally can see through visible spectrum obscurants. To counter that, obscurants that block observation in these other spectral wavelength domains (UV, IR, MW) are required. There has been some successful work in this area. There are obscurants which provide opacity of the smoke cloud to UV and IR detection. Work is continuing on these obscurant agents to not only improve their quality and effectiveness, but also their duration over the target area and extending the approach into the MW portion of the spectrum.

BIOLOGICAL AGENTS

Bioengineering is an open field of infinite possibilities. As the technology expands and improves, so too do the possibilities of cross-matching otherwise presently harmless microorganisms with pathogenic traits. Since the plasmids of microorganisms possess the resistance factors for various antibiotics, the advances in plasmid research and bioengineering can take advantage of antibiotic immunity of one microbe combined with the antigenic stealth of a second and the intense pathogenic abilities of a third. Such a "bug" would in the very beginning not only frustrate medical researchers trying to identify the little critter, but would reek havoc with exposed populations before anything definitive were determined or done about it. And then there are the viruses. Of all the microbes that present a threat to human health and life, the viruses are without doubt the most stealthy and the most difficult to characterize and medically combat. The present problems posed by AIDS or the burst experience with the filoviruses of Ebola is but a glimpse of the problems that bioengineered viruses can present. All such bioengineered creatures (viral or cellular) would constitute technological surprise when employed in a hostile setting. Such microbes as these, in principle, could present a perilous threat to human life on this planet as great if not greater than global nuclear exchanges. Natural mutational processes that occur among microbe populations would only complicate the problems yet further.

LIKELY USERS & TARGETS

The obvious target for any weapon system is a military force. However, in this new world order with the dissolution of the USSR, one can argue that there is no longer a major military threat presented to the US military forces. This is not to say that the weaponry, doctrine and capabilities of the former Warsaw Pact countries have evaporated along with the USSR political system.[48] It is just to say that Eastern Europe may no longer feel the U.S. the "threat" to themselves individually as Moscow once claimed and characterized us to them. And, of course, the lack of a credible threat to U.S. military forces presupposes that we will not find ourselves facing off with France, England, Germany or of all adversaries, Japan, yet again.[49] So, if there are no significant threats to the US military what possible targets are there for CBWT? CIVILIAN! The easiest, most vulnerable target of any war.

Operation Desert Storm erased a decades old question of American ability, determination and political will to stand-up for national interests. This question had always been foremost in the minds of U.S. adversaries since the end of the Korean War[50] and it acquired greater significance as a result of the outcome of the Vietnam War and the disastrous performance of the U.S. military and U.S. government's foreign policy.[51] Operation Desert Storm clearly and unquestionably revealed the technical capabilities and muscle of U.S. military might and weaponry. Even though we were part of a coalition, we were the major component. We did demonstrate that we do have the ability to use force in our interests, though some may reasonably argue that we regularly stand-up to the lesser adversaries but have not done so, militarily, against the former USSR.[52] And in spite of the fact that we were not engaged with a quality adversary, we did unquestionably demonstrate the quality of our arms if not our national metal. The effectiveness of our technology in the Persian Gulf was a lesson not lost on our future adversaries waiting in the wings.[53] Clearly, to go head-to-head, toe-to-toe with

---

[48] Communism, like capitalism, is not a political system, rather an economic system. However, just as capitalism requires some reasonable degree of democracy to really function as the theory of capitalism demands, so too, the requirements of communism as practiced by the former Soviet leaders required a "political" component. I am not an economist nor political scientist, so I will bow out of this topic as gracefully as the professionals of these fields will let me...

[49] The U.S. military have many plans drawn up, called contingency plans, for waging war at any level with various potential foreign threats directly from or originating in any country or continent, including France, England, Germany and yes, Japan.

[50] The reader may recall the phrase "paper tiger" was used to describe the U.S.

[51] The performance of the American troops is not derided here, rather the performance of their political leaders and the highest military ranks.

[52] Recall our incursions into Panama and Grenada as two other examples. Of course, the USSR was a nuclear power and no one in their right mind would argue we should risk nuclear war over say the KAL flight that the USSR shot down. However, our *ease* or *rapidity* to take third world nations to task for real or perceived infractions against us has not helped our image as the "slayer of bullies." I suspect that some of our actions have come across more like those of the LA police that overreacted to Rodney King, beating our puny transgressor to an unnecessary pulp, and accomplishing nothing substantive (politically) for the effort.

[53] We may not have heard the last from the likes of Iran which is actively building up its military forces and of course Syria has always bothered a number of Middle East watchers. The existing diminishment in U.S. resolve to hold Iraq's feet to the fire, so-to-speak, in adhering to the letter and spirit of the cease-fire in Operation Desert Storm legitimately raises questions that we may well have not heard nor seen the last of Saddam Hussein and his thirst for power in the region. Especially true since Operation Desert Storm, his lust for revenge against the U.S. undoubtedly is high. As long as he is in power or in influence of any kind in that region, he will be a threat to the region and "we the people." Keep in mind that if he will kill thousands of his own people for whatever

U.S. military might is now demonstrably suicidal. The only option is covert/terrorist operations, and not directed directly against U.S. military forces, but rather against U.S. citizens-- civilian population centers.[54] We are a people ripe for the slaughter.

There are ominous rumblings from nongovernment intelligence and strategic analysts that voice concern over Iran's activities in rebuilding her military. This zealously proud Aryan nation with a strong sense of history is not just rebuilding her conventional forces decimated as they were at the end of the Iran-Iraq eight years war.[55] She is also actively purchasing entire systems applicable in the development of nuclear, chemical and biological weapons systems. One particular supplier according to intelligence sources (read that essentially CIA) is Communist China. The affront to U.S. honor experienced in 1979 with the taking of the U.S. embassy in Teheran may worsen beyond the recent desert encounter with Iraq in 1990. Iran witnessed the build-up of U.S. forces for five months under the very noses of Iraqi officials, who unexplicably remained passive through it all. The inaction of Iraq in countering this build-up was the single most important factor to the (hindsight) ease of Iraq's defeat by the U.S. and its coalition forces. Such a lesson is not lost on Iranian officials nor on any other nation of that Gulf region hostile towards the U.S., including Iraq or Syria. Any repeat attempt by the U.S. to insert itself militarily *en mass* in the region to counter a real or perceived threat to us or our interests in world peace and oil flow again most likely will not enjoy a single day's build-up honeymoon window.

In Chapter 13 we had considered the civilian vulnerabilities to biological attack. We had noted that a foreign agent could, under cover of diplomatic immunity, bring a biological agent into the U.S. and disseminate the agent in a well crowded area. Airports are particularly well suited areas as they bring together people from all over the U.S. into one confined location. Those people will return to their home cities and spread the agent there as well.

Even if we do not have diplomatic relations with a foreign government, they do have diplomatic people in the U.S. through the United Nations. Several years ago, Yassar Arafat, considered by many, including U.S. officials, to be nothing more than a terrorist was permitted to enter the U.S. to address the UN. He could not have entered the U.S. any other way except as a recognized leader of a national government, though true, he has by many been considered the representative of the Palestinian community. The UN then represents the means by which those who have no diplomatic means of entry into the U.S. as official emissaries to the U.S. may enter the country. Under UN associated diplomatic immunity, anything they bring in is opaque to U.S. inspection and scrutiny!

In spite of the best efforts of the U.S. Customs and INS[56], our borders are indeed very porous. The border with Mexico represents the most porous sieve through which those without papers[57] may

---

indiscriminate reason, he certainly will have no qualms about killing thousands of Americans if he can find a way...

[54] Remember the 1993 NYC World Trade Center bombing?

[55] Remember, we helped Iraq in that war. Iran has little reason to love Uncle Sam.

[56] Immigration and Naturalization Service

[57] At the turn of the century, the U.S. saw a large influx of immigrants. Many were from the south European regions such as Italy and Sicily. Most of those were without papers as classified by INS-- WOP-- the origin of what became a derogatory term designating a Southern European and more specifically an Italian.

surreptitiously enter the U.S. If tens of thousands of Mexican nationals with no field craft skills[58] can enter the U.S. illegally and anonymously, a trained foreign operative certainly will have no problem!

One may rightly ask why would we not have early warning of a terrorist CBW attack? After all with all the intelligence agencies of the U.S.-- CIA, FBI, DIA, NSA, etc.-- we surely would know if something was afoot. Not necessarily so. We learned during the late 1970s and into the 1980s that terrorists were very skillful in their covert operations against the western nations. The reader may recall at the height of the hijackings of aircraft and hostage abductions particularly throughout the Middle East that our intelligence chiefs told the President, Congress and the news media that we have very little ground assets in the region. That means few if any agents or spies (HUMINT) working within these groups. Furthermore the most significant reason given for this was the close-knit nature of these groups. They consist of members who are relatives or very close childhood friends. Everyone knows everyone else. The insertion of an outsider just does not happen and most certainly, not with any timely ease.

To be sure, with the demise of the Soviet Union and the clear lack of capital by the now splintered and independent states that have reemerged from the old Soviet block ashes, it is doubtful that these countries will supply the weapons and explosives to such terrorist groups as long as they have a chance to gain U.S. funds to support their disarrayed economies. However, should the aid they seek not come or prove insufficient for their needs, they certainly do still have the weaponry and technology in hand to sell for the purposes of raising hard cash. The impetus to do so will be heightened should the present Middle East Peace process, begun at the conclusion of the Iraq-Kuwaiti Persian Gulf Conflict, collapse. It is on very thin ice as it is. The oil reserves of the region can and certainly will in time provide the capital for these terrorist groups to acquire their needs if a seller can be found. As seen recently, there is no shortage of sellers if you have the cash. Can the world keep selected weaponry out of the wrong hands? Paraphrasing Shakespeare: *To be* (successful) *or not to be* (successful), that is the question for the twenty-first century and the so-called *new world order*.

---

[58] Field craft skills is a term popularized in many spy novels such as those by Tom Clancy in referring to the training and skills required to be a spy or agent in a hostile enemy country.

CHAPTER 23

CIVILIAN DEFENSE

Foreknowledge is power.
-Auguste Comte, 1798-1857[1]

GENERAL

In April, 1960, The American Chemical Society held its 137th meeting. A symposium titled "Nonmilitary Defense, Chemical and Biological Defense in Perspective" was held. It was published in July 1960 as part of the Society's Advances in Chemistry Series, numbered 26. It examines in nontechnical terms the view, held then, concerning the threat of chemical and biological warfare to the U.S. and the civilian population. This work, developed before the 1962 Cuban Missile Crisis, indicates the seriousness attached to CBW preparedness of the U.S. population as seen by one of the most prestigious chemical science authorities in the world. However, even after the Cuban Missile Crisis, the importance of CBW preparedness still held the attention of some in government.

In 1965, the Food and Drug Administration published a booklet titled "Civil Defense Information for Food and Drug Officials". Part I includes sections on the removal of chemical and biological contamination and Part II has three sections addressing chemical, biological agents and sabotage in food plants. The importance of preparedness and the vulnerability of civilian populations to a covert CB threat is evident, but also clearly stated in these works.

There are several published short works on chemical and biological attack of civilian population centers. The magazine published by the U.S. Army Chemical School at Ft. McClellan, Alabama, *Army Chemical Review*, carried an article by George Schecter and Amnon Birenzvige which originally appeared in *Army Magazine*. They addressed the vulnerability of cities to chemical attack.[2] More recently, Kupperman & Smith wrote a White Paper for the Federal Emergency Management Agency addressing the ease and vulnerability of the American population to biological agent attack.[3]

The title of this chapter is not misstated. I do mean civilian defense, not civil defense. Following WWII and the advent of intercontinental nuclear war, civil defense primarily applied to those measures taken to protect population centers against heavy loss of life and massive real property and infrastructure destruction in the event of a nuclear attack. It was a masses approach rather than an individual approach. With the end of Federal Government interest in such protection for the U.S. population, civil defense has taken on or rather reverted back to what it once was before nuclear bombs and ICBMs existed. Though by no means insignificant in importance, civil defense has

---

[1] In *The Harvest of a Quiet Eye*, p. 38

[2] Cities: Inviting Targets for Chemical Attack, *Army Chemical Review*, September 1987, pp. 40-43

[3] Coping with Biological Terrorism, 22 August 1991.

become essentially, effectively, and practically concerned with natural disasters such as flood, earthquake, hurricane or tornado effects. It is true that plans exist for various man-made disasters such as nuclear, chemical and biological events. The point of civilian defense here is that the individual must assume sole responsibility for his own defense against man made causes of harm and to recognize personal risks as they arise. The actions the individual can or must take on his or her own behalf within the material, intellectual, and legal capabilities available to the individual definitively constitute his or her state of preparedness.

The ability of an individual to actively provide for his or her own self defense or that of a loved one is directly related to the level of knowledge and physical ability. Clearly, the first requirement in self defense is the recognition of the threat. The ability to prepare and deal with that threat depends upon what materials and knowledge (or training) the person has. It also depends upon what laws will allow a person to do or to have in his or her possession to provide the tools readily at hand for self defense preparedness. Finally, preparedness depends upon the cost. This is no less true for the individual than it is for government sponsored and financed defense, the so-called bang for the buck principle.

To be sure, the government at all levels points to emergency plans in bound volumes ready for implementation. As anyone who has planned a vacation knows, the plans as written and as executed often bear no resemblance to each other. It is in the execution of a plan that problems unforeseen are uncovered, defects in assumptions arise or resources counted upon show their real availability. Given the history of foreign attack and invasion in the U.S., when was the last time we had a national level exercise to test a civil defense preparedness plan, all so neatly and authoritatively gathering dust on the shelves of civil defense offices? We haven't, of course. And, in our society, as conformist as it is in so many respects, such specific conformity demand of the public to test a national emergency plan would probably prove disastrous at best. All the more reason for the individual to have some idea and concept of the realistic threats posed and reasonable and workable measures to implement if and when the threat materializes. But where to start?

Any library probably has some written material concerning most any disaster you can think of. By checking references of the particular written material, additional sources can be uncovered. Many Federal, State and even local government agencies can provide literature on various emergency situations (see Appendices for a few of the more likely). A good start is a small handbook put out by the Federal Emergency Management Agency titled "Are You Ready?", H-34 September 1990. Another booklet compiled by the U.S. Department of Transportation lists common hazardous chemical substances and the minimum precautions to be taken in the event of an accidental (or perhaps, as the case may be, not so accidental) spill. This booklet is titled "1990 Emergency Response Guidebook" DOT P 5800.5. Having a good First Aid manual on hand is an excellent idea.

In the sections that follow, it may be more apparent to view a chemical threat as arising not from a terrorist or foreign military attack, but rather, from a chemical plant just down the road or from a chemical tank truck or rail car passing close by. Another possibility is the military installation involved in the handling, processing, storage or even research in chemical and biological agents.

CHEMICAL AGENTS

In chapter 2, I noted a few common household chemical agents. Few people recognize the hazard posed by household chemicals since few people have had any formal chemical education. This is regrettable in a nation that asserts the availability of education to all, yet does not establish universally enforceable educational requirements of its citizens to live and function in a very technological world.

The vast majority of household chemicals are, for the most part, relatively safe to use. A few are quite dangerous if minimum safety and use precautions are not followed. As an example, few people really recognize the potential hazards inherent in the use of bleach as a general cleaning agent. In its commercial form, it is a very serious respiratory and skin hazard. Another potential hazard concerns the practice of commercial businesses in cleaning drain pipes. Certain acids must be avoided. Though hydrochloric acid[4] has and can be used, such acids as sulfuric and nitric must not. Concentrated sulfuric and nitric acids are strong oxidizing acids. Concentrated sulfuric acid when in contact with organic matter, releases hydrogen sulfide gas. This gas with its characteristic rotten egg odor, is very poisonous. In enclosed, poorly ventilated areas the concentrations can build to lethal levels. Additionally, the gas is responsible for the nose's loss in ability to detect it,[5] and the lethal concentrations can build with no further indication beyond the initial odor warning. Nitric acid can release nitrogen dioxide, a common air pollutant and responsible for the reddish brown haze often seen hovering over a major city such as San Francisco when viewed from a plane on its approach. Nitrogen dioxide is a powerful lung irritant.

The threat is not the use of household cleaning agents. Most people recognize irritations of the eyes, nose and throat, signaling over exposure to these materials. They leave the room for fresh air. The problem is with industrial and other toxic chemicals on the tank farms, in chemical plants or in the railroad cars on a siding. Many of these chemicals are suffocating, odorous, pungent, etc. and their presence is usually evident in the event of a leak or accidental spill. On the other hand, many industrial chemicals have little or no odor. Because of the varied volatility of the different chemicals, major accidental spills can discharge large concentrations into the air which carries the fumes on the wind for significant distances. By the time a general warning is made and effective evacuation plans implemented, vast areas of the countryside or community can be under the vapor cloud.

DETECTION

Man has always at one time or another relied upon his sense of smell for distinguishing between odors. As high-tech as man is today, he still sniffs his food at the finest restaurant as though complying with some prehistoric instinct, searching the odors and fragrances for signs of fine food, or tainted food. It is his detection of the odorant[6] added to natural gas that alerts him to a leak in the gas stove.

An alert sense of smell remains the least expensive and most sensitive detector available to the person on the street. The odor of burning wood in a neighborhood always triggers a look around. Is it a fireplace or a house on fire? One must not dismiss the human sense of smell as a detector. The detection of odors that are not normally present in the area is a potential warning. As in the odor of burning wood, if one smells burning wood in July, it most likely is not a fireplace. Is it someone burning brush? Is it possibly a house on fire? One investigates. One searches the sky in the vicinity for large black plumes of smoke.

If a chemical plant or a chemical storage facility is upwind of you, do you know what their chemicals are? What do those chemicals smell like? How poisonous are those chemicals? Can you

---

[4] Commercially known as muriatic acid.

[5] technically known as olfactory fatigue

[6] Methanethiol

tell the signs of potentially lethal doses? Do you know what first aid can be administered. Are you prepared to protect yourself and your family from further exposure? Do you have the equipment and materials to do so? Do you know of and is there a less traveled road out of your community or do you follow the herd to the traffic jam? Do you know how to determine the wind direction?

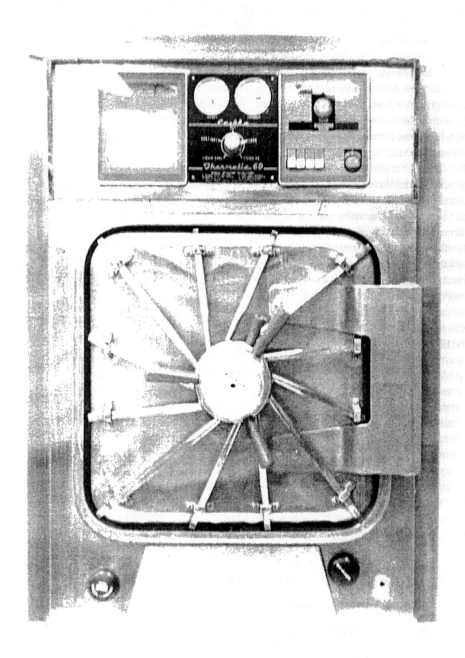

FIGURE 23-1 A close-up view of a research laboratory autoclave. The dials indicate temperature, time of operation and pressure within the autoclave.

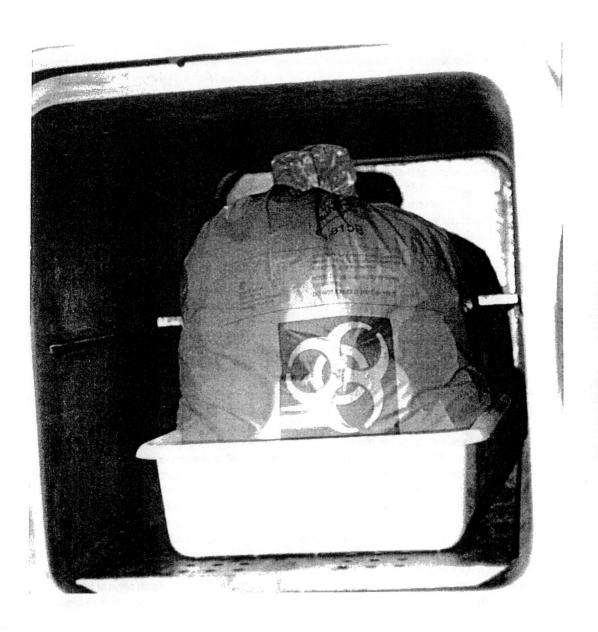

FIGURE 23-2 Inside view of a research laboratory autoclave showing a *BIOHAZARD* bag containing various petri dishes and test tubes for sterilization before discarding.

PROTECTION

The first element of preparedness and therefore protection is to know what the threat is, what you may be confronting in an emergency situation.[7] It is a good idea to contact the chemical plant manager and ascertain what kinds of chemicals they are using? What odors do those chemicals have? However, in this day and age of concern over criminal activities and terrorist activities, a chemical plant may not wish to be very cooperative with your inquiries. You may be able to determine what the major precursor chemicals are from trade journals, industrial magazines, commercial product reports and such in your local library or a university library. Observing the tank trucks entering the plant and looking for any signs on them indicating flammability and type of chemical also may work out. Once you have some idea or identified the chemical types on the premises, consult a book on poisoning or your physician[8] concerning symptoms of exposure to such chemicals and the first aid treatment to take until medical experts can take over. Though an accident will presumably result in authorities alerting the public and even ordering an evacuation of the immediate area, accidental leaks and releases of chemical vapors may also occur before anyone in authority or responsibility knows about it. This is particularly true of chemicals which have very little or no odor. Monitoring equipment on site at the plant is nice, but not foolproof or invulnerable to breakdown. Explosions on site (accidental or sabotage) release toxic clouds which travel down wind rapidly. A warning to evacuate may be too late in the sense of preventing exposure and perhaps hospitalization. Few people can hold their breath for even two minutes let alone a half an hour or more (humanly impossible) during the time required to evacuate. Traffic flow is far from expeditious during an emergency, unplanned evacuation. A protective mask for each householder with the appropriate filter elements for the chemical fumes hazard at hand is the best insurance at warning against inhalation during the evacuation process. A good set of eye sealing goggles is also a must to protect the eyes against exposure to and absorption of the chemical hazard. Topical chemical exposures generally are slower acting. They can be dealt with as much as an hour later if unable to be handled immediately. Usually, flushing the exposed area with water is good enough for the short term. Inhalation or eyes exposed to hazardous chemical vapors are potentially very rapid acting hazards. In the case of inhalation, exposure is potentially life threatening within minutes depending upon the nature of the chemical agent and the level of exposure. Protective masks which protect the nose and lungs are not fashionable wear, but then, if it is necessary, you'll be the envy of your neighbors.

At the first warning of a chemical spill requiring you to evacuate your home, close all closet doors (seal the threshold with a towel jam), drawers, bedroom doors (seal with a towel jam), windows and vents allowing air to enter these spaces or the home. Turn off all heating and A/C units and blowers. Cover aquariums with a plastic trash bag. Infants should be carried out in one of those handle-equipped carriers and a blanket placed over them to protect them from aerosol in the air. In the car, keep windows rolled up, air vents closed. In warm weather the tendency will be to run the car

---

[7] Anticipation of a possible threat is not by any means easy. In Cameroon, Africa a deadly cloud of carbon dioxide was emitted from Lake Nyos in August 1986. The cloud of CO_2 killed more than 1700 people and over 3000 head of livestock. [Curt Stager, *National Geographic* **172(3)**, September 1987 (404-420)]

[8] This advice of contacting your physician for information is often cited in commercials, ads, etc. The fact is when it comes to chemical hazards, most physicians probably don't know very much about the hundreds of chemical types available. The general practitioner is not a chemist or biochemist. But he (or she) is a good place to start for the vast majority of the public which know even less. A good book on industrial chemicals probably will provide more information in a concise form.

A/C. This is not a good idea from the standpoint that as the inside air cools, it contracts, creating a slight drop in interior pressure which is balanced by outside air seeping in, bring in chemically contaminated air. The interior of the car will warm up, but that creates an overpressure which attempts to equilibrate with the outside air by seeping from the interior to the outside.

The use of rubberized raincoats, boots, mittens and such is very good temporary protection against aerosolic vapors and particles in the air. If you see clouds, fog or mists in the area of an emergency chemical incident, then assume the air is contaminated and wear whatever you can to protect yourself in your evacuation.

Upon return at the all clear, open all windows, ventilation vents and building doors to air the building out in the event that some vapors seeped in during your absence. Leave the closet and bedroom doors closed until you have washed surfaces and appliances, etc., of the main rooms such as the living room, dining room, kitchen. Remember to replace the air filter(s) on the heating/AC system. It may be contaminated also.

DECONTAMINATION

There is no substitute for consulting a physician as to what should be done for particular chemical exposures. Under the law, only a physician may prescribe. But there are some lower level actions one can take as preliminary precautions until a physician is consulted. For topical exposures of a minor, nonlethal level agent some common household solutions may be useful. What should be on hand for decontamination and first aid treatment of chemical exposure hazards. One should have vinegar (5% acetic acid); baking soda; baking soda solution (5%, about 1.5 ounces in a quart or liter of water); powdered laundry detergent; strong, grease dissolving/cutting dish detergent.

For splashes of acid or alkali on the skin, copious flushing with water is the first action to take. Application of baking soda is effective as a paste against skin acid contacts. Acid fumes are quite sharp to the breath and usually induce an involuntary, even violent cough and halting of the breath. The fumes are corrosive to the mucous tissues such as the eyes, nose, throat and lungs. Opening windows and doors for maximum fresh air exchange and flow is necessary.

For alkali splashes[9] on the skin and eyes, copious rinsing with water is the first step. . Washing the exposed skin with a vinegar soak is good for removing any liquid alkali that has seeped into pores or adheres to skin hairs. Any reddening of the skin means some kind of injury has occurred and a physician should be consulted as soon as possible. Any eye contact leading to pain, itching, etc. should result in immediate consultation with a physician.

Since most hazardous chemicals are organic and generally water insoluble, their decontamination from surfaces, clothing, etc. can be accomplished by washing in very strong or concentrated detergents. Bleach is an effective cleaner since it oxidizes materials. Most any oily cleaner such as pine oil will serve to dissolve organic chemical contaminants from surfaces followed by a washing with a water soluble strong detergent which removes the residue of the pine oil cleaner and any contaminant therein. For fabrics such as upholstery and carpet, a strong cleaner such as a concentrated

---

[9] A likely hazard of alkali accident in the home is the use of various drain cleaners such as DRAINO®. Most if not all such drain cleaners contain lye, sodium hydroxide (NaOH). The solid cleaners are perhaps the more likely ones to pose an accident. When the solid lye makes contact with water, the resulting reaction with water liberates huge quantities of heat which in the confines of the drain sump can build up rapidly leading to a spattering boiling of the water in the sump. The unwise user standing over the drain looking down it, may be tortuously surprised by the eruption of the drain contents into the eyes.

rug cleaner solution should do well. Finally, wash the bedroom and closet doors leading from the main building rooms before opening. Remove the vents of the heating/AC ducts and wash the vent and duct surfaces as far in as you can reach. Since these surfaces are metal, a combination detergent and bleach solution should work well. If nothing else, the dilute bleach solution will help in removing mildew that may be in the vents. Always wear rubber gloves to protect your hands against the bleach. Rinse the cleaned surfaces well with fresh water after the cleaner treatment. Wash all dishes, cooking utensils, pots and pans and eating utensils. If you have a basement, remember, chemical vapors seek the lowest point. This area will also require venting and similar thorough cleaning particularly if it is drafty. Always wear some type of rubber dishwashing gloves when performing these decontamination/cleaning procedures.

Don't overlook foods. Open foods and drinks should be discarded. Any canned goods can be decontaminated by washing and rinsing of the can. Food storage containers that are sealed can be externally washed and the contents retained. Nonsealed food storage containers such as the counter-top canisters for coffee, sugar, flour etc., should be cleaned inside and out and the contents discarded.

Don't forget the car! You probably traveled through a chemical vapor cloud on your way out. A good car washing at the local car wash will do the outside surfaces well. The inside can be washed down with an upholstery detergent. As a minimum, use a garden hose and if you have such, a detergent adaptor with soap in it. Use a general cleaner designed for the upholstery interior of your car and wash those surfaces down as well.

If you have an infant and carried the little crumb-snatcher out in a carrier of some kind, that, too, must be thoroughly cleaned. Wash all clothes and blankets used as covering.

These measures are certainly necessary if a strong chemical odor is detected in the home upon return form an evacuation in a chemical accident scenario. But even if no unusual odors are apparent, it does not mean that hazardous chemical vapors have not seeped into the home. Judgment is necessary and sometimes misleading. The risk to your home depends upon a multitude of factors such as proximity to the accident spill site, the direction of the wind, the quantity of the spill (often unknown to the resident), the nature of the chemical involved, etc. We all make judgments in our daily lives and the determination of when to be concerned about contamination in the home is just another judgment.

BIOLOGICAL AGENTS

The detection and identification of microorganisms requires a corresponding technical ability and facilities as for the detection of chemical agents. Since the general public does not have possession of or access to such sophisticated facilities, the best approach is that of prevention of infection. This is no small task in light of the remarkable ability of microbes to survive otherwise intolerable conditions for humans.

Microorganisms exhibit remarkable adaptability to the varied environmental conditions found on Earth. Certain microorganisms can live in or very near to the hot geyser vents such as those at Yellowstone National Park. The temperatures there or at the ocean floor where hot vents also exist rise as high as 180°F.[10] Additionally, microorganisms populate the ice and tundra of the Arctic and Antarctic regions illustrating why freezer kept food does not last indefinitely in freezer storage. With

[10] The temperature of the normal hot water supply of a home is about 120°-140°F, hot enough to cause severe scalding burns of the skin.

such tenacious ability to survive under conditions that would otherwise kill man, how does one control the populations of microbes, particularly the pathogenic variety? Would you believe through a kind of chemical warfare?

Every time you wash your hands with soap you are using a chemical agent to kill, inhibit the growth of, or remove microbes.[11] Rubbing alcohol also is effective as an antiseptic against microorganisms[12] on human skin. However, these and other agents are effective on what is termed vegetative microbes, that is, actively living cells undergoing metabolism, growth, etc. Spores are a different matter and are not affected by such topical agents. Bacterial and fungal spores require sporicides, special chemical compounds that can penetrate the near impenetrable external coating of such spores, or extreme physical conditions such as prolonged boiling, even in a pressure cooker, to destroy the spores.

There are two major types of cleansing. One is called disinfection and the other is called sterilization. They are not the same thing, though generally used interchangeably by those not understanding the difference. Disinfection is a cleaning process utilizing soaps, detergents, perhaps bleach as well, that kill sufficient populations of potential pathogenic bacteria on a surface thus reducing the numbers of such pathogens and rendering the surface less infective. Since infection requires a minimum number of pathogenic bacteria to illicit the infection and subsequent disease, this type of cleaning is in fact what is done around the home as a result of general cleaning. Sterilization is very different. Sterilization kills all bacteria, viruses, etc, pathogenic or nonpathogenic. It also entails the complete removal of their bodies so to speak from the surface. This is the process utilized by hospitals for the cleaning of surgical hardware and gowns. Typically a special pressure cooker called an autoclave is used to perform this procedure. Households as a rule do not have autoclaves available. Thus, your cleaning activity is geared at disinfection, not sterilization.

General cleaning is disinfection with the use of a sanitizer or disinfectant. Sanitizers are formulations such as soaps or detergents that permit a thorough washing of objects. The term is used in context of commercial cleaning of cooking utensils and food handling or processing equipment. Disinfectants[13] are also used on objects and kill microorganisms but do not have any effect on spores. In both cases, microorganisms are not completely killed or removed to the very last creature. Such agents only significantly reduce the numbers of vegetative microbes remaining to levels which reduce the pathogenic or disease producing hazards they pose. To absolutely kill and even remove the microbes from an object requires sterilization.

Sterilization requires extreme conditions such as very high temperatures and pressures[14] or very potent and lethal chemical agents. Germicides are capable of killing microorganisms quickly but may

---

[11] The reader may find it useful to check the glossary for the definitions of the following terms: disinfectant, disinfection, antiseptic, bacteriostatic, bactericide, sterilization, germicide, fungicide, viricide, sporicide.

[12] Rubbing alcohol, technically named 2-propanol, is toxic to humans when ingested. However, it is not absorbed through the skin such as methanol (wood alcohol) or ethanol (grain or drinking alcohol). It is because rubbing alcohol is not easily absorbed through the skin that it is an effective germicide for topical application.

[13] One of the oldest known disinfectants is phenol a.k.a. carbolic acid.

[14] The pressure cooker is an example of a home tool for sterilization that operates on the principle of very high temperatures (over 100°C) and pressures (greater than atmospheric pressure). The high pressure has no effect on microbes but does allow the attainment of the high temperatures.

be specific for certain kinds of microbes while only inhibiting others. Bactericides, for example, kill only bacteria while fungicides kill only fungi and viricides kill viruses.

The means by which chemical agents kill microorganisms depends upon the type of microbe targeted and the agent used. Chemical agents used as disinfectants affect microbes in one of several ways: attack proteins, attack membranes, or attack other cellular components. The antimicrobial chemical agents are grouped into at least nine categories: soaps and detergents, acids and alkalis, heavy metals, halogens, alcohols, phenols, oxidizers, alkylators, dyes. The action of chemical agents on the cell was discussed with respect to antibiotics. The reader may find it useful to review chapter 12 for the cellular morphology of the microbial cell and the viruses. Many of the methods discussed below are applicable to home use. A few are not because of significant inherent hazards they pose to the user. They are presented for a fuller understanding of the methods available to those in public facilities and institutions requiring varying degrees of microbial population death. The overriding purpose of soaps and detergents is not to kill microbes, but rather solvate or solubilize the dirt, grit and grime that harbor such microbes, thus permitting these dirt materials and associated microbes to be rinsed down the drain.

ANTIMICROBIAL CHEMICAL AGENTS

Soaps and detergents are undoubtedly the most common and least expensive of the antimicrobial chemical agents. They also are the least hazardous to human use and contact. Soaps in their simplest chemical form are salts of a base such as sodium hydroxide and a long-chain fatty acid. As a consequence, soaps contain alkali which will in some instances kill many species of Streptococcus, Micrococcus and Neisseria. Detergents, though also consisting of long-chain fatty acids in a salt form, are often a bit more complex. Detergents generally are alkylated aromatics with inorganic acid components such as sulfuric or phosphoric acids. Detergents once possessed phosphates which enhanced their ability to saturate materials capable of absorbing water and thus harboring bacteria. Additionally, the phosphates were used as "padding." The phosphates added bulk to the product so the box of detergent appeared full. Since the ecological problems associated with phosphate detergents came to light, present day detergents possess no phosphate. For a while, a substitute "padding" component called sodium nitrilotriacetate, NTA, was used. This material was thought nontoxic to humans but was later found to be toxic in combination with the heavy metals cadmium and mercury, themselves common waste water pollutants. The use of NTA is restricted to only laundry detergents. It may not be used in preparations such as shampoos or oral washes which make contact with skin. A substitute for the phosphate is the sulfate group or a variant leading to sulfonated detergents. Additionally, many detergents possess what are called quaternary ammonium moieties. Because the quaternary ammonium moieties are positively charged, such detergents are referred to as cationic detergents. Those with negatively charged groups, such as the phosphate or sulfate type, are anionic detergents.

These materials are primarily hydrophobic (like gasoline or oil, nonwater) substances though they also possess a hydrophilic (water-like) component in their molecular structure. This "biphasic" property allows soaps and detergents to solubilize water nonsoluble materials such as grease and oils in water. The hydrophobic portion of the soap or detergent "dissolves" the grease or oil material by forming what is called a micelle, a spherical object suspended in water. The dirt, grime or grease with microbes are within the interior of the micelle. The hydrophilic portion of the soap or detergent is soluble in water.

Soaps act by solubilizing greasy, oily and gritty substances and the microbes associated with these materials. The agitation by mechanical means such as rubbing the hands together serves to dislodge such hydrophobic materials for removal by rinsing. Detergents because of their wetting ability, that is, the ability to penetrate fatty or greasy materials or between fibers of materials, also solubilize the debris and microbes. Additionally they tend to foam in low concentrations and this also serves as a mechanical means for removal of the debris and microbes. Furthermore, cationic detergents also disrupt membrane structure, upsetting its selective permeability and lead to the lysis of the cell.[15] Because bacterial cell walls possess negative charges, the anionic detergents appear less effective in cleansing materials of microbes. Cationic detergents appear better suited to the task of killing bacterial cells, but they are more toxic particularly to the eyes. Still, they are effective in "killing"[16] some viruses.

All microbes have an optimum pH at which they perform their life's processes quite well. If the pH of the environment is altered, the ability of the microbe to function is diminished. This is principally due to the microbial enzymes secreted into the immediate environment about them. These enzymes are pH sensitive. As a result, acids or bases added to a microbial medium will lower or raise the pH, respectively. Many foods have acid or alkali added to alter the pH and thus retard microbial growth. Soft drinks, catsup and margarine often have benzoic acid added for this reason to prevent fungal growth. The importance of this principle has direct application in the pickling[17] of various home canned foods.

Heavy metals such as silver, mercury, lead and arsenic are very effective in killing microbes. However, they have very restricted use in human medicine owing to their highly poisonous nature to humans as well. Arsenic was discussed previously in chapters 8, 11 and 18. The same basic concepts of arsenic toxicity also carry over to such heavy metals as silver, mercury and lead. These materials, notably silver and mercury, are restricted to topical applications for disinfection. Silver nitrate is useful in cleansing the eyes of newborn infants against gonococcal infection, while mercury in the form of Mercurochrome and merthiolate are used for surface skin wounds. Silver based antibiotics also find significant use in the treatment of third degree thermal burns. However, spores are resistant to many if not all the heavy metal agents. Selenium, found in many antidandruff shampoo preparations, is effective not only against fungal infection but also spores. Copper is an effective algicide and in the form of copper sulfate is commonly used to treat the water within the waterbed mattress to inhibit such growth.

Halogens are elements of group VIIA of the periodic chart of the elements. Chlorine, iodine, and bromine are the more commonly encountered halogens. Chlorine is gaseous at room temperature and pressure; iodine is solid and bromine is a liquid. Chlorine is used to treat municipal water systems. Adding it to water forms hypochlorous acid (see chapter 7). Sodium hypochlorite is the active

---

[15] Examples of cationic detergents are Phemerol, Bactine, Ceepryn and Zepharin (a presurgical scrub agent).

[16] Viruses are not "killed" in the sense that one understands the word kill. Viruses are not living organisms such as bacteria, dogs or elephants. All "living" organisms participate in a wide range of functions which have become characteristic of living things. All living organisms require food, reproduce themselves (by means resident to the organisms), discharge waste products of metabolic reactions and so on. Viruses do none of these processes by themselves as stand alone organisms. They require residence within another cell and utilize the cell's own biochemical "machinery" to do the reproduction of the virus particles. Viruses don't require food, or discharge waste products of metabolism because they have no metabolism of their own.

[17] Pickling is accomplished by acetic acid, or vinegar when in a 5% solution.

ingredient of household bleach (about a 5% solution). The hypochlorous acid is an oxidizing agent. It can be used to disinfect objects not chemically attacked by bleach. Some organic matter is oxidized by the hypochlorous acid. Stains on clothing are organic matter and when oxidized by the acid or bleach, the discoloration of the stain disappears. The acid also oxidizes the organic components of cells and some viruses thus destroying the microbe.

Iodine has been a useful topical antiseptic for decades and one of the first to come into use in the form of tincture of iodine (an alcoholic solution). Iodine also is formulated in various other organic molecules to provide a slow release of iodine. Betadine and Isodine are only two such examples. These antiseptics find use in cleansing human skin before surgery. Properly speaking, they do not sterilize skin, only disinfect it.

Alcohols are organic compounds with a hydroxyl group. The common alcohols are rubbing alcohol (2-propanol) and drinking alcohol (ethanol). Both act by denaturation of microbial proteins (see chapter 2). Rubbing alcohol is effective as an antiseptic in the concentration range of 70% to 90% alcohol. It does not sterilize skin but does disinfect it. It only acts on vegetative surface microbes and does not affect microbes deep in pores or spores themselves.

Phenols are aromatic alcohols. The most common and oldest used member of this group is phenol (a.k.a carbolic acid). This was the agent employed by Lister in the first surgical procedures employing a disinfectant during surgery. Phenols act on microbes by denaturation of proteins, enzymes and membrane disruption. They can be used on a wide variety of objects and surfaces and in dilute concentrations on skin. Other phenols are halogenated to enhance their antimicrobial effects. Such phenols are quite effective disinfectants against staphylococci and fungi.

Oxidizing agents are powerful antimicrobials since they oxidize microbial proteins and other susceptible membrane components. They can disrupt the normal disulfide linkages of proteins (see chapter 2) and in the case of membrane bound proteins, disrupt the membranes. Sodium hypochlorite (bleach) is an effective oxidizing agent for surface disinfection as well as for other materials such as clothing. Bleach is an effective disinfectant for viruses including the AIDS virus.

Hydrogen peroxide (30% solution) is also an effective oxidizing agent for cleansing wounds. Wounds, particularly puncture wounds, are very susceptible to infection by anaerobic pathogens. The hydrogen peroxide releases superoxide (O^{2-}) upon contact with the tissue. This superoxide decomposes to release oxygen which is lethal to anaerobic microbes.

Other oxidizing agents are chlorine gas, potassium permanganate ($KMnO_4$) and potassium dichromate ($K_2Cr_2O_7$). In dilute solutions, potassium permanganate has found use in disinfecting skin. These last three materials are very dangerous to handle and the last two are fire hazards in dry form when brought into contact with organic matter. Upon oxidizing of the organic material, potassium permanganate yields insoluble manganese dioxide (MnO_2), a brownish-black solid. Potassium dichromate upon oxidizing substances yields cationic chromium (typically Cr^{+3}) in salt form, which is water soluble. Chromium is a suspected chemical carcinogen and for that reason dichromate salt use on human skin is medically inadvisable.

Alkylating agents are compounds that add small molecular components to another molecule. They are varied in nature and one example discussed in this book is the military mustard agents (see chapters 4 and 8). More common compounds of this type are formaldehyde (methanal), glutaraldehyde, β-propiolactone and ethylene oxide.

Alkylating agents attack proteins and nucleic acids. The action on nucleic acids forms the basis of chemical carcinogenicity. Formaldehyde inactivates viruses and microbial toxins as well as the microbes. Concentrated formaldehyde is essentially an embalming fluid. It is very effective at dehydrating dead tissue, including microbial cells. Denying water to bacteria and molds prevents their growth. Glutaraldehyde kills all types of microorganisms and spores as well. The β-propiolactone is effective against hepatitis viruses. Ethylene oxide is a gaseous substance which exhibits remarkable penetration ability. It finds use in sterilizing a wide range of materials including rubber, plastics, and various bedding materials which cannot sustain high temperature techniques. These materials are quite toxic and should be avoided by the chemically inexperienced and ill-equipped individual.

Various dyes (organic compounds of intense color) have been used for decades by biologists to stain and thus highlight various cellular components. These materials chemically interact with a specific cellular component and thus alter the physicochemical properties of the component. Some can be used in disinfecting wounds. Acridine, methylene blue and crystal violet are but a few of the many dyes in usage. These materials are themselves toxic and their use is best left in the hands of experts knowledgeable of their specific applications and hazards. This is so because many dyes are aromatic compounds and they are potential mutagens, carcinogens or teratogens.

There are many over-the-counter cleaners that also exhibit varying degrees of disinfection properties. Household ammonia can be used to cut grease and grit from surfaces which harbor microbes. Pine oil cleaners are popular and they too solubilize the grimy hydrophobic materials associated with dirty surfaces where microbes abound. Lysol is another commercial cleaner effective as a disinfectant. A number of cleaner formulations are defined in the book *Household and Industrial Chemical Specialties*, 2nd Ed., Vol. 2, Chapter 3 by Chalmers & Bathe.

ANTIMICROBIAL NONCHEMICAL METHODS

Antimicrobial nonchemical methods are: heat (dry vs moist), freezing, drying, pasteurization and radiation (UV, ionizing, sunlight). As can be anticipated by the methods, some require very specialized facilities. Also apparent, these methods are not suitable for use on human tissue.

For its low cost and ease of application, heat is by far the most preferred method. However, heat is useful only on materials that are not themselves destroyed by heat. Heat's advantage is that it can penetrate where chemical agents cannot and it requires the simplest of equipment available in any home as far as general heat treatment is concerned. There are two kinds of heat applicable in sterilization-- dry and wet.

Dry heat (absence of water) penetrates more slowly than wet heat. Its method of destroying microbes is most likely by oxidizing biomolecules with oxygen present in the air.[18] Such heating methods are useful on objects made of metal or glass. Objects sterilized by dry heat require exposure to the heat for an hour or more at temperatures at least 121°C.[19] This method if done properly will kill all microbes, viruses and spores. An hour of heating at 171°C is sufficient. Lower temperatures require a longer time of heating at that temperature.

Wet heat is the heating of materials in the presence of water or the water content of the material itself. Boiling water is the commonly used technique. Such heating penetrates materials quite well and is effective against vegetative microbial cells and inactivates some viruses. It is not to be trusted for destruction of spores[20] since many spores are resistant to such wet heat treatment. Water boils at 100°C at one atmosphere pressure. The temperature of the boiling water can be increased by the

---

[18] This is essentially a burning of the organic matter to carbon dioxide and water in extreme cases.

[19] Water boils at 100°C at sea level atmospheric pressure. At higher elevations, the temperature is much less than 100°C and such (wet) heating requires much longer times.

[20] Spores do not contain water.

addition of salts such as table salt (sodium chloride) or baking soda (sodium bicarbonate). Addition of several tablespoons full of these salts will raise the temperature only a fraction of a degree at best above the normal boiling point. One way to increase the temperature significantly, and thus the heat in wet heat sterilization, is to increase the pressure over the material being heated. In laboratories and industry, autoclaves are used. These are nothing more than sophisticated pressure cookers of home use.[21] By doubling the pressure in a pressure cooker and heating at 121 °C for at least 20 minutes, all vegetative microbial cells, spores and viruses (disruption of their nucleic acids) are destroyed. The increased pressure does not cause the destruction. The increased pressure only allows for the attainment of higher temperatures, which are the killing agent.

Pasteurization is also a method of disinfection applied to various liquid food products, the most common being milk and beers. Essentially the liquid product is heated to about 72 °C for 15 seconds or 63 °C for 30 minutes. Pasteurization does not sterilize a liquid product. It only disinfects. Pasteurization derives its name from the French microbiologist Louis Pasteur who developed the process for treatment of the wines in the French wine industry. It quickly became useful for other liquid products, particularly milk, which in the raw state harbor *Salmonella and Mycobacterium*. The incidence of tuberculosis in children who drank raw milk prompted the application of pasteurization to milk. Canned and evaporated milk are sterilized by a process of pressurized steam treatment.

There has been some interest in using microwave systems for the sterilization of materials. The microwave unit as found in the home heats substances up by exciting the water content. The water molecules undergo excited oscillations and this energy is dissipated as heat. As a practical matter for the home user, present microwave technology available in the home effectively cooks foods but does not sterilize them. Research in this application is ongoing.

Freezing, drying or freeze-drying are not sterilization or disinfection methods. Rather, such methods function to inhibit microbial growth by depriving the microbes of the essential conditions for growth, namely, warmth and moisture. Freezing is useful for short term preservation of food stuffs which would otherwise spoil. Bacterial growth is slowed since the enzymatic reactions of bacteria are temperature dependent. Freezing only slows these processes down, it does not completely stop them.

Drying and freeze-drying[22] are methods used to remove moisture from materials such as food stuffs. These methods require some sophisticated equipment to perform the technique properly and in some instances such as freeze-drying, extremely cold liquids such as liquid carbon dioxide or liquid nitrogen. The materials so frozen under these liquefied gases are then subjected to a high vacuum which removes the moisture from the substances while in the frozen state. You may notice that some foods left in the home freezer for an extended time, if not completely sealed well, show signs of what is called freezer burn. This freezer burn is a freeze drying.

Radiation is another method for disinfecting and even sterilizing materials. There are three types of radiations used: ultraviolet light (short wave), strong visible light (sunlight with its associated short wave UV) and ionizing radiation (X-rays, gamma rays). Of the three, strong visible light as achieved by exposure to sunlight is the least hazardous to humans for general use. The advent of the clothes dryer has larger replaced the practice of hanging clothes out in the sun for drying, and as a result, no benefit of disinfection from sunlight accrues.

Sunlight does possess some short wave ultraviolet light which is responsible for countless cases of sun burns annually. Additionally, such extreme exposure is a principal suspected cause of various

---

[21] Autoclaves generally employ a steam bath medium around the objects to be sterilized rather than the water bath associated with home pressure cookers.

[22] also known as lyophilization

skin cancers.[23] The common practice of hanging the cloths out on a line in the sun is the best example of this method put to practical use. The strong bacteriocidal properties of sunlight is directly attributed to its ultraviolet light frequencies. The UV can oxidize UV-sensitive biomolecules such as the riboflavins and porphyrins (important components of oxidative enzymes) and perhaps as well the nucleic acid components such as thymine (yielding thymine dimers).

Ionizing radiation is the most hazardous to handle. The most common type with which the general public has experience is the X-ray (by order of either a physician or a dentist). In small, controlled doses, the risk of any harm is minuscule, as for example in X-rays of body regions or of the teeth. Rapidly growing and dividing cells are, however, very susceptible to damage by even these low level radiations and for this reason, X-rays of a pregnant woman requires protective, lead-lined cloth shielding over the lower portion of her abdomen to shield the womb and its fetus from this radiation.

Ionizing radiation derives its name because the radiation can dislodge an electron from biomolecules creating ions. The most susceptible molecule to ionization by such radiations is water, the most common and plentiful molecule of living cells. These ions can damage DNA and also produce powerful oxidizing agents known as peroxides within tissues. In high doses this X-ray radiation can cause massive ionizations within microbial cells, viruses and spores leading to their death or inactivation. Ionizing radiation treatment of medical equipment and plastics is an effective sterilization method. It does require specialized facilities for such practices. The sterilization of foods by irradiation with X-rays or gamma rays is also effective in sterilizing certain foodstuffs. There is no radiation contamination of the foodstuff as a result of such treatment. The ions that arise in such foodstuffs very quickly disappear in reacting with other molecules. The time frame for the life of such ionic species is on the order of nanoseconds (10^{-9} seconds). As a method for home sterilization purposes, it is not available for clearly obvious reasons.

DECONTAMINATION

Decontamination of biological hazards is perhaps less likely a need than from an industrial chemical accident. The most likely scenario, however, concerns virulent disease organisms in epidemic cases. Surfaces are the most likely sites for harboring pathogens. Coughing, sneezing, vomiting, etc. can eject pathogens into the air as aerosols. These aerosols will hang in the air for varying periods of time depending on their particle size. They will eventually collide with an object, be it a person or a surface. General hygienic habits are the key to minimization of spread of infections. Many of the methods discussed above are suitable in general cleaning as well as specific attempts to minimize spread of particularly virulent pathogens. Washing of the hands with soap and hot water is perhaps the first and simplest personal protection. Thorough washing of all food handling utensils and hardware in strong detergents is a second step. Complete washing of clothing and bedding, in bleach where possible, is a third means of minimizing pathogen spread and exposure. As the adage says: "an ounce of prevention is worth a pound of cure."

Finally a word about foods and storage. Most everyone has been sick with vomiting overnight and then felt much better and recovered about one day later. This type of illness has probably happened to everyone at least once in their life. These illnesses are dismissed as 24-hour viruses. These so-called 24-hour viruses do not exist. Usually the cause of such sudden and short lived illnesses is a case of mild food poisoning caused by bacterial contaminants such as *salmonella* or

---

[23] A serious problem for those possessing the autosomal recessive gene for *Xeroderma Pigmentosum*.

some other agent such as a chemical contaminant. That is to say, the food ingested was spoiled though the nose or palate did not detect it and the stomach objected to the insult.

Such illnesses are most probably due to improper storage or processing of the food item. This could have occurred with the vendor or at home. Since microorganisms that cause illness are pathogenic by definition, and since such microbes can be found almost anywhere on earth including in the home, foods provide excellent growth media for such creatures. A little care and caution in the storage, handling, and processing of foodstuffs goes a long way to preventing these "24-hour virus" occurrences. A concise book on the subject was authored by Walter D. Batchelor titled *Gateway to Survival is Storage*. This book discusses the correct way to store various types of foods and even contains a section on Civil Defense.

SEALED ROOM DESIGN

During the 1950s much commercial activity occurred concerning the design of home as well as public fallout shelters. The design of shelters intended to provide shielding against various ionizing radiations associated with nuclear detonations was based principally on the most penetrating radiation, that of gamma rays. One of the most important considerations that went into such shelter designs was that of ventilation. In any sealed room where no exchange of air with the outside is possible, carbon dioxide levels can build up very quickly. Carbon dioxide in high concentrations is poisonous to any air breathing animal including humans. Thus, ventilation is a factor that must be built into a shelter of any kind. With the demise of the Soviet Union and the possible reduction of world nuclear arms stocks, a fallout shelter may not be considered a necessity any longer, even by those who have them.

A shelter for other disasters may have more value such as a shelter from tornadoes. Even in the consideration of a shelter for lethal chemical accidents, the best choice is to vacate the area completely. In the event of a deliberate chemical attack upon a civilian population center, any place you go to may be encompassed by the chemical vapor cloud. Just such a problem confronted the Israelis during the Iraq-Kuwait Gulf Crisis. Thus, many Israeli citizens had what can be called a sealed room shelter within their homes. Of course, the wisdom of such shelter availability fits the hostile climate of the region in which they find themselves, a case that has not had historical application in the U.S. and perhaps, is not a significantly likely problem for the U.S. in the future.

There are many books and much printed literature by the U.S. government on shelter design and construction which, for those interested, maps out in detail, the necessary requirements for a shelter or sealed room environment. Included are necessary materials and food and drinking supplies advisable and amenable to long term storage. The reader is directed to those sources for such information and details.

A dated but nonetheless excellent work on Civilian Defense is a book titled *Handbook of Civilian Protection* put forward by the Civilian Defense Council, The College of the City of New York, 1942. Though written very early in the years of U.S. involvement in WWII, the book covers a number of hazards facing a civilian population during total war. The risks faced by civilians even in these modern times may not be any less, though a declared war need not be the case, and since the end of WWII, we've had several nondeclared wars to contend with. Chapter V covers poison gas. Another book of interesting reading is that titled *Civil Defense in the Soviet Union*, 1962. This is interesting reading as compared with what little national awareness and preparation exists in the U.S., even at the height of the Cold War.

CHAPTER 24

CONVENTIONS, TREATIES, RULE OF LAW AND TERRORISTS

*The number one security challenge in the United
States now and probably for years ahead is to prevent
these weapons of mass destruction, whether chemical,
biological or nuclear-- and the scientific knowledge
of how to make them-- from going all over the world,
to rogue groups, to terrorist groups, to rogue nations.*
- Sam Nunn, member of the Senate Armed Services Committee,
appearing on *Face the Nation*, 15 October 1995

GENERAL

Can it be done? In absolute terms, probably not. There's an old saying, often used derisively against someone, that goes "a little bit of knowledge is dangerous." Another saying goes, "if you had a brain, you'd be dangerous." One last such saying is "knowledge is power". The fact of the matter is that terrorists do have "the little bit of knowledge" and "a brain" to be very dangerous. Setting out to kill someone is not a benign or benevolent undertaking, and certainly no accident when well planned. Anyone, if dedicated enough to the act, and willing to risk even certain self death, can plan and execute the murder of someone else, no matter how well protected the target is. Terrorists are dedicated, and certainly the underlings we've seen carrying out these infamous acts, have been willing to sacrifice their own lives for successful accomplishment of their chosen or assigned mission.

To effectively succeed at Senator Nunn's stated challenge for the US, we as a nation must embark upon actions which, by their very nature, may well cripple education, international intercourse, technological and medical advance. How so you ask? Consider the field of chemistry.

The importance of chemistry in modern society is transparent to those who have little or no understanding of chemistry. They do not see the pervasive presence of chemistry in their daily lives. The best indication of chemistry's importance to modern western civilization is found in viewing the plight of societies where chemistry is essentially absent, no chemical industry, the so-called Third World countries such as Ethiopia or Somalia to name a few. Such societies live a primitive existence. Sanitation is one of the most important contributions to a modern society. More important than plastics, diodes, computers, etc. No doubt you have seen reports on the evening news of the refugee camps in Ethiopia or Somalia or some other African country torn by internal power struggles between warlords. The conditions of the camps is such that sanitation is merely a word. Cholera has always struck such environments. We westerners take the toilet for granted. We take the water treatment plant for granted. The use of chlorine and chlorinated water treatment compounds never crosses our minds unless we have a swimming pool. The chemicals and the PVC plumbing lines are a product of a chemically advanced society and knowledgeable chemists and chemical engineers. A standard of living has emerged and exists in part from the genius or insight of our physical scientists and engineers, not the least important are our chemists and chemical engineers, the knowledge and know-how they uncovered and its use by industry and medicine. What about biology?

Biology, and in today's world biochemistry, microbiology and molecular biology, has held center stage to advances in medicine. But today's biology is mostly a delving into the chemical differences among species, the chemical defenses of microbes and sea animals, and the gene. Medicine also is dependent upon chemistry. Biochemistry, the chemistry of life, is chemistry. The development of antibiotics is dependent upon researchers understanding the biochemistry of the human cell and the biochemistry of the pathogen, and the differences between the two. Organ transplants are possible because of our knowledge of the biochemistry of the immune system- chemistry. The cloning of the sheep Dolly also has its roots in knowledge of (bio)chemistry. The development of artificial components for hearts, kidney machines, an artificial bone glue for repair of fractures, and so on are directly related to chemistry.

So what does this have to do with Senator Nunn's statement?

One of many subjects for high school and college freshman level introductory chemistry courses is that of REDOX reactions. REDOX reactions (oxidation-reduction) are a major means by which living cells derive energy, produce proteins, genes, and so forth. REDOX reactions are at the heart of countless thousands of chemical reactions taking place in the air, soil, living cells, and the depths of the Pacific Ocean. With a knowledge of REDOX reaction principles, one also has one of the foundation knowledge concerning life and to devise explosives. The truly dedicated chemistry student learns REDOX principles well since they bear such importance in future and higher levels of chemistry study.

If the knowledge of REDOX reactions can be used to make bombs, and a decision is made to eliminate the study of REDOX reactions from the chemistry curriculum because of a fear of that knowledge being criminally utilized to make explosives, you cripple the study of chemistry, the education of chemists, the advances made at Dupont, Dow, etc. You end significant advances in biology and particularly medicine and physicians training suffers for that lack of knowledge.

The subject of REDOX reactions is but one area of chemistry where the opportunity exists to use that knowledge beneficently or maliciously. Others include organosulfur chemistry, organophosphate chemistry, organohalogen chemistry, organonitro chemistry and so on. Knowledge of these and other areas of chemistry can be used to make plastics, computer chips, medicinals, or highly poisonous substances and yes, chemical weapons and explosives. The choice, as always, rests with the user.[1] The flip side of this coin is how can you recognize the inherent peaceful or criminal use of a chemical if not educated to its properties, spectrum of reactions and uses? Does not the knowledge of the multiple uses provide government with the means to recognize a misuse in progress? We know of organophosphates (the nerve agents) because of (1) the pesticide industry and (2) the experiences from accidents with humans who have absorbed them in accidents. An interesting fact enters the picture here. Organophosphates were one of the chemicals used to understand the workings of nerves and the action of neurotransmitters. This has had significant importance in advances in biochemistry and medicine. Nerve agents as weapons, however, were never used as weapons in war.

The other consideration is that of international intercourse. Trade, education again, and so on. If we as a nation, under orders from government officials, begin classifying subjects of chemistry,

---

[1] What are governments' responsibility for harnessing such knowledge for geopolitical reasons of conquest, offense, or defense. Remember, it was Albert Einstein who alerted FDR to the potential uses of the atom's internal energy as a weapon of unparalleled destruction. It was government that actually set about to harness that energy for war. So who is at fault? The messenger or government?

biology, or physics because someone on high has decided that knowledge is too easily misused, then logically, we can't teach it to our own students, and we must not admit foreign students to our educational institutions. How will that play with the nations of the world I leave to the social and political science researchers. However, a unilateral domestic restriction has no bearing on foreign educational practices. We may be harming ourselves in matters of trade competition with foreign researchers and national security because they know about the subjects we restrict if not ban outright domestically. And it is what we don't know that our competitors or adversaries do know that is dangerous to us.

Realistically, the knowledge base is already out there. Between the millions of chemistry textbooks, the Internet, World Wide Web, and word of mouth dissemination, no amount of government effort to classify and restrict access to arbitrarily declared sensitive chemical knowledge will work. We can't even keep illicit drugs off our streets, how are we going to police ideas or knowledge and expect to be any more successful there?

The other problem is determining who is and who isn't a potential threat. Governments have a curious history here themselves. In WWII the Russians and the US were allies, buddies. After the war, we were near mortal enemies. Around 1989, the Russians and the US were back on the buddies track again. The US and Iraq at one time were close friends. Adhering to the principle "the enemy of my enemy is my friend", we supplied Iraq with much military hardware because Iraq at the time was locked tooth and jowl in war with Iran, a former friend, but then enemy. It seems that friendships in the Middle East change with the wind blown sands. So how does a government decide that this foreign national of that government may learn these things about our sciences, and we not regret it several months or years later? Who's minding the store so to speak? Can it really be minded? Supposedly there is a watchdog of sorts.

The lead agency of the United States in addressing weapons of mass destruction technology and controls is the US Arms Control and Disarmament Agency (ACDA). Headquartered in the US State Department building, the ACDA consists of some 250 people. Its organization is:

DIRECTOR
    Office of Advanced Projects
    Executive Secretary & Advisor for Internal Affairs
    Office of the Chief Science Advisor
    Office of Military Affairs
    Counselor
    Scientific & Policy Advisory Committee
DEPUTY DIRECTOR
    Office of Equal Employment Opportunity
STAFF
    Office of Administration
    Office of Congressional Affairs
    Office of the General Counsel
    Office of Public Affairs
BUREAUS
    Intelligence, Verification & Information Management Bureau
    Multilateral Affairs Bureau
        US Representatives to the Conference on Disarmament
    Nonproliferation Bureau
    Strategic & Eurasian Affairs Bureau
        Joint Compliance Inspection Commission

Standing Consultative Commission
Special Verification Commission

The mission of ACDA *is to strengthen the national security of the United States by formulating, advocating, negotiating, implementing and verifying effective arms control, nonproliferation, and disarmament policies, strategies, and agreements. In so doing, ACDA (attempts to) ensures that arms control is fully integrated into the development and conduct of United States national security policy.* ACDA's 1997 fiscal budget was $41.5 million. Its fiscal 1998 requested budget is $42.2 million.

The Director of ACDA is the principal advisor to the President, the National Security Council, and the Secretary of State on arms control matters. A concise list of the broad and diverse concerns for ACDA is embodied in the points of concern raised by President Clinton in his address before the United Nations General Assembly:

1. ratification of the Chemical Weapons Convention,
2. negotiation of a Fissile Material Cut-off Treaty,
3. implementation of START II and negotiation of further cuts to the nuclear arsenal with Russia,
4. strengthening the Nuclear Non-Proliferation Treaty and increasing the number of signatories,
5. giving the Biological Weapons Convention teeth for on-site inspections when there are suspected violations,
6. negotiating a worldwide ban on the use, stockpiling, production and transfer of antipersonnel landmines.

The scope of ACDA's concerns are seen in the numbers. Some 40 countries now have the technical and material resources to develop nuclear weapons. About 20 countries have chemical weapons programs in place, and roughly 15 have the capability and motivation to develop a chemical weapons program. Many of these countries are not fond of the US. About 39 treaties, conventions and agreements have been or are pending completion under the direction of ACDA. Most are concerned with questions of nuclear proliferation, technology transfers, and fissile material handling and usage. One is concerned with Biological Weapons and another concerns Chemical Weapons.

Historically, the first attempt to prohibit the use of chemical and biological weapons was made on 17 June 1925 in Geneva, Switzerland. The Protocol for the Prohibition of the Use in War of Asphyxiating, Poisonous or Other Gases, and of Bacteriological Methods of Warfare was the instrument. Another milestone was on 10 April 1972 with the signing of the Convention on the Prohibition of the Development, Production and Stockpiling of Bacteriological (Biological) and Toxin Weapons in London, Moscow and Washington. A major shortcoming of these agreements is the lack of any real effective means to police violations (verification and punishment for violations). It is principally that issue that has led to the drive for a more robust agreement in each weapon category separately. The Convention on Biological Weapons and the Convention on Chemical Weapons are the offered solutions.

Some political scholars do not agree that effective verification is possible and even more so disagree that an effective means of enforcement can be devised. The driving argument for these agreements boils down to this: we must start somewhere. The bottom line goal of each convention is the total ban of production, acquisition, stockpiling, and use of chemical or biological weapons. The

Convention on Biological Weapons[2] was proclaimed in force by the US on 26 March 1975.

The issues of verification and enforcement are not simple. It is not my intent to delve into the complexities of the proposed conventions as that is a work in itself. But one stipulation of the Convention on Chemical Weapons is that of resolution of disputes. That calls into play the United Nations General Assembly, the UN Security Council and the International Court of Justice, aka the World Court. As the UN was born of the ashes of the League of Nations, its record in maintaining and resolving world peace disorders is open to debate and question. But treaty questions historically were and are resolved by the World Court.

The governing rules for the World Court's procedures were adopted on 11 April 1978. The procedures include (1) a written phase in which parties submit and exchange pleas and, (2) an oral phase of public hearings before the sitting Court (Article 43). The judgement is final and no appeal is permitted (Articles 59 & 60), unless new evidence not previously heard by the Court arises (Article 60). Should one of the participants fail to respect or abide the Court's ruling, the other may secure recourse in the Security Council of the United Nations. The basis of all World Court decisions is international treaties and conventions in force, international customs, general principles of law and secondary principles such as judicial decisions and teachings of the most highly qualified jurists and legal publicists. Now comes the fly in the ointment. Though a nation state may be a duly recognized member of the United Nations, it does not have to submit to the jurisdiction of the World Court. Presently, several nations do not recognize World Court authority over them in disputes between them and other nations. The problem of enforcement now becomes orders of magnitude greater and stickier. Thus, two UN members may be signators to the Convention, yet any one or both may refuse World Court jurisdiction over them by virtue of refusal to submit to World Court authority in disputes involving them. If the World Court is one of the means of enforcement, that enforcement is then already on shaky ground.

However, the Chemical Weapons Convention specifically states that the UN Security Council is the final arbiter of disputes and issues of violation. But, a few of the members states of the Security Council are adversaries of the US. A veto of a single member state can invalidate any proposed action or decree offered by the Security Council. That's the second fly in the ointment.

The Chemical Weapons Convention is a document some 130 pages long. In its numerous Articles, many concerns are addressed but others are not. One of the most sensible statements of what such a treaty should accomplish was advanced by Baker Spring of the Heritage Foundation[3]. In the report five litmus tests should guide the merit of any treaty concerning chemical weapons that the US wishes to enter into. Those five tests are:

1. will the Chemical Weapons Convention (CWC) reduce the risk of war?
2. Are the CWC's requirements consistent with America's global responsibilities?
3. Is the CWC adequately verifiable?
4. Are the provisions of the CWC enforceable?
5. Does the CWC enhance US national security?

The analysis by Mr. Spring is interesting reading but too lengthy to develop here. He does offer

---

[2] The full title is Convention on the Prohibition of the Development, Production and Stockpiling of Bacteriological (Biological) and Toxin Weapons and on Their Destruction.

[3] Baker Spring, Senior Policy Analyst, The Heritage Foundation, Committee Brief No. 25, A Special Report to the Senate Foreign Relations Committee, April 15, 1996.

his view of improvements to the CWC. They are:

1. Modeling the CWC after the Nuclear Non-proliferation Treaty.
2. Formulate a new policy to deter chemical attacks.
3. Improving US defenses against chemical weapons.
4. Improving US ability to destroy chemical weapons production and storage facilities, and enhancing deployment of chemical weapons forces in the event such are used against the US.
5. Strengthening the CWC enforcement means by:
    a. avoiding the UN Security Council authority where potential hostile nations have veto power over any Security council decisions
    b. providing for strong military measures against those that do not sign and ratify the CWC and who may be inclined to use chemical weapons.

What is worth noting about the present CWC ban on even US chemical weapons stocks is then the potential requirement on the US, locked toe-to-toe with a chemical weapons capable foe, to resort to the nuclear card in response to an unprovoked, first use chemical attack. Is a nuclear retaliation considered a reasonable and proportionate response for a localized chemical attack?

Article XX, paragraph 3 is in my view a very dangerous requirement on the US as a participant of the CWC. Article XX, paragraph 3 states:

Each State Party undertakes to facilitate, and shall have the right to participate in, the fullest possible exchange of equipment, material and scientific and technological information concerning means of protection against chemical weapons.

What that passage requires is that the US must reveal to all other nation states, friend and foe alike, any and all information, technology, and doctrine on defense against chemical weapons. It is giving your enemy your plans and counter weapons systems. Such information in the hands of a foe permits that foe to develop measures to overcome or circumvent your defenses. How would you like to go up against an enemy who knows how to frustrate your defense against him?

Another point of interest in the current CWC is Article XXII which states:

The Articles of this Convention shall not be subject to reservations. The Annexes of this Convention shall not be subject to reservations incompatible with its object and purpose.

Those two sentences have rendered null and void the power of the US Senate to advise and consent on the CWC. The US Senate, in its capacity to judge the merit of a treaty and to approve it with whatever reservations for future alterations of action or wording, must object to Article XXII. Such an Article usurps US sovereignty, self defense considerations, actions and policies, and removes our ability to react freely and measurably to a first use chemical attack directed against the US. In other words, if chemically attacked, the US may not retaliate in kind, but must either resort to a nuclear response or accept chemical attacks.

These and other considerations not withstanding, the US Senate ratified the CWC and the President signed it on 25 April 1997. The CWC goes into effect on 27 April 1997. A done deal.

However, the CWC is concerned for the most part (of necessity) with nation states. Terrorists are not so legally bound. Aside from the political basis for terrorist actions, how do terrorists operate. Under what principles do they seem to so unerringly succeed against the mighty array of military and policing strength of the west. They follow military principles of war.

PRINCIPALS OF WAR (AND TERRORISM)

Much of the discussion in previous chapters has been geared to organized military forces of nation states. Terrorist groups are organized, however loosely that may be, and they certainly undergo a form of military training. So, they are in effect a military force without a country. One area of military training, particularly for the US officer corps includes a close study of the Principles of War many of which were compiled by British Major General J.F.C. Fuller for training of British officers in WWI. The Principles of War are a concise list of paramount guidance for the commander in the conduct and waging of war. Keep in mind, terrorism is a war directed against the defenseless, but a war or military action nonetheless. The Principles of War are reduced to an acronym for easier memorization: MOSSCOMES.

M	Mass
O	Offensive
S	Surprise
S	Security
C	Command Unity
O	Objective
M	Maneuver
E	Economy of Force
S	Simplicity

As an ROTC student I had to learn, know, and understand these principles as a future officer and leader of men. Though their meaning and discussion in all military texts examines them in light of recognized and formal military organizations, we will examine them here in light of the terrorist as well.

MASS

Historically, mass is seen to mean having overwhelming numbers of troops arrayed against the enemy formations. This is no less important in modern warfare as the public learned in Desert Storm. We amassed over 500,000 troops against the Iraqi forces. However, the mass principle was employed at particular points of focus, i.e. Iraqi weak points. Today, modern military doctrine examines mass with a corollary. It also means overwhelming firepower. A woman confronted by an attacker employs mass against him, not by her own presence, but with a handgun against his knife. Overwhelming firepower-mass.

Terrorists also employ mass. Not so much as in numbers of terrorists but in their being well armed against an unarmed number of hostages. In fact any weapon, be it firearm, bomb, etc. is mass by virtue of the lack of means of defense of the target- civilians.

OFFENSIVE

Offensive means seize, retain and exploit the initiative. Victory depends upon offense. We did not win WWII or the Gulf War by remaining defensive or static. We took the initiative. We brought the conflict to the doorstep of the foe. Contrast our actions of WWII and the Gulf War with our approach in Vietnam. There we waged an essentially defensive war, while the Viet Cong and the NVA (North Vietnamese Army) waged an offensive war. We tried to hold (defend) cities, fire bases, rice paddies. The enemy attacked. It was in fact the conduct of the Vietnam War that led to the determination to do it differently in the Gulf War with Saddam of Iraq.

Terrorists execute offense also. They strike. They bring the conflict to the target, again the defenseless. They seize buildings (as the Japanese Embassy in Peru) or hostages and actually both. They retain what they took. They exploit the situation. They make demands which may include release of comrades imprisoned, money, transportation means of escape. They fortify their position. Though this latter element may seem defense rather than offense, it is an exploitation of their gains. They seek to make it very difficult if not impossible for government forces to counterattack. Certainly they seek to make it very costly if government forces do attack-- costly for the defenseless hostages that is. Offense may require a modification to mass above.

The Peruvian terrorists in seizing the Japanese Embassy initially held between 300 to 500 hostages. There were only about 15 or so of the terrorists. That's a 20 or more to 1 ratio of hostages to terrorists. Control becomes a critical feature in offense. By releasing all but about 75 hostages over several days, they consolidated their control over the hostages establishing a ratio of about 5 to 1. They also scored a political gain, by appearing humanitarian. Of course, what's humane about taking anyone hostage let alone at gun point?

A point about military command and control is that a single leader can not effectively control and be responsible for more than five or six people. If you look at the organization of say the US military forces, they follow this ratio in the structure of units. The terrorists in Peru set up an effective control ratio of hostages to terrorist members by releasing many others.

SURPRISE

Common criminals such as burglars or muggers execute surprise against their victim. There is no better way to engage an enemy than when he least expects it. Surprise him. Hit him when and where he least expects and is least prepared for the attack. Terrorist employ surprise with uncanny precision. It goes without saying that every successful attack from the Japanese Subways to the World Trade Center Bombings to the Oklahoma Federal Building bombing were unqualified surprises and effective terrorist successes. Deception is an element of surprise as it leads a foe to believe you are going to zig when in fact you plan to zag.

The time of day or the time of the year for an attack can be an element of surprise. On 16 December 1944, the German *Wehrmacht* launched a surprise attack against the Allied forces in Europe massed along the German border. Becoming famous as the Battle of the Bulge and one of the most hotly contested battles in WWII, the time of the year and the belief by Allied intelligence that the German war machine was effectively spent, the attack by the Germans caught the Allies by dumb founded surprise.

The Peruvian terrorists took the Japanese Embassy by surprise. Masquerading as caterers they entered and seized the embassy with virtually no resistance or opposition. They took advantage of the day's activities, the innate confusion such large affairs invariably attend (there was a major party going on at the Embassy), and the numerous strangers coming and going.

Perhaps the premier surprise for the US this century was the 7 December 1941 attack by Japanese Naval air forces against the US naval installation at Pearl Harbor, Hawaii. Two elements of that surprise attack were the time of the week and the time of day. A Sunday. At about 0800 hours local time. In peace time, American forces operate on a relaxed schedule meaning minimum manning of facilities. Civilians too operate on time-of-the-week schedules. Intent on their activities for the day, individuals seldom are aware of what is going on around them.

On the afternoon of 22 April 1997, counter-terrorism forces of the Peruvian government stormed the Japanese Embassy compound, ending with irreversible violence the hold the terrorists exercised for four months since their December 1996 assault. The siege of the Japanese Embassy, instituted by the terrorists, ended with all terrorists killed. Some 72 hostages were released, one killed, some bearing injuries of the lightning quick invasion by Peruvian forces. A few reasons may be offered for the successful surprise assault implemented by the Peruvian forces. Those reasons may be summed up in the words routine, complacency and relaxation.

The Peruvian forces were successful in their surprise assault against the terrorists because of four months of routine established between the Peruvian government and the terrorists. That routine undoubtedly led the terrorists to become complacent in their security and tactical operations, a false sense of confidence in the stand-off envisioned by the terrorists. In other words, their guard was relaxed or let down. The terrorists let tactical security slack or lapse. One news report following the end of the incident supports the previous assertions.[4] The report revealed that the Peruvian forces had dug at least two main tunnels under the Japanese Embassy compound. Explosives set within the tunnels detonated as the signal for government forces to storm the compound. One tunnel was located under a group of six or so terrorists who at the time were playing tennis or some such game. Other terrorists were caught by complete surprise as they were not in immediate possession of their weapons. That relaxation made the surprise invasion by Peruvian counter-terrorist forces work in this instance given the Peruvian government's continued development of tactical knowledge of the situation. In short, when the terrorists weren't looking, the government struck. Surprise cuts both ways for the two adversaries of a face-off.

SECURITY

Security means that a military force does all that is possible to avoid itself being surprised by the enemy. The only way to do that is to have effective and efficient intelligence. Since the end of WWII with the emergence of electronics and from that satellite communications and surveillance, Western nations have come to rely heavily on such intelligence means called SIGINT (signals intelligence) and SATINT (satellite intelligence). The one area of intelligence that has suffered, particularly with respect to foreign inspired terrorists is HUMINT (human intelligence).

HUMINT is having a person on the scene able to gather information that just can not come across signals or satellites. That intelligence is intentions. Not only what the foe is planning but what he is thinking and why? Many of the terrorists are of Middle Eastern origin. They consist of members who come from the same villages, the same tribes, they know each other. They very seldom take in strangers within there own intimate ranks if at all. Planting a mole is very difficult if not impossible within these groups. Their successes have been a testament to their own security measures and practices. Probably the most effective intelligence group with the best record of securing HUMINT is the Israeli intelligence serves, one arm being the MOSSAD.

Security for a terrorist group means also minimizing the number of people who know what is planned and going on. A saying goes "a secret known by two is not a secret". By tying and blindfolding hostages, terrorists increase their own operational and individual security. Such hostages cannot resist, oppose, observe, note, count, or identify anything. Even when released they can provide

---

[4] McNeil Report, PBS, 24 April, 1997

only sketchy details to authorities- the minimum. It also increases the terror factor for the hostages (offense again).

COMMAND UNITY

Command Unity or Unity of Command is simple and straight forward. Essentially it means one boss, one guy in total complete control and responsibility for the unit, the operation. This is summed up by the acronym C^3I which means command, control, communications and intelligence. There is some question concerning the unity of command among terrorist groups. They all seem to operate for the most part independently of each other. That actually works to the advantage of the rest of us because they are then effectively divided among themselves and that division automatically limits their effectiveness and capabilities. Should various terrorist groups unite in a common and orchestrated front, we are in big trouble then.

Command Unity within terrorist groups is localized. As isolated and separately acting entities, they do not have as yet a single overall "head terrorist". There certainly have been attempts among the more sinister nation states such as Iran, Iraq and Syria and even in Egypt during the reign of Nassar for the heads of these states to set themselves up as *the* leader of the Arabic or Islamic states. Such efforts to establish a particular state head as the leader of the to be aligned and unified countries has been the basis in part for many of the wars that sprang up in the Middle East since the end of WWII. The common and unifying enemy has been Israel. Just as with western history, wars against Israel have served as a means of diverting popular opinion and awareness away from troubled domestic waters toward foreign threats and helped to retain if not permanently entrench the ruling party, powers, officials, politicians, bureaucrats, what have you.

A good example of the effectiveness of foreign conflict temporarily erasing domestic concerns was in WWII with FDR and the Depression versus a real threat of Nazi Germany's and Imperial Japan's military expansionism, the temporary focus on the stated threat of world communist expansionism via the Vietnam war under Lyndon B. Johnson, and the tremendous support enjoyed by George Bush with Desert Storm against Saddam Hussein of Iraq. Of course, the economic troubles of the US reemerged after conclusion of hostilities and Bush's success in war didn't carry any capital with the voters in the presidential elections.

Within the terrorist groups there is considerable reliance on the C^3I. Such important terrorist personalities as Abu Nidal exist and exert considerable influence and command control on their own little group. Communications and control within and of the group takes considerable advantage of their own intelligence network, particularly drawing on broadcast news of ongoing operations. The news media indirectly augments their intelligence gathering by its free broadcast of activities surrounding the terrorist operation under way and government actions in response. A well educated and experienced intelligence official can gather much information from news broadcasts from both what is said as well as what is not said relative to what is said. Silence, the best practice for effective security is not the norm in a free press society. Nor should it be, but some restraint during and under the "heat of battle" to balance the ever present scoop mania is sorely needed. The public does have a right to know. More probably than present national security laws and practices allow, but when innocent, noncombatant lives or the lives of friendly forces is hanging in the balance, the public's right to know is not "right now".

Even the comments and answers by hostages to questions by terrorists is compromising of their own safety and an aid to terrorist security and their C^3I. Projecting ignorance may be the best course of action in such circumstances. That is an individual. on site call.

OBJECTIVE

For military units, nothing is more important than having a clear objective. Unlike the popular TV show *Mission Impossible*, the military commander's mission (he will accept it) is to succeed. He will seize the ground, building, destroy the tanks, take the hill, knock out the machine gun nest, etc. Refusal or failure is not an electable option. In assigning a mission to a commander, he may be tasked with achieving more than one objective. The multiple objectives may be dependent or independent. Regardless of the number of objectives, they must be clearly defined, and attainable with the resources available to the unit tasked with the job. This last point is open to considerable opinion concerning the ability of a unit to perform its assigned mission with the resources at hand. There have been cases where a unit was required to perform an assigned mission that at the outset appeared beyond its capabilities. There have also been cases where a mission assigned quickly grew to dimensions that the responsible commander must certainly have had doubts about the chances to perform the mission once committed. The attainment of multiple objectives may be ordered. That is to say, he must achieve objective one since that objective must be secured before he can go after objective two. On the other hand, they may not be dependent though proximally related in space or time.

Clear objectives, or goal(s) to achieve, are critical as they define the who, what, when, where, (why) and how the commander and tasked unit will accomplish the mission. Clear objectives require a plan. Plans in the US military for assigning a mission (objective) come in the form of a mission order or operations order. You may note that in the list above, the why was qualified with parentheses. That is because the why may not be necessary for the unit to know, and in fact, it may not be wise to reveal the why to the commander and his unit in the event they are captured. The mission order also tells the tasked commander what other assets outside his own unit he may draw upon to assist him in achieving the mission.

During WWII, small detachments were sent throughout the European Theater of operations searching for documents and scientists. Various small combat units assisted these small contingents of specially trained teams in performing their unique mission. The units assigned to assist were not told why. Reason: the special operations units were searching for documents and scientists working for or under German control that or who revealed the state of German research and development of nuclear weaponry.

Terrorists also operate with defined objectives. It may be difficult to determine what the objective is since they do not readily brief the opposition on such delicate matters. The Peruvian terrorists that took the Japanese Embassy clearly had as an objective the seizure of the building, the grounds, and as many hostages (as they feel they can effectively control). That objective serves to enable them to achieve a second objective. The reason for doing so is to secure the release of comrades held in Peruvian prisons. Were those the only two objectives? Since no other terrorist act followed in the wake of the Peruvian incident, it seems safe to say that the Japanese Embassy attack was itself not part of a larger plan or objective. Yet the bombing of the World Trade Center may have been the opening round for a yet larger objective that was foiled by the rapid arrest of the perpetrators and its tactical leadership, all still within US borders at the time.

This raises the question of the rank of the objective. By that I mean is the objective purely a tactical objective or a strategic objective. An explosive device and even chemical agent use can only be seen as a means to achieving a tactical objective, an objective of short term, localized gain or advantage. The very nature of nuclear or biological weapons, however, is more appropriately seen as a means to attaining a strategic objective, accomplishment of a very long term, broad impact goal, say a national level event.

MANEUVER

Maneuver means to make movements in order to gain an advantage. This necessarily means that mobility is a key element in a military unit's repertoire for success in battle. Taking the high ground is a classic military goal and doing so requires maneuvering an enemy force so you get it before he does. In Desert Storm much emphasis was made of General Schwartzkopf's Hail Mary maneuver to the west of Iraqi positions. By so doing he outflanked the Iraqi positions and was able to attack from the back door so-to-speak, hitting them where they were the weakest (mass again) and where they didn't expect an attack (surprise) because of a well orchestrated diversionary attack by Navy Seals and Marines off the coast of Kuwait (surprise again by deception). It is often common that maneuver employs other Principles of War to achieve victory.

Maneuver requires the means of mobility such as land based vehicles or aircraft. Since Vietnam, US Army doctrine recognizes the great advantage of what is called air mobile operations. The WWII use of paratroopers has been replaced with troop helicopter assault forces. Classic envelopment operations such as that executed by General Schwartzkopf in his Hail Mary maneuver are now second to the vertical envelopment meaning helicopter inserted troops behind enemy front lines.

Terrorists take advantage of maneuver by virtue of the multiplicity of target opportunities they have. However, as in the case of the Peruvian terrorists, once joined in a set piece action as holding the Japanese Embassy, they have lost the advantage of maneuver in a classic sense, certainly as far as any further ground positioning is concerned. Now maneuver becomes more a psychological action rather than a physical action. The release of hostages over several days is also a kind of maneuver. However, here too the options are diminished and limited. Only so many hostages can be released and still retain any as leverage against a certain counter attack by government forces.

In the heyday of terrorist commercial jet aircraft highjackings, a favorite ploy was to land, refuel, take off and fly to yet another country. This was a maneuver in the truest sense and it was rather effective since it offered little time on the ground in hostile territory (from the terrorists point of view) for any attempt to rescue the hostages. And it placed the terrorists on ground of their choosing, which after all is one of the reasons for maneuver by any military force- the selection of the ground on which you make your stand.

ECONOMY OF FORCE

Economy of Force actually has two meanings. The first as it classically applies to military Principles of War and the conduct of war itself means that combat strength is reserved for the attainment of the major and primary objective and only a minimum of combat force is allocated to secondary objectives. Thus in post WWII or Cold War doctrine and planning, US military commanders planned for fighting a two-front war (much as was the case in WWII against Japan in the Pacific and Germany in Europe). The application of economy of force in a dual engagement scenario is that sufficient combat power be possessed and held in reserve for the engagement of a second conflict outbreak even as the forces begin confronting the first conflict. This typically can mean that a judgement be made as to the priority or relative importance between the two conflicts. Again, in WWII, Germany was viewed as the more pressing and dangerous foe, requiring a major (offensive) effort directed against her all the while operations against Japan were for the most part defensive and delaying until the primary enemy is weakened and or neutralized. However as regards the war against Japan as a second theater of operations, as US industrial might began sustained production of war materiel at unprecedented levels, sufficient materiel became available to begin but tactically critical offensive operations against her in June 1942. The island hopping campaigns exemplify this switch from defensive, delaying actions to offensive actions, employing mass, surprise (including deception) and unity of command which implemented a focused set of objectives.

The second meaning of economy of force is simply put, the biggest bang for the effort. That is to say, you apply only that force required to achieve the goal- victory. An excellent example of this principle's implementation is in special operations. Very small units of highly trained, highly skilled soldiers can raise havoc with an enemy force much larger than themselves. Economy of force is embodied in the various special operations units such as the Army's Special Forces (Green Beret), the Navy's Seals, the Air Force's Special Operations Wing, and the USMC's Recon Platoons. Such units can and do employ several of the other Principles of War (surprise foremost among them) in their operations by virtue of their small size, but potent combat ability and efficiency.

Terrorists make use of economy of force in two ways. First they select targets which by their very nature (civilian) offer no resistance. Second, they use a small force of dedicated individuals who are prepared to make any sacrifice necessary to achieve their goal. By using a small number of people they also minimize possible detection before they strike and insure operational surprise and security.

SIMPLICITY

Simplicity is perhaps the key to implementation and gaining full advantage of the other mentioned Principles of War. Mission or operations orders are an attempt to not only spell out the mission in full, such as objective, resources available, coordination with supporting units, and so on, but also a deliberate attempt to reduce all factors to the simplest terms for maximum understanding and greatest probability of accomplishment.

The one salient feature of any mission or operations order is that they each must be kept simple, clearly defined, and achievable within the assets available to the executing unit. In formulating plans another military axiom comes into play. It is KISS. Keep It Simple, Stupid. The more complicated or intricate the plan, the more potential exists for a failure in any one of the plan components, and by default, failure in accomplishing the mission. As has been said by various military commanders, no plan survives contact with the enemy. Intricate and complicated plans are the surest way to invite Murphy's law to intercede on the side of the enemy.

Though with terrorist groups it is impossible to necessarily delineate a set of overall objectives they have for what they initiate, what can be said is that their essential goal and the plans they implement to achieve those goals are quite simple. Create a maximum of terror, death, destruction or chaos with a minimum of assets, both personnel and materiel. This they do very expertly indeed. And it is not in principle difficult to do against an unarmed, defenseless civilian population or target. When was the last time you read of a terrorist attack directed against a military installation or forces?

As terrorists become more sophisticated in their ability to take advantage of technology such as communications security, explosives technology, chemical and biological weapons technology, not to mention nuclear technology, they will undoubtedly do so and do so with even greater effective terror for the public and to the consternation of government law enforcement and counter-terrorist organs. Treaties and laws to the contrary, the knowledge is out there. Terrorists will eventually assimilate it, develop it, and use it. So long as they perceive the socio-political forces driving them as such they will be compelled to do so. Their greatest weapon is terror. And that weapon is so effective because ignorance nurtures terror.

Terrorist groups may not be officially viewed as military or paramilitary in nature, organization or standing. They may be viewed as simply criminal misfits. That is a dangerous view. They are every bit as committed to their cause as US Armed Forces and their Special Operations forces are dedicated to a free and secure American people. Terrorist do operate as a military force. They may not adhere to the Geneva Convention or the Uniform Code of Military Justice, but they do adhere to military Principles of War. They do use them. The public needs to recognize that as the first step toward its own defense against terrorist attack. Each individual is first and foremost responsible for his or her own defense. Calling 911 will not be a workable option under all circumstances. Knowing the vulnerabilities of potential targets, and the signs of attack by terrorist units particularly in absence of explosions and gunfire is the key to the first step in self defense- recognizing the threat. If the hairs on your neck stand up, pay heed. Act accordingly.

The question on one's mind at this point may be that if the former Soviet Union was a prime mover behind terrorist groups, with its demise, is it not less likely that such renegade groups will have the means to embark on a chemical and certainly biological weapons program? Yes and no, perhaps. Crystal balls are not good predictors of the future. Even in the present climate, backing of terrorist groups is not necessarily diminishing. It may only become more subtle. After all Lybia learned the hard way what support for terrorist groups can mean. Then President Reagan sent a message to the Libyan leadership that they could not fail to receive and others of that ilk have certainly taken notice as a result of Desert Storm. Support for terrorists, let alone terrorist actions will be more so carefully planned and executed than ever before.

Aside from the Fundamentalist states such as Iran, or the totalitarian states like Iraq or Syria, what other possible support might the more organized and better led terrorist groups receive? The answer hinges on the word possible. What about the international drug trade cartels?

International drug trade is a multibillion dollar a year business. Any cursory examination of the efforts and success rate of the international community to even inhibit illicit drug activities let alone stop it reveals a rather dismal record of what can only be called minuscule achievements. With increased pressures on host governments with drug cartels within their borders to clean things up, pressure on these drug groups is building also. There are some well established organizations in South America, Southeast Asia, the Middle East, Japan and a growing faction in the Russian Federation. Only a fraction of a percent of the billions of dollars these combined drug cartels pull in if invested with a receptive terrorist group in a remote (politically, culturally, geographically) state could provide the funds for very serious efforts. Combined with the education in the western universities of foreign nationals in the sciences and engineering, only a few of these educated individuals with anti-American, anti-west feelings could do serious damage. The only stumbling block to such an alliance is the innate greed of the drug cartels whose idea of investment is much like business: short term, profit now, not later, and the fractionalization of the terrorist groups among themselves. But if they ever combined forces, we would have a very different two front war on our hands.

Man has always feared that which he does not understand or can not see. Terrorists, in their self-declared war on innocent, defenseless civilians, employing chemical, biological or nuclear weapons, capitalize on their two greatest assets: ignorance and terror.

CHAPTER 25

CONCLUSIONS

The greater the power, the more
dangerous the abuse.
-Edmund Burke, 1729-1797[1]

The use of chemical weapons requires a minimum of technical know-how compared to nuclear weapons development. The technology required is either already in the hands of most of the world's nations or it is available. The most significant demand for chemical weapons development is technically qualified and knowledgeable personnel. As most Western Nations already provide the opportunity for foreign nationals to enroll in their universities and colleges, that demand is being met. The Western Nations provide the education for the masters and Ph.D. level students of foreign nations in chemistry; biochemistry; physics; metallurgy; biology; microbiology; chemical, electrical, computer, and mechanical engineering as well as a wide range of other technical fields. Additionally, the U.S. government sanctions foreign nation's military officers' education in the U.S. in a range of U.S. service schools as well as the service academies.[2] This open friendliness is not to be criticized except to say that in so doing, we must not be surprised, though perhaps outraged, when our hand, extended in friendship, is bitten at a later date. It has been many times in the past and will be in the future.

The events in Operation Desert Storm with the Iraqis is but one example of the saying: yesterday's friend, today's enemy (and probably after a suitable interval, tomorrow's friend again). Such is the way of governments and it seems necessary to relearn each and every time (on the political level any way).

The outrage at German companies as well as other nations' business leaders for selling CBW hardware and technology to Saddam Hussein is as much a part of capitalism as the check in the mail. U.S. companies may be partially excused if only by citing the U.S. Department of Commerce's encouragement and approval of technology and hardware sales to Iraq prior to August 1990 before the Persian Gulf Crisis became a crisis. These sales were over the strong objections of the U.S. Department of Defense. The bigger the government, the less its left hand knows what the right hand is doing and the less effective any oversight responsibility is. But, one must realize the geopolitical position Iraq and Saddam Hussein held for the US before August 1990. After 3 August 1990, they were out. As a result, the U.S. Department of Commerce put the lock on the technology leaving U.S. shores for Iraq. Too little and too late. U.S. Forces and their Arabic Allies faced much of the technology that Commerce (over Defense objections) permitted (as in permit or license) to leave the

---

[1] Dictionary of Quotations, The Oxford University Press, Cresent Books, New York, 1985, p 101

[2] U.S. Military Academy, West Point, NY of the U.S. Army, U.S. Naval Academy, Annapolis, MD of the U.S. Navy, and The U.S. Air Force Academy, Colorado Springs, CO.

U.S. Politics makes strange bed fellows, but the divorce proceedings between the U.S. and Iraq in the Persian Gulf have proven devastating to the area's ecology as well as lethal to men, women, children and wildlife.

Training and education are the only ways to prepare people for the rigors of inhumanity that is war. As disquieting as it may be, most people must be untrained as civilians. Obeying cardinal laws of "thou shalt not kill" can be lethal in combat. The Johnny's and Jimmy's down the street may be able to handle themselves in a fist fight, but combat is not so tame. What is otherwise in civilian life called dirty fighting is in war the norm if not the rule, and those who do not adapt to and adopt it may be short lived in the first combat engagement. There is no substitute for training: hard, hands-on, in the field training. Though one of the most unpleasant peacetime activities of the soldier, it is his wartime primer and intended to be his salvation. Training is his lifeline to actual combat survival. There is no such thing as overtraining a soldier. Under training him can cost him his life. And so it is with NBC training. It's not enough. It's not realistic enough. It's not regular enough. The fear and in trepidation that was evident among the U.S. forces, their families at home, and the US political leaders during Operation Desert Shield and into Desert Storm, was understandable. NBC is dangerous, most particularly to those uninitiated to its nature, practices and principles.

The same character of fear and concern is not evident with respect to conventional warfare. Why? Fear of the unknown. That's why. There is ample understanding and experience with conventional warfare. Conventional warfare training accounts for what is expected. It is so commonly understood and taken for granted, that it is almost, almost accepted as inevitable. Not so with chemical and biological warfare. The difference in the concern expressed over chemical casualties versus conventional fire casualties speaks loudly to the problem. The training isn't as good as it should be. It's missing something. It's missing a confidence component that far exceeds the teargas chamber exercise. It's missing the same dogged, determined, intensive attention that conventional weapon training enjoys.

With the waning of the cold war, the collapse of the Soviet Union and the Eastern Block countries, vast stores of military hardware, technology and personnel are essentially footloose and searching for an identity and a belonging, and perhaps a regular pay check. Though immediate emphasis has been placed upon the securing of nuclear weapons, technology and personnel so they don't fall into the hands of unscrupulous nations, the threat of NBC technology and expertise also must be considered. The specter of a renegade national leader sending agents armed with biological weapons to a targeted nation is not paranoia or science fiction. One only has to consider the historical impact of naturally spread diseases such as the flu or even in today's world, AIDS, or the potential of Ebola outbreaks to perceive the potential harm and threat posed to a targeted nation.

The threat to civilian populations to CBWT is exemplified in their vulnerability to conventional bomb terrorist attacks and the recent (March 1995) Sarin nerve agent attack directed against Tokyo, Japan subway commuters. Bans against possession of critically suspect chemical or biological material, equipment, etc. will not serve as the ultimate insurance policy against such exposure and threat. Laws, both national and international, against any number of other abhorrent offenses are broken daily if not hourly. What is needed is a better understanding in the public's mind of just what the threats are, the tactical and strategic implications of such attacks and that knowledge must come from an educational process encouraged and advanced by governments. Just as we are asked to help police in recognizing the more mundane criminal signals and activities of the common criminal, we as a people must also be educated to the signals of the more heinous and yet subtle fingerprints of CBWT activities. Though a call to 911 is the advice of government, one is ultimately responsible for one's own safety. Awareness is the key to that safety. Education is the key to that awareness. This is not suggesting or encouraging paranoia. As FDR once said in a fireside chat to pre-WWII America, all we have to fear is fear itself. Let's know what the fear (threat) is and educate ourselves about it.

As biotechnology advances in the western and other technologically advancing nations, the spread of that technology to other nations with less moral inhibitions will enable them to develop systems for covert attacks upon their enemies, real or imagined. Though nuclear or even chemical terrorism attacks are in principle somewhat containable, biological attacks are not. How do you advance the state of man's knowledge for his improvement and at the same time keep that knowledge out of the hands of the unscrupulous? I certainly don't have a canned answer...

RADIOLOGICAL THREATS

NBC which is the US Army acronym for Nuclear, Biological and Chemical warfare subject matter has as a historically and critically important component the nuclear concern. The US Army Chemical Corps personnel are charged with responsibilities in this area of unconventional weapons defense and employment also. As for the question of terrorist activities involving nuclear materials, considerable concern, interest and effort is expended by US officials in intelligence and defense arms of the government as well as law enforcement agencies such as the FBI.

The likelihood of a terrorist group procuring a nuclear device and detonating it in a western country is not necessarily remote, but not impossible, either. With the demise of the USSR and the rather spotty, haphazard or questionable controls on nuclear weapons in former Soviet satellite states with centuries-old hatreds among those peoples, the concern for such a loose device finding its way to a rogue nation state or terrorist group, by theft, misplacement, or sale, harbors serious consequences for most any country on the wrong side of such a nuclear device possessing group.

Coupled with the uncertainties of nuclear security in these former Soviet affiliates and the vast sums of money derived from oil producing states (not to mention international drug cartels) and the economic and political uncertainties of the Russian Federation, there is little reason for confidence in the absolute accountability and security of those weapons. The development of nuclear capabilities attributed to Israel is thought by some to come form acquisition of small quantities of weapons grade fissile material over time on the sly.

Nuclear explosions instigated at the hands of terrorists are not the only concern as relates to nuclear terrorism. Spreading fissile or other highly radioactive material around densely populated cities of the world spells as much trouble as the mushroom cloud and fireball only on a less spectacular scale. The hazards are in the ionizing radiations.

One primary, lead agency of government charged with the responsibility to respond to any nuclear emergency (threat) is the NEST, the Nuclear Emergency Search Team. The NEST is an arm of the Department of Energy (DOE), headquartered in Nevada as part of the Nevada Operations Office, under the authority of the DOE's Director of the Office of Military Applications (OMA). The NEST is specifically charged with the following:

1. search for and assist in the recovery of lost nuclear weapons or materials,
2. assist the FBI in events of criminal theft or alleged theft of nuclear weapons, improvised nuclear device (IND), or
3. a radiation dispersal device (RDD), or
4. involving any other aspect of nuclear weapons, explosives, devices, or such nuclear materials use

NEST members are personnel with special training, expertise, and equipment for performing the above cited tasks. Specific details of means for detection of nuclear radiation sources, either ground or air surveillance, specifications of equipment, including limitations are classified as part of the national emergency response plan.

There are three kinds of ionizing radiations associated with nuclear materials. The first is beta radiation. The second is alpha radiation. The third is gamma radiation. The second is the least troublesome, technically speaking, while the last is the most dangerous.

Alpha radiation, or more specifically alpha particles, is helium atoms without their electrons. Thus alpha particles are doubly positively charged helium nuclei. They are the slowest moving and the least penetrating radiation.

Beta radiation (beta particles) is high energy electrons emitted (ejected) from the nucleus of certain atoms. Beta particles travel at about 85 to 90% to speed of light. They are slightly more penetrating than alpha particles.

Gamma rays are basically very high energy electromagnetic radiation (very high energy light, invisible to the human eye). These rays (not particles) travel at the speed of light and are the most penetrating and thus the most dangerous of the three radiations. These rays can pass through the human body, but not without causing serious tissue harm in doses.

As with chemical or biological agents, it is the level or dose absorbed of radiation that determines the extent of harm done. Topical exposure of skin is serious, but if the radioactive dust particles are washed off immediately, damage can be minimized. Inhalation of the radioactive dust presents a more serious problem. The use of masks in such cases does not protect you from the radiation, but it will filter out radioactive aerosols, dust and such which prevents the material from entering the lungs.

The only way to detect such radiations is with instruments such as a Geiger counter, or film badges which must be developed and assessed for the amount of exposure. One point of radiation exposure that is important to understand is that it damages living tissues, not dead tissues, and that damage is generally due to the interaction of water of the cell with the radiation. The ionized products of water interaction are what lead to damage of the cells. The most significant cellular component of concern is the DNA which is the genetic store of the organism. The effects on the DNA are complicated (not necessarily well understood either) and beyond discussion here.

A second point of radiation concerns exposure as a function of distance from the source. An example familiar to all will convey the principle considered here. At night if you observe a porch light on, you undoubtedly notice that the further away from the light you are the less brightly lit the area where you are appears. As you approach the light, the brighter the area you are in becomes. This is because the light intensity decreases with the distance from the source. This same principle applies to radiation. The further away from the source, the less intense and therefore the less a dose you absorb with time of exposure.

A simple way to explain this is to consider a bicycle wheel removed from the bicycle and laid on the ground with its spokes radiating out from the axle. Consider for our purposes that the spokes represent "particles of radiation" radiating (traveling) out from the source (the axle). In close to the axle, the spokes are more densely packed or clustered in appearance. Yet at the tire end, the spokes are further apart from each other or less densely clustered. Consider the number of spokes as the intensity. The close clustering near the axle is the intensity at the source. The widely spaced clustering further away represents the intensity at a distance from the source. Now if you imagine that we extend the length of the spokes for several hundred feet, it is possible for you to stand in between these extended spokes at a distance of a few hundred feet from the axle. The "spoke" intensity is much less so far out from the axle (source) than it is in close to it.

Radiation exposure follows a similar principle as relates to distance from the source. The closer you are, the more exposed and the more radiation you will receive. The further away from the source, the less exposed, and the less radiation you will receive. The level of radiation received is a function of $1/r^2$ where r is the distance from the source and is commonly referred to in physics as the inverse square law. The increased distance represents a kind of physical dilution of the intensity due to increasing distance. The following table of distance and level of reduction in radiation exposure illustrates the import of the inverse square law concerning exposure to radiation. Let's assume you are at a distance of X feet from a radiation source. If you like, say X is 10 feet. For each doubling of the distance from the source, your exposure is reduced by 1/4 of the previous distance as shown:

Distance	$1/r^2$	Level of Exposure	Reduction/doubling
X	$1/X^2$	1	
2X	$1/4X^2$	1/4	1/4 of previous level
4X	$1/16X^2$	1/16	1/4 of previous level
8X	$1/64X^2$	1/64	1/4 of previous level
16X	$1/256X^2$	1/256	1/4 of previous level

The point? The further away from an ionizing radiation source you are, the less radiation injury you will suffer.

FURTHER READINGS

Most of the references cited are rather technical for the general reader. For those with more chemical and biological sciences background, the direct technical sources are very useful for further, in depth reading.

AGRICULTURE

The Biochemistry and Physiology of Infectious Plant Diseases, Robert N. Goodman, Zoltan Kiraly & Milton Zaitlin, D. Van Nostrand Co., Inc., Princeton, NJ, 1967
Famine on the Wind: Man's Battle Against Plant Disease, G.L. Carefoot and E.R. Sprott, Rand McNally & Co., 1967

Field Crop Disease Handbook, Robert F. Nyvall, AVI Publishing Co., Inc., Westport, CT, 1979

Introduction to Plant Diseases: Identification and Management, G.B. Lucas, C.L. Campbell and L.T. Lucas, AVI Publishing Co., Inc. Westport, CT, 1985

Plant Diseases and Vectors, Ecology and Epidemiology, Karl Maramorosch & Kerry F. Harris, Academic Press, New York, 1981

ANTIBIOTICS

Antibiotics and Chemotherapy, Vol. 20, Acquired Resistance of Microorganisms to Chemotherapeutic Drugs, F.E. Hahn, Ed., S. Karger, New York, 1976

Antibiotics: Mechanism of Action of Antibacterial Agents, Vol. V, Pt. 1, Fred E. Hahn, Ed., Springer-Verlag, New York, 1979

Biochemistry of Antimicrobial Action, 3rd. Ed., T.J. Franklin & G.A. Snow, Chapman & Hall, New York, 1981

Encyclopaedia of Antibiotics, 2nd. Ed., John S. Glasby, John Wiley & Sons, New York, 1979

Manual of Antibiotics and Infectious Diseases, 4th Ed., John E. Conte, Jr. & Steven L. Barriere, Lea & Febiger, Philadelphia, 1981

The Molecular Basis of Antibiotic Action, 2nd. Ed., E.F. Gale, E. Cundliffe, P.E. Reynolds, M.H. Richmond and M.J.Waring, John Wiley & Sons, New York, 1972

Wonder Drugs: A History of Antibiotics, Helmuth M. Boettcher, Translated from the German by Einhart Kawerau, J.B. Lippincott Co., New York, 1963

BIOCHEMISTRY & PHYSIOLOGY

The Biochemical Basis of Neuropharmacology, 5th Ed., Jack R. Cooper, Floyd E. Bloom and Robert H. Roth, Oxford University Press, New York, 1986.

Biochemistry, 3rd Ed., Lubert Stryer, W. H. Freeman & Co., New York, 1988. [Textbook]

Biochemistry of Endotoxins, Christian R.H. Raetz, in *Ann. Rev. Biochem.* **59**, 129-170 (1990)

Biochemistry of Interferons and Their Action, Peter Lengyel, in *Ann. Rev. Biochem.* **51**, 251-282 (1982)

The Fine Structure of the Nervous System, Alan Peters, Sanford L. Palay & Henry DeF. Webster, Oxford University press, New York, 1991

Fundamentals of Enzymology, 2nd Ed., Nicholas C. Price and Lewis Stevens, Oxford Science Books, New York, 1989.

Hemoglobin and Myoglobin in Their Functions with Ligands, E. Antonini & M. Brunori, North-Holland Publishing Co., Amsterdam, 1971.

Human Anatomy and Physiology, John W. Hole, Jr., William C. Brown Publishers, Dubuque, Iowa, 1978. [Textbook]

Influence of Particle Size upon the Retention of Particulate Matter in the Human Lung, J.H. Brown, K.M. Cook, F.G. Ney and Theodore Hatch, *American Journal of Public Health* **40**, 450-458 (1950).

Interferons and Their Actions, Sidney Pestka, Jerome A. Lenger, Kathryn C. Zoon & Charles E. Samuel, in *Ann. Rev. Biochem.* **56**, 727-777 (1987)

Mechanisms of free Energy Coupling in Active Transport, Charles Tanford, *Ann. Rev. Biochem.* **52**, 379-490 (1983)

Membrane Receptors for Hormones and Neurotransmitters, C. Ronald Kahn, *Journal of Cell Biology*, **70**, 261-286 (1976).

Mitochondria, Alexander Tzagoloff, Plenum Press, New York, 1982.

The Mitochondrial Electron Transport and Oxidative Phosphorylation System, Youssef Hatefi, in *Annual Reviews in Biochemistry* **54**, 1015-1069 (1985).

The Molecular Basis of Communication Between Cells, Solomon H. Snyder, *Scientific American* **253(4)**, 132-141 (1985).

A Molecular Description of Nerve Terminal Function, Louis F. Reichardt & Regis B. Kelly, in *Annual Reviews in Biochemistry* **52**, 871-926 (1983).

The Molecular Organization of Membranes, S. J. Singer in *Ann. Rev. Biochem.* **43**, 805-833 (1974)

Pathophysiology: Clinical Concepts of Disease Processes, Sylvia Anderson Price and Loraine McCarty Wilson, McGraw-Hill Book Co., New York, 1978.

Physiological Psychology, Mark R. Rosenzweig and Arnold L. Leiman, D.C. Heath and Company, Lexington, MA 1982. [Textbook]

Structure and Function of Cytochrome c Oxidase, Roderick A. Capaldi, in *Annual Reviews in Biochemistry* **59**, 569-596 (1990).

Three-Dimensional Structure of Membrane and Surface Proteins, David Eisenberg, in *Ann. Rev. Biochem.* **53**, 595-623 (1984)

Topography of Membrane Proteins, Michael L. Jennings, in *Ann. Rev. Biochem.* **58**, 999-1027 (1989)

Transmembrane Transport of Diphtheria Toxin, Related Toxins and Colicins, David M. Neville, Jr. and Thomas H. Hudson, in *Ann. Rev. Biochem.* **55**, 195-224 (1986)

BIOLOGICAL WARFARE

Bacillus anthracis on Gruinard Island, R.J. Manchee, M.G. Broster, J. Melling, R.M. Henstridge & A.J. Stagg, *Nature(London)* **294**, 254-255 (1981).

Biological Weapons Treaty Review, Melissa Hendricks, *ASM News*, **57(7)**, 358-361 (1991)

Biomedical Aspects of Botulism, George E. Lewis, Jr., Ed., Academic Press, New York, 1981.

Experimental Air-Borne Infection, Theodor Rosebury, Williams & Wilkins Co., Baltimore, 1947.

Gene Wars: Military Control Over the New Genetic Technologies, Charles Piller & Keith R. Yamamoto, Beech Tree Books/William Morrow, New York, 1988.

Japan's Secret Weapon, Barclay Newman, Current Publishing Co., 1944.

The Microbiologist and Biological Defense Research: Ethics, Politics and International Security, Vol.

666, Raymond A. Zilinskas, James A. Poupard & Linda A. Miller, *New York Academy of Sciences*, 1992.

CHEMICAL WARFARE

Active Carbon, John W. Hassler, Chemical Publishing Co., Inc., New York, 1951.

Chemical Reactions of Diphosgene of Biological Significance, E.S.G. Barron, G. Bartel, G.B. Miller and J. Meyer, in *Fasciculus on Chemical Warfare Medicine*, Vol II, Respiratory Tract, National Research Council, Committee on Treatment of Gas Casualties, Washington, D.C. 1945

Chemical Warfare, Edward M. Spiers, University of Illinois Press, Urbana and Chicago, 1986.

Chemical Warfare Agents, Satu M. Somani, Global Professional Publications, Irvine, CA, 1992.

Chemical Warfare and Disarmament, Mathew Meselson and Julian Perry Robinson, *Scientific American* **242(4)**, 38-47 (1980).

Chemical Warfare: A Study in Restraints, Frederic J. Brown, Princeton University Press, Princeton, NJ, 1968.

Chemical Warfare, Pyrotechnics and the Fireworks Industry, T.F. Watkins, J.C. Cackett and R.G. Hall, Pergamon Press, New York, 1968.

Chlorine and Hydrogen Chloride, Committee on Medical and Biologic Effects of Environmental Pollutants, National Academy of Sciences, Washington, DC, 1976

Cities: Inviting Targets for Chemical Attack, George Schecter & Amnon Birenzvige, *Army Chemical review*, US Army Chemical School, Ft. McClellan, Al, September 1987, pp. 40-43

Gas Rattles- Early Devices Cheap, Effective, TE Tragle, Jr. & JW Williams, *Army Chemical Review*, US Army Chemical School, Ft. McClellan, Al, September 1987, pp. 22-24

Gas Warfare, Brigadier General Alden H. Waitt, Duell, Sloan & Pearce, New York, 1944.

Harvest of Death, J.B. Neilands, Gordon H. Orians, E.W. Pfeiffer, Alje Vennema and Arthur H. Westing, Free Press, New York, 1972.

The War Gases, Chemistry and Analysis, Mario Sartori, D. Van Nostrand Co., Inc., New York, 1940.

Recent Research on Respiratory Irritants, Chapter XXXVII, R.W. Gerard, in *Science in World War II*, Vol. II, Advances in Military, Ed. E.C. Andrus, Little, Brown and Co., Boston, 1948

Smoke and Obscurants- Cheap Countermeasures to High Tech Weapons, LTC Robert E. Thornton, *Army Chemical Review*, US Army Chemical School, Ft. McClellan, AL, September, 1987, pp. 5-9

Toxic Chemical Training, CPT Chris Parker, *Army Chemical Review*, US Army Chemical School, Ft. McClellan, Al, September 1987, pp. 15-17

New Equipment- To Carry, Wear, Use, CPT Cathy Hampton, *Army Chemical Review*, US Army Chemical School, Ft. McClellan, Al., September 1987, pp. 25-29

CHEMICAL & BIOLOGICAL WARFARE

Doomsday Weapons in the Hands of Many: The Arms Control Challenge of the '90s, Kathleen Bailey, University of Illinois Press, Urbana, 1991, Chapters 4-7

A Higher Form of Killing, Robert Harris & Jeremy Paxman, Hill & Wang, New York, 1982.

Military Chemical and Biological Agents: Chemical and Toxicological Properties, James A. F. Compton, The Telford Press, Caldwell, NJ, 1987

No Fire, No Thunder: The Threat of Chemical & Biological Weapons, Sean Murphy, Alastair Hay and Steven Rose, Monthly Review Press, New York, 1984.

The Problem of Chemical and Biological Warfare, Vol. I: The Rise of CB Weapons; Vol. II: CB Weapons Today; Vol. III: CBW and the Law of War; Vol. IV: CBW Disarmament Negotiations, 1920-1970; Vol. V: The Prevention of CBW; Vol. VI: Technical Aspects of Early Warning and Verification, Stockholm International Peace Research Institute, Humanities Press, New York, 1971

A Survey of Chemical and Biological Warfare, John Cookson and Judith Nottingham, Monthly Review Press, New York, 1969.

Tomorrow's Weapons: Chemical and Biological, J.H. Rothschild, McGraw-Hill Book Company, New York, 1964.

Chemical and Bacteriological (Biological) Weapons and the Effects of Their Possible Use, United Nations Report No. E.69.I.24, Ballantine Books, New York, 1970

CIVIL DEFENSE

Are You Ready?, Federal Emergency Management Agency (FEMA), H-34 September 1990

Civil Defense Information for Food and Drug Officials, 2nd Ed., U.S. Department of Health,

Education and Welfare, Food and Drug Administration, Washington, D.C., 1965

Civil Defense in the Soviet Union, Leon Gouré, University of California Press, Berkeley, 1962

First Aid Manual for Chemical Accidents, Marc J. Lefèure, Dowden, Hutchinson & Ross, Inc., Stroudsburg, PA, 1980

Gateway to Survival is Storage, Walter D. Batchelor, Hawkes Publishing, Inc., Salt Lake City, 1974

Handbook of Civilian Protection, Civilian Defense Council, The College of the City of New York, McGraw-Hill Book Co., 1942

Hazardous and Toxic Effects of Industrial Chemicals, Marshall Sittig, Noyes Data Corp., Park Ridge, NJ, 1979

Nonmilitary Defense: Chemical and Biological Defenses in Perspective, Advances in Chemistry Series, No. 26, American Chemical Society, Washington, D.C., 1960

Coping with Biological Terrorism, Robert H. Kupperman & David M. Smith, FEMA White Paper, 22 August 1991

ELECTRONIC CHEMICAL DETECTOR PRINCIPLES

Electrochemical Detectors: Fundamental Aspects and Analytical Applications, T. H. Ryan, Ed., Plenum Press, New York, NY, 1984.

Fundamentals and Applications of Chemical Sensors, ACS Symposium Series **309**, Dennis Schuetzle, Robert Hammerle, and James W. Butler, Eds., American Chemical Society, Washington, D.C., 1986.

INCENDIARIES

Incendiary Weapons, Stockholm International Peace Research Institute, MIT Press, Cambridge, MA, 1975

Army Talks About Napalm, Chemical & Engineering News, **32**, 2690 (1954)

The Flaming Bayonet-Achieving Tactical Surprise Not So Easy To Achieve, James W. Williams, *Army Chemical review*, US Army Chemical School, Ft. McClellan, Al, September 1987, pp. 36-38

MEDICAL HISTORY

Chemistry: A History of the Chemistry Components of the National Defense Research Committee, 1940-1946, Ed. W. A. Noyes, Jr., Little, Brown and Company, Boston, 1948

Cholera: The American Scientific Experience, 1947-1980, W.E. Heyningen and John R. Seal, Westview Press, Boulder, CO., 1983

A History of Plague in the United States, Vernon B. Link, Public Health Service, Public Health Monograph No. 26, U.S. Department of Health, Education and Welfare, Washington, D.C., 1955

MICROBIOLOGY

Basic Medical Microbiology, 4th Ed., Robert F. Boyd and Byran G. Hoerl, Little, Brown and Co., Boston, 1991 [Textbook]

Biology of Microorganisms, Thomas D. Brock, Prentice-Hall, Inc., Engelwood Cliffs, NJ, 1970 [Textbook]

Essentials of Medical Virology, Robert W. Pumper and Herbert M. Yamashiroya, W.B. Saunders Co., Philiadelphia, PA, 1975

Medical Microbiology, 3rd Ed., Samuel Baron, Churchill Livingstone, New York, 1991

Microbiology: Principles & Applications, Joan G. Creager, Jacquelyn G. Black & Vee E. Davison, Prentice Hall, Englewood Cliffs, New Jersey, 1990. [Textbook]

Zinsser Microbiology, 9th Ed., Wolfgang K. Joklik, Hilda P. Willett, D. Bernard Amos, and Catherine M. Wilfert, Appleton & Lange, Norwalk, Ct., 1988 [Textbook]

MILITARY HISTORY & SCIENCE

The Army Almanac, Department of the Army, Superintendent of Documents, Government Printing Office, Washington, D.C., 1950

Booklet, Weapons Systems, U.S. Army, March 1991

Brochure, Chemical Research, Development and Engineering Center, U.S. Army, 1991

The Chemical Warfare Service: Chemicals in Combat, Brooks E. Kleber and Dale Birdsell, Office of the Chief of Military History, U.S. Army, Washington, D.C., 1966

The Chemical Warfare Service: From Laboratory to Field, Leo P. Brophy, Wyndham D. Miles and Rexmond C. Cochrane, Office of the Chief of Military History, Department of the Army, Washington, D.C. 1959

The Chemical Warfare Service: Organizing for War, Leo P. Brophy and George J. B. Fisher, Office of the Chief of Military History, Department of the Army, Washington, D.C. 1959

Chemistry, W.A. Noyes, Jr., Editor, Atlantic, Little and Brown, Boston, 1948.

Chemistry in Warfare: Its Strategic Importance, F.A. Hessel, M.S. Hessel & Wellford Martin, Hastings House, New York, 1940

Cities: Inviting Targets for Chemical Attack, George Schecter and Amnon Birenzvige, Army Chemical Review, p. 40, September 1987

Countering the Chemical Threat, Tom Jones, Army Chemical Review, p. 4, September 1987 Equipping the U.S. Army and Statement to the Congress, FY92, Army RDT&E and Procurement Appropriations, March 1991

FIELD MANUALS

FM 3-3, Tactical Employment of Herbicides, U.S. Army, December 1971

FM 3-5, Charateristics and Employment of Ground Chemical Munitions, U.S. Army, May 1946

FM 3-5, Chemical, Biological and Radiological (CBR) Operations, U.S. Army, September 1961

FM 3-5, Tactics and Techniques of Chemical, Biological and Radiological (CBR) Warfare, U.S. Army, November 1958

FM 3-50, Chemical Smoke Generator Units and Smoke Operations, U.S. Army, April 1967

FM 8-285, Treatment of Chemical Agent Casualties and Conventional Military Chemical Injuries, U.S. Army, February 1990 [also U.S. Navy NAVMED P-5041 and U.S. Air Force AFM 160-11]

FM 21-40, NBC (Nuclear, Biological and Chemical) Defense, U.S. Army, October 1977

TECHNICAL MANUALS

TM 3-215, Military Chemistry and Chemical Agents, U.S. Army, April 1942

TM 3-220, Chemical Decontamination Equipment & Materials, U.S. Army, March 1942

TM 3-366, Flamethrower and Fire Bomb Fuels, U.S. Army, March 1958

TM 3-4240-279-10, Operator's Manual, ABC-M17 Mask, Chemical-Biological: Field, U.S. Army, March 1983 w/C1

TM 3-6665-225-12, Operator's and Organizational Maintenance Manual, Alarm, Chemical Agent, Automatic: Portable, U.S. Army, August 1975

TM 8-285, Treatment of Casualties From Chemical Agents, U.S. Army, July 1941

TECHNICAL MEMORANDA

USAMRICD Technical Memorandum 90-1, Clinical Notes on Chemical Casualty Care, U.S. Army Medical Research Institute of Chemical Defense, Aberdeen Proving Ground, MD

USAMRICD Technical Memorandum 90-2, Clinical Notes on Chemical Casualty Care, U.S. Army Medical Research Institute of Chemical Defense, Aberdeen Proving Ground, MD

USAMRICD Technical Memorandum 90-3, Clinical Notes on Chemical Casualty Care, U.S. Army Medical Research Institute of Chemical Defense, Aberdeen Proving Ground, MD

USAMRICD Technical Memorandum 90-4, Clinical Notes on Chemical Casualty Care, U.S. Army Medical Research Institute of Chemical Defense, Aberdeen Proving Ground, MD

MISCELLANEOUS

Hazardous Chemicals Desk Reference, 2nd Ed., Richard J. Lewis, Sr., Global Professional Publications, Irvine, CA, 1990

Disinfection by Chlorine: Theoretical Aspects,O. Wyss, *Water & Sewage Works* **109**, 12155-12158 (1962)

The Chemistry of Poison Ivy, Charles R. Dawson, *Trans. NY Acad. Sci.* **18(II)**, 427-443 (1956)

Emergency Response Guidebook, Department of Transportation (US), DOT P 5800.5, Washington, D.C.. 1990

Introductory Medicinal Chemistry, J.B. Taylor & P.D. Kennewell, John Wiley & Sons, New York, 1985.

Vibrios in the Environment, Rita R. Colwell, John Wiley & Sons, New York, 1984, Chapters 36-39.

The New Book of World Rankings, George Thomas Kurian, Facts on File, Inc., New York, 1984

Organophosphorus Pesticides: Organic and Biochemical Chemistry, Morifusa Eto, CRC Press, Inc., Cleveland, OH, 1974.

Organophosphorus Poisons, D. F. Heath, Pergamon Press, New York, 1961

Health Assessment Document for Phosgene (Review Draft) Environmental Protection Agency (US), EPA/600/8-86/022A (This document as a draft is not official and not intended for citation or quotation. It does, however, provide an indication of the interest and direction of thinking of the Federal Government concerning this industrial air pollutant.)

Phosphorus Chemistry in Everyday Living, Arthur D.F. Toy, American Chemical Society, Washington, D.C., 1976, Chapters 1, 2, 17-19

The Plant World, Harry J. Fuller, Zane B. Carothers, Willard W. Payne, Margaret K. Balbach; Holt, Rinehart and Winston, Inc., New York, 1972

Windborne Pests and Diseases: Meteorology of Airborne Organisms, David E. Pedgley, Halsted Press, New York, 1982

PESTICIDES

Acute Toxicity of Pesticides, Thomas B. Gaines, *Toxicol. Appl. Pharmacol.* **14**, 515 (1969)

Biochemical Insect Control: Its Impact on Economy, Environment and Natural Selection, M. Sayeed Quraishi, John Wiley & Sons, New York, 1977.

Insecticides: Action and Metabolism, R. D. O'Brien, Academic Press, New York, 1967.

Organic Insecticides: Their Chemistry and Mode of Action, Robert L. Metcalf, Interscience Publishers, Inc., New York, 1955.

Pesticides: Theory and Application, George W. Ware, W.H. Freeman & Co., San Francisco, 1983

Rapid Detection System for Organophosphates and Carbamate Insecticides in Water, Thomas B. Hoover, Office of Research and Monitoring, U.S. Environmental Protection Agency,

Washington, D.C., 1972.

Toxicology of Insecticides, Fumino Matsumura, Plenum Press, New York, 1975.

PHYSICOCHEMICAL PROPERTIES

CRC Handbook of Chemistry & Physics, 57th Ed., CRC Press, Cleveland, OH, 1976.

The Merck Index: An Encyclopedia of Chemicals and Drugs, 10th Ed., Merck & Co., Inc., Rahway, NJ, 1983.

PSYCOACTIVE AGENTS

The Botany and Chemistry of Hallucinogens, Richard Evans Schultes & Albert Hofmann, Charles C. Thomas Publisher, Springfield, Il., 1973

Chemical Psychoses, Leo E. Hollister, Charles C. Thomas Publisher, Springfield, Il., 1968

Neuropoisons: Their Pathophysiological Actions, Vol. 2- Poisons of Plant Origin, L.L. Simpson & D.R. Curtis, Eds., Plenum Press, New York, 1974

A Primer of Drug Action, 3rd Ed., Robert M. Julien, W.H. Freeman Co., San Francisco, CA, 1981

Psychotropic Drugs and Related Compounds, Earl Usdin & Daniel H. Efron, US Department of Health, Education and Welfare, Washington, DC, Publication No. 1589, 1967

TOXICOLOGY

Active Sites of Biological Macromolecules and Their Interactions with Heavy Metals, G.L. Eichhorn, in *Ecological Toxicology Research: Effects of Heavy Metal and Organohalogen Compounds*, A.D. McIntyre and C.F. Mills, Eds., Plenum press, New York, 1978

Atropine and/or Diazepam Therapy Protects Against Soman-Induced Neural and Cardiac Pathology, John H. McDonough, Jr, Nancy K. Jaax, Renee A. Crowley, Mary Z. Mays and Harold E. Modrow, *Fundament. Appl. Toxicol.* **13**, 256 (1989)

Chemistry and Biochemistry of Thiocyanic Acid and its Derivatives, A.A. Newman, Ed., Academic Press, New York, 1975, pp. 169-211

The Chemistry of Cyanates and Their Thio Derivatives, Pt. II, Chaps. 20, 22, Saul Patai, Ed., John Wiley & Sons, New York, 1977

The Chemistry of Industrial Toxicology, 2nd. Ed., Harvey B. Elkins, John Wiley & Sons, New York, 1959

Cholinesterases and Anticholinesterase Agents, George B. Koelle, Ed.,Springer-Verlag, Berlin, 1963

Clinical Observation and Comparison of the Effectiveness of Several Oxime Cholinesterase Reactivators, SZ Xue, XJ Ding, & Y Ding, Scand. J. Work Environ. Health 11, Suppl. 4, 46-48 (1985)

A Colour Atlas of Poisonous Plants, D. Frone and H. J. Pfänder, Wolfe Publishing, Ltd., London, 1984

Countering the Chemical Threat- Providing Medical Countermeasures to Chemical Weapons, Tom Jones, Army Chemical Review, US Army Chemical School, Ft. McClellan, Al, Septemeber 1987. p. 4

Dangerous Marine Animals of the Indo-Pacific Region, Dr. Carl Edmonds, Wedneil Publications, Newport, Australia, 1975

Detoxication Mechanisms, 2nd Ed., R. Tecwyn Williams, John Wiley & Sons, New York, 1959

Disposition of Toxic Drugs and Chemicals in Man, 2nd Ed., Randall C. Baselt, Biomedical Publications, Davis, CA., 1982

Effect of Benzodiazepine Derivatives on Soman-Induced Seizure Activity and Convulsions in the Monkey, J.A. Lipp, Arch. int. Pharmacodyn. 202, 244 (1973)

Effect of Electrolytes on Cholinesterase Inhibition, David K. Myers, Arch. Biochem. & Biophys. 27, 341 (1950)

Effect of Nicotinhydroxamic Acid Methiodide on Human Plasma Cholinesterase Inhibited by Organophosphates Containing a Dialkylphosphato Group, F. Hobbiger, Brit. J. Pharmacol. 10, 356 (1955)

Effectiveness of Pyridostigmine in Reversing Neuromuscular Blockage Produced by Soman, P. Dirnhuber and D.M. Green, J. Pharm. Pharmac. 30, 419 (1978)

The Effects of Some Oximes in Sarin Poisoning, J. P. Rutland, Brit. J. Pharmacol. 13, 399 (1958)

First Aid Manual for Chemical Accidents, Marc J. Lefèvre, Dowden, Hutchinson & Ross, Inc., Stroudsburg, PA, 1980

Fluorescent Phosphonate Labels for Serine Hydrolases, Harvey A. Berman, Dennis F. Olshefski, Mark Gilbert and M. M. Decker, J. Biol. Chem. 260(6), 3462-3468 (1985)

Handbook of Industrial Toxicology, 3rd Ed., E.R. Plunkett, Chemical Publishing Co., Inc., New York, NY, 1987.

Handbook of Poisoning, Robert H. Dreisbach, Lange Medical Publications, Los Altos, CA, 1983.

Interactions Between Nerve Agent Pretreatment and Drugs Commonly Used in Combat Anesthesia, Jill R. Keeler (LTC, AN), *Military Medicine* **155(11)**, 527-533 (1990)

The Mechanism of Action of Phosgene and Diphosgene, A. M. Potts, F. P. Simon and R. W. Gerard, *Arch. Biochem.* **24**, 329 (1949)

Medical Defense Against Mustard gas: Toxic Mechanisms and Pharmacological Implications, Bruno Papirmeister, Alan J. Feister, Sabina I. Robinson, and Robert D. Ford, CRC Press, Boston, 1991

Metabolic Disposition of the Alkylphosphate Antagonist, 1,1'-trimethylenebis(4-aldoximinopyridinium) ion (TMB-4), in the Rat. III. Trimethylene-1-(4-aldoximinopyridinium)-1'-(4-carboxamidopyridinium) ion., RL Morgan, GE Burrows, MH Yen, & JL Way, *Drug Metab. Dispos.* **10(5)**, 491-494 (1982)

Oximes and Hydroxamic Acids as Antidotes in Anticholinesterase Poisoning, Beryl M. Askew, *Brit. J. Pharmacol.* **11**, 417 (1956)

Oxime Induced Decarbamylation of Pyridostigmine Inhibited Acetylcholinesterase, L. Harris, B. Talbot, D. Anderson, W. Lennox and M.D. Green, *Proc. West. Pharmacol. Soc.* **28**, 281 (1985)

Pathogenesis of Phosgene Poisoning, W.F. Diller, in Phosgene Induced Edema: Diagnosis and Therapeutic Countermeasures, *Toxicol. Ind. Health* **1**, 7 (1985)

Poisonous and Venomous Marine Animals of the World, Bruce W. Halstead, Darwin Press, Inc., Princeton, 1978

Poisons & Overdose, Marc J. Bayer and Barry H. Rumack, Aspen Systems Corp., Rockville, MD, 1983.

Progress in Medical Defense Against Nerve Agents, Michael A. Dunn (Col., MC) and Frederick R. Sidell, *J. Amer. Med. Assoc.* **262(5)**, 649-652 (1989)

Properties and Behavior of Purified Human Plasma Cholinesterase. III. Competitive Inhibition by Prostigmine and Other Alkaloids with Special Reference to Differences in Kinetic Behavior, Avram Goldstein, *Arch. Biochem. & Biophys.* **34**, 169 (1951)

Prophylactic and Antidotal Effects of Hexamethylenetetramine Against Phosgene Poisoning in Rabbits, M. F. Frosolono, in Phosgene Induced Edema: Diagnosis and Therapeutic Countermeasures, *Toxicol. Ind. Health* **1**, 101 (1985)

The Protection of Animals Against Organophosphate Poisoning by Pretreatment with a Carbamate,

J.J. Gordon, L. Leadbeater and M.P. Maidment, *Toxicol. Appl. Pharmacol.* **43**, 207 (1978)

Protection of Cholinesterase Against Irreversible Inactivation by Di-isopropyl Fluorophosphates in Vitro, George B. Koelle, *J. Pharmacol. Exptl. Therapeut.* **88**, 232 (1946)

Protective Effect of Diazepam Pretreatment on Soman-Induced Brain Lesion Formation, Lee J. Martin, Jeffrey A. Doebler, Tsung-Ming Shih and Adam Anthony, *Brain Rsch.* **325**, 287 (1985)

Response of the Pulmonary Surfactant System to Phosgene, M.F. Frosolono and William D. Currie, in Phosgene Induced Edema: Diagnosis and Therapeutic Countermeasures, *Toxicol. Ind. Health* **1**, 29 (1985)

Reversible and Irreversible Inhibition of Rat Brain Muscarinic Receptors Is Related to Different Substitutions on Bisquaternary Pyridinium Oximes, Y Kloog, R Galron, D Balderman, & M Sokolovsky, *Arch. Toxicol.* **58(1)**, 37-39 (1985)

A Specific Antidote against Lethal Alkyl Phosphate Intoxication. IV. Effects in Brain, Helmut Kewitz and David Nachmansohn, *Archiv. Biochem & Biophys.* **66**, 271-283 (1957)

Studies on Cholinesterase 10. Return of Cholinesterase Activity in the Rat After Inhibition by Carbamoyl Fluorides, D. K. Myers, *Biochem. J.* **62**, 556 (1956)

Studies on a Group of Oximes as Therapeutic Compounds in Sarin Poisoning, L. Dultz, M.A. Epstein, G. Freeman, E.H. Gray and W.B. Weil, *J. Pharmacol. Exptl. Therap.* **119**, 522 (1957)

Survey of Contemporary Toxicology, Vol. 1, Anthony T. Tu, John Wiley & Sons, New York, 1980

Therapeutic Strategy in Phosgene Poisoning, Werner F. Diller, in Phosgene Induced Edema: Diagnosis and Therapeutic Countermeasures, *Toxicol. Ind. Health* **1**, 93 (1985)

Toxicologic Emergencies, Marc J. Bayer, Barry H. Rumack, and Lee A. Wanke, Robert J. Brady Co., Bowie, MD, 1984.

The Use of Therapeutic Mixtures in the Treatment of Cholinesterase Inhibition, David Gall, *Fundament. Appl. Toxicol.* **1**, 214 (1981)

WEATHER

Descriptive Micrometeorology, R. E. Munn, Academic Press, New York, 1966

The Atmosphere, 3rd Ed., Richard A. Anthes, Merrill, Columbus, OH, 1981

GLOSSARY

The many of the following definitions of the terms listed can be found in most any common dictionary or medical dictionary. Most of the medical specific definitions cited are taken (with kind permission of the publisher) in whole or in part from Stedman's Medical Dictionary, 25th Edition. Others are generally defined by the author. Brackets, [ ], enclose further supplementary explanatory information added by the author. Military definitions generally apply to U.S. Armed Forces and specifically to the U.S. Army.

A

Absorption-- the taking in, incorporation, or reception of gases, liquids, light or heat.

AC-- US Army symbol for hydrogen cyanide, a blood agent.

Adsorption-- the property of a solid substance to attract and hold to its surface a gas, liquid, or a substance in solution or in suspension.

Acetylcholine-- the acetic acid [vinegar] ester of choline. It is released by preganglionic and postganglionic endings of parasympathetic fibers and from preganglionic sympathetic fibers as a result of nerve injuries, whereupon it acts as a transmitter on the effector organ [example: muscle].

Acetylcholinesterase-- the cholinesterase that hydrolyzes acetylcholine to acetic acid and choline within the central nervous system and at peripheral neuroeffector junctions [example: motor endings and autonomic ganglia].

Aerobic-- living in air [utilizing oxygen].

Aerosol-- a liquid or solution dispersed in air in the form of a fine mist for therapeutic, insecticidal, or other purposes.

Agent Blue-- U.S. military name for defoliant agent grade sodium cacodylate.

Agent Orange-- U.S. military name for defoliant agent grade mixture of 2,4-D and 2,4,5-T.

Agent White-- U.S. military name for defoliant agent grade mixture of 2,4-D and picloram.

Alkaloids-- basic, heterocyclic nitrogenous compounds of plant origin which possess pharmacological activity and whose nongeneric names usually end in -ine.

Alveoli-- (singular: alveolus) the terminal saclike structures in the lungs. They appear as a cluster of miniature balloons. They are the site of oxygen transfer and uptake [across the capillaries] by the blood.

Amino Acid-- an organic acid in which one of the C-H bonds is replaced with an amino group

Amyl Nitrite-- an obsolete military blood agent antidote.

Anaerobic-- living without oxygen. Many anaerobic microorganisms cannot tolerate oxygen and are significantly impeded in growth or are killed by it.

Anorexia-- diminished appetite; aversion to food

Anthrax-- a disease in [domestic animals and] man caused by infection of subcutaneous tissues with *Bacillus anthracis*; marked by hemorrhage and serous effusions in various organs and body cavities and by symptoms of extreme prostration.

Antibiotic-- a soluble compound usually derived from a mold or bacterium that inhibits the growth of other microorganisms

Antidote-- an agent that neutralizes a poison or counteracts its effects

Antigen-- [antigenic] a substance that, as a result of coming in contact with appropriate tissues of an animal body, induces a state of sensitivity and/or resistance to infection or toxic substances after a latent period (8 to 14 days) and which reacts in a demonstrated way with tissues and/or antibody of the sensitized subject *in vivo* or *in vitro*.

Antineoplastic-- preventing the development, maturation, or spread of new cell growth or tumors.

Antiseptic-- a chemical substance used externally to destroy or inhibit the growth of microorganisms.

Army-- as a military field, combat organization composed of two or more Corps and associated support units such as transportation battalions, air defense brigades, field artillery brigades, medical battalions, etc., commanded usually by a general (four-star).

Arsenicals-- compounds formulated on the element arsenic. They are as a rule, very poisonous, often being significant systemic poisons.

Atom-- the smallest indivisible particle of an element possessing all the properties of that element

Atropine-- an alkaloid chemical compound obtained from *Atropa belladonna* and used as an antispasmodic, anticholinergic drug.

B

Bactericide-- an agent (chemical or physical) that kills bacteria. Some chemical bactericides may not be effective in the killing of spores.

BAL-- British AntiLewisite: antidote for Lewisite agent poisoning.

Bacteriostatic-- a substance that inhibits bacterial growth.

Battalion-- typically an infantry unit composed of three or more maneuvering rifle companies and a headquarters company of support personnel, commanded by a lieutenant colonel; the senior NCO is a sergeant major; consisting of about 800 men

BBC-- military symbol for Camite, bromobenzyl cyanide, an incapacitant agent.

Blistering Agent-- a vesicant, organic compounds formulated usually on the atom of sulfur [mustards] or nitrogen [nitrogen mustards] and in some cases on arsenic [arsenicals] which are chemically reactive with human skin and cause chemical burns (blistering).

Blood Agent-- a misnomer, compounds, usually inorganic in nature, which were thought to act directly on the blood itself, hence their name. Carbon monoxide is a true blood agent in this vein. The so-called military blood agents are not. The most effective action of military designated blood agent is on the enzyme system [cytochrome c oxidase found in mitochondria] that is responsible for the transfer of electrons from metabolic processes to oxygen to form water. The cyanide moiety binds to the enzyme in place of oxygen, thus preventing this electron transfer as no oxygen is in place to receive them. Cyanide is the only such agent of concern to military forces and the use of the term blood agent is generally discontinued except for history reference purposes.

Botulinum Toxin-- (botulin) a neurotoxic protein of some 1500 amino acid residues and molecular weight of about 150,000 daltons, secreted by the anaerobic soil borne bacteria *Clostridium botulinum*. A substance so toxic that 0.03 ng/Kg will kill a mouse. Proteolytic digestive enzymes do not destroy the toxin though boiling does. Most always formed by bacterial spore germination in anaerobic canned food preparations that were not thoroughly sterilized by high heat, pressure cooking.

Brigade-- typically an infantry unit composed of three or more maneuvering battalions and associated support personnel including perhaps an aviation company, a field artillery company, commanded usually by a colonel though an independent operating brigade may be commanded by a brigadier general; senior NCO is a sergeant major; consisting of about 3000 men.

Brigadier General-- lowest ranked general officer, one-star, serves as a brigade commander for an independently operating brigade, a deputy commander of a division, or staff officer of higher echelon units.

BW-- common abbreviation in the literature for Biological Warfare.

BZ-- U.S. military symbol for the psychoactive incapacitant 3-quinuclidinyl benzilate.

C

C-- chemical symbol for carbon.

CA— tear gas agent bromobenzylcyanide

CBT— author's abbreviation for chemical and biological terrorism

CBW-- common abbreviation in the literature for Chemical and Biological Warfare

CBWT— author's abbreviation for chemical and biological warfare and terrorism

Carbamate-- a salt or ester of carbamic acid

Carcinogenesis-- the origin or production of cancer, including carcinomas and other malignant neoplasms

Casualty Agent-- a material of such physical and chemical characteristics that a dangerous or killing concentration can be set up under conditions encountered in the field. Casualty agents are therefore used directly against personnel for the primary purpose of producing casualties [TM 3-215].

Catalyst-- a substance that accelerates a chemical reaction but is itself not consumed in the reaction it facilitates

CG-- U.S. military symbol for the military choking agent phosgene.

Chelating Agent-- a chemical used to form a complex with a metal which then acts as a single chemical entity. An example is that of the iron associated with the porphyrin ring system of hemoglobin. Therapeutically speaking, a chelating agent binds the offending metal ion enabling it to be removed from the body through some other extraction means. A method of removing poisonous metals from the body.

Chemical Agent-- a substance useful in war which, by its ordinary and direct chemical action, produces a toxic effect, a screening smoke or an incendiary action [TM 3-215].

Chemical Corps-- A branch of the United States Army that is responsible for all matters pertaining to the use, defense, employment, R&D, training, etc. of chemicals, biological microorganisms, and radiological operations of the U.S. Army.

Chlorine Trifluoride-- an incendiary chemical agent.

Chlorosulfuric Acid-- a component of a smoke/obscurant agent.

Choking Agent-- now called pulmonary agents, usually inorganic gaseous or dense vapor compounds which dissolve in the moisture of the lungs and hydrolyze to release highly irritating byproducts which can severely damage capillaries of the alveoli (air sacs) of the lungs, leading to fluid buildup, coughing, sputum discharge, choking (hence the name) and death in severe cases.

Cholera-- a disease of the gastrointestinal tract, caused by a bacterium, *Vibrio cholerae*, marked by excessive loss of fluid through the small intestine, evidenced by uncontrollable, clear-colored, watery diarrhea.

CK-- U.S. military symbol for the military blood agent cyanogen chloride.

Cl-- both the chemical and military symbol for chlorine.

CN-- U.S. military symbol for MACE, chloroacetophenone, a tear gas agent.

Coccoid-- a round, spheroidal shaped body applied to bacterial cell shape.

Colloid-- a mixture in which atomic or molecular aggregates are suspended in solution and generally stable. The aggregate species are larger than simple individual ions or molecules. They range in size from 0.001 to 1 μm, too small to be seen with a light microscope. Example: Milk. [Contrast with emulsion]

Company-- typically an infantry unit composed of three maneuvering platoons and a weapons platoon, commanded by a captain [not the same as a Navy captain which is equivalent to an Army colonel]; the senior NCO is a First Sergeant; consisting of about 200 men.

Compound-- the covalent or ionic combination of two or more elements to form a substance of distinct properties different from the individual components comprising it.

Conformation-- relating to the shape of a molecule.

Corps (Army)-- typically composed of three or more divisions, including perhaps an aviation battalion, field artillery brigade, associated air defense brigade, commanded by a lieutenant general (three-star), consisting of about 50,000 men.

Covalent Adduction-- the adding of a chemical specie to another with the formation of a covalent bond between them.

Covalent Bond-- denoting an interatomic bond characterized by the sharing of 2, 4, or 6 electrons.

Cristae-- (of mitochondria) enfoldings of the inner membrane of a mitochondrion

CS-- U.S. military symbol for a tear gas agent o-chlorobenzylidene malonitrile.

CW-- common abbreviation in the literature for Chemical Warfare.

CX— the blistering agent phosgene oxime

Cyanosis-- a dark bluish or purplish coloration of the skin and mucous membranes due to deficient oxygenation of the blood.

Cytochromes-- a class of hemoprotein whose principal biological function is electron and/or hydrogen transport by virtue of a reversible valency change of the heme iron.

D

DA-- U.S. military symbol for the arsenical incapacitating (vomiting) agent diphenylchloroarsine.

DC-- U.S. military symbol for the arsenical incapacitating (vomiting) agent diphenylcyanarsine.

Denaturation-- the process that results in the altering of the structure of proteins or nucleic acids by the agency of heat, acids, bases, organic solvents or salt solutions

Dengue fever-- a subtropical or tropical disease of the epidermis [of the skin] caused by a virus which is spread by a vector, usually the mosquito *Aedes aegypti or albopictus*. Another variant known as hemorrhagic dengue fever is much more pathogenic with numerous occurrences in the Pacific basin.

Density-- the compactness of a substance; the ratio of mass to volume, usually expressed a g/ml (kg/m^3 in the SI system).

Dioxin-- a contaminant in the manufacture of 2,4-D and 2,4,5-T, Agent Orange of the Vietnam War fame.

Diphtheria-- a disease caused by *Corynebacterium diphtheriae* and its highly toxic toxin which degeneratively affects the mucous membranes of the throat, nose, tracheobronchial tree with simultaneous damage to the peripheral nerves, cardiac muscles and lesser tissues.

Disinfectant-- a chemical substance useful for the destruction of microorganisms on inanimate objects. Disinfectants may not necessarily kill spores.

Disinfection- the process by which the number of pathogenic microorganisms is reduced such that the remaining numbers present no risk of disease.

Division-- typically an infantry unit composed of three or more brigades and associated elements such as aviation company, field artillery battalion, air defense battalion, usually commanded by a major general (two-star), consisting of about 9,000 to 15,000 men depending upon its organization as an airborne or heavy division.

DM-- U.S. military symbol for the vomiting incapacitating (vomiting) agent Adamsite.

DNA-- **D**eoxyribo**N**ucleic Acid, the type of nucleic acid containing deoxyribose as the sugar component and found principally in the nuclei (chromatin, chromosomes) of animal and vegetable cells, usually loosely bound to protein; considered to be the autoreproducing component of chromosomes and of many viruses, and the repository of hereditary characteristics.

DP-- U.S. military symbol for the choking agent diphosgene.

E

ED-- U.S. military symbol for the blistering agent ethyldichlorarsine, an arsenical.

Edema-- an accumulation of an excessive amount of watery fluid in cells, tissues, or serous cavities

Element-- a substance consisting of only atoms of one kind

Emulsion-- the mixture of two immiscible liquids in which one is completely dispersed in the other in the form of small droplets. Emulsions are of two types: oil-in-water and water-in-oil. [Contrast with colloid]

Endoplasmic Reticulum-- ER, a net like system of double membranes located in the cytoplasm of eukaryotic cells. The ER appears to be continuous with the outer membrane of the eukaryotic nucleus and with the secretory system of the cell (the Golgi apparatus). If associated with ribosomes it is termed rough ER, otherwise, smooth.

Endospore(s)-- a spore formed within a vegetative bacterium especially of the *Bacillus & Clostridium* genera. Also pertaining to the spore formed within a vegetative fungus cell, or other fungal structure.

Enzyme-- an organic catalyst; a protein, secreted by cells, that acts as a catalyst to induce chemical changes in other substances, itself remaining apparently unchanged by the process.

Ergotism-- a poisoned condition due to the toxins secreted by a fungus, *Claviceps purpura*, frequently associated with contamination of rye, resulting in the necrosis of the extremities.

Eukaryotic-- designating the characteristic of a class of cells which possess a membrane bound nucleus with chromosomes of DNA, RNA, and protein.

Extracellular-- outside of the cell.

F

Fasciculation-- involuntary contractions, or twitchings of groups of muscle fibers (fasciculi), a coarser form of muscular contraction than fibrillation.

FEBA-- Forward Edge of the Battle Area

FM-- U.S. military symbol for the smoke/obscurant titanium tetrachloride.

FS-- U.S. military symbol for the smoke/obscurant mixture of sulfur trioxide and chlorosulfuric acid.

Fungicide-- a substance that kills fungi.

G

GA-- U.S. military symbol for the military nerve agent TABUN.

Ganglia-- (singular: ganglion) an aggregation of nerve cell bodies in the central or peripheral nervous system.

Gas-- a chemical agent which, in field concentrations, produces a toxic or powerful irritant effect. The term includes irritant smokes [TM 3-215].

GB-- U.S. military symbol for the military nerve agent SARIN.

GD-- U.S. military symbol for the military nerve agent SOMAN.

General-- A four-star general officer, commander of an Army, or member of the Joint Chiefs of Staff, or service chief of the Army (or Air Force).

Germicide-- a rapidly acting chemical substance that kills microorganisms. Some germicides kill one type of microorganism but only inhibit growth of others.

GF— obsolete US Nerve agent, a cyclohexylmethylphosphonofluoride

Gram-- a unit of mass equivalent to about 1/28th of an ounce.

Gram-negative-- a designation given to certain bacteria when treated with a dye (crystal violet) in which such organisms stain pink in color and used to distinguish between different types of bacteria on the basis of taxonomy, identification, and indicative of fundamental differences in cell wall structure.

H

Harassing Agent-- any agent used to force masking and thus retard military operations. Only those agents which produce this result with the expenditure of small quantities of ammunition are considered primarily as harassing agents. Irritant gases are the principal agents of this type [TM 3-215].

HD-- U.S. military symbol for the sulfur mustard agent bis(2-chloroethyl)-sulfide, distilled mustard.

HE-- military abbreviation for High Explosive.

Heme-- an organometallic complex of iron and tetrapyrrole, responsible for the color of blood and the oxygen carrying moiety of the hemoglobin molecule residing within the red blood cells [erythrocytes].

Hemoglobin-- a higher level complex of the heme group and the protein globin. It is actually a tetramer structure itself, each hemoglobin unit possessing four iron [oxygen binding] atoms, or hemes, and four globin protein units.

Hepatitis-- a generic condition afflicting the liver typified by inflammation, usually virally caused, though toxic agents also can produce the condition.

HN-1 — nitrogen mustard one, U.S. military nitrogen mustard agent bis-(2-chloroethyl)-N-ethylamine

HN-2 -- nitrogen mustard two, U.S. military symbol for the nitrogen mustard agent 2-chloro-N-(2-chloroethyl)-N-methylethanamine

HN-3 — nitrogen mustard three, U.S. military nitrogen mustard agent tri-(2-chloroethyl)amine

HS-- a formulation mixture variant of HD.

Hydrogen Bond-- a very weak bond arising from the sharing of a hydrogen atom covalently bonded to a nitrogen or oxygen atom with another nitrogen or oxygen atom

Hydrolysis-- a chemical reaction between a compound and water in which the compound is split into two or more simpler molecules by the uptake of the H atom and OH group of water as components of the simpler molecules formed

Hydrophilic Interaction-- interactions between molecules in which water [or other polar substance] is attracted.

Hydrophobic Interaction-- interactions between molecules in which water [or other polar substance] is excluded.

Hyperbaric-- pertaining to pressure of ambient gases greater than one atmosphere.

I

Immiscible-- two liquids which are not soluble in each other at all. Example: water and gasoline. [Contrast with miscible]

Incapacitant-- a substance designed and intended to impede physical or mental activity, without causing harm or death.

Incendiary-- a material which, upon exposure to the air, or upon ignition followed by the rupture of the container, generates sufficient heat to cause the ignition of combustible substances with which the agent is in contact [TM 3-215].

Influenza-- flu; an acute respiratory infection caused by the genus *orthomyxoviridae* which attack the epithelial cells of the lungs.

Interferon-- a class of small glycoproteins which possess antiviral properties

Intracytoplasmically-- meaning inside [intra] the cytoplasm [cytoplasmic] or cell sap, but separate and external from the nucleus of a eukaryotic cell.

in vitro-- used to refer to processes that take place outside of the body (cell) such as in a test tube.

in vivo-- used to refer to a process that takes place inside of the body (cell).

Ionic Bond-- relating to an ion, the property of possessing a charge, either positive (from loss of one or more electrons) or negative (from the gain of one or more electrons).

Irritant-- a nonlethal, nonpersistent gas characterized by an intensely irritating physiological reaction [TM 3-215].

Irritant Gas-- a chemical agent whose toxicity, in concentrations producible in the open, will not cause death [TM 3-215].

Irritant Smoke-- The common designation of a sternutator type of irritant gas that can be disseminated as extremely small solid (or liquid) particles in the air [TM 3-215].

K

Kg-- kilogram, a unit of mass, also 1000 g, equivalent to about 2.2 lbs.

L

L-- U.S. military symbol for the arsenical blistering agent Lewisite, an arsenical.

Lachrymator(y)-- an irritant that causes copious flow of tears and intense, though temporary, eye irritation [TM 3-215].

LD_{50}-- the lethal dose for 50% of the test specimens exposed. Usage: mg/Kg means mg poison per Kg body mass.

Lieutenant General-- a three-star general officer, typically commander of an Army Corps.

Lipid-- a term describing chemical solubility and solvent extractability of certain compounds by nonpolar or "fat solvents"

LSD-- Abbreviation for the hallucinogen Lysergic Acid Diethylamide.

M

M-1-- Another military symbol for Lewisite.

Major General-- A two star general officer, typically a division commander, or deputy commander of an Army Corps.

MD— the blistering agent methyldichloroarsine, an arsenical.

Membrane-- (biol.) a lipid material of living cells consisting of two layers aligned such that the interior is hydrophobic and the exterior is hydrophilic. Membranes form the "sack" of a cell that confines and encloses the fluids and systems of the cell

Metallic Bond-- a bond arising from the delocalized electrons in a metal that gives the characteristic shine and the conductive properties of the metal

mg-- a unit of mass equal to 1/1000th of a gram.

Miosis-- contraction of the pupil. Not to be confused with meiosis.

Miscible-- two liquids soluble in each other in all proportions. Example: water and drinking alcohol. [Contrast with immiscible]

Mitochondrion-- (plural: mitochondria) an organelle of the cell cytoplasm consisting of two sets of membranes, a smooth continuous outer coat and an inner membrane arranged in tubules or more often in folds that form plate-like double membranes called cristae; mitochondria are the principal energy source of the cell and contain the cytochrome enzymes of the terminal electron transport and the enzymes of the citric acid cycle, fatty oxidation and oxidative phosphorylation.

Molecule-- the smallest component of a di-, tri- or polyatomic substance, possessing all of the properties of the substance

Motile-- having the power or ability of spontaneous movement.

Muscarinic-- of or pertaining to the production of effects upon binding of muscarine that resemble acetylcholine binding. Cholinergic.

Mustards-- generally known as blistering agents, but usually designating the chloro-organo sulfur based compounds of that characteristic.

Mutation-- a change in the character of a gene that is perpetuated in subsequent divisions of the cell in which it occurs; a change in the sequence of base pairs in the chromosomal molecule.

N

Napalm-- a U.S. military incendiary oil-base mixture of hydrocarbon compounds formulated principally on naphthenic and palmitic acids (hence its name).

NBC-- Nuclear, Biological and Chemical; an abbreviation currently in use, replacing the older CBR, Chemical, Biological and Radiological terminology in the United States Army. Pertaining to such warfare.

NCO-- military abbreviation for Non Commissioned Officer.

NCOIC-- Non Commissioned Officer In Charge.

Necrosis-- pathogenic death of one or more cells, or of a portion of tissue or organ, resulting from irreversible damage.

Nerve Agent-- organophosphate [or certain carbamate] compounds which possess significant and rapid neuromuscular inhibitory activity and lethal to life of nervous system possessing animals. Specifically they interfere with the transmission of nerve impulses to voluntary and other muscles under nervous system control by binding to the enzymes responsible for regulation of impulse transmissions [example: acetylcholinesterase].

Neuroeffector-- chemical compounds which stimulate or regulate neurological cells or tissues. Neurotransmitter-- Any specific chemical agent released by a presynaptic cell, upon excitation, that crosses the synapse to stimulate or inhibit the postsynaptic cell.

ng-- nanogram, a unit of mass equal to 10^{-9} grams.

Nicotinic-- of or pertaining to the production of effects similar to nicotine upon binding of a substance. Initial stimulation (small doses) and then depressed activity.

Nonmotile-- not capable of independent, spontaneous movement.

O

OIC-- Officer In Charge.

Organometallic-- pertaining to the chemical association of metallic elements with organic compound species.

Organophosphate-- organic compounds covalently associated with phosphate and possessing a very reactive or labile atom covalently bonded to the phosphorus atom such as fluorine or sulfur and possess significant neurotoxicity.

P

Parasitic-- an organism that lives on or within another and derives its nutritional needs from the host organism.

Pathogenic-- capable of causing disease.

PD— the blistering agent phenyldichloroarsine, an arsenical

Persistency-- Characteristic length of time an agent will maintain an effective concentration in the air at the point of release. If the remaining concentration, under conditions favorable for use of that agent, is sufficiently great at the end of ten minutes to require protection of any kind, that substance is said to be a persistent agent. When no protection is needed after ten minutes have elapsed, the agent is said to be nonpersistent [TM 3-215].

Phagocytosis-- a general process in which specific immune system cells ingest and digest solid substances, other (pathogenic) cells such as bacteria, dead tissue bits, or other foreign particles.

Physical Association-- in chemistry, a noncovalent interaction between two or more molecules, mediated by weaker forces such as hydrogen bonding, hydrophobic or hydrophilic interactions.

Pinocytosis-- a process in which a portion of a cell membrane engulfs fluid in an invagination manner and forming a vesicle within the host cell. Similar to phagocytosis.

Plague-- a disease of ancient experience a.k.a Black Death, caused by the bacteria of *Yersinia pestis*, transmitted by vectors borne by rodents and characterized in four forms: bubonic, septicemic, pneumonic and ambulant.

Platoon-- typically an infantry unit composed of four squads, commanded by usually a second lieutenant, senior NCO is a sergeant first class, consisting of about 45 men.

Pleomorphic-- (polymorphic), pertaining to fungi, having two or more spore forms.

Poison-- Any substance, either taken internally or applied externally, that is injurious to health or dangerous to life. [Poisons are to be regarded as substances that are not made by other plants or animals and can be inorganic or organic substances. See toxin]

Postsynaptic-- pertaining to the area on the distal side of the synaptic cleft.

Presynaptic-- pertaining to the area on the proximal side of a synaptic cleft.

Primary Structure-- refers to the sequence of amino acids that comprise a protein of polypeptide.

Prokaryotic-- an organism (usually applied to bacteria as an example) which possesses no nucleus.

Protein-- a polymer made up of biological α-amino acid joined together in a sequence by amide linkages (peptide) that result from the covalent bonding of the carboxyl end of one amino acid unit to the amino group of the following amino acid throughout the chain's length.

PS-- U.S. military symbol for the incapacitating agent chloropicrin.

Psychochemical-- a chemical which affects the mind, perception of reality, or ability to interact with the environment or social circumstances about.

Psychoactive Agent-- a psychochemical

Psychotomimetic-- a chemical compound which produces conditions resembling psychosis, that is, psychological and/or behavioral changes.

Psychotropic-- that which affects the mind, drugs used for the treatment of mental disorders

Pulmonary-- relating to the lungs, to the pulmonary artery, or to the aperture leading from the right ventricle [of the heart] into the pulmonary artery.

Pulmonary Agent— formerly called choking agent.

Pyrolysis-- decomposition of a substance by heat.

Q

Q— blistering agent (obsolete) bis(methylchloroethyl) sulfide

Q-Fever-- a pathology caused by *Coxiella burnetii* in humans, transmitted by asymptomatic sheep and cattle.

Quaternary Structure-- a reference the level of protein structure in which the combining of two or more separate protein molecules form a larger, unified structure which functions as a biological single unit.

R

Receptor-- a structural protein molecule on the cell surface or within the cytoplasm that binds to a specific factor, such as a hormone, antigen, or neurotransmitter.

Red Phosphorus-- a form of elemental phosphorus commonly found as an ingredient of kitchen matches.

S

SA— military blood agent arsine, an arsenical

Sanitizer-- typically referring simply to a soap or detergent for use in the reduction of bacterial numbers (sanitization) for compliance with health laws. Sanitizers are used on equipment used in food handling such as eating utensils, pots, dishes, etc.

Saprophytic-- an organism that grows on dead plant or animal matter.

SARIN-- a U.S. nerve agent, methylphosphonofluoridic acid, 1-methylethyl ester.

Screening Agent-- a substance which when burned, hydrolyzed or atomized produces a dense obscuring smoke in the air [TM 3-215].

Screening Smoke-- a chemical agent whose principal effect is to produce an obscuring smoke [TM 3-215].

Secondary Structure-- a reference to the level of protein structure which characterizes the results of hydrogen bonding between distally placed amino acids along the native chain. Such structure typically refers to α-helical or β-pleated sheet organization of the protein chain.

Serous-- relating to, containing, or producing serum or a substance having a watery consistency.

SHAPE-- an explosive charge in a geometric shape which directs a concentrated, high temperature explosive focus usually used against road surfaces, bridges, building and in civilian blasting applications. Composed of C4 plastique explosive.

Smoking Agent-- see screening agent

Sodium Nitrite-- an antidote for blood agent poisoning.

Sodium Thiosulfate-- an antidote for blood agent poisoning.

SOMAN-- a U.S. nerve agent, methylphosphonofluoridic acid, S-[2-[bis(1-methylethyl)amino]].

Sporicide-- a chemical agent that is intended to kill bacterial endospores of fungal spores.

Squad-- typically an infantry unit composed of about eleven men, headed by an NCO (staff sergeant), organized into two fire teams of about five men each.

Sterilization-- the complete removal or death of all microorganism on or in a material or object.

Sternutator-- an irritant which when breathed in extremely low concentrations causes coughing, sneezing, or headache, followed by nausea and temporary physical disability [TM 3-215].

Steroids-- A large family of chemical compounds comprising many hormones, vitamin D, body constituents, and drugs, each derived structurally from cholesterol.

Substernal-- deep to the sternum, or breast bone.

Sulfur Trioxide-- a component of a smoke/obscurant agent.

Synapse-- The functional membrane-to-membrane contact of the nerve cell with another nerve cell, an effector (muscle, gland) cell, or a sensory receptor cell. The site between two such cells in which neurotransmitter is released to bring about a desired effect such as muscular contraction.

Systemic Poison-- Substance which directly affects the heart action, nerve reflexes, or interferes with absorption and assimilation of oxygen by the body [TM 3-215].

T

T— blistering agent (obsolete) bis(2-chloroethyl sulfide) monoxide

TABUN-- a U.S. nerve agent, dimethylphosphoramidocyanidic acid, ethyl ester.

Tertiary Structure-- a reference to the level of organization of a protein's three dimensional shape assumed by its folding on itself.

TH-- U.S. military symbol for the incendiary mixture called THERMITE.

Thermit(e)-- an mixture of aluminum and a metal oxides (normally of iron or manganese) which burns with extremely high temperature and used militarily as an incendiary ingredient of bombs and other such munitions.

Titanium Tetrachloride-- a smoke/obscurant, $TiCl_4$.

Toxin-- a poisonous substance that is formed or elaborated either as an integral part of the cell or tissue, as an extracellular product (exotoxin), or as a combination of the two, during the metabolism and growth of certain microorganisms and some higher plants and animal species. [Toxins are to be regarded specifically as poisons of plant or animal origin. However, the use of the word toxin or toxic often is used in connection with poisons that are not of animal or plant origin. See poison]

Trench Fever-- an uncommon disease caused by the rickettsial organism *Rochalimaea quintans*, transmitted by the louse *Pediculus humanus*. The disease exhibits chills, fever, myalgia of the back and legs, headache, and malaise. The earliest significant occurrence of the disease was during WWI and arose among the troops who were for the most part occupying trenches, hence the name.

Typhoid Fever-- an acute disease caused by the bacteria of *Salmonella typhi* exhibiting high fever increments, rosy spots of the chest and abdomen and severe physical and mental depression.

U

Uranium-- A heavy metal of the Actinide series of elements. Its radioactive isotopes are used in the manufacture of nuclear weapons and the fuel for nuclear power plants. The depleted (nonradioactive) metal is used also in the manufacture of incendiary projectiles such as the 30 mm guns of antitank aircraft weapons.

Urticant-- a substance that upon contact with skin produces intense itching, reddened rash or welts

V

Vaccine-- a general term applied to the use of specifically prepared components (killed or attenuated) of pathological microorganisms, injected intramuscularly or taken orally, and intended to confer (acquired) immunity from infection and disease of the specific microbe.

Vacuole-- a clear space in the substance [cytoplasm] of a cell, sometimes degenerative in character, sometimes surrounding an englobed foreign body and serving as a temporary cell stomach for the digestion of the body.

Vapor-- Molecules in the gaseous phase. A visible emanation of fine particles of a liquid.

Variation-- deviation from the type, especially the parent type, in structure, form, physiology, or behavior.

VE— obsolete U.S. Military nerve agent, persistent

Vector-- As applied to medicine, an invertebrate animal [tick, mite, mosquito, bloodsucking fly] capable of transmitting an infectious agent among vertebrates.

Vesicant-- a chemical agent which is readily absorbed , or dissolved, in both the exterior and interior parts of the human body, followed by the production of inflammation, burns and the destruction of tissue [TM 3-215].

Viricide-- an agent effective in the inactivation (killing) of viruses

VX— U.S. military nerve agent, persistent

W

White Phosphorus-- a form of the element phosphorus which is yellowish to whitish (hence its name) which is highly reactive in air, spontaneously igniting into flames and setting fire to combustibles with which it is in contact. Also quite toxic to living cells.

WP-- U.S. military symbol for the incendiary white phosphorus. Also referred to by servicemen as Willie Pete(r).

Z

Zirconium-- (Zr) a transition metal with incendiary properties (sparks) when struck with instantly sharp force. Used in many incendiary applications as an ignitor or initiator of other incendiary devices.

ADDRESSES OF DIRECT SOURCES

1. FEMA: Federal Emergency Management Agency, 500 C Street SW, Washington, D.C. 20472

2. U.S. Department of Health and Human Services, Food and Drug Administration, 5600 Fishers Lane, Rockville, MD 20857

3. American Chemical Society, 1155 Sixteenth St., N.W., Washington, D.C. 20036

4. Commandant, U.S. Army Chemical School, Attn: ATZN-CM-FI, Ft. McClellan, Al. 36205-5020

5. Department of the Army, Headquarters, U.S. Army Armament, Munitions and Chemical Command, Attn: AMSMC-GCS (R), Rock Island, IL. 61299-6000

6. U.S. Department of Health and Human Services, Centers for Disease Control and Prevention (CDC), 1600 Clifton Road NE, Atlanta, GA 30333

7. Chemical Corps Museum, Building 2299, Ft. McClellan, AL. 36205

8. National Archives and Records Administration, Reference Service Branch (NNIR), Washington, D.C. 20408

9. U.S. Military History Institute, Carlisle Barracks, Carlisle, PA. 17013

10. Interlibrary Loans, U.S. Army War College, AWC Library, Root Hall, Carlisle Barracks, Carlisle, PA. 17013

11. Commander, U.S. Army Chemical Research, Development and Engineering Center, Aberdeen Proving Ground, Maryland 21010-5423

12. Commander, U.S. Army Medical Research Institute of Chemical Defense (USAMRICD), Attn: SGRD-UV-ZA, 3100 Ricketts Point Road, Aberdeen Proving Ground, MD 21010-5425

13. US-EPA, U.S. Environmental Protection Agency, 401 M Street SW, Washington, D.C. 20460

14. Chemical Manufactures Association 2501 M Street, NW Washington, DC 20037

15. US Arms Control and Disarmament Agency (ACDA), 320 21st St., N.W., Washington, D.C. 20451

HOW TO READ CHEMICAL STRUCTURAL FORMULAS

STRUCTURES KEYED TO CHAPTERS

Each structure cited in a chapter appears with a Roman Numeral bounded in brackets. The name of the structure or a brief explanation is given.

Those in the chemical sciences convey much information about a chemical substance by referring to its composition. For chemical compounds, chemical formulas are used and there are no formulas as informative as the structural chemical formula. The inorganic formulas utilize the chemical symbol of the elements comprising the molecules of the compound and dashes represent (covalent) bonds between the atoms for covalent substances. If ionic systems are depicted, the formula (unit) is noted by the chemical symbols of the elements comprising the unit and negative (⁻) or positive (⁺) signs are associated with the appropriately charged atom or the polyatomic specie.

For organic compounds the major element is carbon which is for the most part covalently bonded with perhaps, in some cases, ionic components. The same general approach for depiction as noted above applies. Additionally, certain short hand notations are used. As was explained in Chapter 2, Chemical Formula Notations & Conventions, certain structures employ geometric shapes to represent the basic structure. Pentagons represent cyclopentane rings, hexagons, cyclohexane rings, etc. Cyclic ring structures which have no inscribed circles or lines are termed saturated, that is, the vertices of the ring system represent carbon atoms which are tetravalent (having four single bonds to carbon). As each vertex of the geometric figure has two lines (bonds) an integral part of the geometric structure, the remaining two bonds are to other atoms external to the ring system. Usually, when no other element symbol is shown exocyclically (meaning not part of the ring, external to the ring), the two bonds not shown are to two undrawn hydrogens. If another atom such as nitrogen is attached exocyclically to the ring, the symbol of that atom such as N for nitrogen is written with a dash line to the carbon to which it is bonded. If the other noncarbon atom is endocyclic (meaning it is part of the ring) the symbol of that atom is written such as a nitrogen N. Such structures with atoms other than carbon making up the ring system are generally referred to as heterocyclic ring systems.

Two lines drawn between two vertices of a ring structure represent a double bond, a.k.a. an unsaturated site. The number of bonds on a given carbon may **NEVER** be more than four though multiple bonds between two carbons are permitted to a maximum of three bonds. If a cyclic structure shows a double bond between two adjacent vertices (carbons) the number of exocyclic bonds remaining is one on each carbon (vertex of the ring structure). Thus only a hydrogen or other element may be singly bonded to such a double bonded carbon.

Some cyclohexane rings are drawn either with alternating single and double bonds or as a cyclohexane ring with an inscribed circle. These as were pointed out in Chapter 2 represent a special class of organic compounds, the aromatics typified by the designated hexagonal figure with inscribed circle known as benzene. Each vertex of the benzene ring structure has associated with it only one exocyclic single bond site which bonds a hydrogen when only the hexagon with inscribed ring is shown. Other atoms including carbon may be exocyclically bonded to the benzene ring system.

In characterizing ionic organic species it is often customary to represent the polyatomic component in brackets [ ] with an appropriate charge sign outside and to the upper right of the brackets which completely bound the polyatomic component-- [ ] ˙ or [ ] ⁺.

The structures that follow are keyed by Roman Numerals within brackets [ ] to the appropriate chapter. Each chapter for which structures are cited has its own structures Romanly numbered in sequence: [I], [II], [III], ...

STRUCTURES FOR CHAPTER 2

BIOLOGICAL MOLECULES

[I]   Cyclopentane ring. Shown are the three ways it may appear in structural representations. Each vertex of the geometric figure represents a carbon atom. Each single line between vertices is a single bond consisting of two electrons which bind or "glue" the two atoms together. Conventionally, any hydrogens attached generally are not explicitly written. Cyclopentane is not a planar ring system but rather bent much like a small envelope. See [VI]

[II]   Cyclohexane ring. Shown are the two ways it may appear in structural formulas. See [I] for explanation of bonds and atoms represented. The ring of cyclohexane is not planar but adopts to shapes: the boat or the chair form. See [VII]

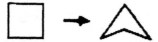

[III], [V] Cyclobutane ring. In [V] the right figure illustrates that the cyclobutane ring is not planar but bend about its diagonal.

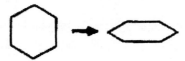

[IV]   Cyclopropane ring. This is the only cyclic ring system that is actually planar.

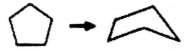

[VI]   The cyclopentane ring shown is its normal bent form depiction.

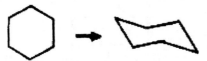

[VII] Cyclohexane rign shown in its chair form depiction.

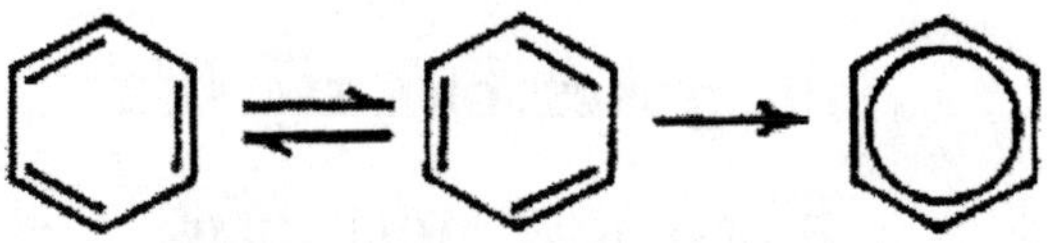

[VIII] The aromatic benzene ring. The double lines [IX],represent double bonds (4 electrons) which are [X] in alternation with single bonds (single lines). These single and double bonds may change positions (called resonance by chemists) and because they do so the far right structure shows the normal form written for benzene as a hexagon ring with an inscribed circle to represent the resonance of the electrons holding the carbons together.

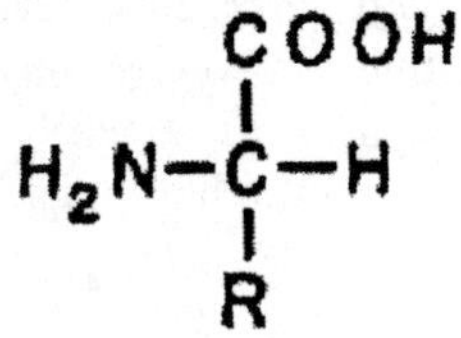

$$\begin{array}{c} \text{COOH} \\ | \\ \text{H}_2\text{N}-\text{C}-\text{H} \\ | \\ \text{R} \end{array}$$

[XI] The general structure of an amino acid, the building block of proteins. The "R" represents different chemical groups which distinguish the common 20 amino acids from each other.

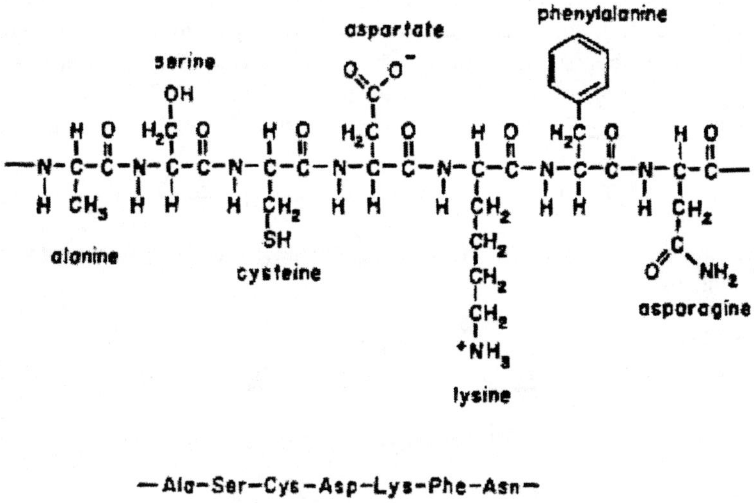

— Ala–Ser–Cys–Asp–Lys–Phe–Asn —

[XII]

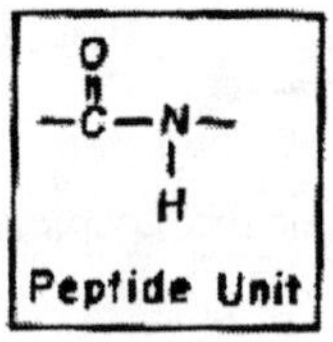

Peptide Unit

[XII] a heptapeptide (7) amino acid sequence protein fragment. The fragment shown in the box is the peptide unit from which the term (poly)peptide comes.

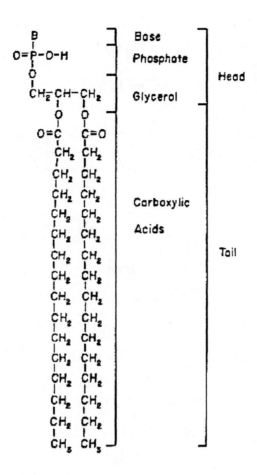

[XIII]   A general structure of a phospholipid, a common component from which membranes of cells are made. The component marked "B" for base may be several different chemical types as shown in [XIV], [XV], [XVI], and [XVII].

$$HO-CH_2-CH_2-\overset{+}{N}H_3$$

[XIV]   An ethanolamine component base of phospholipids [XIII].

$$HO-CH_2-CH_2-\overset{+}{N}(CH_3)_3$$

[XV]   The choline base component of some phospholipids [XIII].

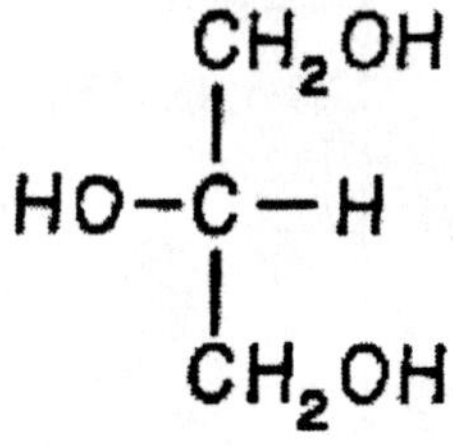

$$CH_2OH$$
$$|$$
$$HO-C-H$$
$$|$$
$$CH_2OH$$

[XVI]   Glycerol, a component of body fat (triglycerides) as well as a component of more complex phospholipids of the heart.

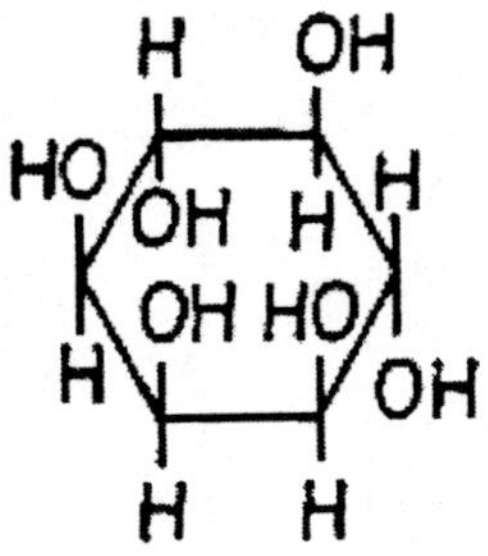

[XVII]   Inositol base component of certain phospholipids [XIII].

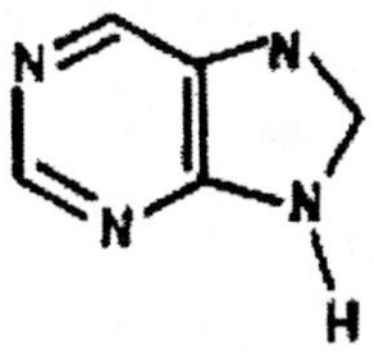

[XVIII] The purine ring, the parent compound of the DNA and RNA bases adenine and guanine.

[XIX]   The pyrimidine rig, the parent ring of the DNA and RNA bases cytosine, thymine and uracil.

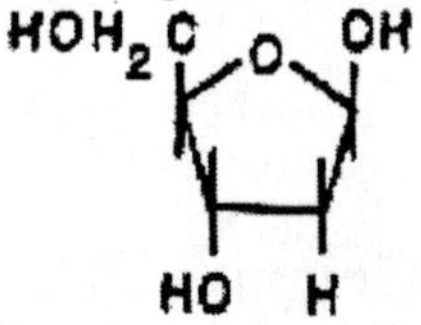

[XX]   The five-carbon sugar (aldopentose) deoxyribose, the sugar of the DNA polymer backbone.

[XXI]   The five-carbon sugar ribose, the sugar of the RNA polymer backbone.

[XXII] An AT (adenine-thymine) base pair common in DNA. The dots represent the hydrogen
        bonds between the AT pair.

guanine   cytosine

[XXIII] A GC (guanine-cytosine) base pair common to DNA. The dots represent the hydrogen bonds
        between the GC pair.

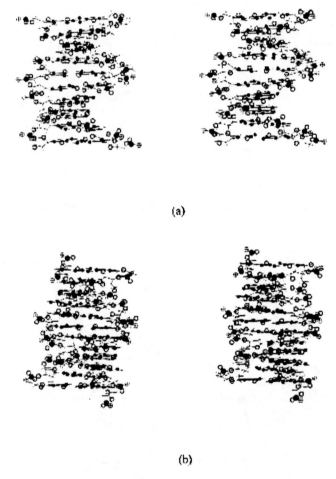

[XXIV] The pyrimidine base uracil found only in RNA.

(a)

(b)

[XXV]   a. Stereoview of a segment of one conformational form of DNA (B-form) of a eukaryotic
          cell. b. Stereoview of another conformational form of DNA (Z-form).

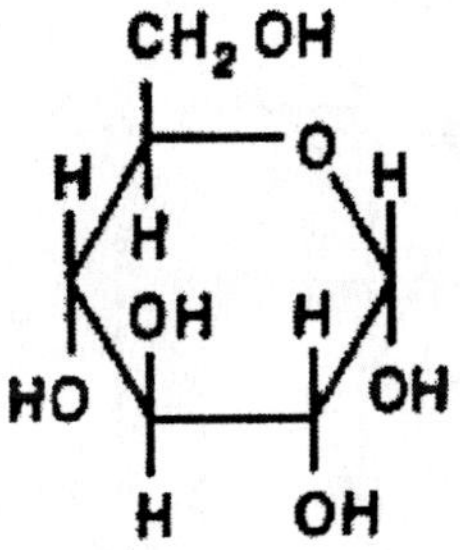

CH₂ OH

α-ᴅ-Glucopyranose

[XXVI] The cyclic form of glucose. Starch and cellulose are biological polymers of glucose. Animal starch called glycogen is stored in both human liver and muscle.

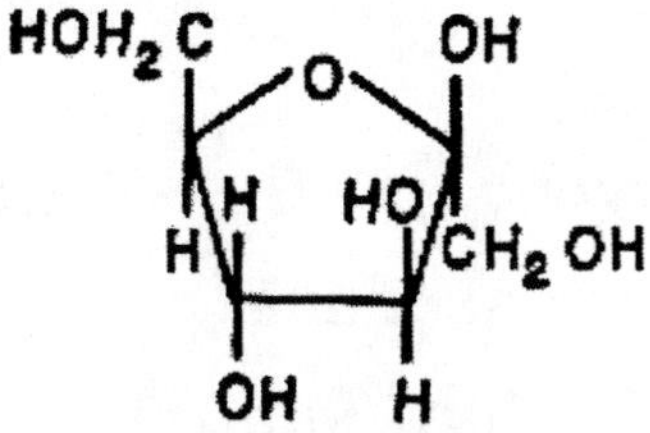

β-ᴅ-Fructofuranose

[XXVII] The cyclic form of fructose, a fruit sugar.

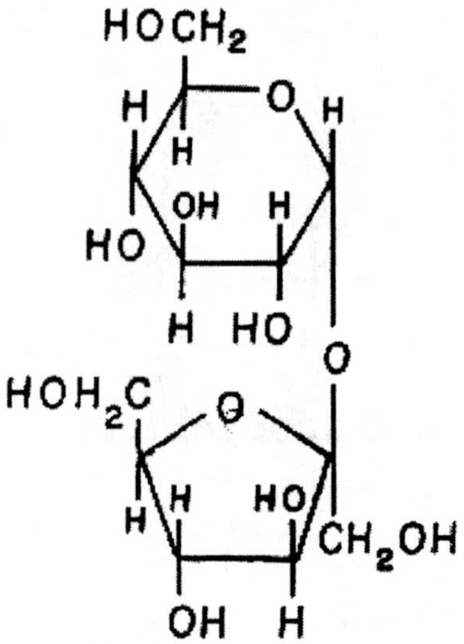

α -D -glucopyranosyl - β- D- fructofuranoside

sucrose

(Table Sugar)

[XXVIII] The structure of table sugar, sucrose. The chemical name of sucrose is also given.

STRUCTURES FOR CHAPTER 3

CHEMICALS

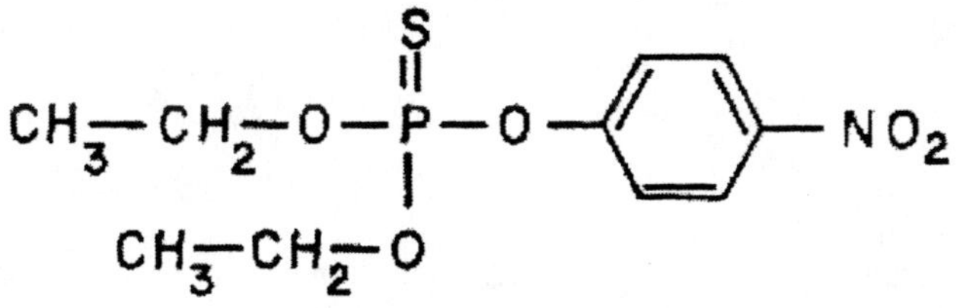

$$CH_3-CH_2-O-\overset{\overset{\displaystyle S}{\|}}{\underset{\underset{\displaystyle CH_3-CH_2-O}{|}}{P}}-O-\bigcirc-NO_2$$

Parathion

[I]   The organophosphate insecticide Parathion. Note the aromatic benzene ring comprising part of the structure of this poisonous molecule.

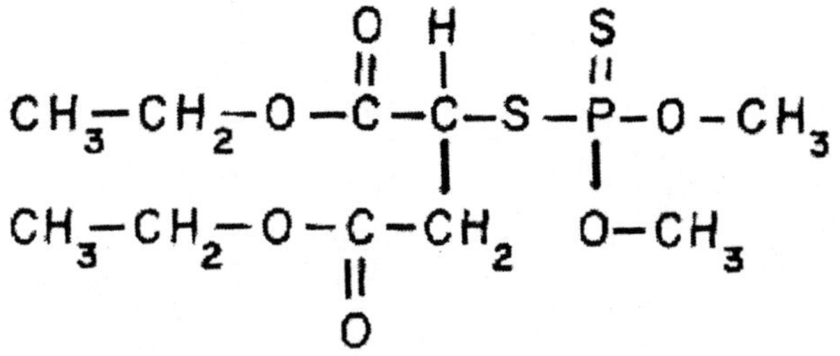

$$CH_3-CH_2-O-\overset{\overset{\displaystyle O}{\|}}{C}-\overset{\overset{\displaystyle H}{|}}{\underset{\underset{\displaystyle CH_3-CH_2-O-\overset{\displaystyle C}{\underset{\overset{\displaystyle \|}{\displaystyle O}}{}}-CH_2}{|}}{C}}-S-\overset{\overset{\displaystyle S}{\|}}{\underset{\underset{\displaystyle O-CH_3}{|}}{P}}-O-CH_3$$

Malathion

[II]   The organophosphate Malathion.

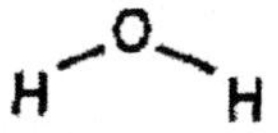

$$H^{\diagup O}\diagdown H$$

[III]   The chemical structure of water, the liquid of life itself.

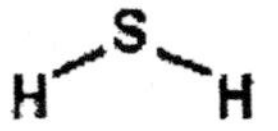

$$H^{\diagup S}\diagdown H$$

[IV]   The chemical structure of hydrogen sulfide, the chemical with the rotten egg odor. This is a deadly poisonous gas every bit as lethal as cyanide.

$$Na^+\ [OCl]^-$$

[V]   The ionic chemical structure of sodium hypochlorite, bleach in 5% solution.

$$NH_3\ +\ HOH\ \rightleftharpoons\ NH_4^+\ +\ OH^-$$

[VI]   the reaction of ammonia with water. The OH⁻ is the hydroxide ion and what makes ammonia solutions basic.

$$CH_3\text{-}CH_2\text{-}CH_2\text{-}SH$$

[VII]   Propanethiol, the tearing agent of onions

[VIII]   Urushiol, parent compound of poison plant skin irritants of ivy, oak and Sumac. Each specific type irritant is distinguished by a different "R" group

STRUCTURES FOR CHAPTER 4

TOXIC AGENTS

$$H-\overset{\overset{\displaystyle H}{|}}{N}-\overset{\overset{\displaystyle O}{\|}}{C}\diagdown_{O-H}$$

[I]   Carbamic acid

$$H-C\equiv N$$

[II]   The chemical structure of hydrogen cyanide, a deadly poisonous gas used in the California gas chamber and a WWI chemical gas weapon, originally classified as a blood agent.

$$Cl-C\equiv N$$

[III]   The structure of cyanogen chloride, a potential chemical weapon agent, originally classified as a blood agent.

$$^-O-\overset{\overset{\displaystyle O}{\|}}{\underset{\underset{\displaystyle O_-}{|}}{P}}\sim O-\overset{\overset{\displaystyle O}{\|}}{\underset{\underset{\displaystyle O_-}{|}}{P}}\sim O-\overset{\overset{\displaystyle O}{\|}}{\underset{\underset{\displaystyle O_-}{|}}{P}}-O-H_2C$$

[IV]   The chemical structure of ATP (adenosine triphosphate), the energy molecule of life, and produced in the mitochondria by the enzyme ATP synthase.

$$\overset{\displaystyle Cl}{\underset{\displaystyle Cl}{}}C=N-O-H \qquad \sim high\ energy\ bond$$

[V]   The structure of phosgene oxime, a potential chemical weapon agent originally classified as a chocking agent, now classified as a pulmonary agent in modern classification schemes.

STRUCTURES FOR CHAPTER 5

NERVE AGENTS

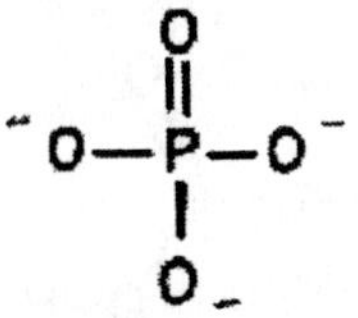

$$^-O-\overset{\overset{\displaystyle O}{\|}}{\underset{\underset{\displaystyle O_-}{|}}{P}}-O^-$$

[I]   The inorganic phosphate group, from phosphoric acid, and a common component of DNA, RNA, ATP, and other phosphorylated compounds of the cell.

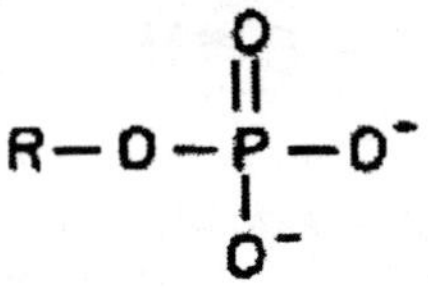

$$R-O-\overset{\overset{\displaystyle O}{\|}}{\underset{\underset{\displaystyle O^-}{|}}{P}}-O^-$$

[II]   Typical general structure of a normal cellular organophosphate

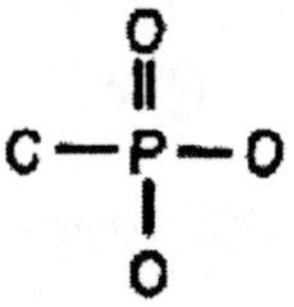

$$C-\overset{\overset{\displaystyle O}{\|}}{\underset{\underset{\displaystyle O}{|}}{P}}-O$$

[III]   A direct carbon-phosphorus bonded, nonbiological organophosphate of toxic property to a cell

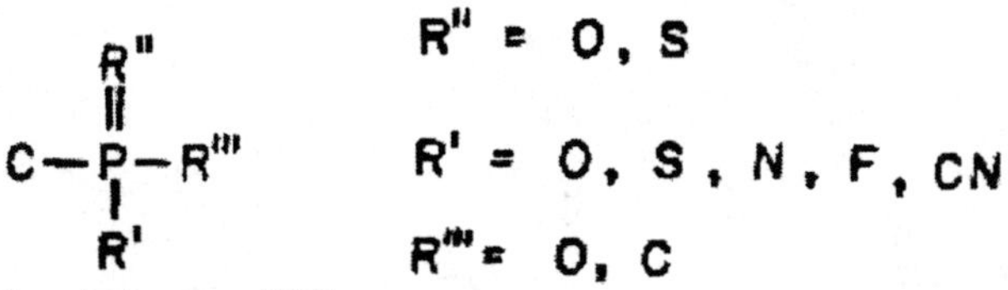

$$C-\overset{\overset{\displaystyle R''}{\|}}{\underset{\underset{\displaystyle R'}{|}}{P}}-R'''$$

R" = O, S

R' = O, S, N, F, CN

R''' = O, C

[IV]   Derivatized variations on [III]

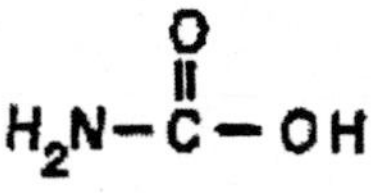

$$H_2N-\overset{\overset{\displaystyle O}{\|}}{C}-OH$$

[V]   Carbamic acid, parent carbamate compound

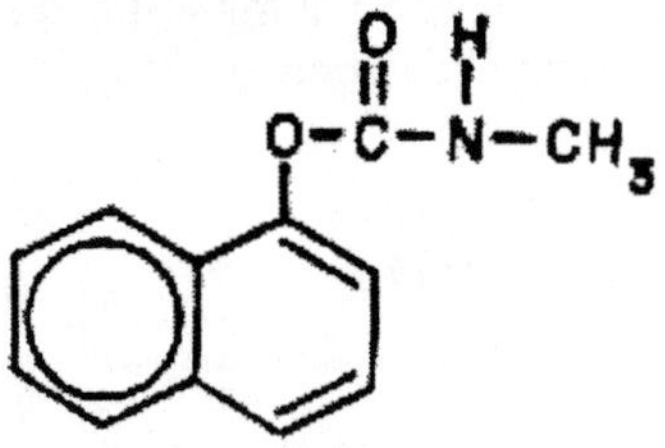

$$O-\overset{\overset{\displaystyle O}{\|}}{C}-\overset{\overset{\displaystyle H}{|}}{N}-CH_3$$

[VI]   Insecticide carbamate- Sevin

$$\underset{+N(CH_3)_3}{\underset{\displaystyle |}{\bigcirc}}\!\!-O-\overset{\displaystyle O}{\overset{\displaystyle \|}{C}}-N(CH_3)_2$$

[VII]   The carbamate Prostigmine

$$H_3C-\underset{\underset{H_3C}{|}}{\overset{\overset{H_3C}{|}}{C}}-\underset{\underset{H}{|}}{\overset{\overset{CH_3}{|}}{C}}-O-\underset{\underset{CH_3}{|}}{\overset{\overset{O}{\|}}{P}}-F$$

[VIII]   Military organophosphate (nerve agent) Soman (GD)

$$H_3C-\underset{\underset{H}{|}}{\overset{\overset{CH_3}{|}}{C}}-O-\underset{\underset{CH_3}{|}}{\overset{\overset{O}{\|}}{P}}-F$$

[IX]   Military organophosphate (nerve agent) Sarin (GB)

$$CH_3-CH_2-O-\underset{\underset{CH_3}{|}}{\overset{\overset{O}{\|}}{P}}-S-CH_2-CH_2-N\!\!\begin{array}{l}\diagup CH-CH_3 \;(CH_3)\\[2pt]\diagdown CH-CH_3 \\[2pt] \qquad\; CH_3\end{array}$$

[X]   Military organophosphate (nerve agent) VX

$$\begin{array}{c}CH_3\\ \diagdown\\ N-\overset{\overset{\displaystyle O}{\|}}{\underset{\underset{CN}{|}}{P}}-O-CH_2-CH_3\\ \diagup\\ CH_3\end{array}$$

[XI]   Military organophosphate (nerve agent) Tabun (GA)

[XII]   Structure of carbamate observed to be 30 times more poisonous than Sarin

[XIII]   Organophosphate insecticide Diazinon

STRUCTURES FOR CHAPTER 6

BLOOD AGENTS

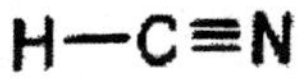

$$H - C \equiv N$$

[I] Hydrogen cyanide

$$Cl - C \equiv N$$

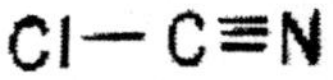

[II] Cyanogen chloride

STRUCTURES FOR CHAPTER 7

CHOKING AGENTS

$$O = C \begin{matrix} Cl \\ Cl \end{matrix}$$

[I]   Choking (pulmonary) agent Phosgene

$$Cl-Cl$$

[II]   The structure of chlorine (gas).

$$Cl-\underset{\|}{C}-O-\underset{|}{\underset{|}{C}}-Cl$$

[III]   Choking (pulmonary) agent Diphosgene

$$CH_2 = C = O$$

[IV]   Ketene, the model structure used to determine chemical action of phosgene on lungs

$$H-Cl$$

[V]   Hydrogen chloride, dissolved in water, hydrochloric acid. Hydrochloric acid is stomach acid.

$$H \overset{O}{\diagup} \diagdown Cl$$

[VI]   The structure of hypochlorous acid, a component of chlorine dissolving in water.

$$Cl \overset{O}{\diagup} \diagdown Cl$$

[VII]   Dichlorine oxide

$$CH_3(CH_2)_{14}\overset{\overset{O}{\|}}{C}-O-CH_2$$

$$CH_3(CH_2)_{14}\underset{\underset{O}{\|}}{C}-O-CH_2$$

$$CH_2-O-\overset{\overset{O}{\|}}{\underset{\underset{O_-}{|}}{P}}-O-CH_2-CH_2\overset{+}{N}-CH_3$$

with CH_3 groups on N.

[VIII]   Dipalmitoylphosphatidylcholine, a common biological membrane lipid

$$CH_3-(CH_2)_{12}-\overset{\overset{H}{|}}{C}=C-CH-CH-CH_2-O-\overset{\overset{O}{\|}}{\underset{\underset{O-}{|}}{P}}-O-CH_2-CH_2-\overset{+}{N}(CH_3)_3$$

with H, OH, NH beneath, and

$$O\overset{C}{\diagdown}(CH_2)_{16}-CH_3$$

[IX]   Sphingomyelin, the only phosphorylated sphingolipid and biological membrane component associated with nervous tissue cells

STRUCTURES FOR CHAPTER 8

BLISTERING AGENTS

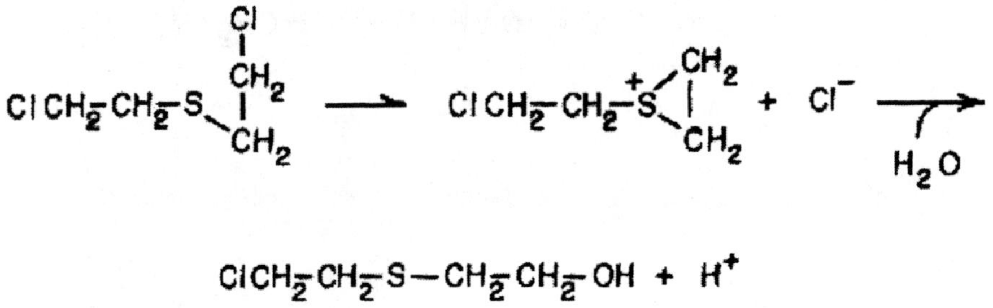

$$CICH_2CH_2S\underset{\overset{|}{CH_2}}{\overset{\overset{Cl}{|}}{\underset{}{CH_2}}} \longrightarrow CICH_2CH_2\overset{+}{S}\underset{CH_2}{\overset{CH_2}{\diagdown}} + \ CI^- \xrightarrow[H_2O]{}$$

$$CICH_2CH_2S-CH_2CH_2OH \ + \ H^+$$

[I]   Harmful mustard gas intermediate believed formed prior to reaction with cellular tissue

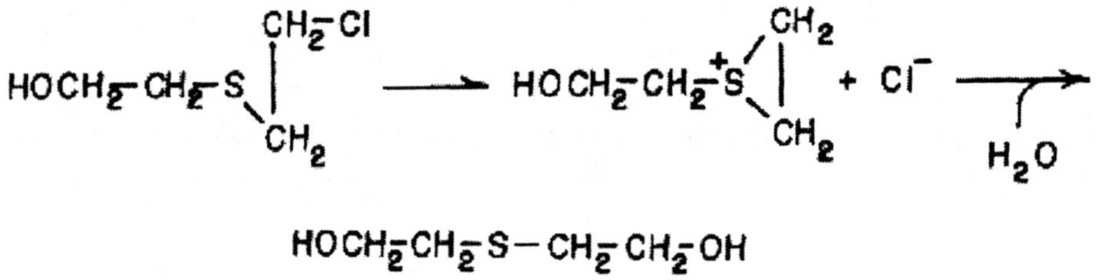

$$HOCH_2CH_2S\underset{\overset{|}{CH_2}}{\overset{\overset{CH_2Cl}{|}}{\underset{}{}}} \longrightarrow HOCH_2CH_2\overset{+}{S}\underset{CH_2}{\overset{CH_2}{\diagdown}} + \ CI^- \xrightarrow[H_2O]{}$$

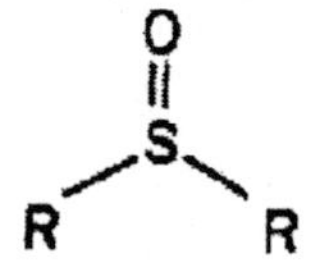

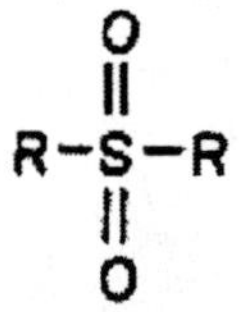

$$HOCH_2CH_2S-CH_2CH_2OH$$

[II]   Thiodiglycol

$$\underset{R\qquad R}{\overset{\overset{\textstyle O}{\|}}{S}}$$

[III] A sulfoxide

$$\overset{\overset{\textstyle O}{\|}}{\underset{\underset{\textstyle O}{\|}}{R-S-R}}$$

[IV]   A sulfone

$$CI-CH_2CH_2S-CH_2CH_2Cl$$

[V]   The original mustard gas, a blistering or vesicant agent used in WWI with considerable
       success in spreading injury, chaos and terror among troops receiving the gassing.

$$Cl-CH_2-CH_2-N-CH_2-CH_2-Cl$$
$$|$$
$$CH_3$$

[VI]   A nitrogen mustard agent. No know record of use in war exists, but these agents have seen some limited medical related curiosity.

$$\overset{\displaystyle O}{\underset{\displaystyle CH_3}{\overset{\displaystyle \|}{H_3C-As-O^-\ ^+Na}}}$$

[VII]   Sodium cacodylate, an arsenical

$$CH_3-CH_2-As\overset{\displaystyle Cl}{\underset{\displaystyle Cl}{}}$$

[VIII] ethyldichlorarsine, an arsenical

$$\overset{H}{\underset{Cl}{}}C=C\overset{H}{\underset{As}{}}\overset{Cl}{\underset{Cl}{}}$$

[IX]   Lewisite

[X]   Adamsite, an arsenical vomiting agent

$$\overset{\displaystyle OH}{\underset{}{HO-As-OH}}$$

$$HO-\overset{\displaystyle O}{\underset{\displaystyle OH}{\overset{\displaystyle \|}{As}}}-OH$$

$$HO-\overset{\displaystyle O}{\underset{\displaystyle OH}{\overset{\displaystyle \|}{P}}}-OH$$

[XI]   Arsenious acid   [XII] Arsenic acid   [XIII] Phosphoric acid

CH$_2$—SH
|
CH$_2$
|
CH—SH
|
(CH$_2$)$_4$
|
C=O
|
NH
|
Lys
|

$$\xrightleftharpoons[\text{[H]}]{\text{[O]}}$$

S
S
(CH$_2$)$_4$
|
C=O
|
NH
|
Lys
|

[XIV]   Lipoic acid, reduced form   [XV]   Lipoic acid, oxidized form

CH$_2$—SH
|
CH$_2$
|
CH$_2$—NH$_2$

[XVI]   β-mercaptoethyleneamine

STRUCTURES FOR CHAPTER 9

INCAPACITANTS & DEFOLIANTS

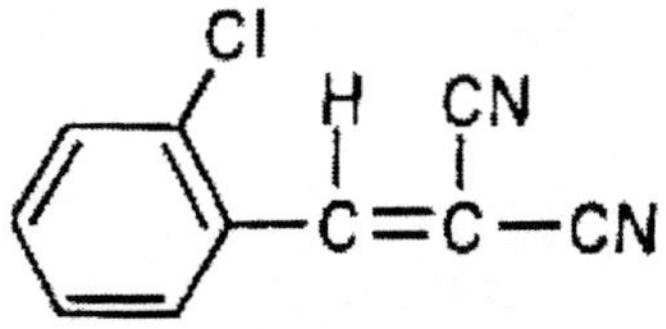

[I] o-chlorobenzylidenemalononitrile

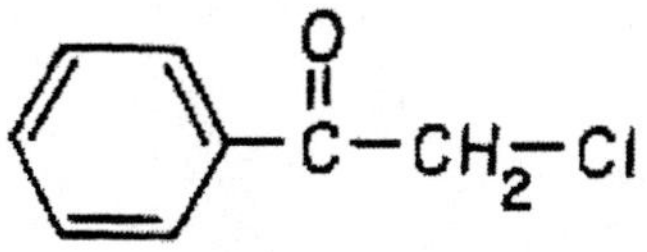

[II] 2-chloroacetophenone

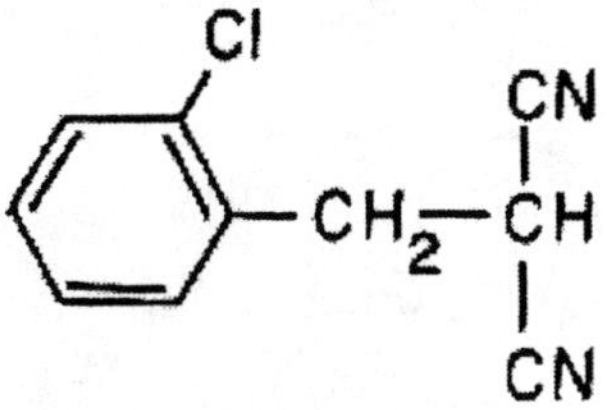

[III] o-chlorobenzylmalononitrile

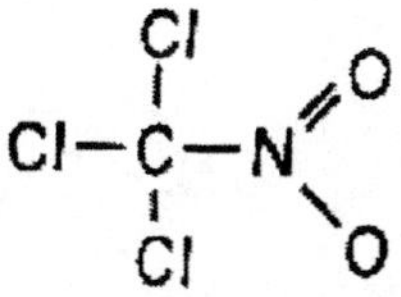

[IV] Chloropicrin

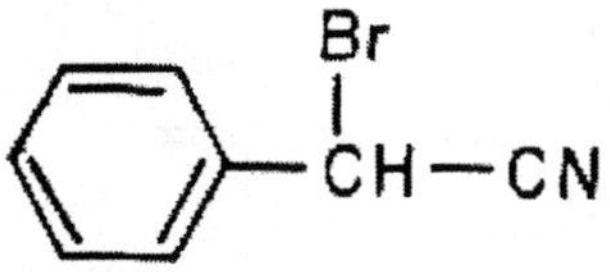

[V] Bromobenzyl cyanide

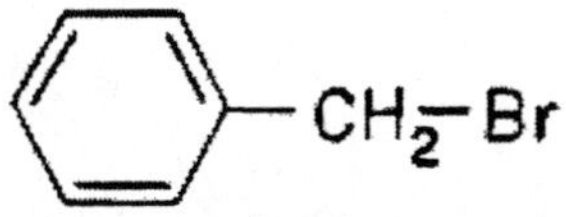

[VI] Benzylbromide

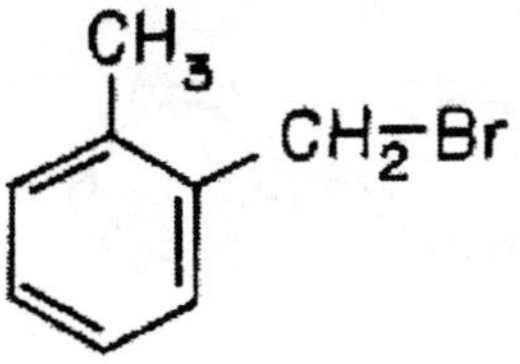

[VII]a o-xylylbromide

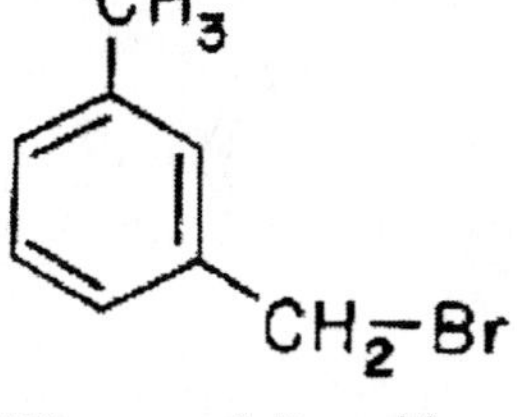

[VII]b m-xylylbromide

[VIII]   Adamsite, a vomiting agent and arsenical

[IX]   LSD, Lysergic acid diethylamide

[X] a-f   various bipyridyl structures

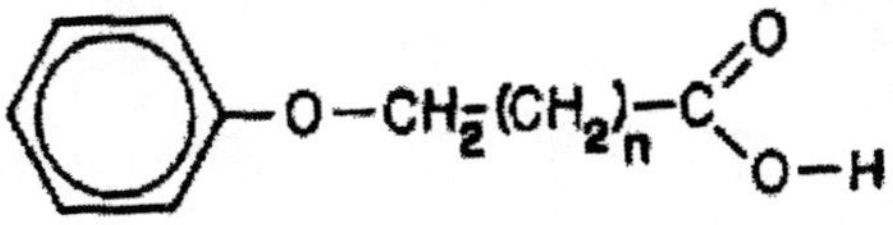

[XI]   A phenoxyaliphatic acid

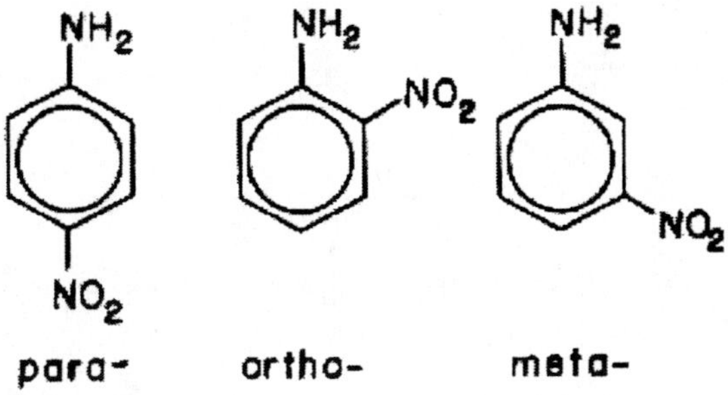

para-   ortho-   meta-

(a)   (b)   (c)

[XII]   a-c various nitroanilines

$$R-C\equiv N$$

[XIII]   A general nitrile

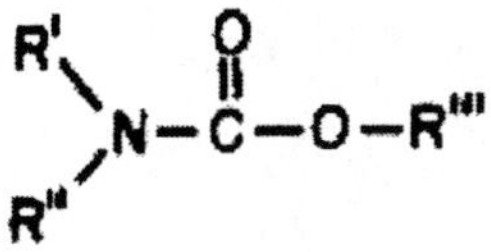

[XIV]   A carbamic acid ester 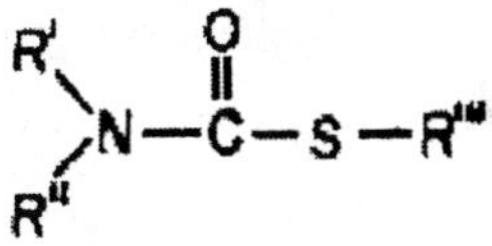   [XV]   A thiocarbamic acid ester

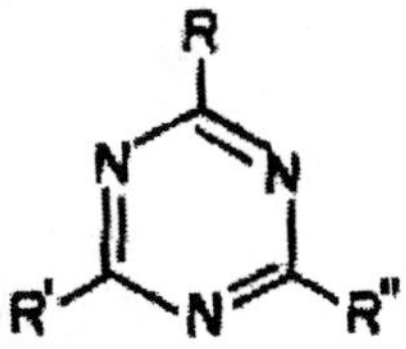

[XVI]   Triazine

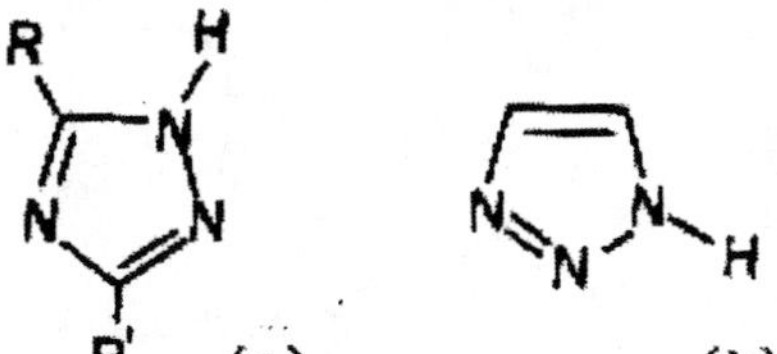

R'   (a)   (b)

[XVII] a,b Various triazoles

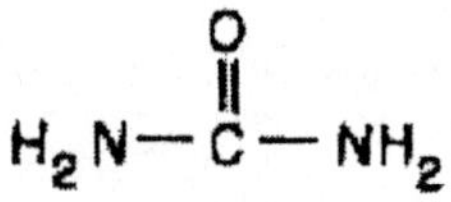

$$H_2N-\overset{\overset{\displaystyle O}{\|}}{C}-NH_2$$

[XVIII] Urea, a compound used to remove ammonia from the animal body

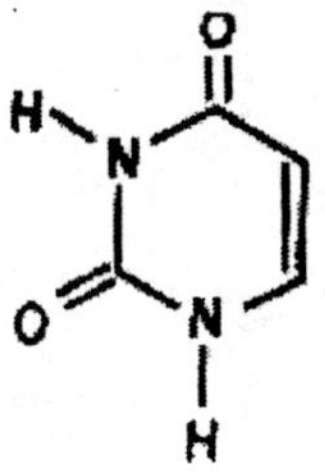

[XIX] Uracil

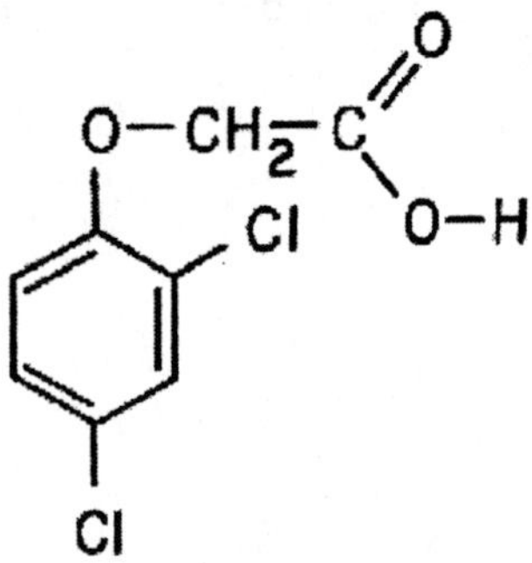

[XX] (2,4-dichlorophenoxy)acetic acid

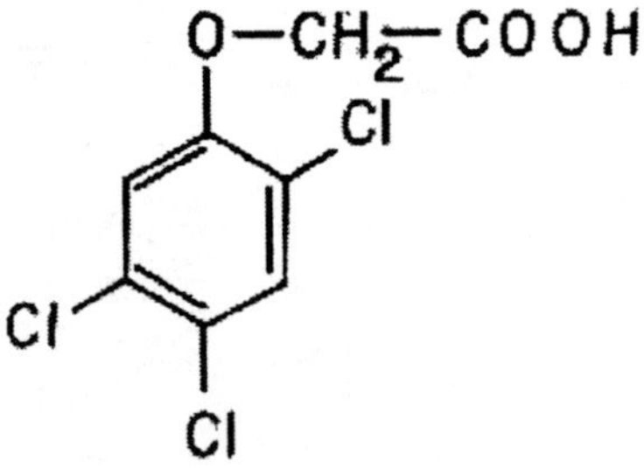

[XXI] (2,4,5-trichlorophenoxy)acetic acid

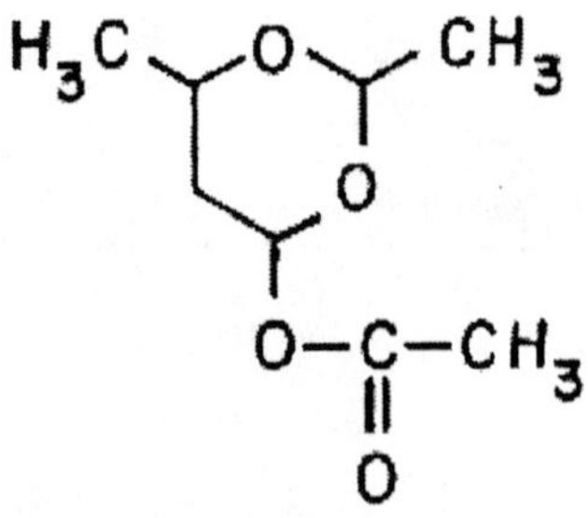

[XXII] Dioxin

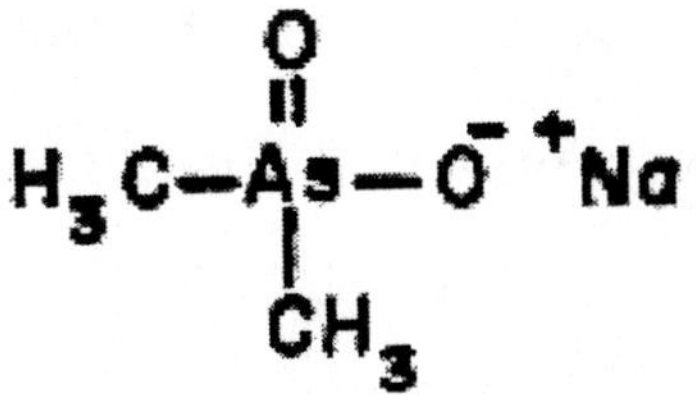

$$H_3C-\overset{\overset{\displaystyle O}{\|}}{\underset{\underset{\displaystyle CH_3}{|}}{As}}-\overset{-}{O}\ ^+Na$$

[XXIII] Sodium cacodylate

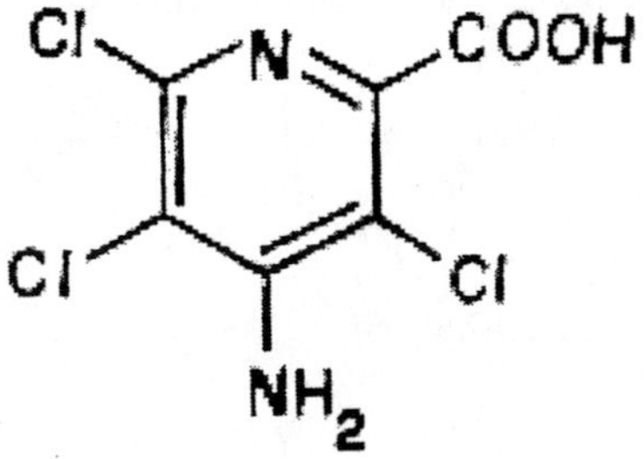

$$\begin{array}{c} \text{Cl} \\ \\ \text{Cl} \end{array} \quad \begin{array}{c} \text{N} \quad \text{COOH} \\ \\ \text{NH}_2 \quad \text{Cl} \end{array}$$

[XXIV] Picloram

$$\begin{array}{c} \text{OH} \\ | \\ H_3C-C-CH_3 \\ H_3C \quad | \quad CH_3 \\ | \qquad | \qquad | \\ HO-C-N-C-OH \\ | \qquad | \\ CH_3 \quad CH_3 \end{array}$$

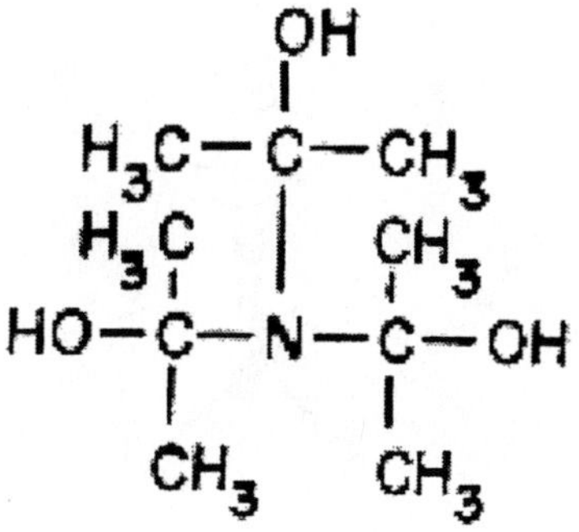

[XXV] Triisopropanolamine

STRUCTURES FOR CHAPTER 10

INCENDIARIES & OBSCURANTS

[I]   Molecular structure of White Phosphorus, spontaneously ignited with contact with air

$$F$$
$$|$$
$$Cl$$
$$F \quad \quad F$$

[II]   Trifluorochlorine, chlorine trifluoride

$$Cl$$
$$|$$
$$Cl-Ti-Cl$$
$$|$$
$$Cl$$

[III]   Titanium tetrachloride

$$O$$
$$\|$$
$$S$$
$$O \quad \quad O$$

[IV]   Sulfur trioxide

$$O$$
$$\|$$
$$Cl-S-O-H$$
$$\|$$
$$O$$

[V]   Chlorosulfuric acid

STRUCTURES FOR CHAPTER 11

ANTIDOTES

[I]   Atropine, nerve agent antidote   [II]   Pyridine-2-aldoxime methylchloride

[III]   Sodium Nitrite, Blood agent antidote

[IV]   Sodium Thiosulfate, Blood agent antidote

$$N \equiv C - S - R$$

[V]   Thiocyanate

[VI]   BAL, British AntiLewisite, 2,3-dimercaptopropanol

$$CH_3-CH_2-As\begin{cases} Cl \\ Cl \end{cases}$$

[VII]   Dichloroethylarsine

[VIII]   Chlorodiphenylarsine

STRUCTURES FOR CHAPTER 14

ANTIBIOTICS

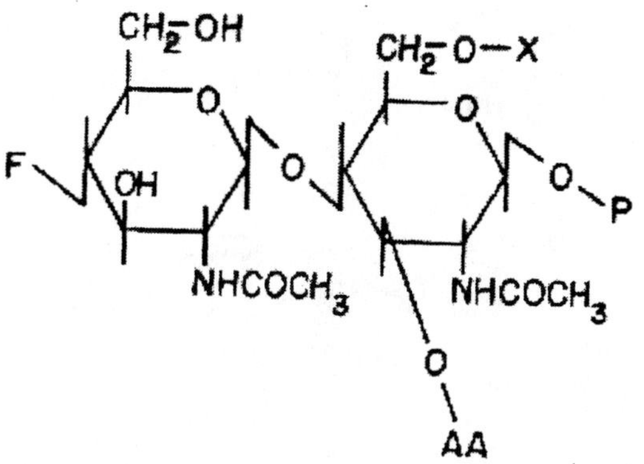

P = preceding unit
F = following unit
AA = amino acid units
X = polysaccharide unit

[I] Peptidoglycan repeat unit of bacterial cell wall

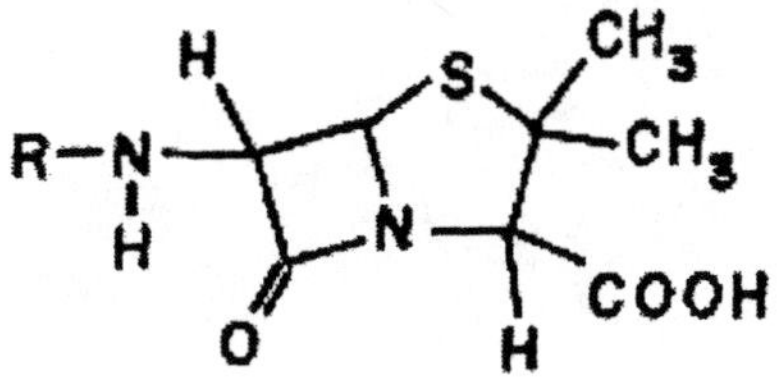

[II]

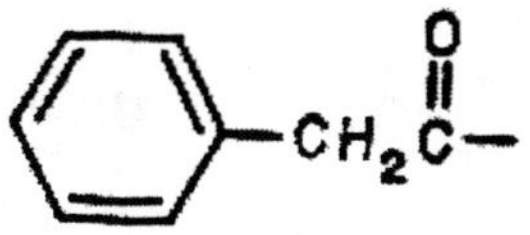

(a)

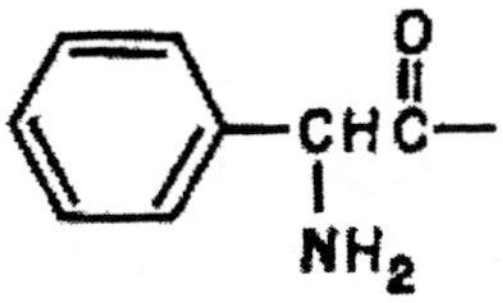

(b)

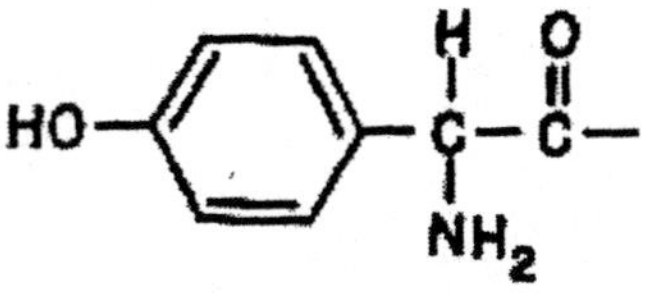

(c)

[II] Penicillin nucleus, R groups: (a) penicillin G, (b) ampicillin, (c) amoxicillin

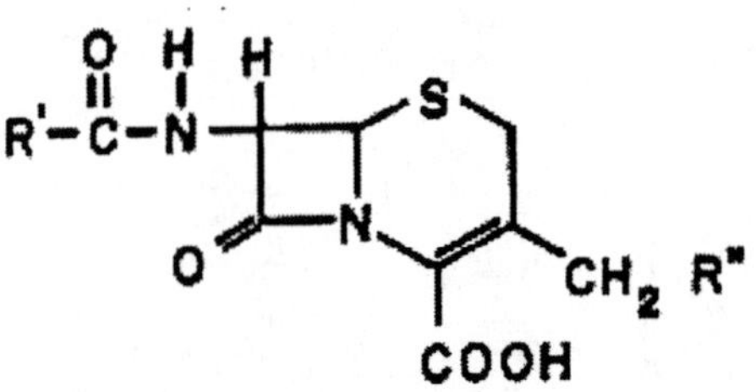

[III]   A cephalosporin

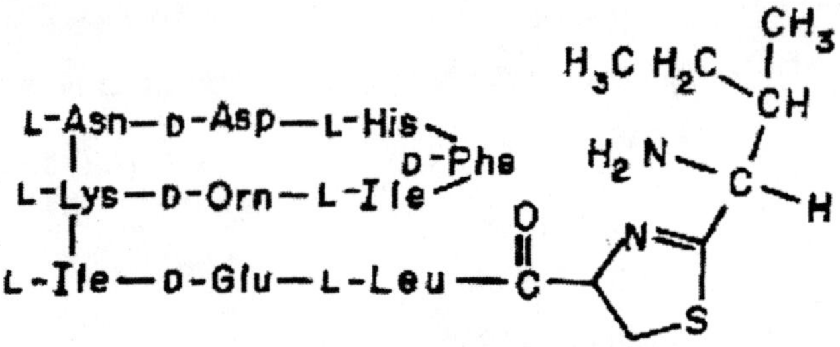

[IV]   Bacitracin

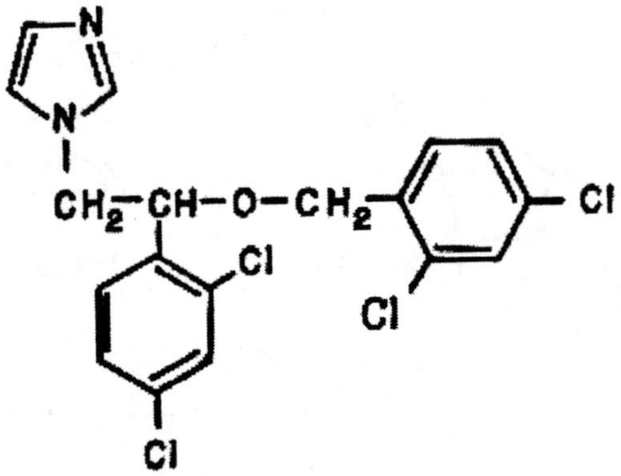

[V]   Miconizole

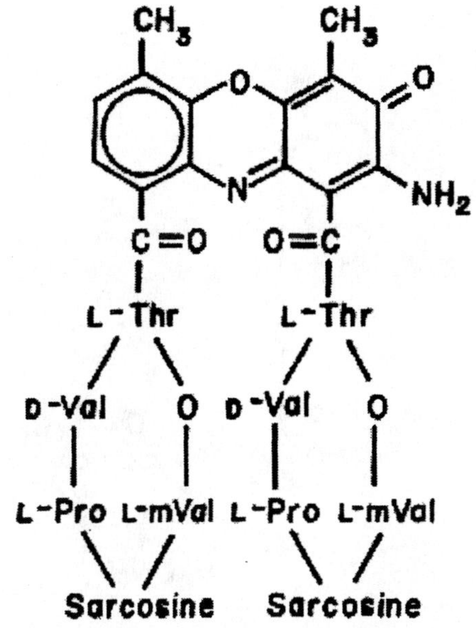

[VI] Actinomycin D

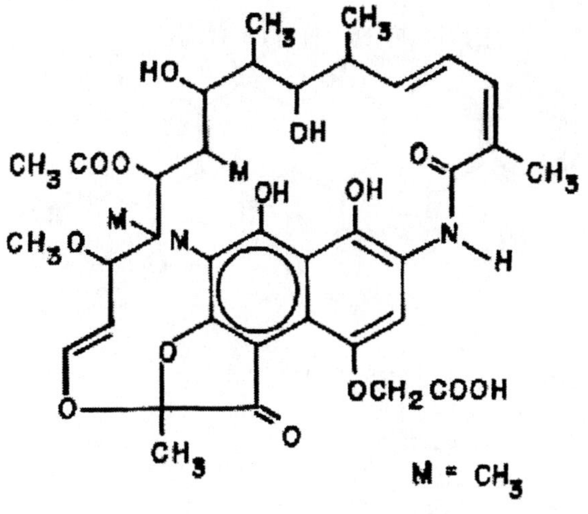

[VII] Rifampicin

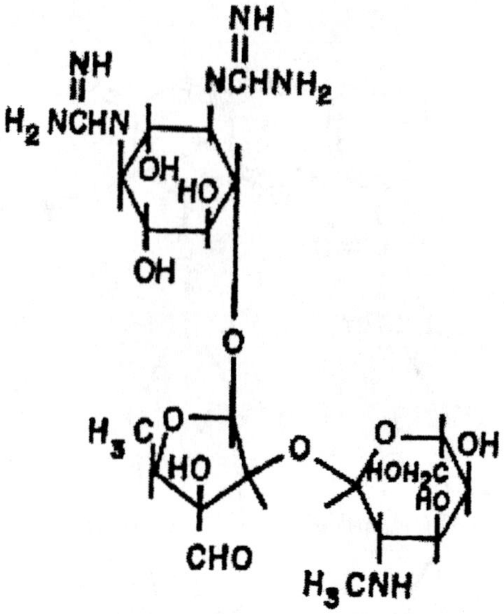

[VIII]   Streptomycin

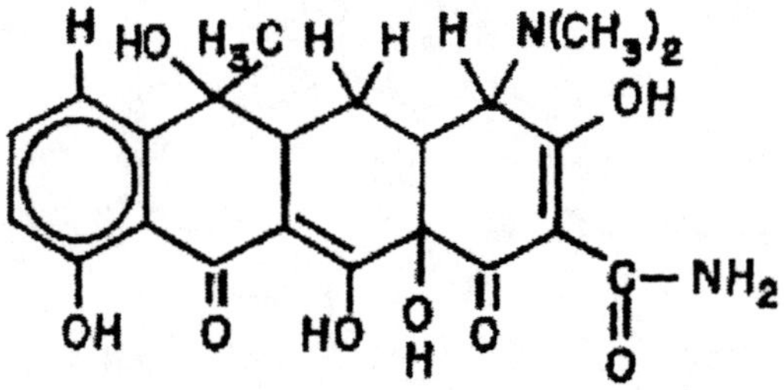

[IX]   Tetracycline

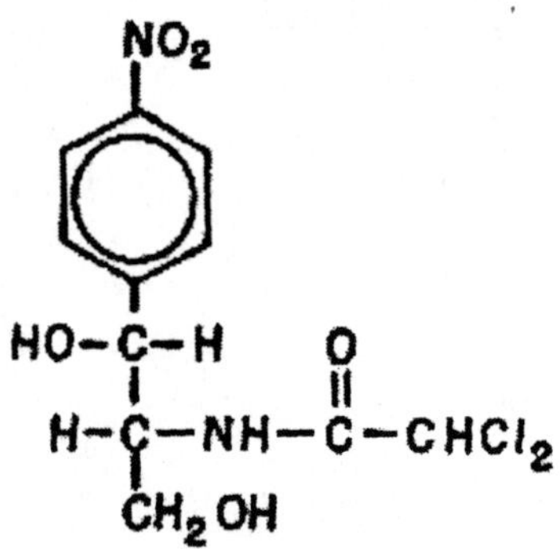

[X]   Chloramphenicol

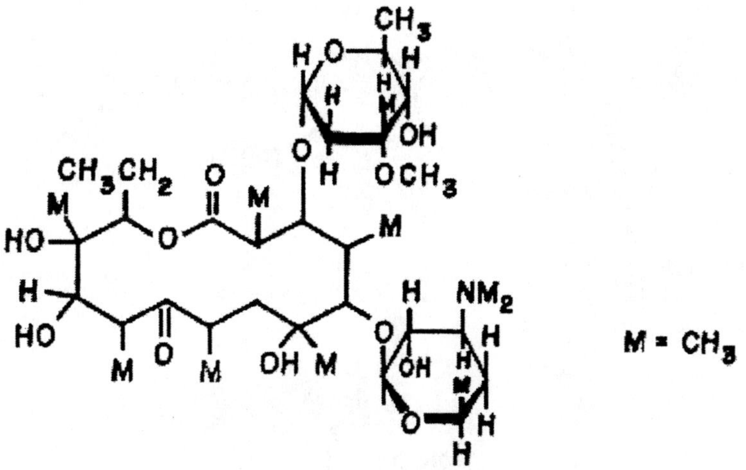

[XI]   Erythromycin

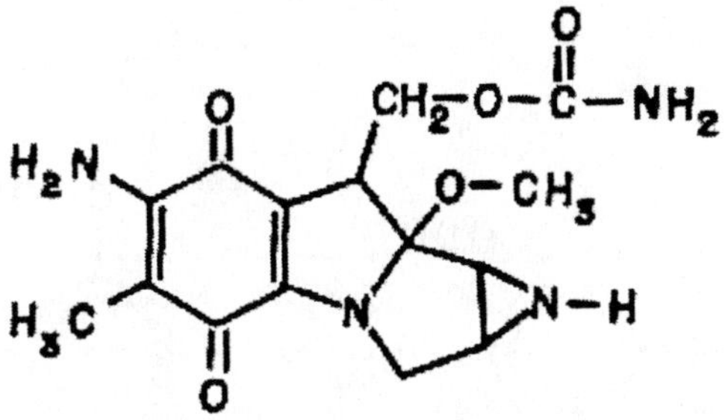

[XII]   Mitomycin

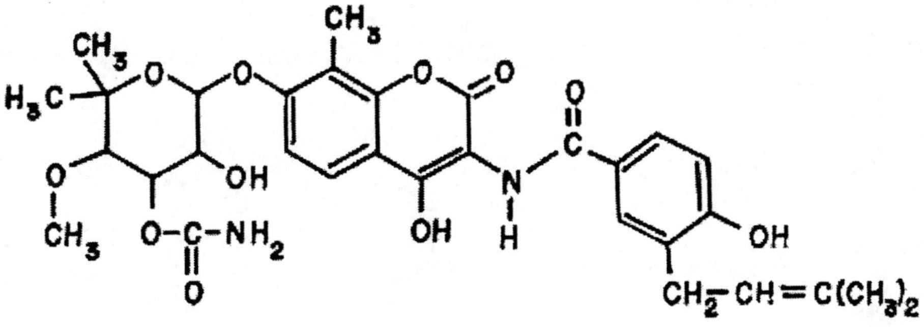

[XIII]   Novobiocin

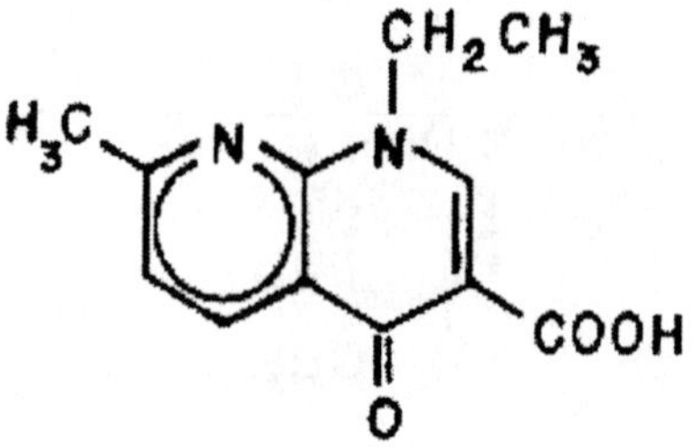

[XIV]   Nalidixic acid

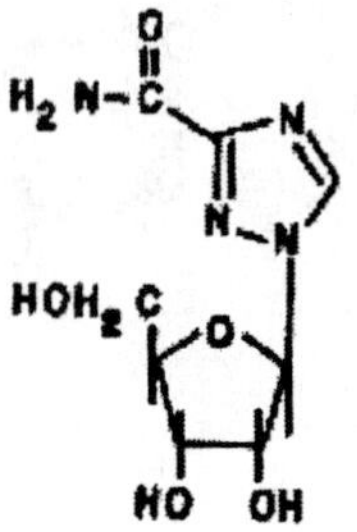

[XV]   Ribavirin

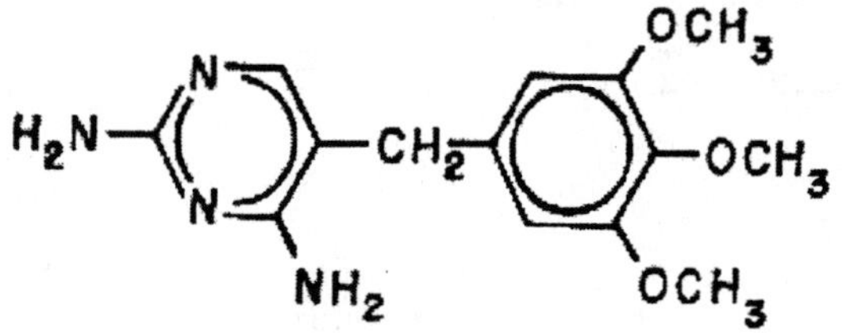

[XVI]   Trimethoprim 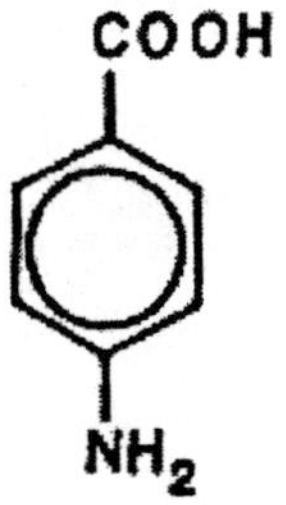   [XVII]   PABA, p-aminobenzoic acid

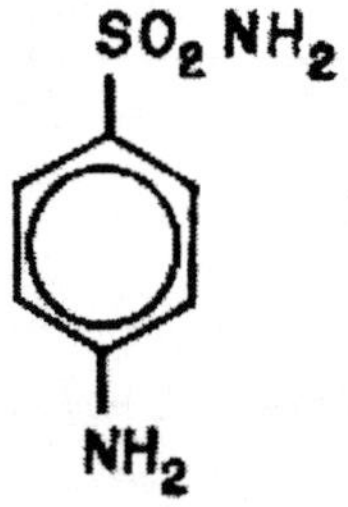

[XVIII] Sulfanilamide 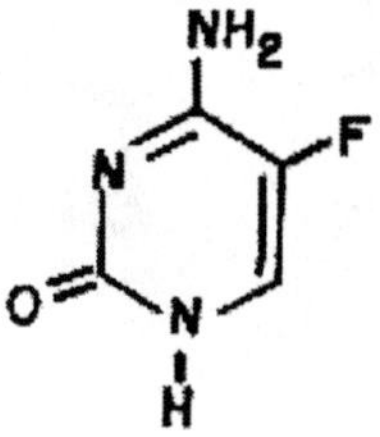   [XIX]   Flucytosine

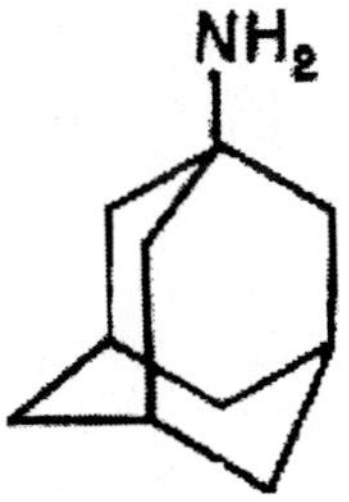

[XX]   Amantadine

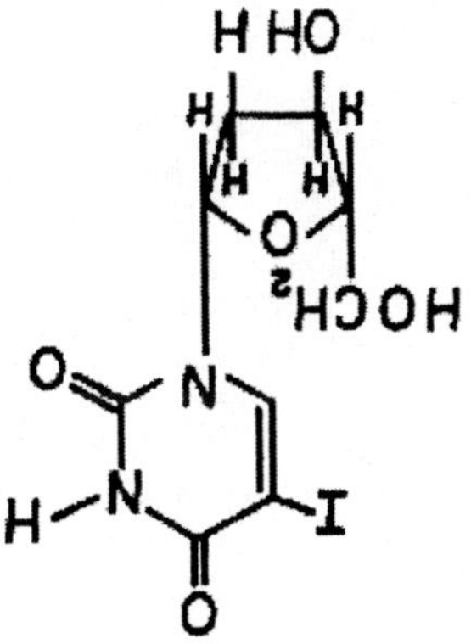

[XXI]   IDU, 5-iododeoxyuridine

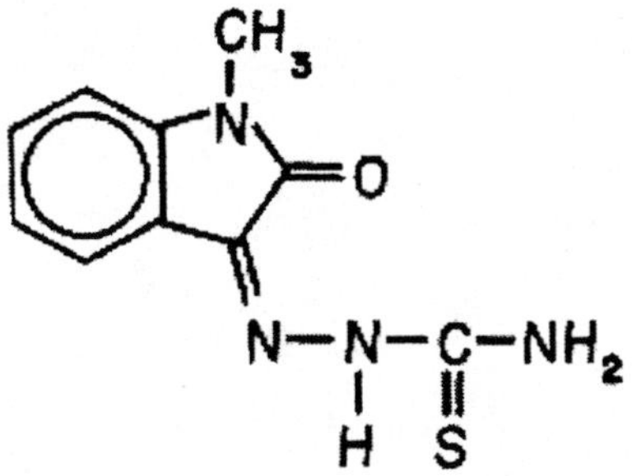

[XXII]   Methisazone

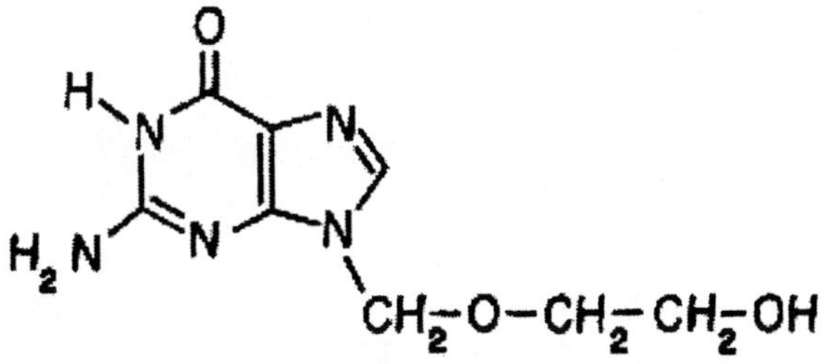

[XXIII] Acyclovir

[XXIV] araC, 1-β-D-arabinosycytosine

STRUCTURES FOR CHAPTER 18

TREATMENT

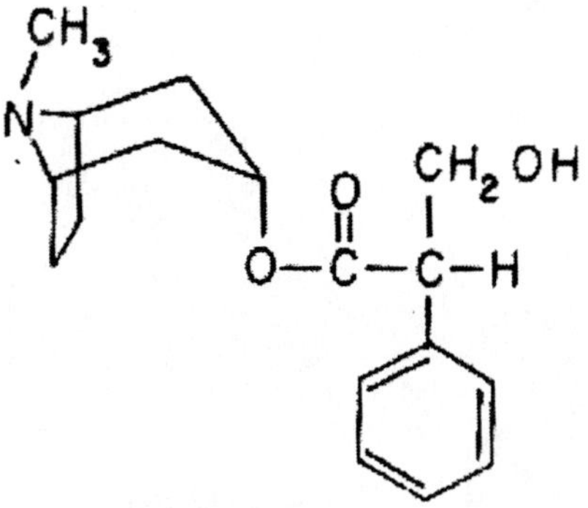

[I]   Atropine Sulfate

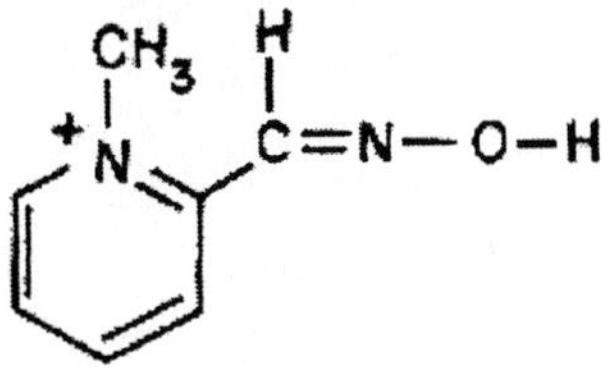

$$X^- = Cl^-, I^-, CH_3SO_3^-$$

[II]   2-PAM Chloride

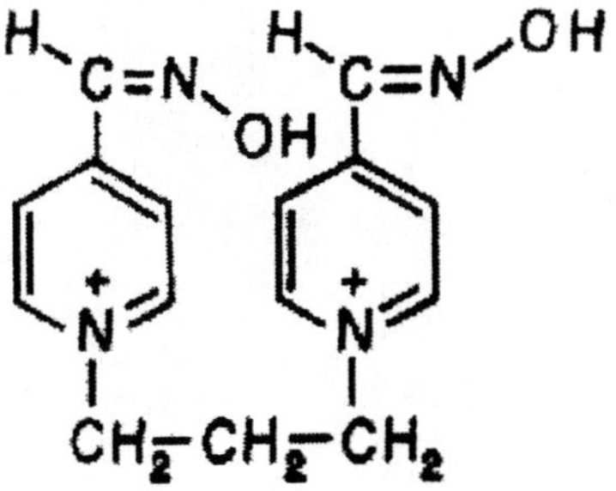

[III]   Trimedoxime

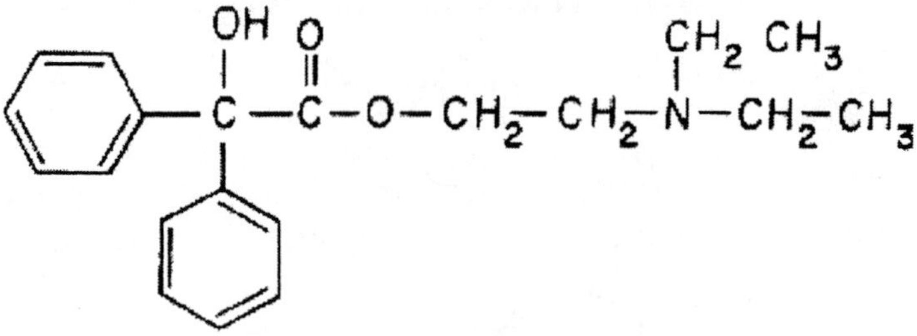

[IV]   Benactyzine

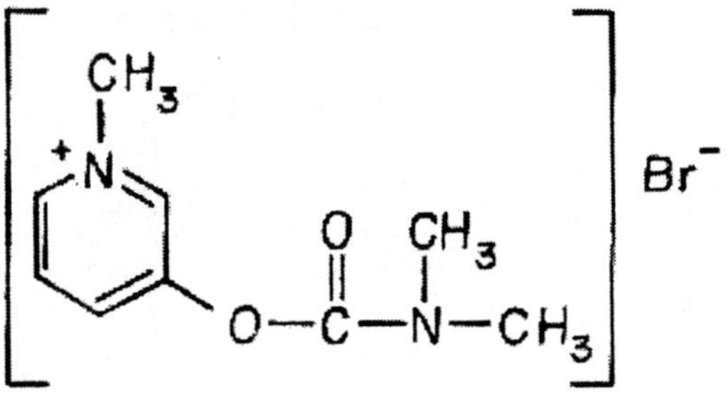

[V]   Pyridostigmine

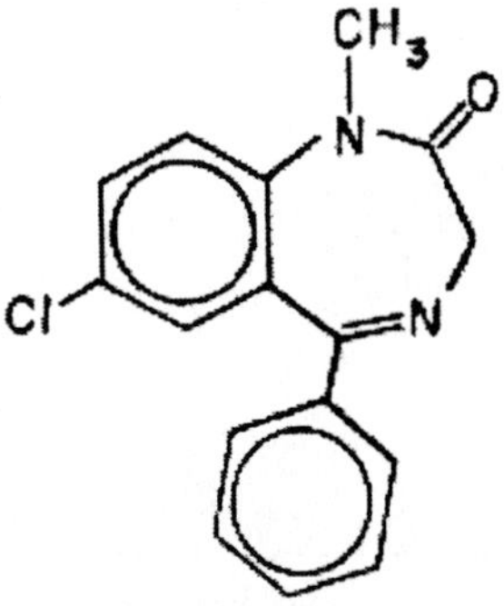

[VI]   Diazepam

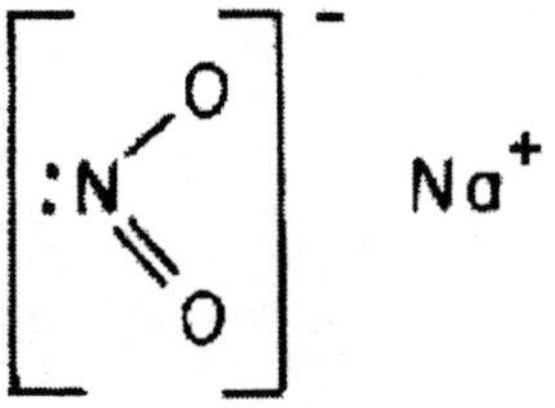

[VII]   Sodium Nitrite

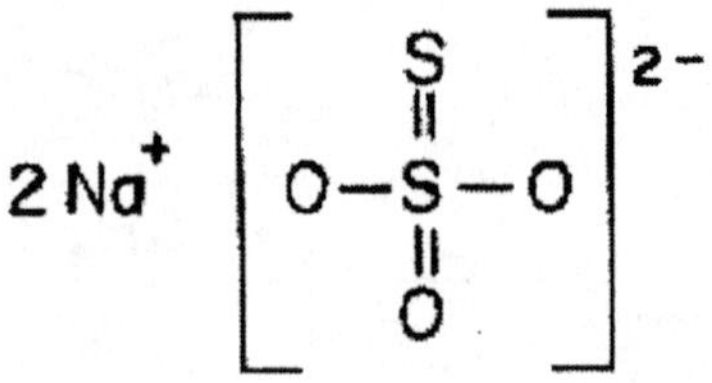

[VIII]   Sodium Thiosulfate

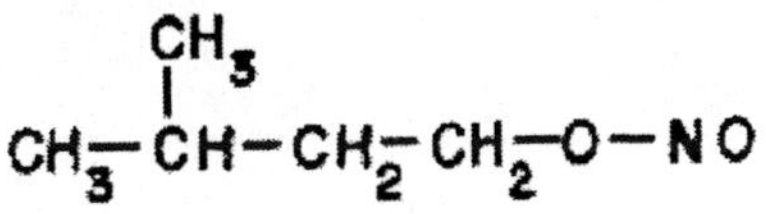

$$\underset{\mathbf{3}}{CH_3}-\underset{}{\overset{\overset{CH_3}{|}}{CH}}-\underset{\mathbf{2}}{CH_2}-\underset{\mathbf{2}}{CH_2}-O-NO$$

[IX]   Amyl Nitrite

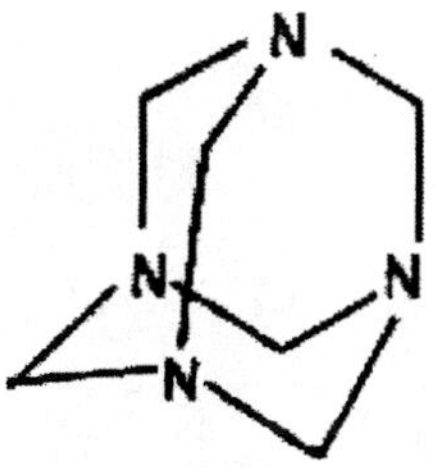

[X]   HMT, Hexamethylenetetramine

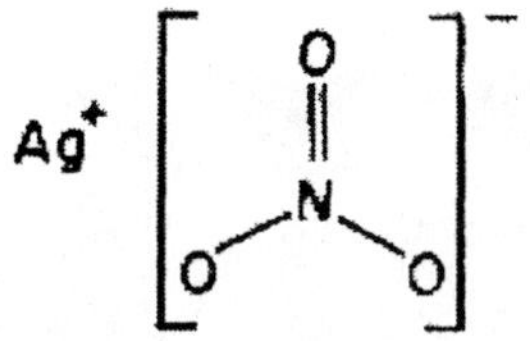

$$Ag^+ \left[\overset{O}{\underset{O}{\overset{\|}{\underset{}{N}}}} \right]^-$$

[XI]   Silver Nitrate

$$\underset{H-C-SH}{\overset{CH_2-SH}{|}}$$
$$CH_2-OH$$

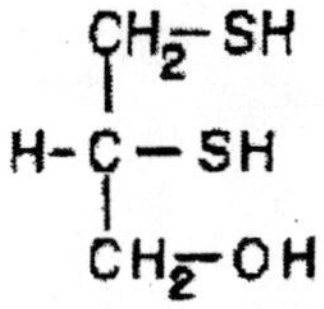

[XII]   BAL, British AntiLewisite

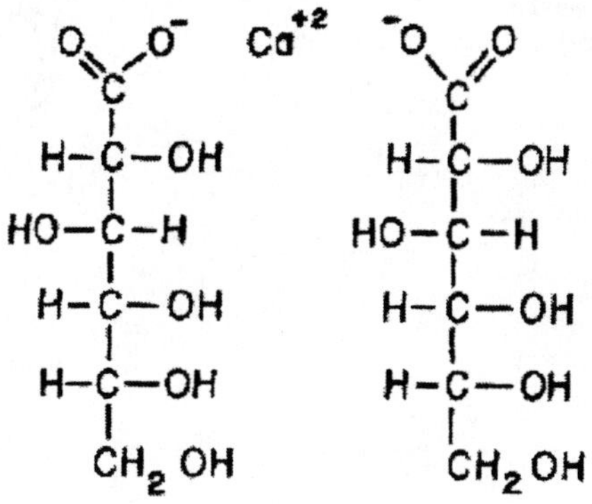

$$
\begin{array}{c}
\underset{C}{\overset{O}{\diagup}}\overset{O^-}{\diagdown} \qquad Ca^{+2} \qquad \overset{-O}{\diagdown}\underset{C}{\overset{O}{\diagup}} \\
H-C-OH \qquad\qquad H-C-OH \\
HO-C-H \qquad\qquad HO-C-H \\
H-C-OH \qquad\qquad H-C-OH \\
H-C-OH \qquad\qquad H-C-OH \\
CH_2OH \qquad\qquad CH_2OH
\end{array}
$$

[XIII]   Calcium Gluconate

STRUCTURES FOR CHAPTER 22

FUTURE OUTLOOK: 21ST CENTURY AGENTS

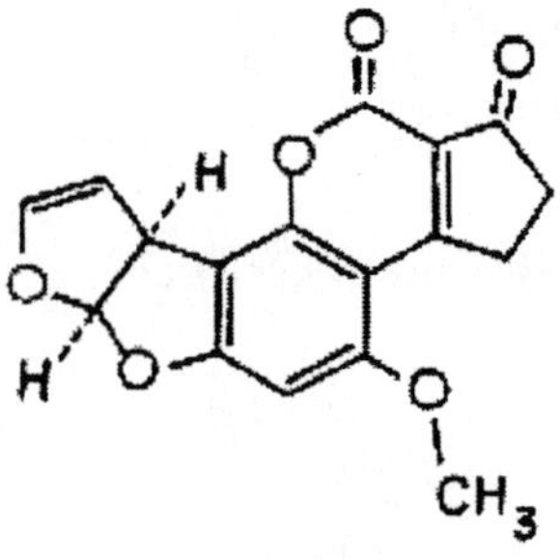

[I]   Aflatoxin

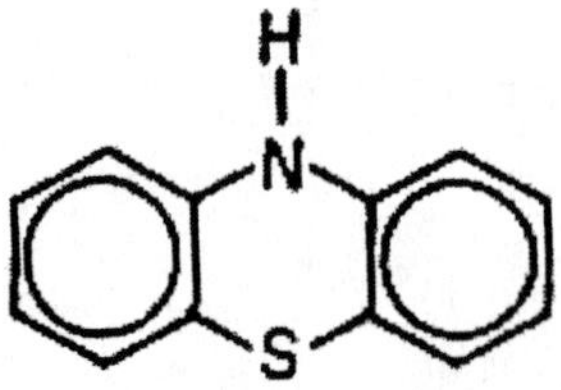

[II]   Phenothiazine

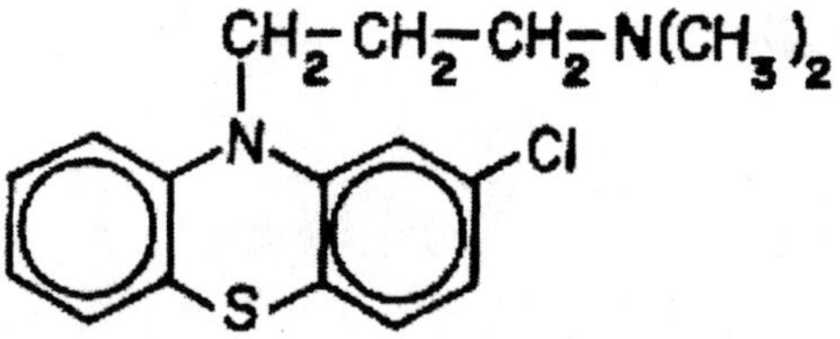

$CH_2-CH_2-CH_2-N(CH_3)_2$

[III]   Thorazine

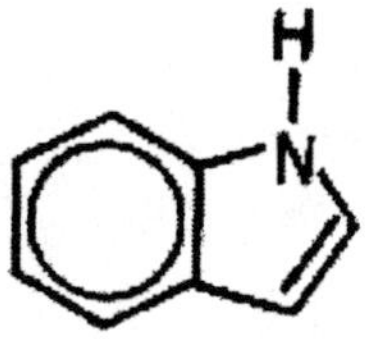

[IV]   Indole

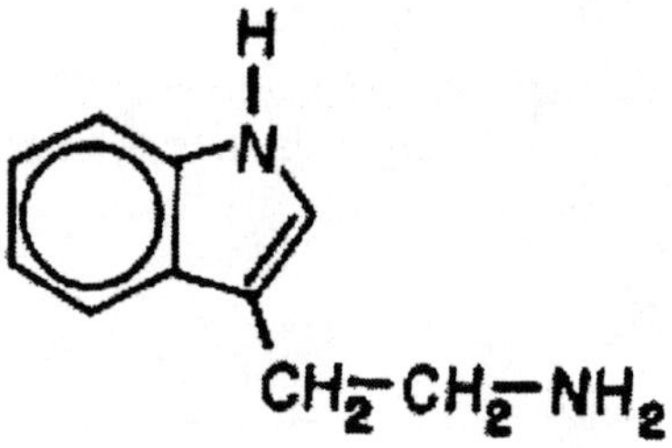

$CH_2-CH_2-NH_2$

[V]   Tryptamine

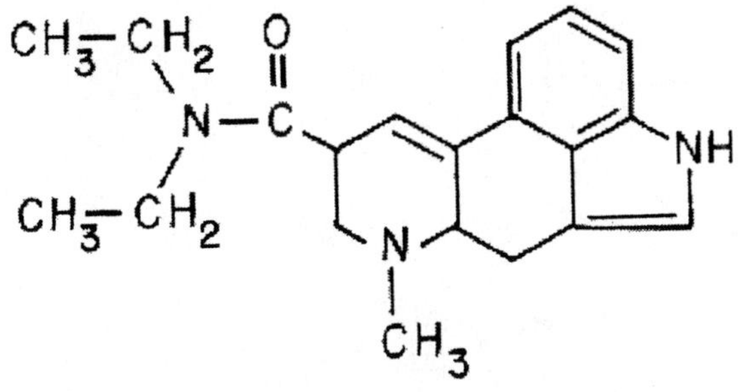

[VI]   LSD, Lysergic Acid Diethylamide

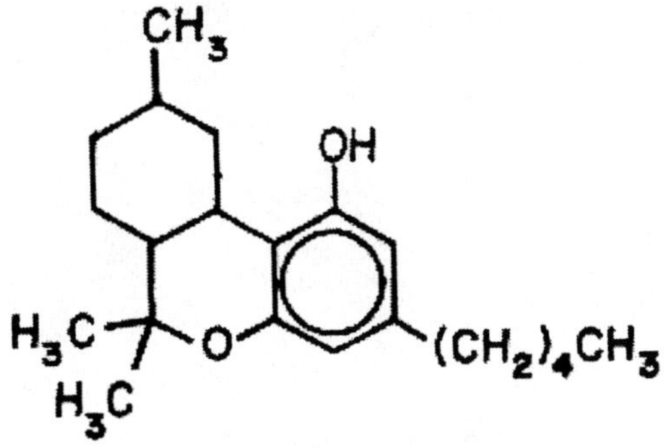

[VII]   THC, Tetrahydrocannabinol

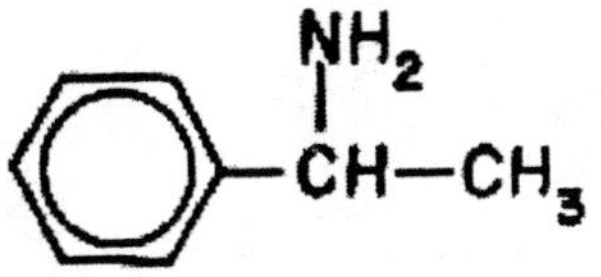

[VIII]   Phenylethylamine

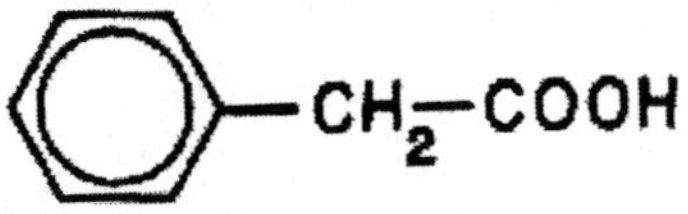

[IX]   Phenylacetic acid

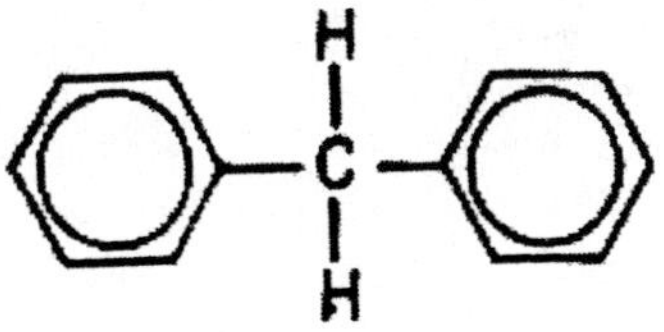

[X]   Diphenylmethane

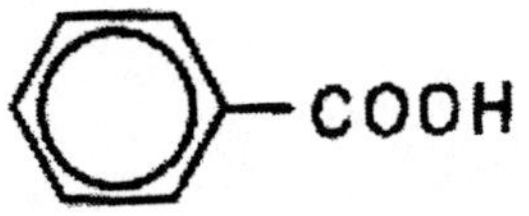

[XI]   Benzoic acid

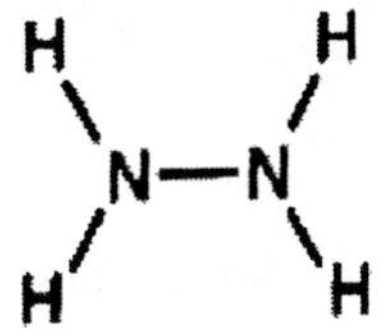

[XII]   Hydrazine

[XIII]   BZ

INDEX

2,3-Dimercapto-1-propanol, 120
2-PAM, 62, 117, 120, 216, 224

Abbreviations, Amino Acids, 13, 14
Absorption, 30, 38, 39, 40, 42-45, 49, 51, 54, 55, 74, 85, 107, 109, 116, 143, 154, 171, 186, 198, 224-226, 241, 267, 269, 286, 331, 346
Abyssinian Campaign, 4
AC, 49, 68, 287, 288, 331
Acetyl Group, 62
Acetylcholine, 21, 62, 63, 66, 68, 69, 116, 149, 216, 331, 341
Acetylcholinesterase, 21, 40, 61, 88, 115, 216, 331
Acetyl-CoA, 91
Acetylene, 10
Acid/Base, 20, 30
Acidic Group, 34
Acidic Molecule, 33
acidophilus, 138
Acidosis, 83
Actinomycin D, 171, 177
Activated Charcoal, 205-208, 227, 230
Active Site, 18, 21, 35, 60, 62, 88, 90, 173, 265
Active Transport, 34
Acyl Transferase, 82
Acylation, 61, 62, 77, 78, 259
Adamsite, 90, 95, 101, 115, 232, 336
Adenine, 15, 22, 73, 173
Adenosine, 12, 48, 59, 71
Adsorption, 206, 207, 331
Aerobic, 137, 182, 331
Aerosol, 37, 38, 39, 95, 108, 156, 163, 187, 195, 197, 204-207, 213, 230, 243, 247, 266, 267, 286, 331
Aflatoxin, 69, 263, 270
Agent Blue, 99, 104, 331
Agent Orange, 96, 99, 104, 331, 336
Agent Selection, 195
Agent White, 103, 331
Aging, 117, 161

Agricultural Diseases, 157, 164
AIDS, 136, 139, 141, 143, 164, 247, 276, 292, 312
Aircraft, 7, 12, 18-20, 96, 106, 107, 109, 112, 189, 203, 207, 208, 211, 255, 262, 263, 279, 308, 347
Alcohol, 59, 78, 99, 131, 240, 274, 289, 292, 341
Alkaloid, 116, 332
Alkylation, 18, 52, 88
Allergenic, 169, 170
Alveoli, 50, 77, 80, 82, 83, 152, 269, 332, 335
Amide, 13, 34, 78, 80, 91, 344
Amino Group, 10, 62, 78, 91, 332, 344
Ammonia, 4, 9, 24, 33, 52, 57, 204, 208, 257, 293
Amoxicillin, 170, 180
Amphotericin B, 177
Ampicillin, 170, 180
Amyl Nitrite, 49, 120, 224, 225, 332
Anaerobic, 125, 137, 150, 292, 332, 333
Angle, 10
Anionic Site, 61, 62, 116
Anorexia, 41, 332
Anoxia, 71, 151, 225
Anthrax, 5, 144, 147, 151, 152, 164, 165, 175, 213, 233, 332
Antibodies, 13, 16, 130, 150, 174, 176
Anticholinergic, 21, 40, 42-45, 60, 62, 116, 216, 265, 274, 332
Anticholinesterase, 59, 61
Antigen, 130, 332, 344
Antigenic Mutation, 143
Antigenicity, 176
Antineoplastic, 25, 172, 184, 332
APC, 198, 211
Apolar, 17
Aristotle, 157
Armor-Piercing, 107
Arsenic Acid, 90
Arsenic, 54, 85, 91, 95, 98, 99, 104, 115, 118, 119, 226, 291, 332, 333
Arsenical Agents, 118, 239

Arsenicals, 53, 85, 90, 98, 115, 226, 232, 239, 332
Arsenious Acid, 90
Arsenolysis, 90, 98
Asexual, Spores, 123, 139
Asphyxia, 57, 217
Athlete's Foot, 138, 139
Atom, 7, 10, 11, 13, 21, 24, 27-30, 59, 60, 62, 74, 77, 78, 117, 119, 269, 332, 333, 339, 343
ATP Synthase, 74, 75
ATP, 9, 12, 15, 16, 48, 71-75, 90, 91, 117
Atropa belladonna, 116, 332
Atropine, 41-45, 62, 116, 117, 120, 199, 210, 216, 224, 265, 332
Atropinization, 216, 274
Auxin-like, 97, 98

β (1-3), 12
β (1-4), 12
β-Mercaptoethyleneamine, 91
β-Oxidation, 71, 267
Bacillus anthracis, 147, 151, 165, 332
Bacillus, 123, 125, 127, 137, 147, 151, 165, 177, 332, 337
Bacitracin, 170, 177
Bacteria, 5, 121-123, 125-128, 130-132, 137-140, 143, 144, 147, 149-154, 160, 161, 169, 170, 174, 177, 179, 180, 226, 232, 233, 239, 240, 289-292, 294, 333, 338, 343, 344, 347
Bacteriocidal, 174, 295
BAL, 54, 55, 101, 104, 115, 118, 120, 226, 333
Basic Molecule, 33
Basic Salt, 30
Basis of Pathogenicity, 129
BBC, 100, 333
BDU, 208, 218, 262
Benactyzine, 216
Benzene, 11, 12, 106, 120
Benzyl, 170
Benzyl, 95, 102
Biological War, 163, 233
Biological, 1-3, 5-8, 9-11, 15, 17, 29-32, 34, 38, 59, 60, 62, 68, 71, 74, 79, 82, 87, 89, 91, 117, 126, 129, 130, 135-137, 139, 140, 142, 144-150, 155-157, 159, 162-167, 171, 173, 175, 185-192, 195, 196, 197-199, 203, 205, 207, 211-213, 215, 232-234, 235-237, 239, 241-243, 246, 247, 259-261, 263, 264, 266, 267, 270, 275, 276, 278,

281, 282, 288, 295, 297, 300, 301, 307, 309, 310, 312-314, 333, 334, 336, 342, 344
Black Bain, 151
Black Death, 147, 343
Black Eschar, 152
Bleach, 24, 32, 33, 44, 45, 48, 50, 51, 80, 81, 108, 236, 238-240, 257, 283, 287-289, 292, 295
Blepharospasm, 56
Blinding Smoke, 109
Blistering Agent, 21, 24, 40, 52, 54, 55, 52, 53, 85, 87, 89, 115, 199, 208, 226, 238, 240, 259, 333, 335, 337, 340, 341, 343, 344, 346
Blistering, 4, 21, 24, 25, 31, 38, 40, 52-57, 85-87, 89, 93, 115, 199, 208-210, 226, 238, 240, 259, 333, 335, 337, 340, 341, 343, 344, 346
Blood Agent(s), 45, 46, 48, 49, 71, 73-75, 115-117, 120, 188, 187, 195, 196, 199, 200, 224, 225, 238, 259, 270, 331-333, 335, 345
Blood, 1, 11, 13, 14, 16, 17, 31-33, 35, 38, 41, 45, 46, 48-50, 57, 60, 71, 73-75, 82, 83, 85, 86, 93, 115-117, 119, 120, 125, 126, 131, 132, 138, 143, 144, 150, 152, 154-156, 166, 169, 170, 174, 186-188, 195, 196, 197, 199, 200, 215, 224, 225, 232, 235, 238, 255, 259, 265, 268-270, 272, 273, 331-333, 335, 336, 339, 345
botulinum, 5, 138, 149, 150, 175, 259, 263, 267, 270, 333
Botulism, 5, 131, 138, 149-151, 164
Breathing Rate, 82, 83, 265
British AntiLewisite, 54, 115, 226, 333
Bromobenzyl Cyanide, 95, 100, 333
Bronchi, 56, 82, 89
Bronchioli, 82
Bronchopneumonia, 52, 56, 226
Brucella abortus, 131
Bubonic Plague, 5, 147
Budding, 129
bulgaricus, 138
Burns, 21, 31, 32, 52, 85, 94, 95, 107, 215, 226, 232, 288, 291, 294, 333, 346, 347
BW, 2, 148, 150, 158, 159, 333
BZ, 103, 272, 274, 334

Cacodylate, 90, 99, 104, 331
CADNET, 198
Calcium Gluconate, 232
Camite. 100. 333

CANA, 224
Candida albicans, 133, 138, 178
Capsid, 128, 129, 140
Carbamic Acid, 40, 61, 334
Carbohydrates, 12, 16, 21, 22, 31, 126
Carbon Dioxide Fixation, 98
Carbon Disulfide, 107
Carbon Monoxide, 46, 57, 71, 333
Carbon, 9-11, 16, 17, 20, 24, 27, 30, 36, 46, 57, 59, 60, 71, 77, 80, 82, 83, 98, 107, 118, 122, 131, 173, 174, 188, 204, 205, 238, 259, 265, 267, 286, 293, 294, 296, 333, 334
Carcinogenesis, 33, 334
Casualty Agent, 334
Catalase, 74
Catalyst, 34, 334, 337
Cation, 19, 27, 85, 119
Cationic, 15, 17, 19, 27, 29, 62, 122, 290-292
Cause of Symptoms, 131
CBPS, 212
Cell Membrane Disruption, 171
Cell Membrane, 15, 124-129, 170, 171, 177, 343
Cell Wall Disruption, 170
Cell Wall, 81, 123-127, 137, 160, 170, 171, 173, 177, 178, 180, 181, 338
Cellulose, 12, 16, 123, 139
Centoxin, 213
Central Dogma of Molecular Biology, 129, 141
Cephalosporin, 170, 177
Cerium, 107
CG, 51, 77, 334
Charbon, 151
Charring, 20, 28, 31
Chelating Agent, 119, 334
Chemical Agents, 2, 4, 5, 11, 14, 15, 18, 21-23, 25, 31-38, 39-41, 61, 71, 93, 95, 108, 109, 115, 137, 165, 186, 187, 191, 192, 199, 203, 208, 209, 211, 216, 236, 237, 243, 248, 256, 259, 260, 263, 264, 267, 269, 272, 282, 288-290, 293
Chemical Bonds, 26, 31
Chemical Burns, 21, 32, 52, 85, 107, 333
Chemical Corps, 241-243, 248, 313, 334
Chemical Indicators, 197, 200
Chemical Injuries, 26
Chemical Reactions, 11, 19, 26, 30, 34, 35, 79, 115, 298
Chemical Structures, 59, 270
Chemical War, 18, 23, 25-27, 40, 185, 242
Chemiotaxic, 129

Chemoreceptors, 83
Chemotherapy, 118, 133, 151, 172
Chitin, 123, 139, 170
Chloramphenicol, 152, 154, 172, 175, 178
Chlorine Monoxide, 81
Chlorine Trifluoride, 108, 112, 334
Chlorine, 3, 4, 27, 30, 41, 50, 51, 60, 77, 78, 80, 81, 85, 108, 112, 205, 225, 235, 238, 291, 292, 297, 334, 335
Chloropicrin, 95, 102, 239, 344
Chlorosulfuric Acid, 109, 113, 239, 334, 338
Choking Agents, 50, 51, 77, 78, 83, 115, 196, 197, 199, 225, 235, 238, 259
Choking, 3, 4, 24, 38, 41, 50, 51, 77, 78, 83, 93, 102, 115, 195-197, 199, 225, 235, 238, 259, 264, 334, 335, 337, 344
Cholera, 131, 138, 144, 150, 153, 154, 164, 165, 297, 335
Cholesterol, 12, 14, 15, 346
Chromium, 205, 292
Civilian Masks, 208
Civilian Vulnerabilities, 146, 164, 278
Cl, 51, 77-79, 81, 88, 101, 335
Clostridium, 5, 125, 138, 149, 150, 270, 333, 337
CN, 41, 46, 60, 74, 80, 95, 98, 100, 116, 118, 238, 239, 335
Coagulase, 132
Coccobacillus, 123
Coccoid, 127, 140, 335
Coccus, 123, 137
cochlearium, 150
Coenzyme A, 91
Collagen, 33, 40, 132
Collagenase, 132
Color, 33, 36, 37, 42-45, 49-51, 54, 55, 74, 81, 98-104, 111-113, 155, 158, 197, 200, 207, 293, 338, 339
Combination Chemical Reactions, 24, 27, 30, 34, 59, 73, 146, 212, 216, 272, 288, 290, 335, 346
Conformation, 10, 15, 35, 90, 130, 172, 335
Conjugation, 86, 125
Conjunctivitis, 56, 89, 144
Conventional, 2, 38, 95, 148, 162, 188, 189, 195, 196, 212, 255, 262, 278, 312
Copper Sulfate, 232, 291
Copper, 73, 74, 205, 232, 291
Corn, 51, 159, 160, 162-164
Cortisone Acetate, 225
Covalent Adduction, 34, 35, 335
Covalent Bond, 9, 17, 21, 22, 28, 34, 35, 69, 172, 335

Coxiella burnetii, 127, 167, 344
CPE, 198, 212
CPFU, 212
Creatine, 59
Cristae, 335, 341
Cross-Linking, 78, 88
Crypts, 154
CS, 41, 95, 100, 255, 335
Cutaneous Anthrax, 151, 152
Cutaneous, 151, 152
CW, 2, 335
Cyanide, 3, 4, 23, 24, 41, 46, 48, 49, 74, 95,
     100, 116-118, 188, 195, 199, 205, 238,
     270, 331, 333
Cyanmethemoglobin, 117
Cyano Group, 60, 116, 238
Cyanogen Chloride, 48, 49, 74, 195, 200, 205,
     335
Cyanosis, 41, 49, 51, 152, 336
Cysteine, 9, 13, 14, 17, 74, 79, 88, 90, 118
Cytochrome P450, 69
Cytoplasm, 17, 33, 36, 64, 71, 74, 86, 122,
     123, 127, 129, 170, 337, 340, 341, 344
Cytosine, 15, 21
Cytosol, 71, 127

DA, 101, 239, 336
DC, 101, 239, 336
Decarbamylation, 63
Decomposition, 2, 30, 42-45, 49, 51, 54, 55,
     100-104, 137, 187, 196, 200, 203, 209,
     218, 235-240, 243, 244, 246-248, 255,
     256, 266, 267, 287, 288, 295, 344
Defoliants, 5, 96-98
Denaturation, 18, 20-22, 33, 34, 90, 98, 142,
     176, 292, 336
Density, 28, 36-38, 42-45, 48, 49, 51, 54, 55,
     60, 77, 100-102, 108, 111-113, 172, 186,
     188, 191, 336
Deoxyribose, 15, 16, 59, 336
Dephosphorylation, 62
Dermis, 85, 86, 144
Detection, 147, 163, 196, 197-201, 248, 255,
     263, 264, 268, 269, 276, 283, 288, 309,
     314
Diazepam, 224, 232, 265
Diazinon, 45, 69
Dichlorine Oxide, 81
Digestive Tract, 17, 36, 38, 142, 150, 165, 166
Dihydrofolate Reductase, 173
Dihydrolipoyl Dehydrogenase, 91
Dinitrogen Tetroxide, 57, 58
Dioxin, 99, 104, 336

Dipalmitoylphosphatidylcholine, 82
Diphenylchlorarsine, 101, 119, 239
Diphosgene, 51, 77-79, 238, 337
Disease, 25, 118, 121, 129-131, 135-145, 147,
     148, 150-167, 169, 174, 176, 213, 233,
     246, 247, 259, 267, 274, 289, 295, 332,
     335, 336, 343, 346, 347
Displacement, 30
Disruption, 18-21, 29, 34, 90, 97, 170, 171,
     292, 294
Dissemination, 52, 112, 160, 162, 187, 188,
     190, 209, 247, 264, 266, 299
Disulfide, 17, 90, 107, 292
Divalent, 9
DM, 101, 336
DNA, 9, 12, 15-18, 20-22, 28, 29, 31-33, 52,
     53, 59, 88, 89, 122, 123, 127-129, 140-
     142, 148, 171-176, 178, 179, 182, 184,
     204, 264, 295, 314, 336, 337
DP, 51, 77, 237, 337
Drug Resistance, 174, 175
DS2, 108, 235-237, 266
Dummy, 112
Dyspnea, 56, 57

Ebola, 108, 136, 155, 156, 234, 246-248, 261,
     276, 312
ED, 26, 55, 149, 293, 337
Edema, 56-58, 78, 225, 232, 337
Edematous, 56
EDTA, 119
Electron Transport, 69, 71-75, 98, 117, 341
Electronegativity, 28, 29, 60, 78
Element, 9-11, 19, 24, 28, 29, 52, 60, 95, 97,
     111, 130, 205-208, 219, 221, 222, 228-
     230, 241, 243, 286, 304, 308, 332, 337,
     348
Elongation, 98, 172
Employment, 2-5, 39, 96, 146, 148, 185, 187,
     189, 191, 195, 211, 248, 253, 267, 299,
     313, 334
Endoplasmic Reticulum, 337
Endospore(s), 337
Endotoxin, 126
Enzyme-Inhibitor Complex, 62
Enzyme-Substrate Complex, 62
Epidermis, 86, 336
Epidermophyton floccosum, 138
Epistaxis, 56
Epsom Salts, 27
Ergot, 131, 163
Erythema, 56, 85
Erythromycin, 152, 172

Eschar, 152
Escherichia coli, 138
Eserine, 116
Esteratic Site, 62
Ethyldichlorarsine, 55, 90, 119, 238, 337
Ethylene, 10, 85, 235, 292
Ethylenediamminetetraacetic Acid, 119
Eukaryotes, 122, 123, 172
Excision, 172
Exoskeleton, 61, 123, 126, 170
Exotoxin, 151, 153, 346
Extracellular, 131, 337, 346

Facilitated Invasion, 132
fallax, 150
Fasciculation, 41, 337
FEBA, 109, 112, 337
Filter Element, 205-208, 219, 221, 222, 228-230
Fimbriae, 125
Fire, 1, 3, 5, 6, 37, 68, 83, 97, 105, 108, 109, 112, 145, 148, 161, 189, 196, 200, 205, 213, 225, 226, 232, 253-255, 260, 277, 283, 292, 304, 312, 345, 348
First Aid, 215, 230, 248, 282, 284, 286, 287
First Degree Thermal Burns, 32
First Flight, 150
Flagella, 125, 153
Flares, 112
Flu, 145, 147, 312, 340
Flucytosine, 174, 178
Fluid-Mosaic Model, 126
Fluoride, 60, 343
FM, 91, 109, 112, 338
Folic Acid, 174
Formic Acid, 118
Fougasse, 107
Fructose, 12, 16
Fruiting Bodies, 123
Fuel-Air Weapons, 108
Fuel-Air, 108
Fumigants, 23
Fungi, 121-123, 125, 131, 133, 137, 139, 144, 160, 177, 178, 232, 290, 292, 338, 343

GA, 249, 338, 4, 42
Ganglia, 338
Gas Mask, 203, 205
Gastrointestinal Anthrax, 144, 151, 152
Gastrointestinal, 41, 107, 143, 144, 151-154, 335
Gatling Gun, 1
GB, 4, 39, 42, 61, 248, 338,

GD, 4, 43, 61 265, 338
Genetic Exchange, 174
Genetic Mutation, 174
Geneva Disarmament Conference, 6
Geneva Protocol, 6
Gentamicin, 152
Germany, 105, 156, 158, 164, 185, 198, 247, 249, 270, 272, 275, 277, 308
GF, 4
Globin, 13, 33, 339
Glucose, 12, 16, 34, 86, 91, 265, 267
Glucuronic Acid, 132
Glutathione, 86, 88
Glycerol, 15, 35, 59
Glycine, 13, 14, 173
Glycogen, 12, 16, 265
Gram Stain, 125
Gram-Negative, 124-127, 140, 233, 264, 338
Gram-Positive, 124-126, 232, 264
Gruinard Island, 147
Guanine, 15, 21, 22, 88, 173

Hannibal, 3
HANTA Virus, 156
Harassing Agent, 338
Hawaii, 249, 304
HC, 112
HCN, 42, 49, 60
HE, 1, 3, 6-8, 41, 105, 107, 130, 135, 136, 145, 147, 150, 153, 163, 187, 188, 195, 197, 203, 210, 215, 216, 233, 238, 242, 253-256, 259, 262, 272, 274, 277, 278, 283, 286, 301, 304, 305, 307, 308, 310, 339
Heat Exhaustion, 209
Heat Stroke, 209
Helper Virus, 140
Hematemesis, 152
Heme, 13, 73, 74, 336, 339
Hemoglobin, 13, 46, 57, 71, 73, 74, 117, 334, 339
Heteroaliphatic, 85
Heteronuclear, 11
Hexamethylenetetramine, 225, 264
Hexavalent, 9
HF, 60
Hiroshima, 105, 106, 162, 263
History, 1, 3, 135, 137, 145, 151, 158, 163, 188, 233, 262, 278, 282, 299, 306, 333
HMT, 225, 264
HN, 55, 339
Hot Vents, 137, 288
Household Agents, 24

Hyaluronic Acid, 132
Hyaluronidase, 132
Hydrazine, 24, 257, 274
Hydrochloric Acid, 19, 50, 77, 78, 81, 86, 238, 239, 283
Hydrogen Chloride, 77, 78, 83, 205, 208, 238, 239
Hydrogen Cyanide, 4, 46, 48, 49, 116, 118, 188, 195, 205, 238, 331
Hydrogen Peroxide, 74, 97, 292
Hydrogen Sulfide, 24, 57, 204, 208, 257, 283
Hydrolysis, 16, 30, 34, 42-45, 49, 51, 52, 54, 55, 60, 62, 63, 68, 77, 81, 83, 85, 95, 100-104, 113, 115, 119, 142, 190, 210, 232, 236, 238, 239, 261, 265, 266, 339
Hydrophilic Interactions, 17, 29, 343
Hydrophilic, 14, 15, 17, 19, 26, 29, 33-35, 127, 290, 339, 341, 343
Hydrophobic Interactions, 15, 17, 26, 29
Hydrophobic, 14, 15, 17, 19, 20, 26, 29, 34-36, 40, 115, 127, 290, 291, 293, 339, 341, 343
Hydroxocobalamin, 118
Hyperbaric, 225, 339
Hyperventilation, 83
Hyphae, 122
Hypochlorous Acid, 48, 80, 81, 238, 291, 292

I-BAL, 226
ICBAD/DAM, 236
Ileum, 153
Imino Group, 10
Iminothiazolidinecarboxylic Acid, 118
Immune System, 13, 16, 25, 130-132, 174, 261, 298, 343
Impermeable, 212, 217, 218
In Vitro, 332, 340
In Vivo, 332, 340
Incapacitating Agents, 2, 93, 230, 239, 260, 269
Incendiaries, 2, 93, 105-108, 112, 232
Indirect, 1, 5, 162
Infectious Process, 130
Infectious Risks, 143
Influenza, 144, 147, 166, 183, 340
Inhibitor, 49, 62, 68, 69, 149, 171, 173, 174, 183, 216
Initiation, 68, 172
Inositol, 15, 35
Installations, 97, 162, 163, 173, 191, 192, 211, 212, 242, 268
Instrumentation, 197
Intercalation, 171

Interference, 21, 48, 98, 107, 149, 170-173, 175
Intermediate Metabolites, 9
Intermolecular Forces, 16, 122
Intracytoplasmically, 140, 340
Intramolecular Forces, 16, 18, 21
Ionic bonds, 18, 26-30, 59, 73, 85, 97, 119, 268, 295, 335, 340
Italians, 4
IUPAC, 10
Ivy, 24, 25

Jejunum, 153

Keratin, 33, 86
Keratinized, 33, 86, 89
Ketene, 78
KGB, 7
Kilogram (Kg), 42-44, 49, 54, 55, 104, 150, 157, 225, 226, 232, 333, 336, 340
Krebs Cycle, 91

Lacrimators, 4, 94, 95
Lactobacillus, 138
Large Area, 112v
LASSA Virus, 157, 234
LD_{50}, 24, 36, 49, 90, 224, 268, 340
Lead, 17-19, 21, 31-33, 36, 50, 52, 63, 69, 71, 83, 90, 95, 107, 108, 118, 144, 148, 152, 155, 172, 191, 232, 233, 246, 254, 271, 274, 291, 295, 299, 313, 314
Leprosy, 138
Lesion, 31, 85, 88, 172
Lewisite, 41, 53, 54, 56, 57, 85, 90, 115, 118, 119, 200, 226, 236, 238, 333, 340, 341
Lipid Bilayer, 31, 126
Lipids, 12, 14-16, 20-22, 31, 35, 82, 126, 127
Lipoic Acid, 91
LSD, 95, 103, 271-274, 341
Lysine, 13, 14, 17, 19, 78, 91
Lysis, 21, 31, 36, 128, 170, 177, 291

M17 Series, 207
M25 Series, 208
MACE, 100, 335
Machine gun, 1, 189, 307
MAD, 8, 142, 186
Maintenance, 17, 37, 151, 198, 210, 254
Major General, 105, 241, 242, 303, 336, 341
Malathion, 23, 44, 59
Malignant Pustule, 151, 152
MANAA, 224
Maps, 97, 191, 192, 249, 251, 296

MASH, 211, 212, 225
MCPE, 212
Mechanism of Reaction, 61
Medicine, 7, 25, 52, 61, 79, 147, 151, 152, 171, 233, 265, 271, 291, 298, 347
Meninges, 152
Meningitis, 138, 144, 152
Mercury, 90, 118, 169, 290, 291
Metal, 3, 13, 20, 27, 30, 59, 74, 90, 106, 107, 112, 111, 119, 226, 232, 240, 277, 288, 291, 293, 334, 341, 346-348
Metallic Bond, 341
Metallic, 26-28, 341, 342
Methane, 10
Methemoglobin, 117
Methionine, 9, 13, 14, 88, 173
Methyl Group, 10
Methylene Group, 10
Metric Ton, 157
MICAD, 198
Miconazole, 171, 178
Microvilli, 154
MIDS, 198
Military Vulnerabilities, 145
Military, 2-4, 7, 8, 18, 23, 25, 38, 39, 41-45, 49, 51-55, 57, 59-61, 64, 68, 77, 93, 95-97, 99-104, 107, 108, 112, 111-113, 118, 119, 129, 136, 145, 146, 148, 149, 162-164, 173, 185-188, 190-192, 195, 197-199, 203, 205, 207-213, 215, 228, 235-237, 239, 241, 243, 246-248, 253-256, 260, 261, 263-265, 267, 268, 270-278, 282, 292, 299, 302-310, 311-313, 331-342, 344-348
Milk, 18-20, 257, 294, 335
Milligram (mg), 42-44, 49, 54, 55, 61, 100, 117, 150, 152, 177-183, 216, 225, 226, 232, 340, 341
Miosis, 41, 341
Miscellaneous, 38, 57, 83, 200, 209, 212
Mission, 105, 112, 242, 243, 254, 297, 300, 307, 309
Mitochondria, 46, 48, 71, 72, 74, 335, 341
Mitomycin C, 172, 173, 179
Mixed Function Oxidases, 69, 75, 90
Molecule, 11, 14, 16, 18, 19, 24, 29, 33-35, 48, 59, 62, 71, 73, 77, 85, 119, 129, 142, 204, 267, 269, 292, 295, 335, 339, 341, 342, 344
Monovalent, 9
Motile, 137, 341
Multiple, 10, 125, 175, 298, 307
Munition Packaging, 186, 187
Murrain, 151

Mustard Agent, 21, 85, 88, 338, 339
Mutation, 143, 174, 342
Myalgia, 152, 346
Mycelium, 122
Mycobacteria, 121, 123, 126, 139
Mycobacterium leprae, 138
Mycoplasmas, 160, 161, 170

N-Acetylglucosamine, 125, 126, 132, 170
N-Acetylmuramic Acid, 125, 126
NAD+, 15, 73
NADPH, 69
Nagasaki, 39, 105, 106, 263
Nalidixic Acid, 172, 173, 179
Napalm, 3, 5, 41, 106, 112, 342
Natural gas, 10, 283
NBC, 198, 212, 241-243, 248, 249, 254-256, 260, 275, 312, 313, 342
NCO, 333, 335, 342, 343, 345
Necrosis, 32, 56, 152, 337, 342
Nematodes, 160, 161
Nerve Agents, 4, 21, 23, 35, 40-46, 52, 53, 59-61, 64, 68, 90, 116, 120, 186, 189, 195, 199, 200, 209, 210, 216, 224, 236, 237, 248, 259, 267, 269, 270, 298
Neuroeffector, 331, 342
Neurotransmitter, 62, 64, 66, 68, 69, 116, 216, 342, 344, 346
Neutralization, 30, 151
New York City, 148
ng, 333, 342
Nicotine, 116, 273, 342
Nitric Oxide, 57, 58
Nitrogen Dioxide, 57, 58, 283
Nitrogen Mustard, 53, 55, 238, 339
Nitrogen, 4, 9-11, 19, 28, 32, 52, 53, 55, 57, 58, 60, 61, 78, 80, 85, 88, 90, 161, 188, 204, 208, 236, 238, 283, 294, 333, 339
Nomenclature, 10
Nonmotile, 137, 342
Nonvegetative, 125, 151
notatum, 139
Novobiocin, 172, 173, 179
Nuclear War, 2, 8, 277, 281
Nucleic Acid Synthesis, 128, 170, 172, 173
Nucleic Acids, 9, 12, 15, 18, 20, 22, 31, 59, 121, 128, 141, 176, 292, 294, 336
Nucleus, 18, 31, 64, 89, 122, 123, 129, 269, 314, 337, 340, 344

Oak, 24, 25
Obscurants, 105, 109, 112, 243, 245, 269, 276
o-Chlorobenzylmalononitrile, 95

Odor, 11, 24, 36, 42-46, 49-55, 57, 58, 77, 100-104, 111-113, 195, 199, 200, 225, 226, 283, 286, 288

Oil-Based, 106, 107

Oil-Metal, 106, 107

Opacification, 89

Organization, 18, 19, 97, 121, 127, 136, 162, 173, 235, 242, 246, 253, 299, 304, 309, 332, 336, 345, 346

Organometallic, 339, 342

Origins, 23, 241, 246, 270

Oxazolidine-2,5-dione, 80

Oxidation, 30, 31, 33, 57, 71, 74, 81, 86, 90, 106, 107, 118, 150, 266, 267, 298, 341

Oxidative Phosphorylation, 71, 74, 75, 90, 98, 117, 341

Oxidizing Agent, 17, 32, 74, 80, 97, 292

Oximes, 42-45, 62, 116, 117, 216

Oxygen, 9-11, 13, 19, 24, 27, 28, 34, 36, 41, 46, 48, 57, 59, 60, 62, 71-74, 78, 82, 97, 116, 117, 149, 150, 199, 204, 206, 208, 211, 215, 217, 224, 225, 259, 292, 293, 332, 333, 339, 346

PABA, 174

p-Aminobenzoic Acid, 174

Papule, 152

parabotulinum, 138

parahaemolyticus, 153

Parasitic, 137, 140, 343

Parathion, 23, 44, 69

Pasteurella pestis, 137

Pathogenic, 121-123, 125, 126, 128, 131, 132, 136-142, 144, 153, 161, 163, 165, 169, 171, 175, 176, 213, 233, 247, 264, 276, 289, 296, 336, 342, 343

Penicillium, 139, 180

Pentavalent, 9, 59, 90, 118

Peptide, 13, 20, 34, 78, 126, 344

Peptidoglycan, 124-126, 170

perfringens, 150

Permeable, 208, 209

Permissive Infection, 128, 139

Persistence, 38, 161, 195

Pesticides, 23, 24, 59

pH, 60, 82, 86, 161, 243, 291, 311

Phagocytosis, 128, 130, 343

Phosgene Oxime, 53, 335

Phosgene, 4, 41, 50, 51, 53, 58, 77-80, 82, 83, 195, 200, 205, 225, 226, 238, 264, 334, 335

Phosphate, 9, 15, 20, 21, 35, 48, 59, 62, 71, 90, 98, 290, 343

Phosphoric Acid, 59, 62, 90, 107, 232

Phosphorus, 3, 5, 9, 59, 60, 62, 94, 98, 107, 109, 111, 161, 215, 343, 345, 348

Phosphorylation, 16, 60-62, 71, 74, 75, 90, 98, 117, 341

Physical Association, 35, 343

Physical State, 36, 37, 42-45, 49, 51, 54, 55, 100-104, 111-113, 195

Phytophthora infestans, 158, 167

Pili, 125

Pinocytosis, 128, 343

Plague, 5, 137, 138, 147, 166, 275, 343

Plasma membrane, 126

Pleomorphic, 140, 343

Poison, 1-3, 5, 24, 25, 53, 60, 69, 91, 95, 99, 101, 104, 115, 153, 215, 216, 232, 239, 268, 296, 332, 340, 343, 346

Polar, 13, 17, 19, 27, 29, 119, 339

Polyatomic, 10, 59, 269, 341

Polyenes, 171, 177

Polymerization, 13, 48

Polymixins, 171

Polypeptide, 13, 18-20, 171, 172, 344

Polyribosomes, 127

Porphyrins, 295

Portal of Entry, 36-38

Potato, 74, 140, 158, 161, 167

Primary Structure, 13, 18-20, 344

Prion, 121, 140-143

Procaine, 152

Prokaryotes, 123, 128, 172

Propanethiol, 24

Prostigmine, 61

Protection, 1, 37, 38, 87, 93, 109, 132, 146, 159, 170, 176, 198, 203, 205, 208, 209, 211-213, 218, 224, 227, 243, 247, 261, 265, 281, 286, 287, 295, 296, 302

Protective Clothing, 208-210, 248, 255

Protein Coat, 86, 87, 128, 129, 140, 150, 160, 341

Protein Synthesis, 12, 127, 141, 170-176, 178, 183

Proteins, 11-15, 17-22, 28, 29, 31, 33-36, 64, 73, 74, 78, 81, 83, 88, 90, 98, 115, 121, 122, 129, 130, 140-142, 153, 155, 174-176, 267, 290, 292, 298, 336

prowazekii, 138

PS, 102, 344

Psychoactive Agents, 96, 271, 273-275

Psychoactive, 95, 96, 103, 232, 271, 273-275, 334, 344

Psychotomimetic, 274, 344

Psychotropic, 274, 344

Pulmonary Anthrax, 151, 152, 233
Pulmonary Edema, 56-58, 225, 232
Pulmonary, 56-58, 77, 89, 144, 151, 152, 156, 225, 232, 233, 335, 344
Pyridostigmine, 224, 265
Pyridostigmine, 61
Pyrogels, 107
Pyrolysis, 20, 31, 77, 225, 344
Pyrophorics, 106
Pyruvate Dehydrogenase, 91

Quaternary Nitrogen, 61
Quaternary Structure, 18, 29, 344
Quaternary, 17, 18, 20, 29, 55, 61, 62, 64, 290, 344

R&D, 4, 136, 234, 242, 246, 260, 262, 265, 270, 334
Receptor, 62, 64, 68, 69, 116, 130, 175, 243, 267, 344, 346
Red phosphorus, 107, 345
Reduction, 17, 30, 74, 91, 97, 173, 265, 296, 298, 315, 345,
Replacement, 23, 24, 30, 89, 154, 157, 197, 208, 210
Replication, 15, 88, 128, 140, 172, 179
Resistance, 93, 94, 97, 123, 135, 144, 145, 174, 175, 207, 233, 261, 274, 276, 304, 309, 332
Resonance, 11, 85, 263
Reverse Transcriptase, 129
Rhinorrhea, 56
Rhodanese, 117
Ribavirin, 173, 181, 213
Ribose, 15, 16, 59
Rice, 159, 160, 304
Rickettsia, 121, 123, 127, 138, 140, 160, 232
Rifampicin, 172, 182
RNA, 9, 12, 15, 16, 31, 59, 98, 128, 129, 140-142, 160, 171, 172, 174-178, 182, 337
Rusts, 158

S. Korea, 249
Saccharomyces cervisiae, 139
Salt Formation, 17
Salvarsan, 118, 169
San Francisco, 7, 147, 261, 283
Saprophytic, 125, 137, 345
Sarin, 4, 41, 42, 61, 151, 165, 185, 188, 224, 234, 312, 338, 345
Saturated, 10, 74
Second Degree Thermal Burns, 31
Secondary Infections, 56, 85, 156

Secondary Structure, 13, 17, 345
Selective Permeability, 36, 127, 291
Septicemia, 138, 144, 152, 213
Serine Series Enzymes, 21
Serine, 13, 14, 19, 21, 60-62, 78, 173, 265
Serous, 56, 332, 337, 345
Sevin, 61
Sexual, Spores, 123, 139
SHAPE, 10, 18, 29, 32, 34, 35, 68, 124, 126, 137, 141, 142, 160, 172, 335, 345, 346
Shigella dysenteriae, 175
Silvadene, 226
Silver Nitrate, 226, 291
Silver, 111, 205, 226, 291
SIPE, 209, 262
SK, 66
Skin, 11, 18, 24, 31-33, 36, 38, 39, 40, 42-45, 49, 51, 52, 54-58, 85-90, 95, 100-102, 107, 112, 113, 132, 133, 135, 137, 143, 144, 151, 152, 154, 155, 165, 167, 186, 199, 208, 210, 213, 215, 226, 230, 232, 235, 236, 238-240, 246, 259, 272, 274, 283, 287-292, 295, 314, 333, 336, 347
Small Area Smoke Screens, 112
Small Intestine, 153, 154, 335
Smoke Pot, 112
Smokers, 116, 137
Smuts, 158
Sodium Nitrite, 49, 117, 120, 224, 225, 345
Sodium Pyrophosphate, 48
Sodium Thiosulfate, 55, 117, 120, 224, 225, 236, 238, 345
Soman, 4, 41, 43, 61, 338, 345
Somme Offensive, 4
Spartans, 3
Spirillum, 123, 124
Spirochetes, 123, 124, 137, 233
Spiroplasmas, 160
Splenic Fever, 151
Spores, 123, 125, 144, 147, 150-152, 158, 160, 161, 167, 240, 289, 291-295, 333, 336, 345
Sporulation, 123, 125
-S-S-, 17, 90
Staphylococcal, 152, 181
Starch, 12, 16
STB, 108, 235-237
Sternutator, 340, 346
Stratum Corneum, 86
Stratum Germinativum, 86
Stratum Granulosum, 86
Stratum lucidum, 86
Stratum Malpighii, 86

Streptococcus lactis, 138
Streptokinase, 132
Streptomycin, 154, 172, 175, 182
Substance, 5, 24-28, 30, 34, 62, 69, 77, 86,
    108, 115, 116, 130, 131, 169, 216, 259,
    266, 267, 272-274, 292, 331-339, 341-347
Substernal, 41, 346
Substrate, 18, 35, 60, 62, 73, 91, 173, 197,
    216
Sucrose, 12, 16
Sulfadiazine, 226
Sulfanilamide, 174, 175, 182
Sulfonamide, 174
Sulfur Trioxide, 109, 113, 239, 338, 346
Sulfur, 3, 9-11, 24, 27, 52, 53, 57, 60, 73, 74,
    78, 85, 86, 88, 90, 109, 113, 118, 204, 208,
    239, 333, 338, 341, 343, 346
Sumac, 24, 25
Supercoiling, 173
Symbiosis, 129
Synapse, 342, 346
Synthesis Interference, 171, 172
Synthesis, 12, 15, 16, 82, 90, 91, 118, 126-
    129, 141, 142, 169-184, 270
Syphilis, 7, 169, 273
Systemic Poison, 53, 91, 95, 99, 101, 104,
    239, 346
Systemic Toxicity, 90, 238

TAB, 216
Tabun, 4, 5, 41, 42, 61, 200, 338, 346
Tachypnea, 49, 56
Tank, 1, 107, 108, 186, 211, 237, 244, 255,
    256, 262, 263, 282, 283, 286
Tartars, 5
Tear Gas, 95, 100, 334, 335
Termination, 157, 172
Termination, 68
Terrain, 38, 91, 97, 186, 188-191, 195
Tertiary Structure, 17-20, 346
Tertiary, 17-20, 29, 90, 346
tetani, 138, 150, 270
Tetanus, 131, 138, 150, 175, 259, 267, 270
Tetracycline, 152, 154, 172, 175, 182
Tetrahydrofolate, 173
Tetrapeptide, 126
Tetraphosphorus Decoxide, 107, 232
Tetravalent, 9
Thallus, 122
Thermal Burns, 31, 32, 232, 291
Thermal Effects, 190, 191
Thermite, 3, 5, 41, 106, 113, 346
THF, 173, 174

Thioester, 80
Thiosulfate Sulfurtransferase, 117
Third Degree Thermal Burns, 31, 107, 226,
    291
Thymine, 15, 295
Tissue, 16, 21, 28, 31-33, 36, 40, 50, 57, 64,
    78, 80, 81, 83, 87-89, 95, 97, 98, 107, 127,
    132, 143, 144, 155, 161, 165-167, 170,
    225, 236, 264, 267, 292, 293, 314, 342,
    343, 346, 347
Titanium Tetrachloride, 109, 112, 239, 338,
    346
Toxic Agents, 21, 35, 39, 85, 93, 196, 200,
    201, 207, 261, 265, 266, 269, 271, 339
Toxic Metabolites, 131
Toxin, 5, 69, 115, 130, 131, 149-154, 175,
    259, 263, 267, 270, 300, 301, 333, 336,
    346
Tracheobronchitis, 56
Transcription, 12, 15, 171
Translation, 12, 171, 172, 175
Treatment, 6, 17, 19, 20, 28, 35, 52, 115, 116,
    118, 119, 127, 133, 137, 143, 147-152,
    154, 155, 157, 163-167, 169, 205, 208,
    212, 213, 215, 216, 224-226, 230, 232,
    233, 239, 246-248, 256, 263-266, 269,
    271, 286-288, 291, 293-295, 297, 344
Tricarboxylic Acid Cycle, 71, 91
Triisopropanolamine, 99
Trimedoxime, 216
Trimethoprim, 173, 183
Trivalent, 9, 90, 118
tsutsugamushi, 138
typhi, 138, 167, 347
Typhus, 5, 138, 140

Uncoupling, 90, 98
Unsaturated, 10, 11, 80, 81
Uracil, 15, 98
Uranium, 41, 107, 108, 111, 347
Urea, 18, 98
Urticant, 24, 53, 347
Urushiol,
USA, 191, 192, 211

Vapor, 37, 39, 41, 43, 48, 83, 91, 95, 108,
    111, 112, 187, 188, 190, 195, 197, 198,
    205, 208, 212, 227, 235, 283, 288, 296,
    335, 347
Variation, 143, 191, 347
Vegetative, 122, 125, 190, 240, 289, 292-294,
    337
Vibrio cholerae, 138, 153, 165, 335

Vibrio, 123, 138, 153, 165, 335
Vicksburg, 5
Viet Cong, 6, 96, 254, 304
Villi, 154
Viricide, 173, 289, 347
Viroids, 121, 140, 160
Virulence, 145, 147, 162, 164, 176
Viruses, 29, 121, 128, 129, 137-144, 155, 156,
    160, 161, 173, 175, 176, 213, 232-234,
    246-248, 264, 276, 289-295, 337, 347
Vitamin B12, 118
Vomiting Agents, 5, 94, 95, 232
Vomiting, 5, 38, 41, 49, 51, 56, 94, 95, 101,
    144, 150, 152, 154, 155, 199, 232, 274,
    295, 336
vulnificus, 153
VX, 4, 39, 41, 43, 61, 248

Warfare, 1-5, 24, 25, 39, 40, 79, 107, 135,
    137, 145-149, 159, 162, 163, 185, 187,
    189, 195, 198, 200, 207, 212, 224, 241-
    243, 246, 256, 259, 260, 263, 267, 270,
    273, 281, 289, 300, 303, 312, 313, 333-
    335, 342
Warning, 2, 129, 130, 162, 197, 198, 200,
    201, 203, 226, 247, 263, 264, 268, 279,
    283, 286
Weather, 91, 158, 161, 185, 186, 189-191,
    195, 207, 261, 268, 286
Wheat, 157, 159-161, 163, 164
White Phosphorus, 94, 107, 109, 111, 348
Wind Effects, 191
Wind Patterns, 190
WP, 107, 111, 232, 348

Xylyl Bromides, 95

Yeasts, 121, 122, 133, 139, 170
Yemen, 5
Yogurt, 138
Ypres, Belgium, 4

Zirconium, 107, 111
Zirconium, 348